© 2013 Michael Day and Laverock Publishing

ISBN 978-0-9576306-0-4

Published in the United Kingdom by Laverock Publishing,
21 Moor Park Avenue, Huddersfield. HD4 7AL.

Laverock Publishing

Printed by The Amadeus Press, Ezra House, West 26 Business Park, Cleckheaton, BD19 4TQ.

CONTENTS

CHAPTER ONE	From Home Production to Mills	1
CHAPTER TWO	The Coming of Machinery	13
CHAPTER THREE	Revolution, Riots and Reform	23
CHAPTER FOUR	The Employment of Children	29
CHAPTER FIVE	Trade Unions, Disputes and Wages	36
CHAPTER SIX	From Clothiers to Manufacturers	45
CHAPTER SEVEN	Floods	55
CHAPTER EIGHT	Holme to Hinchliffe Mill	79
CHAPTER NINE	Bottoms mill to Holmfirth	115
CHAPTER TEN	Holme Styes to Holmfirth	149
CHAPTER ELEVEN	Holmfirth to Mytholmbridge	176
CHAPTER TWELVE	Upper House to New Mill	217
CHAPTER THIRTEEN	Wooldale to Mytholmbridge	243
CHAPTER FOURTEEN	Mytholmbridge to Honley	268
CHAPTER FIFTEEEN	Honley and the Mag Valley	307
GLOSSARY		338
BIBLIOGRAPHY		341
INDEX OF NAMES		344
INDEX OF SUBJECTS		368

WOOL & WORSIT

A HISTORY OF TEXTILES IN THE HOLME VALLEY

Michael Day

Laverock Publishing, Huddersfield

Front Cover Picture: 'The Story of Wool': from the sheep through the mill
                       to become finished cloth

Back Cover Pictures:

1   Tumming Stocks for hand carding wool

2   'Fly Shuttle' for a hand loom

3   Chain for a powered Pattern Loom plus gear wheel

4   Spindle for hand spinning

5   Shears for cropping cloth or shearing sheep

6   Control cylinder for a Witch

7   Notched Shuttle Stick for a handloom

8   Roving Brush for handraising woollen cloth

9   Portable Bobbin Winder

10   Shuttle for power looms

INTRODUCTION

This book is the result of seven years of research into the history of Textiles in Holme Valley, which began when I realised that there were at least two generations growing up in the district with no knowledge of what the area and life in it was like when all the mills were working. Woollen textiles have been responsible for shaping our corner of the West Riding over many centuries, and also of forming the characteristics of its inhabitants. Initially the production of yarn and cloth was carried on by families within their own homes, but as demand grew and machinery was introduced mills came into being, changing the pattern of work and society from domestic to industrial.

The first six chapters give a brief outline of domestic production and the gradual industrialisation that took place, also some of the problems experienced by manufacturers and workers; the seventh chapter covers the many floods that have occurred in the district over the centuries. Chapters eight to fifteen cover the mills of the area, plus details of some, but by no means all, of the many dyehouses, weaving shops, dressing shops and warehouses that existed. The plans shown on the title pages of these chapters are not accurate reproductions of Ordinance Survey maps and are not to scale, but are intended only to give an indication of the positions of the various mills relative to the main rivers and streams.

I have, where possible, given the earliest information available on many of the mills, obtained by examining the Wakefield Court Rolls from the earliest roll still in existence dating from 1274 through to the late nineteenth century. I have also examined a large number of legal documents relating to the mills of the district stored at the West Yorkshire Archive Service's Kirklees office in Huddersfield, also the offices in Leeds and Wakefield. Copies of early newspapers from the towns throughout Kirklees, also Leeds and Halifax are available on microfilm and can be studied in the Local History section of Huddersfield Library. These studies have led to numerous discoveries, some surprising, some incredulous, while others produced feelings of joy or sadness. I trust that readers will also experience similar emotions.

Should any reader wish to obtain more detail about the information given in the book on any of the mills please refer to the references at the end of each chapter, a copy of my notes is also available for perusal from the West Yorkshire Archive Service office to be found with the Local Studies library on the first floor of the Library building in Huddersfield. This will provide information about the original sources.

What is Worsit? It was a word that was in regular use during the 1940s and '50s, but it seems to be missing from many people's vocabulary today. It is a colloquialism for Worsted.

ACKNOWLEDGMENTS

I wish to record my sincere thanks for all the help that I have received from a large number of sources. Particularly Mr. Alan J Brooke of Honley for allowing me to utilise the fruits of his extensive research into the mills of Huddersfield and district, also his generous provision of many original images of his photographs. I also wish to record my thanks to Mrs. J.M. Ford of Honley for allowing me to use information from her unpublished Dissertation on the Mill Buildings of the Upper Holme Valley, completed in 1973. My thanks also go to Mr. Peter Sandford of Lancaster, for providing a large amount of genealogical information on various families of the district. The contribution by Mrs. M. Beardsell of Clayton West of the manuscript of Isaac Beardsell's diary written between 1844 and 1846 also added much to my knowledge of the period.

My thanks also go to the Directors and staff of Messrs. Moxon's, at Yew Tree Mill for allowing me to photograph processes and cloth in the mill, and to Messrs Bower Roebuck of Glendale mill New Mill for the insight and information that they provided.

Sincere thanks go to all the staff of the Local Studies Library in Huddersfield, and to the staff of the Kirklees branch of the West Yorkshire Archive Service for their infinite patience and helpful assistance over several years. My gratitude also goes to the Archivists, Librarians and other officers of the Yorkshire Archaeological Society in Leeds for all their assistance. I also thank the staff of the Colne Valley Museum Golcar, and the Industrial Museums of Bradford, and Helmshore near Rawtenstall Lancashire, for their generosity in allowing me to take photographs and publish them in this book. My thanks also go to the many residents of the district who have helped in any way.

CHAPTER ONE

From Home Production to Mills

The manufacture of textiles is one of the earliest crafts known to mankind, being second only to agriculture. The sheep indigenous to Britain from at least the Bronze Age were similar in breed and characteristics to the Soay sheep of today, one of their attributes being that they naturally shed their fleece in June or July. By collecting the loose wool, which can be plucked from the sheep at the right time or collected from bushes and hedgerows, then spinning it into yarn before weaving it into cloth, early Britons could keep themselves warm without the need to kill the animal in order to be able to wear its skin. Subsequent cross breeding of sheep over time, firstly to improve the fleece, and subsequently to produce larger animals, has led to the large variety of breeds to be seen in the fields and on the fells of Britain today.

From the early medieval period onwards the major industry in England was the production and export to Europe of wool. Every bale of wool exported attracted a tax, known as a 'subsidy', which contributed to the income of the reigning monarch. The size and importance of this trade between Britain and Europe can be appreciated from there being Frisian wool merchants resident in York in the mid eighth century. The trade grew over the next 600 years to the extent that by 1421 wool exports accounted for 74 percent of England's entire customs revenue.[1] These exports were principally raw wool, the relatively small amount of woven cloth that was produced at this time being mainly for use in the home market.

Cloth manufacture was carried on throughout Britain; as production increased some towns and cities established trade gilds which regulated their particular trade in their area. Beverley and York both had gilds governing textiles; in 1164 Henry II granted a Charter to the York weavers giving them the sole right, on payment of ten pounds per annum[a] to produce striped and coloured cloth in Yorkshire. The ban did not apply to other royal boroughs such as Beverley, but did apply throughout the West Riding. The size of the levy suggests that twelfth century York was a major centre for textiles with many weavers, as they were paying more than the cities of Lincoln, Winchester or Oxford.[2]

Gilds set standards of work, regulated prices charged, numbers of apprentices, checked the credentials of newcomers wanting to work in the trade, and inspected the premises and quality of work of members, they also oversaw the distribution of work to ensure that all members prospered equally. Additionally they influenced the religious observance of members, and each gild took part in the annual Corpus Christi procession and pageants. The weavers, along with other gilds in York, found that due to a multitude of reasons trade became extremely difficult. Despite the Royal Charter they were finding increasing competition from other areas, particularly the West Riding, not only for plain white cloth, but also for striped and coloured cloths. A York writer summed up the problems of the city's weavers in 1561:

> The cause of the decay of the ...weavers and loomes for woollen [cloth] within the sayd cite as I doe understand and learne is the lak of cloth making in the sayd cite as was in old time accustomed,

---

a   The equivalent amount in 2011 would be around £6,930.

> *whiche is now encreased and used in the towns of Halyfaxe, Leedes, and Wakefield, for that not only the commodytie of the water-mylnes is ther nigh at hand, but also the poor folk as speynners, carders, and other necessary work-folkes for the sayd webbing, may ther beside ther hand labor, have rye, fyre, and other relief good cheape, which is in this citie very deare and wanting.[3]*

The gilds managed to continue by combining memberships, the woollen weavers had combined with the linen weavers by 1548. The last meeting of the weavers gild was in 1796 when no indication was recorded that it would not continue, neither was an explanation of their demise offered from other sources.

Production of cloth outside cities continued to flourish; the domestic system operating in the Cotswolds and West Country during the 16th and 17th centuries was organised around the 'putting out' system, where a wealthy Merchant commissioned weavers living in a concentrated area to produce cloth for which he would supply the yarn, after which he would take the cloth elsewhere to be dyed and finished. The average number of weavers working for one merchant was about ten, although there were exceptions to this, one example is John Winchcombe, known as Jack of Newbury who, according to the ballad, employed 100 weavers in the early sixteenth century, all accommodated in one room. Each weaver had an assistant, suggesting that they were weaving wide looms; the ballad also maintains that 'Jack' employed some 560 other men, women and children to card and spin the wool, and to dye and finish the cloth; there was also William Stumpe of Malmesbury, who rented Osney Abbey in 1546 where he reputedly employed up to 2,000 people making cloth.[4].

Textile manufacture in the West Riding, and throughout much of the country, was a family affair, involving every member of the family from at least the age of four upwards, and sometimes younger children as well. An example was given by the son of Samuel Crompton inventor of the spinning mule, who said that he remembered when he was a child, shortly after he could stand up his mother, holding up his petticoats – boys were not 'breeched' until they were about 5 or 6 years of age, would stand him in a wooden tub containing raw cotton in water for him to tread down. As he trod she would add more cotton, putting a chair beside the tub for him to hold onto so that he would not fall out as the amount of cotton in the tub grew.[5] The mother was presumably attempting to strengthen his legs to avoid rickets, but he was also performing a necessary function in the production of cotton yarn.

Daniel Defoe, writing of the area around 'Hallifax and Huthersfield' in 1724 confirmed whole family involvement when he wrote:

> *Among the manufacturers houses are likewise scattered an infinite number of cottages or small dwellings, in which dwell the workmen which are employed, the women and children of whom, are always busy carding, spinning &c. so that no hands being unemploy'd, all can gain their bread, even from the youngest to the antient; hardly any thing above four years old, but its hands are sufficient to it self.[6]*

Defoe can be seen as suggesting that the workers were employed by 'manufacturers' who owned the materials and employed others to make the cloth for which they received wages, whereas in reality, during the fifteenth and sixteenth centuries virtually all clothier families in the West Riding were independent, the father would be the master weaver, with sons being either journeymen weavers, or apprenticed to him or another weaver; while the mother, daughters and younger sons would sort, pick, card and spin the wool into yarn. Clothiers bought their wool from middlemen known in the north as Wool Drivers or Wool Chapmen, and as Wool Staplers elsewhere in the country. As demand grew and wool prices rose clothiers blamed the people from whom they bought their supplies, the Wool Drivers. Animosity towards them rose to such a high level that in 1552 an Act of Parliament limited Wool Drivers to buying wool only for export, and forcing clothiers to buy their supplies direct from the wool producers. Because the weavers of this area had neither the time nor the means to visit fairs and farms to buy wool, they were disadvantaged to such an extent that in 1555 Parliament passed the 'Halifax Act'. The preamble to the act is as follows:

Forasmuche as the Paryshe of Halyfaxe and other places thereonto adjoyning, beyng planted in the grete waste and moores, where the Fertilite of Grounde ys not apte to bring forth any Corne nor good Grasse, but in rare Places, and by exceedinge and greate industrye of the inhabitants, and the same inhabitants altogether doo lyve by clothe making, for the greate parte of them neyther gettethe Corne nor ys hable to keepe a Horse to carry Woolles, nor yet to bye much woolle att once, but hath ever used onelie to repayre to the Towne of Halifaxe, and some other nigh theronto, and ther to bye upon the Woolldryver, some a stone, some twoo, and some three or foure according to theyre habilitee, and to carrye the same to theire houses, some iij, iiij, v, and vj myles of, upon theire Headdes and Backes, and so to make and converte the same eyther into Yarne or Clothe, and to sell the same, and so to bye more Woolle of the Wooll-dryver, by means of whiche Industrye the barreyn Gronde in those partes be nowe muche inhabyted, and above five hundrethe householdes there newly encreased within theis fourtye yeares past.[7]

Weavers in other parts of the north were eventually granted similar permission.

There were two principle types of cloth woven in our area; one was the Kersey, which takes its name from the village of Kersey in Suffolk, this was a fairly heavy woollen cloth particularly suited to making outer garments and also Army uniforms. The second was the Cassimere or Kerseymere, a finer twilled woollen cloth, that sometimes incorporated a mixture of wool and silk, originally woven in the West of England around Bradford on Avon, which retained its popularity for many years until being ousted by Worsteds. There was still a steady demand for both Kerseys and Cassimeres at Huddersfield's Cloth Hall in the mid nineteenth century. In the Huddersfield area during the sixteenth and seventeenth centuries both these cloths were usually woven on narrow looms approximately 36 inches wide, which could be woven by one person, whereas other areas such as Leeds favoured the wider loom producing cloth around 54 to 60 inches wide and needing two people to pass the shuttle from one side of the cloth to the other through the warp. The length of pieces from either loom was usually around 12 yards and became known as 'Northern Dozens'.

Wuzzing Holes. © Colne Valley Museum Golcar

If the family were starting with a full fleece, it would be opened out and spread on hurdles to raise it from the ground and be beaten with sticks to remove dirt and dust, after which it would be picked over to remove dark fibres, bits of grass or leaves and any wool contaminated with tar or pitch used by the farmer to brand his flock. The next process would be to sort the wool by length (staple) and thickness, as several grades of wool are to be found in one fleece, the wool from the underbelly and neck being finer and softer than the wool from the animal's back. The sorted wool could be washed before spinning, in which case after washing it would need to be spun or wuzzed. The wet wool would be put into a basket suspended from a rod, one end of which was pressed against a firm upright, often a door jamb; holding the other end of the horizontal rod the operator would rotate the stick and basket to expel the water in a similar manner to a spin dryer. This eventually drilled holes in the stone; 'wuzzing holes' can still be found in the walls of weaver's houses, often close to the doorway.

Alternatively the wool could be left 'in the grease', in which case it would be washed after it came off the loom. Whether washed or unwashed, the wool would next be carded, usually by the children, to ensure that each strand was laid in the same direction as the rest, after which it was ready for spinning, which would be undertaken by the mother and older daughters.

The oldest method of spinning is with the distaff and spindle. The distaff (or 'rock') is a stick about a yard in length with a forked top on which the sliver of wool, called the 'lint' or 'tow' was loosely wound. It could be held under the left arm, or tucked into the girdle of the spinner to allow greater freedom for the hands. The method of spinning was to draw a continuous supply of fibres through the left hand, and twist it between the forefinger and thumb of the right with the aid of the pendant spindle. The spindle was a slender rod, made from reed or wood, around 8 to 12 inches in length. An incision in the top allowed the thread to be attached to the spindle; as the spindle revolved it twisted the yarn in addition to stretching it into a finer thread. The lower end of the spindle carried a circular fairly flat whorl, often made from stone. This acted as a flywheel giving the spindle momentum, the weight of the whorl keeping the spindle revolving on its axis. When the length of the spun thread allowed the spindle to touch the ground the spinner wound the spun thread round the spindle, re-notched the thread, and carried on. The problem with hand spinning is the difficulty of spinning a thread which is consistent in both thickness and tension while controlling each element of the operation. An advantage of the distaff and spindle over the spinning wheel is that it allows the spinner freedom of movement; she is not confined to one spot. Even in the late twentieth century, women in many parts of the world spin using the distaff and spindle, as, for example, when they walk from their villages to the local market and back again.

A Great spinning wheel and a Saxony Treadle wheel. © Colne Valley Museum Golcar.

Spinning wheels were virtually unknown in England before the 14th Century; the early spinning wheels, known eventually as the 'Great' wheel due to their size, were powered by the spinner pushing round the large wheel by hand, which restricted her control of the spinning process. In comparison with the distaff and spindle, this wheel doubled a spinner's output. The invention of the smaller Saxony wheel with its addition of a foot treadle allowed the spinner continuous use of both hands giving her greater control over the thickness and tension of the thread, and increased output still further. One handloom weaver working full time would consume the output of up to ten spinners, and this consumption would increase after the adoption of the 'fly shuttle'; therefore it would be likely that one family could not supply sufficient spun yarn to keep a weaver fully occupied, making it necessary to enlist relatives, friends and neighbours.[8] Having obtained a sufficient amount of yarn, the next task was to make a warp.

Ben Turner was a trade unionist, Alderman and MP who, as a child, lived at either Booth House or Burnlee, his first job was as a reacher-in for a handloom weaver. He writes that the yarn to be used for the warp was first treated with size, which would coat the surface of the yarn and stop threads catching together and snagging during weaving, and possibly give some additional strength to the yarn. Each thread would need to be slightly longer than the finished length of the piece to allow the new warp to be fastened to the end of the previous one, plus some to leave in the loom to fasten the next warp onto. Ben Turner continues: "Then, on very fine days…there was a regular performance of putting sticks into the wall every few yards, and laying the warp out on it, putting in the raddle to run it over the warp to straighten or dress it, and put it ready for running on the warp beam ready for the loom."[9]

Warping Woof. © Colne Valley Museum, Raddle (inset), © Bradford Industrial Museum

In the event of inclement weather, the warp would be prepared inside the house, using the warping-woof, which is a frame, fastened to the wall, with holes for pegs to be put in so that the yarn can be wound back and forth across the frame to the required length, this operation would be repeated many times until sufficient warp threads were prepared, after which it would be run through the raddle to ensure that strands did not cross one another, as it was wound onto the beam.

When the warp was completed the beam would be lifted into the back of the loom and the threads of the new warp would be joined to the ends of the old warp in the correct order, after which the new warp would be drawn through the healds and slay so that weaving could commence. Yarn for the weft was wound onto a bobbin or a notched shuttle stick which would then be passed, by hand, from side to side between the warp threads to make the piece. After each weft pass the position of the warp threads would be altered by either raising or lowering them, to trap the weft thread in place.

Warping stone (inset); Warping wall in Field Head Lane, Holme. © Author
The Warping wall is set back from the road to allow the warper to work unhindered by traffic.

The preparation of the wool, plus carding and spinning would all be carried out on the ground floor of the house, whereas the warping, beaming and weaving would be done in the 'weaving chamber' on the top floor of the house, which also often doubled as the bedroom. This room was usually reached by an outside staircase known as 'taking-in steps', most of which have now disappeared. The photograph of Fulling Stocks at Helmshore mill (*page 10*) also shows Urine pots. One of these pots was often to be found on the landing at the top of taking-in steps. They were collected weekly and the householder would be paid 1d for a full pot, or if the family were tea-total, the price would be 1½d as the contents were considered to be of a higher quality.

After weaving the piece and taking it from the loom, the weaver would carry the piece outside where 'weeting', a mixture of urine and swine's dung that had been strained through straw, would be used to coat the cloth, after which it was folded and trampled to ensure full penetration, and left overnight. The object of this delightfully fragrant operation was to break down any natural or applied oils in the cloth, and loosen any other foreign matter. Eventually, the mixture of dung and urine used in this part of the fulling process was replaced by absorbent clay that became known as Fuller's Earth.

The next phase was to wash the cloth; before fulling mills this was done manually, sometimes by

Taking-in Steps, High Kinders. © Author

hand but more usually by putting the cloth in a tub, or series of tubs, containing water where it would be 'walked' (trampled) barefoot by the fuller[b]. The majority of kerseys were woven white, after the first fulling the cloth could be taken to a nearby dyehouse and dyed, but many were actually sold white, which would enable the buyer to determine the colour of the cloth. If the finished cloth was required to have a 'nap', a furry texture, it would then be treated with soap and fulled for a much longer period. This exploited the scaly construction of the wool by 'felting' it, raising and thickening the individual fibres, which then locked together; thus decreasing the overall dimensions of the cloth, but increasing its thickness, improving both its waterproofing and warmth.

When fulled, the cloth needed to be dried, which entailed stretching and fixing the cloth to tenter hooks on a row of tenter posts in the open air and leaving it to allow the breeze to blow through it. The 6 inch Ordinance Survey maps of the district printed in the 1850s show a great many rows of tenter posts in each community, however, there were no tenter posts marked on the 25 inch Ordinance Survey maps printed in the 1890s, indicating that an alternative method of tentering had been devised. This took the form of the hot room or 'stove', which had several benefits for the clothier over the outdoor tenter posts; firstly, the drying process was not subject to the vagaries of the British weather, neither was the cloth as likely to be stolen, five yards was a popular length to steal, but in some cases the full piece was taken. The people of Halifax obtained royal ascent to erect a Gibbet which was very similar to the French Guillotine, this is mentioned in the Wakefield Court Roll of 1360, and was also mentioned by James Ryder in a memorandum to Lord Burleigh in 1588 that its use as a deterrent continued to be necessary as cloth left drying on tenter posts overnight was likely to disappear.[10] Fifty-two people were beheaded for theft in Halifax between 1541 and 1650, which possibly gave rise to the saying "From Hull, Hell and Halifax, good Lord deliver us".

Tenter Posts, Marsden.© Author.

The fulling process produced a thicker cloth, but a more randomly hairy one. To get an overall smoother finish it was necessary to crop the cloth with shears. There were two processes involved, namely roving and cropping. Roving involved raising the nap on the surface of the cloth by scratching it with teasels fixed in a hand frame not unlike the cards used for hand-carding wool.

---

b   Fulling is thought to be the origin of the surname Walker.

The second process consisted of cutting the raised fibres level by shearing the cloth using large shears, to give the surface an even finish. Someone who was inexperienced could inflict a great deal of damage on the cloth. Shearmen or Croppers, either title covers the same operation, served an apprenticeship to learn their trade and considered themselves the elite of the textile community. Attempts to mechanise both processes met with fierce resistance, which will be addressed later.

The final act was to take the piece to market and sell it. Henry de Lacy Earl of Lincoln, had been granted the right to hold a market in Almondbury in 1294, but as time progressed the importance of Almondbury declined and that of Huddersfield rose. Huddersfield's Market Charter dates from 1671, and for almost one hundred years prior to the erecting of the Cloth Hall, cloth, which was the largest commodity in the market, was initially offered for sale

Teazel raising brush. Used by Croppers to raise cloth by hand. © Helmshore Ind. Museum Armley.

in the market place, but due to the volume being brought, some from as far away as Saddleworth, it was also shown on the walls and possibly some of the gravestones of the churchyard of St. Peter's in Kirkgate. There was no guarantee that a weaver would sell his piece on the first day he offered it for sale. The Rev. Robert Meake recorded in his diary on 18 April, 1694:

> *I heard a poor man talking to my landlady under the window, and telling her he had been four days at market with a piece, and could yet receive no money; that he was forced to buy bean-meal to make bread, oatmeal being dear; and nothing almost got for work.*[11]

The main market day was originally Tuesday, but it is likely that cloth was also on show on other days of the week. As will be seen later, some clothiers, like James Beardsell, went to enormous lengths to sell their wares.

Early mills

The structure of West Yorkshire's moors and hills coupled with an abundant, almost year-round, supply of rain ensured a plentiful supply of soft water for washing and dyeing wool; plus power to drive machinery; although many of the smaller water courses had only a sufficient volume of water to drive a water wheel for six to nine months of the year. Consequently early mills were built beside rivers that could supply large continuous volumes of water, which often meant building them in the valley bottoms.

The earliest mills were Corn mills, these were Soke or Manorial mills held by the Lord of the Manor, who let the mill to a lesser landowner or to a group of tenants, who appointed the miller, although in some instances the miller was himself one of the fee-farm holders. The Manor of Wakefield, which included the Graveship of Holme, was granted to William de Warrenne Earl of Surrey, by Henry I in 1112 or thereabouts. The lettings of the mills were recorded in the Wakefield Court Rolls; the earliest roll still in existence is the one for 1274-75, which records that the only mill within the Graveship of Holme was in the township of Cartworth. The court rolls give no indication of the actual location of the mill, which has been the subject of much speculation over a long period. The Court Roll for 1274 carries the following entry:

> *18 Oct. 1274, Richard the Grave of Scholes, Richard the Grave of Birkes, Hannah of Wlvedale, John son of Mary of Wlvedale, William de Thwong, Addam of Heppeworth, Nicholas Kenward, and Nicholas the Millener, give 20 marks [£13 6s 8d] for having the Mill at Cartewrth this year, under their own pledge, payable half on St. Giles's Day [1ˢᵗ Sept.] and half at Michaelmas [29 Sept].*

It was the duty of every tenant to have their grain ground at the Lord's mill which explains the high rent, any household found to possess their own quern stones would be fined and the stones broken. The fee for grinding the grain in the thirteenth century was about one seventeenth of the amount ground, this had dropped to one twenty-fourth by 1650; it was this flour that made the fee-farm holders their profit.

In 1313 Cartworth mill was damaged by flood waters, along with the dam and the miller's house. Being the only mill within the Graveship at that time its destruction must have presented the population with the problem of where to get their grain ground; it would also mean a loss of revenue for the lord. Cartworth mill was subsequently repaired, additionally, after the flood a second mill was built, possibly as a consequence of the floods, or perhaps increased demand. The Court Roll for 1316 records that at the court held at Byrton [Kirkburton] on the Wednesday after the Feast of St. Luke the Evangelist [18th October]:

> *The mill of Cartwrth and the new mill of Holnefrith are let to farm this year to Richard of Byrton, Richard son of Michael, William the Forester, Jordan the Milner, Adam his son, Richard Child, Richard del Bothe, and William Strekeyes, for £26. 13s 4d. besides the suit of foreigners coming to the new mill, which is reserved to the lord the Earl. Pledge each of them for one another, &, besides them, Adam son of Jordan found Henry Wade as pledge, and Jordan the Milner found John son of Michael, and John son of Loukes, and William the Forester to answer for the profit of foreigners.*

Although referred to as the 'new mill', it seems likely that it was in the woodland in the valley bottom, which eventually became Holmfirth centre and was in the township of Wooldale, not actually at New Mill. References to the 'new mill' disappear within a matter of a few years, and are replaced by 'the mills of Cartworth', or 'the mills of Holne'. Cartworth mill needed fairly extensive repairs in 1426, whether this was due to another flood or to wear and tear is not stated, but it was necessary to buy the trunks of 26 Oak trees from Honley wood, and also use 32 Oaks from Holme Wood for the work. Although the entry says that the timber from Honley was bought, the cost is given as nothing, suggesting that the cost was probably repaid in labour. The bark from the trees, which was not wanted, was sold at a profit of 3s 4d.[12]

Despite Cartworth mill appearing in the court rolls on an almost annual basis for many years, no indication of it whereabouts is given. Specific references to the mills ended around the mid sixteenth century when they were let by deed, probably to the Allot family of Bentley Grange who held them until the Eighteenth century; although there is a reference to the 'mills of Holmfirth' in the rolls during the mid seventeenth century.

The Kirkburton Parish Register of Baptisms lists twelve families and one unmarried woman giving their 'place of abode' as Cartworth mill between the years of 1729 and 1827. The first of these families, that of Jonathon Worsley, gives Cartworth mill as their abode on the first entry in 1729, and the Walk mill at Cartworth on the second entry in 1732, suggesting that both sites remained. Perusal of the rolls throughout the period indicates that the families named all lived in the Arunden and Cartworth area. Although the actual mills had disappeared by this time, their presence was obviously well remembered. The mills would have been on the Cartworth side of the river, probably in the area between Washpit and Dover mills. The stream forms the boundary between the townships of Cartworth and Wooldale, Choppards being on the opposite bank is in the township of Wooldale.

The earliest mention of a corn mill at New Mill comes much later, and is in the Court Roll for 1456:

> *29 October 1456, William Moorehous and Richard Castell came here in court and took from the lord three parts of two mills within the graveship of Holme, of which one is called Cartworthmylne and the other Nwemylne, and John Sykes came here in court and took from the lord the fourth part of the two mills, to have and to hold the two mills with their appurtenances to the aforesaid William Richard and John from the feast of St Michael the Archangel last past before the date of this court until the end of*

the term of seven years next following and fully completed. Paying thence to the lord annually during the whole term abovesaid 76s 8d for rent/farm at the feasts of Easter and St. Michael by equal portions etc. And the lord will repair and keep up the said mills during the aforesaid term at his own costs and expenses except for Cogges and Spyndils etc.

The community that grew up around this new mill also became known as New Mill, making the name of the mill New Mill mill. Whereas during the thirteenth and fourteenth centuries it had been the practise of the court to let a mill annually for quite a high rent, the increasing number of mills in the area probably meant that despite a rising population, the revenue received by each mill was reducing, which arguably encouraged both the lord and his tenant to agree terms for longer leases.

The first textile process to be mechanised was that of Fulling, with large wooden hammers driven by the power of the water wheel replacing the pounding action of the fuller's feet. Fulling mills existed in some parts of the country from the twelfth century; although they were few in number, at the beginning of the fourteenth century there were only eleven fulling mills in the West Riding of Yorkshire, one was in Wakefield, and there was also a fulling mill listed in Almondbury.[13]

Fulling Stocks © Helmshore Mill nr. Haslingden.
The pots beside the stocks held Urine.

The earliest indication of a fulling mill within the Graveship of Holme is in the Court Roll of 1329, when: the Lord's Fulling Mill at Cartworth [which would place it near to the Cartworth corn mill] is let to John the Walker and his heirs for   [blank]   years at 15s per year. From the huge differential between the rents for corn mills and the rent for the fulling mill, it would seem that at that time, unlike some manors, the lord did not insist that all cloth should be taken to his mill to be fulled, leaving the manual fullers to continue plying their trade. Eventually there was also an early fulling mill near the corn mill in Holmfirth which also belonged to the lord, but as yet, no specific early reference to it has been found.

The revenue to be gleaned from fulling does not appear to have been protected by the lord as closely as that from corn-milling, as the Hinchecliff family, who were fee-farmers at the lords mill at Cartworth in 1402, were later permitted to build their own fulling mill nearby. The date of construction is not known, the earliest reference to it is in the court roll for 1503, and is after the death of the man who probably had the mill built and would have been the first to work it. The entry records:

> *18 October 1503, Holme, William Hynchecliff son and heir of William Hynchecliff came here in the Tourne and gave to the lord 3s 4d of fine for a licence of heriot for one parcel of water in Cartworthmere at a certain place called Braithfurthe with one fulling mill built on the same with appurtenances in the Graveship of Holme after the death of the aforesaid William the father to the aforesaid William the son to hold to himself and his heirs by services according to the custom of the manor.*

The probable meaning of Braithefurth is 'broad furrow', which applies to the location of the mill as the valley bottom widens in this vicinity; another interpretation of Braithefurth is 'broad ford', which would also be an apt description. As with New Mill, the community that grew up around the mill would become known as Hinchliffe Mill; the above information refers to the original mill that was upstream of the bridge at Damhead, a building still exists on the site but is no longer a mill. The earliest reference to a fulling mill near the New Mill is in the court roll of 1539 to 1540, which shows:

> *9 January 1540, HOLME: John Rowler by Thomas Coldwell, tenant and sworn, surrendered into the lord's hands one rood of land and water in the water called Newmillwater with a certain pond for a fulling mill built and established there with appurtenances: to the use of Stephen Rowley son of the said John Rowley and his heirs forever. Agreed. Entry fine 4d.*

The corn mill was on the site of New Mill mill, therefore the fulling mill was probably built where Ing Nook mill eventually stood, now known as Glendale mill.

A sixteenth century survey of the Graveship records that: 'Edward Booth holdeth by copy two Messuages one Fullinge Milne & 23 acres and one rood and payeth by yeare 12s 1½d'[14] This entry is in the district headed 'Overthong', now known as Upperthong; the description also occurs several times in later years within the Court Rolls and refers to what is now known as Bridge Mills. The survey is not dated, but makes mention of the 'Queen's Mill in Holnefrith', indicating that it was written after 1553 but before 1603, during the reign of either Queen Mary or her sister Elizabeth I. The number of fulling mills gradually increased, the Wakefield Court Roll for 1640 gives details of the mill that became known as the Upper Mill or Prickleden Mill:

> *22 May 1640, HOLME – Thomas Haigh of Hadfield in Derbyshire by William Dernilee, lord's tenant and sworn, surrendered an interest and title in a close of arable land called Lathecroft, another called Rydinge, a house in the same two closes called Pense bothomes, a close called Holme adjoining a fulling mill, a piece of wood and land called Prickmoore banke (now divided into three), another close called Tentercrofte, 2 barns, a little backside adjoining (saving an access way at all times for repair of the fulling mill) and all rents associated in Overthwong and Cartworth in the Graveship of Holme, now occupied by Edward Batty or his assigns at a lord's rent of 2s 6d and certain fine: to the use of Nicholas Haigh of Hadfield in Derbyshire his heirs etc. Agreed: entry fine of 3s 9d. Compounded for by Edward Batty, John West, and Martyn Allott.*

The Batty family appear to have tenanted the mill for some considerable time, an entry in September 1751 records the passing of this mill along with a second fulling mill which is presumably the one that became Lower Mill, from Joseph and Thomas Batty to James and Jonathon Batty who were likely to be their sons.

Honley and Brockholes were outside the Manor of Wakefield, and consequently the mills in that area are not covered by Court Rolls. Much of the land in that area belonged to the Earl of Dartmouth. Mary Jagger wrote that in 1344 there was a corn mill in existence at Honley, and a fulling mill at Steps; but documentary evidence confirming this is non-existent. A manuscript copy of 'A book of several transactions of the Kaye's of Woodsome from Queen Elizabeth's days to 1642' originally compiled by Sir John Kaye, and transcribed by a Mr. Wilson, records that Sir Robert Stapylton Knight, sold to Sir John Kaye the 'Corn Mylne in Honley and the Walke Mylne at one tyme, and Helayhowsse and Bess Wilsons XXVILi' [£26]; Mr. Wilson recorded in brackets 'he gave XIILi [£12] for Honley mills'.[15] The corn mill presumably stood just downstream from Honley Bridge, and the fulling mill would also be on the River Holme at Steps. The entry does not, unfortunately, carry a date, but took place in the mid to late 16th century. There is a record in the book of rents received by the Kaye family from the two mills in Honley for 1594: Richard Ratclyff grain mill and house £6 13s 4d; George Wilson fulling mill and house 16s 8d.

Whether the lords of the manor realised the income potential provided by fulling mills or not, the state certainly did; they introduced a tax on all cloth being fulled from 1393-4. The tax, called Ulnage, was to be collected by the fuller, who kept a record of all the cloth fulled; this was checked by the tax collector, known as the Ulnager or Aulnager, who then collected the tax from the fuller. The tax on a full piece of cloth was 4d; however, the kerseys and cassimeres woven in this area were classed as one quarter of a piece, consequently Ulnage was 1d.[16] Clothiers disliked paying the tax and tried various means to avoid it; they gradually increased the length of their pieces from 12yds to 24, and, despite protests from the Ulnagers, refused to pay more than the 1d per piece. The Ulnagers took the dispute to law in 1613, and tried various arguments to win the case but failed, the clothiers maintaining that if they were to pay a higher levy they would be unable to continue to support the aged and infirm of the area, neither would they be able to support the parish priests, or keep up their vigilance against recusants. A second trial brought by the Ulnagers in 1637 was eventually abandoned; they apparently having decided that even if they won, the costs of the case would be greater than the increased revenue.[17] As trade increased the fulling mills could not cope with demand and consequently began working on Sundays, which was against the law, in an attempt to catch up. In 1739 it was put to the Quarter Sessions in Pontefract that:

> *It is, and for many years last past hath been, a common Practice to mill Narrow Cloth upon Sundays, and that the Clothmakers are now arrived to such a Scandalous and Shocking Degree of profaning the Sabbath this way, that they contrive to bring more cloths to be milled upon a Sunday than any other day, whereby both Masters and Servants are guilty of a public Neglect of the Holy Duties of the day, and by certain Consequence are insensibly drawn into all manner of Sin and Wickedness, to the great displeasure of Almighty God, the scandal of the Kingdom, the evil example of their Neighbours, and the breach of the Laws, both divine and human.*[18]

The court forbade mills to work from midnight on Saturdays to Midnight on Sundays, and Justices of the Peace were ordered to be very vigilant and severely punish anyone who engaged in any textile occupation on Sundays. One reason why clothiers had taken cloth to be fulled on Sundays was that many fullers did not record the pieces fulled on that day, and consequently did not charge ulnage.

As will be seen in ensuing chapters, the number of mills in the district greatly increased during the coming years; with many but not all, surviving into the latter half of the twentieth century.

Notes

1   Heaton p.3, also Lipson p. 87.
2   Heaton p. 3
3   York Corporation Minute Books, xxiii, f. 20a, 8 June, 1561. Quoted in Heaton, pp 54-5.
4   Cunningham pp 514-5.
5   Lipson, p. 70
6   Defoe, Vol. 2, p. 195.
7   Heaton, p. 94.
8   Catling, p. 106.
9   *Holmfirth Express;* 9 June, 1923.
10   Roth Ling, pp. 190-206, 280-281.
11   Sykes, p. 284. .
12   W.C.R. 1426.
13   E.M. Carus-Wilson, An Industrial Revolution… p.49.
14   Kirklees Archive Service, Ref. KC175 p. 3.
15   M. Jagger, p. 6; also Yorkshire Archaeological Society, MS 178, p. 13.
16   Heaton, p. 69
17   Ponting in Baines, pp. 26-28
18   *Quarter Sessions Order Book U,* p. 141. Pontefract, May 1, 1739. Quoted in Heaton, p. 343.

CHAPTER 2

The Coming of Machinery

The latter half of the eighteenth century and the first half of the nineteenth are often referred to as the time of the Industrial Revolution; but as far as wool textiles are concerned it would be better described as evolution. The demand for British made wool and cotton goods increased considerably during the seventeenth and eighteenth centuries, and while wool exports doubled in that time, the demand for cotton rose around 800 times over the same period vastly outstripping the former supremacy of wool. This stimulated many mechanically minded men, both within the textile community and outside it, to attempt to design and build machinery that would process the raw materials into cloth. The majority of the inventions were developed to process cotton, and had to be adapted in order to be suitable for the woollen industry, which took time.

Many people working in textiles do not appear to have realised the rate at which demand for their products was growing, and invariably objected to any new innovation, sometimes with force, fearing that increased production by some would lead to unemployment for many. One of the earliest inventions was that of the 'fly shuttle', a means of passing weft between the warp threads without the weaver having to pass it from one hand to the other, or in the case of a wide loom from one person to another. It was invented and patented by John Kay in 1733, and was condemned by

Hand Loom. © Bradford Industrial Museum
The suspended cord across the loom operates the fly shuttle

the people it was meant to help due to their fears of unemployment; weavers in Lancashire and East Anglia were particularly hostile towards it.

The shuttle was propelled across the loom between the warp threads by the weaver quickly pulling a cord that was attached to a 'picker' at each end of the batten to send the shuttle in the direction that he wanted it to travel. The use of this system increased the output of both broad and narrow looms, and dispensed with the need for an assistant when weaving a broad loom. It was readily taken up by the handloom weavers of Yorkshire, particularly in the Leeds area where most weavers used a wide loom. It would appear that many weavers were using the fly shuttle illegally, as the following announcement appeared in the *Leeds Mercury* on August 27th 1737:

> '*Whereas John Kay of Bury…having obtained a patent for his new invented shuttle for weaving of broad cloths, and dyvers clothiers within the West Riding…have made use of the said shuttle without the lycense of the said John Kay, contrary to the prohibition of the said patent. This is to give notice that if any person will come to Mr. John Lazenby in Leeds, and lodge an information against a sufficient number of clothiers, &c….*'

A reward was offered for information and the following year Kay brought a case against several weavers, but the costs of the case were so great that he was financially ruined, and had to abandon it.[1]

The process of taking the raw wool and straightening the fibres ready for spinning comprises two processes, the first is 'scribbling', which separates thicker fibres from finer ones, after which the fibres are carded. The two processes were initially carried out on separate machines, but were eventually combined in one machine named a Condenser. Attempts to produce a mechanised form of scribbling and carding fibres began in the 1740s; both Daniel Bourne and Lewis Paul patented mechanical methods in 1748, which imitated the hand operations. Paul's invention enjoyed limited success in Leominster and Wigan, but seems to have disappeared after Richard Arkwright patented his carding machine in 1775. Arkwright also invented a machine that would roll the carded wool into rovings ready for spinning; this was called the 'Slubbing Billy'.

The huge increase in demand for cloth coupled with faster production due to the growing use of

Early Carding machines. © Helmshore Ind. Museum, Haslingden.

the fly shuttle, particularly in Lancashire, put pressure on spinners to increase yarn production. There were several attempts to mechanise the spinning process to enable one person to concurrently spin multiple threads. The first machine to spin fibres into yarn without the aid of human fingers was patented in 1739 by Lewis Paul of Birmingham. The description of his machine reads:

> 'the sliver is put between a pair of rollers, and being turned round by their motion, draws in the raw mass of wool or cotton to be spun in proportion to the velocity of such rollers. A succession of other rollers moving proportionately faster than the rest, draw the rope, thread, or sliver, into any degree of fineness that may be required.[2]

This machine had some flaws in its design and construction and was soon abandoned. There were several other people who produced machines to spin multiple threads around the same time. Lawrence Earnshaw of Mottram in Cheshire invented a spinning machine that he showed to friends before scrapping it because he was afraid that it would cause unemployment and unnecessary hardship. In 1764 Thomas Highs, a reed-maker of Leigh, invented a machine to simultaneously spin six threads of wool or cotton, which he reputedly named 'Jenny' after his daughter, the yarn spun by this machine was particularly good for weft, but was too soft for warp. There is a suggestion, but no proof, that Highs handed his invention to James Hargreaves of Blackburn, who then claimed to have invented a similar machine in 1767, which he also called a Jenny, producing fear of unemployment in the local spinners to the extent that he was driven from the town.

Hand operated Spinning Jenny with 28 spindles. © Colne Valley Museum, Golcar.

Highs turned his attention to the production of a firmer yarn on a power-driven machine, which, with the help of John Kay, a clock maker of Warrington, he appears to have achieved by 1767. The original machine was made from wood, Highs asked Kay to make a metal model which he did. Richard Arkwright, a wig maker, then befriended Kay and learned the secrets of the powered machine. Highs was unable to fully exploit his inventions due to a lack of money; Arkwright found someone in Preston who was prepared to back him in setting up his business, when he claimed to have invented the machine that he called the water frame, which he patented in 1769. He built a factory in Nottingham, and one at Cromford in Derbyshire that was very successful. There were several court cases disputing Arkwright's patents, at the final one, *Rex V Arkwright* in 1785, Highs, Kay, and Hargreaves' widow all claimed that Arkwright had stolen their inventions, and his patents were withdrawn.[3] When the water frame was connected to a steam engine it emitted a low whistle or humming sound, and became known as the 'throstle'; this machine was particularly suited to spinning yarn for use in warps.

It was now possible to convert raw wool or cotton into yarn ready to be used as warp or weft without using human fingers. The yarns produced by these machines proved to be superior to hand spun yarns in that they were of equal thickness and elasticity throughout their length, and consequently were less likely to break. Secondly, the woven cloth had a more even texture and appearance making it more pleasing to the eye, and therefore more saleable. These scribbling and carding processes were readily taken up by West Riding manufacturers from the late eighteenth century onwards. Many fulling mills added scribbling and carding engines, while other manufacturers built mills specifically to take raw wool and convert it into yarn. There were around 38 scribbling mills in Yorkshire in 1790, which had increased to at least 243 by 1800.[4] All these were powered by water or steam; there were also an unknown number of other scribbling mills that were powered by hand, horse, or wind. In 1794, Ben North had installed the first scribbling engine at Shelley Woodhouse mill, which was powered by two Asses working in a treadmill rather than the more usual method of a horse-gin.[5]

In spinning, the outstanding invention of the era came in 1774 when Samuel Crompton combined the draft-against-twist of the jenny with the drafting rollers of the water frame, resulting in what became known as the mule.

Crompton achieved this by mounting the spindles, driving bands and drum on a moveable carriage travelling back and forth on rails. The mule was particularly suited to spinning yarn for weft. He did not patent his invention and was pestered by other spinners to reveal how it worked, which he agreed to do in November 1780 by surrendering his machine. He should have been paid the sum of £70 9s 6d, which was the total to be contributed by eighty-two firms for the information. He actually received £60, which barely covered the cost of his machine. Within a period of some seventy years

Spinning mule with the 'Jenny' open. © Helmshore Mill near Haslingden.

the spinning of fibre into yarn had progressed from one spinster with one wheel spinning one thread, to the point where one person operating a mule with two hundred spindles could spin around five to six hundred times as much yarn, as the mule worked at three times the speed of a spinning wheel. Compared with the distaff and spindle, production had increased one thousand fold. Industrial action by spinners after the repeal of the Combination Act in 1825 encouraged employers to commission Richard Roberts to completely automate the mule. He achieved this and patented his new machine known as the 'self-acting' mule in 1830, which was so successful in its operation that it was possible to extend the number of spindles on one machine to one thousand.

The processing of worsted fibres into yarn differs from that of woollen or cotton fibres in that the length of worsted fibre makes it impossible to card; it must therefore be combed. The teeth of the worsted hand comb are much longer than those on the wool cards, and there are fewer of them. In hand combing one worsted comb is fixed to a post and some fibre attached, a second comb is pulled through the fibres transferring some of the wool to the second comb, until each comb contains a roughly equal amount. Each bunch of fibres would then be combed for a second time to straighten them, after which the long fibres would be taken off the combs and rolled into a ball, and are known as 'tops', which are subsequently spun into worsted yarn; the medium length fibres would be added to the next lot of fibre to be combed; and the shortest fibres, known as 'noils', would be consigned to the woollen trade. The invention of mechanical combing proved to be difficult; the Rev. Edmund Cartwright patented his first combing machine on 27 April 1790, which attempted to replicate the method of hand combing. He made several alterations between 1790 and 1792 when he patented his third combing machine. Several other people subsequently invented combing machines, notable amongst these were Platt & Collier in 1827, Heilmann in 1846, and Lister & Donisthorpe in 1851, with the most widely used being the one invented by James Noble and patented in 1853, but the others were useful for specialised fibres.[6]

Production of worsted fabrics was initially carried out in East Anglia, taking its name from the village of Worstead in Norfolk, but, as with woollens, it eventually became concentrated in West

Noble Worsted Combing machine. © Bradford Industrial Museum

Yorkshire, chiefly in the areas around Bradford, Leeds, Keighley and Skipton, spreading to the Huddersfield area in the late nineteenth and early twentieth centuries. After combing, worsted fibres would be spun into yarn in a similar way to woollen; however, worsted yarn, due to its longer staple, makes a much finer yarn and consequently a much finer cloth.

In order to take advantage of the automated methods of producing yarn, many scribbling mills were built during the late eighteenth and early nineteenth centuries as a result of small groups of yarn manufacturers combining their resources of capital; with each individual taking a floor, or part of one floor, as his manufactory. Other mills were built by landowners who then let them to manufacturers; Lord Dartmouth had built twenty three mills on his estates in Yorkshire by 1805, which were all let to tenants; some of them being multi occupancy. Should one of the occupants be very successful and wish to expand, he may choose to build a mill of his own and move in, leaving his former premises empty. Conversely, should a business fail the premises would again be left empty. If no-one in the building wanted to take over the empty space, the situation was remedied by advertising 'Room and Power to let' to obtain a new tenant, a practice that continued well into the twentieth century. Some mills that were multi occupancy over long periods were Holmfirth Mill, Bridge Mills, Thongsbridge Mills, and Crossley/Neiley Mills in Honley, there were also many others.

As the number of spinning companies increased, the need for hand-spun yarn diminished; but, for a weaver to buy machine-spun yarn rather than loose wool to be spun by the family increased the family's capital outlay and left the female members and younger sons without work. The spinning companies needed people to operate the machines, which gave wives and older children, girls in particular, the opportunity to earn wages, which helped to redress the balance. A woman who worked as a spinner would need an assistant, called a piecer, often referred to locally as a 'piecener', a mother who had a young child that was old enough to start to help at home would take the child with her to the mill, where he or she would be introduced to the working environment. This represented a major change, as mill workers had set hours of work and had to walk to and from their place of work in their own time, whereas when working at home hours of work were more flexible, and 'travelling time' was unnecessary.

There were also subtle changes taking place in the structure of the trade. Instead of the weaver buying wool to be spun, or in some cases buying spun yarn, which he would weave into cloth, have it fulled, and then sell the cloth, the spinner would supply yarn for a warp and weft to a weaver, who would return it to the spinner as woven cloth, for which he would be paid an agreed amount. In effect, the weaver became an outworking wage earner as he still worked at home, rather than a self-employed clothier. An advantage to the weaver of this system was that he could accept work from more than one spinner in order to keep himself fully employed. John Charlesworth a handloom weaver was living on Water Street in Hinchliffe Mill in 1852. He had two handlooms that were unfortunately washed away in the flood. Each loom contained a partly woven piece; one belonged to James Brooke & Son, Bridge Mills; and the other to Richard Bower of Green Lane Mill, near Choppards.[7] A potential disadvantage to the weaver was that the spinner could influence the weaver's work pattern by specifying a completion date; failure to comply may prejudice future relations.

In the early part of the nineteenth century many mills were still water powered, and were necessarily built on or near to the banks of rivers or streams. The long established fulling mills had taken the best positions; therefore some new mills had to be sited in positions where it was necessary to build long goits to a dam or dams in order to get a water supply sufficient to turn the water wheel. Some small mills were built alongside the higher reaches of relatively small streams where, in warm dry summers and also in cold hard winters the water supply must have diminished to a mere trickle, which would stop the mills from working. By the 1840s, an increasing number of mills were adding coal fired boilers and steam engines to supplement their water wheels in dry weather. Some of the mills had coal mines close by, which was a point emphasised by estate agents should the mill be put up for sale, or its tenancy become vacant. Stoney Bank Mill in New Mill was advertised as having coal workings within 100 yards of the mill; Winney Bank Mill near Wooldale was advertised as being within 1 ½ miles of several beds of excellent coal; and George Haigh who was a partner at Woodroyd Mill Honley and owned Grove mill, was also a coal-owner, and at one time had a pit at Marsh in Honley.

Many weavers were still living in their long established villages and homesteads on or near the tops of the hills in the nineteenth century. As many of the spinning mills were in the valley bottoms it was a daunting prospect for a weaver to have to walk to the mill carrying his woven piece, and walk back home carrying his yarn for the new warp and weft plus the gears needed for his loom, which were often the property of the manufacturer. Although a power loom had been invented by Edmund Cartwright in 1785, it was slow and difficult to operate. Early power looms were virtually a cast-iron version of the wooden handloom, automated to throw the shuttle between the warp threads, raise and lower the healds in the correct order, and beat up the newly inserted weft thread with the batten; eventually being modified to let off the warp roller and take up the cloth roller keeping a consistent tension on the warp threads. William Horrocks brought out a much improved power loom in 1813, which he had further improved by 1821.

The cotton and worsted trades adopted the use of the power loom fairly readily, but it was of limited use in the woollen trade as the need to use a soft-spun yarn in order to allow the wool to 'felt' when fulled meant that the necessary tension that had to be applied to the warp threads in power looms often caused them to break, slowing down production and necessitating a great deal of mending to get rid of the knots; consequently it was not taken up by woollen manufacturers. Secondly, to have weavers on the mill premises would entail building and equipping a weaving shop, which required space, capital, and inclination, which many manufacturers did not have. Mr. Law Atkinson, a Huddersfield manufacturer and merchant, said when interviewed by Factory Commissioners in 1832, that provided that he could trust the honesty of the weaver, he would rather have his cloth woven in the weaver's home than in the mill. As out-workers were only paid for the actual work that they completed, and were contracted to weave one piece at a time, manufacturers could, to some degree, increase or decrease the number of weavers they employed as necessary. During the early nineteenth century, due to disruptions such as the Napoleonic wars, and the American War of Independence, there were dire shortages of orders for cloth, which was an added deterrent to manufacturers to install power looms. In 1835, the number of power looms installed in mills throughout Yorkshire totalled 3,544 of which only 688 were used for weaving woollen cloth; the other 2,856 being used for worsteds or cotton.

In the ensuing years handloom weavers found increasing difficulty in competing against power looms as these looms became both more efficient and more versatile. Manufacturers who installed power looms began to employ women weavers, who were inevitably paid less than their male colleagues, but they were not expected to carry out minor adjustments to the mechanical parts of their loom, or to single–handedly carry woven pieces, as the men were.

In order to keep working, if they were weaving a piece that could be woven more quickly on a power loom, handloom weavers had to submit to reductions in wages; or they had to resort to weaving ever more complex designs by using the 'witch', this sits atop the loom and is connected to each of the healds. A roller runs alongside the bars controlling the healds, this roller has holes drilled in it in line with the heald bars, into which pegs can be inserted that raise or lower the bars in the required order. The roller is operated by the weaver depressing a foot-pedal that moves the roller one notch at a time. These were not available for power looms at the time.

In 1828, the Weavers' Union estimated that the minimum amount to keep a man, his wife, and three children was 15s 8d per week, this included rent, food, fuel and candles, and an allowance for shoes but no clothing. Richard Oastler, who lived at Fixby Hall for a time, said that he had met men and women, who had to walk eight or nine miles to fetch their work by carrying it on their backs, and were only making between 4s 6d and 5s 2d a week clear wages.[8] It was therefore inevitable that some handloom weavers would become power loom weavers out of necessity. Most of these would be younger men probably with young families; older men would be more reluctant to give up

'Witch' ©Bradford Industrial Museum.

a trade which they had followed for many years, and which they considered to be superior to that of power loom weaver, also some mills would be reluctant to take them as they would take longer to train and would be less receptive to change.

    Woollen manufacturers in the Huddersfield area began installing power looms in their mills in the

Dobcross power loom with 4 drop boxes for shuttles. © Bradford Industrial Museum

first half of the nineteenth century; bringing a gradual migration of the population towards the bottom of the valleys and nearer to the mills. This caused the diminution of some upland communities, and coupled with the irregularity of the upland water supply, to the loss of some of the upland mills. Those that appear to have been affected in this way are the two mills at Upper House between Scholes and Hade Edge, Winney Bank Mill above Wooldale, and possibly Rake Mill at Holme.

Work towards greater versatility and full automation of the power loom continued; drop boxes at each end of the batten allowed the use of multiple shuttles and more intricate designs, and the loom would stop automatically to avoid the warp threads breaking if the shuttle failed to completely cross the batten. A device was added, in the centre of the batten, to stop the loom should the weft thread break or run out; and metal forks sitting on each of the warp threads, known as 'dollies', stopped the loom should one of the warp threads break. These innovations allowed one weaver to look after two or more looms. The introduction of the American Northrop loom into Britain in 1902, which mechanically changed the bobbin in the shuttle and re-threaded it, threatened to revolutionise the industry as it allowed one weaver to supervise up to twenty-four looms. The main disadvantage of this loom was its cost, which was three times that of its counterpart. Not many were installed in local mills.

After the Second World War several developments in weft insertion took place, by rapier, by water jet, and by air jet, all of which speeded up the weaving process, to the point where a full width piece, sixty to seventy yards in length can be woven in one day; the time taken to weave the same piece on a Dobcross or Hattersley loom in the first half of the twentieth century would probably be between three and four days.

Mechanisation had a profound effect on the way that woven cloth was treated after it came off the loom. The fulling mill was replaced by the 'scouring' or 'wet finishing' room, where a piece would be washed with soap and water to remove oil and grease deposited on it by the various machines through which it had passed; after which, if it was woollen rather than worsted and was intended for overcoats or something similar, it would be milled between rollers, which had a similar effect to the fulling stocks but was quicker. The cloth would then be dried in a Tenter.

One end of the cloth was stretched between two arms equipped with endless belts of spikes to keep the cloth taut while it was carried to the top of the arms and into the main body of the machine which was fitted with rows of steam pipes. The cloth snaked its way over, around and under the

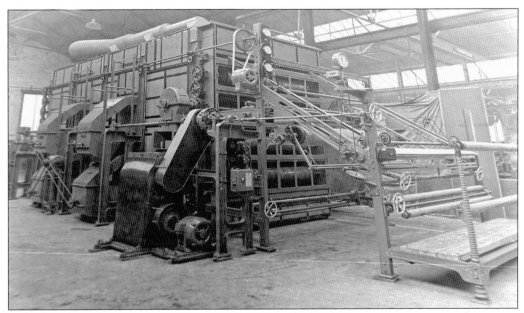

Tentering machine, made by Whiteley's of Huddersfield. Author's collection

steam pipes until it emerged at the bottom, dried. The local manufacturers of Tenters, Whiteley's of Lockwood, claimed that one machine, operated by one man and a boy, could process 2,500yds of cloth per day. With the possible exception of the Press, the Tenter was the largest and probably the most expensive machine in a mill, and always commanded a good price in a nineteenth-century auction of textile machinery.

Cropping machine c.1950s. Author's collection

Next came the dry finishing processes; if a woollen piece required a longer nap than the milling machine could produce it would be put on a gig mill, also known as a raising gig. This was the mechanisation of 'roving'; the gig consisted of a large cylindrical drum covered originally with rows of teasels, but later with rows of teeth very similar to those on carding machines. The cloth was draped fairly tightly over the drum, and the drum travelled in one direction while the cloth travelled in the other, with care being needed to ensure that the cloth was not torn. Worsted cloth was hardly if ever milled or raised as it usually required as smooth a finish as possible. The cloth was then steamed and brushed, the steam raised the nap and any loose fibres, and the brush removed any loose fluff from both the face and back of the cloth, after which it was cropped.

The first cropping frame was constructed by the Rev. James Harmer in Sheffield in 1784, by setting several pairs of hand shears in a frame and connecting them together with a crank. He made a series of adjustments and improvements to the frame; and in 1794 obtained several patents. The first cropping machine with a cylindrical blade was developed in America by Samuel Dore (or Dorr), and was also patented in England in 1794, but, for some unknown reason, was not taken up and developed. The first rotary cropping frame to be successfully used in England was patented by James Lewis of Briscombe, near Stroud, in 1815. Plans of the machine invented by Dore had been brought to England in 1811, and it is possible that Lewis had seen them; in fairness to him, Lewis never claimed that his machine was entirely his own invention. The original machine had a fairly narrow rotary blade that travelled across the cloth from selvedge to selvedge, requiring repositioning of both blade and cloth after each traverse. It was not until the blade was turned ninety degrees, and extended to cover the entire width of the piece that cropping became a continuous operation.

One of Lewis's employees saw that the same principle could be applied to mowing lawns, which until then had been trimmed with a scythe, or failing that with a goat. Having obtained permission from Lewis, he sold the idea to a maker of agricultural machinery and the rotary lawnmower came into being. The difference between the two machines being that with the lawnmower it is the machine that moves, whereas with the cropping machine it is the 'lawn'. Cropping with hand shears was a highly skilled operation; whereas cropping using a cropping frame, whichever type, was faster and could be carried out by someone who was semi-skilled, to which skilled croppers objected on two counts in the early nineteenth century. Firstly, it downgraded their profession; and secondly, it was likely to create unemployment as a semi-skilled man on a cropping frame could crop the same amount of cloth in one day as ten skilled hand croppers. Installation of gig mills and cropping frames in mills created havoc and mayhem in most textile areas throughout England.

Notes

1   Heaton pp. 340-1
2   E. Lipson, pp 145-6.
3   Baines, Cotton Manufacture, ?
4   Jenkins & Ponting, p. 28.
5   Deeds Registry, RD.DN 415:550. 1794.
6   J.G. Jenkins, pp. 90-100.
7   Kirklees Archive Service, T/H/F/36 Schedule of Loss Ledger.
8   E. Lipson, p. 188, also pp. 196-7.

Chapter 3

Revolution, Riots & Reform

The late eighteenth and early nineteenth centuries were troubled and difficult times in Britain and much of Europe. The American War of Independence (1775–1783) was followed six years later by the French Revolution (1789–1792), and in 1793 ten thousand British soldiers fought alongside Austrian troops against France in Flanders. The Napoleonic Wars (1796–1815) followed, during which time France and her allies banned all trade with Britain and closed their ports to British Shipping.[1] Poor harvests in Britain forced imports of foodstuffs and rising prices, which when coupled with restricted export opportunities for manufactured goods brought particular hardship to the working classes.

Food riots during times of shortage, often led by women, had been a feature of English life since at least the early sixteenth century.[2] During the eighteenth century weavers in Leeds had threatened strikes, and also returned unwoven weft to clothiers, in attempts to improve their rates of pay. The fear of unemployment due to the spread of machinery led to cotton workers attacking the house of James Hargreaves in 1768-9; and the premises of Richard Arkwright at Birkacre near Chorley, were attacked on October 4th 1779, when machines were destroyed, and the factory burned to the ground; at least one man was killed, with the damage being estimated to be around £4,000.[3] In both these attacks the machines that were destroyed were large ones that needed power to operate them; smaller machines suitable for hand workers were left untouched. Grimshaw's had built a factory in Manchester in 1790 and had reportedly installed some five hundred power looms made by Cartwright's. In 1792 handloom weavers burnt it to the ground; an action which was said to have inhibited the progress of power loom weaving in the area for several years to come.[4]

It was during this turbulent period that clothing manufacturers began to attempt to introduce Gig Mills to mechanically raise the nap on cloth, and also Cropping Frames which would speed up the finishing process. There were riots by croppers in Wiltshire and Somerset in 1802 against the installation of gig mills, due to fears of unemployment. The use of machines named 'gig mills' had been banned by law in the Tudor period, although as neither designs nor examples of the sixteenth century machines existed in the nineteenth century, it is not clear whether the new machines closely resembled the banned machines or not. After combining with small clothiers from Yorkshire, with whom the government had considerable sympathy, the cloth workers of Wiltshire petitioned Parliament to enforce the old statute banning gig mills. The petition failed due, at least in part, to the Government Select Committee pointing out that had the ban on machinery been enforced for even the previous fifty years the woollen textile industry would not have increased at anything like the rate at which it had.[5]

Attempts by manufacturers in Leeds to install gig mills were met with strikes, and by croppers refusing to shear cloth that had not been raised by hand. The reason for the objection to gig mills was that one man and two boys operating a gig mill could produce the same amount of raised cloth as eighteen men and six boys using wire cards or teasels to raise the cloth by hand. Again, the objections were driven by the fear of unemployment. The Leeds manufacturer and merchant

Cloth in a Teazel Raising Gig. © Leeds Ind. Museum

Benjamin Gott employed two fifteen year old boys as apprentice croppers in September 1802. The other croppers in his factory objected to this on the grounds that the two would not be fully trained when they reached their 21st birthday, and would then be expected to do a mans work on an apprentice's pay. As each cropper finished the piece he was working on, he left Gott's employment. No other croppers in the city would work on Gott's cloth, bringing production to a standstill. Mr. Gott complained about his croppers that: "Their power and influence has grown out of their high wages, which enables them to make deposits [savings], that puts them beyond all fear of inconvenience and misconduct".[6] In an attempt to replace the striking croppers an advertisement appeared in Wiltshire before the end of September:

WANTED IMMEDIATELY at LEEDS in YORKSHIRE A NUMBER OF JOURNEYMEN SHEARMEN

sober, steady, good workmen will meet with constant employ and good wages by applying to Messrs. Wormald, Gott and Wormald, at their manufactory near Leeds.

There is no evidence to suggest that any croppers from Wiltshire responded to the advertisement, and production at the factory was brought to a standstill, putting around 1,000 people out of work. The matter was put to arbitration, and the magistrates got all the employers to agree not to take on any boy as an apprentice after his fifteenth birthday, or for a period of less than seven years. Ultimately, workers benefited little from these actions due to the Government's introduction of Annual Suspending Acts from 1803 until the general repeal of legislation governing wages and working conditions in 1809. The poverty and degradation suffered by the working class during this period coupled with high food prices and scarcity of work, along with their determination to survive, fuelled their anger.

One of the earliest attacks against machinery in Yorkshire took place in 1803 in Marsden, where Shearing Frames made by Enoch Taylor and his brother, the local blacksmiths, had been installed in Ottiwells Mill owned by William Horsfall. Croppers broke into the mill, smashed the frames with a

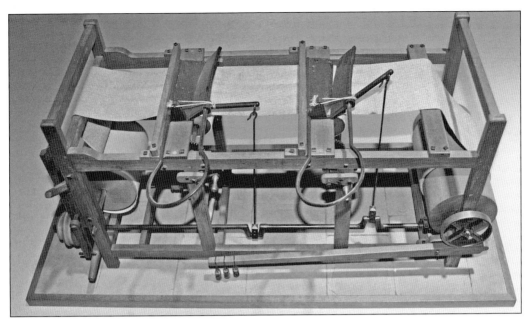

Model of an early Cropping Frame. © Kirklees Museums

large hammer and set fire to the mill. They christened the hammer Enoch, saying: "Enoch doth make 'em, and Enoch shall break 'em".

The term 'Luddite' was first applied to Frame Knitters in the East Midlands who, in 1811, reacted to a reduction in the number of knitters, coupled with a reduction in the wages of those in employment, by breaking knitting frames; around 1,000 frames were smashed between March 1811 and February 1812. The name was taken from a report in the *Nottingham Review* of 20 December 1811 about a young frame knitter from Anstey Leicestershire, named Nedd Ludd. He was averse to work and, following a complaint to a magistrate by his employer, Ludd was ordered to be thrashed. In response, Ludd took a hammer and smashed the hated frame.[7]

1812 was the year when Luddite activity in the West Riding was at its height, with attacks on cropping shops in various areas around Huddersfield taking place during February, March and April of that year. One of the largest bands of men to attack premises occurred on 9 April, when up to 300 men, some of them from Huddersfield, did extensive damage to the cropping shop and scribbling mill owned by Joseph Foster in Ossett. Two days later, on 11 April, around 100 men attacked Rawfolds mill at Cleckheaton owned by William Cartwright, but failed to gain entry to the premises as it was defended by five soldiers, plus the owner and some of his men, who were all armed. Two of the raiders were killed. Cropping machinery was being delivered to the mill, supposedly secretly, in February of that year, the loaded wagons were waylaid on Hartshead Moor and the frames smashed. Replacements had apparently been delivered in the meantime.

Enoch' Hammer.
© Colne Valley Museum

The attack on William Horsfall, which resulted in his eventual death, took place at Crosland Moor on 28 April 1812. After having his shearing frames broken in 1803 Horsfall had been very outspoken about his enthusiasm for machinery and his dislike of Croppers, and had encouraged all manufacturers to follow his example and install machinery in their mills. He said that "he was determined to fill Ottiwells Mill with machinery, even if he had to ride up to his girth straps in Luddite blood to do it" George Mellor, the leader of the group that waylaid Horsfall and shot him, was possibly looking for revenge as Horsfall had reportedly struck Mellor across the face with his riding crop while Mellor was attempting to comfort a poor woman whose infant had died from starvation.[8]

It has, in the past, been suggested that Holmfirth was a hotbed of Luddism; the reason put forward for this is that evidence was supposedly given to the magistrates by someone named Barrowclough about Luddite activity in the area, resulting in a detachment of Scots Greys searching the town for weapons on 9th July 1812, but they appear to have found little or nothing. Other evidence would suggest that rather than being a Luddite stronghold, the opposite was nearer the truth, that there were some Luddite sympathisers in Holmfirth, but not many. In May 1812, John Schofield of Netherthong, a Cropper, had met John Hinchliffe, a clothier of Upperthong whom he knew, in Upperthong Lane and had asked him if he was a 'Ludd'. Hinchliffe said that he was not, and Schofield asked him to join as they were trying to get a group

Cropper using manual cropping shears. © Kirklees Museums

together in Holmfirth similar to the one in Huddersfield and in other places, so that they could "all rise up together and overturn the government", a desire held by many working people at that time. On July 20th Schofield accused Hinchliffe of informing against him to the Holmfirth constable Mr. Blyth, which Hinchliffe denied, but he did admit to having told two men, Mr. Keeling and Mr. Charlesworth, of the conversation. Schofield was later charged with shooting at Hinchliffe in an attempt to kill him at around midnight on July 22nd, which he denied. A Reward Poster dated 27 July 1812, offered a reward of 200 guineas for information leading to the conviction of two felons, and/or a reward of 20 guineas to anyone who would apprehend John Scholefield[a] of Netherthong, and lodge him in any of His Majesty's Prisons. He had apparently absconded. It also says that John Hinchliffe sustained a wound in the attack, 'of which wound he lies in a dangerous state', and from which he lost the sight in one eye, but he appears to have recovered before the trial. In his evidence Hinchliffe said that two men armed with pistols had come to his house at Wickens and woken him, he recognised the voice of one of them as being Schofield, who, he said, had subsequently shot at him. Schofield produced several witnesses who said that they had seen him at his father's house on the evening in question, some of whom swore that they had seen Schofield and his wife in bed together between ten and midnight. Schofield was found not guilty.[9]

Riots against the installation of machinery continued into the 1820s and 1830s, but those who carried them out did not claim to be Luddites. It is fair to say that the incidents only temporarily delayed the installation of machines, and in some instances possibly hastened it. Public disorder during the early nineteenth century affected many parts of the country to the consternation of the middling sort and the upper class. An indication of the degree of fear and uncertainty that gripped

---

a   Both Sykes and Stevenson use the name Schofield, but the poster names him John Scholefield.

magistrates, politicians, and officials throughout the country at that time can be gauged by looking at the meeting held in St. Peter's Fields in Manchester on the 16th of August 1819, where a crowd numbering around 60,000 had gathered from many towns in South Lancashire to hear a particularly popular speaker, Mr. Henry Hunt, known as 'Orator' Hunt. Despite the crowd being quiet, orderly and even cheerful, with no hint of any disturbance, as soon as Mr. Hunt appeared the magistrates decided 'that the whole bore the appearance of insurrection'. The Deputy Constable of Manchester was told to execute a warrant [obviously previously prepared] for Hunt's arrest, and forty yeomen cavalry, some wielding sabres, broke into the tightly packed crowd. Hunt was arrested and removed, and, as the yeomen were now trapped in the crowd, the Hussars were called in. Panic ensued, many people were trampled and others were beaten, sabred or slashed by the troops. In less than fifteen minutes eleven people were killed, and 400 injured; all of which was unnecessary. Coming, as it did, fairly soon after Wellington's victory at Waterloo, the incident became known as the Peterloo massacre.[10]

Increase in political awareness by the working classes was a recent phenomenon, which grew stronger in the early nineteenth century due, in part, to the shenanigans of members of parliament, particularly the Tories, who were very much against any reduction of their powers or their privileged position. A piece of legislation that was particularly damaging to the poorer classes was the introduction of the first of the Corn Laws in 1815. Intended to preserve the high price paid for grain to Britain's landowners during the Napoleonic wars by excluding imports until the price of home produced wheat rose to over 80s per quarter ton; it resulted in working people having to spend the majority of their income on food, and, in consequence, contributed to the rise in popularity of potatoes.[11] It also reduced their ability to buy manufactured goods. Secondly, excluding grain imports directly affected Britain's exports by reducing the ability and inclination of foreign buyers to buy British made goods. The slump in manufacturing between 1816 and 1819 brought widespread unemployment.[12] The highest price for wheat, which was 112s per quarter ton had been reached in April/May 1812, before the imposition of the Corn Law, and coincided with the peak of Luddite activity in our area. While it cannot be considered to be a decisive factor in the unrest, it no doubt contributed to it.

The 1832 Parliamentary Reform Act increased representation of the people in most industrial towns and cities, but because prospective MPs had to fund their own campaigns, and successful MPs were given neither salaries nor expenses making a substantial private income essential; the majority of MPs still came from the landed gentry. The property requirement for anyone wishing to be added to the Voting Register remained unchanged, excluding the vast majority of the population from taking part in the election process.

In an attempt to rectify some of the perceived shortcomings of the 1832 Act, William Lovett a cabinet maker, and Francis Place a master tailor, devised the 'People's Charter' in 1838. This called for universal manhood suffrage, annual parliaments, votes by secret ballot [at that time the preferences of individual voters were printed in the newspapers], the abolition of property qualifications, equal electoral districts and payment for MPs, but was not welcomed by MP's at that time. Despite a petition urging acceptance of the Charter signed by 3.3 million people, the House of Commons refused to hear a second reading of it, effectively putting an end to it. Active support for the Chartist movement came principally from South Lancashire and West Yorkshire. A serious depression in trade coupled with high food prices made 1842 one of the most disturbed years of the century. In March, the Home Secretary said that ten percent of Britain's workers were on poor relief. Not all were actually unemployed, wages had fallen to such low levels that in order to stay alive families were forced to apply for parish relief. One factory inspector reported that workers had a choice of 'employment on any terms, or starvation'; Sykes records that the average wage of many families in Huddersfield was 'not more than a shilling per head per week'.[13] Two meetings took place in Manchester in August 1842, the National Charter Association was one, and a conference of Trades Union delegates was the other. Supporters joined forces and, in a bid to increase support marched on mills and factories drawing boiler plugs and draining dams. The march became known as the 'Plug Riots' and affected not only South Lancashire and Cheshire, but much of the West Riding. Details of the mills affected in our area will be found in the relevant chapters.

Some employers were paying their workers by 'truck', a form of payment in kind where workers were given goods; or vouchers that could be exchanged in specified shops, instead of money. The problem with this system was that employers tended to grossly over-value the goods, or under-value the vouchers, thereby short changing their workers. There is evidence that various authorities had attempted to abolish the practice since the early fifteenth century, but at times of hardship it tended to reappear.

The Corn Laws had been enacted to deliberately protect the livelihoods of landowners, with no thought for the plight of those in 'trade' or their workers, who found increasing difficulty in buying food due to continually rising prices and shrinking markets. Anti-Corn Law Associations appeared in Nottingham and Sheffield in the 1830s and spread to Manchester, Leeds, Huddersfield, Carlisle and Leicester by the early 1840s. The Anti-Corn Law League, whose headquarters was in Manchester, was established in 1839 as a national organisation intended to draw the individual associations together to form a cohesive force. A bill put forward by Charles Villiers in the same year for the abolition of the Corn Laws was rejected by the commons with only 195 votes for the motion, but almost twice that number against. 1839 also saw the third bad harvest in succession, not only in Britain, but also in Europe, therefore, even had the motion for repeal been carried there would have been no surplus European grain to import. The debate continued while the Anti-Corn Law League contested parliamentary by-elections with some success, slowly increasing support for repeal. Prime Minister Robert Peel saw the repeal as essential to his ideal of complete free trade, and also "to elevate the social condition of that class of people with whom we are brought into no direct relationship by the exercise of the elective franchise", namely the working class.

The Irish potato famine of 1845 coupled with yet another poor grain harvest, further exacerbated the plight of underfed workers increasing the necessity of repeal of the Corn Laws, which was eventually passed by the Commons in February 1846.[14] Jonathon Heap a weaver of Hepworth, who was 84 years of age in 1912, was asked about 'the old days', he said: "Before the repeal of the Corn Laws life was hard and trade was slack. After the repeal, trade began to move and changes came fast".[15]

Notes

1   F. O'Gorman pp. 236-7.
2   J. Stevenson, p. 91.
3   Fitton & Wadsworth, pp. 79-80
4   J. Stevenson, p. 118.
5   Ponting in Baines pp. 48-50.
6   K. Laybourn, p.19.
7   Hammond & Hammond p. 259.
8   K. Binfield, pp.201-3
9   J. Cowgill, pp. 81-8; D.F.E. Sykes, p. 315.
10   J. Stevenson, pp. 214-5.
11   E.P Thompson, p.348.
12   E.J. Evans, pp.227-8.
13   J. Stevenson, p. 262; D.F.E. Sykes, p. 326.
14   E.J. Evans, pp. 320-339.
15   *Holmfirth Express*, 20 July 1912.

CHAPTER 4

The Employment of Children

There was a widely held belief in England towards the end of the eighteenth century in the inborn sinfulness of humanity – original sin; and that to overcome this it was essential to inculcate habits of industry in children from an early age.[1] This attitude was to influence all levels of governance for at least the next half century. The domestic system of textile production allowed children to be introduced gradually to the world of work taking account of their age and capabilities, while mills and factories did not. The introduction of mills in the late eighteenth century heralded the beginning of the industrialisation of textiles, and consigned the domestic system to a slow lingering demise. The mechanisation of scribbling and spinning, followed by the building of mills to accommodate the machines, needed workers to operate the machinery.

There was an initial reluctance by families, who were used to working in their own homes, to take on a completely different way of life by going out to work. One way of overcoming the reluctance of local people to work in the new mills adopted by some manufacturers was to obtain numbers of Parish Apprentices from the Poor Guardians of larger cities.[2] All towns and cities had orphaned or abandoned children who, along with the infirm and destitute, were put into Workhouses, from where the authorities would attempt to place the children with tradesmen, as portrayed by Charles Dickens in *Oliver Twist*. A person from Gloucester, where the wool trade was not as buoyant as that in Yorkshire, reported to the *Annals of Agriculture* in 1791:

> A Gentleman from York passed through this city a few days ago, who gave us a new confirmation of the flourishing state of the woollen trade in that county. He says that although so many machines have been erected, yet the trade has thereby been encreased to that degree, that at this time no less than seventy additional machines are now setting up in the neighbourhood of Leeds, Bradford, and Huddersfield. One manufacturer assured this gentleman, that he was in such want of hands as to be driven to the expedient of procuring from the workhouses in London, 500 poor children to be employed in his workshops'.[3]

The need for large numbers of children by industrialists in many parts of the country must have been welcomed by those parishes that had numbers of children available; not only did it remove the burden of the upkeep of those children, but often, in addition the parish received a bounty of around 5s a head from the manufacturer. The practice of mills and factories taking children from workhouses seems to have been at its height between 1785 and 1815, although there is evidence to suggest that it continued in a reduced form until the late nineteenth century. One mill in the Huddersfield district that employed parish apprentices was Haigh's of Marsden who had some 90 apprentices in a total workforce of about 100; most of their apprentices came from the Westminster area of London. They lived at Throstle Nest in a building 'as big as a small factory', and worked at 'The Factory', a cotton mill close to Warehouse Hill. In addition to their accommodation they were also fed and clothed, but did not receive wages. Some of the apprentices died while working in Marsden, while at least 14 ran away, there is no indication that efforts were made to find the runaways and their subsequent fate is not known. The Factory closed in 1805 and the remaining apprentices, being destitute, were dependant on the local Parish; at least some appear to have stayed in the area and intermarried, as D.F.E. Sykes records: 'They bred after their kind, and it threatened to be a breed that would never become extinct'.[4] The diet that the apprentices enjoyed seems to have been very similar to that of the children of local families interviewed by Commissioners in their 1832 *Inquiry into the Employment of Children in Factories,* published in 1833, which was Porridge made with water or milk for breakfast; bread with tea or coffee, or occasionally a small amount of meat at midday; with more porridge for supper.[5] This would become very monotonous when repeated day after day.

As the number of mills grew and produced ever greater quantities of yarn of consistent quality and at a greater speed than was possible by hand, the numbers of local people who needed to work in the mills in order to survive also grew. The men who ran the machinery working as Slubbers and Spinners needed assistants to act as 'layers on' or 'piecers'; as mentioned in Chapter 2, many took their own children to work with them. Children were considered ideal for the job due to their size, their delicate and nimble fingers and their ability to crawl under some machines to retrieve fallen wool. Due to the rapidly rising population in the late 18th and early 19th centuries, 49 percent of the population were under 20, and half of those were between 5 and 14 years of age, therefore children were both plentiful and cheap.[6]

Slubbers and spinners were paid piece rates for the amount of wool processed and it was their responsibility to pay their layer-on or piecer. If the men employed their own children all the money earned stayed within the family, if not the family's income diminished. A large family increased the need for children capable of work to go out and earn money to increase the family's total income, which could, in some instances, raise their standard of living above subsistence level.

The first legislation was the Health and Morals of Apprentices Act of 1802, which applied to pauper apprentices, and had originally been intended to include all factories, but was eventually amended to apply only to Cotton mills. This Act was ineffective as it was largely ignored by all manufacturers. The first Factory Bill was introduced in 1818, one of its proposals was to reduce the working hours of children, and was again intended to apply to all factories. There were numerous objections put forward to the Bill, some maintained that the Bill was unnecessary and had been proposed due to the disappointment and commercial jealousy of its proposers; others said that the Bill was inquisitorial, interfered with free labour, with parental authority, and would affect the labour of adults because they would not be able to work without the children; and conversely, others argued that under the new law mills would employ adults who could work longer hours, leaving children unemployed. It was also suggested that due to the proposed restrictions British goods would be excluded from foreign markets as they would be less competitive; that due to shorter hours mills using water wheels would suffer greater depravation in dry periods of the year compared with those using steam; also that manufacturers would institute the changes themselves by their realisation that this would be mutually beneficial to all; and finally, that the existing system promoted industry and good order in people, whereas shorter hours would promote indolence and profligacy by giving people time to go to public houses at night and be otherwise disorderly.

The resulting Factory Act of 1819, although intended to apply to all mills and factories, was again amended to apply only to Cotton mills; it set the minimum age for the employment of children at 9 years, and restricted the hours of employment to 10 per day, plus mealtimes; and also prohibited children under 16 years old from working at night. This Act was also largely ignored by manufacturers as it contained no proposals for its enforcement. There was, by this time, growing concern throughout the country for the health and wellbeing of everyone, particularly children, who worked in the nation's mills and factories.

On reading the reports of the evidence supplied by workers to the Commissioners in 1832, there is a clear indication that some children had started work at the age of five, but the majority started at seven years old. They worked the same hours as adults, usually from 6am to 7pm although some mills worked longer, one man said he had started work around 1812 when he was nine years old, and the mill where he worked at that time started at 5am and worked until 9pm; if the mill had been stopped during the day due to the lack of water they would work one hour longer in the evening to make up the lost time. If the mill had been stopped for a number of hours the lost time would be made up by working an extra hour a day over several days; although one person giving evidence to the Commissioners claimed that one particular mill in the Huddersfield area had, on at least one occasion, made their employees work all night to make up lost time, but this was emphatically denied by other witnesses who had worked in the same mill and at the same time as the first witness. There is the possibility that people supporting the reduction of working hours encouraged children who were selected to meet the Commissioners to make the mills appear to be 'hellish institutions'.[7] There is also some suggestion that certain individual interviewees received payment to encourage them to exaggerate their evidence.

Abraham Whitehead a clothier of Scholes was interviewed by the Commission, in his evidence he said that children were never employed under five years of age, Children were on their feet all day, the only time that they had to rest was the time allowed for dinner, and they could be employed until 10pm, by which time their actions were automatic, their fingers were piecing although they had nothing in their hands. He said that a boy who worked at Smithy Place mill as a piecer had hanged himself some years earlier; he had said that he preferred to be dead rather than work so many hours in a day as he had done.[8]

The machinery would be stopped at midday to allow the workers to eat a meal; the length of time allowed for the meal varied between mills, and could be anything from thirty minutes to one hour. It was the practice in many mills that children would be delegated in turn to clean the machinery while it was stopped; these children were not allowed extra time to eat their meal. Some children who lived close to the mill went home for their midday meal; others brought their meal with them and could, if necessary, usually warm it in an oven, or by placing it on a hot steam pipe. In the majority of mills the machinery was not stopped for either Breakfast or 'Drinking' when people had to carry on working while they ate; one of the overlookers who gave evidence said that due to the increased number of spindles that each child had to look after he had seen them taking their breakfast back home at lunchtime as they had not had time to eat it.

Discipline was the responsibility of the overlooker and was invariably maintained by using a strap, one girl said that in the department in which she was employed the overlooker was her grandfather, who used the strap to discipline other children, but hit her with his hand. A 15 year old boy said that at one time he had received regular beatings on Monday mornings for not attending Sunday School. He would be held over a broad wooden beam by four men and be beaten with a 'great thick strap'; alternatively they were made to clean out the 'necessaries', or they were each fined 3d from their wages which was distributed by the employer to the Sunday Schools in the district. The boy told the commissioners that he would have happily attended Sunday school had he possessed suitable clothing.

In some mills it was not unknown for the overlooker to use a spindle from one of the machines to discipline children; particularly boys, who seem to have been dealt with more harshly than girls; one man, who was an overlooker, said that he had occasionally seen girls of 15 or 16 strapped, and on one occasion a woman of 20, although he thought that he had not strapped any girl over the age of 14. The same man said that he had sometimes seen parents of boys come to the mill and complain to either the overlooker concerned, or in some instances the employer, about excessive beating. He also said that he thought many parents did not complain about excessive beatings because they were afraid that it would encourage the overlooker concerned to find a reason to dismiss the child as quickly as possible. Interestingly, the majority of children giving evidence did not appear to feel aggrieved at having been beaten. Lateness by any employee was dealt with by deducting money from wages.

The degree of concern for the plight of people employed in mills and factories and particularly for the plight of young children gradually increased to the point where government found it necessary to legislate against some of the excessive practices of manufacturers. In 1832, the Commissioners sent a list of questions to manufacturers throughout the country asking for details of the processes which were carried out, the type and amount of power, hours of work, numbers and ages of employees, amounts paid to employees in wages, plus other questions. Nineteen manufacturers from the Holme Valley replied, all but three employed children under 10 years of age; the majority of mills worked from 6am to 8pm in Summer, but slightly less in winter, although J & G Gartside at Holmfirth Mill worked from 5am to 9pm when they had sufficient work; Joshua Robinson of Smithy Place Mills employed all his workers on piece rate paying them for work completed, he had no set hours, all his employees set their own hours of work.

Joshua Cuttell & Brothers at Cuttell Mill, Underbank, Holmfirth, justified their reason for starting one hour later in winter than in summer, i.e. 7am instead of 6am, by explaining: "because in winter, we think it a pity to call them from their warm, comfortable beds so soon"; others explained that the shorter hours were an attempt to save money on lighting the interior of the mill, and to reduce the fire risk. All the replies indicated that children were employed as piecers and layers-on; several said that children under 12 were better for that work than older children as they were faster and more enthusiastic.

One question asked the manufacturer whether they had ever employed more than one set of children to relieve each other during the day, while employing one set of adults. The reaction from the manufacturers was almost unanimous; they all replied that it would be impossible to recruit double the number of children employed as there were not sufficient children available; that parents would object to it as the wages of children would be halved, reducing the families to poverty and forcing them to apply for Parish Relief. Some manufacturers seem to have assumed that the Commissioners were implying that work made children unhealthy, J. Wrigley & Sons, Cocking Steps Mill, Honley, replied that they had not had two sets of children, and continued: 'We find the workmen and children are quite satisfied with the present plan; and think it is not more than pleasant and healthful for them. Indeed, we do not know the same number of children any where more healthy than those we have in our mill'. Joshua Robinson of Smithy Place Mill, included in his answer to the same question: 'No children are healthier on earth'. Joshua Cuttell said that working part time would unsettle the children, making them less attentive to work, which would result in machinery being adapted so that children would not be needed, reducing the family income and causing distress.

The final question asked whether the manufacturer had any observations to make on Parliament restricting the hours of labour. The general response was that an Act restricting mills and factories to working 12 hours a day would be acceptable, and some suggested that Saturday work could be restricted to 10 hours. Hinchliffe & Horncastle, Green Lane Mill, Holmfirth thought that to reduce the working hours of children 'would deprive the poor widow in numberless instances of her dependence, except parish allowance, which would take away one half of her own and her fatherless children's bread.' They also said that to reduce the working hours of children to 10 per day would destroy the existing system, as it would necessitate employing two sets of children, raising overheads beyond reach. D. Shaw & Co. Crossley and Neiley Mills Honley wrote that: 'A Bill restricting hours to less than twelve would be injurious to both manufacturers and operatives, and would be a bounty to foreign manufacturers who could operate machinery any length of time they pleased.' [9]

Despite the assurances given by manufacturers of the good health enjoyed by the children in their employ, the evidence given by Doctors to the Commissioners shows that many children suffered deformities, mostly of the legs, knees and ankles, which was attributed to the long hours that they worked standing at the machines, with no possibility of sitting down. The medical practitioner who oversaw the examinations of workers carried out in the North Eastern section of the country was Dr. Loudon; in his conclusions he said that the hours worked by children not only caused deformities, but in some cases contributed to their premature death. In his opinion, no child under fourteen should work more than 8 hours a day, and that from fourteen upwards no-one should work more than 12 hours a day, although he would prefer the maximum to be set at 10 hours. Dr. Loudon went on to suggest that every mill should have a medical practitioner appointed to oversee the health of all employees, in addition to examining every child before they were employed to ensure their suitability.[10]

In our area one of the foremost advocates of factory reform was Richard Oastler, who was Land Steward to Thomas Thornhill and lived at Fixby Hall. He and his supporters were instrumental in setting up the Short Time Committees which pressed for a ten-hour day for children and adults. They hoped that by restricting the hours of 10 to 13 year olds, a crucial part of the labour force, the reduced hours would be applied to everyone. They were convinced that reduced hours would reduce production, creating increased employment; whereas manufacturers saw it as threatening Britain's position in world markets. Lord Ashley, along with other Tory humanitarians believed that it was the duty of the ruling class to care for those who could not care for themselves, which obviously included children. Others argued, with some justification, that excessive work would damage the health of young people, reducing their working life as adults; and that their lack of opportunity for education stunted their intellectual development.

William Cobbett MP, in deploring the greed of industrialists, sarcastically suggested that Britain's wealth was due to "the labours of 300,000 little girls in Lancashire", and that should these little girls work 2 hours a day less it would allow the other nations of the world to bring an end to our industrial wealth.[11] Richard Oastler wrote to the press after attending a meeting in Leeds which was addressed by William Wilberforce the Hull MP who led the campaign for the abolition of slavery. Oastler pointed out that while he campaigned against the wrongs of adult slavery in the West Indies and elsewhere, Wilberforce was ignoring the 'slavery' of thousands of young children in the mills and factories of the north of England.[12] A meeting of Cotton Spinners, held in Manchester, on the 25-26 August 1832, was addressed by Richard Oastler and Mr. M.J. Sadler. Richard Oastler said that children working in cotton mills in England worked longer than criminals who were imprisoned and sentenced to hard labour; and longer than the slaves working in the cotton fields of the West Indies, who worked 9 hours a day; whereas Lancashire employers, who professed Christianity, thought nothing of working children for twelve hours or more a day. Mr. Sadler said that a reduction in the working hours of children was essential to give them the opportunity to acquire 'useful and pious knowledge', and to destroy the system that tended to destroy the limbs of its unhappy victims who were doomed to premature old age. He agreed wholeheartedly that it was necessary to eradicate slavery anywhere in the world, but charity began at home, and it was necessary to end the slavery of children in our mills and factories.[13] There is a bitter irony in the contrast of the conviction held by many manufacturers that slavery in the West Indies and the Americas should be abolished, and their apparent disregard for the health and wellbeing of the young children employed in their own mills.

The Factory Bill of 1832 was introduced in the House of Commons by M.J. Sadler; the major proposal at that time was that the working day for all employees should be reduced to 10 hours. This motion was lost in a vote in June 1833, but an amended motion restricting the hours worked by children aged 9 to 13 years to 8 per day, and the hours worked by older children up to 18 years to be not more than 9 per day was passed. Other requirements of the Act were: 1½ hours per day to be allowed for meals, this was additional to the hours of work, making a total of up to 10½ hours for older children; no child under the age of 9 to be employed; children working less than 8 hours a day in one mill could not then work in another; all working children must have been examined by a Surgeon who would supply a certificate as to the child's strength and appearance; Inspectors were to be appointed; children working in factories must attend school for 2 hours each working day, employers could deduct up to 1d per shilling of wages to pay school fees; interior walls and ceilings of mills to be lime-washed yearly; time lost due to lack or excess of water could be made up in one hour segments to a maximum of three hours per week. Mill owners were liable to penalties if children stayed on mill premises longer than 9 hours, presumably plus mealtimes; parents were liable to a fine of 20s if their children worked longer than the legal limit. Four Factory Inspectors were appointed to cover the country; the sub-inspector for our part of the North of England was Mr. James Bates of Winney Bank, Wooldale.

The clause restricting children to a maximum of 9 hours on mill premises could potentially cause problems as not all departments started and finished work at the same time, and some children who had worked their full time were in the habit of waiting until their brother or sister finished work, perhaps one hour later, so that they could walk home together; thereby contravening the 9 hour rule. An illustration of this is given in the evidence given to the Enquiry; one boy who worked from 6am to 7pm as a piecer, then waited for his younger sister, who worked in the Roving room and did not finish until 8pm, to walk her home.

The education of children was also a potentially contentious issue. The Sunday School system was well established, which gave children a basis on which to build by teaching them to read and, in some areas, to write as well. Rather than allow children to attend a local school, some manufacturers employing a good number of children fulfilled the education requirement of the Act by setting aside one room in the mill to act as the schoolroom, and appointing someone to be the teacher. Some of those appointed were not particularly well educated, and had no training in, or little concept of, imparting knowledge to others. This shortcoming was addressed in the Act of 1844, which gave Factory Inspectors the power to terminate the contract of any teacher whom the Inspector found to be unfit due to ignorance.

The Factory Bill of 1843 was particularly concerned with education and attempted to address some of the perceived shortcomings of previous Acts. One of the suggestions, which caused a considerable protest from both MPs and others, was that every school where 'factory children' were being educated should be under the jurisdiction of the local Church of England clergyman, who was to be chairman of the school governors in addition to being responsible for religious education, which all the children would receive on Sundays by attending the day-school for three hours. This was seen by many as Parliament handing over the education of the nation to the Church of England, as only schools fulfilling both the temporal and religious requirements of the Act would be able to issue the certificates of attendance that every child worker had to hand over to his or her employer every Monday morning before starting work. Had the clause been included in the Act it would have closed a large number of schools which were already well established and delivering a good standard of education to their pupils. It would also have had a deleterious effect on any Sunday school that was not under the jurisdiction of the Anglican Church.

The ensuing Act of 1844 makes no mention of those suggestions indicating that the protests were successful, but there were several changes; the age from which children could be employed to work in mills and factories was reduced from 9 to 8 years, and the Act sets out two alternative work schedules for children under the age of 13. The first gives a working time of 6½ hours plus 3 hours of lessons per day, while the second sets out three 10 hour days of work on alternate days, interspersed with three 5 hour days of lessons. The reason put forward for reducing the age at which a child could start work was that it would at least partly compensate poorer families for the loss of income brought about by children attending school.

Children working and attending school each day worked mornings and attended school in the afternoon for a month, followed by school in the morning and work in the afternoon in the second month, alternating *ad infinitum*. Manufacturers gradually realised that there were benefits for both workers and employers from children attending school and becoming literate and numerate. Other regulations included in the Act were that drive wheels and mechanisms including belts that transmitted the power from the drive shafts to the machines should be fenced to avoid injury, and also included penalties for employers who failed to comply of fines from £5 to £20. On reading the information that I have accumulated on the development of the various mills in Holme Valley given in succeeding chapters, it will be seen that there were a number of mills that initially did not take adequate safety precautions. The Act of 1844 only applied to Textile factories, as time progressed the regulations were extended to include other trades such as pottery, hosiery, match making and some metal working.

It was not until 1867 on the introduction of the Workshops Regulations Act that businesses in all the above trades with less than 50 employees, came under the regulations; after which many small employers reduced the number of children under the age of thirteen working for them, forcing those children to find work in agriculture, brick making, domestic service or street trading, all of which were unregulated. The firms then employed boys and girls over 13 or women instead, which would increase the wages bill slightly. By the 1870s attitudes of authorities to part time employment plus education were beginning to change. It was realised that part time working was primarily a means of perpetuating juvenile labour, whereas the emphasis should be on providing children with an adequate education.

The enquiry undertaken prior to the 1874 Act pointed out that children receiving a part time education while working needed to have been given a preliminary education previously, in order to be able to keep up with children in full time education. The Act also made provision for children who were judged to be inadequately educated at the age of thirteen to continue part time education for a further year. The minimum age of employment in textile mills rose to 10 years in 1874, and was introduced into factories in other trades some 4 years later. In the late eighteenth and early nineteenth centuries childhood had been regarded as a time of preparation for the world of work; towards the end of the nineteenth century some people had realised that childhood up to the age of thirteen, was a period in life with its own dynamics and culture; and that education was a prime necessity.[14]

Despite this, part time work for children under thirteen continued as the Huddersfield Bye-laws of 1913, based on the 1903 Employment of Children Act, show.[15] They state that no child under the age of twelve shall be employed, (which was a further improvement on the 1874 Act); that children attending school must not work more than 20 hours a week during school terms; that children not at school could not work more than 9½ hours a day excluding meals, (which made their working week around 52 to 54 hours); and that children must not work between 8pm and 7am.

The wording of the 1913 bye-laws indicates that not all children continued in education until their thirteenth birthday. Those children considered by their Head Teacher to have attained a sufficiently high standard of education at their twelfth birthday could, on production of the appropriate certificate, get a job and work full time. The practice of part time work for children under thirteen continued until at least 1918. Another contentious issue that gained momentum during the eighteenth and nineteenth centuries was that of workers rights.

Notes

1   P. Horn, p. 1.
2   E.P. Thompson, p.369.
3   Hammond & Hammond, p.150.
4   J. Thorpe, Marsden Children, pp. 10-15; D.F.E. Sykes, History of the Colne Valley; p.173.
5   Some information on Parish Apprentices is taken from a talk by Prof. Katrina Honeyman of Leeds University entitled Off the Parish given at Huddersfield University on 17 March, 2010.
6   E.J. Evans, p. 157.
7   C. Nardinelli, quoted in P. Horn, p. 17.
8   Factory Inquiry Commission, First Report on Information on the Employment of Children in Factories; (printed 28 June 1833).
9   Factory Inquiry Commission, Supplementary Report into the Employment of Children in Factories and as to the Propriety and Means of Curtailing the Hours of their Labour, Part 1. (25 March, 1834).
10 Factory Inquiry Commission, Second Report into the Employment of Children in Factories and as to the Propriety and Means of Curtailing the Hours of their Labour; (15 July, 1833).
11 P. Horn, pp36-38.
12 Leeds Mercury, 16 Oct. 1830.
13 Ibid, 1 Sept. 1832.
14 P. Horn, p.69. Also, Information on the employment of children can be found in the Minutes of Evidence from various Select Committees of Enquiry into Factory conditions, and copies of the Acts that followed, available from the National Archives in Kew; plus A.J. Brooke's unpublished thesis, The Social and Political Response to Industrialisation in the Huddersfield Area 1790-1850; (1988). A copy of which is available for perusal in the Local Studies section of Huddersfield Library.
15 A copy of these Bye-laws is held in the University of Huddersfield's Archive.

CHAPTER 5

Trade Unions, Disputes and Wages

Organisations intent on safeguarding the rights of workers were being formed by the early eighteenth century. In order to conceal their true identity they took the form of Friendly Societies to which members paid contributions of 2d a week, and from which they would receive around 6s per week if they succumbed to illness. Some of the names on the Union Ancestors website indicate the concealment: Huddersfield and District Cloth Pressers Benevolent and Burial Society; or the Healders and Twisters Trade and Friendly Society; both of these were trade unions in addition to their other activities.[1] Members inevitably discussed any grievances that they had, some of which were taken up by the society on their members' behalf. Disagreement between the societies and the employers sometimes led to violence eventually resulting, in 1726, in an Act of Parliament forbidding combinations of workers on pain of imprisonment. The Act did not however preclude employers from combining to determine rates of pay, which they continued to do.

A succession of Acts forbidding combinations failed to achieve their objective; the Act of 1799 prohibited both employers and employees from combinations, which was followed by another Act in 1800. By the end of the Eighteenth Century there were more than 40 Acts of Parliament intended to stop workmen from combining; despite this, in the early nineteenth century it was discovered that cloth workers in the West of England and the West Riding of Yorkshire had formed union branches which issued membership tickets common to all, allowing members to move freely between branches in order to find work. This co-operation was no doubt instrumental in bringing about Benjamin Gott's failure to obtain replacement croppers when his own walked out in September 1802; see Chapter 3.

Government and employers were aware that despite legislation trade unions existed, and that attempts to ban them were futile, which was arguably one of the factors that led to the repeal of the Combination Acts in 1824. It can also be argued that the workers' struggle for recognition contributed strongly towards their politicisation.[2] The repeal of the Combination Acts can be seen as either Government's acceptance that workers needed a combined voice in order to overcome their subjugation by employers; or that attempts to prohibit combinations had totally failed, and should be abandoned.

The repeal of the Acts did not initially alter the attitude of manufacturers towards Trade Unions; some employers coerced workers, particularly during periods when trade was sparse, to renounce their union membership or face dismissal. One of the practices that early weavers' unions attempted to eliminate was the use by manufacturers of the 'long measure'. The weaver would measure the piece of cloth when he took it from the loom, and the manufacturer would measure it again when it arrived at the mill. There was invariably a discrepancy, with the manufacturer's length being shortest; which was the length used to calculate how much the weaver should be paid. In an attempt to overcome some of the disagreements a meeting between manufacturers and weavers was held in 1826. William Norton of Clayton West who was said to employ 300 weavers, claimed that "there is no such thing as a yard; we have forty inches composed of thirty-seven inches and a thumb". Many other manufacturers were using similar methods of calculation.

Manufacturers were also known, particularly during difficult trading, to reduce the price per yard for weaving a piece while it was actually on the loom. The length of time taken to weave a piece of cloth on a handloom would probably be between one and two weeks; one weaver complained that although he had initially agreed to weave a piece at 5d a yard, while it was being woven the manufacturer had reduced the price in 3 stages to 3d a yard; a reduction of 40 percent.[3] There was little that the weaver could do at that time but accept the situation.

A Government Select Committee set up in the 1830s to examine the problems faced by Handloom Weavers points out that the belief that although weavers' wages had dropped between 1797 and 1834, they were not really worse off as the price of food and other commodities had also dropped, was actually a fallacy. They give figures for 1797 when a weaver's average wage was 26s 8d per week, which would buy 238 lbs of food; by 1832 the weaver's average wage was 5s 6d, which would buy only 83 lbs of food. Property rents had also increased during the period, to illustrate this the committee wrote that in 1797 a weaver would need to weave 7 pieces in order to pay his rent for the year, by 1832 that figure had increased to 25.[4]

After 1824, Trade Unions became more overt, but were not necessarily more successful. Unions would bring their members out on strike, but often the result was that workers eventually returned to work either at the original rates of pay or less, depending on the degree of desperation that their plight had reached. During a strike employer's tended to bring in fresh workers to replace the strikers in order to keep the factory running. Even when the union managed to stop this the outcome was the same, no increase in wages. In cases where fresh workers had been employed there is evidence to show that wage reductions followed the return to work of the original employees due to the amount of surplus labour available, which defeated the object of calling the strike.[5]

Richard Oastler wrote in favour of trade unions in 1834, he pointed out that employers were blaming unions for their difficulties, whereas it was the need for workers to protect themselves against the stringencies imposed by the employers that had led to the unions being formed. He condemned attempts by employers to coerce workers to sign agreements not to 'combine' by joining a trade union; arguing that it was the employers who were acting illegally by combining against their workers. Another point about which Oastler was convinced was the need for workers to all be paid a realistic wage; he pointed out that manufacturers could not expect to sell their products if the country's working population could not afford to buy them.[6]

Workers in the Holmfirth area were joining Trade Unions in the late 1820s and 1830s, much against the wishes of the manufacturers. Peter and Isaac Beardsell record some events, from their point of view, in 1832. Peter gives the first indication of an impending struggle by his entry of Monday June 11, 'Hinchliffe's of New Fold have notice to advance the wages of their workpeople or else a strike is anticipated'. On Wednesday June 20th he wrote 'Harpins Mill [Bottoms Mill] people turned out this morning because they set on a Slubber to work that was not in the Union'.

The major conflict was, as ever, between the manufacturers and the weavers, however, the eventual resolution included, at least initially, all millworkers. The accepted standard weight of wool used in one piece of cloth was 48lbs, for which each worker received an agreed amount depending on their part in the process. Much of the work at that time was done on a commission basis, where a manufacturer would supply a quantity of raw wool to be made into yarn. Some manufacturers instead of giving 48lbs of wool, were giving up to 58 or 60lbs. of wool for a piece, but were only paying the 48lb. rate, this practice was continued when the yarn was given to the weaver; which was virtually a repetition of how clothiers had gradually extended the length of Kerseys in an attempt to reduce the amount of Ulnage. (See Chapter 1). Isaac Beardsell wrote that the manufacturers agreed that they would pay by the weight of wool used, but that they would not employ Union members.

Peter gives a more detailed account in his diary, he wrote on Wednesday July 4th 'I have been at a meeting of the Manufacturers about weights. Nothing done worth noting. People seem very backward in giving their opinion on the subject unless they are compelled to do'. This is followed one week later on July 11th by 'There has been a meeting of the Association at Boothroyd's and a very strong resolution was passed, that is, that all men which are in the employ of any member of this Association [if they were Union members] shall be turned off on Saturday night except they promise to retract from the Union. I should expect it will be put into force'. On Friday 13th, 'It is now generally known that there will be a turn out of their men throughout the neighbourhood of Holmfirth'. Followed on Saturday by 'There is a general turn out. As soon as the workmen knew that they must not stop at their work if they were in the Union. It was a complete turnout at Holmfirth and there has been a meeting held of the Union. It is reported there will be soldiers in Holmfirth before Tuesday night'. Peter wrote on Monday 16th: 'Joseph has been over at Mill to turn off John Charlesworth from his work because he is in the Union, and a sad differ Jos. and him have had.' Peter's account continues: 'Such turning out as never was seen in this dale before nor do I wish to see such again....By far the largest part of the workmen are turned off to go and get their livelihood from their new Master, John Powlett', who was the Secretary of the Operatives' Union. 'Our Finishers in Holme Banks have left their work and I think we have about 12 makers in [the union] or may be more. There has been a Committee Meeting of the Masters tonight and they have received a letter from the Union Committee wishing to come to reconciliation for the public good. There will be another meeting on Wednesday and then we shall know more about it.'

Wednesday July 18th: 'All the talk in this Country is the Union. There has been another meeting of the Manufacturers and a deputation from the Union Committee has been to meet them. No terms of reconciliation can be come to.' Peter records that at least two manufacturers agreed terms with their workers and returned to work in early August, but, apart from those two, no other mills returned to work. Isaac suggests that a gradual return took place in late January or early February 1833, but Peter's only comment in that year was made on February 7th, when he wrote 'The Holmfirth concern is not yet settled, I mean the Union business'. Were the majority of the mills in the Holmfirth district closed for seven months, or were they working at a reduced rate by employing non-union labour? The eventual return to work must have been gradual as there was no indication in the press that it had taken place, which probably indicates that neither workers nor manufacturers gained by the dispute. The Unions, at that time, used the term 'Black Sheep' for workers who accepted employment when union members were on strike, which was eventually amended to 'Blackleg'.

Power loom weavers were again dissatisfied with their rates of pay in 1872, they held a meeting at the Waggon & Horses Inn, Norridge Bottom Holmfirth, in June 1872 to work out new rates that were acceptable to them, which they forwarded to manufacturers on June 17th. As the manufacturers had not replied the weavers held a mass open-air meeting at Cinder Hills on 24 June attended by around 1,000 weavers from 37 firms. It was decided that weavers who had unfinished warps in their looms should return and finish them before going on strike. While they were working men were asked to contribute 6d per day and women 3d towards the maintenance of those already on strike. They should not, under any circumstances, start a new warp unless the manufacturer had agreed to pay the new rates. Other demands to manufacturers were that all pieces should be woven to a standard length; that pick measures should be one standard inch; and that pieces should be measured correctly. Bills were to be posted throughout the district asking power-loom weavers not to work at mills where weavers were already on strike; and manufacturers were to be asked to advance wages to enable strikers to pay their house rent and buy coal and other necessities. Although this dispute began by weavers walking out and asking for higher pay it effectively became a lockout, which Ben Turner [Alderman and MP] maintained was due to the failure of Holmfirth manufacturers to realise that consumer demand was moving away from woollens and towards worsteds. Huddersfield manufacturers had already begun to produce worsted cloths, and Turner writes that during the dispute many weavers left Holmfirth to find work in Huddersfield, Dewsbury, Batley and Leeds. The dispute continued through July, August and into September; during that time a couple of manufacturers had come to an agreement with their weavers and resumed work, but the majority of weavers remained inactive. A meeting between employers and weavers took place in early September at Joseph Mellor & Sons, Thongsbridge, where rates that proved acceptable to all were agreed and the weavers returned to work on Thursday September12th.[7]

Bills were posted in Holmfirth by manufacturers in mid April 1878, giving notice of wage reductions from May 1st. Some employers had agreed to continue paying the old rates until a new agreement could be reached, but many began paying the reduced rates after 1st May causing weavers to stop work when they downed their current piece. Some employers closed their mills from June 1st, by which time at least 50 weavers had found work in Huddersfield. On 8 June eleven mills were closed, they were J. Barber & Sons Holmbridge; George Charlesworth Hinchliffe Mill; H. Bower & Son Lower Mill; J.T. Taylor & Co. Ribbleden Mill; Lockwood Bros. Lee Mill; Ed. Hirst & Son Wildspur Mill; Chas. Lockwood & Sons New Mill mill; Booth, Pitt & Co. Sude Hill mill; plus one in Shepley and two in Birdsedge. In several other mills weavers were in the process of leaving as they finished their warps; it was estimated that 300 weavers were now idle, plus many other workers who were locked out of the closed mills. The dispute continued into July, by which time individual employers were reaching agreements with their workers and resuming work. On the 27th of July, at which time the dispute had been running 12 weeks, all but five firms had reached agreement and resumed work. Presumably these five companies resolved their problems quickly, as no further reports appeared.[8]

The difficulty in reaching an agreement that would be acceptable to all manufacturers and workers in an area is demonstrated in the report of a meeting of employers and union representatives held at the George Hotel Huddersfield in March 1883, during a strike affecting some 2,000 weavers in the Huddersfield area. Mr. Alfred Sykes, an employer, [possibly from Rock Mill, Brockholes] gave some examples of the amounts weavers working in different mills would earn by weaving a particular piece. A weaver working on a slow loom at Martin's Mill in Lindley would earn 5s 3d in a week; whereas a weaver weaving the same piece on the much faster looms installed at Middlemost's Mill in Birkby would earn six times that amount, which was 31s 6d. Weavers in other mills weaving the same quality of cloth but on different looms would earn amounts between those two extremes.[9] Writing on trade unions, T. S. Cree maintained that their function was to improve the pay and working conditions of members by arbitrating between the workers and their employers; however, at that time, unions had no means of calculating the correct rate of pay for any job, their strategy was to argue that whatever the current rate of pay, it should be higher. He also pointed out that the rate of pay for any job would fluctuate according to the demand, or lack of it, for the end product.[10]

Unions grew in size in two ways, firstly by holding recruiting meetings, and secondly by amalgamating with other unions in the same or allied trades. The West Riding of Yorkshire Power Loom Weavers Association, which had a branch in Huddersfield, held their first meeting in Honley on 28 November 1889, the President Mr. J.W. Downing, told the assembly that they had received numerous requests from weavers in Holme Valley to start a branch in the valley, but the meeting appears to have been the result of a letter sent by a weaver to the Yorkshire Factory Times, asking why the Association held meetings all over the West Riding, but, despite numerous requests from potential members, never came to Holme Valley. The result of the meeting was that: 'A goodly number joined the Association'. The Association also held a meeting in Holmfirth a few days later on 4th December, when it was reported that 40 men joined the Association.

One of the speakers, Mr. W.H. Greasley, suggested that the number of married women weavers in the district were a 'great drawback'. He had no objection to widows or women whose husbands were unable to work going out to work, but he would boycott the employment of wives whose husbands were in a good trade; the oft-quoted reason for this attitude was that married women were more interested in the wellbeing of their family than work, and were consequently reluctant to support the union. This was a recurring theme by textile trade union officials until the mid twentieth century; the numbers of women workers being frequently given to explain why men's wages could not be improved.

The union reported at a meeting on 14 March 1890 that membership in Holmfirth had risen to 214; however, at a meeting on 21 January 1894 in Holmfirth Town Hall, the chairman Mr. Downing said that membership of the union had dropped considerably. This was probably due to a lack of work, as the speakers went on to criticise weavers in some areas for agreeing to work for what were described as 'women's rates', rather than combining together to stand up to the employers. It was again suggested that the problem was due to the numbers of married women who were working as weavers.

Despite continual attempts by trade unions to enrol new members, the various textile unions throughout the district never seem to have attained the position where a majority of the textile workers were members of a union, which limited their effectiveness when negotiating with employers. Union delegates from mills met with the officials of the General Union of Weavers and Textile Workers in October 1906 to discuss wage rates being paid to weavers of 100 pick looms. Throughout the district the rates varied between 7½ and 17½ percent lower than the rates being paid for weaving slower looms. The union officials were unable to offer a collective plan, and urged the delegates to go back to their mills and negotiate individually with their employers.

Union activity was not restricted to negotiations on wage and employment conditions; it sometimes embraced a lighter side. The National Society of Dyers and Finishers held what was described as a 'demonstration' in Holmfirth town centre on the afternoon of 10 October 1908, followed by a Tea in the Socialist's Hall at a cost of 6d a ticket; after which the assembled company enjoyed a 'Grand Social and Jovial Evening'. The intention of the organisers was to increase the membership of the Society.

A meeting of delegates of all Willyers and Fettlers in the Huddersfield area was held at the Friendly & Trades Club, Northumberland Street, Huddersfield, in early June 1910, when there were 511 votes for strike action, with only 25 against. One manufacturer estimated that a strike would affect a total of 15,000 workers in the area. Union representatives met with manufacturers on 13 June, and after 7 hours of negotiation an agreement was reached. A meeting of workers voted to accept the new agreement, which still meant them working a 58 hour week, but they would receive overtime rates after working for 55½ hours taking their wages from £1 4s 2d, to £1 6s 9½d per week.

Also in 1910 the General Union of Weavers and Textile Workers began a series of meetings between Manufacturers Associations and their union members, in an attempt to raise wage rates across the industry. It was not until November 1913 that union members voted to accept the terms offered by manufacturers, rather than strike. The rate of pay for Dyers Labourers rose to 6¼d per hour, giving them a weekly wage of £1 9s 6d. Scourers, Willyers, Fettlers, Rag packers, Tag shakers and Carbonisers, 6d an hour or £1 7s 6d a week. Firemen, Greasers and under-engine men, an increase of 1s per week, to a maximum wage of 27s per week, Weft men currently receiving 24s per week or less to receive 1s per week increase. Weavers' wages were to be negotiated by union representatives and management of each mill, but to be in excess of rates set for women in 1888, with a percentage addition for men similar to that already in existence. No-one was to receive less than their present earnings. The agreement was dated 5 November, 1913.

One year later the disruption of world trade created by the Great War considerably increased the cost of living. To counteract this, a system of war bonuses was agreed between the General Union of Weavers and Textile Workers and the Employers Association to be paid to all workers for the duration of war and for 3 months after it ended.

In 1919 there was a mood in the country that it was time to shed the restrictions of war and get back to the prosperity of pre-1914; coupled with the conviction that the world was hungry for British produced goods. One of the first decisions was that Britain would relinquish the gold standard, for 6 years, at least initially. Sterling had been fixed at a rate of $4.86 to the pound; after leaving the gold standard the pound dropped to $3.50 increasing the cost of imports, but reducing the price of British goods abroad. This action also led to a rapid increase in prices, so rapid that prices rose at double that of the war years; this was followed by an equally rapid increase in wages.[11] Post-war business had initially increased in many industries including textiles but the 'boom' was short-lived, and unemployment ensued. The root cause of the unemployment problem dates back to before the First World War, when Britain's old establish industries of textiles, iron and steel, engineering and shipbuilding were facing heavy competition from France, Germany and the United States.[12] The war forced our industry to concentrate on production for the home market and the armed forces; the neglect of export markets during that time exacerbated the problem as consuming countries had sought other suppliers, and in some instances had begun manufacturing industries of their own.

This lack of demand rapidly led to growing unemployment. The gravity of the situation is evident from the decision of the GUWTW, in March 1921, to reduce the length of time members would receive unemployment pay in a twelve month period from 8 weeks to 2 weeks. The reason given for this decision was 'the slump in trade from August 1920'. Unemployment pay had been introduced in 1914 to help workers who were unavoidably 'playing for materials' due to the war. The downturn in trade from August 1920, coupled with unemployment of textile workers due to strikes by Miners and Railway workers, had resulted in the union paying out many thousands of pounds in benefits during the year, which they could no longer afford to do.

An indication of the amount by which wages had increased between 1913 and 1921 is given in the announcement by the National Wool Textile Industrial Council, consisting of representatives of Manufacturers and Workers, on 12 May 1921, that the weekly wage for adult males including scourers, millers, weavers, dyers and finishers, employed on a time basis should be reduced from 78s 1½d, to 60s 5d. Female time workers should be reduced from 45s 11½d, to 35s 7d, a drop of some 22.5 per cent in both cases. Male piece rate workers would lose between 18s and 20s per week, and females from 10s 6d to 12s per week. In April 1922 the Board of Trade announced a 'Drop in the Cost of Living', the average of retail prices on April 1st, including food, rent, clothing, fuel, lighting etc. was 82 percent above the July 1914 figure; compared with 86 percent on March 1st, and 133 percent on 1st April 1921; that figure for April 1922 was the lowest since October 1917. At a meeting in Bradford in July 1924, the National Wool and Allied Industries Council agreed to continue paying wages at 72½ percent above the 1914 cost of living rate for another year. Although wages had increased considerably in the previous decade, there is little indication that, due to the increased cost of living, even those who managed to find work and feed their families were materially better off.

Since leaving the gold standard in 1919 there had been an increasing belief amongst politicians, financiers and manufacturers that to return to it would solve many of the country's problems; this view was also expressed by the Cunliffe Committee on Currency and Foreign Exchanges after the War. The pound had steadily increased in value against foreign currencies since 1919, giving Winston Churchill, the Chancellor of the Exchequer, the opportunity to announce in his budget speech in April 1925 that Britain was returning to the gold standard, he said that "no responsible authority had advocated any other system"; and that "all members of the gold standard would rise and fall together". This would have been the case had all countries traded on equal terms, but Britain re-entered not at $4.30 to the pound, the rate at which the pound was then trading, but at the original rate of $4.86; making imports cheap, but considerably over valuing exports. The intention was to reduce exports and encourage imports, creating a balance of payments deficit, which would be redressed by Britain paying in gold and bullion, this would have the effect of forcing down domestic prices, which would make British goods more competitive and raise exports, which foreign buyers would pay for in gold. The gold standard was seen as being a self regulating mechanism; put simply, the policy failed.[13] Had the government set the rate of exchange at $4.30 to the pound it may have been more successful.

1925 was a difficult year for employers and workers, there was talk of wage reductions in the early part of the year; in June the National Union of Textile Workers announced that membership was at its lowest figure since 1912, having fallen by almost 90,000 during the previous year to 830,300; the reduction was probably due to workers leaving textiles and moving to other industries, in addition to those leaving the union due to disaffection. Wage reductions which would come into force in July would affect 200,000 textile workers in West Yorkshire, where some 135,000 workers were already on strike.[14] In early August the press reported that Holmfirth's streets were thronged with unemployed textile workers, due to a number of mills being closed owing to strike action against the reduction in wages. After intense negotiation many mills resumed work on Monday 17 August, to await the deliberations of a Court of Investigation that was to be set up. The Court began its investigation, but on September 26th it announced that it would adjourn for three weeks; mills continued to work, and no further announcements appeared in the Holmfirth Express. At the Annual Meeting of the National Union of Textile Workers in January 1926, it was announced that 'there had been no justification for the employers to reduce wages, which had been proved by an impartial tribunal'; this presumably refers to the dispute of the previous year. 1926 was the year of the National Strike, which took place over nine days in May, although the textile industry was not directly involved. The failure of the strike to resolve the original dispute between the miners and their employers obviously affected supplies of coal to all mills and factories, reducing output.

Employers, mainly in the Leeds and Bradford districts, were again proposing wage reductions of 8.3 percent in October 1929. A ballot of workers showed that 79.67 percent were against the reductions, resulting in a strike that was expected to affect up to 200,000 workers. The Government set up an inquiry, chaired by Lord Macmillan, to look into the problem in January 1930, which reported in March that textile workers wages should be reduced by 9.249 percent for time workers, a reduction of 1s 10½d in the pound; and 8.776 percent for piece workers, equal to 1s 9d in the pound. The inquiry considered that the wool textile industry was in a grave position, and that the reductions were imperative if the industry was to survive. The effect of this announcement on workers in the local textile industry was to bring them out on strike. It was reported on Saturday 12 April that 'Thousands of workers in the West Riding came out on strike on Thursday, and thousands more ceased work yesterday evening.[15] Three courses of action had been adopted in Holme Valley: (1) in some mills workpeople were continuing to work at the old rates; (2) in other mills work was continuing at the reduced rates; (3) alternatively, the mills had closed. It was also reported that some workers wanted to return to work, but could not due to the absence of others. While the strike was in progress, W.H. & J. Barber of Holmbridge Mill, advertised for weavers and a tuner at Macmillan rates; Graham & Pott also advertised that they were recommencing work on May 5th at 9am, and needed winders, warpers, healders, twisters and weavers, pay would be as the Macmillan award, 'old employees may apply'.

In early May the Union view was reported as 'More unions were becoming involved, engine-men, firemen, transport workers, engineers and dyers have decided to support the strikers'; whereas the Employers view was that 'More workers were returning to work'.[16] The dispute continued throughout April and May, which was having a devastating effect on Union finances. It was reported on 31 May that strike pay during weeks 7 and 8 had been 12s for men, 8s for women, and 6s for juveniles; however, from the beginning of the ninth week it would be lowered to 6d per day for men, 5d a day for women and 3d a day for juveniles. The unions had announced on May 30th that they were prepared to accept a phasing in of the Macmillan Award over a period of nine months; the reaction of the employers was that it was 'all or nothing'.

Individual unions began negotiating with employers in early June, it was reported that agreements of reductions greater than 5.8 percent, but less than the full amount of 9.24 percent suggested by Macmillan, would be acceptable to unions. Workers began their return on Wednesday June 11th, mainly for wages reduced by the full amount recommended by Macmillan. The dispute was effectively over, the workers had lost. As if to add insult to injury, those people involved in the strike were told by Government in September that they would not be credited with the cost of unpaid National Insurance contributions as they could not prove that they had been available for work but unable to do so, due to the strike. This could eventually have an adverse effect on their pensions.

Despite all the amalgamations that had taken place between the various trade unions, there were still around 40 different unions in the wool textile trade in October 1930, when Ben Turner urged them to amalgamate in order to increase their effectiveness. Had they done so and become one National Textile Union with a louder voice, it is debateable whether they would have achieved more for their members, or whether, due to militancy, they would have brought about the industry's demise at an even earlier date.

Trade was difficult in the early 1930s due to the aftermath of the Wall Street Crash, which induced a worldwide recession. This is particularly apparent from the lack of advertisements in the Situations Vacant columns of the local papers at that time, and also from the way manufacturers who were members of the Huddersfield Woollen and Worsted Federation were urging Local Authorities to review the wage rates of their employees. They pointed out that many unskilled labourers working for local Councils were earning higher wages than skilled men working in the local mills and factories, the implication being that the manufacturers were worried about losing skilled workers who may apply for jobs as unskilled labourers purely to increase their income.

In April 1933 the number of unemployed in the country was 2,776,184 which amounted to 29.5 percent of the insured workforce.[17] In an attempt to find gainful employment for at least some of that number the Government brought in various job creation schemes throughout the country. I believe that one such scheme in our area was the building of the Penistone by-pass road from Scout Dike to Thurgoland. There was a slow recovery in trade through the 1930s with the numbers of unemployed gradually reducing, although the occurrence of advertisements for workers in the Situations Vacant columns remained low. One explanation for this is that many who were out of work would stand at the mill gates in the hope that should a vacancy arise in their field of expertise they would be employed.

Wages became linked to the cost of living index, the National Association of Textile Trade Unions wrote to the Wool and Allied Textile Employers Council asking for wage increases in all trades due to increased turnover in July 1939; the employers replied in September saying that they would consider an increase when the index reached 60, it was then at 55. The index presumably reached 60 by November 1939, as wages for time workers were to be increased by 11.4 percent for men, taking their wage from £2 8s 4d to £2 14s 1d per week, and women's wages from £1 8s 5d to £1 11s 9d per week. Piece rates were not mentioned. Wages continued to rise and fall in line with the cost of living index throughout the period of the Second World War.

Conscription claimed many able bodied men working in textiles for the armed forces or as 'Bevin Boys' for the coal mines, some of the vacancies being filled by employing more women. Textiles were given the status of an essential industry in 1942, which gave employees a guaranteed wage for a 48 hour week and increased job security; but also imposed restrictions on people changing jobs. In April 1942, 300 workers at Josiah France's, Queens Square Mill Honley, went on strike objecting to what was described as an 'embargo' by the Employers Federation. When a person applied for work with a different employer the prospective employer would contact the current employer and ask if that person could be spared. If the answer was negative the person stayed with the same company. Workers presumably saw this as a form of victimisation. Work was resumed on the assurance that negotiations between workers, unions and management would begin immediately.

Owing to the restriction of the amounts of coal available for all heating, generation of electricity and the supply of industrial power, in late 1941 the government were reviewing the numbers of employees and the amount of space available in mills and factories with a view towards consolidation of industry to save fuel and power. At least two local mills reported that they had been approached; they were Bower Roebuck & Co. of Glendale Mill, and Copley, Marshall & Co. of Wildspur Mill, both in New Mill. It was subsequently announced that production would cease at Bower Roebuck & Co. on 1 February 1942; most workers found other employment locally, but some were transferred to the parent company W. E. Yates of Bramley, Leeds; Glendale Mill did not reopen until 1945. The overall numbers of employees in the industry fell during the war years by some 31.7 percent.[18]

Post war textile production probably increased somewhat, in 1956 Mr. E. C. Behrens, chairman of the Wool Textile Executive said "Since the war ended, British wool textiles have earned more dollars than any other single industry"; but overall production was lower than pre-war, and considerably lower than during the first decade of the twentieth century. The value of the cloth being produced post war was greater as companies were finding that in order to stay in business rather than producing 'run of the mill' goods, they had to appeal to the more discerning buyers by producing higher qualities, a trend which has continued to the present day.

Notes

1   See http://www.unionancestors.co.uk/AtoZ%

2   Information on the Combination Laws and workers struggle for recognition can be found in Carpenter, *Trade Unions in the Early 1830s*; Laybourn, *A History of British Trade Unionism*; Turner, *A Short History of the General Union of Textile Workers*.

3   A. Brooke, *The Handloom Fancy Weavers*; pp.15 & 16.

4   *Minutes of Evidence of the Report from the Select Committee on Handloom Weavers*; 1835, p.xiii.

5   E.C. Tufnell, pp.40-66.

6   K.E. Carpenter, *Trade Unions in the Early 1830s*; see 'A few words to the Friends and Enemies of Trade Unions', and 'A Serious Address to the Millowners and Manufacturers…'

7   Information taken from editions of *The Holmfirth Express* between 6 July and 14 Sept. 1872.

8   See *Huddersfield Examiner* and *Holmfirth Express* between 4 May and 27 July 1872.

9   *Huddersfield Examiner*, 17 March 1883.

10 T.S. Cree, *A Criticism of the Theory of Trade Unions*; (1895). A copy of which is held in Huddersfield University Archive.

11 A.J.P. Taylor, *English History 1914-1945*, pp.139-140.

12 K. Laybourn, *Britain on the Breadline*; p.8.

13 *Ibid*, pp.13-15.

14 *Holmfirth Express*, 25 July, 1925.

15 *Ibid*, 12 April, 1930.

16 *Ibid*, 3 May, 1930.

17 *Ibid*, 8 April, 1933.

18 M.T. Wild, p.228.

CHAPTER 6

From Clothiers to Manufacturers

There were many families in the district who, over a period of years, made the transition from being clothiers to becoming manufacturers. The difference between the two terms is that a clothier, in the West Riding, worked from home, possibly recruiting help from other branches of the family or from neighbours also working in their own homes, to produce yarn or cloth that could be sold at a profit. Whereas a manufacturer had premises in a specially constructed building, a mill or factory, where he employed workers to run machines to whom he paid wages, to carry out the same operations that had formerly been carried out at home, to produce the yarn or cloth. One such family, for whom a reasonable amount of information is available, was that of James and Mary Beardsell of Holme.

James was born in 1764; he was the son of Joshua Beardsell, a spinner, who also lived in Holme. James attended the village school that was run by the curate of Woodhead until he was seven years old, when the curate said to him: "James, thou must go home now and learn to spin." Although he left school with only a basic education, James continued to educate himself to the point where he was capable of running a successful business. It has previously been written that James introduced the first spinning jenny into Holme in 1776, when he would have been only twelve years old. A Mr. Holmes gave a talk to the Holmfirth Literary and Philosophical Society in 1837, in which he said that the first Spinning Jenny was introduced into Holmfirth by a man named William Hanson in 1776, and was used in New Fold, that jenny had 18 spindles.[1] Crump & Ghorbal record that as a young man James Beardsell introduced the first jenny into Holme, which had twenty-four spindles.[2] Time has possibly conflated the two events. After its introduction, Spinning Jennies were developed with up to 60 spindles

James married Mary (or Mally) Clough on 25 October 1792, they moved into what is currently known as Holme House. In addition to the living accommodation the building had a large room at the top which was used as a warehouse for wool and cloth storage, and became known as 'the garret'; there are also signs that something was fixed to upright posts in some of the first floor rooms, but whether it was for storage or possibly hand-driven machinery is not known. There was probably a flight of 'taking-in' steps on the south-western gable end of the building to facilitate access to the business part of the premises, but these no longer exist. There were many weavers living in Holme whom James could have employed to weave his yarn into cloth, before he took it to the market in Huddersfield to sell it. James said that he took cloth to the Cloth Hall in Huddersfield for thirteen consecutive weeks without selling a piece; after which he took his cloth to Stockport and on to Manchester in order to sell it. He continued to travel to other towns selling his cloth, eventually going to Birmingham and on to London, Maidstone and Deal. The journey to London by Stage Coach took two days and one night, or two nights and one day, and was fairly dangerous as well as being uncomfortable. James was away from home for at least two months and often up to three months at a time, when presumably his wife Mary and, as they grew older, his sons would undertake the day-to-day running of the business. Mary provided James with four sons and one daughter; Joseph was born in 1793, Charles in 1799, Peter in 1802, Isaac in 1806, and Mary in 1815.

James took his four sons into partnership in 1828, but apart from the record of Mary's baptism in 1815 no other information about her seems to exist.[3] James' journeys to London and Kent not only allowed him to sell his cloth, but benefited his business and that of other manufacturers in the district, by introducing him to Southdown wool and German Botany wool which was being imported into London, both of which he is credited with introducing into our area. These, along with ideas for different colour combinations and designs gained from seeing cloths produced in different parts of the country gave him the opportunity to introduce many innovations to overcome competition. James was 64 years old when he took his sons into partnership, putting his entire capital and stock-in-trade into the business, which he estimated at £5,000. All four sons already worked in the family business, but Joseph and Peter also had enterprises of their own which they managed to conduct while working for their father. Isaac, who wrote an account of the first nine years of the business, was convinced that it was principally their mother's influence that made James put forward the suggestion of the partnership, as she was always concerned for the well-being of her sons. The trading name of the company was James Beardsell & Sons.

Joseph was 35 years old in 1828, and in addition to working for his father, had been buying wool, having it processed, and selling the finished cloth; but it would appear that he had not been particularly successful in the venture. Due to his experience the younger brothers looked to Joseph for guidance, believing that he would have learned from his past mistakes, consequently Joseph was responsible for buying wool, obtaining orders from buyers and selling the finished cloth; however, some wool merchants refused to accept orders from Joseph, presumably as a result of his previous business record. It was also Joseph's responsibility to determine which wool was to be used for which pieces, and to determine the weights and colours for dyeing.

Charles was 29 in 1828, he had been responsible for the finishing of the cloth, which was carried out at Lower Brow Bottom Mill off Holme Banks, and he continued this responsibility. Peter who was 26, in addition to working for his father was also in partnership with one Amon Dearnley making cloth and successfully selling it in Huddersfield's Cloth Hall. Isaac does not record whether this partnership continued after 1828, it presumably terminated, but the firm continued to produce yarn for Amon until at least 1844.

Isaac was 22 in 1828 he, like Charles, just worked for his father. Along with Peter, Isaac was responsible for the dyeing of the wool, giving out warps and weft to, and receiving woven pieces from, the handloom weavers; getting the cloth milled or fulled, and burled, and assisting in the drying stove. Isaac also sorted the various grades of wool from whole fleeces when necessary; while Peter also looked after the family's herd of cattle.

In the early days most of the wool was dyed in what Isaac describes as: 'a little pan set in an old hole opposite to Benjamin Broadhurst's house end'. This pan would hold a maximum of 128 lbs of wool, but was larger than the original pan which 'only held 112lbs when crammed in so that a man might walk across it without sinking.' Isaac records that at the time he wrote this, which was obviously later as he uses only past tense, their original dyehouse was being used 'by John Kaye as a coal hole', which gives an indication of how small it actually was. During the first year of the partnership the family built the drying stove; originally intended as a single storey building for drying loose wool. Before its completion they decided on a two storey building that could be used for drying wool on the ground floor, and had the capacity to dry scoured pieces on the top floor. The cloth would be stretched out on tenter posts, as it would have been in the open air, but drying would be much quicker. Stoves at that time were in short supply, which created a demand from other clothiers, consequently the family dried wool and cloth for others as well as for themselves. The busiest day for tentering was Monday in order to have the cloth ready to take to market on Tuesday;

on occasions there was such a demand that preparation started on Sunday evening. The precise location of the stove is not given, but it was presumably fairly close to Holme House, possibly in its grounds, as Isaac writes that he had been out one Sunday evening and on his return around midnight, he went to lay down on the ground floor of the stove and could hear his brothers walking about on the floor above as they fixed the cloth to the tenter posts. The total cost of building and equipping the stove was £219 11s.

In July or August 1830 Joseph went to see Abel and Solomon Garlick at Meal Hill, Holme, and negotiated with them to buy two houses, some old outbuildings and some land, which the Garlick's owned in Meal Hill Road, in order to build a new dyehouse. The land adjoined an already established water supply that provided a plentiful supply of 'very good water'. The dyehouse, which again does not seem to have been very large, was virtually finished and ready for use by Christmas of that year. It was presumably built of stone but the roof was covered with thatch, whether it was of straw or heather is not recorded. In September 1845 Isaac records in his diary that the thatch was in need of replacing, they had it removed and replaced by slates. The total cost of the houses, land etc, also building and equipping the dyehouse and making a dam for the water supply was around £560. As the business grew, it becomes apparent that even this dyehouse could not cope with the demand. A letter dated January 1832 written to James, who was in London at the time, by his wife Mary, mentions that they would be paying about £200 to George and Hobson Farrar, who were at Prickleden and Lower Mills, for Dyeing and Scribbling work carried out in the previous month.

At the commencement of the partnership in 1828 the business that they were doing was chiefly in London, with some cloth being sold in Kent, from orders obtained by James Beardsell. This business amounted to an average of five pieces per week in that year. After the formation of the partnership Joseph began attending the Cloth Hall in Huddersfield and also travelled to Stockport market, with a consequent increase in the number of pieces made to 14 per week in 1829, rising to around 20 pieces per week in 1830. Towards the end of 1831 trade became more difficult, although they managed to keep going mainly due to Isaac's design capabilities. He produced a great variety of designs by combining different colours which, it appears, no-one else was doing at that time; this kept them in business.

In November 1831 they took stock for the first time since the formation of the partnership 3½ years earlier. What prompted this is not recorded, but the outcome was regarded as unsatisfactory. After calculating the assets of wool, cloth, dyewares etc. held by them, plus stocks of cloth held in London, Huddersfield and Stockport, plus goods delivered to customers but not yet paid for, the total amounted to over £7,000; from which they deducted amounts owed to their suppliers, reducing their net capital to £5,120. It appeared that although they had increased their output considerably, their net capital had increased by less than £40 per year. Isaac records two reasons for this; firstly, that Joseph was buying quantities of wool at too high a price from companies that would allow them extended credit, and that when he bought wool at a competitive price the selling price that Joseph asked for the cloth was under that which other manufacturers were asking, leaving virtually no margin for profit in either case. Secondly, although James was selling his cloth in London at a good profit, the slow payment by some customers coupled with a large failure rate amongst the tailoring trade considerably reduced the net profit on that business. There were also other factors which the family do not appear to have taken into account; firstly, the business was valued at £5,000 at the commencement of the partnership, this was purely an estimate, Isaac writes more than once that he wonders if his father over-valued his assets, there does not appear to be any written evidence to back James' assessment. Secondly, although they had built the stove and the dyehouse at a total cost of around £800, these do not appear to have been included in the assets. Thirdly, they had no book-keeping system, although they had a notebook in which they recorded expenditure, they had no record of moneys received; each of the partners appears to have kept whatever money they received from customers and taken their personal remuneration from it, with no central check on income or expenditure, therefore it was virtually impossible to arrive at a true valuation of the company. The realisation that despite the effort and hard work put in by all the partners since the formation of the company they had made virtually no headway put a strain on relationships within the family.

James wrote two letters from London in February 1832 in which he complains about the way in which his sons manage the business. He had no confidence in the way that Joseph managed the buying and selling, being convinced that he would run them into debts from which they would not be able to escape. Charles appears to have taken no interest in any branch of the business other than the finishing of the cloth, which he continued to manage. Isaac and Peter were both concerned about the way that the business was being run, they expressed a desire to either take a greater part in the running of the business, or, if that was not possible, to leave the partnership. Isaac writes that they made an attempt to set up in business on their own account, which failed, but gives no details of how, where, or when they attempted to do this. Isaac does give one example of the pricing of goods. They were taking the first piece from a batch of black Cassimere's to the market, which Joseph was proposing to sell at 5s per yard. Isaac thought that they were worth at least 5s 3d per yard and James agreed with him; Joseph continued to argue that they would show a profit at 5s per yard. The first person to look at the cloth bought it at 5s 3d per yard, which set the price for the rest of the batch.

In addition to the difficulty in obtaining orders, the insecurity from the lack of profit, and the potential unrest throughout the country brought about by the Parliamentary Reform Act; or arguably due to that unrest and insecurity, 1832 was the year that many weavers decided to form themselves into a Union. Weavers had been dissatisfied for years with the amounts that manufacturers paid for work done. The manufacturer would find a reason to reduce the rate, or would measure a piece to be shorter than the weaver had measured it, in order to reduce the amount paid for weaving. By 1832 there was a system in operation where a 'standard' piece took 48lbs of wool and attracted a fixed rate for weaving, with heavier cloths attracting a higher rate; but some manufacturers were insisting on paying the standard rate for any piece regardless of weight, even those that weighed up to 20lbs more. The weavers were also insisting that manufacturers should not employ any weaver who was not a trade union member. In retaliation, the manufacturers formed their own Association, where they agreed to pay the weavers by the weight of the piece, but also agreed that no Association member would employ any worker who was a trade union member. The association members implemented these rules from 14 July 1832, putting many people out of work, however, by early August solidarity amongst the manufacturers was weakening, Peter and Isaac attended an association meeting on Friday 3rd August when they heard that one manufacturer had resigned from the association and agreed to pay workers union rates, and a second manufacturer left the association on 8th August expecting to resume working immediately. If these manufacturers had orders that they needed to complete, it is understandable that they wanted to get the work done as soon as possible; Peter recorded on July 25th that the *Leeds Mercury* reported: 'nothing but complaints are heard among Merchants, Manufacturers, Shop-keepers and Workmen due to public debt, the Corn Laws and cholera; while in Germany the woollen trade is good with full employment.' Apart from the two instances mentioned, no other manufacturer appears to have withdrawn from the Association. The laid off weavers were supported by donations from other unions, but as the months dragged on these donations became smaller, and the strikers had spent their savings.

Trade improved considerably in January 1833, which, as Isaac records, is not surprising when we take into account that due to the dispute trade had been at a standstill for many months. Due to diminishing support by the unions for the strikers many of the men who had been laid off were virtually forced to return to work and accept the rates that the manufacturers had offered to pay in the previous July. The price of wool and other commodities increased; Isaac writes that by 5 March they did not have a single piece of cloth in the Cloth Hall to sell, and that they continued to sell all they could make throughout the summer. Employers were selective when re-employing workers but, due to the high demand for cloth, the majority of the strikers found work.

Despite the demand for cloth Isaac felt that they were making less profit than they should, he attributed this to Joseph's policy of selling cloth at marginally above cost rather than assessing its true worth. Although the result of their first stock taking showed that the business was profitable, James was convinced that they were heading for bankruptcy. Mary, James' wife, told the brothers that James frequently said to her that he wished he had never taken his sons into partnership as he felt that he would have prospered well enough on his own, whereas now he was convinced that he would be taken to jail for debt. To allay James' fears they took stock for a second time in April 1833, the results showed that their total capital stood at £3,804, which pacified James by proving that they were still solvent; but made Isaac very uneasy as he realised that their capital had diminished in the last eighteen months.

Joseph began to take a lesser role in the running of the business, leaving the organisation of the work entirely to Isaac and Peter. He would consult with his brothers on Monday evenings to determine the costs of production, and would then fix the selling price in his usual manner in readiness for taking the finished cloth to market on Tuesday morning. This caused disputes between the brothers which made Isaac very uncomfortable. Isaac writes that his father encouraged him to stand up to Joseph on the issue of pricing as James 'would always rather set someone else to dispute a matter, rather than do it himself'. Isaac also raises, for the second time, his frustration that the family do not keep any record of cash received by any of the family members, nor of how much each family member appropriates to his own use. From 1828 they had kept a record of amounts spent, particularly on capital projects such as the building of the stove, also of the house built for Isaac and Ruth, and building and equipping the new dyehouse, a practise that had lapsed in 1832 and was not restarted, but as there was no record of cash received that the expenditure could be set against it was of little value. The family had several meetings during which they attempted to devise a system where receipts and expenses were recorded and balanced each month; but nothing came from them, even though James and Mary were much in favour of it, as were Peter and Isaac; whereas Joseph and Charles showed no interest in the idea at all. A possible reason for the lack of interest by the elder brothers is family size: in 1833 Joseph had a total of 9 children by his two wives Hannah and Sarah, and Charles and Lydia had 7 children; while Peter and Rachel were childless, and Isaac and Ruth had just 2 children at that time. It would be much more expensive to house, feed and cloth the families of Joseph and Charles than those of Peter, Isaac and James.

Mary became ill with influenza around the middle of 1833; she seemed unable to shake off the infection which gradually worsened to the point where she passed away on the 5th of September. All the family felt a keen sense of loss at her passing, and, as is often the case, they had not fully appreciated her until she was no longer with them. Towards the end of the year the firm experienced a decline in orders, this could be due, at least in part, to one of their principle customers, a Mr. Noble, having met with a serious riding accident, putting him out of business for some months. Over that year they produced an average of sixteen pieces per week, using 65lbs. of wool per piece. The price of wool was fairly high, possibly because Joseph was still in charge of the buying and bought most of the wool at prices that were not competitive, but came from a firm that would allow them extended credit, which would probably not have been necessary had they used a more comprehensive accounting system.

James' visits to London not only allowed the company to sell their established qualities, designs and colours, but gave them an insight into what would be in demand in the future. In a letter written by Mary to James in January 1832 she asks him to call on Cooper of Bond Street 'and get him to give you samples of things he thinks will be selling for spring trade, and ask him if stripes are likely to take the lead'. This insight would give them a slight advantage over their competitors. Some innovations in design took place in early 1834, diagonal twill became popular, initially made as a bold heavy twill it was soon modified to a finer neat twill with no nap that became known as Buckskin, which sold well until the warmer months of the year. By November, plaid Cassimere's had become popular along with Buckskins and Fancy Mixtures; these were followed by Striped Buckskins. Along with a steady demand for plain cloths they achieved a total production of 728 pieces for the year, or an average of fourteen pieces per week. At this time Isaac knew little or nothing about either weaving or design, but by educating himself in the 'mystery' of the art he soon became more expert than many of the weavers who worked for them. By cooperating with John Clough, one of their more knowledgeable weavers, Isaac was able to produce experiments using various combinations of colour, design and weave to produce patterns that were unique to James Beardsell & Sons, thereby expanding both their production and customer base. James continued to voice his misgivings saying: "there was sure to be a *monce* [bad job] with those ugly things when they stopped". In reality, they were increasing production and, due to their unique designs, commanding better prices, thereby increasing their profits.

A second tragic death occurred in May 1835, when Peter, the third brother, died. He had ridden out to meet the candidates for the West Riding in a forthcoming election, who were coming to speak in Holmfirth. It was a very cold day and Peter was without a coat; after being out for several hours he was probably suffering from Hypothermia. Isaac writes that in the evening he had 'a glass or two of spirits' which made his condition worse. Despite the best efforts of the family and his doctors, Peter died eight days later. In addition to the grief and loss felt by the family it was necessary to reorganise the business responsibilities of the three remaining brothers. Joseph had ceased to take any active part in the manufacturing processes, although he did attend the Cloth Hall in Huddersfield every Tuesday and kept a record of the sales there; he also took over the management of the horses and cattle, which included all the other farming duties. Charles continued to be responsible for finishing the cloth, the fancy cloths that now formed the bulk of the production all had to be finished, considerably increasing Charles' workload. Isaac took over the responsibility for all the other processes; this allowed him to introduce new systems so that he could keep track of orders and production to a higher degree. He maintained that 1835 was the first year of the partnership during which they had really made money, he attributed this to the increased volume of business and the better prices realised for their cloth due to them having their own designs. Production for the year amounted to 1,000 pieces, averaging about 20 per week. 1836 proved to be equally busy and profitable, with production holding steady at the average of 20 pieces per week.

Trade declined somewhat in early 1837, giving the brothers the opportunity to take stock again. Isaac was very pleased with the result as it showed that their capital had risen from £3,800 to just over £7,000; although he complains about deficiencies in the keeping of customer's accounts, principally by Joseph, and records his gratitude to their customers for their honesty when he found it necessary to ask the customers to supply details of how much they owed to Beardsells. One positive aspect to emerge from their discussions on the state of the business was an agreement that the brothers should keep account of moneys received from customers, amounts spent, and amounts taken by each brother for use by their own family. There was a greater decline in trade from March 1837 onwards, the price of wool had dropped by 6½d per lb since the previous September, and Isaac records that patterns and qualities that had previously sold at 5s 6d or 5s 8d per yard were fetching only 4s 8d or 4s 10d per yard. This appears to have been caused principally by a decline in the American market. The lowest point was reached in late June and early July; trade began to rally in August and continued until the end of that year. Most of their trade for the year was in 'fancies' which averaged about 20 pieces per week, plus 80 pieces of Kersey during the year.

The firm took over at least part of Upper Digley Mill around the 9 October 1837, on a lease for 12 or possibly 13 years. Isaac does not indicate which processes were carried out there, presumably carding, spinning, and dyeing were probably all done there, and the finishing was moved there from Holme Banks; whilst weaving was still done by outworkers. Wool prices began to increase in 1838 and the demand for 'fancies' held up, but the prices for finished cloth did not return to their previous maximum, most sold at between 4s 6d and 4s 9d per yard. This account by Isaac ends, literally mid-sentence, on February 27th 1838.

I have also been privileged to read a diary written by Isaac between 18 January 1844 and July 1846. Several changes had taken place in the intervening years, James, the father, had moved out of Holme House to Upperthong, and Isaac, Ruth and family had moved in; Charles, Lydia and their family were now living in Holme rather than Holme Banks, possibly in the adjoining house to Isaac's although this is not certain. Joseph and his family also lived in the village but where is not stated. All their families had grown, Joseph now had a total of thirteen children, three had been born to his first wife Hannah, and ten to Sarah. Sarah apparently died in June 1841, her last daughter, Sarah Lucy, was born at the end of February in that year, and there is a record of a child of that name dying in December of that year, but it is not necessarily the same child. Charles and Lydia had twelve children; while Isaac and Ruth had six, with their seventh child Ruth Hannah being born in 1845.

Each of the brothers had virtually the same responsibilities as in the 1830s, although Joseph attended Huddersfield's Cloth Hall only occasionally, spending almost all his time looking after their farming interests, which must have been quite considerable as Isaac records that at one point they had nineteen acres of grass cut for hay. Charles continued to be responsible for cloth finishing, which had been moved to Upper Digley Mill, and Isaac divided his time between Holme House, where they stored both wool and cloth, and where they possibly had some pattern looms, and Upper Digley Mill. They also had some wool scribbled, carded and spun at Farrar's Lower Mill and some dyeing carried out at Farrar's Upper Mill at Prickleden. Isaac continued to visit the Cloth Hall every Tuesday to meet customers and suppliers. An oft-voiced complaint from Isaac, particularly when he had visited a friend or competitor at their mill lower down the valley, was the disadvantage that Beardsell's were under being based in Holme rather than being nearer Huddersfield. On January 18th 1844, the first day of this diary, he writes that he went to see Joe Mellor who had recently negotiated to rent Mytholm Bridge Mill:

> *'Situated below Holmfirth with all the advantage of good roads, near to Coals, near to Market, and the land of a superior quality up to here, as it is with us with all the disadvantages of heavy roads, a long way from Coals, from Mills and Markets and in a colder and a more uncongenial climate. I could not help thinking how much worse we are situated as manufacturers than those who are below Holmfirth, and I felt a wish to remove. I regretted we had laid out so much money in Land and Buildings when we might have had as much Land of a better quality and as much building for the same or less cost and in a far superior situation.'*

Despite these feelings, Isaac was a committed member of the community in Holme, he was an official at the Sunday School, and served at least two years as village constable. He was also an official at Lane Independent Chapel; and a member of the committee of manufacturers formed to reduce the amount of embezzlement by outworkers. Although he reiterates his feelings about being based in Holme, in the diary rather than to another person virtually every time he visits another manufacturer, he continues to live in Holme and maintain the manufacturing processes at the same premises until 1848. At this time he seems either unwilling or unable to resolve the conflict between his loyalty to his father and brothers, and his desire for the freedom, as he sees it, of being his own master and running his own business from more conveniently situated premises. A problem that was slow to reach resolution.

Isaac set the wheels in motion for his breakaway when his father and brothers agreed to him purchasing Hagg House at Thongsbridge for the sum of £830 including the 8 acres of pasture, 2 acres of woodland, and the stream; although it was several years later before he lived there. Isaac saw the land alongside the stream between the house and Woodhead Road as being an ideal place to build a mill, but this never materialised. The purchase was completed on 30th June 1844, after which Isaac let the house to Mr. John Hobson who later sublet, with Isaac's agreement, part of the property to Samuel Mellor. Isaac spent quite a lot of money on the house, grounds and land, in repairs to the house, setting out the gardens and buying shrubs and plants, also repairing and renewing walls, fences and water courses.

The brothers had eventually agreed, in 1837, that they would each keep a record of the amounts of money taken out of the business for personal and family use. They arranged to meet to compare and discuss the amounts in March 1844; Joseph was unable to produce any figures at all, and was apparently reduced to tears; Charles said that his accounts were not up to date but he thought he could make them out. They had carried out another stock-take in late February, and Isaac had completed the calculations in early March. He was able to show his brothers that they had a 'Floating Capital' of £10,200, made up of stocks of wool and cloth, plus moneys owing to them, less money which they owed; plus, for the first time, an amount for 'Fixed Capital' of £3,400, which included machinery and land, but whether it includes buildings owned is not stated.

Since the reorganisation of responsibilities after the death of Peter in 1835, Isaac had taken over buying the wool, which he usually incorporated into his visits to the Cloth Hall in Huddersfield on Tuesdays, when he would buy perhaps 3 or 4 bales most weeks. As the company's output grew there was the opportunity to buy greater quantities of wool at better prices. Isaac's first venture was to visit Mr. Wright Rhodes at New Delph in Saddleworth, wool merchant and fellow manufacturer, from whom he bought 12 bales of wool. 1844 was a good year for the wool textile trade, the volume of orders, particularly from America, in spite of the competition from American manufacturers, was so great that cloth merchants were refusing to accept any more orders as they could not guarantee delivery dates. It was also a very dry summer, which reduced the volume of water available to drive water wheels, fill dyepans or supply fulling stocks etc. increasing the frustration of manufacturers who found that although they had plenty of orders they could not get the work completed. This was a particular problem with regard to orders for the American market, as the cloth had to be despatched in time to catch sailings on specific dates. The drought came to an end on Saturday July 13th, when Isaac noted in his diary: '*It set in wet this afternoon, and by night we could all run Stocks at Mill, something we had not been able to do for months*'; giving them the opportunity to complete the orders and despatch them before the deadlines arrived. The American market was a difficult one, apart from the deadlines for despatch manufacturers faced the uncertainties of the American government's protectionist policies such as the imposition of import tariffs, which were designed to price foreign competition out of their markets.

Buying wool at importer's wool sales, rather than from local wool merchants would increase the firm's competitiveness. The main wool sales in the country took place in London and Liverpool; in order to be able to take full advantage of the opportunity to improve their purchasing power they needed a bank account. Their first bank account was with the Huddersfield Banking Company, and was opened on 21 May 1844; in addition to the normal day-to-day banking business the account also allowed them to obtain Letters of Credit and would give them an overdraft facility if needed. All transactions prior to that date had been conducted in cash. The first visit to a wool sale was in early July at Liverpool when Isaac, in the company of David Brook and John Hirst, fellow manufacturers, left Holme in a horse-drawn vehicle and travelled to Glossop, where they caught a train to Manchester, then a second train to Liverpool, which took them about five hours in total. Isaac bought 18 bales on that occasion; he does not say whether, in view of the cost of travel and accommodation for two nights, he considered it a financial success by comparison with prices charged by Huddersfield merchants for similar qualities; but the experience gained would be priceless.

The spread of the railway network throughout Britain greatly improved communications for both passengers and freight, by increasing passenger comfort and considerably reducing journey times. However, in the 1840s the network was still undergoing construction. Whereas, on their first trip to Liverpool, Isaac and friends had travelled to Glossop to catch the train; from 8th August 1844, it was possible to catch a train from Woodhead to Manchester, when that part of the Sheffield to Manchester line opened. The section from Sheffield to Dunford Bridge did not open until 14 July 1845, but was still not complete as the tunnel between Dunford Bridge and Woodhead was not yet built. That part of the journey was covered by either Coach or Omnibus, both horse-drawn; the tunnel was completed and the line fully opened on 27th December 1845. On one journey from Woodhead to Liverpool, Isaac writes that the third class fare was 4s 2d.

His first journey to London was in October 1844, travelling from Huddersfield via Normanton, Derby and Rugby, which took him 11 hours from leaving home, at a cost of 38s. In addition to attending the wool sales where he bought about 32 bales of wool, he also took the opportunity to call on some of his father's old customers, at least two of which still owed them money. He does not record the amounts that were owing, or how long the debts had been outstanding, but they still stood at the same level when he left. Isaac also called at several cloth merchants that had been recommended to him by friends, he does not appear to have secured many orders on his first visit, but contact had been established and could be built on. The connections that he established with merchants in London would eventually prove to be very rewarding as the business done with them expanded, while the number of orders from American buyers contracted. He also spent some time sight-seeing, spending a Sunday in Brighton; a morning on the Thames visiting Woolwich dockyard, and Saturday morning in Windsor. Having spent 9 days and nights in London, he left there in the evening travelling via Derby then on to Barnsley, where he arrived before dawn. His brother Charles came to meet him at an Inn, where Isaac had managed to get a few hours sleep, and take him home. The line between Huddersfield and Penistone, giving rail access to Barnsley and Sheffield, was originally intended to open in 1848 but, due to delays did not open until 1st July 1850, by which time the branch line to Holmfirth was also completed and opened on the same day.

In December 1844 the part of Holmfirth Mill that had previously been occupied by George Gartside (now deceased), was available to rent. Isaac and Charles went to look round the property on Dec. 28th, followed by a meeting between the three brothers and James the father two days later. Isaac said that if they were to take the mill they would need to move homes in order to be nearer to it, to which James answered 'those might leave that would, but he should never leave until he was carried away', he described Holmfirth as 'a low crowded place'. Isaac had calculated the probable earnings and expenses and said that they should make around £400 a year profit if they moved there. He followed this in his diary, by reiterating his preference for discontinuing the partnership and going into business on his own, as he would prefer to be able to make his own decisions and act upon them rather than having to seek agreement from others. He also said that he felt that the ratio of profit to capital employed was greater where the amount of capital was small. As an example he said that if the three brothers were to each set up and run their own businesses, they could each expect to turn over more than one third of the turnover of the present company. Charles made the point that both Joseph and Isaac had property held in their names which, apart from any income that they derived from it, qualified them for inclusion on the register of electors in national elections, whereas, he Charles, 'was a Slave yet'. Isaac reminded them that he had previously suggested to his father that the land that the family held at Statham should be put into Charles' name to bring Charles into line as a property owner with Joseph and himself, and give Charles the opportunity to vote in West Riding elections, which James had agreed with, but had apparently not acted upon. The foregoing gives some indication as to why Isaac felt he would rather leave the partnership and 'do for himself' as he puts it.

Charles and Isaac actually made an offer to rent the property at Holmfirth Mill on January 2nd 1845, to Joshua Moorhouse who was the person dealing with it on behalf of Mrs. Gartside. They asked him what was the lowest rent that he would accept, he said £440; they offered £400. Moorhouse pointed out that there was someone else who was interested in the property and asked if they would increase their offer, which they declined to do despite misgivings on the way home that they may lose it. Isaac and Charles were both disappointed and annoyed to learn the following day that the mill had been let to Nathan Thewlis without them having another opportunity to increase their offer.

In the ensuing weeks they had discussions with Joshua and William Batty about renting part or all of Brown Hill Mills, Battys offered to let Lower Brow Bottom Mill to them, which they declined; they also talked to Sydney Moorhouse who would have rented Wildspur Mill at New Mill to them at £300 a year, but they decided it was too far away from Holme; and they also talked to Thomas and Edward Butterworth about renting space in Hinchliffe Mill mill, but the Butterworths were not prepared to rent them the amount of space that they required. Despite these enquiries Isaac continues to maintain that he would prefer to leave the partnership and be entirely independent.

The family continued in business in Holme and at Upper Digley Mill probably until after the death of the elder brother Joseph on 8 April 1848, in his 55th year. James, the father, was still alive and living in Upperthong, he would be at least 83 years old, and took no active part in the running of the business. After Joseph's death Charles and Isaac appear to have wound up the family business, and each gone their separate ways. Charles took premises in Brownhill mills and undertook all the processes of manufacturing cloth rather than just the finishing of it, trading as Charles Beardsell & Sons. The date when Isaac took up residence in Hagg House is unclear, he was definitely there by the later part of 1848, when he took premises in Smithy Place mill and began trading in the name of Beardsell & Co. Both brothers continued to run their businesses until their respective deaths, after which they were both succeeded by their sons.

Notes

1   Yorkshire Archaeological Society archive, MS514/A-Y; cutting from a newspaper giving a report of the talk, fixed into a copy of The History and
     Topography of the Parish of Kirkburton and the Graveship of Holme; by Henry James Morehouse.

2   Crump and Ghorbal, p. 67.

3   All the genealogy of the family quoted here is taken from the Baptism records of Lane Chapel, Holmfirth; available from the Local Studies library
     Huddersfield, and other sources.

CHAPTER 7

Floods

The streams and rivers of the Holme Valley certainly provided the inhabitants of the area with an ample supply of soft clean water and the power with which to manufacture cloth; but on some occasions the volume of water in those streams and rivers was so great that it became destructive rather than productive. The earliest record outside the Wakefield Court Rolls, although certainly not the earliest flood, was a thunder storm that occurred on the morning of Sunday May 7th 1738, and caused what was described as a 'cloud burst' over Scholes Moor. Most of the water found its way into the stream in the Ribbleden valley, which 'acquired an enormous bulk' as it carried the water towards the centre of Holmfirth, where it entered the Parish Church while the congregation were attending evensong. The water reportedly rose to a depth of five feet within the church much to the consternation of the assembled congregation, and roads and property in the town centre were damaged.[1]

A more disastrous flood occurred on July 23rd 1777, affecting both Holme and Colne valleys. A report in the *Leeds* Mercury of 29 July suggests that the rain began about 8pm, causing much damage to buildings and crops in Colne Valley, with much hay and corn being swept away. An eye-witness to the devastation in Holmfirth wrote that:

'In the middle of the afternoon, a tremendous thunder-storm burst on the hills above Holmfirth, accompanied with such torrents of rain as almost instantly to fill all the small rivulets and brooks, which, on uniting with the main stream, formed a vast body of water, spreading far beyond its accustomed channel, sweeping away wears[sic], walls and hedges; inundating the adjacent lands, tearing up trees, carrying away haystacks, timber &c.; yet those apparent impediments only added to its gigantic and irresistible force. By the time it reached Holmfirth it rolled down with a breast of several yards perpendicular, sweeping before it, or crushing down by its enormous force, wears, bridges, mills, and houses; in short everything within its reach was either swept away or gutted and made a complete wreck.

At the upper part of the town, what is usually called Lower Mill, with its dwelling house and furniture &c., were instantly overwhelmed and swept away, with the single exception of the waterwheel. Holmfirth Mill, then a corn mill, was completely gutted; not a window or a door left, though the walls remained; but of the fulling mill, now on the site of Messrs. Gartsides' dyehouse, only a few yards below on the same side of the river, scarcely a vestige remained. Many of the other mills in the district suffered in a similar manner; and together with the loss of cattle, sheep, &c., the destruction of property was very great.

But the most melancholy part of the story remains to be told. Three men were carried off Mill-hill, in the middle of the town, in the site of hundreds of trembling spectators, who were unable to render them the slightest assistance, or even make their warnings heard, from the roaring of the torrent. Their names were Elkanah Hinchliff, publican, John Booth, of Scholes, and ---- Lindley, carpenter, Holmfirth. Booth was afterwards found in a tree near Bridge Mill; Lindley was found near the King's

Mill, Huddersfield; and Hinchliff was found near Horbury. Several bodies were also washed out of their graves in the parochial burial ground. All the level ground on the banks of the river were covered with mud, stone, and wreck, like the bottom of a torrent, over which was spread broken furniture, machinery, and timber.

This awful visitation came so suddenly, that several persons could with difficulty be got out of their houses; and in some instances were only saved by breaking through the roof, either themselves or by their neighbours.

Had this calamity occurred in the night, many persons in these exposed situations must have been surprised in their beds, and the loss of life would have been far greater.'²

Estimates put the cost of the damage caused by the flood at £10,000. A distress fund was launched, and the not inconsiderable proceeds distributed amongst the sufferers. Holmfirth parish church suffered some damage in this flood, in addition to that sustained in the flood of 1738. The church was not considered adequate for the needs of the congregation at that time; consequently the parish took the opportunity in 1778 to enlarge it to its present size.

Some forty-four years later another, but less serious, flood occurred on the evening of Friday, September 21ˢᵗ, 1821, the *Leeds Mercury* of September 29ᵗʰ carried the following account:

'The public have observed with much concern and apprehension the influence of the rainy weather upon the harvest, but in the neighbourhood of Holmfirth it has produced other disastrous consequences. The rivulets had considerably increased without attracting much observation until Friday evening, the 21ˢᵗ inst., when the reservoir above Black Sike mill broke, and a prodigious volume of water rolled down the valley, with rapid course and overwhelming violence. At first the water ran over the top, which indicated the danger, and warned those who were in the mill, and in the adjoining houses, to escape. They had just time enough to save their lives, but they saved nothing else. Immediately the side burst, the water rushed forth, the buildings were swept away, and all their property perished before their eyes. Amidst the horror of this awful scene, with amiable presence of mind, they ran downwards to give the alarm to the workmen at the dyehouse at Burnlee, who instantly fled, and it soon appeared that a moment's delay would have been fatal to them. The middle part of the dyehouse was bourn down by the inundation, but the two ends which were recently and more strongly built, stood the shock. The devastation here was much less injurious than could have been supposed, for all the account books, most of the dyeing wares and a part of the wool were saved from the wreck. Through Holmfirth the water filled the cellars in many houses, and rose three or four feet high on the ground floor. The low grounds were covered to considerable distances from the water courses, the bridges were carried away by the torrent, and the wear [sic] at Bridge Mill was destroyed, besides much other damage. The flood began at six o'clockᵃ in the evening, it was at the height a little after seven, by ten it had subsided; but the agitation and fear were such that some of the people never went to bed that night, The ensuing morning exhibited an affecting scene of desolation; mud, stones, timber, fragments of furniture, pieces of work-tools, and trees torn up by the roots, were spread over the fields. Thousands have since been to visit the ruins, who, although they deplored the havoc, rejoiced that no lives were lost on this dreadful occasion.'

The valley's inhabitants were less fortunate when the next inundation occurred. The latter part of 1851 and January 1852 were particularly wet, a paragraph in the *Huddersfield Chronicle* of 31 January under the news from Holmfirth begins:

'The Weather – During the present week we have had in this neighbourhood frequent strong gales of wind, and an unusual quantity of rain….We now frequently hear very old people remark that they cannot remember so wet a January on the whole as this has been.' There are then a few lines about the winter in general, and the last line reads: *'At least no serious results have attended its course as yet.'*

---

a　　Other reports say that the reservoir overflowed at seven o'clock; all agree that it was over by ten.

The most serious flood was to occur some five days later during the night of February 4th to 5th. An indication of the amount of rain that must have fallen before the flood can be gained from an account by George Sykes who, in 1851-2 was 13 years old, when on February 2nd he attended the funeral of a family friend at the Holmfirth Wesleyan Burial Ground, which was near to the site of Holmfirth Mill, but on the opposite side of the river and slightly downstream. When the mourners arrived at the graveside, they found the grave was full of water, 'the ground was so wet and the rain so continuous that the water could not be baled out, and the coffin had to be lowered into the water in the grave'. He also records that as he was going to work on the morning of the 4th, crossing Victoria Bridge he looked over the parapet and saw that the water was so high that it filled the arch, and had he put his hand over the parapet he could have touched the water.[3]

During the flood, damage to both persons and property was probably greater than if Bilberry Reservoir had not been built, due to the embankment bursting and releasing a considerable volume of water and debris into the already swollen River Holme. The reasoning behind the building of the reservoirs in the hills above Holmfirth was to conserve water to ensure a year round regular supply to drive the water wheels of the mills and factories along the banks of the several streams and rivers during the drier summer months.

The Holme Reservoirs Act of 1837 provided for the building of a total of eight reservoirs in the district. In the event it was decided to build three, which were Bilberry Reservoir to supply Digley Dike and the River Holme; Holme Styes Reservoir to supply the Ribbleden Valley and the River Holme; and Bowshaw Whams Reservoir to supply Upper House Dike, then New Mill Dike, which also joins the River Holme. The Act allowed the Holme Reservoir Commissioners to raise the sum of £40,000 to cover the cost of building the three reservoirs. The people who invested the money, known as Subscribers, were to receive interest at five percent per annum on their loans. The commissioners, who were elected, were drawn from the major Mill Owners or Mill Occupiers of the district, who had little or no specialist knowledge of Civil Engineering. Initially, attendances at meetings of the commissioners were good, but numbers dwindled over time and even though there were at least twenty-six commissioners, in January 1847 the minutes show that there were only five or six attending some meetings, and on at least three occasions only one commissioner turned up. After the flood and its ensuing publicity, there was a much improved attendance, with almost every commissioner attending each meeting.

Having negotiated with the landowners of the areas where the reservoirs were to be built, in June 1838 the commissioners wrote to Mr. George Leather of Leeds, who was a highly regarded Civil Engineer in business with his son under the title George Leather & Son. The type of work that he had previously undertaken was the Surrey Iron Railway, and the Pocklington Canal; he had also been consulting engineer to the Aire and Calder Navigation Authority since 1920, and had built several bridges across the Aire and Trent rivers. In 1837 he was also the consulting engineer to the Leeds Waterworks Company concerned with the building of Eccup Reservoir.[4] The letter asked him to 'undertake the management of the making of the three Reservoirs', and told him that the commissioners would employ a Surveyor to oversee the day to day building, and that he would only have to give directions and come to Holmfirth 'now and then as circumstances might require'. The commissioners were presumably trying to save the expense that would be incurred by George Leather visiting the area. The Huddersfield to Penistone railway line with its branch line to Holmfirth did not open until 1850; therefore, before that date, the journey would be undertaken on horseback, or in a horse-drawn carriage or coach, which would be fairly slow and also expensive. This lack of supervision was, arguably, one of the major failings of the project, which became evident at the inquest that was held in Holmfirth shortly after the flood.

George Leather drew up plans and specifications for all three reservoirs, and submitted them along with his estimates of costs to the commissioners in October 1838. He had calculated the cost of building Bilberry Reservoir to be £13,000; the commissioners gave the contract to Daniel Sharpe & Son of Dewsbury, who had tendered a price of £9,324, which George Leather told the commissioners was too low; however, they appear to have ignored him. Was this another example of their desire to save money?

The top of the embankment of Bilberry Reservoir was to be sixty-seven feet above the stream bed, and would stretch three hundred and forty feet across the valley. In 1838 there were only seven reservoirs in the whole country with embankments higher than sixty-one feet, George Leather had not worked on any of them, and neither did the Holme Reservoir Commissioners consult anyone who had. It is possible that no-one at the forefront of the project appreciated the enormity of the undertaking. Regulation of the water supply to the mills was through a pipe that contained two 'shuttles', or sliding valves, set towards the bottom of the fifty-nine feet high waste pit which was fifteen feet in diameter, with a 12 feet wide open shaft down the centre to carry away excess water. The winding gear to raise and lower the shuttles was on top of the waste pit.

Sharpe & Son were awarded the contract on 26 October 1838, and work commenced shortly afterwards. George Leather received repeated communications from the overseer complaining about the difficulty of getting the contractor to carry out the work in accordance with the plans and specifications, but he does not appear to have been asked to attend the site. The Embankment was to have a central core of clay running across from side to side, and from five feet below the level of the stream bed to within around two feet of the top; it had to be sixteen feet thick at its base, tapering to eight feet at the top. It did not add any strength; its purpose was to waterproof the embankment to ensure that no water leaked through. When the contractors were digging the trench below the valley bottom they found that midway between the valley sides the shale bed was spongy, digging down another four feet they uncovered a spring; a witness at the 1852 inquest described the flow of water from the spring as being "as thick as my arm". Sharpe & Son decided that it was not necessary to construct anything to carry that water away, that by covering the spring with the clay puddle trench, the spring water would be forced down into its original course and would not create a problem. This was to prove to be a major mistake. The son of Daniel Sharpe said, at the inquest, that they thought that they could contain the spring by putting puddle clay on top of it, but "the spring followed us up the puddle bank, I cannot say to what height, and then washed its way out at the low side of the embankment". At no time did they attempt to carry the water away. Mr. Joseph Whiteley, one of the commissioners, said that he had spoken to several commissioners when at the reservoir about the spring, and that he had raised the subject on at least three occasions at commissioners' meetings, but on every occasion he had been ignored.

George Leather maintained that he was never told about this spring; he did say that he had been told in 1841 about a leak of muddy water at the base of the embankment, [that it contained mud showed that the water had come through the puddle core], which was reported to him again in August 1843 and in 1844, also he said that when the reservoir started to fill, clean water was leaking from the north side of the embankment. That this water was clean indicates that it was not coming through the embankment, but probably through fissures in the rocks of the reservoir side. John Tait, overseer, and James Morton, stone mason of Holmfirth, both said in evidence that George Leather and his clerk Mr. Falshaw had seen the spring in the bottom of the puddle trench, which Leather strenuously denied; he maintained that had he been aware of it he would have insisted that it be carried away in a solid masonry culvert, which would have cost between £12 and £15 to build. An indication of the force behind the spring water was given by James Morton, who said that even when the puddle was two or three yards thick the water pushed it up. On 25 November 1842, the commissioners ordered that: 'measures be taken to stop the runs in the Bilberry Mill Reservoir and that the same be done under the superintendence of Mr. George Hirst' who was the owner and occupier of Lower Digley Mill and a Commissioner. If any attempts were made to stop the leaks at that time they were unsuccessful.

The minutes of the commissioners on 4 January 1843, record that Daniel Sharpe & Son had constructed part of the Valve Pit and Embankment 'in an improper and unsatisfactory manner', which should be put right immediately. From evidence given at the inquest by Joseph Sharpe, son of Daniel

Sharpe, they left the project in 1843 having completed the construction of the embankment and the waste pit to George Leather's specifications. George Leather having inspected the embankment, recommended that part of the embankment should be removed and replaced, and that the base of the valve pit and the culvert should be rebuilt. Sharpe & Son do not appear to have carried out any corrective work, as the commissioners advertised for tenders from other builders in August of that year, and gave the job to David & George Porter of Fartown, Huddersfield on 5 September.

David Porter said in evidence at the inquest that while they were carrying out these repairs they were also instructed to extend the culvert to a hollow place in the centre of the embankment; [this was presumably caused by the action of the spring water, and the reason for muddy water escaping through the embankment] but they were stopped from completing this by the overseer Jonathon Thorpe. Told to fill in openings in the embankment, David Porter refused due to the amount of water that the openings contained. Nine [unnamed] commissioners ordered Porter's men to fill in the holes; at times these men were working up to their knees in water; Porter told the commissioners that it would not cure the problem, and later complained to Mr. John Harpin, a commissioner who often chaired the commissioners' meetings, who told him 'he must attend to Thorpe's orders'. Porter continued: "The embankment sank two or three inches every morning – the puddle sank several inches daily at the end of the masonry – the stream of water running against the puddle made it very thin". George Leather made more suggestions for correcting the problems, which David Porter spoke to Mr. Harpin about. Harpin's response was "We have been Leather'd hard enough". David Porter's assessment was that had the culvert been extended as George Leather had suggested, the problem would have been resolved and the embankment would have held; but due to the intervention of the overseer and nine commissioners they were prevented from doing the work. It would appear that again, the primary concern of the commissioners was to save expense.

In November 1845, George Leather was asked to supply a plan and estimate for repairing Bilberry Reservoir, but he did not reply; the request was repeated in January 1846, but still, he did not reply. At the inquest he said: "I considered myself the Engineer from the commencement of the work up to September 1844, the last time I visited the works". He had visited the site in July 1844 and found that the puddle lining was not satisfactory. He explained to some of the commissioners that the reservoir would not hold water unless the puddle core was complete, and he had also explained what needed to be done. He had given orders to the overseer to have the water drained to enable the work to be done, but when he visited the site in September he found that nothing had been done and the overseer Jonathon Thorpe told him that Mr. Littlewood, a commissioner, had countermanded the order. He never visited the site again and considered that his connection with the project had terminated. He had obviously omitted to convey these feelings to the commissioners, who possibly had some inkling of how he felt, as when they had asked him for the estimate the second time in January 1846, they also asked Mr. George Crowther of Milnsbridge to supply one, which he declined to do.

On January 28th they instructed the clerk to write to Mr. Joshua Hall and ask him for an estimate; the minutes do not record whether one was ever received. It is possible that by this date the Holme Reservoir Commissioners were getting a bad reputation in Civil Engineering circles due to them having to replace contractors and also for not paying accounts promptly. The costs of repairs to Bilberry Reservoir in the two and a half years between October 1843 and May 1846 amounted to £6,378 17s 9d; the building of the reservoir was completed in 1846, but that was not the end of its problems.

In the original Act of 1837, Parliament had given permission for £40,000 to be raised, which had been done. The estimates tendered by the contractors who were appointed to build the three reservoirs totalled just under £25,000; but, due to the problems encountered, and the lack of expertise by the original contractors, for which the commissioners had to engage other contractors at additional expense, by 1844 the commissioners were experiencing great financial difficulty. Daniel Sharpe & Son had submitted an account for work 'completed' for £3,405 10s 4d, which the commissioners refused to pay as George Leather would not give his approval to it. Sharpe's had commenced court action to recover payment in January 1844, and by 27th of October had taken their case to the Chancery Court, involving the commissioners in yet more expense in defending the action. In addition to this, some mill owners or occupiers, some of whom were also commissioners, were refusing to pay the water rates levied by the commission, which restricted the commission's income, and their ability to pay the annual interest due to Subscribers. In 1846, in an attempt to reduce the opposition by mill owners to the water rate system, the commissioners suggested that each side should appoint a qualified representative, and those two would then jointly appoint a third person. The mill owners appointed Mr. George Crowther of Milnsbridge, the commissioners tried for three weeks, from 12 May to 2 June, but no-one would agree to represent them, so the attempt failed.

In March 1846 Porters' brought court action against the commission for money owing; George Leather had also submitted an account for £257 12s 6d, and by April 1850 was asking for payment. The commissioners told him that they had no money, nor prospect of receiving any for some time. From 1846 the Commission was effectively bankrupt; the Subscribers had not been receiving interest payments on their investments in the project. A letter from the Subscribers legal representatives pointed out that many of the people who had invested in the scheme were elderly ladies who relied on the interest payments for their day-to-day living. The commissioners felt that to attempt to raise income by increasing the water rates would be counter productive, as it would reduce income by encouraging mill owners to convert wholly to steam power rather than relying on their water wheels. It was decided to apply to government for permission to raise an additional loan. This was met with disdain in some quarters, as is shown by an article in the *Leeds Mercury* in 1849:

'Opposition to the Reservoirs – We are glad to hear that many millowners and occupiers are coming forward to oppose the mortgagees (who have given notice of their intention to apply to parliament this session) in getting further powers. It is an acknowledged fact that these reservoirs are of very little use, if any. The one at Bilberry is a mere apology for one: upwards of £20,000 have been expended upon this one reservoir and yet it is worthless: the embankment which was always leaky has been very much injured by the late heavy rains'[5]

In 1852 after the flood, a letter dated 14 November was sent to the Subscribers telling them that the mill owners and occupiers would not agree to an increase in the water rate to cover the 2½ percent per annum interest due on the unpaid interest arrears. The commissioners asked the subscribers to agree that all unpaid interest should be cancelled, and that future interest should be calculated not at the 5 percent to which they were legally entitled, but at 2½ percent. The commissioners also wanted to raise more money; an additional £7,000, which they expected the subscribers to provide at 4 percent per annum interest. If the current subscribers were not prepared to advance the additional money, they should be prepared for the new subscribers to be given preference on interest payments. From the tone of the reply in late January 1853, the subscribers were very unhappy, but did reluctantly agree to abandon their claim to the arrears of interest, provided that the new rate of 2½ percent interest was 'fully and absolutely secured'. No doubt a contributory factor in the subscribers decision was the flood and the bursting of Bilberry Reservoir embankment the previous February.

The additional £7,000 that the commissioners wanted to raise was not to repair the damage to the reservoir embankment, as the Holmfirth Flood Relief Fund had put £7,000 in the hands of Trustees to cover that cost. The extra money was needed to pay off outstanding creditors, and to carry out repairs to the embankment of Holme Styes Reservoir, which had been reported as unsafe in 1850, due to cracks opening in it. From that time it was not allowed to fill to a depth greater than 40 feet. The contract to repair Holme Styes was awarded to John Kirk in January 1857; his tendered price was £2,150. The Bill to raise the extra £7,000 had been submitted to Parliament in 1853, the cost of preparing, drafting and presenting the Bill to Parliament amounted to £3,465 4s 1d; that, plus the £2,150 for repairing Home Styes, only left £1,400 for everything else.

To return to the problem of Bilberry reservoir embankment: in 1846 the spring under the puddle trench was still running and continued to wash out the puddle core, resulting in the top of the embankment getting lower and lower to the point where instead of the waste pit being eight feet lower than the top of the embankment, the opposite had occurred. In March 1846 after the commissioners and George Leather had ceased communications, but before the settlement in the embankment had become disastrous, the commissioners contacted Mr. Bateman of Manchester, who had recently acted as Civil Engineer in the building of a reservoir in Glossop, and asked him to inspect Bilberry reservoir which he did between 14 and 21 April. Possibly as a result of his recommendations, the commissioners ordered that an opening be made in the waste pit 18 feet above the top of the shuttles to limit the amount of water in the reservoir, and appointed Joshua Littlewood, a commissioner and Architect, to see that the work was carried out. He then appointed Jonathon Thorpe & Co. to do the work. Thorpe subsequently told Littlewood that when he went to the reservoir to ascertain what equipment was needed to do the job, a number of commissioners questioned him and told him that should he attempt to undertake the work, they would resist by force if necessary. Littlewood took no further steps to get the work done, and neither did he report the incident at a commissioners meeting. William Jacomb, Clerk to the commissioners said at the inquest that he had no idea, until the flood, that the order to make the opening in the waste pit had not been carried out, or that the top of the waste pit was higher than the lowest part of the embankment. If the last statement was correct, why had Jacomb written to Mr. Littlewood to appoint him to oversee the making of the opening in the waste pit to restrict the depth of the water? The Commissioners must have been aware of the leaks in the embankment, although they denied that.

Charles Battye, Cloth Miller at Bilberry Mill, was appointed 'drawer' on 11 February 1846. He took his orders from two commissioners, John Roebuck of Bank End Mill, and George Hirst of Lower Digley Mill. In his evidence at the inquest he said that he was told to allow enough water through the shuttles to supply Bilberry Mill whether they were working full time or not, as "that, with the runs [leaks] would supply the other mills"; they presumably meant the mills down to Holmbridge, where the water from Bilberry would then be supplemented by Rake Dike and Dobb Dike. Battye also said that the waste pit was higher than the embankment when he first became drawer, and that in the last six years it had settled about another ten feet. Battye also said that both John Roebuck and George Hirst were aware of the settlement; and that George Hirst had told him to limit the water in the reservoir to a depth of thirty feet, as he did not consider it safe above that depth.

The drawer before February 1846 was Jonathon Woodcock of Hoobram Bottom, he said that he had been supplied with a set of printed rules which said that he could leave the shuttles down for a fortnight together, and the leakage from the embankment and the water from the wood on the north side were sufficient to supply the mills below. He also said that the embankment began to show signs of sinking as soon as the contractors left. The unusually high volume of rainfall in January and early February 1852, plus the fact that only one of the two shuttles at the base of the waste pit would function, and that the embankment was, at its lowest point, some eight or ten feet below the level of the overflow, was a bodeful combination.

The shuttle that did not function was supposedly fully open, but something was restricting the passage of the water. The two shuttles were located in the same pipe, one behind the other; closing either of them would stop water passing through the pipe. A year prior to the flood a submerged tree-trunk was found to be wedged in one of the shuttles, which was cleared, but no measures had been taken to prevent a recurrence. At that time several trees were floating in the reservoir, having been washed down from where they had been felled. It is possible that another submerged tree or other object had been drawn to the outlet and become wedged. With no other means of increasing the outflow of water, it was inevitable that the reservoir would fill and overflow.

The state of the reservoir was common knowledge amongst the people living near, and in the days before the flood many people came to see how full it was getting. Charles Battye lived in a house at Bilberry Mill, John Roebuck advised him to get his family and belongings out of the house as the reservoir would be sure to burst if the rain continued. By 9pm on the evening of February 4th there was about nine feet of masonry showing on the inside slope of the embankment, corresponding to about three feet vertical height, with the water visibly rising. Having previously moved his wife and family out of his house, Charles Battye began moving his belongings around 10pm. John Woodcock was on the embankment about 11pm by which time the water had almost reached the top. John Roebuck was also there, he told Woodcock that: "he would see such a scene as he had never seen in his life, before 2 o'clock. There would not be a mill left in the valley". Woodcock and Roebuck stood watching until the embankment broke. Woodcock said:

> *"The embankment did not give way all at once, the water first began to flow over near the middle of the bank, the water washed into the middle of the settlement and then over it, and then washed part of the embankment away. The water first lodged in the settlement about twenty minutes past eleven, about half an hour after that the water came over the outside – the hollow would be about six feet deep – on the outside of that hollow the embankment first gave way. In a short time the embankment began to give way all along the top, in the middle of the embankment the water boiled up and it swam away the embankment in great parts at once, it washed away nearly to the bottom [of the soil], close to the puddle bed, we were then aware of the consequence that would ensue and left the place. The embankment gave way and Bilberry Mill was washed away in less than five minutes after the outer embankment was washed away. The puddle bank was standing for a short time, not five minutes before it gave way, I might have got 100 yards off when I heard the noise of the bursting. Before the bursting two persons started off to give warning to people below, they were John Whitely and Benjamin Bray."*

John Whiteley of Green Gates Farm, who was a weaver at Bank End Mill, said he went to give warning about 12.30am. The first time he was aware of the water following was when he got to Victoria Mill. He carried on towards Holmfirth and arrived at Upper Bridge where he met people that he knew, and where he collapsed from exhaustion. In spite of the warnings people living near to the river did not have time to get clear. There was considerable damage to livestock, property, and also around 80 people died.[b] Many people had had misgivings about the state of Bilberry Reservoir for some time, probably for too long, as people who voiced their concerns in the days running up to the flood were accused of crying 'Wolf'.

The Inquest

The inquest into the tragedy was opened in Holmfirth on Friday 6 February, the jury, having already viewed the dead, were sworn in, but the Coroner, Mr. George Dyson, said that he did not propose to hear any evidence that day as he wanted the jury to visit the reservoir, and that he also wanted to give the Government the opportunity to appoint a qualified engineer to inspect the reservoir should they so desire. The bodies of victims that had been recovered were released for burial. The inquest reopened on Wednesday February 18th, ostensibly to determine the cause of death of Eliza Marsden of Hinchliffe Mill, who was one of the victims, but in reality to determine the cause of the reservoir's collapse. Hearing the evidence was to take two and a half days. The coroner recommended that the inquiry should be divided into two parts: firstly, the state of the reservoir prior to February 5th; and secondly, whether or not the accident had arisen from culpable negligence. An affirmative answer to the second question could result in charges of manslaughter.

Captain Moody of the Royal Engineers was present at the inquest on behalf of the Government. In his evidence Captain Moody said that the cause of the tragedy was that the top of the embankment was lower than the rim of the waste pit. Regardless of the number of leaks through the embankment, or the quantity and quality of the puddle core, where the top of the embankment was lower than the waste pit, that was the point where an excess of water would escape. Due to the type of embankment, this would result in the water washing away the grass and soil from the top and outer

---

b   The number of deaths and the amount of damage vary slightly depending on which report one reads.

side of the embankment, which would lead to its eventual collapse. Had the puddle core been of a better construction, the collapse although inevitable, would have occurred more slowly rather than a sudden breach, but would have still resulted in a flood. The shuttles in the lower wall of the waste pit were only to regulate the flow of water to the mills; they were not intended to regulate the amount of water in the reservoir. Captain Moody criticised the design of the waste pit and shuttles, which he knew was in common use in the area; but was not a suitable design for the terrain in which Bilberry reservoir was built, with steep sided valleys and ravines where 'obstructions of various kinds may be expected to be continually brought down, particularly in heavy floods of rain'. The flow of water towards the outlet would draw the potential obstructions towards the shuttles where, without any metal guards to keep them away, they were likely to stay. When he examined the reservoir after the flood, he had the water that remained in the reservoir drained, and found a large stone measuring twenty inches by seventeen inches and five inches thick obstructing the shuttle opening which was eighteen inches square. This explains why Charles Battye thought that the volume of water passing through them was reduced.

The dimensions of the waste pit were sufficient to allow excess water to escape had the embankment remained at its full height. However, Captain Moody said that he preferred the overflow to be cut into the embankment at one or both ends, where, of course, it can be seen and can be easily kept clear of obstruction. The dimensions of the embankment were adequate, had the quality of the materials and construction been of a sufficiently high standard. Unfortunately, this was not the case. The outer part of the embankment should have been constructed from heavy materials including stones which, together with the puddle core, would more than equal the weight of the water in the reservoir pushing against them. Where the earth in both the inner and outer walls meet the puddle core it should be well rammed so that the density of the soil equals that of the clay puddle, to ensure that water is unable to penetrate. The puddle core should be of a dense and even consistency. The soil used in the embankment at Bilberry was loose in nature, the inner wall being permeable throughout, with a dry rubble wall running up both sides of the puddle core that would allow water to spread through the entire embankment and work on any cavities or porous areas with which it came into contact. The puddle used in the embankment was an uneven mixture of clay and gravel, but the Captain could not say that it was necessarily detrimental. He stressed the need to convey any springs of water safely away, and to cut the puddle core into the rocks at the sides of the valley to ensure that all faults and fissures were effectively stopped up.

In his summing up of the evidence the Coroner said that it was perfectly clear that before the flood the embankment was 'in an improper state and a danger to the public, and that the commissioners knew this to be the case. The commissioners had made several attempts to correct the faults, which had been largely unsuccessful. He was not convinced by their protestations about the lack of money, because if they were criminally responsible the want of funds would not have saved them. Although the construction of the embankment was not ideal, the cause of the accident was that the overflow in the waste pit was higher than the embankment; and there had been ample opportunity since the initial building work was completed for an opening in the waste pit that was below the level of the embankment to be made'. The 1837 Holme Reservoirs Act declared the commissioners to be a corporate body, which meant that they were a corporation, and as such the commissioners could not be individually held liable for the accident. Neither could George Leather the Civil Engineer; Daniel Sharpe & Son, or Porters, be held criminally responsible. Regarding the order from the commissioners that an opening should be made in the waste pit eighteen feet above the shuttles that was countermanded by a group of commissioners who threatened resistance, Mr. Dyson said that he did not think that the threat amounted to a criminal act; there would have had to be actual resistance. However, he was critical of Mr. Littlewood's failure to bring the abandonment of the work to the notice of the commissioners. Had that work been undertaken, from Captain Moody's evidence the accident would have been avoided. The Coroner also put the onus onto the commissioners for their failure to order that the spring discovered in the base of the puddle trench should be carried away, which, 'for the want of a few shillings' would have avoided the accident. As to criminal neglect:

> '*It appeared to him from this enquiry that there had been very gross and culpable negligence on the part of the commissioners, and he did not think from what they had said in evidence, notwithstanding their applications to parliament, that there was anything that could excuse their negligence. It was a negligence of the most gross kind, and had they been individuals, instead of a corporate body, it would have called for and justified a verdict of manslaughter*'.

The jury made up of eight manufacturers, two schoolmasters, a clock maker, a saddler, a linen draper, a shopkeeper, a bookseller, and a gentleman; retired to consider the evidence and decide upon their verdict. After two and a half hours they returned, only one juror dissented from the verdict read out by the foreman.

> '*We find that Eliza Marsden came to her death by drowning, caused by the bursting of the Bilberry Reservoir.* [This was consistent with the verdicts on all the other fatalities caused by the flood]. *We also find that the Bilberry Reservoir was defective in its original construction, and that the Commissioners, engineers and overlookers were greatly culpable in not seeing to the proper regulations of the works; and we also find that the Commissioners, in permitting the Bilberry Reservoir to remain for several years in a dangerous state, with a full knowledge thereof, and not lowering the waste pit, have been guilty of gross and culpable negligence; and we regret that the reservoirs being under the management of a corporation, prevents us bringing in a verdict of manslaughter, as we are convinced that the gross and culpable negligence of the Commissioners would have subjected them to such a verdict had they been in the position of a private individual, or a firm; we also hope that the legislature will take into its most serious consideration the propriety of making provision for the protection of the lives and properties of her Majesty's subjects exposed to danger from reservoirs placed by corporations in situations similar to those under the charge of the Holme Reservoir Commissioners.*'

Captain Moody had also been requested to make some observations on the state of Holme Styes Reservoir. He said that he had inspected the reservoir, which had a valve pit with the same type and arrangement of shuttles as those at Bilberry which, if one could not be opened would cause the reservoir to fill and overflow. There was a leak in the valve pit that was larger than the one at Bilberry, and also a leak on the outside of the masonry of the culvert. Holme Styes did have a byewash at one side, but a wall had been built across it that would restrict the water from flowing over should the reservoir become full. Had Holme Styes reservoir filled to a slightly higher level than it had on February 4th, it would have flowed over the embankment, with a similar result to that at Bilberry; resulting in a much greater inundation in Holme Valley. The Captain suggested that whoever had built the wall across the byewash was 'insane'. Despite stressing the urgent need for the repairs, they were not carried out until 1857. The censure of George Leather by Captain Moody and the Coroner dealt such great blows to his reputation that he retired from business in 1855.

The Aftermath

The scene in the Holme Valley in the aftermath of the flood was one of devastation, destruction, and despair. Many buildings, both houses and workplaces were destroyed, countless others damaged. A meeting was called for Saturday February 7th to form a Committee to coordinate relief and restoration, its title was the Holmfirth Flood Relief Committee. People from Huddersfield, who had already formed a Relief Committee, attended the meeting and were able to report that, in the two days since the flood, donations to the Relief Fund already amounted to £1,600, which was in an account at the Huddersfield Banking Company. The committee formulated a letter to be sent to mill owners and occupiers suggesting that men who had been put out of work due to damage done by the flood should be given the opportunity to work in retrieving salvageable goods and machinery, for which the committee would pay: Children under 14 – 4d per day; from 14 to 18 – 9d per day; men over 18 – 1s 6d per day. A weekly return listing names, ages, and occupations was to be submitted by the mill owner or occupier every Friday. The committee considered this method to be a better form of relief than actual charity. The weekly returns indicate that men were employed on clearance work until late June, or possibly into July. Many houses near to rivers had cellars that were full of water, on the 11th of February members of the committee were delegated to oversee the emptying and clearing of these cellars in an attempt to minimise the spread of fever and disease. One man who died from Typhus was the husband of Ann Cartwright, he had been working at Mytholmbridge on salvage recovery for Charles Bashforth.

Not all the people who were missing after the flood had been accounted for; also on the 11th the committee asked that men should be employed to search water courses and flooded cellars looking for bodies, these men would be paid 2s 6d a day. There is an item in the accounts which reads: 'Searching for and laying out dead bodies £19 9s 9d', although it does not record how many, if any, were found.

The compassion felt by the rest of the country for the people of Holme Valley was not expressed solely in the form of monetary gifts; another entry in the minute book, also on February 11th gives details of a letter received by the committee from 24 men in Oldham, who describe themselves as 'mechanics', offering the services of each of them free of charge for four days. The minute books do not appear to give any indication of their offer being accepted, or for that matter, declined. The committee in Huddersfield did an extraordinary job in appealing to the rest of the country for relief funds. They obtained 2,000 to 2,500 copies of the *Huddersfield Examiner* and *Huddersfield Chronicle* newspapers containing the reports of the flood and sent them to towns and cities throughout Britain, accompanied by a letter saying that donations could be paid into any Bank that had a connection with Huddersfield Banking Company for transfer to the Flood Relief Fund. The response to the appeal was overwhelming; donations totalled over £50,000. On 2nd November 1852, the Flood Relief Committee set aside £7,000 in the hands of Trustees, for the use of the Holme Reservoir Commissioners in rebuilding the reservoir. Whether this was a justifiable use of money that had been donated for the relief of those damaged or made destitute by the bursting of the original reservoir is a debateable issue, particularly in view of the assessments of culpability given at the inquest. The total of the donations, slightly over £50,300, actually exceeded the requirements, and the committee began returning money to donors before the end of 1852, the amount refunded was approximately 43.33 percent, equal to 8s 8d in the pound. This was made regardless of amount, a contribution of 2d given by 'a poor person' shows a refund of 1d. The total amount returned is shown as £16,952 9s 10d.

Householders, mill owners or occupiers, and small business proprietors completed schedules showing losses and damage to their property. The claims varied in size from around ten pounds to over ten thousand pounds, depending on what was involved. The amount of money paid to claimants from the Relief Fund was, in many cases, much less than the amount originally claimed. An example of this is the claim submitted by the executors of the late George Hirst who owned and ran Lower Digley mill, which was destroyed by the flood. The total claim for the extensive range of mill buildings, farm buildings, houses and cottages, water wheel, steam engine and boiler, machinery, wool, cloth, dyestuffs, and farm stock amounted to £10, 500. The amount paid by the fund was £4,628 12s 5d. The claim submitted by the executors of George Farrar for Lower mill totalled £2,000; an independent valuation put the claim at £1,889. The amount paid by the fund in full settlement was £1,246 13s 2d. There are no reasons given to explain why the payments were smaller, it is possible that part of the claims were covered by insurance, which had not been taken into account by the claimants, or that some machinery, wool, or cloth was salvaged and possibly reused or sold, but the size of the discrepancies is surprising. There is evidence that some goods were sold, but the amounts realised were well below their true value. William Day Martin was a watch and clock maker in Holmfirth. His claim for the loss of stock, fixtures and fittings came to £766 8s 10d. An auction sale on 27 March of 170 small lots realised a total of £13 6s 11d. This did not, by any means, represent all his stock, but the average price raised per lot was just over 1s 6d, far less than their true value.

The claims give us some insight into the integration and cooperation between competing manufacturers; the multiple occupancy of some mills, and how some manufacturers in addition to their own work, were carrying out commission work for others. John Roebuck of Bank End mill Holmbridge also had five fulling stocks in Bilberry Mill higher up the valley, which was occupied by Joseph Broadhead & Co. Pieces would be transported between the two premises by horse and cart. Lower Mill in Holmfirth was occupied principally by George Farrar's son James Hobson Farrar; and in addition, Messrs. Pogson, Iron Founders of Round Bottom mill had a counting house and smith's shop in Lower mill; Mr. Thewlis occupied the dyehouse; Benjamin Mellor, who later occupied Albert mill, had finishing rooms, a raising house, and other rooms in the mill; John Furniss of Upper Digley mill who, at the time of the flood, was in liquidation, had recently occupied a warehouse; and Joshua and Eli Hoyle had their spinning rooms there. Lower Mytholmbridge mill owned by Lord Dartmouth, was let to four different enterprises. Firstly James & George Robinson; secondly, J. Beardsell & Co., Joshua Heap & sons, John Littlewood & Sons, Mark and Frederick Heap, and George Brook; thirdly, Robert Hallas & Co; fourthly, Joseph Mellor & Sons. There were many other mills throughout the district that were also multi occupancy.

The *Huddersfield Chronicle* of 25 June 1853, reports on a discussion that took place in Parliament prior to the third reading of the Bill to sanction the rebuilding of Bilberry Reservoir. Three petitions had been received by Parliament: one was signed by 1,200 residents of Holmfirth and district; one was from the Chairman of a public meeting called in Holmfirth to discuss the rebuilding; and the third was signed by six mill owners and fourteen occupiers of mills in the district. All three petitions were requesting that permission for the rebuilding should be refused. It was pointed out by Mr. Richard Cobden that the reservoir was no longer essential to the running of the mills, as virtually every mill in the district had a steam engine to provide power for machinery. There was, understandably, considerable concern in the district that if the reservoir was rebuilt there could be a recurrence of the 1852 disaster. Mr. H. Denison, Chairman of the Parliamentary Committee, said that the committee were unanimously in favour of the bill. After the third reading the voting was: those in favour 129, those against 29.

The Flood Relief Committee had set aside a sum of money for the rebuilding of the reservoir; initially £7,000, although about the time that the commissioners were prevailing upon the subscribers to forego the unpaid interest that they were owed, and agree that in future, they would accept half the amount to which they were entitled, the Relief Committee reduced the rebuilding fund by £1,000 to £6,000. There is nothing to suggest that the two things are linked, but it does seem rather more than a coincidence.

The request for tenders for rebuilding the reservoir went out in 1854, the former overseer John Kirk formed a partnership with a William Mellor from the Manchester area, and they tendered a price of £6,100. After a meeting with the commissioners, Kirk and Mellor amended their price to £5,600. They were finally awarded the contract on 12 September 1854, having revised their price yet again to £5,500. The new embankment was moved upstream some thirty feet, which would take most of it clear of the spring that had been the cause of much of the damage. The height of the embankment was reduced to fifty-three feet, with a waste pit still with a hollow interior to carry away excess water, that was to be forty-nine feet high; and there was also to be a waste weir on the Hoobram Hill [north] side of the dam. Any springs that were discovered had to be turned into a two-foot barrel culvert that ran through the base of the embankment. The smaller area that the reservoir covered, and the reduction in the height of the embankment, reduced the reservoir's capacity; but the work was well executed and there were few problems after its completion.[6]

Heavy rains on the evening of 15 November 1866 and throughout most of the following day caused flooding in both Yorkshire and Lancashire. In our area there was damage at Bilberry mill, the new Digley mill, flooding at Hinchliffe Mill and between Bottoms and Victoria where Black Sike Dike joined the river. Property was damaged at Round Bottom mill, part of the retaining wall for the road collapsed at Victoria, and the dam at Farrar's Upper mill was damaged. There was also flooding further downstream between Smithy Place and Honley Bridge; Mag Dike was also in flood, but there were no reports of casualties.[7]

For the next fifty-five years all appears to have gone well until on September 5th 1931, the following report appeared in the *Holmfirth Express*:

> : *'GIANT FLOODS IN HOLME VALLEY' Due to heavy rains on Thursday and Friday September 3rd & 4th ; water came to within 18 inches of the roadway of Victoria Bridge, and overran Higgin Bridge in front of the Rose & Crown. James Lancaster's at Lower Mytholmbridge had water in the ground floor of the mill, but due to the foresight of the workers they had moved as much material as possible before the water entered. The same applied at Joseph Sykes' at Rock mill, and James Robinson's at Smithy Place. A number of houses close to the river were also flooded on the ground floor. An area of the main road below Honley was flooded to a depth of between two feet six inches and three feet, which held up traffic for a time. Some flooding also occurred in Berry Brow, and forty employees at Lockwood mill had to escape through a window; and workers at a mill in Waterloo left the premises when their premises became flooded to a depth of six to eight feet.*

The rain on this occasion affected a wider area than Holme Valley, as the report also records that a goods train on the Manchester to Sheffield line came to a stop in the Woodhead Tunnel when the water became deep enough to dowse the fire; the train had to be hauled out.

An annual event that was eagerly anticipated by many children in Holme Valley was the School Feast, when you were able to walk in procession with your Sunday school wearing your new clothes. During the 1940s, due to the war, clothing and footwear were often in short supply, but even if the shop had what you wanted, and you (or your mum) had enough money to pay for it, if you did not have the clothing coupons you could not have it. Many areas had their School Feast around Whitsuntide, and in Lancashire they were known as the Whit Walks. Holmbridge Parish Church, Hinchliffe Mill Methodist, and Hall (Austonley) Sunday schools each 'walked round' headed by a banner and a Brass Band on the Saturday before Whitsuntide, and came together, originally in St. Thomas' Square but later at Dam Head, both in Hinchliffe Mill, for their 'united sing'. Holmfirth Sunday schools walked round on Whit Monday, and met in Victoria Park for their 'sing'. Whit Monday, 29 May, 1944 was a beautiful warm and sunny day, and a large crowd gathered in the park for the sing at 2.30 pm. Before the event was over rumblings of thunder could be heard, and some people who had a fair way to walk home began to leave. In the Holmbridge area the rain and thunderstorm started before tea-time; but from the newspaper report the Sunday School children in Holmfirth went to their respective Sunday Schools for tea, before going to play games in a field next to the cricket field, where Holmfirth were playing Honley. The rain in Holmbridge got gradually heavier and the river began to rise; a cloudburst occurred just after 6pm centred over Good Bent the hill to the west of Bilberry, which received a considerable amount of water, most of which ran off into the two streams that border the hill and feed directly into the reservoir. The storm was very localised, it was calculated that at least five inches of rain fell on that area in a very short time; whereas less than two miles away at Yateholme the rain gauge showed just 1.66 inches of rainfall. The water level in Bilberry reservoir on the morning of the 29th was 12 feet 4 inches below the level of the overflow, equating to a storage capacity of some twelve million gallons. The amount of rainfall even before the cloudburst was considerable, as water began running over the reservoir bye wash at 5.30pm, reaching its maximum about one hour later. Two Air Raid wardens, who were near the reservoir, said that eventually some water flowed over each end of the embankment, which held firm.

The water flowing from the reservoir was much increased by water running off the fields in torrents, increasing the volume of the river many times over until it became a highly destructive force. The flow of water was at its height in the area of the reservoir at around 6.30 pm, and peaked in the centre of Holmfirth about 7 pm. Trees, vegetation, rocks, stones and soil were washed down, some of which became caught under bridges, causing a large build up of water behind them; eventually, the weight of the water became great enough to force the detritus to overwhelm the bridge and carry on downstream, releasing a large wave of water that helped to demolish river banks and retaining walls. The parapet of the bridge at Holmbridge was swept away, and the retaining wall for the land at the Parish Hall was damaged, the parapet of the bridge at Dam Head in Hinchliffe Mill was also destroyed. Several mills were damaged, including W.H. & J. Barber's Clarence Mill at Holmbridge, where the water dislodged concrete floors and flooded the ground floor; at Whiteley & Green's in Hichliffe Mill, the finishing shed was badly damaged and silted up; at T. & J. Tinker's Bottoms Mill, the water undermined the mill foundations next to the river and flooded the offices and a shed. The water had risen high enough inside the mill to stop the time-clock at 6.20 pm. After leaving Bottoms Mill, the water became diverted across the fields to R. H. Dark & Co. Riverside Mill, where it demolished some sheds and swept many bales of Rabbit fur and other materials along its course. These caused much havoc, as they became wedged under bridges, and were carried into other premises where they caused additional damage. At W.W. Battye & Sons Ltd. Victoria Mill, the two lower floors were flooded, leaving around five feet of sludge on each floor, here the time clock stopped at 6.25 pm;

W. Greenwood & Sons, Perseverance Mill was also flooded. At Victoria, the river runs alongside Woodhead Road, albeit several feet below road level. The volume of water and debris demolished the retaining wall for the road, and washed away a large semi-circle of roadway virtually outside the Victoria Inn, reaching almost to the opposite pavement and making the road impassable for vehicles. For several weeks busses for Holmbridge and Holme were diverted up Greenfield Road to Parkhead, where a shuttle service of single deck busses, which could get under the bridge across the road at Birks House, took passengers through Burnlee to Bottoms and up Woodhead Road to their destination. What had formerly been known as Farrar's Upper Mill at Prickleden was, in 1944, the premises of Wright Hinchliffe & Co. Ltd., and was known as Valley Dyeworks, here the whole premises were flooded and covered with sludge. Downstream from here were the premises of H. & S. Butterworth Ltd., Lower Mill, where part of the mill formed a bridge over the river, this part collapsed and the rest of the mill was flooded, causing extensive damage. From the mill towards the centre of Holmfirth, the water reached a depth of thirty feet.

Damage caused by water and debris at Lower Mill. © Mrs. J. Bray

Just below Lower Mill is Upper Bridge, which also lost its parapets, from here the river ran alongside Hollow Gate, with concrete bridges crossing the river to what were at that time two

Garages, the first one belonging to G.W. Castle Ltd. car dealers and taxis; the second one being Baddeley Bros Ltd., 'bus operators and taxis. Both bridges, which were concrete, withstood the deluge, but both premises were flooded, and some cars were washed away. The next bridge downstream was Victoria Bridge at the bottom of Victoria Street, which at that time had shops built on it on the upstream side, all of which were demolished. The first to go was the branch of Wallaces Grocers, which had a dwelling house over, the report from Holmfirth Council records that it collapsed into the river in 'two seconds', the whole of the building disappearing. Next was the Yorkshire Penny Bank, which subsided into the river much more slowly. The Huddersfield Building Society branch was next to Messrs. Gledhill & Brook, which was built on firm ground. The report says that the Building Society moved some six inches away from Gledhill & Brook before it collapsed into the river, again disappearing in 'two seconds'. The parapet on the downstream side also collapsed. The Valley Cinema was open for business, patrons were evacuated via the side and rear entrances into Norridge Bottom, from where they were able to make their way to safety. Some sixty shops were affected in total, damage varied from flooded cellars and loss of stock, to total demolition.

Albert Mill, was where the Co-op. supermarket now stands, and was the home of B. Mellor & Son, Ltd.; just across Bridge Lane is J. & J.W. Longbottom's Iron Foundry, both these premises were flooded; the bridge here, along with the one at Smithy Place in Brockholes, were the only two to survive the deluge unscathed. In Thongsbridge, the premises of R.L. Robinson and Boothroyd Rugs, both in Thongsbridge Mills along with John Woodhead Ltd. of Albion Mills, were flooded on the ground floors, and a considerable amount of sludge and debris was deposited. The bridge here was destroyed. J. Lancaster & Sons Ltd. at Lower Mytholmbridge Mill and Joseph Sykes & Co. of Rock Mill Brockholes, suffered extensive damage from flooding and deposits of debris. Lancaster's also had damage to weaving sheds, while Sykes's lost parts of new machinery. It is obvious that as the flood waters passed Holmfirth and moved northwards, and the valley widened, the water was slowing. It still carried debris and soil, but the larger stones and the rocks weighing up to one ton had been left behind, therefore the damage done by the flood diminished. The candle works of Kaye and Messenger Ltd. at Neiley, and Cooper Liversidge & Wood's dyeworks, also at Neiley, along with Allen Thornton & Co Ltd., Crossley Mills, and A.C. Wickman Ltd. of Reins Mill both in Honley, were all flooded, but apart from debris little damage was done.

Unlike the 1852 flood, although 109 houses were affected by the flood waters and some people had to be evacuated, damage to housing property was not as bad. People living in Waterside, and Ford Gate in Hinchliffe Mill; Scar Fold, Upperbridge, Hollowgate, Victoria Square, and Towngate in Holmfirth; and Rock Terrace in Brockholes were evacuated by the Police and Air-Raid Wardens. 122 people were given temporary accommodation. Those from Holmfirth were taken to Lane Congregational Church, but before nightfall they had all managed to find accommodation with relatives or friends. Unfortunately, there was some loss of life due to this flood. The first tragedy took place close to Riverside Mill, when Miss Maude E. Wimpenny, aged 76, got into difficulties in the rising flood water. She was seen by Geoffrey Riley aged 14, who attempted to save her, but was unable to pull her from the water. His father, Donald Riley also joined in the rescue attempt, but was also drawn into the rising water. Mr. Riley and Miss Wimpenny both drowned; Geoffrey was pulled from the water about a quarter of a mile downstream, near Valley Dyeworks, by a Mr. Willis, using the hose of a stirrup pump. The *Holmfirth Express* dated 7th October, reported that for the bravery he had shown in the rescue attempt, Geoffrey was to be awarded the Albert Medal. The third fatality occurred in Holmfirth, two employees of Baddeley Bros. who had been working, Mrs. Dorothea Schofield, a part-time clerk; and Mr. Lewis Hirst, a bus driver, had climbed onto a wall to try to escape the flood waters. One of the bales of rabbit fur belonging to R.H. Dark & Co. struck the wall and demolished it, throwing both people into the water. Mr. Hirst managed to hold onto the bale and was eventually rescued by the fire brigade; but Mrs. Schofield drowned.

A marked difference between the flood of 1852 and the one of 1944 was in the way in which they were reported, which was due to the war. The *Huddersfield Daily Examiner* of Friday 9 June

1944 carried the following notice immediately under its headline about the destruction caused by the flood in Holmfirth on 29 May:

> *'In order that the enemy may not be helped to forecast the weather by knowing what is taking place over Britain, no mention may be publicly made of meteorological conditions or happenings – except in the Straits of Dover – until ten days have elapsed.'*

The first reports in the press gave brief details about the people who had drowned, but no details of how it had come about, or of the devastation that had been caused. It is probable that most people in Huddersfield knew the details of the flood from friends and relatives living in the Holmfirth area well before June 9th; but to the people of West Yorkshire and the rest of the country, ten days after the event its newsworthiness would be considerably diminished.

The task of cleaning up began the following morning, the 30th, with Civil Defence, the Fire Brigade, and other organisations giving help where possible. There was a considerable amount of sludge and debris to be cleared from the streets and buildings affected by the flood water, the efforts of the workers and volunteers were hampered somewhat by the amount of rain that fell for several days after the flood, which severely restricted the ability to dry furnishings or equipment in the open air. It was necessary for shops and businesses to reopen as soon as possible, principally to overcome any feelings of despondency that may have existed, victory over the elements was a step towards winning the war; and speedy resumption of trade would help to ensure the continuity of businesses, in addition to boosting morale. The Valley Cinema reopened for business on Monday June 19th, although the restoration was not entirely completed. Clearing obstructions from the river bed was also a priority, particularly in the area around bridges, as deposits of silt and stones had reduced the head room under bridges, increasing the possibility of a recurrence of the flood.

The capacity of Bilberry reservoir was considerably reduced; silt had raised the bottom of the reservoir until it was only about fourteen feet below the rim of the waste pit. To rectify this, a steel tower was built on the Hoobram side of the reservoir, from where steel hawsers were stretched across to a concrete anchorage on the opposite bank. A manoeuvrable grab was suspended from these wires that could be lowered into the reservoir, take up silt, and be brought to the side to be unloaded into a lorry. The concrete base for the tower and the anchorage still exist in situ.

There were several differences between the 1852 flood, and the one in 1944. Firstly, in 1852 the flood began around midnight on a dark night in February, after days or even weeks of rain; whereas in 1944, it began around 6pm in May, with more hours of daylight and when the ground was not waterlogged. The major difference between the two events was the embankment; in 1852 it collapsed, whereas in 1944 it held, even though some water flowed over it. It was no doubt the surge of water created by the collapse of the embankment that was the cause of much of the destruction to property and the large loss of life in 1852. Publicity of the two events was also very different; in 1852 the details were widely reported, many people published illustrated pamphlets, and *The Illustrated London News* published an article with drawings of the reservoir before and after the collapse of the embankment, and some of the devastation that ensued. Due to the restrictions of wartime, the publicity was much less widespread in 1944. Despite the lack of publicity, Private Harry Kenworthy who was in a military hospital somewhere in North Africa wrote to the *Holmfirth Express* enclosing a donation to the Flood Relief Fund. He had received a copy of the paper from a relative containing some details of the flood, and wished to contribute to the fund. On the 21st of October the total contributions had reached £20,232; the final total was given (in 1946) as £22, 814 19s 4d.

There was a much less serious event in 1946: heavy rain began on the night of Thursday 19 September, which continued all day Friday, raising the water level in the River Holme. Water entered some buildings in Holme village, and three houses in Water Street in Hinchliffe Mill had flooded cellars. The river overflowed into several fields just below Bottoms mill; a house at Victoria Buildings was flooded, probably due to a blocked drain, and the residents from one house at Lower Victoria had to be evacuated. H & S Butterworth, Lower Mill, stopped work at lunchtime on Friday when the level of the water in the river was just below the weaving shed floor, and some water entered the weaving shed as the river level rose higher. Victoria Bridge, which was in the process of being rebuilt after the 1944 flood, had much of the repair work undone and timber and equipment were washed away. The landlord of the Rose and Crown (the Nook) had to cancel a delivery of beer as his cellar was flooded. R.L Robinson, Thongsbridge Mill, had lost buildings in the 1944 flood, which had recently been rebuilt; these were washed away again. The adjoining premises of John Woodhead were also affected.

The only fatality was that of Edward Brook Addy, 44, of Hope Bank. He was standing on a plank that spanned the river, attempting to 'rescue' some chickens that had taken refuge in the branches of a tree, when he lost his footing and fell into the racing water; he was a non swimmer. A neighbour ran down the bank in the hope of offering Addy assistance, but Addy disappeared below the water and did not reappear. His body was found the following morning in the river below Lockwood Cricket Field.

At Neiley the recently re-erected premises of Messrs. Messenger, candle makers, were again washed away; Allen Thornton & Sons, Crossley Mills, and James Beaumont & Sons, Bridge Dyeworks both had to stop work due to flooding. The bus service between Holme Valley and Huddersfield was interrupted when the police declared Lockwood Bridge unsafe. Buses to Huddersfield were turning round at Salford and returning to Holme Valley, passengers wanting to continue to Huddersfield presumably had to cross the bridge on foot and then catch another bus at Lockwood Bar. The water was subsiding by 4pm.

There has been no recurrence of serious flooding of the River Holme since the building of Digley reservoir in the 1950s. The reservoirs of the Ramsden and Digley valleys seem to have had the capacity to contain inundations, although other areas have not been quite so lucky.

Heavy rain on 30 July 2002 caused flash floods that affected Jackson Bridge, New Mill, Holmfirth and Honley, when two thirds of the month's average rainfall fell in one day. A resident of Jackson Bridge said that at one point water was pouring off the hills and washing over the roofs of cottages below while the residents were trapped inside. New Mill dike became a raging torrent; Bower Roebuck's mill was flooded to a depth of three feet with considerable damage to stock, machinery, and office furnishings etc, with some items being carried by the water into the centre of New Mill. Water running down Kirkbridge Lane swept Mrs. Kathleen Devenish into the main torrent which was some 8 feet deep at Kirk Bridge and carried her downstream. She managed to catch hold of overhanging branches and hung on until she was rescued by neighbours who had seen her washed away and came to her aid.

Woodhead road above Holmfirth was shut near to the Victoria pub by a tree that had fallen across the roadway; the surface of Dunford Road was washed away, and one woman motorist who was driving up the road reported having to dodge boulders that were being carried towards her by the water. Several shops and businesses in Holmfirth town centre were affected by flooding.

The water level of Mag dike rose considerably washing away one bridge, and water entered the premises of DP Dyers at Thirstin Dyeworks. Electric motors affected by the flood waters had to be dried out and thoroughly checked before being re-connected to their machines, causing some delay in production. The rain continued on the 31st although not as heavily; Emley Show, due to take place on Saturday August 3rd, had to be cancelled due to the site being waterlogged.[8]

Notes

1   H.J. Morehouse, p. 228.
2   This account was written in 1838 by Mr. Joseph Holmes, and is recorded in H.J. Morehouse, pp. 228-9.
3   From George Sykes' 'Memoirs', published in the Holmfirth Express between Dec. 1923 – Feb. 1924.
4   G.M. Binnie, pp. 44-5.
5   Leeds Mercury 3 Feb. 1849.
6   Reservoir Commissioners Minute Books and other records, including details of claims submitted, can be viewed at the Kirklees Archive office in Huddersfield Library building. Newspaper and other accounts are available in the Local History section of the Library.
7   Huddersfield Examiner, 17 Nov. 1866.
8   Huddersfield Examiner 31 July 2002 and subsequent days.

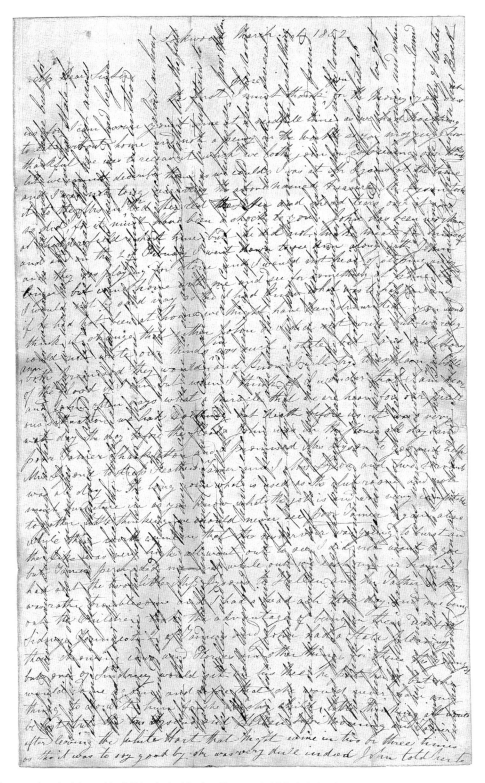

Letter written by John and Lydia Tait who had lived on Towngate in Holmfirth, in a house opposite the White Hart. It is written on 3 pages, each page had to be read firstly from top to bottom, after reading all 3 they were then turned ninety degrees and read again; making effectively six pages in total. The photograph is of pages 1 and 4.

Transcript of a letter written by Lydia and John Tait to Mrs. Tait's sister,

Mrs. Smith of Cartmell Lancashire telling her of their ordeal in the Flood of 1852.

(Spelling is as originally written)

Lockwood, March 10th 1852.

My Dear Sister,

In the first place I must thank you for the money you sent us, for I can assure you it came at a needful time, as we had nothing to eat, without home, and with not a penny in the world, so you may juge how thankful we was to receive it, which we both join in expressing our thanks, but we cannot describe them as we could. I was at Mr. Dyson's at the time, and I was not long receaving the above named treasure. Mr. Dyson took it to the Mrs. in her bed and they read the letter and shed tears over it, and so did I, for it must have been a shock to you. John has been working at Huddersfield a short time but he did not make meat for himself, and on 2 February I went down to see Ann along with John, as they was playing for stone, and I would not hear of stopping any longer, but come home with me and see for something at home and I would not be said nay, as tho' I had know what was to happen and if he had not been at home we might have been drownded. You would think it strange that either John or I did not write, but we really could not write – our minds was in such a state – but Jane and Mary Ann both promised they would, and now I will try to explain a little of the flood if I can, but when I think of it I wonder that I am hear, and John often says what a miracle that we are hear, doe our perilous situation we had nothing but death before us. It was a very wet day the day before the flood. John was in the house all day, and poor Tamer Shackleton and I promised Mrs. Dyson to goe and help Mrs. Dyson to Dress Feathers. Tamer and I, Mrs. Dyson and the two servants was all day in the long room what is used as the club very comfortable together, little thinking we should never see poor Tamer again alive. While there, word came in that the reservoir was going to burst, and the Dike was very high. All went out to see. I did not want to go, but Tamer persuaded me, and while out we each ran in home. I had sent the two little Miss Dysons to Hellen and her Father as they was rather troublesome, and I had a headache that day, and me being out the Children took advantage of being in. Thear was 4 of Sidney's, Youngest 2 of Tamer's, and John had a Slate pleasing them drawing cows and Horses and other things for them. The youngest but one of Sydney's would sit on his Nee, he put her of but she would come again, and before that she would never have anything to do with him, for she was a shy child. little thinking all would be lost but the two Dysons and Hellen before morning, and Tamer after leaving the White Hart that night came in two or three times as tho' it was to sy good by. She was very dull indeed John told her to keep up her spirits as we should have to goe before her and call of her, little thinking that when we was rescued from our perelious situation that Sydney's 7 out of 11 gone and the 4 that was saved climed on our Roof, but poor Tamer and all her Family gone, no one left to give the least account of anyway. Mrs. Hartley held the Baby up out of the water, 10 weeks old. It cried very much. She bid farewell to them all 3 times and said she could not help them. Sydney might have been saved but was trying to help the younger children. Juge our feelings when we came to ourselves – neither a home, nothing to eat, not a penny, and what is saved is completely spoiled, which are only a few of my better dresses. We had none of us stockings, shoes left, Bonnet, not cap, cuffs, collars and all our general wearing close and nothing in the furniture line but 3 chairs and the bed we stuck to and was saved on it and two Boxes. All our Bed table linen work Boxes Teachests and all my Julyry Books and all John's Books drawing instruments. We dug a few pots out of the reck and few tins and kettle and a few trifleing things, but I can assure you we have a Miserable Home, but it is better to have a harth of our own. You would see us different if you was to come now, for we was comfortable then and we have great reasons to thank the Allmighty that we are hear. Bur I must drop it for a short time for my hart is to full to say more and John is going to write a few lines for me.

Dear Sister,

You must allow me to call you by that Name, for if I had no other right to your kindness to us on the present occasion is sufficient to endear you to me as such. (Yours respectfully, J.T.)

As Lydia has hardly got her mind sufficiently settled yet for writing (and I have just finished the one we are sending to Scotland) for we have had no chance of writing to any one before this, she wishes me to help her through with this, so I must Just begin where she left off. She has not described our situation in the flood yet so I will try and give you as good an idea of it as I possibly can. Although we had heard a rumour that the reservoir was going to burst the night before (there had been so many so many of the same sort at other times that we took no notice of that one more than others) so we went to bed about ½ past 10 that night as careless as ever, little thinking what was to happen before morning. You may form some idea of our situation and feelings when about 20 minutes past one Lydia was awakened by a strange rushing noise outside and went to the window after getting up to see the cause. When she saw the water running through the fold in front of the door she immediately woke me saying John the reservoir has burst and the flood's coming. I went to the window to see for myself, and to my surprise saw in that short time it had got up to the window head downstairs and the dyehouses and stove opposite all leveled to the ground. I next looked up the valley in the direction the water was coming from and saw the warehouse next door but one to ours falling onto the stream. We then heard poor little Hellen cry Father from the back room and tried to open the door to get her beside us but could not move it for the Building had got a shake and fastened the door. In another minute Lydia was nearly up to her neck and I up to the middle in water and the Bed, chairs and Boxes rolling about the room as if they had been on the troubled Sea. We then felt the floor giving way under our feet and as we heard no more of Hellen we had given her up as lost and got again onto the Bed as the only thing we could see to take hold of, and was on that but a few seconds when we saw the front of the next house and a great part of our own fall into the water, and expected every Moment the remainder falling about our heads and either smothering us at the place or launching us out into the Boiling Current that surrounded us. We could see Firth's chairs, Boxes, Drawers and Bed, and a many of our own things go off with the stream; But cared not for them as we thought we should never want such things as them again for we had no other thought or hope but for Salvation of our souls in another world, But we were not kept long in that state of suspense for just at that moment I could see a piece of board that had got across the end of our room which the water had left that it was at its height and had begun to lower again. Then hope revived, for if the portion of the Building we were in stood we would be safe, and it was so. But we had to remain in that predicament about an hour before the water lowered that anyone could come to our assistance. Firth's father was the first that came and helped him down (and he then came and helped us) I then went upstairs to see for Hellen, and Lydia stood till Mr. Dyson came and carried her to her house. Poor Hellen! I shall never forget her narrow escape, for when I got upstairs I could not open her room door, for it was driven across its frame. I also saw the wood partition was broke in several places, so I went along the passage to try and force my way into the room and the first thing I trod on was something soft so I put my hand down to ascertain what it was and found it was her feet and legs. She was laying part in the passage and her head and sholders in the room. I then Broke the partition down, and as soon as I took the weight of wood off her chest I heard her give a sob, so I got her out and sent for Mr. Beeley who stopped with her about two hours, and then left her to go and see if he was wanted elsewhere, he could not say if she would come round again or not, But told us to keep her on her Back and keep putting a little whiskey and water into her mouth. As soon as he was gone I found great difficulty to keep her on her Back as she seemed to lay easier on her left side so I let her lay in that position about half an hour as she fell into a sleep, and when I awoke her she knew me but seemed inclined to sleep again and I let her do so for another hour and when I woke her again she could tell me about the water coming into her room. And I can assure you we was very glad to see she was getting so nicely round again. She appeared to be as well as ever during the time we remained at Holmfirth, But after we moved to Lockwood she began to droop again. She had been confined to her Bed from Friday last up to Monday that we thought we was going to loose her after all. She seem now to be coming round again But is still very weakly. She is only able to remain up 2 or 3 hours each day But as there is a sign of mending we hope she will gather strength daily and soon get well again. It is now a fortnight now since we removed down to Lockwood with a few things we had left, and have been kept so Busy cleaning them again fit for use (and with people calling to see us) that we have not had time to put pen to paper to any one to the present that I trust you will excuse us for not writing you before this. We have recieved some assistance from the subscription fund. Lydia went to Holmfirth on Saturday last, when they gave her seven pound which had enabled us to get a few chairs and a Table and several other small things that we beging to feel ourselves at home again.

I have not been able to meet with any work since we removed But have the promise of some work Monday next. I hope with proper care to be soon able to alter our circumstances. Your Mother is in very good heal;th at present, and Mary Anne sends her love to you and tells that she hopes you will excuse her writing this time as she considers we are sending you all the news and they are getting rather Busy at present. Jane or Mrs. Jonathon I am sorry to inform you is not so well at present. She has been complaining for a fortnight Back. and Mr. Nathan Littlewood I am sorry to have to tell you is at present very dangerous Ill of a liver complaint. He has been laid up for a week, and has had sometimes three Doctors with him as many as four times a day and they can't say yet if he will get over it or not. Poor Tommy Castle and several other of o That you are acquainted with had very near escapes for their lives, and I can safely say I never saw such a sense of confusion and dirt in all my life before I saw that morning. I believe I have given you all the News I am possessed of at present. I thought Lydia would have a great lot more to have supplied me with, But she is fast asleep in her chair that it is impossible to get another word from her. Poor Boddy she has almost knocked herself up with working so hard. I therefore am forced to conclude for this time, and believe me to be,

> Dear Maddam
> Yours Sincerely and Truly,
> John Tait.

P.S. Write soon and Direct for us J.R., Mason, Salford, Lockwood Nr. Huddersfield.

P.S. I forgot to tell you that the two Houses below our (viz) Sid Hartley and Dick Shackletons where entirely washed away and 7 drowned from Hartleys and 5 from Shackletons (they only found poor Dick's Boddy yesterday floating down as far as Ferry Bridge.

There was 80 drowned altogether and as far as I can learn there is 5 that has not been found yet. J.T.

> Sent to
> Mrs. Smith
> with Mrs. Machell
> Broughton Grove
> Nr. Cartmell
> Lancashire

Photographs taken from a brochure produ
showing various processes used in the

Teazing loose wool to open up the fibres and remove unwanted rubbish

Weaving shed

Carding woollen fibre prior to spinning

Drawing worsted yarn

Preparing warp

by Messrs W.H. & J. Barber of Holmbridge
duction of woollen and worsted cloth

Spinning woollen fibre into yarn

Menders removing knots and repairing flaws

prior to weaving

Finishing the cloth. Piles of finished cloth are shown in the foreground

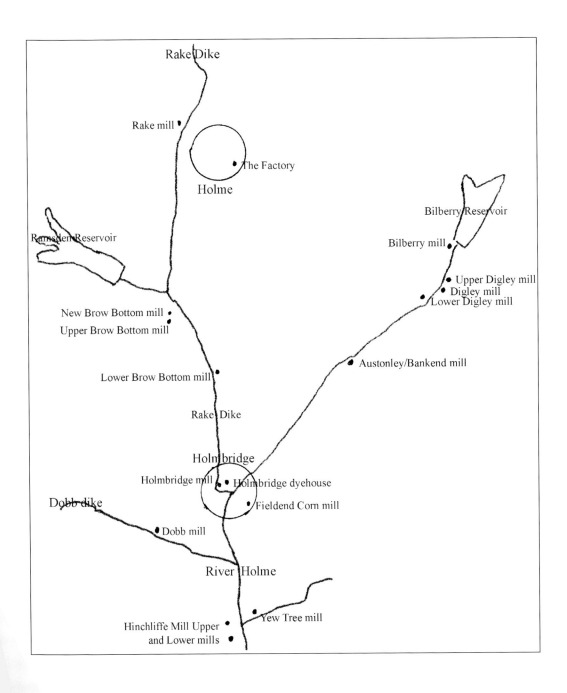

Rake Dike

Rake mill

The Factory

Holme

Bilberry Reservoir

Bilberry mill

Ramsden Reservoir

Upper Digley mill
Digley mill
Lower Digley mill

New Brow Bottom mill
Upper Brow Bottom mill

Austonley/Bankend mill

Lower Brow Bottom mill

Rake Dike

Holmbridge

Holmbridge mill   Holmbridge dyehouse

Dobb dike   Fieldend Corn mill

Dobb mill

River Holme

Yew Tree mill

Hinchliffe Mill Upper
and Lower mills

CHAPTER 8

Holme to Hinchliffe Mill

Rake Dike – Rake mill, Holme

This is one of the earlier mills of the industrial period, probably being built in the 1780s. The earliest written reference that exists for the mill is in the *Holm Rentals* of 1790 when it was recorded as having an annual value of £3. An entry in the *Wakefield Court Rolls* of 1802 shows that the owner of the property at that time was Mr. John Varley of Slaithwaite. The following year William Leake of Ramsden purchased from John Varley and his wife Mary, the Messuage or tenement at Ripper Lane, and closes called the Nether Croft, the Croft under the House, the Middle Croft, the Croft Head, the Intake, the two Round Hills, the Rough Ing, the Round Close, the close of Nederley, and the Heald Gate Sike, totalling 40 days work or approx. 40 acres, which at that time were occupied by Aaron and Jonas Hinchliffe; and also the Scribbling Mill at Lane in Holme, with the Water Wheel, Gear, Machines, Cards and Engines therein, then in the possession of Aaron Hinchliffe, Joseph Leake, John Howard and Joseph Barber. The purchase price for the whole was £1,150.

In 1808 the occupant of the mill was Joseph Sykes, who, for £16 1s, purchased from William Leake and his wife Rachel 321sq.yds. of land called the Upper Stone Pit Hill, with permission to take water from a spring called Spink Well through 2 closes called the Upper and Lower Stone Pit Hills, and to have a footpath through both closes to and from Rake Mill. The Leake family reserved the right to take soot, ashes and manure from any cottages that were subsequently built on the land.

A return submitted to the Factory Commissioners in 1832 shows that power was provided by a 6hp water wheel, and that 9 males and 4 females, whose ages are not given were employed at the mill, which, at that time, was probably being run by William and Edward Leake, who in 1836 were fined for infringing the 1833 Factory Act, dealing with the employment of children. The infringement was not considered serious, and was probably a breech of the hours that children were allowed to work. The monetary fine imposed was partly mitigated, and the Factory Inspector who brought the case said that the money from the fine would be distributed amongst the Sunday Schools of the district.

William Leake the elder died in 1837, he divided the ownership of the mill equally between his two sons William and John, also Thomas Wain Leake and Edmund Leake his nephews; giving them each a quarter share. The sons and nephews do not all appear to have shared their father and uncle's enthusiasm for the mill or the other property, as in 1838 Edmund and Sarah Leake sold a house with outbuildings and land, plus a quarter share in Rake Mill to George Starkey of Huddersfield; and later in the year John Cuttell of Long Walls bought a quantity of land along with a house at Ings, and a quarter share in the mill from John Leake of Ramsden; in each case the purchase price was £600. Moses Howard, described as a manufacturer and small farmer, was in business at Rake mill as a scribbling miller along with William and John Leake, and the trustees of Caleb Howard deceased. Moses had got into debt and was incarcerated in York Gaol between 4 September and 22 October 1852.[1]

In March 1855 a quarter share in Rake Mill, which was then occupied by George Tinker and James Charlesworth, was offered for sale by auction, as was the Peacock Inn, a beer house at Ing, own----

by the Leake family but tenanted at the time by William Askham. The mill was again advertised for sale in November 1856, when the occupants were given as George Tinker and James France; also offered for sale was a property at Ing described as a dwelling house with barn, stable, and dyehouse, plus a cottage and garden. This was possibly the former Peacock Inn which was no longer being used as a beer house. The mill was offered for sale yet again in May 1857, when it was described as having 3 scribblers; 3 carders; 3 billeys; 1 willey; and many sundries. In July of the same year, a one quarter share in the mill along with a quarter share in a nearby dwelling house was to be auctioned, the mill was presumably not working at that time, as it was described as being 'lately occupied by Messrs. Tinker and France'.

A second report to the Factory Inspectors in 1858 records that power was from a 4hp water wheel, and that the mill still had 13 employees, made up of 11 males and 2 females. A one quarter share in the mill was again offered for sale in May 1859, when the occupants were James Hinchliffe and James Booth. The Holm Rentals of 1860 record the owner of the mill as being Mr. Thomas Wain Leake, with Hinchliffe and Booth as the occupiers; however, they had left the mill before 1866. In February 1866 John Cuttell of Holmbridge and Thomas Wain Leake of Holme were summoned for the recovery of £3 6s unpaid rate for the mill. The overseer responsible for collecting the rate said that he had previously collected rates from Mr Cuttell, which Cuttell disputed. The overseer said that he could provide dates when he had collected property tax from Cuttell which the Bench said was a different matter from rates. Cuttell agreed that as part owner of the mill he had paid the property tax, but insisted that Leake was responsible for the Rates. Leake said that he was also a part owner of the mill and had undertaken to use it provided the wheel did not break down, but part way through a job the wheel broke and the mill had been unusable since then. The question was put: was the rate due even though the mill was unusable? Mr. R. Meller, appearing for the overseers, said that the rate was due for the full year, firstly because there was machinery in the mill, and secondly because if the mill ran for only one day the full rate was payable. The Chairman of the bench said

Rake Mill Holme front view. Photograph provided by Mr. G. Hallas

that he felt that principle should give way to practice, which was to make some allowance in these cases. The bench ruled that the full rate was due, but recommended the overseer to make a suitable allowance.

Possibly as a result of this case coupled with a falling off in demand from weavers for the mill to scribble and card their wool, the machinery was offered for sale in March 1866, consisting of 1 scribbler, 1 carder, a piecing machine described as 'almost new', a billey, plus a teazer with a fan, 1 spinning mule, and 33ft of wrought iron shafting, also various sundries. Whether this constituted all the remaining machinery; or whether the additional equipment listed in 1857 remained is not known, but no existing or future occupants are named.

In November 1876 a one quarter share in the mill along with a 13acre farm were offered for sale, outcome unknown; followed in July 1887 by the offer of three undivided quarter shares in the mill, along with the adjacent cottage, outbuildings and land, the whole being bought by Mr. H. Hebblethwaite for £20. This would suggest that the mill, and possibly the cottage, were not only empty, but partly derelict. The mill was demolished between 1912 and 1914, but some of the building materials apparently remained on the site as in 1918 the Holme U.D.C. purchased some spare roofing slates for the sum of £15.

A ratepayers meeting held in Holme Sunday School on 22 March 1915, resolved that the Holme U.D.C. should not oppose the new Holme Electricity Company supplying electricity to the area, and recommended the Council to provide at least thirty street lights along the roads in the district; the number that were eventually erected was twenty. The power was to be generated by installing a turbine in a newly erected building on the left bank of Rake Dike where the mill had stood. Poles were erected to convey the power from the turbine to a distribution and storage centre built at Corn Hey Farm, from where it would be distributed to every house in the village and the street lights. The official opening of the service was on Saturday 13 November 1915, Holme was the first area in the Holme Valley to have electricity. Consumption was not metered, each house was allowed up to three thirty-watt bulbs, at the fixed cost of £1 10s per year.[2] Application could be made to use additional bulbs, which would incur an annual charge of 4s per bulb. The Holme Electricity Company was eventually taken over by Holme U.D.C. which continued to supply electricity to the district until late 1933, by which time, due to advances in the number and types of electrical appliances that were available, the turbine was unable to supply sufficient power to fulfil customers' needs. The electricity supply for the area was taken over by Holmfirth U.D.C. on January 1, 1934; the turbine was sold 'as it stands' to Mr. J.R. Dunkley for £25 in 1937, bringing the use of the mill site to its conclusion.

'The Factory' Holme

The firm of James Beardsell & Sons, who were initially based in what is now Holme House, had a small dyehouse somewhere in the village which, as the business expanded, became inadequate for their needs. As recorded in Chapter 6, in 1830 they bought land and property in Meal Hill Road from Abel and Solomon Garlick, consisting of two houses, some old outbuildings and some ground adjoining a water supply, which offered a very good situation for a dyehouse. The cost of the land and property was £315; plus the cost of building and equipping the dyehouse, which was another £250, although this does not appear to include the cost of the dyepan. It was this building that eventually became known as 'the factory'. It continued to be used as a dyehouse well into the 1840s, when Isaac recorded in his diary that the original thatched roof needed repairing, and would be replaced with slates; it was possibly at this time that it was converted into a three storey weaving shop, with a basement that contained a gas making plant to provide light, rather than the hearths and brickwork for dyepans. After they had taken space in Upper Digley Mill in 1837, which was where Isaac, who was in charge of the dyeing, was based, it would be more efficient to dye the yarn in the mill.

When the sale of plant and machinery belonging to the firm of Charles Beardsell & Sons of Brow Bottom Mill, was advertised in 1867, it included 22 narrow handlooms and 4 broad handlooms complete with 3-shuttle boxes and witches that were shown as being in premises in Holme. The building remained in the Beardsell family, and was next occupied by Charles Beardsell's son Alfred, who in 1874 was experiencing problems of liquidity. His machinery, which consisted of 8 looms, both broad and narrow, with gearing, a warping woof and creel, 2 winding-on frames, 2 platform weighing machines and various sundries were offered for sale by auction.

The family also built a second building next to the factory in 1839, which is still standing and is currently the home of Holme Club, which they also possibly used as a weaving shop. Alfred had managed to retain the premises, as he sold them to the Trustees of Holme Liberal Club in October 1884. A former resident of Holme, James Battye, used to claim, in later life, that at the age of 11 he had been the Beardsell family's 'gas manager' at the Factory.[3]

There is also evidence of another **Dyehouse** in Holme during the 1830s and 1840s. The Court Rolls record that on 29 December 1837, Jonathon William Roberts of Farnley Tyas bought two dwelling houses with two barns, stable and mistal in the possession of Caleb Heward and Charles Brearley, with the stove, dyehouse and a butcher's shop near to the houses, in the possession of Caleb Heward and John Bray; and also five cottages in the possession of David Kaye, John Crosland, Ruth Kaye, Jonathon Beardsell and Edward Heward. And three closes of land containing 2 acres 2 roods 5 perches in the possession of Caleb Heward, plus 2 acres and 20 perches of land at Meal Hill.

The Court Roll entry dated 4 March 1843 records that the two houses were then occupied by Caleb Howard and Edward Howard, and the stove, dyehouse and butchers shop near the houses were occupied by Caleb Howard and Richard Brown, along with a steam boiler, dyepan, steam pipes, and tenters. These were all bought by Abraham Sanderson.

Brow Bottom / Brownhill Mills

There were originally two mills that were known as Brow Bottom Mills; one was Upper Brow Bottom Mill, which was situated on the hillside between Brown Hill and Rake Dike, the second was Lower Brow Bottom Mill which was also on the right bank of Rake Dike, but on the flat land between Holme Banks and Kilnhouse Bank, near to where the original filter house for Brown Hill

Brow Bottom mill. Postcard.

Reservoir eventually stood. There was subsequently a third mill, called New Brow Bottom Mill, which was built close to the upper mill. It was possibly around the time that this mill was built that the name changed to Brownhill mills.

The upper and lower mills were probably built in the 1790s; the water supply for the upper mill came via a long goit, from a dam built at the confluence of Ramsden and Rake dikes. The Wakefield Court Roll for 1802 shows that John Batty of Hinchliffe Mill bought 1 rood of land from John and George Roberts of Brown Hill for £35 so that he could raise the level of that dam, known as Batty's dam, and increase the flow of water to the mill, which was already in existence. The Court Roll for 1825 records that John Batty's seven sons bought 2 acres 1 rood 35 perches of land in the area of the mills from John and George Roberts of Brown Hill for the sum of £350, which was probably the land on which the third mill known as New Brow Bottom mill was built. On the death of John Batty senior, the ownership of the mills passed to his seven sons, James, Joshua, Jonathon, Thomas, George, John and William. The father also held a quarter share in Holme Styes Mill which was to be divided equally between James, Jonathon, George and William. Someone broke into one of the mills early on the morning of 17 June 1844, and stole one piece of doeskin cloth, unmilled. J. Battye & Bros. offered a reward of ten guineas (£10 10s) for information leading to a conviction.

Charles Beardsell returned to one of the upper mills in 1848, after the breakup of the original company started by his father twenty years earlier. He began trading as C. Beardsell & Sons, and appears to have embraced all the processing of manufacturing woollen cloth rather than concentrating on just its finishing. On 31 December 1850, a man called Allen Hollingworth broke into Brownhill mill, with the intention of stealing cloth. The Beardsell's had thought for some time that lengths of cloth were going missing and the sons had been taking turns to keep watch at the mill overnight. On hearing a noise the brother keeping watch shouted and went towards the sound. He eventually found a man hiding under a table and dragged him out. During the struggle that followed the man managed to break free, leaving part of his waistcoat in Mr. Beardsell's hand. Mr. Beardsell had a pistol, and as the man made his escape he fired the pistol, the ball passing through the man's thigh. Asked for his name, the man had said that he was Joseph Battye of Hinchliffe Mill, but Mr. Beardsell did not believe him, having recognised him as Allen Hollingworth. Two constables went to the house of Hollingworth's father at the top of Brownhill Lane, where they found a large quantity of cloth of various qualities and lengths. More cloth was found on top of a haystack at Ramsden. Allen Hollingworth was apprehended at mid-day on Thursday; he was taken to Huddersfield where he received medical attention for the bullet wound, and was expected to appear in court on Saturday 4th January 1851. Father and son, who were both called Allen Hollingworth, appeared in court on the 4th, the son was charged with stealing the cloth, and his father with receiving stolen property; the charges having been proved, the pair were sent for trial at Wakefield Assizes.

Charles Beardsell died on January 25th 1852 and the running of the company was taken over by his eldest son James. The original company, James Beardsell & Sons, had gained a reputation for their innovative designs, which the younger James appears to have thought were copyright to the family, as he brought a case against the firm of Firth and William Hobson, who also occupied one of Brownhill mills, for infringing a registered design. James produced his grandfather, James Beardsell the head of the original company, as a witness, who claimed that it was their original design, and that it had formed part of their prize-winning display in the Great Exhibition of 1851. The defendants claimed that the design was not new and produced as a witness Mr. John Donkersley of Crosland Moor, a designer who had worked for D. Shaw & Sons of Honley, he said that Shaw's had been weaving that design since 1846. The magistrates agreed with the defendants and dismissed the case, which had created a wide interest. The court was crowded, with 'a great portion being the principle manufacturers of the neighbourhood'. All of whom would be interested in, and could be affected by, the outcome.

In August 1855 Tom Battye fulling miller, had a young son called Alfred who was playing near the mill dam when he fell in. His sister had seen him fall and immediately ran for help, but when she returned she was unsure precisely where her brother had entered the water. He was eventually found lying on the dam bottom, but was dead when they got him out. Heavy rain on 9 August 1856 increased the amount of water in Ramsden and Rake dikes to the extent that all three dams serving the mills were breached; and caused some damage at Holmbridge mill. Bilberry reservoir was filled and some water penetrated the upper part of the embankment, giving rise to fears that it would breach. Damage was also caused to land and property at Bottoms, Victoria and Thongsbridge, and a recently constructed bridge at Mytholmbridge was washed away.

C. Beardsell & Sons gave their workers a day's holiday on 10 October 1857, and treated them to a visit to the Art Treasures Exhibition held in Manchester. The firm paid for about 200 people to travel to Manchester by train via Dunford Bridge.

There were several suicides in the dams of the mills in 1857-8. The body of William Kaye apprentice joiner aged 20, son of Jonathon Kaye of Holme, was found in the dam of the upper mill on 21 November 1857 in an advanced state of decomposition. He was said to be suffering from depression, and had gone missing about 1 month earlier. In January 1858, Betty Heward aged 18, had left home in a distressed state after being taunted about meeting her 'sweetheart'. Her family began searching for her about 2½ hours later; and eventually found her in one of the dams. The report says: 'the inquest recorded a verdict in accordance with the above facts'. The body of David Lawton aged 25, described as 'a person of weak intellect' was found in the dam of the upper mill on Tuesday 13 April 1858. He lived with his parents in Hinchliffe Mill and had been heard to say that he would put an end to his life; but as he was prone to eccentric habits no-one took any notice. A woman had seen him throwing snowballs into the dam during the afternoon, and he was later seen struggling in the water. Help was summoned and he was taken out of the dam but was found to be dead. A fire in the drying stove at the mill in 1859 burned some wool, but did little else; damage was estimated at £20 to £30.[4]

The Beardsell's must have been finding business difficult in 1867, as a Deed of Assignment dated 2 August was issued against James Beardsell and Alfred Beardsell both of Holme, and William Henry Beardsell of Brownhill, trading as Charles Beardsell & Sons, conveying all their estate and effects to Henry Wilde of Huddersfield an Accountant, to the benefit of their creditors. Over 100 pieces of plain and fancy woollen coatings and trouserings were to be sold by tender, sealed tenders to be in by 11 October; and a large quantity of machinery was advertised for sale on 16 and 17 October, consisting of dyepans and equipment, dyestuffs, spinning mules, warping equipment, wet and dry finishing equipment, cloth presses, plus a large quantity of wool; also the broad and narrow looms that were in 'The Factory' in Holme village. This was followed in February 1868 by the sale of 4,000lbs of first class quality wool cops ready for use, and 1,000lbs of Mungo, waste and rags, along with a considerable quantity of dyewares. The *London Gazette* announced in September 1870 that a meeting of creditors would be held on 26 September to give details of money held but not yet distributed, and also of the personal estate of William Henry Beardsell. Possibly the firm may not have closed down completely in 1867, as the finishing equipment was advertised again in 1871, although the advertisement for that sale gives the vendor as T. Battye & Bros.

Tedbur and John Tinker moved from Upper Digley Mill with their twelve employees into part of the upper mill complex in 1863, and were here for some years prior to moving to Bankend Mills. In 1868 the part of the mills not being used by T & J Tinker was advertised to let 'with machinery and two reservoirs, capable of dyeing the most delicate colours; water power for a considerable portion of the year, also steam power'; this was possibly taken by J. C. Walker, who was in bankruptcy in November 1870, when his looms, yarn and wool were offered for sale by auction.

The land and property was sold to Batley Corporation in 1871, which would allow the corporation to extend their series of reservoirs downstream from Yateholme. Batley Corporation let the upper mills to Richard Ross Heap and Alexander Heap, which coincided with T & J Tinker leaving and moving to Bankend mill. One of the textile directories shows that Heaps were still in the mills in 1881 along with George Lawton who was a yarn spinner. Richard Ross Heap trading as R.R. & A. Heape, was in financial difficulty in 1884 when, at a creditors meeting on 21 April, Mr. John Haigh the official receiver, presented a statement showing that Heap had liabilities amounting to £12,168 16s 6d; his total assets amounted to £2,648 19s, less £722 4s 3d to be deducted for rent, rates, taxes and wages; leaving a deficiency of £10,292 1s 9d. The failure was attributed to trade expenses, rent and wages being too high. The creditors decided that Mr. Heap should be adjudged bankrupt. His discharge from debt was granted on 24 April, 1885.

In 1886 Thomas Campbell of Chapel-en-le-Frith was looking for textile premises in Holmbridge; having been told that Brownhill mills were empty, he applied to Batley Corporation for a lease on one of the buildings. The corporation refused to accommodate him saying that the land was needed for a reservoir.[5] Work on Brownhill Reservoir did not commence until the 1920s, but the mills remained empty until they were demolished. The site occupied by the Upper and New Brow Bottom mills is under the waters of the reservoir, on the Brownhill side, about one third of the length of the reservoir above the embankment.

Lower Brow Bottom mill

As stated above, this mill was situated on the right bank of Rake Dike, but nearer to Holmbridge. It was built by the Batty family about the same time as the Upper mill (1790s), and in 1810 was described as a: "Mill or Building with the machinery therein called or commonly known by the name of Batty Lower Mill, together with all and every Barns, streams of water, dams, goits, wheels, water races, tumbling shafts, going gear."

The tenants at that time are not known. The water supply came from Rake Dike but in two streams; surplus water from the upper mills was channelled into the dam for the lower mill, with a second channel from the dike straight into the dam. Isaac Beardsell wrote that in the late 1820s his brother Charles attended to the finishing of their cloth "at Holme Banks", which was presumably carried out in this mill, Charles and his wife Lydia lived in Holme Banks, and there is no other record of a finishing shop in Holme Banks besides this mill. After the family rented part of Upper Digley Mill in 1837 the cloth finishing would also be transferred. However, the partnership appears to have ended in 1848, possibly brought about by the death of Joseph the eldest brother, after which, Isaac set up in business on his own in part of Smithy Place Mills in Brockholes, while Charles returned to Brow Bottom Mills, but to one of the upper mills.

In October 1850 Luke Beardsell of Holme, who was not a descendant of James Beardsell or his sons, but had married Martha the third daughter of Joseph Beardsell in 1845, was a tenant of the mill, as was James Gardiner, also from Holme. On 7 October the stove used by Luke Beardsell became overheated causing pieces drying in there to begin to smoulder. The problem was discovered at 5am and the fire put out. Three pieces were damaged or destroyed, but there was only slight damage to the building.[6] Luke appears to have moved from here to Victoria mill Holmfirth by 1852; James Gardiner moved to Spring Lane mill. As with the upper mills, this mill appears to have remained empty until it was demolished as part of the reservoir development. In 1925, the author of the Nature Notes in the *Holmfirth Express* wrote that the deserted mill was a haven for owls and starlings.

Holmbridge mill

The mill stood on the left bank of Rake Dike at the bottom of Holme Banks. In his reply to the Factory Commission Enquiry in 1833, Joseph Barber described the original building on the site as 'ancient', with the principal part of the mill having been rebuilt in 1823. Documentation for the mill exists from 1778, when, on 29 July, Benjamin Green of Austonley took over ownership of the fulling mill at Holmbridge on the death of his mother; the mill was occupied at the time by James and Edmund Green. In addition to the mill, the family also owned the farm at Field End, plus the barns, stables and other buildings there; the tan yard and tan pits below Field End, (now on Digley Road), and the fields surrounding these properties. After the death of Benjamin Green the property was to pass to William Gartside of Cumberworth, a clothier, in trust for Benjamin Gartside and his wife Mary of Denby Dikeside in Penistone parish. Mary Gartside was Benjamin Green's daughter. A plan of the three storey mill built at Holmbridge during the late eighteenth or early nineteenth century by Benjamin Gartside who is shown as being the owner of the property in the 1790 Land Tax returns, is reproduced below. It shows a building about 70ft long by 25ft wide, which at that time was powered by two water wheels that drove 5 fulling stocks and 1 Teaser on the ground floor; plus 4 scribbling 'Ingens' and a 40-spindle Billey on the first floor, there was also an area that is designated as a 'Dwelling House' on that floor; plus a floor above known as the Garrit used for wool storage. The land tax returns show that the mill was occupied by John Kenion in 1792, but changes to Widow Kennion from 1793 to 1797.

The Barber family's involvement with Holmbridge Mill had already begun by 1798 when Benjamin

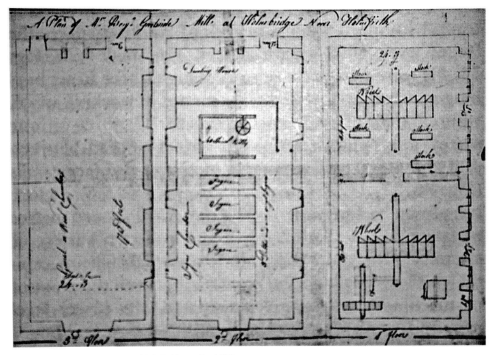

Holmbridge mill c.1800. Photographed by the Author Jan. 2011
The plan shows 3 floors: Right, ground floor; Centre, first floor; Left, top floor

Gartside's will was registered in the manor court. The will gives Joshua and Joseph Barber along with Widow Kenyon[c] as being tenants. The Barbers and Widow Kenion appear to have shared the building equally until at least 1805, as they are shown as paying 10s 11d each in annual land tax; from 1809 the occupier is recorded as Joshua Barber. A new lease dated 20 November 1819, between Firth Gartside of Holm Banks (son of Benjamin Gartside), and Joshua Barber the elder of Field End and Joshua Barber the younger of Bank Bottom Cartworth, quotes the rent as £200 per annum.

Firth Gartside registered his will in the Manor Court in 1820, when the occupants of the mill are given as Joshua Barber & Co. and also Edmund Sykes of Long Ing, Austonley, Joseph Charlesworth the elder of Upper Bridge Holmfirth, David Charlesworth of Yew Tree, Joseph Charlesworth junior Holmfirth, and Joshua Charlesworth of Yew Tree, who were also in business as J. Charlesworth & Sons, cloth dressers, at Holmfirth Mill.

Joshua Barber & Co. answered the questionnaire sent out by the Factory Commission in 1832,

c   The spelling of her name alters in the records from year to year.

the return was probably completed and signed by Joseph, as the company is recorded as Joseph Barber & Co; they were occupied in the scribbling, carding and slubbing of wool, and milling of cloth. Power was supplied by two water wheels delivering 18hp; and by a steam engine of 14hp, which was only used in cases of extreme drought. They employed 29 people: 2 boys and 3 girls under 10 earning 4s 6d; 5 boys and 3 girls under 12 earning 4s 6d or 5s; 4 boys and 1 girl under 14 earning 6s; 1 boy under 16 earning 14s; 1 boy under 18 earning 18s; 2 men under 21 earning 18s; 5 men and 2 women over 21, 3 earning 24s, the earnings of the other 4 are not given. All amounts are weekly wages. Twenty seven workers were paid via the person for whom they worked rather than directly by their employer. During the summer work began at 6 am, until 8 pm; the working day was shorter in winter due to having less demand, but the hours are not given. Two hours less were worked on Saturdays than weekdays. There was a half hour break at 8am for breakfast, one hour from 12 to 1 for dinner, and 30 minutes for 'drinking' at 4.30pm. 'Two individuals have to work during breakfast and afternoon meal, but are relieved'. These would be children, who probably took it in turn to work through the breaks. Joseph Charlesworth & Sons were in Holmfirth Mill, but also had some men working at Holmbridge Mill, presumably running the fulling stocks; there is a reference in the wages section of Barber's return to six persons being employed in the fulling mill but no other details are given. The remains of the original mill at Holmbridge and the one built in the1790s were pulled down and replaced with a four storey mill in 1840, with a new weaving shed for the installation of power looms being added in the 1850s.

Firth Gartside died in 1847, leaving his property to be divided equally between his four daughters: Mary Ann was married to Joshua Charlesworth described as a Gentleman, but possibly a partner in the firm of J. Charlesworth & Sons; Sarah was married to John Wood a Fancy manufacturer of Denby Dale; Fanny was married to John Barber of Holmbridge Mill; and Cassandra was married to Richard Hinchliff an Agent living in Huddersfield. An Indenture of Settlement dated 23 May 1848 shows that Joshua and Mary Ann Charlesworth passed their quarter share to James Charlesworth (Joshua's nephew), and Thomas Lister Charlesworth (James's son and Joshua's great-nephew), both of Upperbridge, Holmfirth. The property is described as all the "buildings, barns, stables, kilns, tan-yards, tan-pits, closes, lands, grounds and other appurtenances recited in the surrender of 29 July 1778 and in the Mill, dwelling houses and other buildings and improvements erected on the said ground…and in the wheels, engines, machinery and going-gear in the said mill and other buildings, which were then more commonly known as All that Fulling and Scribbling Mill called Holme Bridge Mill situate at Holmbridge in Austonley with the Spinning Rooms, Drying Stove, Engine House, Boiler House and other buildings near thereto, and the wheels, engines, machinery and going-gear to the same belonging.…Also all those two cottages or dwellinghouses, garden and several parcels of land or ground thereto belonging containing by estimation including the site of the Mill and buildings and Reservoir, 1 acre, 2 roods, 36 perches, in the occupation of Messrs Joshua Barber & Co". Joshua and Mary Ann also assigned their quarter share in the 'Steam and other Engines, Boilers, Water and other wheels, scribbling and carding engines, billies, drums, shafts, willows and machinery in and about the said mill' to James and Thomas Lister Charlesworth.

The Barber family were well established in Holmbridge, the 1851 Census shows that Joshua Barber aged 60, of Bank Bottoms, Kilnhouse Bank, was a Woollen Manufacturer employing 100 men, which was a large increase from the 29 shown on the 1834 return to the Factory Commissioners; (he also had a servant in his house). Others of the family in the Kilnhouse Bank area were Henry Barber aged 31, woollen manufacturer; John Barber, Bank Cottage, aged 30, woollen manufacturer and merchant, (also with a servant); John Barber of Holmbridge, aged 54, woollen manufacturer, and his son Joe Barber aged 20, woollen manufacturer; also Thomas Barber aged 27, woollen manufacturer.

Despite the mill's proximity to Digley Dike it was not affected by the severe flood in 1852, as it drew its water from Rake Dike, and was above the level of the flood water raging downstream from Bilberry reservoir; however, property owned by Joshua Barber in Water Street, Hinchliffe Mill was destroyed. The property consisted of a row of six houses on the river bank, which were washed away with a large loss of life; the families in all six houses were occupied in the textile industry in some way. Of the 44 people living in those houses, 36 lost their lives due to the flood. Joshua Barber's executors submitted a claim for £1,400, which was reduced to £600, with £302 10s 7d being paid. In 1853 the Reservoir Commissioners list the occupants of the mill as Joshua Barber, John Barber, Edmund Barber, Joseph Barber, John Earnshaw and Uriah Wimpenny.

John Bates, Factory Inspector, charged Barber's with offences against the Factory Regulations in August 1853: William Brown aged 15, had climbed onto a bale of wool that was positioned underneath a rotating horizontal shaft 7ft from the floor which was not protected. The boy's clothing became caught carrying him around the shaft injuring him quite severely. The firm were fined £3 for not having the shafting fenced, but this was withheld as the incident led to a more serious, but unspecified, offence against a different part of the act that attracted a fine of £10; they also had to pay the costs of the case involving William Brown. Other charges were: allowing Elizabeth Chatterton, who was under 13, to work without her name being entered in the register; allowing Hugh Hinchliffe, again under 13, to work without a surgeon's certificate; and allowing Hinchliffe and four other boys to work without a schoolmaster's certificate. Barber's admitted liability on all the charges, consequently only costs were levied. Joseph Chatterton, father of Elizabeth, was charged with allowing his daughter to work full time while under the age of 13, and for not sending her to school as the Act required; he was also charged with using a false surgeon's certificate. Chatterton admitted the offences, and consequently was only charged costs.

There were rejoicings throughout the country in 1856 when the Crimean War ended. In Holmbridge the employees of Barber's, Wimpenny's, Earnshaw's and Midgeleys along with their families met together on 10 May to enjoy a dinner of Roast Beef and Plum Pudding served in Holmbridge Dyehouse; this was followed by a procession around the district headed by a large flag and Beaumont's Sax-Horn Band; which was succeeded by a 'meeting' with many speeches and toasts. A large flag representing England, France, Turkey and Sardinia was stretched across the main road between the mill and the dyehouse.[7]

Barbers bought two pieces of land known as Hutch Bottom and The Wood in 1856 from James Shaw Esq. for £161 1s; and within the next three years built their first weaving shed on it, this was later extended to become Clarence Mill. The installation of power looms in the mill would mark the beginning of the end for the local handloom weavers who, up to that point, had turned all the company's yarn into cloth.

A fire was discovered in the stove about 5am on Tuesday 1 September 1857; the alarm was raised and someone went to get the Unity brigade, but the fire was brought under control before they arrived. The roof of the building had collapsed, and damage was fairly extensive, but no estimate of the damage was given.

About 100 of the older members of Barber's workforce were given tickets in August 1858 for a rail excursion to Liverpool, along with another 700 or so people from Thongsbridge; while the younger members of the workforce were treated to a good dinner at the mill. The number employed by Joshua Barber & Sons had risen to 164 by January 1859, when they enjoyed a treat at the New Inn Hinchliffe Mill on the 8th.

There had been more minor alterations in the ownership of the buildings, Richard and Cassandra Hinchliff had passed their quarter share to Joshua Charlesworth of South House Holmfirth, Edward Hill a builder of Huddersfield, and James Hinchliff a manufacturer in Meltham; and in 1859 Joshua and Fanny Barber transferred their quarter share to John Barber, Joshua Barber (junior) and Able Thewlis.

The firm's employees enjoyed another treat at the New Inn to celebrate the marriage of Mr. John Barber's second daughter to Mr. George Brook the son of Mr. David Brook manufacturer of Spring Bank House. The 100 men enjoyed their treat on Saturday 22 August 1863; while the 60 women had theirs on Tuesday 25th.

The firm found it necessary to take court action against Mr. James Turner Prince in October

1864, whom they had employed for about 18 months, up to October 1863, as a commercial traveller. They found that he had been given cash by some customers that he had not passed on to the firm. He was accused of embezzling over £150 from various sources as far afield as London and Bristol. Prince was committed to the assizes, and was presumably held in custody as bail was refused. A slight accident occurred in June 1865, when a 30 year old woman named Thewlis put her arm between the spokes of a slow moving wheel in an attempt to connect two pulleys together with a strap. The wheel through which she had placed her arm trapped and mutilated it. She was seen by Dr. Trotter who recommended that she should be taken to the Infirmary for treatment.

A scheme had been put forward by some manufacturers to purchase a second fire engine for the district. It had been suggested that manufacturers should contribute £1 for each slubbing billey that they possessed; this proposal met with indifference from some and opposition from many. However, Turners of Bridge mill and Barber's of Holmbridge mill built their own machines to their own designs, and met on Saturday 9 June 1864 at Prickleden mill dam in a contest to determine whose machine was best. Barber's machine pumped a greater volume of water, and threw it further with 12 men pumping than Turner's could with twenty. At a meeting between all the brigades in Huddersfield and District held at Dalton on Whit. Monday, Barber's machine again proved to be the best. It was designed by Robert Bentley the mechanic at the mill, and built under his supervision.

Everything appears to have been going well for the company; in 1872 there was an extensive re-equipping with new machinery and the old machinery being sold off. However, due to the deaths of John, Joshua and Edmund Barber in the late 1870s and early 1880s leaving the company without any directors, by 1886 the company was in dire financial straits. Sarah Barber and Annie Rachel Barber agreed, with the concurrence of the Accountant and the Yorkshire Banking Corporation, to sell the two parcels of land mentioned above plus the weaving shed and engine house to James Hirst of Rochfield, Lockwood, for £725 to clear the debt.

In November 1887 Joseph Brook Norcliffe, a manufacturer of Huddersfield paid Reuben Hirst of Lockwood £750 for the large shed at Holmbridge mill and began business in the mill with his partner Noah Jessop, trading as Norcliffe & Jessop, making seal skin. The opening of the Huddersfield to Penistone railway line in 1850 with its branch line to Holmfirth, allowed people to look further afield for work than had previously been possible. Norcliffe & Jessop employed at least one woman weaver from the Huddersfield area; a Miss Roberts, who lived in Dalton. She would probably need to walk from her home to Huddersfield station, catch a train to Holmfirth and then walk the two miles to Holmbridge; consequently she did not arrive until after breakfast time. It was accepted practise for weavers to throw off the drive belt for their loom from the top drive pulley, which was on the shafting suspended from the ceiling, before cleaning their loom on Saturday afternoons. The belt would then be left slack round the shaft until early Monday morning, when either the weaver or tuner would put it back round the drive pulley ready for the mill engine being started. On the morning of Monday 16 April 1888, the mill engine was already running when Miss Roberts arrived. As the tuner was busy elsewhere she asked a fellow weaver, Josh Boothroyd aged 22 who had previously helped his father to install the looms, if he would put the drive belt for her loom round the top pulley for her, which he agreed to do. Instead of getting the ladder that was kept for that purpose, he climbed onto the loom, and balancing on one leg attempted to put the belt over the pulley. When the belt started to move it caught his jacket and took him up and round the shafting, crushing him between the shafting and the ceiling joists. The shafting was stopped as quickly as possible and Boothroyd was taken down, but he was found to be dead. The subsequent inquest returned a verdict of accidental death.

J. B. Norcliffe died on May 2nd 1888, at the age of 55; which was probably the deciding factor in the Halifax Joint Stock Banking Company demanding repayment of loans in 1890 that had previously been made to Norcliffe & Jessop, which appears to have instigated the firm's demise.

Joshua Thristle Barber, who had established himself in Bankend Mill in 1889, in conjunction with William Henry Barber and John Barber who were previously in Bottoms Mill, paid £920 in June 1890, for the land and buildings known as Clarence Mill. Joshua Thristle Barber was not directly related to William Henry and John Barber; but was a descendant of the Barbers of Fieldend, whereas William Henry and John Barber were cousins and were descended from the Barbers of Kilnhouse Bank. W.H. & J. Barber were charged with contravening the Factory Act in 1891; Mr. J.D. Prior the Factory Inspector said in evidence that the Act allowed firms to employ young people between the hours of 6.30am and 5.30pm. On 5 February he had visited Clarence Mill at 6.15pm and found a girl named Mary H. Hollingworth working on the lower floor; he then went upstairs and found the gas lights lit and obvious signs that workers had hastily decamped. He subsequently took statements from ten employees; he could have interviewed thirty, but felt that ten were sufficient to prove his case. Mr. W.H. Barber appeared for the company, and pleaded guilty to the charges, saying that re-sighting of machinery had brought about serious delays in production, and due to the firm having received several letters of complaint about late delivery and threatening to cancel orders they were attempting to make up the time lost. The bench imposed a fine of 3s plus costs of 9s 1½d for each offence; a total of £6 1s 3d.[8]

In 1892/3 both firms gave a treat to their workers, W.H. & J. Barber gave over 100 people a knife

Holmbridge mill Aerial Photograph July 1985. © Crown Copyright. EH

and fork tea followed by dancing, games and songs on 28th December; while J.T. Barber provided a similar meal and entertainment for 50 people on the following Saturday 4th January. Joshua Thristle Barber's tenancy within Clarence mill was due to expire in December 1897; a sale of machinery was advertised to be held on 3 November, comprising 3 condenser sets, 2 pairs of self-acting mules, 2 patent warping mills, an iron beaming frame, warping woofs and creels, bobbin winding frames, burling tables, 3 twisting frames fitted for knopping, a burring machine, a 48in Fearnought, 2 milling machines, sizing machine, shoddy cleaner and various sundries.

W.H. & J. Barber bought the 5 storey mill, with the dam and other buildings situated at the bottom of Holme Banks for £1,000 in August 1900; this was followed in 1903 by the purchase of Holmbridge Dyehouse with the dwelling house and other buildings that went with it, along with 6 closes of land, for £775. The tenant of the Dyehouse was Mr. F.W. Midgeley; the purchase also included the cottage then known as 'Old Tan Yard' on Digley Road. The company continued to prosper, a new engine house, and a new boiler house were added in 1905 and 1909 respectively. The Yorkshire Textile Directory for 1910 lists the company as manufacturing fancy worsteds and trouserings; in that year the firm applied to Holmfirth Council for permission to build new offices and add a new weaving shed to Clarence Mill.

After Lehane, MacKenzie & Shand Ltd. commenced work on the building of Brown Hill Reservoir for Batley Corporation in 1924, Barber's had problems with their water supply from Rake Dike. The major complaint was that one piece of cloth, when being given its final inspection, was found to be considerably off shade, samples enclosed with the archived documents show that the cloth was much lighter than it should have been; they had also been forced to completely refinish 45 other pieces, and had needed to use far more soap when scouring pieces than had normally been the case. All of which they found was due to a much higher level of lime in the water than usual. On investigation it turned out that the workmen on the reservoir sight were in the habit of washing any tools and equipment, particularly those used in mixing and placing concrete, in the waters of the dike, which subsequently ran into the mill dam. Barber's also complained that they had to employ a youth to fetch buckets of water for at least two hours a day from a local well, to be used for making drinks in the canteen for the workpeople, as the usual supply from the mill dam was undrinkable. The outcome of this complaint to Batley Corporation is not recorded, but Barber's were presumably compensated for any losses incurred. In 1926, Barber's made application to Holmfirth Council to build a new spinning mill for worsted yarns onto the eastern end of Clarence Mill, which was approved. In 1938, the company bought the business of B. Vickerman & Sons Ltd. which had begun before 1800, and had been at Thongsbridge Mill since 1887, their production was transferred to Holmbridge. A new mending room, built at Clarence Mill on the side nearest the river, was added in 1939.

The flood on 29 May 1944, Whit Monday, washed away the parapets of the road bridge and the retaining wall on the left side of the river opposite Clarence mill, but left the mill buildings virtually undamaged. Water did get into the ground floor of Clarence Mill, and some pieces of cloth suffered water damage, but apart from this the mill appears to have escaped unharmed. Some two and a half years later, in January 1947, thieves stole over 50 pieces of cloth valued at £3,000; that amount of cloth would make at least 1,000 suits.

The company continued in business, despite worsening trading conditions, until October 1975, when they announced their closure due to a lack of orders; they also cited the high level of inflation prevailing at the time. Even though trade was difficult, 118 people were employed in the mill at that time. Butterworth & Roberts, of Yew Tree Mill, took over the worsted spinning plant in March 1976, which they ran for about 4 years spinning worsted yarn for use at Yew Tree.[9]

Clarence mill was split into units and occupied by a variety of businesses, the majority of which were non textile, although a company by the name of Barramatch Fabrics were there in 1988, and placed advertisements for staff in the *Holmfirth Express*. The five storey mill along with its surrounding buildings were demolished in 1994 and have since been replaced with housing.

Digley Dike – Lum(b) Bank / Billberry mill

This mill stood on the right bank of Digley Dike, virtually opposite Hoobram House, very close to the original reservoir embankment. Water was brought from the outflow of the reservoir via a goit to the mill. The history of this mill is distinctive due to the number of changes in ownership of the property in its early years. The earliest information is given in the Wakefield Court Roll of 1781, before the mill was built. John Whiteley took two closes of land called the Lum Bank in Holme and the Upper Bottom in Austonley from Mary Littlewood and her son John of Honley. In 1806 John Whiteley raised a mortgage from John Barber of Norland nr. Halifax on the 2 closes of land called the Lum Bank and the Upper Bottom totalling 5 acres, also the recently built Fulling Mill on the Upper Bottom, plus land and a building at Hoowood. The mill on Lum Bank was marked and staked out by 28 October 1807, and was possibly being built. In the same year John Whiteley surrendered a moiety (half share) in the mill for a period of 21 years to Joseph Broadhead of White Walls Austonley; after which they passed the use of the mill (the income from rent etc), to the Rev. Joseph Broadhurst of Holme. John Whiteley repaid the mortgage taken from John Barber of Norland in 1806 by raising a mortgage of £320 in 1809 from William Barker a worsted manufacturer of Sowerby, for the two closes and the mill at Lum Bank, and also for two closes at Hoowood called Greenowlers and Middle Hirst.

In 1820 the occupant of the mill was Joseph Broadhead; a half share in the land and mill at Lumb Bank and the house and land at Green Owlers was sold to John France of Slaithwaite; the money then being paid to William Barker of Sowerby. This half share was then sold the following year to the executors of William Kinder's estate in Meltham. The moiety changed hands again in 1829, being bought by James Wells of Wakefield; the occupants of the mill at that time were Joseph Broadhead and John Whiteley. Joseph Broadhead subsequently died, leaving his moiety in the mill and a dwelling house in Holme occupied by James Beardsell to his son James. In 1836 it was reported that Joseph

Bilberry mill after rebuilding of the reservoir

Beardsell and James Broadhead had committed a minor offence against the Factory Act; the fine was mitigated and was to be distributed amongst the local Sunday Schools; which suggests that a child had been employed longer than the permitted number of hours, or possibly did not possess a surgeon's certificate.

Being situated on the hillside a few yards downstream from Bilberry Reservoir the mill was quite badly damaged in the flood of 1852. Ten yards of the mill building was washed away, along with the fulling stocks and other machinery; fortunately no-one was hurt, Charles Batty, the fulling miller at the mill, lived in the mill cottage, he along with his wife and six children had left before the embankment burst; but, due to the damage, some 20 people were subsequently unemployed. Joseph Broadhead & Co. submitted a claim for damage to the buildings, goit, dam, machinery and stock amounting to a total of £1,609 10s, which the claims inspectors reduced to £1,129. Broadhead's were paid £754 12s 3d in full settlement. The year after the flood the Reservoir Commissioners charged the Broadheads with refusing to pay £21 0s 0½d water rate for the year 1 August 1852 to 31st July 1853. The Broadheads said in their defence that due to the flood the mill was not useable until March 1853, therefore they were only liable for 5 months water rate. The case was adjourned by the Bench in September, with the magistrates ordering that an equitable offer should be considered; it was reconvened in October when the Commissioners said that they could not accept anything less than a full year's rate, arguing that the defendants still held the fall, even if they did not occupy or employ it. The magistrate refused to pass judgement, saying that he would consult with other members of the bench with a view to dismissal.

When the new reservoir embankment was built it was moved about 30 yards upstream, taking it well away from the spring that had been the cause of most of the trouble. Due to the death of John Whiteley, his moiety in the mill was offered for sale on 24 August 1855; this was followed by a sale of machinery that was advertised to take place at the mill on 21 September 1855; followed by an auction sale of at least part of the mill on 27 September, described as a three storey building, with a floor and framework for a fourth floor, partly occupied as a dwelling house and partly as a workshop with room for woollen machinery. There was also a kitchen, cellar and coal place; plus a separate 2 storey building to the west of the mill, used for teazing and scribbling, along with a pan house, engine house, chimney and other outbuildings. Additionally, there was the road to the mill with 2,568sq.yds. of land. The buyer would be expected to take the steam engine, boiler and other machinery in the mill at its valuation, which would be given at the time of the sale. The mill was again advertised in June 1856 as being either to let or for sale, having been recently owned and occupied by John Rodgers; no other details are given.

David Broadhead, who lived at Stubbin, had been using the mill until he fell on hard times in 1865, when his goods were assigned to his creditors in October of that year. A sale of yarns etc. was advertised to take place at the mill on the morning of 28 October, which would be followed by a sale of his farm stock at Stubbin at 2pm the same day.

Heavy rain on the evening of 15 November 1866, which continued throughout the night and most of the next day, damaged the goit taking water to the mill due to the volume of water trying to travel along it. In late June 1869, a fire on the ground floor of the mill burned through to the floor above, damage was estimated at £220; the occupants at the time were Messrs. Broadhead & Mason. In August of that year the mill was advertised to let with 3 billies and mules to follow, stocks and all required for fulling, also a dyehouse and stove.

The next occupants were the Hirst family, with Edward Hirst being named as the person in charge in 1872. In June of that year Jane Hirst a 14 year old girl, but apparently not a relative of Edward's, was in charge of a teazing machine, she was clearing some waste when her arm slipped and was drawn into the teeth of the machine. She was taken to Huddersfield Infirmary where it was found that her arm was broken above the elbow, the elbow joint was crushed, the ligaments were torn, the flesh lacerated and her wrist and hand were badly crushed. Despite the seriousness of the injuries, her father persistently refused to allow her arm to be amputated. The girl was said to be in great pain and some danger, after having had two pieces of bone removed from the damaged elbow. It is possible that she eventually recovered, as there does not appear to be any notification of her death in the succeeding weeks.

The running of the business was taken over by Mr. Thomas Hirst; in October 1873 the mill was all but destroyed by a serious fire. The four storey mill had been locked at 6pm on Monday October 20th; at 1.30am on the Tuesday morning Mr. Hirst was awoken by the loud barking of his dog. He found that the part of the mill containing the engine house was on fire. The alarm was raised and about an hour later W.H & J. Barber's 'Integrity' fire engine arrived and began to direct water jets onto the building, but the fire had such a good hold it could not be extinguished. Damage to the building, which was owned by Fred Shaw of Huddersfield and Dyson Whiteley of Green Owlers, was estimated at £1,300, only part of which was covered by insurance; damage to the machinery, owned by Mr. Hirst, much of which had been installed recently, was put at £2,500 and was mostly covered by insurance. A 'salvage sale' of some machinery and a horse and cart was advertised to take place the following month, but was possibly postponed, as it was not until August 1874 that Joseph Holroyd, a machine broker of Huddersfield sued John Dyson Whiteley for £3 3s 6d, which was expense incurred in sending men and a cart to the mill to remove a machine that Holroyd claimed he had bought in the sale. Whiteley said that the machine was part of the fixtures of the mill and could not have been sold as it did not belong to Hirst. The judge ruled that Holroyd had no claim against Whiteley, and should take up his complaint with Hirst.

The mill was rebuilt during 1875 and early 1876, and was advertised 'To Let' as a water powered mill in March 1876. It does not seem to have attracted a tenant, as it was re-advertised in January 1877, and again in July and December 1878, when it was described as having 4 storeys and an attic, a stove and a 3 pan dyehouse; all fitted with new shafting. The mill was finally let to J. Greenwood Sons & Co. who were also occupying the recently built third Digley Mill. In 1882 they submitted plans to build a new boiler house and long chimney, they were obviously converting the mill to steam power, also a tentering room, which were all approved. An unfortunate accident occurred in March 1887; the *Holmfirth Express* printed the following account:

> *Accident: on 26th Feb. John Moorhouse a bobbin carrier, had been sent up to the fourth floor of the mill by James Smith mill manager, to get a skep of bobbins. When he went into that room he saw Charlie Alderson aged 10 years 9 months, also employed as a bobbin carrier, standing by the crane door and asked for his help. They pulled the full skep to the door which Charlie opened, and fixed the crane hooks to the skep handles. Charlie pulled the lever to operate the crane then took hold of the strap holding down the lid of the skep. As the skep left the floor it swung out of the doorway taking the boy with it, and, letting go of the strap he fell about thirty feet to the ground, where he was found to be dead. James Smith said that the boys should not have lowered the skep, they should have asked the foreman Mr. Ayre to do it, but they had not looked for him. When asked why they did not look for Mr. Ayre, Moorhouse said that it was about 12.25pm and they wanted to get the skep down before the wheel stopped for the dinner break at 12.30. The factory inspector said that he had inspected the premises and the crane doors complied fully with the Factory Act regulations. The jury's verdict was that: "The deceased was accidentally killed by falling from a crane doorway; no blame was attached to anyone".*

Greenwood's carried on with their businesses at both Bilberry mill and Digley, with the workpeople at Bilberry joining their colleagues from Digley in a day out to Cleethorpes in September 1891. Some damage to Bilberry mill was sustained in January 1899 due to a large quantity of water being released from the reservoir, for which Greenwood's claimed £200 in damages from the Reservoir Commissioners.[10] Despite the company going into receivership in 1926, they carried on trading for another ten years until they had to close to allow the premises to be demolished to make way for Digley reservoir, which Huddersfield Corporation had intended to build in the late 1930s, but was delayed due to the Second World War.

Digley mills

There were three mills in total in the area known as Digley

Upper Digley mill

The mill was already built by September 1793, possibly by the same stone mason that built Lower Digley mill for John Hirst, who was Joseph Booth of Meltham. The owner of the mill, and of the acre of land known as the Upper Bottom on which it was built, was John Whiteley of Green Owlers; he paid Joseph Booth for building the mill by raising a Mortgage of £300 from Edmund Green of Austonley. It stood around 300 yards downstream from Bilberry mill on the left bank of Digley Dike (Hoobram side) and was in the township of Austonley. The water supply was taken from the dike upstream of the mill and brought via a goit along the right bank and across an aqueduct over the dike to the mill. In January 1806 John Whiteley took a mortgage from John Barber of Norland Halifax, possibly to repay the loan from Edmund Green, or to allow him to build Bilberry mill. John Whiteley died, probably in 1835. His will is shown in the Wakefield Court Roll on 15 January 1836, he left Upper Digley mill to his two daughters: Ann Whiteley who was then the wife of James Bradbury of Digley mill, and Hannah Whiteley the wife of Joseph Whiteley clothier of Hoobram.

The description of Upper Digley mill in 1852 records it as a stone built mill with a large house, farm buildings and outhouses. Although built around the turn of the century, the first known recorded tenant was James Beardsell & Sons of Holme, who moved into at least part of the mill in October 1837, at a rent of £140 per year. The small amount of water used by the occupants of the mill led to a reduction in the water rate of 25 percent from January 1846, until the amount of machinery using water increased. Beardsell's moved out of this mill in either 1847 or early 1848, and were replaced by John Furniss, who, in 1851, occupied the mill and lived in the recently constructed house with his family.

In the 1851 census John and his wife Ruth are both 28, John is listed as a Woollen Manufacturer, his younger brother George who was a scholar aged 12 was living with them, and they had two children, William aged 1 had been born in Holme, his sister Alice, who was 3 weeks old at the time, was born in Austonley; which suggests that they had moved into the house at the mill during the previous twelve months. Business does not appear to have gone well for the Furniss family, the *London Gazette* records that John Furniss was adjudged bankrupt on 20 December 1851, and ordered to attend the Bankruptcy Court in Leeds on 13 January and 8 February 1852, for public examination. Possibly as a result of the first hearing, the court installed two bailiffs at the mill to secure it for the creditors.

On the 4th of February, the night of the flood, John Furniss was not at home, he could have been held in prison due to the bankruptcy case, as a Mrs. L. Furniss (possibly John's mother) was listed as having to flee the premises along with the rest of the family when the water level in the dike rose. They do not appear to have alerted the two bailiffs, Thomas Miles and William Crompton, who were left in bed. When they realised the danger that they were in, the two had barely time to get dressed and get to higher ground before the reservoir embankment gave way, one of them having to wade through waste deep water. The whole of the ground floor of the mill was inundated; the end of the mill nearest the dike was washed away along with machinery, cloth and wool. The gable end of the house and all the farm buildings were also swept away. The fulling miller lived in a cottage with his wife and three children at the higher end of the mill; due to a back injury he had been confined to bed for seven weeks, fortunately for them the flood waters did not reach their house which allowed them to wait until the following day before being moved out. James Whiteley, William Shaw and the assignees of John Furniss submitted a claim for damage to the buildings, dams and goits totalling £330, which the inspectors reduced to £111, and paid £77 11s in final settlement.

The Reservoir Commissioners list the owners of the upper mill as Joseph Whiteley and William Shaw in 1853; they also give the occupier as James Wood, which suggests that repairs to the building were carried out very quickly; no information exists to suggest what Mr. Wood was making at the mill, nor how long he was there. Salvaged machinery from the mill would be included in the sale that took place on the 19th and 20th of October 1853.[11]

Tedbur and John Tinker first began their business in this mill on 31 October, or 1 November, 1853. They were here for almost ten years before moving to Upper Brow Bottom mill. The upper mill at Digley was later pulled down by the occupants of the third mill, Greenwoods.

Lower Digley mill

As the name implies, this mill was downstream from the upper mill. Built on the right bank of the river in Holme township, and is of a slightly later date than Rake Mill as it was built around 1790. This mill was probably at least twice as big as Rake Mill at that time, as it was recorded in the Holm Rentals as having a value of £7 per annum. The original mill appears to have been built by John Hirst, born 1759 son of Joshua Hirst. The Wakefield Court Roll for 1791 suggests that John Hirst bought 2,224sq. yds. of land in Holme Banks Wood in 1790 from Mary Wimpenny for the sum of £20. He then borrowed £105 from Joseph Booth a mason, Joseph Eastwood a clothier and Jonas Eastwood an Innkeeper, all from Meltham, and John Broadbent a clothier from Meltham Mills, on a mortgage at 4¾ percent interest, which he used to build the mill. There were arguably further extensions to the mill in 1827/8 when John Hirst bought 511sq.yds of Shaw Bank Wood from Joshua Wimpenny of Arrunden for £51. 2s.

At his death in 1831, John Hirst left instructions that the property had to be shared equally between his two sons John and George; this consisted of the Mill, a Drying House and Dyehouse, also 2 small cottages, a Barn, Stable and other outbuilding, plus 2 parcels of land known as the Tenter Banks and the Bottom before the Mill. The family were living in a house on the left, Austonley, side of the river which John left to his wife Hannah.

In their return to the Factory Commissioners enquiry in 1833, Hirst's said that the mill that they were using had been built in 1817, which suggests that the original building had been either extended or replaced at that time; power was supplied by a water wheel and a steam engine, each of them delivering 12hp; they employed 2 boys and 2 girls under 10, each earning 4s per week, 2 boys and 3 girls under 12 also each earning 4s, 1 boy under 14 earning 5s and 2 girls under 14 earning 4s 3d, 2 girls under 16 earning 5s 6d, 2 boys under 18 earning 15s, 2 men over 21 earning 31s and 1 woman earning 22s. The hours of work were 6am to 9pm in summer and 7.30am to 8.30pm in winter, with a total of 2 hours allowed for meals. George and John Hirst said that they would like working hours of 12 hours a day during the week and ten hours on Saturday to become standard practice.

Hirst's were fined for infringing the Factory Act in 1836, as with other manufacturers who were reported at the same time, it was said not to be a serious offence and the fine would be distributed amongst local Sunday Schools, suggesting that it was children being employed for too long a period or without a surgeon's certificate.

John and George Hirst dissolved their partnership on 7 April 1849, and in October 1850 John Hirst left Digley mill and moved to Saddleworth where he set up in business on his own account. He started in a small mill built by his brother-in-law Charles Fozzard in Dobcross called Fozzard Mill; from here he moved to Walk Mill for a time before building Bankfield Mill where the business prospered for some years. John's brother George was running the business at Digley, but he died in March 1851 leaving his executors, along with his wife Mary and son-in-law Henry Beardsell to run the mill. Henry Beardsell was the son of Joseph the eldest of the four Beardsell brothers from Holme. Henry had married Mary Hirst, the daughter of George and Mary Hirst in mid 1847, but she had died in 1849.

At the time of the flood in February 1852, Mary Hirst senior, was living in a house close by the mill with 6 of her children and 1 grandchild, with Henry Beardsell living next door. Due to their apprehension about the reservoir embankment some of the family had left home to stay with friends or relatives on higher ground. There were seven houses in the vicinity of the mill, all the occupants left before the embankment burst. The flood waters completely destroyed the mill buildings along with the houses and farm buildings nearby, putting 100 people out of work. The flood water also carried the three large boilers from the mill about one mile downstream; the only structure still standing after the flood was the chimney of the main mill in the valley bottom. Although the dyehouse, which was on the left bank of the river along with the dwelling houses, was also completely destroyed, its chimney, which was on higher ground in the wood, remained as a lone sentinel on the hillside above the river, becoming a well-known landmark as it had a tree growing from its top, until it was demolished in the 1950s. Damage was estimated in the press at the time of the flood to be between £15,000 and £20,000; the claim submitted to the Flood Relief Committee was initially for about £11,600, which was reduced to £9, 993 16s 7d, the inspectors reduced it further to £8,295 16s 7d, the amount paid to Mrs. Hirst was £4,628 12s 4d, there is a note on the page saying that they would add £1,000 to that amount if she would rebuild the mill, which she was not inclined to do.

There is a suggestion that, due to the flood, the lack of work in Holme Valley encouraged some people to go to the Saddleworth area, particularly to John Hirst's mill, looking for work. Two names are mentioned, Mr. Jonathan Chambley, who later founded the firm of J. Chambley, Sons & Co., Stone-bottom Mill, Wool Road; and Mr. James Hollingworth who was eventually a cofounder of Hutchinson & Hollingworth the Dobcross Loom builders.[12] The site of the lower mill and the land around it, totalling 13acres 32 perches, was offered for sale in February 1872, but was not sold. The salvage sale that took place in October 1853 included machinery from both the upper and lower mills.

The third Digley mill

The site of the Digley mills was eventually bought by Joseph Greenwood, probably in June 1873, which was possibly why T & J Tinker moved from Upper Digley mill to Upper Brow Bottom mill shortly afterwards. In September 1875 builders, and allied tradesmen, were invited to submit tenders for a 'new mill and engine bed etc.' designed by architect Ben Stocks for Joseph Greenwood Sons &

Digley mill (Greenwoods), probably taken 1920s

Co, who were worsted manufacturers, which was built close to the area formerly occupied by the upper mill, but was much larger. The head of the firm was Joseph Benjamin Hepworth Greenwood, who had been born in Honley in 1817; he was apprenticed as a wool sorter, and later moved into manufacturing at Neiley Mills in Honley. As his business grew he moved to Old Moll mill, and from there to Digley.

The census of 1881 records that Joseph Greenwood was 63 years old and employed 140 people. He was living at Green Owlers by 1878; where he subsequently unexpectedly died on 24th April 1884, one week short of his 67th birthday; his place as head of the firm was filled by two of his sons, Joseph Albert Greenwood aged 26, and his brother Frank who, at that time, was 14 years old.

Joshua Woodcock a weaver at the mill went for a walk with his two youngest sons, one aged 4 years and the other 1 year 10 months, on the evening of 10th December 1886. Two hours later his wife raised the alarm as they had not returned; Woodcock's coat and hat were found on the Bilberry reservoir embankment, and the hats of the two boys were floating in the water. The following day, after draining the reservoir, the bodies of all three were found. The verdict at the inquest was that Woodcock, who had a history of depression and had previously tried to hang himself, had committed suicide, and that he was guilty of the murders of his two youngest children. He left his wife and two older sons both of whom also worked at Greenwoods.

The firm were in need of larger premises by 1890, and submitted plans to the council for a second woollen mill to be built also at Digley, with a new weaving shed, boiler house, stove and offices. In 1891 the workpeople from Digley and Bilberry mills, enjoyed a trip to the seaside at the company's expense; on August 29th 574 people left Holmfirth station at 5.40am and arrived in Cleethorpes at 8.45am where they spent the day looking round Cleethorpes and Grimsby. The special train arrived back in Holmfirth at 11.15pm.

In 1895 a boy called Fred Dollive was working in the mule room at the mill as a piecer when he was struck on the leg by the jenny as it came out. The mule was stopped and Fred was extracted from beneath it; a spinner who was a member of the St. John's Ambulance Brigade rendered first aid, afterwards Fred was taken home by cart and examined by Dr. Trotter, he was found to have a fractured thigh and was reported to be 'progressing as well as could be expected'.[13]

In 1896 the firm were asking for quotes to build a new dam for the mill, it would cover an area of 2,240sq.yds. and was to be sighted near Hoobram, which was where Joseph Albert Greenwood and his wife Lucy (nee Green) lived with their six children. This dam possibly became known as Ellis Pond, now without the dam wall and much overgrown. The firm submitted plans to the Council in the same year to build a new warehouse and offices, plus a house and outbuildings near the mill, which were approved. In June 1897 the Yorkshire Factory Times reported that the 'new erections' at the mill were nearing completion. Other improvements in succeeding years included a new boiler house in 1900 and an additional weaving shed in 1902.

The employees of both mills attended a party in January 1901, held in the Drill Hall in Holmfirth. Some 300 people sat down to a knife and fork tea, which was followed by dancing, songs and recitations, with a substantial supper at 9pm, followed by more dancing.

In November of the same year the company had to attend a special enquiry in Holmfirth to answer questions put to them by a Local Government Board Inspector regarding pollution of Digley Dike. The Rivers Board, maintained in November 1901, that the mill daily discharged 70,000 gallons of polluted water, and they had been trying for at least four years to get Greenwoods to treat all the water used to wash wool, scour pieces, or in dyeing, before allowing it to run into the dike, but without success. No agreement, at least on this occasion, was reached.

A fire in the drying stove was discovered at 2.15am on February 14th 1903 by Harry Coldwell, a member of the mill's fire brigade. In addition to the mill's own brigade, the brigade from Yew Tree mill and the Unity brigade also attended, and the fire was out by 3.30am. Damage was estimated to be £250.

The Yorkshire Trade Directory for 1910 lists the firm as Joseph Greenwood & Sons Ltd, manufacturers of worsted coatings and trouserings, vicunas, coverts, serges and silk mixtures; the Empire Register dated 1923 gives their specialities as plain and fancy Worsteds and Woollen suitings; fine Tweeds, Vicunas, Overcoatings & Fancy Trouserings. The mill had 3,000 spindles and 88 looms.

Lighting at the mill would be from gas or oil lamps as they were on the wrong side of the river to be able to take advantage of the electricity supply from Holme UDC. Holmfirth council had begun generating electricity in July 1916, and had said that they would be able to supply Greenwoods with electricity for lighting by January 1924, however the supply did not materialise. Greenwood's submitted a plan to the council to install a turbine in Bilberry mill to generate their own electricity supply, which was refused.

The company had gone into receivership in August 1926, but due to the intervention of a consortium of benefactors they were able to continue trading until 1936, when as with Bilberry mill they had to close, as Huddersfield Corporation were intending building the Digley Reservoir. The closing party was held on December 18th 1936.[14] Some of the workers went with Norman Marsh, who had been mill manager, to Reins Mill in Honley, where he traded under his own name until 1969 or 1970.

Austonley / Bankend mill

This mill, which was just a few hundred yards downstream from Lower Digley Mill, was erected in 1800. The Wakefield Court Roll records that the cost of building it was borne equally by Joseph Green Armitage of Thick Hollins, formerly known as Joseph Green of Round Green Silkstone; and Christopher Green of Glass Houghton. There was also a row of seven cottages up the bank behind the mill. The roof of the mill collapsed in November 1802, killing three people and injuring several others. No reason for the collapse is given. In addition to their ownership of the mill, the Green family also bought the recently built house at Bank Top at a cost of £400 including 6 closes of land totalling around 30 acres, which adjoined the land on which the mill and cottages were built. The house is described as having a Burling chamber which was presumably on the top floor in the same way that weaving chambers were; it also had a drying stove. As late as the 1950s the only way into the top floor was via a bridge from the bank behind the house to the third floor door.

The mill appears to have been run by the Green family until August 1827 when John Roebuck the elder, with his sons Jonas, John, Jonathon, Eli and William all of Flashouse [sic], rented it for a term of 21 years. The mill is described as having a water wheel, dams and weirs, a stable with hay loft over, a nearby drying stove, five cottages (one of which used to be three), and two closes of land called the Upper and Lower Bank Brows. The Upper Bank Brow was divided into plots by stone walls and used as gardens by the tenants of the cottages; this is the land on the lower side of Bank Top road from the top of Field End Lane to the bottom of Roods Lane. John Roebuck the elder died in October 1832, leaving the mill and other property to his five sons.

The eldest son Jonas appears to have completed the return to the Factory Commission enquiry in 1833, they were engaged in the Scribbling, Slubbing and Spinning of wool, power was supplied by an 8hp water wheel, they employed 1 girl under 10 who was earning 4s a week, 2 boys and 2 girls under 12 each earning 4s a week, 4 girls under 14 earning 5s each, 3 boys and 1 girl under 16 earning 6s each, 1 girl under 18 earning 6s, and 6 men over 21 earning 20s each. 14 of the children were paid by the person for whom they worked. Their hours were 6am to 8pm in summer and from daylight to 9pm in winter. The workers were allowed a total of two hours a day for the three meal breaks when, they said, the machines were all stopped. They also said that children under twelve made the best piecers.

As with other mills in the area, Roebuck's were summoned in Dec.1836 for infringing the Factory Act; in common with the other mills the fine imposed was to be distributed between the local Sunday Schools. Joseph Green Armitage died aged 81 on 3 Oct 1841, leaving his share of the mill to his son James, and legacies to his three daughters.

The 1852 flood destroyed the end of the four storey mill nearest to the river, the straight severance of the upstream wall giving credence to the claim that part of Lower Digley mill had travelled downstream still standing. Many lengths of woven cloth had been removed from the mill for safety before the flood; the lower floor of the mill was virtually cleared of machinery by the force of water, and machines on the upper floors were pushed together in heaps. The dyehouse, which must have been built after the other buildings before mentioned, possibly by the Roebuck's, and the drying stove that was built just downstream of the main mill were completely destroyed. The mill dam ran alongside the river upstream of the mill, the force of the flood waters broke away the embankment allowing the water in the dam to add to the volume of the flood.

Not having fulling stocks at Bankend, Roebuck's used the fulling stocks at Bilberry mill; these were also destroyed adding to their losses, a claim was submitted for £2,735, this was reduced to £2,216, with £1,164 13s 8d being paid in full settlement. All the 40 or so workpeople were thrown out of work. Repercussion from the flood was fairly swift and severe, a petition for bankruptcy was filed in Leeds against John and William Roebuck on September 20th 1852, and a public hearing was set for 25 February 1853. John Roebuck was committed to prison in York and his assets assigned to creditors.[15]

Eli Roebuck must have considered taking over the business, as a draft Lease was produced in February 1853. The Lessors were William Walter Battye of Fulbeck Hall, Lincolnshire, James Bennett of Almondbury, and James Crosland Fenton, solicitor, of Huddersfield, who were all executors for Joseph Green Armitage, also James Green Armitage; the Lessee was to be Eli Roebuck. The lease describes the premises as having been a Scribbling and Fulling mill despite there being no previous mention of fulling stocks, and includes the cottages and land plus a schedule of machinery. The lease was to run for one year, during which time Eli was to rebuild what was referred to as the Old Mill, and install a wool drying and tenter stove 'with the necessary boiler and appurtenances'. He would be allowed to receive the money from the Relief Committee for the flood damage, but had to spend the money allowed for loss or damage to machines on replacing or repairing them. He also had to insure the property and contents, and pay £300 in rent for the year. If, at the end of the year, the owners felt that Eli had fulfilled all the conditions of the lease, he would, at his own expense, be able to take a further lease for 14 years at a rent of £250 a year. The value of the machinery to be left in the building on the expiry of the second lease was to be not less than £740. Surprisingly, or is it? the one year lease does not appear to have been signed.

Rebuilding of the mill began in March 1854 and was completed by June 14th; the work was undertaken by James Ramsden of Austonley for which he was paid £125. This was followed by a second agreement between the owners and the builder dated June 20th to build a goit for the water supply for the sum of £59 2s 9d, which had to be completed by September 15th of the same year, or the owners would deduct £2 for each week that the project overran. There appear to have been problems finding a new tenant for the mill, as in July 1857 it was advertised 'to let' with a £300 grant from the relief committee, to which the owners would add a further £300. The rent required is not given.

The next tenants of the mill were Samuel and James Moorhouse, who were in bankruptcy in 1871, when their machinery was to be sold. It was sold, or was at least offered for sale, on three occasions, the first sale, on 12 August 1871, was for finishing machinery; the second sale, on 6 April 1872, was for scribbling, carding and spinning machinery plus the items that were left from the first sale; the third sale, held on 15 March 1873, was for the remnants of the scribbling, carding and spinning machinery, apparently with additions, as in some instances the quantities on offer were increased.

Ownership of the mill changed before the next lease which is dated March 1873; the owners are given as Charles Hastings of Bradford, Joseph Rayner of Liverpool, Mary Ann Rhodes of Clare Hill Huddersfield, Sarah Lockwood of Spring Grove Austonley, [which was the house in which the Roebuck family lived when they occupied the mill], also James and Elizabeth Hargreaves of Leeds.

The Lessee was George Tinker of Upper Digley; Arthur Tinker was also included in the draft of the lease, but his name is crossed out and a note in the margin states that although Arthur may become a partner at a later date he is not to be included in this agreement. Arthur did eventually become a partner in the firm, as he is recorded as moving from Bankend mill to Bridge mill in late 1889, or very early 1890. The agreement was for the mill with the water wheel, shafting and gearing; also the 7 cottages now occupied as 5 dwellings with the gardens, which were occupied at the time by Samuel Moorhouse, John Armitage, Tom Armitage, Betty Battye and Arthur Tinker. The rent for the mill was £110 a year, plus £25 a year for the cottages. A clause in the agreement required the Lessee to pay £50 a year to Ann Elizabeth Green Armitage during her lifetime [presumably the daughter of Joseph Green Armitage], which was to be deducted from the money paid to the owners. The agreement also allowed George Tinker to build a dyehouse of approved design, costing not more than £120, which he would also be allowed to deduct from the rent over a two year period.

The firm of T & J Tinker joined George Tinker in the mill in 1874, moving from Upper Brow Bottom/Brownhill Mill. They had also taken premises in Upper Mytholmbridge Mill by 1886, and moved out of this mill in 1888 leaving George and Arthur Tinker, trading as Tinker Bros, as sole occupiers. Joshua Thristle Barber was using at least part of the mill in 1889, although he moved to Holmbridge mill with W.H. & J. Barber in 1890. The premises were advertised 'to let' in 1895, but there is no record of an incoming tenant.

In 1902 the mill was advertised for sale by auction, when it was described as a 4 storey mill and attic, plus former dyehouse, shed, boiler house, store shed and chimney. Also land, plantation, site of dam, and valuable water rights. The six cottages plus outbuildings and land were offered as a separate lot.[16] The 'Express' of 19 July reported that the mill was sold for £680 to an unnamed buyer, but makes no mention of the cottages, which could have been bought privately and subsequently withdrawn from the auction. The 25 inch Ordinance Survey map of the area published in 1906 marks the mill as 'disused'; it was later demolished. The cottages continued to be occupied until the early 1950s, after which they too were demolished, the land on which they stood is now used as a garden.

Holmbridge dyehouse

Sited at the foot of Holme Banks, across Woodhead Road from Holmbridge mill, between the road and Digley Dike, this dyehouse was part of the 'appurtenances' that went with Holmbridge mill from at least 1778, although it appears to have become a separate entity from the mill in the early nineteenth century until being bought by W.H. & J. Barber in 1903. While the mill drew virtually all its water from Rake Dike, the dyehouse drew its supply partly from Digley Dike via a long goit; plus some from a small reservoir behind the dyehouse buildings, and partly from the overflow of a well in Holme Banks. In 1822 it was owned by Firth Gartside, a dyer who was living in Holmbanks. The Austonley Tithe published in 1847 gives the occupants as John and Jonathon Midgeley, while the owners are Firth Gartside's executors. A detailed inventory giving a comprehensive description of the premises and contents was compiled in 1871, which shows that during their tenancy the Midgeley's had improved the premises. Inventory of equipment:

> *Boiler House, steam engine and boiler, shafting, stove pipes, iron head on boiler, water gauge, pressure gauge, safety valve and injector. Perforated floor to upper storey used as a stove heated by boiler. Firing place with chamber over.*
>
> *Pan Dyehouse, 8 pans various sizes (3 on entry), a great quantity of steam and water piping, 16 valves, about 20 taps, washing machine, shafting and gearing. 8hp engine on ashlar foundations, wooden cistern, winch with counter shaft and pulley.*
>
> *Dyeware room, 2 stoves, office and counting house.*
>
> *Blue Dyehouse, 10vats (8 on entry), scour pan and still and iron crane for working same. Scouring machine, shafting, steam and water pipes valves and taps.*

Wheel House water wheel about 10ft diam. 2ft 6in wide, Mr. Midgeley thinks fall is about 8ft; 2 Indigo rockers, large stone cistern, moveable cylinder.

Piece Dyehouse 2 Iron pans, brickwork and winches. Steam and water pipes and valves, shafting and pulleys, 2 wood cisterns.

Dyehouse has dyeing water principally from small reservoir at back, but in dry seasons Mr. Midgeley has to pump water from the goit into reservoir above mentioned, and they also use water out of the goit for the scouring machine and water wheel, but all water (except fouled water from the Dyepans and washing machine) runs to the Mill Dam. Trough in Holme Banks: overflow from it is now intended to be continued for use in dyehouse.

The Midgeleys' also held the property at Field End, comprising 4 cottages, gardens and outbuildings, 2 privies, 2 storage buildings and 3 coal places, tenanted by William Broadhead, Eli Ridgwick, George Starbrook and Mark Hinchliffe. Also the Barn and Mistal at Field End, and the Tan Yard cottage [on Digley Lane] with garden and outbuildings tenanted by Charles Hinchliffe, and some vacant ground.

The goit, dam stones and shuttle head were damaged by the 1852 flood, a claim for £150 was submitted, the only recorded payment was £25 5s 10d for labour. Frederick Midgeley advertised a sale of surplus dyehouse requisites plus agricultural stock in January 1894.[17]

After being bought by Barber's, the dyehouse continued to be used for some time, but by the 1940s the main part was being used as a joinery. Two buildings on the roadside just above the main dyehouse were used by the mill principally for storage. These two buildings still exist.

Fieldend corn mill

This building stood across Woodhead Road from the Wagon & Horses Public House which was at the bottom of Field End Lane; the buildings would have been mostly below road level as the ground falls away towards the river. There is no record of this corn mill being built, but it was presumably after the change of use at Dobb mill, and before 1827. To get water to drive the wheel at the mill was fairly complex as the land between the mill and the river was reasonably flat, and the river bed is lower than the land. This was achieved by building what the documents describe as 'a trunk or tunnel' that collected water from the tail goit of the water wheels at Holmbridge mill and carried that water across the river to the head goit of Field End corn mill. The water wheel at the Corn Mill was driven by water that came from Rake Dike. The 'trunk' was forty one feet long and was made from wood that was apparently five inches thick, as it was thirteen feet wide externally but twelve feet two inches wide internally, with an internal depth of thirteen and three quarter inches, and had a three inch partition running down the centre. It was to be positioned so that the depth of water within it would not exceed ten inches. After crossing the river, the water travelled via a long goit that started just downstream from the road bridge and ran along the field, more or less in line with the river, to the junction with the field that is now the recreation ground, where it turned left, away from the river towards the mill. At this point there was a return to the river, which was intended as a safety valve in case too much water entered the goit; this took the form of a spillway by having a ten inch high rim that would allow any surplus water to escape back to the river. There was a dam in front of the mill, from where the water would drive the wheel, but how this was achieved is something of a mystery. A 'fall' of water is needed to turn the wheel, therefore the return has to be lower than the input; if the two are level there is no flow to turn the wheel. If there was a means of pumping water from the dam to at least half the height of the wheel, then it would turn; or another alternative would be to put the wheel in a pit, with an underground tunnel taking the water back to the river further downstream, but there is no indication of this.

An entry in the Wakefield Court Roll dated 26 Jan. 1827 records that Benjamin Green a miller of Field End, held a newly erected Drying Kiln and Water Corn Mill, with water wheel, going gear and machinery, in a close called the Great Bottom, along with 3 houses at Fieldend, with an adjoining blacksmiths shop, warehouse and stable. In addition to these properties, an entry in the Court Roll of 1830 shows that Benjamin Green also owned the Wagon & Horses Inn [currently the Bridge Tavern], and a Malt House and warehouse.

The flood of 1852 washed away the 'trunk or tunnel' and damaged the goit to the mill, but, even though the water spread across the fields and damaged the Parish Church, it does not appear to have affected the mill buildings. The entry in the Reservoir Commissioners register in 1853 confirms that Benjamin Green was the owner of the mill and that Benjamin and John Green were the occupiers. The occupier of the mill in 1856 is given as Thomas Woodhead, who must have taken it part way through the year as the water rate for that year was to be reduced because the mill had been unoccupied for several months. The Directors allowed a discount of £2 18s 8d, leaving £4 12s 4½d to be paid.

A conveyance dated 1861 records that John Cuttell of Long Walls acquired the drying kiln and water corn mill from the trustees of Mr. and Mrs. Henry Spurr. A property sale in 1873 advertises the sale of the mill with the water wheel, fixed machinery, dams, goits etc. together with the Butchers shop, which must have been a recent innovation as it had not been mentioned previously; also offered for sale is the Commercial Inn, which was the renamed Wagon & Horses.[18] The buyers of the properties were Reuben and James Senior brewers, of Shepley.

The mill must have gradually fallen into disuse, as the 25" Ordinance Survey map of 1893 shows the mill buildings, but the section of the goit from the point where it turned away from the river is missing, as is the dam. The mill was gradually demolished to the point where, in the late 1940s, there were just a couple of small buildings at the foot of the wall opposite the then Commercial Inn, which were used for keeping pigs. These probably disappeared when the ground level was raised to make a car park for the Inn.

Dobb Dike – Dobb mill / dyehouse

This has the distinction of being one of the few mills in Yorkshire that was marked on Jeffery's map printed in 1775. The mill would appear to have been built around 1720, when James Earnshaw paid £10 to John Matthewman and Thomas Haigh of Millsom Edge for two areas of land next to Dob Dike in a close called le Spring, the first was 80 roods (440yds) long and 20 roods (110yds) wide on which to build a dam, the second was 30 roods (165yds) long and 10 roods (55yds) wide on which he could put a building, which could be either a corn mill or a 'furnace house' (bakehouse or oven). Earnshaw could also construct a goit to convey water from the dike to the dam, and also make a carriage-way from the mill to the road.[19] Whether the Earnshaw family lived at and operated the mill is unknown, but is doubtful as James was described as a gentleman. James Earnshaw senior died in 1722, the mill and other assets passed to his son who was also called James.

In 1723, Bryan Allott who held the fee-farm of the lord's mill in Holmfirth, filed 'an information' in the Duchy Court of Lancaster against James Earnshaw of Holme to show why he ground not only his own corn, but also that of other copyholders, at his own mill in the township of Cartworth, thereby defrauding Bryan Allott of his accustomed suite and toll. James submitted in his defence that even before his father built the mill at Dobb, he had been accustomed to taking his corn to be ground at whichever mill he chose. That Bryan Allott brought this case is somewhat puzzling, as he was presumably aware that permission to build the mill had been granted by the manor court, which was the court that would normally have heard Allott's case. That he chose to take his complaint to the Duchy Court of Lancaster suggests that he thought that he had little chance of success in the manor court. The case does not seem to have ever been heard, whether this was because the Duchy Court realised that the Earnshaw's were acting within their legal rights, or whether it was because Allott was entering the Church and decided not to pursue the case is unknown, he subsequently became the Rector of Kirkburton.

In 1781 George Hobson the younger who was a corn miller, lived and worked at the mill, but did not own it; he had moved from the mill to Hillhouse by 1800. In 1793 the owner of the mill was

Joshua Earnshaw who lived in Ossett, in May of that year he passed 'all that water corn mill known as Dob mill with seven acres of land occupied by George Dyson' to the use of the said George Dyson. More evidence of the mill having been used as a corn mill was found by the present owner in the latter half of the twentieth century, when he discovered a pair of grind stones for a corn mill buried in the field that is now his garden. The date on which the water corn mill became a textile mill is unclear, but presumably happened before Fieldend Corn mill was built.

The 6" Ordinance Survey map of 1853 marks the mill as a woollen mill, whereas the 25" map dated 1893 marks it as a dyehouse. The water source changed at some time from the dyke to a spring in the field behind the mill, with water being conveyed via a pipeline to the dam. The 1851 census shows that John Earnshaw who was 66 lived there with his wife and grandson, his occupation is given as a manufacturer employing 41 men, not all of them would necessarily be employed at Dobb; White's Directory of 1853 shows that J. Earnshaw & Sons also had premises at 12 King's Head Yard, Huddersfield, which they were probably using as a warehouse and showroom.

The Cartworth Vestry Minutes show that the occupant of the mill in 1859 was Tedbur Earnshaw, but in 1866 Jonas Hobson was living there, he was also a manufacturer. Ten years later, in addition to Dobb mill Jonas Hobson, along with several other manufacturers, was using premises in Littlewood Buildings, Sargentson Street near to the Cloth Hall in Huddersfield for storage, when a beam holding up the upper floor gave way; bringing the ceiling and contents of the upper floor down onto the floor below. While all the cloth was still intact, every piece would have to be refinished.

Ownership of the property was being contested in the Chancery Court in 1893 in the case Broadhead v Morehouse; the property was auctioned on 13th December when it was described as a Dyehouse with a stove, dyewares room, reservoir, and fittings. It was sold for £500, the name of the purchaser was not disclosed; the tenant at the time was Joe Woodhead.

John Clare Earnshaw Morehouse passed his half share in: 'All that the dwelling house with farm buildings, dyehouse and premises, and the several closes of land occupied therewith, situated at

Hearth pit at Dobb mill. © Mr. J. Brook

Dobb in Cartworth…in the occupation of Joe Woodhead, at the yearly rent of £35; to his sister Mary Beatrice Morehouse on his death in 1901.

There is no record of when it ceased to be used as a dyehouse; during the 1930s and '40s part of it was used as a slaughter house, and by 1958 the building was virtually derelict when Mr. J. Brook bought it from Mrs. Gibbon Barber.

Part of the building still contained the hearths for the fires used to heat the dyepans, although the cast iron pans had been removed. He used it as a garage and workshop for cars until around 1990. During 1992 and '93 he virtually rebuilt the property making it into a dwelling.

Hollin Brigg

Upstream from Dobb mill stands Hollin Brigg house, which was for many years, one of the houses occupied by the Barber family. An accident occurred in 1855 to John Battye, a carter employed by John Barber of Hollin Brigg. Battye was returning to Hollin Brigg with a load of coal in his cart when he stumbled and fell as he crossed the bridge over the river at Hinchliffe Mill. One of the cart's wheels ran over his head killing him. The inquest jury returned a verdict 'in accordance with the evidence'.

In addition to the house there are a good number of outbuildings at Hollin Brigg, at least one of which was being used for the manufacture of hearthrugs in the 1880s. A sale of machinery and stock belonging to Booth, Lockwood & Co. rug manufacturers, was advertised to take place 18 October 1886, 'due to declining business'. The machinery included 12 Hearthrug looms with healds, slays, bobbin wheels, shears etc; a double cylinder vertical steam engine with upright boiler, steam piping and iron shafting. A 'jerry' or rug-cropping machine, 200 hearthrugs, several pieces of tweed, 2 tons of woollen rags in blue, scarlet, orange, green, brown and black, ideal colours for making pegged rugs; also a small quantity of jute warp and weft.[20]

The 25 inch Ordinance Survey map of 1893 marks a small dyehouse on the end of the group of outbuildings furthest from the house. The name of the occupants is not known, nor how long it was in use; but it is not marked on the 1930s map, so had presumably been pulled down by then.

River Holme – Hinchliffe Mill mills

There were, eventually, two mills called Hinchliffe Mill, both on the River Holme near the centre of the village; the earliest one being on the upstream side of the road bridge carrying Dobb Lane, the other downstream below the dam. The original mill was probably built in the late fifteenth century by William Hynchecliff; the earliest record for it is in the Wakefield Court Roll of 1503:

> *18 October, Holme, William Hynchecliff son and heir of William Hynchecliff came here in the Tourne and gave to the lord 3s 4d of fine for a licence to Herriot for one parcel of water in Cartworthmere at a certain place called Braithfurthe with one fulling mill built on the same with appurtenances in the Graveship of Holme after the death of the aforesaid William the father to the aforesaid William the son to hold to himself and his heirs by services according to the custom of the manor.* [Braithfurthe means either a broad furrow or a broad ford]

There is a legend that the Hynchecliff family had been millers at the Lord's mill for some years and wanted to build their own fulling mill, which the lord allowed them to do at Braithfurthe; the area subsequently becoming known as Hinchliffe Mill. An entry in the Court Roll of 1402 records that 'the lord's mill of Holme is let this year to William de Hynchecliffe'; although he was not the fee-farmer in subsequent years. There does not seem to be any mention of the Hynchecliff family being linked with either corn or fulling mills later in that century.

In 1531 William Hynchecliff let the mill and a house with 22 acres of land, for six years to John Bray at an annual rent of 20s. William Hynchecliff died in 1539, when the house, land and mill passed to his son John. The place where the mill stands is still referred to as Braithfurthe at this time.

In the mid eighteenth century the mill was owned by Thomas and Sarah Craven of Dewsbury, who had possibly gifted the income from the mill to the benefit of the curate of Dewsbury at the time, who is named as John Earnshaw. In 1751 Earnshaw was ordered to pay half the annual rent from the mill to John Firth of Yew Tree; the occupier of the mill at this time being given as Joseph Roberts of Hinchcliffe Milne. An Indenture dated 1788 between Rev. Joshua Earnshaw of Ossett, and George and John Batty Cloth Millers of Hinchliffe Mill, states that from the 26 January 1787, the Battys' should take over 2 new dwelling houses situated at or near Hinchliffe Mill, with the Fulling mill, barn, stable and other outbuildings, along with nine acres of land. Whether Rev. Joshua Earnshaw is the same person as the curate John Earnshaw in 1751, or a relative, is not clear. It is worth mentioning that a blue and white Delphware jug inscribed 'George and Abigail Batty Hinchcliffe Mill 1790' was shown on the BBC Television programme *The Antiques Roadshow* in 2008, repeated in early 2011.

Around 1795, ownership of the mill passed to the Greame family of Exley, Halifax; and tenancy of the mill was taken up by the Butterworth family, as Matthew Butterworth of Hillhouse was responsible for paying the Land Tax in that year. A lease for 100 years between Henry Greame of Halifax and Thomas Morehouse of Spring Bottom Netherthong of the first part (owners of the property); and Jonathon Butterworth of Wheatclose, Matthew Butterworth of Hillhouse, Benjamin Butterworth of Hillhouse, Jonathon Butterworth of Bank, Anthony Green of Holme Fields and Thomas Battye of Yew Tree, of the second part (as tenants), for the mill, 2 cottages and 10 acres of land, at a rent of £220 a year, was signed in 1805. The rateable value of the mill was £24 at that time. It seems that George and John Batty had literally 'taken possession' of the two cottages that went with the mill, as they are named in the lease as being the tenants.

The lower mill, a five storey building, was built in 1807, along with a larger dam running between the road bridge and the mill. Both mills relied solely on water power, the water supply for the upper mill was taken from Dobb Dike, via a long goit running parallel with the River Holme to a small dam behind that mill, from where it powered the wheel. The arch through which the water reached the wheel can still be seen by looking over the wall on Dobb Lane, the arch is in the lower part of the end wall of the mill. After powering the wheel, the water continued under the mill via a tail goit that took it to a small dam near the river (now silted up and used as a garden), which then fed into the dam for the new (lower) mill from 1807. From that time Butterworth & Co. used both mills for the scribbling, carding and slubbing of wool.

In 1833 they employed 28 people: 7 boys and 2 girls under 10 earning 3s 9d each, 4 boys and 2 girls under 12 earning 4s each, 1 boy earning 5s and 2 girls earning 4s who were all under 14, 1 boy under 16 earning 6s, 1 boy under 18 earning 10s, and 6 men over 21 earning 23s each. From 1 April to 1 October the mill worked 6am to 8pm; in winter they started at daybreak and worked 12 hours. They had a 30 minute break for Breakfast, and one hour for Dinner, but no time was set aside for the afternoon break. The water wheel was not always stopped at lunchtime when, they say, the machinery was supervised by the overlooker and other adults whilst the children ate. They disliked corporal punishment, but had no regular rule about it, and sometimes the slubbers thought it necessary. On the question of reduced hours, they felt a 10 Hour Act would 'injure the country at large' as it would reduce wages; and that an 11 Hour Act would lower the value of mill property, particularly water mills, unless a law was passed allowing mills to work longer to make up lost time due to water shortage. In common with many manufacturers the Butterworths' were of the opinion that 12 hours work, plus meal breaks, was acceptable to adults and children alike; anything less was a bad thing, as it would allow people time to get into trouble.

During the next fifteen to eighteen years, in the lower mill the water wheel alone seems to have proved inadequate for the amount of power needed, as an engine house was built over the river. This, along with a bridge, were destroyed by the flood of 1852, as were the 6 houses owned by Joshua Barber on the opposite side of the river in Water Street, where 36 people lost their lives. The residents of one of the houses were Jonathon Charlesworth and his eight children, seven of whom were drowned along with their father. The only child to survive was a 22 week old girl who was possibly being cared for by a relative at the time of the flood. Jonathon was a handloom weaver with two looms, each of which had a warp in the process of being woven. One warp belonged to James Brook, the other to Richard Bower. The claim submitted, presumably by relatives, totalled £75 12s 2d, this was reduced to £49 16s 2d, the inspectors paid £40; they also allowed 5s per week to the relatives who were looking after the baby girl; and at the time of the flood Jonathon had debts amounting to £9 4s 4d, for coal, groceries and money borrowed from other family members. The inspectors paid Jonathon's 69 year old father the £2 he was owed because it was an old debt, the rest appear to have been left unpaid.

In 1853 the Reservoir Commissioners recorded the owners of both mills as Thomas Morehouse and John Earnshaw Greame, and the occupiers as Joseph Butterworth, Robert Butterworth, Richard Woofenden Butterworth, Benjamin Butterworth, Edward Butterworth, Thomas Butterworth, Sarah Butterworth, Matthew Butterworth, Anthony Green, Samuel Sandford and his wife Nancy.[21] Samuel Sandford was the father of Jonathon Sandford, who was drowned at Dyson's mill in the 1852 flood, where Samuel is also listed as a tenant in 1853. Samuel and his wife were possibly using part of Hinchliffe Mill mill as Dyson's mill had been destroyed.

A firm called J & T Ellis had taken part of one of the mills in 1856, they gave their workers a treat on 14th May to celebrate the end of the Crimean War. The rate valuation list for 1857 gives the total rate for both mills as £321, a substantial increase from the £24 of 1805.

James Mettrick was using part of the mill making Mungo and shoddy, he filed a petition for liquidation in August 1873. There were discrepancies in the accounts, one example was that Eli Wimpenny of Wimpenny & Bowes, Stoney Bank mill had bought Mungo valued at £47 from Mettrick in July, which had been paid to Mettrick two weeks later in cash when he called at Stoney Bank and asked for the money. However, he was not able to supply information as to how the money had been spent. This was not unusual in these cases, whether the amnesia was genuine or merely convenient can only be guessed at. Mettrick had, at one time, had a partner called Shore who had also been given amounts of money by customers that had not appeared in the accounts; the hearing was adjourned for one week, but no more light was shed on the problems.

Joseph Butterworth & Sons were in liquidation in October 1876, with debts of £1,600. A sale of machinery was held on 20 November, when machinery for turning raw wool into yarn, and then weaving it into cloth were auctioned, along with 1,200lbs of yarn. The Butterworth family continued in business at the mill, with Thomas Butterworth heading the firm. They built a new boiler house in 1884, but do not appear to have installed a steam engine, and in 1888 a fire in the drying stove damaged some wool, but was put out within about twenty minutes. Drying stoves were invariably sited over the boiler house.

George Charlesworth, who had been using part of the mill since 1872 died in September 1882, his wife, who was also his executrix, ordered that his machinery for scribbling, spinning and weaving wool, and his stock-in-trade of 10,000lbs of yarn should be sold.

In June 1890 the weavers of T. Butterworth & Sons held a meeting in the New Inn at Hinchliffe Mill with the officials of the Power Loom Weavers Association Messrs. Gee, Drew and Turner, because they were dissatisfied with the rates that Butterworth's were paying for weaving some qualities. Butterworth's rates of pay were compared with the rates negotiated seven years previously for Huddersfield and District. The rates for lower qualities compared quite well, but rates for higher qualities were much lower than had been agreed. The union said that they would approach the company; the outcome must have been acceptable to all as no further information appeared. Later in the year the weavers were again dissatisfied, saying that work was not being shared equally between weavers of fast and slow looms; also slow looms were gradually being replaced by fast looms, but the weaver's were not being re-employed, others were taking their place. Again, no further information was given.

Butterworth's appear to have found trading difficult in the late 1880s and early 1890s, as J. Butterworth left the partnership in January 1891, and in February 1892 the two remaining partners, Thomas Herbert Butterworth and Percy Barber, went into liquidation/bankruptcy with debts in the region of £3,900. There was an auction of yarn, followed by an auction of plant and machinery, both in March 1892, included in the plant and machinery was the Electric Lighting Plant, consisting of 110 incandescent lamps, which were powered by two 95 volt Dynamos'. From notes made on the sale catalogue at the time, these were sold for £57 10s. This must have been one the earliest mills in the upper Holme Valley to use electric lighting.

Henry Whiteley of Mount Pleasant Holmfirth, and Hurst Green of Scholecroft Holme, formed a partnership and began business, trading as Whiteley & Green, on 1st July 1879, leasing part of the lower mill, and paying themselves a salary of thirty shillings each, (£1 10s), per week. In 1892 they were summoned to the magistrate's court for breaching the Factory Act by employing three children without a surgeon's certificate. In their defence, Mr. Whiteley said that one boy who had been borrowed from H & S Butterworth Lower Mill, had a certificate from Dr. Morehouse to work at Lower Mill. They had approached Dr. Morehouse who had said that he could not see the point of issuing a new certificate for a temporary attachment. Whiteley & Green were fined 5s plus costs on each case.[22]

Plans for a new dyehouse were submitted to Holmfirth Council in January 1895, who returned them with the suggestion that 'refuse water' from the dyehouse should be treated before being put into the river. Despite the West Riding County Council having sued Holmfirth council in the courts in 1893 for not making any provision for the treatment of sewage in the district, they still had no plans to build a treatment plant, but were urging mills and other manufacturers to provide their own means of treating effluent and sewage.

> The mill was advertised for sale by auction in 1897, when it was described as an: 'L shaped 5 storey main mill, used for scribbling, spinning, weaving and finishing. Boiler house and drying stove over; outbuildings, water wheel, main shafting and chimney. In occupation of S. Butterworth & Son, and Whiteley & Green. Also the upper mill, formerly used for milling purposes with water wheel. Together with two reservoirs and highly important water rights. The whole contains about ten acres. Property is let on lease: land from Feb. 1806, buildings from May 1806, for 100 years at £280 per annum'. The mill was withdrawn from the auction when the bidding failed to rise over £1,550.

A fire broke out in the scribbling department at the mill at 12.20am on April 5th 1901, the night shift were working and tried to extinguish the flames with buckets of water, but failed. Hoses from Yew Tree mill arrived at about 12.30am, and the fire bell in Holmfirth Church was rung at 12.35am. The fire engine from Holmbridge mill also attended, and along with Yew Tree attached their hoses to the council hydrants. The 'Unity' engine also arrived and began pumping water from the mill dam, but all were unable to stop the fire spreading to the new part of the mill. The 'Alexandria' engine from Bridge Mills also arrived, followed by the council's hose cart; they concentrated their efforts on saving the cottage in the mill yard where Fred Brook and his family lived, also the boiler house and the other adjoining cottages, which they managed to do. Despite all efforts the interior of the mill was completely destroyed. The mill's gas main caught fire, and as Mr. W.E. Roberts, a gas company employee, was unable to turn it off, he 'biked' to the gas works in Holmfirth and turned it off there. The number of spectators was estimated at 3,000. Damage was thought to be in the region of £12,000, around 300 finished pieces were destroyed, and some 100 people were put out of work. The 'Express' questioned the suitability and efficiency of the council's fire engine and equipment; however, a note in the minutes of the council meeting held on 1 April records that the problem was due to an insufficient supply of water in the council mains. The burned out mill attracted many visitors over the weekend, which happened to be Easter.

Henry Whiteley and Hurst Green bought the mills, houses and land at auction from the

Morehouse family in June 1901 for £2,500. The firm registered as a Limited Company in August of the same year; submitting plans to the council for replacing the fire damaged buildings with ones of a more modern design in October of the same year, which was approved. The mill was rebuilt as a three storey mill, with separate buildings housing weaving, mending, scouring and dyeing. The Yorkshire Textile Directory of 1910 lists Whiteley & Green Ltd. as manufacturers of fancies and Bedford cords, having 1,500 spindles and 36 looms. A small steam engine was installed in 1911, which would supply power to drive the machinery during dry spells when the water level was low. A new finishing room was built in 1913 part of it was over the river; a sewer was also laid from the mill to the main sewer.

Mr. Hurst Green was on his way home for his mid-day meal when he was taken ill and died on 24 May 1914 at the age of 57. As he had no children to succeed him the connection of the Green family with the firm ceased. The First World War kept the wheels of Hinchliffe Mill mill turning day and night, producing Khaki Bedford Cord for the mounted Artillery. A new, more powerful steam engine was installed in 1922, which was capable of running all the machinery throughout the mill, allowing the water wheel and small steam engine to be dismantled. Charles F. Whiteley and Thomas Whiteley, both grandsons of the founder, joined the firm in 1936 and 1937 respectively, and both were called up for military service during the Second World War.

The Managing Director, Mr. Charles Henry Whiteley, died in 1939; as there was no-one to take his place, this resulted in the company being run during the war years by a Board of Management consisting of Mrs. C.H. Whiteley, Mrs. F. Whiteley, the firm's Solicitor, the firm's Accountant, and Mr. H. Marsh company secretary. The Yorkshire Textile Directory of 1942-3 shows that the firm's spinning capacity had increased to 2,400 spindles, and that they now had 40 looms.

The flood of 1944 destroyed the finishing room that had been built over the river and washed part of the machinery from the room downstream. Flood waters had also entered the entire ground floor of the mill, leaving a large deposit of sludge throughout. All the machinery on the ground floor, including the mill engine, had to be stripped, cleaned and reassembled before production could resume. The finishing room was rebuilt as soon as possible after the flood; and automatic looms were installed in 1951; these would be replaced by rapier looms in 1971.

An accident on 10 August 1953, resulted in the death of William Chapman Taylor aged 50 the boiler firer, he was badly injured while trying to change a drive belt from the shafting to a machine without slowing the mill engine. He died from his injuries while being taken to hospital. At the subsequent inquest, the jury returned a verdict of 'accidental death'. The company said that it was not usual to enclose the shafting with safety guards. The *Holmfirth Express* subsequently reported on 17 October that the company had been fined £15 for not having guards on the shafting.

The workforce increased by 25 percent between 1960 and 1968, which, along with the installation of modern faster machinery and the introduction of double day-shift working led to a doubling of production. The firm were producing Bedford Cords, Cavalry Twills and Whipcords, using Merino wool, cotton, nylon, rayon and Terelene; with twenty five percent of production being exported. In common with a number of other manufacturers Whiteley and Green opened a mill shop, from where, in 1983, thieves stole ready made trousers valued at £1,900. Whiteley and Green continued in production until the year 2000, after which a company called W&G Weavertec, commission weavers, were advertising for staff with experience of weaving Somet and Dornier looms, who were prepared to work shifts and weekends.[23]

The importance of the upper mill gradually diminished during the early part of the twentieth century, until it ceased to be used for textiles. In the 1940s and '50s it was used as a workshop and storeroom by Bottomley's plasterers. In 2010 it was being used as a motor vehicle repair shop. Many of the buildings at the lower mill were still standing in 2010, but were empty and vandalised; the mill has since been largely demolished, and is presumably to be replaced by housing.

Stubbin Clough – Yew Tree mill

Of all the textile buildings in the Holme Valley Yew Tree is in a unique position, in that it is the only complex that has remained in the ownership and occupation of the same family almost throughout its history, which is the Roberts family. Jonathon Roberts married Mary Roberts on 10 August 1730 and lived at Brown Hill, they had eight children, the seventh child was also called Jonathon, he married Rachel Littlewood on 7 June, 1772, and lived at Waterside. He is probably the Jonathon Roberts referred to in the Land Tax Returns as owning and occupying land in Cartworth from at least 1781.

The oldest buildings on the present mill site date from the 1770s or 1780s, and by the beginning of the nineteenth century there was a dyehouse plus a storeroom, warehouse, wool store, warping room, weaving room and a burling room; along with cart sheds on the site. The building of the turnpike road in 1809 divided the property, necessitating the building of a tunnel to reconnect the two parts; the tunnel still exists, but is closed at each end. The Austonley Tithe valuation and map shows that on the present mill site, in 1847, there were three houses, with a dyehouse, yard and garden, which were owned by Jonathon Roberts, and were occupied by Jonathon, John and William Roberts.

A fire broke out in a woolstore at the mill on Thursday 26 June 1851; neighbours with buckets and cans first poured water onto the roof of the building, then removed some tiles and poured water onto the wool inside the building. The fire, its origin unknown, caused damage estimated between £90 and £100. Although the mill was not seriously damaged in the 1852 flood, some damage did occur. A claim by Jonathon Roberts for damage to machinery and stock amounting to £138 was submitted and the amount was agreed by the inspectors, but a comment on the page in the claims book reads: 'This is a very wealthy firm' and the claim was marked 'disallowed'.

The majority of the cloth produced in the nineteenth century by the Roberts family was sold through the firm of Butterworth & Sons of Huddersfield, who were part of the Butterworth family

Yew Tree mill, © author.

of Hinchliffe Mill mill, and later at Lower Mill in Holmfirth; Butterworth & Sons were in financial difficulty in 1864 when they called a meeting of creditors. Jonathon Roberts, who was the principal creditor, stood by the firm allowing it to remain in business. Four years later, in 1868, Jonathon's nephew Henry entered into partnership with Robert Butterworth, and the firm of Butterworth & Roberts Woollen Manufacturers and Merchants, came into being. This coincided with the building of the first part of the large five storey mill at Yew Tree, with the second half being added in 1872. Henry Roberts, along with his younger brother Samuel took charge of manufacturing, while Robert Butterworth took responsibility for selling the cloth. Robert Butterworth died in 1883; after this time, although the name remained unchanged, the firm gave up the Merchant side of the business and concentrated solely on cloth production.

The water supply for the mill is taken from the stream in Stubbin Clough, and is stored in two dams immediately behind the mill. The second (upper) dam was built in 1874, possibly by William Armitage & Co; as a specification for building the dam and Armitage's price of £267 10s for doing so still exists. There is no evidence that a water wheel existed at the mill; as the earliest industrial use of the site was for a dyehouse there would be a need for water, but not necessarily for a wheel. When the five storey mill was built the company installed a 25hp steam engine, purchased at a cost of £410, from Tim Bates of Sowerby Bridge, (who later became Pollit & Wigzell Ltd). This was used to power the 3,000 spindles of the spinning mules, and the 50 power looms purchased from Hutchinson & Hollingworth of Dobcross. Some machinery, which was surplus to requirements, was advertised for sale by Private Contract in November 1872.

The principle area of production at that time was probably woollens, as they were also processing waste to make shoddy. In 1874 Sarah Ann Taylor of Booth House was passing a moiter or waste puller, and put her hand on the machine. Her hand was drawn into the mechanism and was pulled out by another woman, to find that four fingers were gone. Mr. Trotter the surgeon was called, after examining the damage he decided that the best course of action was to amputate the entire hand.

Demand for woollens dropped considerably during the 1870s; in common with many other manufacturers Butterworth & Roberts adapted their designs to incorporate a combination of yarns, and from the early 1890s concentrated production on fancy worsteds. In celebration of the Coming of Age of Henry Roberts' eldest son John, Butterworth & Roberts took all their workpeople and tenants to Scarborough for the day. A special train left Holmfirth at 4.30 a.m. on 14 June 1884, with 306 passengers, arriving in Scarborough at 8.15 a.m. After spending the day in the resort, the train with its passengers left Scarborough at 6.45pm arriving back in Holmfirth at about 10.30pm.

In 1891 Herbert Hirst Naylor, aged 13, met with an unfortunate accident when he went into the milling room to get a drink of water. There was no cup in the sink so he went in search of one; finding one about ten yards away which was full of clear liquid, he took a drink. He then asked two men who were working in the room what the liquid was, to be told that it was Vitriol [Sulphuric Acid]. The two men immediately administered an emetic which had the desired effect on the boy making him violently sick. Naylor was seen by a doctor, and was later reported to be recovering well.

All the workpeople enjoyed a visit to Scarborough on Saturday 11 August 1906, in celebration of the wedding of Mr. Arthur Henry Roberts. The train arrived at the seaside in time for Breakfast, and everyone enjoyed the sea, sand and sights for about 12 hours, before re-boarding the train for the return journey, arriving back in Holmfirth about 11.30pm. Plans for a new separate weaving shed were passed in 1906, with the shed being built in 1907. This enlargement also required more power; consequently the original steam engine was replaced by one producing 250hp, ten times the size of the original engine.[24]

A breakaway company was started on the premises in 1937, when Gordon Roberts, the eldest son of Arthur Henry Roberts, formed a company in partnership with his wife Hannah, trading as G & H Roberts Ltd. Woollen Yarn Spinners. They used part of the five storey mill and also an old dyehouse containing cast-iron dyepans, which they used for dyeing loose wool. G. & H. Roberts Ltd.

was, as far as I know, unique amongst manufacturers in the area, in that it was run on the lines of a cooperative, with employees participating in a profit sharing scheme. In 1942 the two companies were listed as: Butterworth & Roberts, making worsted suitings and coatings; and G & H Roberts Ltd. wool and angola yarns, 4,250 spindles. Mr. Gordon Roberts fell foul of the law in 1943 due to his beliefs, when he refused to join the Home Guard saying that war conflicted with the teachings of Christ; he was fined £50. The two companies worked side by side for more than ten years, until in 1947 G & H Roberts Ltd. began the move to new premises in Dalry Scotland, which, as they needed to install new machinery they did not complete until 1949. The move giving both firms the opportunity to expand. G & H Roberts Ltd. continued in business in Dalry until the mid 1970s, when they were taken over by Z. Hinchliffe & Sons Ltd. of Denby Dale, who are still using the Dalry premises to spin yarn.

Butterworth & Roberts abandoned the use of the mill engine to provide power to run machinery in 1950, installing an electricity sub-station and equipping all machines with individual electric motors; this did not completely do away with the need for the boiler however, as steam was still needed to heat dyepans and the drying tenter, also the water for scouring machines.

The following year the firm of W.H. Robinson, who were also using part of Smithy Place mill in Brockholes, took space in the five storey mill; they were yarn spinners and occupied the premises until at least 1959.[25] They had the distinction of being the only firm to occupy premises at Yew Tree, prior to 2000, who were not members of the Roberts family.

In 1975, although many textile businesses in the area were unable to secure enough orders to make continuing in business viable; Butterworth & Roberts, due to their policy of installing modern machinery, being imaginative and innovative in design, and maintaining good relations with customers, were expanding. When W.H. & J. Barber decided to close in October 1975, Mr. John Roberts the Managing Director of Butterworth & Roberts negotiated to take over the worsted spinning plant in Clarence mill to produce worsted yarn for the company's own use. This was partially necessitated by some of their former yarn suppliers going out of business due to their overall customer base diminishing. The spinning plant at Holmbridge re-opened in March or April 1976 and was in use for approximately four years.

In the year 2000 John Roberts sold the business and premises to the company controlling the firm of Moxon's of Huddersfield, Gamma Beta Holdings Ltd, who relocated production to Yew Tree mill in 2003, where they continue to use traditional British made machinery manufacturing high quality Wool and Cashmere cloths in what is the Holme Valley's last remaining vertical mill still in textile production.

Small buildings in the area used for textiles

The 1829 Wakefield Court Roll recorded in October of that year, that Joshua Barber deceased, late of Fieldend, left to his son Joseph 2 messuages occupied as 3 dwellings, with the houses, **dyehouses**, outbuildings utensils etc. situated at Kilnhouse Bank Bottom, already in the tenure of Joseph.

There were also two **Dyehouses** at Kilnhouse Bank; one of them was subsequently converted to a dwelling house.

The **dyehouse** and **stove** at Hillhouse were owned by Edward Butterworth in 1843; they were passed to Abraham Hirst of Huddersfield in the following year.

The Wakefield Court Roll for 1822 records on 30 October, that there was a dwelling house at Carr Green Austonley, with a barn, stable and **dyehouse**. A **stove** appears to have been built by April 1826, as the house, barn, stable, dyehouse and stove were bought by Cookson Stephenson of Holmfirth from Benjamin Chapman of Thurlestone for £500; the occupant at the time was John Charlesworth.

The Court Roll for 1827 notes on 7 November that Edmund Sykes of Long Ing Austonley paid £1,200 to Jonathon Goddard of Holmfirth son and devisee of John Goddard of Boothhouse deceased, for one dwelling house with barn, stable, cowhouse, **dyehouse, stove** and outbuildings at Long Ing, plus 6 acres 1 rood 6 perches of land then in the possession of Edmund Sykes.

There is also mention of a **dyehouse** at Carr Lane Austonley near to four cottages in March 1835. In January 1842, Richard Haigh of Gynn House, Honley paid £400 to Christopher Moorhouse of Holmfirth for the 4 cottages, barn, stable and the dyehouse occupied by Ely Kenyon. Whether these entries all refer to the same property or to two separate ones, is unclear.

John Gartside paid George Goddard £550 in April 1830, for land and property including a dwelling house called New House in Austonley with a barn, **dyehouse, drying house, stove** and workshops formerly occupied by John Wimpenny, but now by George Goddard. By May 1833 George Goddard was insolvent, when Jonathon Roberts paid £1,295 for the messuage, with barn, stable, dyehouse, stove, warehouse, workshops, outbuildings, fold, garden and appurtenances known as New House in Austonley, plus 14½ acres of land, which were then in the possession of John Gartside.

There was an **'old dyehouse'** near Booth House in 1826; which, in 1831 was described as being near the road to Hogley, where two cottages had recently been built.

A **dyehouse** and **stove** at Hogley formerly in the possession of John Wimpenny, passed to the possession of James Haigh in June 1823; he was still the occupant in 1847.

The Court Roll of May 1838 records the existence of a **Stove** at Upper Waterside. There was also a **dyehouse** at Dam Head.

Notes

1 Rake mill
   W.C.R. 26 Oct. 1803; also 1 June 1808; Leeds Mercury, 31 Dec. 1836; W.C.R. 12 May 1837; also 13 April and 25 May 1838; London Gazette, 7 Sept, 27 Sept, and 8 Oct. 1852.
2 See Huddersfield Chronicle in months stated for more details, also 24 Feb. 1866; Huddersfield Examiner 11 Nov. 1876; also Holmfirth Express 9 July 1887; Kirklees Archive, UHO Holme, 1 Oct. 1918; The Worker 26 Jan. & 18 Sept. 1915; Kirklees Archive, WYK1122/3/1
3 The Factory
   Isaac Beardsell's unpublished account of the family partnership; Huddersfield Chronicle 12 Oct. 1867; Huddersfield Weekly Examiner 10 May 1874; Liberal Club Committee minutes 9 Oct. 1884; Holmfirth Express, Article entitled Thoughts on a Valuation List, c.1960s.
4 Brow Bottom mills
   W.C.R. 30 May, 1827; also Leeds Mercury, 27 Jan. 1844. Huddersfield Chronicle, 4 and 11 Jan. 1851; H.J. Morehouse, The History of Kirkburton and the Graveship of Holme; facsimile edition 1894, p.221; Huddersfield Chronicle, 28 May, 1853; 25 Aug. 1855; 18 Aug. 1856; 10 Oct. and 28 Nov. 1857; 23 Jan. and 15 April 1858; 24 Sept. 1859.
5 Huddersfield Examiner, 10 Aug. 1867; Huddersfield Chronicle, 5 and 12 Oct. 1867; 22 Feb. 1868; also 29 July 1871; Holmfirth Express 4 Sept. 1897, also 13 June, 1914; Copy of sale catalogue in Roberts family papers; Huddersfield Examiner, 26 April 1884; London Gazette, 19 May 1885; Kirklees Archive, KC6/9/2 1886.
6 W.C.R. 1810; also Huddersfield Chronicle, 12 Oct. 1850.
7 Holmbridge mill
   Kirklees Archive, KC6/9/3; Information from National Monument Record Centre archive in Swindon; W.C.R. 23 Nov. 1798; W.C.R. 18 Aug. 1820; Supplementary Report into the Employment of Children in Factories and as to the Propriety and Means of Curtailing the Hours of their Labour, Part 1; (25 March, 1834); Holmfirth Express 29 July 1994; Kirklees Archive, T/H/F/36 claim no. 223; Huddersfield Examiner, 6 Aug. 1853; Huddersfield Chronicle, 17 May 1856.
8 NMRC records, Holmbridge Mill, p.14; Huddersfield Chronicle, 5 Sept. 1857; 21 Aug. 1858; 22 Jan 1859; Kirklees Archive, KC6/9/3; Huddersfield Chronicle, 29 Aug. 1863, 12 Nov. 1864, 24 June 1865, 16 June 1866; Kirklees Archive, KC6/9/2; Huddersfield Examiner, 5 Nov. 1887; Holmfirth Express, 28 April 1888; Barber papers, document dated 28 May, 1890, and document dated 1 Aug. 1890, also Holmfirth Express, 14 June 1890; Genealogical information supplied by Mr. P. Sandford; Holmfirth Express, 21 March 1891.
9 Holmfirth Express, 9 and 23 Oct. 1897; Kirklees Archive, KC6/9/2; also UHO 28 July, and 15 Dec. 1910; Kirklees Archive, KC6/2/15; UHO 25 Jan. 1926, and 31 July 1939; Holmfirth Express, 10 June, 1944; 18 Jan. 1947; 4 July, 1975; 26 March 1976.
10 Bilberry mill
   W.C.R. 29 Nov. 1805; 1 Jan. 1806; 28 Oct. 1807; 5 June 1809; 24 Mar. 1820; 8 June 1821; 4 April 1829. Leeds Mercury 31 Dec. 1836; Kirklees Archive, T/H/F/36, claim no. 180; Huddersfield Chronicle 15 Oct. 1853; 21 July, 1855, 15 & 22 Sept. 1855; 7 June 1856; 21 Oct. 1865. 3 July 1869; Huddersfield Examiner 17 Nov. 1866; , 7 Aug. 1869, 22 June, 1872, 25 Oct. 1873; 8 Nov. 1873, 1 Aug. 1874; Holmfirth Express, 5 Mar. 1887; Kirklees Archive, KC6/1/59 Jan. 1899.
11 Upper Digley mill
   W.C.R. 28 May 1794, 2 entries; Isaac Beardsell's account of the family partnership; Kirklees Archive, KC6/1/4 Holme Reservoir Order Book 1837 – 1852; Holmfirth Express, 20 February 1892, reprint of account of flood; Kirklees Archive, T/H/F/36 claim no. 237; Holmfirth Express, 19 April, 1890.

12 Lower Digley Mill
    Information from Mrs K. Bell, Marsh, Huddersfield; W.C.R. 19 Oct. 1791, 30 May, 1827, 1 June 1831; Supplementary Report into the Employment of Children in Factories, Part 1; 25 March 1834; Leeds Mercury, 31 December, 1936; London Gazette, 10 April 1849; Kirklees Archive, KC6/1/34; Information kindly supplied by Peter Sandford of Lancaster; Kirklees Archive, T/H/F/36 claim no. 375; Saddleworth Herald, Obit. of Ben Hirst, 1906. (Information from Peter Sandford).

13 3rd Digley mill
    Huddersfield Examiner, 3 May, 1884; Information supplied by Mrs. A. C. Eastwood, descendant of the Greenwood family; Holmfirth Express, 11 December, and 18 December 1886, 20 Sept. 1890 and Minutes of Austonley Local Board 2 Oct. 1890; Holmfirth Express, 5 Sept. 1891, 29 June 1895.

14 Kirklees Archive, WYK1122/2/5 and KMT4 April 1896; Holmfirth Express, 23 Nov. 1901; 21 Feb. 1903; Council Minutes, 4 Jan. 1924; Kirklees Archive KC6/1/83; Holmfirth Express, 26 Dec. 1936.

15 Austonley/Bankend Mill
    Wakefield Court Roll 18 May 1821; J. Mayhall, Annals of Yorkshire, Vol. 1, p.205; W.C.R. 10 June 1812, 21 Jan. 1820, 30 June 1828, 31 Oct. 1832; Supplementary Report into the Employment of Children in Factories, Part 1; 25 March 1834; Leeds Mercury, 31 Dec. 1836; 9 Oct. 1841; Kirklees Archive, T/H/F/36 claim no. 198; London Gazette, 4 Feb. and 22 Nov. 1853.

16 Kirklees Archive, KC1061, Box 8; Huddersfield Examiner, 14 July 1857; 12 Aug. 1871; 6 Apr. 1872; 15 March 1873; Kirklees Archive KC1061; J.M. Hinchliffe, unpublished dissertation Mills of the Upper Holme Valley; (1973); Huddersfield Examiner, 7 Dec. 1895; Holmfirth Express, 12 July 1902.

17 Holmbridge Dyehouse
    E. Baines, Yorkshire, Vol. 1, (1822) p.452; Kirklees Archive KC6/9/2 (1871); T/H/F/36 claim no. 280; Holmfirth Express, 27 Jan. 1894.

18 Fieldend Corn mill
    West Yorkshire Archaeological Services, Wakefield; Holmbridge Mill documents; The goit and dam are shown on the 6" O.S. map published in 1853; the 25" O.S. map published in 1893 shows that the part from the river towards the mill no longer existed; W.C.R. 26 Jan. 1827; 22 Oct. 1830; Kirklees Archive, KC6/1/5; Holmfirth Express, 23 March 1968; Huddersfield Examiner, 30 Aug. 1873.

19 Dobb Mill
    W.C.R. 4 Nov. 1720; H.J. Morehouse, History of Kirkburton and the Graveship of Holme; pp146-7; W.C.R. 24 Oct. 1781; 11 June 1800; 9 Oct. 1793; Huddersfield Examiner, 29 July 1876; Holmfirth Express, 2 Dec. 1893; Kirklees Archive, KC6/8/42; Anecdotal evidence from Mr. J. Brook, plus photographic evidence taken during the rebuilding.

20 Hollin Brigg
    Huddersfield Chronicle, 24 Nov. 1855; also Huddersfield Examiner, 9 Oct. 1886.

21 Hinchliffe Mill mill
    W.C.R. April 1531; 24 April 1539; 26 April, 1751; 5 April, 1788; Land Tax Returns 1795; Kirklees Archive KC6/8/41. Also W.C.R. 11 Sept. 1807; Supplementary Report into the Employment of Children in Factories and as to the Propriety and Means of Curtailing the Hours of their Labour, Part 1; (25 March 1834); Holmfirth Express, 30 April 1892, reprints of flood details; Kirklees Archive, T/H/F/36 claim nos. 65 and 223; KC6/1/33.

22 Genealogical information by P. Sandford; Huddersfield Chronicle, 21 May 1856; Huddersfield Examiner, 1, 8 Nov. 1873; 14 Oct, 11 Nov. 1876; Cartworth Local Board Minutes 2 Sept 1884, and Huddersfield Examiner 10 Nov. 1888; Holmfirth Express, 28 June, 1890; also Yorkshire Factory Times 8 Aug. 1890; Textile Manufacturer, Jan. 1891, Feb. 1892; Holmfirth Express, 5 March 1892; Roberts family papers; Whiteley & Green's Centenary booklet 1979; Holmfirth Express, 1 Oct. 1892.

23 Kirklees Archive, KMT4 17 Jan. 1895; Holmfirth Express, 17 July, 1897, , 6 Apr. 1901; Kirklees Archive KC6/8/41; Textile Manufacturer, 1 Aug. 1901; Kirklees Archive, KMT4, 27 Oct. 1901; 25 Aug. 1913; Holmfirth Express, 16 Feb. 1979, also 17 June 1994, 15 Aug. 1953, 8 June 1968, 23 Feb 1983, £ Nov. 2000; Whiteley & Green's Centenary booklet, 1979.

24 Yew Tree Mill
    Genealogical information P. Sandford; J.M. Hinchliffe, 1973; Kirklees Archive, Austonley Tithe, 1847; Huddersfield Chronicle 28 June, 1851; Kirklees Archive, T/H/F/36, claim no. 346; Butterworth & Roberts centenary booklet, 1968; Roberts family papers; J.M. Hinchliffe 1973; Huddersfield Chronicle, 9 Nov. 1872; Huddersfield Examiner, 21 March, 1874; 21 June 1884; Holmfirth Express, 20 June, 1891; 18 Aug. 1906; Kirklees Archive, UHO 16 Aug. 1906; J.M. Hinchliffe.

25 Yorkshire Textile Industry Directory, 1942-3; Butterworth & Roberts centenary booklet, 1968; and Holmfirth Express, 5 Mar. 1949; Anecdotal evidence supplied by Z. Hinchliffe & Sons Ltd. 22 Nov. 2011; Kirklees Archive, UHO 12 June, 1950; Holmfirth Express, 30 June 1951, and 3 May 1958.

CHAPTER 9

Bottoms Mill to Holmfirth

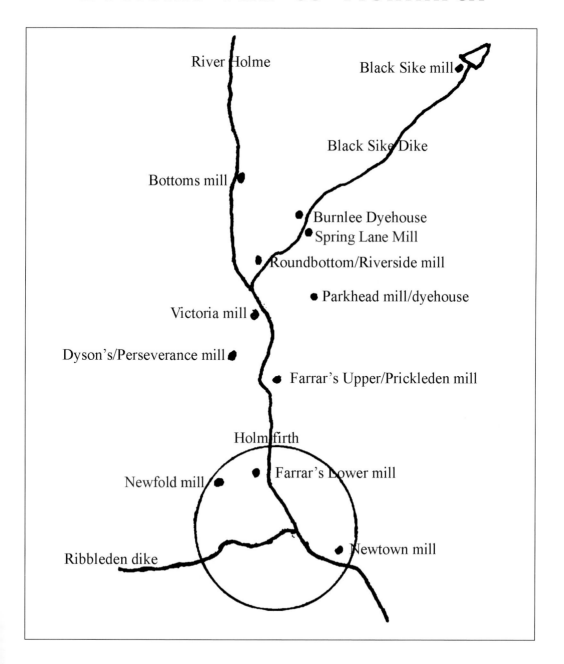

River Holme – Bottoms mill

Bottoms mill. © A.J. Brooke

John Harpin told the Factory Commission in 1833 that the mill had been built in 1825. This is confirmed by an entry in the Wakefield Court Rolls on 13 June 1826, showing that James Shaw of Stubbin Austonley, and Robert Shaw of Shaleys Upperthong, leased to John Harpin dyer of Burnlee, Joseph Barber clothier of Kilnhouse Bank, and Edward Butterworth clothier of Hillhouse, the newly erected mill with 3 storeys and attic, with two water wheels, wheel race, dam, goits etc. and two closes of land called the Bottoms and the Lower Hanging Royd, containing 8 acres 1 rood 14 perches in total; for a term of 99 years from 2 November 1825, at a rent of £300 per annum. In 1828 John Harpin, Joseph Barber and Edward Butterworth took a narrow strip of land 200 yards in length to make a goit from Hinchliffe Mill to the dam at Bottoms.

There was some friction with the workforce in June 1832, as they came out on strike in protest that a Slubber had been employed that was not in the trade union. The problem was presumably resolved quickly as no further reference is made to it. In his answers to the Factory Commissioners John Harpin said that the mill was used for the scribbling, carding, slubbing and spinning of wool, and for fulling woollen cloth. Power was provided by two water wheels delivering about fifteen horsepower each, which were supplemented by a twenty horse power steam engine during times of water shortage. Fifty two people were employed at the mill: 2 boys and 3 girls under 10, earning 4s each; 6 boys and 5 girls under 12, each earning 4s; 5 boys and 7 girls under 14, also earning 4s each; 5 boys and 4 girls under 16, earning 5s each, 1 boy under 18, earning 5s, 1 boy and 1 girl under 21, earning 12s each; 12 men over 21 each earned 21s. Of the 52 employees, 47 were reliant on the other five for their wages. In summer the hours of work were 6am to 8pm, in winter from daylight 'and work about twelve hours'. The mill worked about 2 hours less on Saturdays. The machinery was stopped during the midday break of one hour, but the scribbling machines continued to run during the two half hour breaks. Holidays were three days at Christmas, three days at the feast (late May or early June), half a day on Shrove Tuesday, and one day for Easter. Mr. Harpin felt that children of 9 or 10 were most suited for piecing cardings, which was what most of the younger children were employed to do.

William Lockwood clothier, of Burnlee bought a one-sixth share in the mill and land in December 1834; he presumably also took space in this mill, as he is listed as a tenant in 1853. John Harpin died on 8 May, 1849, and was succeeded by his son also called John. The valley widens below Hinchliffe Mill allowing the flood waters of 1852 to spread their volume over a wider area, reducing both their velocity and potential for destruction. The mill survived the onslaught, although water entered the mill and damaged machinery and goods, and gave a severe fright to five fullers who, as was their custom, were sleeping at the mill. They managed to climb onto the rafters of the upper floor and were able to wait for the water to subside. Three houses beside the mill were less fortunate; built on a slope with one gable end towards the river, the family in the lowest house broke through the dividing wall to the house next door and, joined by that family, then broke through to the third house. All three families went to the upper floor, and managed to escape by lowering a ladder through the window in the upper gable, just minutes before all three houses were swept away. John and Joseph Barber, trading as Barber & Co. submitted a claim for damage to machinery and cloth totalling £95, the inspectors reduced this to £73, it was then marked 'disallowed' and nothing was paid. Firth Barber & Co. submitted a claim for damage to buildings, machinery and cloth totalling £396, which was reduced to £280 by the inspectors, with just £74 1s 8d being paid. The trustees of John Harpin submitted a claim for £311 for damage to buildings and machinery, this was reduced to £291, with £128 11s 6d being paid. In 1853 the Reservoir Commissioners list the owner of the mill as James Shaw, with the occupiers being Edward Butterworth, William Lockwood, Firth, John, George and Joseph Barber.

Fire broke out in the stove on the evening of Monday April 13th, 1857. The bell in the tower of Holmfirth church was rung and the brigade quickly arrived on the scene. The fire was soon extinguished, although the building suffered some damage; no mention is made of the building's contents which were presumably destroyed. The mill was being enlarged in July 1859, and the mill roof had been removed in preparation for the work to begin. A heavy thunderstorm with large hailstones on the evening of Monday 18 July took its toll on machines and cloth.

On Tuesday 9 August 1859, a young man called Hinchliffe was trying to put the drive belt of a machine over the pulley on the shafting when his clothing became caught and he was whirled round, fracturing one arm and injuring his head and body. He was taken to Huddersfield Infirmary where he was said to be in a precarious state.

J. B Hirst had taken space in the mill, but business had not gone well for him, as he was made bankrupt. The sale of his goods and machinery was advertised to take place at the mill on January 17th 1861, consisting of Spinning Mules with 480 spindles, gas fittings, broitches, a warping woof and creels, 4,600lbs of yarn for warp and weft on cops, black slubbing, 149lbs of mungo, 800lbs of waste and cotton, plus casks of oil. The unusual aspect of this sale, apart from the small amount of machinery, was that it included personal and household items such as a gold pocket watch with an additional silver case, a mahogany box containing 36 sets of knives and forks with carvers, various other items of furniture and 8 bound volumes of *The History of England* by Hulme and Smollett. A one-sixth share in the mill, land and machinery was advertised for sale in 1866, with 50 years of the lease remaining, the name of the vendor is not given, but it was possibly William Lockwood selling his share in the property.[1]

New buildings had been gradually added to the mill over the years, and in 1868 one of them caught fire. In the early hours of July 23rd a building used as a warehouse by Joshua Barber, H & S Wimpenny, and C & W Bashforth was burning. The alarm was raised and fire brigades from Turners of Bridge Mill, G. Mellor of Thongsbridge, J. Barber of Holmbridge, and the Unity brigade attended and managed to restrict the blaze to the one building, which contained wool waste, cops, and a number of pieces of cloth. The fire was thought to have started in some wool waste stored in the part of the building used by Wimpenny's. Losses were estimated at between £1,000 and £2,000, only part of which was covered by insurance; Messrs. Bashforth having no insurance cover at all. The Joshua Barber who was in Bottoms Mill lived at Well House, and also used Holme Styes mill. He should not be confused with Joshua Barber of Holmbridge Mill, who was from a different family. The

1871 census shows that Joshua Barber of Well House employed a total of 54 people, made up of 30 men, 10 boys and 14 women, presumably between the two mills. The firm were declared bankrupt in December 1873, with the sale of machinery and cloth being on January 5th 1874. It was a fairly large sale and included: scribblers, carders, piecing machines, billies, hand mules; 16 broad power looms, 2 narrow power looms, bobbin winding machine, broad drying balloon, sizing machine, loom gearing, shafting, drums etc; burling tables, office fittings. Wool, Mungo, Shoddy, also yarns on cops. The sale included some additional machinery, which may have been from Holme Styes mill: including scribblers, carders, piecing machines, and billies; along with around 260 pieces of woollen cloth. While the sale was in progress, a portion of the shoddy room floor gave way and Mr. Henry Tinker the auctioneer, and about twelve other people fell through to the floor below. Some people were slightly injured. After the bankruptcy proceedings were completed, Joshua with his wife and family moved to Saddleworth, and apparently left the textile trade.

There is a record in the council minutes for 1876 of Firth Barber & Co. being in occupation of part of the mill and being reported for having a 'nuisance', which could indicate that something had been left on the carriage-way that the Nuisance Inspector thought inappropriate. In 1878, Charles Bashforth of C & W Bashforth was working on a wringing machine when his right hand became caught in the rollers, removing the thumb and fourth finger of that hand.

W.H. & J. Barber probably began their partnership in Bottoms mill, although when they first moved into the premises is unclear. They were certainly installed by 1887, when they gave a treat to their 60 workers with a knife and fork tea.

Also moving into part of the mill at about that time were Messrs. Brook & Brownson, who gave a treat for their 80 workers in 1891. Later in that year they were in distraint for non payment of rent, and their machinery was to be sold. In January 1892 they were declared bankrupt, with debts of at least £5,800. At their creditors meeting Arthur Wilkinson Brook of Spring Bank Holmfirth, and Thomas Brownson of Binns Wood Holmfirth, were declared bankrupt with debts of £6,106. The sale of their machinery was fixed for 17th February 1892, consisting of scribbling, carding, spinning and weaving machinery, also a felt hating plant, and a narrow fire engine 'Industry', suitable for one or two horses. At the Huddersfield Bankruptcy Court hearing on 22 February, Mr. Brook said that they had commenced business in 1883 with £1,800 capital, as woollen manufacturers. About 2 years ago they began manufacturing hating felt, making little profit in their first year. Mr. W.H. Armitage [Accountant] had taken stock last year and found that they were insolvent with a deficiency of £6,106 0s 8d, which was largely rent arrears for which they had been sued by the mill company. He attributed their failure to losses, bad trade and the action of the mill company. It was announced in the *London Gazette* in November 1892, that a final dividend of 1s 9¼d in the £ would be paid by the company, plus a dividend of 9s 10d in the £ from A.W. Brook's personal estate, which would be available for payment to creditors from November 22nd.

A notice in *Textile Manufacturer* in May 1893 announced that the five storey mill with its two water wheels and steam engine was to be let, but it would seem that no-one took up the opportunity, as the whole site was offered for sale in 1896, when it was described as: 'being of substantial build, though several of the main buildings require repair. The main building is five stories high with attic, 114ft by 54ft; the rooms are lofty and well lighted on all four sides. The adjoining buildings comprise – an engine and boiler house, wool warehouse, chimney shaft, smithy, four cottages, waste shed, store rooms and outbuildings. The fixed machinery comprises a pair of water wheels 28ft diameter by 7ft wide, with gearing in working order; a beam engine, 2 boilers, gas, steam and water piping, 400ft of wrought iron shafting with numerous drums and pulleys'. There was also the mill dam and goit, plus land totalling 19 acres 1rood 36 perches. The estate was bought by Mr. John Tinker senior, for his sons Tedbur and John, for the sum of £2,800.

The *Yorkshire Factory Times* wrote, on 21 August 1896, 'The alterations and additions will make Bottoms Mill a structure, if not quite up-to-date, certainly a great improvement on the old times'.

They also reported that the renovations were completed in June 1897, at which time the mill had been empty for most of the previous decade. A 200hp engine was installed in September of the same year and christened 'Spider' by Mrs. Charles Tinker. Prior to this time T & J Tinker were using Mytholmbridge mill, which they continued to do for some years. Before acquiring Bottoms mill Tinkers had produced everlasting tweeds; whereas their production at Bottoms was predominantly worsteds with some serges. Mr. Charles Tinker was summoned in 1899 for unlawfully employing four women and two young persons at 5.30am. It was unlawful to employ anyone before 'daylight' which was officially 6am. Mr. Tinker pleaded guilty and was fined £1 with 7s 6d costs on each count. Plans for additional buildings were passed by the council in 1902 and 1909; the *Yorkshire Textile Directory* of 1910 lists the occupants of the mill as T & J Tinker, worsted manufacturers; and also J. Thristle Barber as manufacturers of stockinet's and fancy woollens, with 6 looms. Charley Tinker, John Tinker and Albert Tinker junior, became partners in T & J Tinker in 1911 for a term of fourteen years.[2]

A fatality occurred near the mill at some time during the night of 4th to 5th February 1911; a trainee teacher who was studying in Sheffield had come home to visit her family in Hinchliffe Mill. She had got up during the night, dressed and gone out without disturbing her sisters who were asleep in the same room. Her body was found in the goit leading to the mill dam on the morning of Sunday 5th. The Inquest jury returned a verdict of: 'death caused by drowning, but with no evidence to show how she had entered the water'.

Mr. John Tinker senior gave every employee at both Bottoms and Mytholmbridge 10s. on October 31st 1913, on the fiftieth anniversary of him going into partnership with his brother Tedbur, and commencing business at Upper Digley Mill. A gesture that cost him a total of £170 10s.

In 1919 the *Yorkshire Textile Directory* gives T & J Tinker as sole occupants of the mill, they are described as woollen and worsted manufacturers, making stockinet's and puttees, suggesting that they had taken over the business and machinery of J. Thristle Barber, and that they had been involved in manufacturing uniforms for the British Army. The Factory Inspector had reported to Holmfirth Council in 1903 that provision for escape from the upper floors of the big mill was inadequate; an observation which was repeated in 1907, and again in 1910. The complaint was reiterated in 1914, when the firm said that work to correct the problem was in progress. In 1920 the Inspector said that he was still not satisfied with the means of escape from the upper floors, which was through windows onto the fire escape; the problem appears to have been solved as there is no further evidence of complaints.

In late October or early November 1929, James Alfred Booth aged 43, a teazer and fettler, caught his finger in a teazing machine, he was treated by his doctor, but infection set in and he was admitted to Elmwood hospital, where he died from Tetanus two weeks after the accident. John Tinker of Morefield Thongsbridge, son of one of the founders, died in August 1938 at the age of 61. His coffin was carried into the church by employees; the service was attended by 'hundreds'.

The flood of 1944 covered the ground floor premises throughout the mill to a depth of about 5ft 6in, leaving mud and silt in its wake. Much of the water entered through the offices, damaging furnishings and destroying records. Spinning and weaving departments were unable to produce anything for at least a week, and it took longer in the finishing department until all the machinery had been cleaned and checked.

Fire broke out in the 5 storey mill on the evening of 18th July 1958. It was noticed by Robert Beaumont about 11pm who immediately rang the fire brigade. The Holmfirth brigade arrived seven minutes after receiving the call, by which time heat had smashed the glass in the first floor windows and flames were shooting through. They were joined by fire engines from Meltham, Marsden, Slaithwaite, Huddersfield, Brighouse, Mirfield, Skelmanthorpe, Cleckheaton and Penistone, with 78 firemen being involved. Water was drawn from the dams at Bottoms and Victoria mills. Flames quickly spread to the upper floors via the hoist shaft, and erupted through the roof. The fire brigade managed to contain the fire to that one building, but falling debris smashed roof lights in one single storey shed. Four firemen received slight injuries, but returned to work after being treated at Elmwood hospital. Some forty women and girls working in the spinning and drawing departments, who travelled from Mexborough every day, were put out of work immediately. The fire effectively ended T & J Tinker's business, the mill premises were offered for sale by auction on 4 February 1959, when the auctioneer Mr. Edward Thorp of Eddison Taylor & Booth, withdrew the 14,000 sq. yd. premises at £19,000, saying that he would be prepared to accept private bids later. The machinery was auctioned on February 4th and 5th. The damaged building was restored, but as a three storey building not five.

The mill was taken over by Wm. Brook & Sons (Dyers) Ltd. in June 1959, who transferred their business from Slaithwaite to Holmfirth. Nine of their employees were overcome by Chlorine fumes in 1981, and were taken to hospital as a precaution, but no-one suffered any serious after effects.[3] Brook's were taken over by Premier Hank Dyers in 2001; Paramount Dyers also took premises in the mill around this time, they went into liquidation in 2010 and a new company called Pennine Yarn Dyers emerged. There are also a number of other companies trading there, but non are in textiles.

Black Sike Dike – Black Sike mill

An entry in the Wakefield Court Roll states that: Joshua Charlesworth the younger of Hogley Green clothier, passed 1½ acres of land staked out in Bank Close near to Hogley Green, to David Woofenden clothier of Upperthong, and Joseph Booth stone mason of Meltham, on 23 May 1792. The land had a stream running through it, and the transaction allowed Joseph Booth to dig enough stone in the upper part of Bank Stones Close to build two dwelling houses, a dyehouse and stove; and also to take water from a spring in William Bottom Close to supply his needs. By November 1795 there was at least one house, with a Scribbling mill and water wheel, goit and dam on the 1½ acres of land, which were being used by Christopher Green and David Woofenden. The mill was to be mortgaged, by raising a loan from James Midwood corn factor of Huddersfield, to enable David Harrison clothier of Crosland Edge and John Wimpenny clothier of Hogley, to pay David Woofenden and Joseph Booth the builders, who then surrendered the liberty they had been given to build back to the lord of the manor.

At the turn of the century it is referred to as 'a Fulling and Scribbling mill known by the name of Royds Wood Mill' and was occupied by Thomas Battye. Whereas, in 1805 it is referred to as 'Liphill Bank Mill' and was insured for £400. The occupant at that time was Tom Battye.

Heavy rain in 1821 caused the reservoir above the mill to overflow and wash away its embankment. The devastation which this caused is discussed in Chapter 5, and while no lives were lost, there was great devastation of property and vegetation. Although the mill was damaged there does not appear to be a record of it, or of the repairs that were necessary. Thomas Hardy was still occupying the mill when it was the subject of a mortgage, detailed in the Wakefield Court Roll on 30 January 1829, for £130 borrowed by Hardy and David Hepworth of Lindley, from Elihu Dickinson of Denby.

Ten years later, in May 1839, the Court Roll records that the mill was occupied by John Harpin, when Thomas Hardy surrendered ownership of the land at Black Sike known as the Bank, with the stream and the mill used for spinning wool and finishing cloth with the workshop and cottage, together with the dam, goit, stable and coalplace. Also 3 cottages, a smith's shop, and garden, occupied by William Hardy, Joseph Lee and Samuel Shaw, with a piece of ground formerly waste, with the liberty to extend the goit to Black Sike Bridge. The transaction also gave permission for John Harpin to get stone to extend the mill.

Ben Turner, the Trade Unionist and MP was born in 1843, in his memoirs he says that he was born in the Burnlee – Booth House area but does not say exactly where, it is possible that parts of his early life were spent at Black Sike, as some of his relatives lived in the cottages there. Joshua

Woodhead had been using at least part of the mill, but was declared bankrupt in the early part of 1854. His machinery was advertised for sale in February, consisting of: 3 Scribblers, 4 Carders, 4 Billies, 1 Teazer, and many sundries. This was followed by the sale of a 16hp steam engine in April.

The mill was then occupied by Thomas Barber & Co, Thomas married Elizabeth Thristle, and was the father of Joshua Thristle Barber, who was later at Bankend, Holmbridge and Bottoms mills. There was a fire at the mill on 4 January 1856 when some waste caught fire, but it was quickly brought under control and little damage was done. Thomas seems to have been a forthright man, and was frequently in disputes with his workers. On February 3rd 1864, he had posted a notice in the mill saying that, with immediate effect anyone who was 5 minutes late for work would have one penny deducted from their wages, the amount increased with each additional 5 minutes to a maximum of one shilling for being an hour late. This was said to be equal to half the week's wages for a weaver. After reading the notice all the weavers at the mill downed tools and walked out; several meetings between the weavers and Mr. Barber failed to reach agreement. In an attempt to settle the dispute a special court sitting was held in Holmfirth on Saturday 8th of February, when both sides put their arguments. The magistrates ruled that the case should be dismissed, that the weavers should return to work and complete the warps already being woven, after which each weaver could decide whether they were prepared to continue working at the mill under Mr. Barber's terms. This was standard practise at the time, and had been carried over from the time when all weavers worked at home. The 'contract' between the manufacturer and the weaver was renewed each time the weaver agreed to weave a new piece, and the weaver, for their part, undertook to finish the warp. If he or she did not like the terms offered for weaving a new piece, then they were at liberty to refuse the work and go elsewhere. On 5 January 1870, John Hinchliffe a 45 year old weaver was found drowned in the reservoir behind the mill, he had been missing for three days. Whether he worked at the mill or elsewhere is not stated. His sister gave evidence at the subsequent inquest that he had recently been showing signs of insanity.

By March 1871 Thomas Barber was in financial difficulty, the *Huddersfield Chronicle* advertised

Black Sike Mill c. 1871. © A.J. Brooke — Taken to advertise the premises at the time of the sale.

a sale of about 6,500lbs of assorted yarns and wool and dyewares, on 23 March, by order of the Committee of Inspection. This was followed in May of that year with an advertisement in the *Huddersfield Examiner* for the sale of:

> *"All those valuable leasehold Woollen Mills know as 'Blacksike Mill'…late in the occupation of Messrs. Thomas Barber & Co, comprising a 3 storied stone built scribbling and spinning mill with attic over, and a newly erected finishing mill with a weaving room over it, boiler house containing a new patent steam boiler by Arnold of thirty nominal horse power (quite new), engine house and condensing steam engine of 16 horse power, also the dyehouse, willey house, warehouse, gas house, gasometer, and offices attached thereto. There is also an ample supply of pure water specially adapted for finishing purposes, and on the premises are two large reservoirs…and a powerful turbine. The shafting, goinggear, steam pipes, water pipes, gas piping, will be sold along with this lot. Contains an area of 3 acres. Woollen Machinery: 6 scribblers, 4 condensing carders, 2prs. self acting mules, twisting frames, 20prs. broad looms, hydraulic press, press pump, steam press oven, broad raising gig, broad brushing mill, 2 perpetuals, Whiteley's patent tentering machine, 2 milling machines, washing machine, dyehouse plant, and also good warehouse and office fittings.*

The sale was held on 14 June 1871, but the mill does not appear to have been sold, as it was advertised again in January 1872, with the previous occupant being given as Thomas Barber & Co; the reason for the sales was that T. Barber & Co. was in bankruptcy, they were eventually discharged from bankruptcy on 6 May 1894; by which time Thomas Barber was living in Washford, Somerset.

The next occupants of the mill appear to have been Paul Toepler & Co. who installed a chemical extraction and wool cleaning plant. Whether they were intending to build equipment to sell, or whether they were hoping to undertake wool cleaning and chemical extraction on a commission basis is unclear, but things did not go well for them as in July 1873 they were under distraint for rent, and the sale of 6 cast iron cisterns, piping and valves, plus stone flags, fire bricks and other sundries was advertised for the 17th of the month. This was followed in January 1874 by the sale of 1 large cast iron still 9ft diameter, 2 cast iron stills 6'6" diam. 1 patent steam superheater, 1 agitator 8' x 5' and 6 cast iron cisterns, all recently installed; which appears to have brought an end to their tenancy.[4] There is no evidence of the mill being used again; the only thing remaining today is the upper reservoir, and an indication of where the mill buildings and cottages originally stood.

Burnlee / Bottoms   Dyehouse

This building stood alongside Burnlee Road at Bottoms where the row of houses now stands. It is marked on the 6in. Ordinance Survey map of 1853 as Bottoms Dyehouse; the buildings are also shown on the 25in. map of 1893, but are unnamed, as by this time it was part of Spring Lane mill. The date when the dyehouse was built is not known, but it was before 1821, as some of the workers from Black Sike mill ran to the dyehouse to warn its occupants of the approaching floodwater on 21 September of that year, which destroyed much of the building.

The building was owned by John Harpin of Birks House, and in 1848 was advertised as Lot 2 in a sale of his property. It was described as: the Blue dyehouse with the drying stove, scouring house and spacious warehouse, 3 storeys high plus attic, with large barn and stabling under same. Also 2 reservoirs and fold situated in Burnlee, occupied by Harrop Wrigley and John Harpin's trustees. Also the 3 cottages adjoining the dyehouse occupied by James Radcliffe, Charles Hill and Thomas Bowskin. The water supply was from Black Sike dike and also an artesian well in the scouring house which, the advertisement claimed, delivered a never failing supply of pure water, making the premises suitable for dyeing, manufacturing or brewing. It was advertised for a second time in May 1851.

Jonas Brook & Bros. took over Spring Lane mill and the dyehouse in the late 1880s, and advertised the contents of the dyehouse for sale in December 1887. These consisted of 9 Indigo vats 6ft 3in wide and 7ft 6in deep; 6 dyepans of various sizes, all cast iron; 1 stone cistern; 1 52in washing machine; wringing machine; a 6hp vertical steam engine; 1 12ft 6in by 5ft steam boiler; 1 iron water wheel 12ft by 3ft; cast iron perforated stove plates and bearers; shafting and gearing etc; at Spring Lane mill there were also 2 compound horizontal steam engines by Pollitt & Wigzell for sale. The auction was held on 11 January 1888, after which the dyehouse was demolished, and the site became an extension to Spring Lane mill.

There was also a stove at Burnlee in the 1840s which was near two cottages that were occupied by Mary Wild and Jonathon Sandford, presumably the same Jonathon Sandford who was in partnership with the Roberts brothers at Perseverance mill; there was also a Press Shop in Burnlee at that time, which was occupied by Joseph Mellor.[5] The precise whereabouts of these premises is unknown.

Spring Lane mill

Despite processing wool and cotton, this mill was known locally as 'the Silk mill'. The original buildings on the site were a dyehouse, wool stove, tenter rooms, a warehouse and weaving rooms; the precise dates of their construction are not known, but the owner and occupant of the premises in 1831 was William Lockwood of Hinchliffe Mill. The map and award for the Valuation of Upperthong, surveyed in 1837 and published in 1843, show that there was a long building with one gable end on the roadside, which was presumably the mill and warehouse with the stove attached, plus a dam; also two other buildings on the land towards Burnlee, probably the barn and stable mentioned in the Award. In 1839 William Lockwood appears to have borrowed £3,000 from Joseph Brook a woolstapler of Huddersfield; Charles Brook a cotton spinner of Healey House; Benjamin Wilson Barber a banker of Mirfield and John Wilson Barber of Huddersfield, who were executors of Jonas Brook of Meltham. As security for the loan Lockwood put up 5 acres of land in three closes called the Pingle, the Netherwood and the Acre or Linacre, which were possibly close to Parkhead crossroads, and upon which Lockwood had recently built a house; also the 580sq.yds of land at Spring Lane with the mill, engine house, warehouse, workshops and cottages built on it. The Deed of Covenant does not suggest why Lockwood required the loan, which was probably to allow him to expand his business and premises. Water for the mill was taken from Black Sike Dike, and stored in two reservoirs on the western side of the mill buildings.

The 1851 census shows that he was employing 56 people in the mill. A fire was discovered in a stove at the mill at 4am on the morning of Sunday 30 January 1853, neighbours fought the blaze with buckets of water and managed to contain it within the stove building, but 600lbs of wool and 13 pieces of cloth were damaged or destroyed. The estimated cost of the fire was between thirty and one hundred pounds. This was the second fire in the district in a matter of weeks, and brought comments from the '*Examiner*' editor about the lack of a fire engine in the Holmfirth area, which prompted eleven manufacturers in the area to come together to discuss the formation of a local fire brigade.

Charles Bashforth also rented part of the mill in 1853-4; he gave a treat for his 180 workers in March 1853 at the White Hart Inn, Holmfirth. The report said that the men and boys had Roast Beef, with Plum Pudding to follow, and that the women 'enjoyed an excellent tea'. He gave a second treat for 140 workers in November 1854, in celebration of his recent marriage, where again the men had Roast Beef and Plum Pudding and the woman enjoyed their favourite beverage – tea. Both events would be followed by an evening of songs, glees, recitations and dancing.

In June 1853 it was reported that the damage to the mill from the January fire, was about to be repaired, and that the mill was being enlarged, and in December of that year it was announced that 'Room and Power' was available, consisting of: 2 rooms 27yds x 16yds, 1 room 14½yds x 9yds, and another room if required, also a detached fireproof willow room. The premises were said to be 'well suited to scribbling, spinning, power looms etc'. Entry for the new tenant would be available from 2nd January 1854; applications to be made to Mr. Lockwood. Prospective tenants seem to have been reluctant to commit themselves, as the advertisement appeared again in March 1854. The new tenant was Jonas Brook & Brothers, cotton spinners and manufacturers of sewing thread, who also had a large factory at Meltham Mills. This was possibly a way of redeeming the mortgage of 1839.

Smoke was seen coming from the dust chimney of the willowing machine at 10.30am on October 4th 1854, and flames could be seen inside the building. The engine of the newly formed 'Unity' fire brigade was summoned, and while workers poured water down the chimney, the brigade sprayed burning fibres with water and extinguished the flames. The fire was caused by lumps of burning soot from the chimney of the mill's main boiler falling into the dust chimney and igniting the dust and fibres it contained. Bales of wool in the mill yard were also set on fire by the burning soot. One worker had his face scorched by the soot, while the hair of several others was singed. This was the first time that the new 'Unity' brigade had been called out.

Kaye & Rhodes machine makers had been using part of the mill, their tools and stock in trade were advertised to be auctioned under a deed of assignment on 18 January 1856, including various lathes, gantries, wooden benches, a vice and grindstone. William Lockwood advertised thirteen nearly new narrow power looms 'to let or sell' in October 1856, a possible indicator that the popularity of narrow width cloth was declining.

James Gardiner had moved from Brownhill mill but was finding business difficult, as in August 1857 he was in distraint for rent. His machinery and six pieces of cloth were advertised for sale by Auction on 31 August.

T Hinchliffe & Sons were using part of the mill in 1858, two casks of oil were being transported from Holmfirth Station by horse-drawn lurry; they approached the mill from Parkhead along Burnlee Road, necessitating a sharp left turn into Spring Lane; the lurry upset and the casks burst open. Much of the oil found its way into the 'pleasure dam' in John Harpin's garden at Birks House, from where workpeople from the mill were able to retrieve most of it. However, the loss was said to be serious.

David Brook who lived at Spring Bank House, gave a treat to over 100 of his workers on 22 August 1863, to celebrate the marriage of his eldest son George to the second daughter of John Barber of Joshua Barber & Sons, Holmbridge. The 60 men had 'a good dinner' at the Victoria Hotel Holmfirth, which was followed by speeches and toasts; while the 50 women had a 'first rate tea' at the Wellington Inn Burnlee, followed by dancing to music provided by a fiddler.

William Lockwood possibly retired as a manufacturer in the latter part of 1863, with his section of the mill being taken over by Robert Ellis & Son, who advertised some of the machinery for sale, presumably surplus to their requirements, on February 6th 1864, which consisted of: 1 scribbler, 1 carder, 1 billey, 2prs of mules, 1 shoddy cleaner nearly new, a moiety in 1 willow with fan and dust pipe etc, plus sundries.

Yet another fire broke out at the mill on 12 November 1864, which was also put out by the Unity brigade. The cause of the fire was attributed to spontaneous combustion in some wool, and damage was assessed at around £150. William Lockwood died on 4 November 1865 at the age of 67, and ownership of the mill subsequently passed to Jonas Brook & Brothers of Meltham.

In July 1866 Jonathon and Robert Ellis were declared bankrupt; their machinery for turning loose wool into cloth was offered for sale by auction in July of that year along with 2,100lbs of yarn on cops and slubbings.

A fire in the centre section of the main building on 3 October 1866, which was discovered at 3am, destroyed the scribbling engines, billies, spinning mules and power looms that were in there along with a considerable quantity of wool. The fire bell in the tower of Holmfirth church was rung, and the Unity brigade plus the brigade from Bridge Mill attended. They were able to restrict the fire to the central portion of the mill which was occupied by J. Brook & Bros; their losses of stock and machinery were £4,900, the cost of damage to the building was £1,200; the other tenants were Mr. Joshua Hoyle who lost £280 and Thomas Hinchliffe & Sons lost over £200. The absence of wind had helped the fire fighters to restrict the blaze, but around 150 employees were thrown out of work. The fire prompted Mr. Ben Wood, secretary to the Gaslight Co. to write to the *Examiner*, pointing out the need for a tap to enable the gas supply to mills to be turned off in cases of emergency.

The building of the new mill was a somewhat protracted affair, not being completed until 1869;

it was a large building with a basement that contained the boiler house, and five floors above it. The engine house was a separate building, during its construction while craning up a 3 ½ ton iron beam the rope broke; the falling beam broke two smaller beams and a man's leg. He was taken to Huddersfield Infirmary for treatment. Part of the original building was retained; this was a 4 storey building running at right angles to the new one. Benjamin Brook, a builder's labourer was fixing a large vertical piece of stone in place on September 5th 1870, when it fell crushing his right side. He was taken home where he was seen by a doctor, and was said to be in 'a very precarious state'. When the alterations were complete Jonas Brook & Brothers gave a tea-party at the mill for their workpeople, mostly women, to celebrate the opening of a mill to make cotton thread. 250 sat down to a knife and fork tea followed by songs, recitations and dancing; alterations to the mill included a dining hall for the workpeople with facilities for warming and cooking food. In October 1872 Jonas Brook & Brothers were one of the few mills given permission to summon and dismiss workers by blowing their steam whistle.[6] The restriction on numbers of mills allowed to do this was a form of control on noise pollution.

A fire was discovered at the mill a little before 1am on Monday 2 August 1875, by a police inspector and constable. They aroused the mill manager who discovered a quantity of oily waste burning in a room adjacent to the mill, which was extinguished with a few buckets of water. Thomas Milner of Hill was one of a team of men carrying out some structural alterations at the mill when a large door fell on him; the accident happened on 31 December, 1875, he died at home from his injuries on January 26th 1876.

An occupant of the mill in 1878 was Mr. G. Wilson who had a finishing business. How long he had been at the mill is unclear, as this is the only reference found; his machinery was advertised for sale on 24 July due to declining business; he had a large quantity of equipment, including Brushing Mills, broad Raising Gigs, 1 worsted Raising Gig (an unusual piece of machinery, as worsted usually has a smooth surface), narrow and broad Perpetuals, broad Lewis Cross Cutting machines, 3 Hydraulic Presses, plus pumps and many sundries.

Jonas Brook & Brothers applied for permission to convert a warehouse into two cottages in December 1881, which was passed by Upperthong Local Board. These would be the two cottages that stood on the side of Woodhead Road, between Spring Villa and the 5 storey mill.

There was another fire at the mill on 9 October 1885, which was discovered by Edward Sanderson the mill engineer at 4.30am. He sent Vavince Lockwood to awaken Mr. J.W. Donkersley the mill manager, who lived nearby; while someone else went for the fire brigade. The Unity brigade arrived at 5.20am, they were followed by all the other brigades from the local mills who all set to work to put out the fire which, by this time, had spread to the second and third storey's of the building. Some flooring and machinery fell onto the mill engine, but most of the building was saved; although 270 employees would be out of work for several weeks.

The Local Boards of Cartworth, Upperthong and Wooldale had combined to become the Holmfirth Local Board in November 1884; part of the new board's responsibility was the Unity fire brigade; they sent an account for £5 5s to Jonas Brook & Brothers for the use of the Board's fire fighting equipment. This must have been one of the first, if not the very first, charge for this service.

The workpeople of Jonas Brook & Bros. at Spring Lane gave Mr. Edward Brook, the firm's senior partner, a marble and bronze clock on Friday 28 January 1887 in gratitude for Mr. Brook's generosity in giving all the workers laid off by the fire of 1885 one shilling a day until they were able to go back to work. Business must have been going well for Jonas Brook & Bros. in 1887, as they advertised the sale of a pair of compound horizontal condensing engines that had been specially made for the mill at the works of Pollitt & Wigzell only a few years before, but had to be replaced by a larger engine as the firm needed more power.

Hannah Mary Carter of Bottoms was cleaning a doubling machine in April 1890 while it was in motion; she lost two fingers from one hand. On the morning of 9 May 1891, Mr. Donkersley the mill manager discovered the body of a man in the mill dam. The man was identified by his sister as being

Allen Knight, a 67 year old farm labourer from Parkhead. He had previously given up his house and sold his furniture, and was living on the proceeds of the sale. He had said that when the money ran out he would go to the workhouse. The jury returned a verdict of "found drowned without marks of violence, having probably drowned himself, but there was no evidence to show the state of his mind at the time".

In November 1892 Charles and Mabel Francis Brook were married; they recorded the event by placing details in a bottle and sealing it into a cavity in the mill chimney 100 feet above ground level. It does not appear to have been found when the chimney was finally demolished in 1991.

The company decided, in 1911, that they would introduce a 'one break day', in line with their factory at Meltham Mills. The working day would be from 7.30am to 12noon and from 1pm to 5.30pm on Monday to Friday, and 7.30am to 12noon on Saturday, giving a total working week of 49½ hours. This would replace the existing 56 hour week, giving workers more free time, but also reducing their wages by about 12 percent.

A minute in the records of Holmfirth Council in March 1924, records that Jonas Brook & Bros. were asking when they would be supplied with electricity; some parts of the district had an electricity supply from 1922, but not all, Spring Lane mill was connected to the supply in March 1925.[7] The last entry in the *Yorkshire Textile Industry* directory for Jonas Brook & Bros. appears in 1928.

Synthetic yarns arrived in the district in the 1930s in the shape of the North British Rayon Company; they occupied two mills during their stay here, Fearnought mill, and Spring Lane mill. They were in Spring Lane mill from 1935 until 1950, when they consolidated production at Fearnought mill.[8] The firm were probably in the process of moving into the mill in May 1935, when William Chapman a 33 year old textile fitter was working on the installation of a new lift and asked James

Spring Lane mill. © A.J. Brooke

South of Prickleden to help him. South said that he was on the floor above the lift and slid down the rope to get into the cage through the top, he then took the cover off the motor. Chapman had followed South down the rope, he saw a catch on the motor and tried to open it, eventually using a spanner to prise it open. The mill manager had looked down the shaft and told Chapman that he should not open the catch; when it did open the cage fell to the bottom of the shaft, a distance of about 14 feet. Chapman fell out onto the landing as there was no door on the lift; South sustained a broken ankle. After the accident the lift was examined by a lift inspector, who found that the balance weights were much higher in the shaft than they should have been, and that the ropes were hanging loose, indicating that they had been moved by hand; this would allow the lift to drop. The installation had begun in March and, as far as the inspector was aware, the lift had never been operated under power. North British Rayon was waiting to be told when it would be ready for use. Dr. J.W. Wathews said that Chapman was admitted to Holme Valley Hospital on 5 April, suffering from shock, bruises and a fractured left ankle. He had been progressing well until 18 April when he died from an embolism in the coronary artery caused by a blood clot that had formed at the fracture site. The Inquest returned a verdict of Death by Misadventure.

From the 1950s the mill was used by a variety of smaller companies for varying periods of time. Fearnlea Mending Co. was using part of the mill in 1956; Spring Lane Woollen Spinners were advertising for staff for night work in 1957, and were in the mill until about 1969. Britton Rugs moved into Spring Lane in 1959 after the fire at Dover Mill, their last entry in the *Yorkshire Textile Industry* directory appeared in 1964.

W. Haigh & Son applied to Holmfirth Council to install a machine to crush stone at the mill in 1959, which was granted; although why they needed it and how long they were there is not known. Norhill Yarns were using part of the mill in 1959 and 1960; Dunsley Heating Appliance Co. were using part of the mill possibly from the late 1950s into the 1960s, before moving to Fearnought; Spring Lane Woollen Spinners, whose Managing Director was Mr. C. Holmes, were installed at the mill by 1962, their last advertisement for staff was in 1969, and their last entry in the directory was in 1971.

A company called Spring Lane Woollen Mill were using the premises by 1973 until at least 1980, whether there was a connection between them and Spring Lane Woollen Spinners is unclear. In 1972 Fred Hollingworth & Son bought at least part of the mill and were advertising for sheet metal workers; in the same year D. Adams & Co. Ltd. who were joiners were also advertising for staff.

Terry Sylvester bought part of what was the original mill from Fred Hollingworth in 1978, and moved his motorcycle business from Upper Bridge in Holmfirth to the mill, where, at the time of writing, he is still in business. The main building was bought by Ken. Moorhouse in 1990, for demolition. The previous owner George Warewright Ltd, carders and winders, moved to Marsden taking their workforce of 20 to 30 people with them.[9] The site of the mill and the dams is now covered by housing, with the exception of the small part of the mill being used by Terry Sylvester, which is almost entirely surrounded by the houses.

Round Bottom / Riverside mill

Built on Round Bottom close, this mill has the distinction of not appearing on the 6" Ordinance Survey map printed in 1853, but also had the misfortune to be damaged by the flood waters in 1852. The reason for this was that the map was surveyed around 1850, and the mill was built after the survey, but before the flood. Although it was a four storey building, built in the architectural style of a mill, it was built as a foundry by the Pogson family who were Iron-founders. After the flood Abraham Pogson & Brothers submitted a claim to the Flood Relief Committee for damage to buildings machinery and stock at Round Bottom Ironworks, and machinery at their workshop in Lower Mill, for a total of £291 13s. The inspectors reduced this to £275 10s and the Pogsons' were paid a total of £163 9s 3d.

Although built alongside Black Sike Dike, with the rear wall of the mill forming the right bank of the stream at that point, the mill never had a water wheel; power being supplied by a steam engine. The premises were advertised to be auctioned on 16 October 1867, when they were described as having an Iron foundry, mechanic's and smith's shops, fitting room and joiners shop, pattern and model rooms, stable and shed, engine and boiler house with a 12hp steam engine, 30hp boiler, going gear and shafting; occupied by H.W. Pogson. Also scribbling, carding, weaving and spinning rooms which would be on the upper floors, occupied by Jonas Hobson. Of recent erection and substantially built on 2,587sq.yds.of land. Whether the premises changed hands seems doubtful, as the owners in later years were still the Pogson family. In June 1878 the machinery, steam engine and boiler belonging to F. Hobson (probably the son of Jonas) was advertised for sale. It would appear that the items were not sold, as it was advertised in the following year as being 'to let as a going concern, with excellent steam engine and boiler, 3 sets of machines with self acting mules, looms and stocks to follow. Possession may be had immediately, apply F. Pogson on the premises.

Ben Whiteley took premises in the mill in 1880; a fire broke out in a wooden shed near the mill on Sunday 30 January 1881, which was spotted shortly after 12 o'clock. Attempts were made to put out the fire using buckets of water, which were unsuccessful as, when the Unity fire engine arrived, the shed was completely gutted. The newspaper article gives the name of the premises as Foundry mill.

In March 1882, a 13 year old bobbin winder called Minetia Bray went into the warping room to collect some cops, Walker Worsley a piecer, said he had his back to her when he heard her say "Oh my hair, Oh Walker, Walker", he turned round and saw her being carried round the shafting by her hair and skirts, and the fencing round the shaft was completely broken down. He could not get her down so he went to get the engine tenter. Sandy Mellor a sizer and beamer, said he was about six yards away from the girl when he heard her screams; he tried to get her down but was carried round with her two or three times and his legs were knocked against the wall. Matthew Moorhouse, the engine tenter, said that he heard shouting and stopped the engine and went to the room where he cut her loose; her head was injured and her brains were scattered about. Ben Whiteley told the coroner that the boxing on the shaft was perfect; the mill owner had 'made good' everything when the firm had taken space in the mill two years before, and the box had been tested only two weeks before the accident. A verdict of accidental death was recorded.

Ownership of the mill appears to have passed to Firth Hobson by 1886, when he was again, unsuccessfully, trying to sell his machinery. A sale was advertised for 1 August 1888, offering condenser sets, self-acting mules, hand mules, a bobbin winding machine, power looms, 2 pattern looms (hand), balloon and winding on frame, sizing machine, wooden warping woof, many sundries, also office furnishings. This was followed three weeks later by an advertisement for the mill being either for sale or to let; which was repeated almost a year later.

The mill appears to have remained empty until 1892, but was used in the interim on at least two occasions by William Sykes, auctioneer, to sell quantities of yarn and other raw materials. A sale of machinery was advertised in February 1892, along with 1,500lbs of yarn, presumably woollen, and 200lbs of worsted yarn; the name of the vendor is not given, but the machinery was different from the previous sales, possibly suggesting that these items had been transported there specifically for the sale. In the same month as that sale, the *Textile Manufacturer* magazine reported that Mr. Firth Hobson had registered the Yorkshire Felt Company, manufacturing felt hats, as being resident at the mill, he also changed the name of the building to Riverside Mill. If he was hoping that the change of name would bring a change of fortune he was to be disappointed, as the Yorkshire Felt Company went into liquidation in May 1894. A sale of machinery and stock took place a few days after the announcement, some of the machinery being rather different from that seen in the usual sales: a wool scouring machine with centrifugal pump and 4 possers, wool forming machines, iron grinding frame, shaving lathe, settling machine. 4 and 6 plank batteries, half table cup and cone hardening machine, 4 double flat hardening machines, 3 pairs barrel twisters, plus a stock of dyewares, office and warehouse furnishings, 2,500 hat bodies in various colours, also other materials and sundries.

Riverside mill. © A.J. Brooke

Charlesworth Brothers were occupying part of the mill in 1897, manufacturing fancy worsteds; and in December of that year Wm. Sykes & Co advertised a sale of machinery on behalf of a Mr. B. Coldwell, but no company name or description of the machinery is given.[10] In 1898 the two Charlesworths, J. and H., dissolved their partnership and apparently went out of business, as their names do not recur.

George Batty & Brothers were using the dyehouse at the mill in 1898, but were bankrupt by the following year when a sale of their machinery was advertised to take place on May 1st, when a large quantity of dyehouse equipment and a bay Horse called 'Bob' 16 hands high, 6 years old, with harness, a spring lurry with tow, and many sundries were auctioned.

In July of 1899 John Thornton & Co. were advertising for rug weavers to work at the mill; they were still occupying part of the mill the following year when the premises were offered for sale, being described as a 4 storey mill plus attic, 82ft long and 28ft wide; a dyehouse 39ft by 26ft; a vat room 59ft x 23ft; store rooms, engine house with 20hp beam engine, boiler house, blacksmith's shop, warehouse and other buildings. The mill was sold for £425. Allen Hinchliffe & Sons were occupying the mill in 1907, and were still there in 1910 when they were listed as Scribblers and Rag Pullers, manufacturing woollen and worsted yarns.

The mill then appears to have remained empty for around thirty years, but was occasionally used by Wm. Sykes for auctions. In 1940 R.H. Dark & Co. moved in, having had to leave their premises in the London area due to war damage. They were carders and blenders of wool, hair and waste; and also spinners of rabbit hair, and speciality fibres. At the time of the 1944 flood they had many bales of Rabbit fur and other fibres stored in wooden sheds in the mill yard, which were washed away causing extensive damage to buildings and bridges downstream. R.H. Dark & Co. left the mill after the flood, an entry in the *Yorkshire Textile Directory* in 1945 shows that they had an office in Lion Chambers,

Huddersfield; also a factory and warehouse in Stockport and London. The mill appears to have been empty until around 1952 when William Sykes & Co. took it over to use as a venue for auction sales of cattle etc. The premises eventually becoming the Holmfirth Attested Cattle Market.[11]

Parkhead Dyehouse / Mill

The dyehouse/mill stands between Greenfield road and Burnlee road; the water supply does not come from Black Sike Dike, but from an underground supply emerging below the level of Greenfield road that emanates from the rising ground towards Upperthong. The earliest reference for the buildings is in the Court Roll for 1826 when they were already in existence. John Harpin of Burnlee paid £1,000 to Thomas Armitage of Moorbottom Honley, son of John Armitage deceased of Shaleys Upperthong, and Martha Armitage widow of Moorbottom Honley; for a close of land called Linacre or the Acre containing 1 acre 2 roods 22 perches, late occupied by Joseph Mellor, then Joseph Battye, but now by John Harpin, with a cottage, warehouse and dyehouse.

At some time during the next five years, ownership of the dyehouse passed from John Harpin to William Lockwood of Hinchliffe Mill, who also owned Spring Lane mill. He sold the house, warehouse and other buildings erected on the Acre to George Jessop of Honley, plus two closes called the Pingle and the Netherwood which were next to Spring Lane, for the sum of £500.

Ownership of the dyehouse then passed to Iddo Wood of Spring Lane Upperthong; the rating valuation of 1836 records that in addition to the other buildings, Iddo had built a drying stove. The full valuation published in 1843 shows that there was the dyehouse and stove, plus a house, weaving shop, warehouse, garden, stable and barn on the site, all of which were in the hands of Iddo Wood's executors, as he had died. At the time of his death Iddo was living at Park House, in his will he left his dwelling houses, cottages, dyehouse, stove, weaving shop, warehouse, garden, stable and barn to be shared by his friend John Harpin the younger, and his two brothers Tola and Palti Wood.

Parkhead mill/dyehouse. © the author.

John Bower & Sons were using the premises in 1867, when Upperthong Local Board told them to remove a pile of ashes and refuse, which were across the road from the dyehouse causing a nuisance. Bower's were also using premises in Lower mill at this time.

Thomas Hinchliffe & Sons, who were in financial difficulties, were using the dyehouse in 1878 in addition to being in Victoria mill. The liquidation sale for the dyehouse was held on the 18 March, when 2 cast iron dyepans both with fireboxes and piping were auctioned, along with 1 cast iron scour pan with shell and crane, a stone wash cistern with a perforated cast iron bottom, plus various dyewares and sundries. The sale of their farm stock at Lower Netherhouse farm took place on the same day.[12]

There are no records of the dyehouse being used again; it is shown on the 25inch O.S. map of 1893 as a dyehouse, the buildings appear on later maps but are unmarked. I understand that the dyehouse building is now in the ownership of the Woodhead family, who had the chemical works on the Burnlee to Boothhouse road, and that chemicals were stored in the buildings at Parkhead during the 1950s, but it does not appear to have been used since.

River Holme – Victoria mill, Holmfirth

From a date stone on the wall of the mill it was built in 1837 along with the dam, possibly on the site of a domestic weaving building. Water was taken from the river Holme via a goit to the dam, then to the water wheel that was in the mill wall facing the dam. Although it was one of the last mills in Holme Valley to dismantle its water wheel, a steam engine was also installed not long after it was built. The owner of the mill in 1837 is not recorded, but it could have been Mr. John Harpin of Birks House Burnlee, who in 1848 put all his property on the market, which was advertised in 54 lots, lot 9 being Victoria Mill, which was described as: 'All that newly erected and substantially built woollen mill six stories high, situate at and called 'Victoria Mill', in Upperthong. With the water wheel, going gear, steam engine, reservoir and bank, and parcel of land thereto, now in the possession of Mr. Harpin, containing 3 acres and 18 perches'. Lot 10 was the three two-storey cottages that stood in the mill yard. It appears that much of the property was not sold, as another sale was advertised to take place in May 1851, when this mill was Lot 4, and was occupied by Messrs. Roberts and others.

The mill sustained some damage in the 1852 flood, all the windows on the ground floor were broken by the water, resulting in much of the machinery in the mill being broken or damaged. Six cottages in the course of construction in the mill yard were destroyed, as were the three occupied cottages at the opposite side of the mill yard. Fortunately those three cottages did not collapse until shortly after the occupants had managed to escape. The assessment of the total damage at the mill by the Huddersfield papers was in the region of £1,500. Henry Battye submitted a claim to the Relief Committee for damage to one pair of spinning mules and gas fittings totalling £50, the amount was agreed by the inspectors, and was paid in full plus an amount of £3 1s 6d for wages of employees involved in clearing debris. This claim is unique in that more than the amount of the claim was paid. Jonathon Roberts of Hinchliffe Mill submitted his claim for damage to spinning mules and stock at Victoria mill totalling £35, which was added to his claim for Yew Tree, and shared the same fate, nothing paid. The six cottages were being built by John Hollingworth and John Robinson, but there is no record of a claim for losses by them.

The firm of Thomas Hinchliffe & Sons were using the mill by 1872 when they advertised in the *Huddersfield Chronicle* for a competent scribbling engineer; in addition to this mill, they also had warehouse and showroom premises in Vance's Buildings, Cloth Hall St. Huddersfield, and were using Parkhead dyehouse. In 1878 they were in financial difficulties, with liabilities totalling £6,793 19s 4d, and assets of £3,135 7s 3d. Liquidation sales were held at Vance's Buildings on March 19, when 2 Mahogany topped show tables were offered for sale, plus 70ft of Deal scrays, and a hand-screwed packing press. The sale at Victoria Mill took place on the following day, when a large quantity of machinery covering most of the processes of turning wool into cloth took place. The liquidation also extended to the family's farm in Upperthong.

Victoria mill. © A.J. Brooke

The mill possibly stood empty from 1878, the Upperthong Local Board recorded that the mill was to be sold in March 1890, and in 1892 the sale of wood, a wooden building, and tools, the property of Ford & Co who were possibly joiners, was advertised. The 25 inch Ordinance Survey map published in 1893 marks the premises as 'disused'; and in October of that year the steam boiler and engine were auctioned.

That sale was possibly instigated by the next tenant of the mill who was William W. Battye, an Iron Founder, who would not need steam power. He applied to the council to carry out alterations to the premises in 1895, and also changed the name to Victoria Ironworks by 1896. They made textile machinery, and were known locally as 'Pulley' Battye's. They became a limited liability company in 1911, when their title became W.W. Battye & Sons Ltd; and although they stayed in business until the late 1950s they do not appear to have used all the six floors of the mill as other company names appear from time to time.

In 1920 Cartwright & Sons occupied part of the mill; they were presumably manufacturing cloth rather than yarn, as they advertised for a girl to learn winding. Mr. Moorhouse Cartwright unfortunately died from a fall near his home in Thongsbridge in the same year. In 1924 Hobson Battye & Co. were advertising for weavers; and Lockwood & Turner wanted menders in 1933.

The *Yorkshire Textile Directory* for 1942-3 records that Clough Brothers, a firm of commission weavers with 10 looms were using part of the mill. If they were on one of the upper floors they would avoid the five foot deep mud deposits left on the two lower floors by the waters of the 1944 flood. Clough Bros. continued to occupy part of the mill until about 1950.

In 1959 Mr. F. Booth applied to the council for a change of use of the premises from an Ironworks to a vehicle repair shop, which was granted. This was supplemented in 1961 by the addition of a filling station on Woodhead Road. The council granted an application by Mr. B.W.D. Wickam in 1966, to convert 3 floors of the mill for rearing chickens, whether this was ever carried out is not known.

The mill and garage were offered for sale by auction in December 1969, when the mill was described as having a ground floor workshop and stores approximately 3,750 sq. ft; and the 4 storey mill of approx. 10,000 sq. ft, plus a centrally heated office block. Whether the mill was sold or not was not reported.

A company by the name of VM Fabrications was advertising for an OAP and a boy in 1974, applications to Mr. G. Rollinson. They were in the premises until 1994, when it was reported that they were moving to Barnsley, and that most of the staff would be retained.[13] Kirklees council rejected a proposal to use the site of the mill for housing in late October 1994, as they would prefer to retain the premises for industrial use. This was obviously not forthcoming, and houses have subsequently been built on the site.

Dyson's / Perseverance mill

The earliest mention of a mill on or near this site is in the Wakefield Court roll on 1 June 1739, in conjunction with the Upper and Lower mills downstream; this mill was said to have been 'lately erected' at that time. This mill was upstream of Prickleden, and on the opposite bank, i.e. the Cartworth side, in the area where the mill that became known as Dyson's mill stood; although the two closes of land referred to were across the river in Upperthong township.

In 1788 Edmund Hirst of Upper Bridge took from John Beckitt several messuages and a fulling mill in Upperthong and Cartworth, that had previously been owned by John Beaumont, Thomas Roberts, Matthew Hirst, Elizabeth Wood, John Hinchliffe, John Bower, David Roberts and Edmund Hirst. In the same court roll Hirst surrendered the same house and fulling mill known as Pensall Bottom that had recently been occupied by Thomas Kaye, but was currently occupied by John Beaumont, which was in Cartworth township as mentioned, along with a warehouse used by Joseph Downtry, and a pressing shop used by David Roberts, which were across the river in Upperthong township.

In 1795 the fulling mill was in the possession of Matthew Butterworth, Joshua Moorhouse and Joseph Woofenden; the warehouse was being used by Joseph Daintry, [possibly an alternative spelling], the pressing shop was used by David Roberts and partners.

Major John Dyson, 1st West Yorks. Militia, stationed in Ireland, and Joseph Dyson of Upperbridge Holmfirth, paid £200 to William Sykes cloth dresser of Huddersfield, who was the executor for John Holt of Huddersfield in 1816, for the dwelling house and the second fulling mill at Prickleden, with the land and 4 cottages, also the warehouse now occupied by Joseph Daltry [possibly another alternative spelling], and the dressing shop occupied by David Roberts and partners. Edmund Hirst of Upperbridge died in 1821, leaving his interest in the second fulling mill, the cottages, warehouse and pressing shop, and the land and former teazing mill near lower mill, to his two nephews John and Joseph Dyson; they paid off the final £300 mortgage on the property soon after inheriting it.

The mill was renovated or rebuilt in 1824 by its then owners, who were John Dyson of Dalton and Joseph Dyson of Upperthong, in 1825 they leased the mill, which is referred to in the lease as Battye's Upper Mill, to Jonathon Roberts and Samuel Sandford for a term of 40 years. This is confirmed by an indenture in Kirklees Archive department, between the same parties, giving the rent as £315 per annum. The lease was extended for a further 21 years in 1865, by the then tenants Jonathon and William Roberts.

In their responses to the Factory Commissioners in 1833, Roberts and Sandford said that the mill was built in 1824, and was used by them for scribbling, carding and slubbing of wool, and the fulling of woollen cloth. Their main source of power was the water wheel, except in times of drought when they used the steam engine, both forms each delivered between 14 and 16hp. Part of the power was let to someone else who ran two spinning mules, but no name is given. They had 28 employees, 3 boys and 1 girl under 10 earning 4s each, 5 girls under 12 earning 4s each, 6 boys and 1 girl under 14 earning 6s each, 3 boys and 2 girls under 16 each earning 6s, 4 boys under 21 earning 15s each, and 3 men over 21 each earning 23s. Nine of the children were paid by the person for whom they worked. The working day started at 6am in summer, and 7 or 8am in winter "because it is difficult and unpleasant to rouse the children from bed before it is light". The working day ended at 9pm, except Saturdays, all year round. The machines only stopped for dinner from 12.30 to 1.30, at Breakfast and Drinking everyone worked while they ate. The fulling stocks never stopped, either

Dysons/Perseverance mill. © A.J. Brooke

day or night, but no children were employed in that department. Question 21 asked if they had ever employed more than one set of children so that they could relieve each other. No-one, as far as I am aware, answered yes to this; virtually all said that it would not be practical, mainly because the supply of children was insufficient. In response to the question on corporal punishment, Roberts and Sandford said that they strapped children on the hand to make them diligent and attentive, and also to force obedience. They rarely applied this to anyone over the age of thirteen. In common with most other mills, they said that children under ten made the best piecers. On the question of hours of work for children they said that 12 hours a day was the least that they would consent to, and that children were well able to bear those hours without endangering their health.

On 23 July 1844, James Sykes of Linthwaite was charged with stealing 6lbs of black dyed wool from 'Sandford's mill', Holmfirth. Two inspectors, Mr. Kaye and Mr. Charlesworth, were going through bags of waste known as 'Devil's Dust' when they found the wool hidden in the waste towards the bottom of the sack. Sykes said that he had bought the wool from his brother, and that the transaction had been witnessed by another man; he called them both as witnesses in court and they confirmed his story. The report says that Messrs. Roebuck & Sandford, rather than the correct name of Roberts and Sandford, gave evidence that the wool found in Sykes' possession was identical to 39lbs of wool that had gone missing from their mill. The magistrates chose to believe the manufacturers, and Sykes was fined £20; if he could not pay the fine he would be sent to the house of correction for two months.

The mill and machinery were badly damaged in the 1852 flood, the house in the mill yard which was occupied by Jonathon Sandford, his two young daughters aged 10 and 5, and Ellen Wood their maid was swept away and all four were drowned. The bridge over the river providing access from Woodhead road to the mill was also destroyed. The bodies of the maid and the two girls were found fairly quickly, but Mr. Sandford's body was not found until fifteen days later. 40 employees at the mill would be out of work. A claim for damage to the house and mistal was submitted to the Committee for a total of £480, which was not reduced by the inspectors. The only payment made was for £11 8s 4d, which was for labour in clearing debris. In 1853 the Reservoir Commissioners recorded the owners of the mill as Joseph Dyson and the executors of John Dyson deceased, who were Sydney Morehouse, Joshua Morehouse and Jennett Henry Dyson; the occupants were given as Samuel Sandford, and John, George, Jonathon, William and Joseph Roberts. The Roberts brothers paid Samuel Sandford £1,000 for his half share in the mill; due to the death of his son and granddaughters in the flood he probably wished to severe his connection with the mill.

The mill was enlarged in the 1870s, at a cost exceeding £1,400, when it became a four storey building plus attic, approximately 100ft long by 50ft wide. The Roberts family continued to use the mill until the expiry of their lease in 1886, the machinery belonging to William Roberts was auctioned on 9 September, the main lots included machines for spinning wool, weaving cloth and dyehouse equipment, plus 8,000lbs of yarn. The Machinery belonging to Green Roberts was auctioned 4 days later, it consisted of similar items.[14]

The building was possibly empty from 1886, it was advertised to be sold or let in September of that year, but does not appear to have attracted a tenant, apart from William Sykes, Auctioneer, using 1 room for storage. He held a sale of 8,000lbs of tops and noils there in June 1893; finally vacating the premises on 1 June 1895. The mill continued to remain empty; protracted negotiations with a possible buyer began in October 1900, but were not completed until late April 1901 when Mrs. Elizabeth Dyson, widow of Joseph Dyson, sold the mill plus 2 cottages with outbuildings and 3 closes of land totalling 6 acres 1 rood 21 perches to Mr. Thomas Larder of Brockholes, stone merchant, for £1,150.

The premises were subsequently advertised many times as being 'for sale' or 'to let' but no new tenant appeared until in 1906 Walter Greenwood & Sons, who were dyers, finishers and cloth millers, moved from Bridge Mills to Perseverance, and applied to the council for permission to make some alterations. An inquiry was held in May 1913, about Greenwood's failure to install treatment tanks for trade effluent from the mill. The firm had assured the Rivers Board inspector in 1909 that the work would be done in about 9 months. Apart from digging pits for the tanks no progress had been made. The district inspector said that during the past year he had received complaints from mills downstream from Perseverance about the effluent that Greenwood's were putting into the river. Mr. Greenwood said that work was in hand to correct the problem. The inquiry closed without any conclusion being reached. An advertisement appeared in the *Holmfirth Express* in February of 1912 offering skating on 'beautiful ice' on the pond adjoining the mill for 3d per person. No record exists to show how many people availed themselves of the opportunity.

Twenty four of Greenwood's employees went on strike for higher wages on 16 February 1914. The representatives of their trade union attempted to talk to the company, but Greenwood's refused to negotiate, which prompted the strikers to set up a picket line. The police were called but found everything quiet and orderly, so they took no action. The problem appears to have been resolved fairly quickly as no further reports were made.

In the 1944 flood the volume of water overflowing the natural bed of the river took a large part of the road away almost outside the Victoria Inn, and demolished the parapets of the bridge connecting Perseverance mill to Woodhead Road. The flood waters also entered Perseverance mill, but, as the main volume of water was many yards away, not much damage was done.

Greenwood's were joined in the mill by the firm of K.K. Platt, who were manufacturing cloth on their 10 looms between 1949 and 1966. Business appears to have been good for Greenwood's between the mid 1950s and the 1970s, as they made various improvements and extensions to the mill during that time. One setback that they had was that on returning from the Christmas holiday in 1963, they discovered that someone had broken in and stolen pieces of cloth to the value of around £1,000. As Greenwood's were dyers and finishers, the stolen cloth belonged not to them, but to their customers, possibly providing several manufacturers with problems.

In 1976, it was reported that, in common with many other surviving textile companies, Greenwood's were no longer an independent company but were part of Yorkshire Fine Woollen

Spinners Ltd. who were based in Bradford. Mr. J.F. Greenwood was the director responsible for the management of Alan Thornton & Sons Ltd. dyers and finishers, Crossley mills Honley, and Walter Greenwood & Son. Other local members of the group were John Woodhead Ltd. and Anglo Yarn Spinners Ltd. both of Albion mills Thongsbridge. Greenwood's were finishers of high quality Mohair and Worsted cloth; however, the volume of business was diminishing, which they attributed to cheap imports from Hong Kong and Taiwan. In late 1979 the firm announced that it would be making almost half of its workforce redundant; this would affect twelve people. In the event, the entire workforce was laid off in March 1980, and the firm closed completely.

Vandalism soon became a problem; there was a fire of unknown origin in the Mechanic's shop on 10 April 1980. Proposals to turn the building into a sports centre, or to build houses on the site, were refused by Kirklees, principally because the site was designated for industrial use. At least part of the mill was demolished in 1982, two years later there were complaints that the area was both dangerous and an eyesore, Kirklees council gave assurances that they would make the area safe. There were further proposals to build houses, or an hotel, or a supermarket, all of which were turned down. These were followed by a proposal to turn it into a car and coach park, which was also turned down. In 1987 there was yet another proposal to build 80 houses on the site; but it was not until July 1992, that Kirklees council finally agreed that the site could be used for domestic purposes. Younger Homes submitted plans in 1995 for a supermarket, filling station and garden centre, which Kirklees turned down as they had already decided that it should be used for housing; the builders followed this with plans for 100 houses.[15]

Batty's / Farrar's Upper and Lower Mills

For many years these mills were owned and run by the same families. The older of the two sights is that of the Upper mills which is at Prickleden. The earliest information that I have found dates from 1640, by which time it was already built. The court roll entry is dated 22 May 1640 and reads:

> *Thomas Haigh of Hadfield in Derbyshire by William Dernilee, lord's tenant and sworn, surrendered an interest and title in a close of arable land called Lathecroft, another called Rydinge, a house in the same two closes called Pense bothomes, a close called Holme adjoining a fulling mill, a piece of wood and land called Prickmoore banke (now divided into three), another close called Tentercrofte, 2 barns, a little backside adjoining (saving an access way at all times for repair of the fulling mill) and all rents associated in Overthwong and Cartworth in the Graveship of Holme, now occupied by Edward Batty or his assigns at a lord's rent of 2s 6d and certain fine: to the use of Nicholas Haigh of Hadfield in Derbyshire his heirs etc. Agreed: entry fine of 3s 9d. Compounded for by Edward Batty, John West, and Martyn Allott.*

In 1665 Nicholas Haigh passed ownership of the land and property to 'John Wagstaffe of Gloshopp', the occupant of the mill was now James Batty. The annual rent payable to the lord had halved to 15d, but the entry fine had increased to 11s 3d. Seventy four years later, in 1739, the Batty family had become the owners of the mill rather than just tenants. The occupant was still a James Batty of Milne in Overthwong, who appears to have raised a mortgage on the premises, although the amount is not disclosed; from Richard Matthewman and John Firth both of Shepley. This entry lists a total of three fulling mills; the first is the one adjacent to the close of land called the Holme, which is at Prickleden, the second is the low or lower mill at Upper bridge; the third is upstream from the first and is described as being 'lately erected', this became known as Battye's Upper mill and later Perseverance mill.

James Battye registered his will with the manor court in October 1745, leaving his messuages, fulling milns, goits and dams etc. to two of his sons, Joseph and Thomas Batty. The mills were occupied at that time by James Batty, John Byrom, James Eastwood and Jonathon Batty. In 1751 the occupants of the upper and lower mills are named as James and Jonathon Battye.

The flood of 1777, mentioned in Chapter 7, destroyed the mill and house at Lower mill, but any damage suffered by the Upper mill was not as great. John Fallas of Wood, Upperthong, leased a strip of land 124yds long by 3yds wide from James Harrop in 1792, to make a goit between the upper and lower mills in order to improve the water supply to, and increase the efficiency of, the lower mill.

The Farrar family enter the story in 1795, when James Crosland of Deadmanstone [presumably in Berry Brow] paid £188 to Thomas Farrar leather factor, of Southwark, London, George Farrar dyer, of Wakefield, and James Farrar dyer, of Quick Wood Saddleworth, nephews and devisees of John Hobson, deceased, of Wooldale. The property was a dwelling house at Prickleden with a dyehouse, garden and a close of land, which the Farrars' had inherited from their uncle. There is also mention of a Messuage which was a former Teazing mill, which was on land close to Lower mill, and had been converted into two cottages The upper and lower mills continued to be owned and worked by the Battye family, and by 1800 the description of both had become Fulling and Scribbling mills showing that they were processing raw wool in addition to finishing cloth.

In 1804 Thomas Battye surrendered the fulling mill known as the Upper Mill to George Farrar dyer of Prickleden, James Farrar dyer of Prickleden, James Battye fulling miller of the Upper mill, and James Hinchliffe clothier of Holmfirth, who were also the occupiers of the mill, along with 2 cottages and the close of land known as the Holme, for the term of 21 years from 30 October. In 1806 Thomas Battye gave his share of the income from both the upper and lower mills for at least one year to the Rev. John Taylor of Horbury; the reason for the gift is not stated. In 1807 James and Thomas Battye, along with their respective wives Ann and Mary, raised a mortgage on the upper mill from John Rimmington of Hillsborough Sheffield. Neither the amount borrowed, nor the reason for the loan is given. The occupants of the mill were still George and James Farrar, James Battye and James Hinchliffe, who were paying a rent of £230 per annum. In 1809 James Battye borrowed £650 from Jonathon Depledge of Bretton, giving the lower mill, 2 houses and 2 closes of land as security.

James Battye the elder passed a dwelling house at the upper mill and four closes of land, plus the lower mill with its machinery etc. to Richard and Joseph Battye, and James Battye the younger, who were presumably his sons or nephews, in 1811.

George and James Farrar redeemed the £650 mortgage on the lower mill by paying back the amount borrowed plus £101 interest to Jonathon Depledge in 1813. At some point Thomas Battye had been declared bankrupt as, in 1818, William Stead and Brian Holmes of Thrum Hall, Soyland in Halifax purchased 2 cottages with outbuildings for £100 from Jonathon Kinder of Upper mill, Upperthong, which he had built on land purchased from the assignees of Thomas Battye, a bankrupt.

In 1829 the Farrar family were in need of some money, they borrowed £500 from Sarah Wordsworth of Holmfirth and gave as security a large amount of land and the lower mill. A year later George Farrar paid £2,100 to James Rimmington of Broom Head Hall Ecclesfield, for the return of the upper mill, plus the 2 cottages and land that had been sold by the Battye's in 1807.

George Farrar borrowed £2,000 from Ann Whitacre of Woodhouse Huddersfield in 1831, he gave as security the dwelling house at Prickleden with the gardens, outbuildings, barn, warehouse, stable, cowhouse and yard, also the dyehouse, stoves, dye vats etc. and the four cottages tenanted by Joseph Swallow, Joshua Thewlis, George Taylor and John Coldwell; also the cottage with a yard, barn and shop, adjoining premises occupied by Joseph Kirk and David Roberts, plus the close called the Holme between the goit and the river. Also the fulling and scribbling mill known as the Upper mill, which had been previously pulled down and rebuilt by George Farrar, and was in his possession, and also a close of land near Five Lane Ends called Rother Top. The Rate valuation of 1831 notes the building of a new stove, also the rebuilding of the mill and that its height had been raised. The valuation of 1834 notes that additions had been made to the dyehouse.

George and John Hobson Farrar both put their names to the document that they sent to the Factory Commissioners in 1833, but the answers that they gave appear to concern only the Lower mill. They said that the mill then in use had been built in 1817, which means that the original mill on that site from the 1750s had been replaced; power was supplied by both a water wheel and a steam engine, which could each deliver 10hp, and they were involved in scribbling, carding and slubbing white and coloured wool, implying that the fulling stocks had been dismantled. They employed a total of 29 people, made up of 1 boy and 1 girl under 12 earning 3s 6d each, 6 boys and 3 girls under 14 also earning 3s 6d each, 4 boys and 3 girls under 16 earning 4s each, 2 boys under 18 earning 5s to 8s each and 1 girl under 18 earning 5s; 1 man over 19 earning 20s and 7 men over 21 earning 21s each. Hours of work during summer were 6am to 8pm, and in winter were from 8am to 10pm, with 2 hours allowed in total for meals, during which time the engine was stopped. Their answer to the question about corporal punishment was that they did not allow the children to be punished, only with a strap…to keep them out of mischief. To the question on Government regulation of hours of work they answered: 'We have no objections to an Act of Parliament for twelve hours, and to reject children under 11 years old, as by taking off one sixth of labour, it will likewise take one sixth off all, both adult and children's earnings; at the same time, be a serious reduction on mill property. No children can be healthier than ours, even if they never entered a mill'.

James Hobson Farrar took a half share (a moiety) in the Lower mill and its equipment from George Farrar in 1837. This was followed in 1842 by Mary and Elizabeth Farrar surrendering the scribbling mill known as Upper mill at Prickleden, with the water wheel, steam engine and engine house, boiler and boiler house, and the lately erected building called the Factory, with the Dyehouse, warehouse and stove plus machinery, to John Hobson Farrar. There are two interesting points in this entry, firstly, the omission of the word Fulling implying that the fulling stocks had been superseded by more modern equipment; and secondly, the building of the Factory, which was adjacent to the turnpike road, and was probably the building that subsequently became Holmfirth Laundry.

William Butterworth, described by the *Leeds Mercury* of 3 June 1843 as an 'extensive manufacturer of Hinchliffe Mill' had been using part of the Lower mill during the 1830s and '40s. He had called to check that all the doors were locked one night at the end of May 1843 when he accidentally fell into the river and drowned. He had apparently been drinking in the Elephant & Castle Inn. Also in that year, the partnership of George Farrar & Co. was dissolved, with Mary, Elizabeth and John Hobson Farrar resigning from the firm. Although no reason was given, it was possibly because George Farrar had become mentally ill; in the register of owners and occupiers of mills compiled by the Reservoir Commissioners in 1853, the owners are given as John Hobson Farrar, John Heathcote and Mary his wife; Hugh Roberts and Elizabeth his wife, also Joshua Charlesworth, who were trustees of George Farrar, who is described as 'a lunatic'. The occupier of the mill at that time was John Hobson Farrar; he died on 3 June 1854 aged 43.[16]

Both the upper and lower mills were badly damaged in the flood of 1852, the dyehouse at the upper mill, which was 30 yards long, was destroyed along with two boiler houses. One of the boilers weighing five tons was carried downstream by the flood waters as far as Berry Brow. Damage was estimated to be between £3,000 and £4,000.

Part of the lower mill was built over the river; this was destroyed along with machinery. A boiler from this mill was also carried away by the flood waters and deposited downstream. The major part of the mill was used by James Hobson Farrar, but part of the mill was used by Benjamin Mellor cloth finishers, and part by Jonas Cartwright machine makers, they both sustained losses and damage. The number of people employed at lower mill was about 150. The Farrar's submitted two claims to the Flood Relief Committee, the first was for destruction and damage to buildings, goit, dam, machinery and stock totalling £4,495 7s, this was reduced by the inspectors to £2,911 19s, and payments totalling £1,000 were made. The second claim was for £1,889, the amount was not reduced, and payments totalling £1,246 13s 2d were made. Jonas Cartwright submitted a claim for damage to machinery and stock of £55 10s, this was reduced to £46 8s, and £35 was paid. Benjamin Mellor made a claim for machinery and stock of £156 13s, which was reduced to £150, and he received £120. Owners of the Lower mill in the Reservoir Commissioners records for 1853 are given as Thomas and William Eddlestone, trustees of George Farrar snr. deceased, and James Hobson Farrar; the occupier was James Hobson Farrar.

The writer of John Hobson Farrar's obituary in the *Huddersfield Chronicle* of 10 June 1854 suggests that '*the loss here sustained* [in the flood], *together with other unfortunate circumstances, had so far preyed upon his mind as to affect his frame, and he has gradually sunk under the afflictions*'. The upper mill was advertised as being 'to let from year to year, or for a term of years' in June 1854, the scribbling mill was 4 storeys high, with a water wheel and a steam engine each of 20hp, containing a large quantity of machinery; a large heated wool stove separate from the mill; a second 4 storey building 36yds in length; also a room occupied as a machine makers shop. There was a commodious dyehouse containing dyepans etc. with a warehouse over; also an abundant supply of soft spring water well adapted for scouring and finishing purposes.

A sale of farmstock, cloth and dyewares belonging to J. H. Farrar took place on 9 August 1854, followed in the following year by a large sale of properties, 30 lots, in Holmfirth, Totties, Scammonden, Denby and Leeds belonging to the brothers. Their estates became the subject of a case in the Chancery court, Thewlis v Farrar, which instigated two sales of property in 1857, one in late January, and the other in December.

An accident occurred at the lower mill on 30 July 1858, Phillip Booth of Wooldale, a slubber, became caught in the drive belt of a machine and was carried round the shafting, injuring his head and chest. John Bower & Sons were using at least part of the lower mill in September 1859, when Thomas Sharpe, an 18 year old mule spinner, was attempting to replace a broken strap, which caught his clothes and carried him around the shafting killing him instantly. At the inquest Mr. Jonathon Bower said that he looked after the straps, and Sharpe should have reported the problem to him, but Sharpe had only worked at the mill for a short period. The jury returned a verdict of 'accidental death'.

A man was leaving a meeting about midnight in September 1865, when he smelled smoke at the bottom of Victoria Street, which he traced to the mill. The fire was in a wool warehouse used by Bowers that was separate from the mill, he summoned help and the men broke open the warehouse door and pulled a sheet, containing burning shoddy, into the yard to extinguish the fire. Another fire occurred in the stove used by Bowers at 1am on Friday 23 April 1869. The Unity brigade soon arrived, but several pieces of cloth and a quantity of wool were destroyed. Damage was estimated at around £200, and was partly covered by insurance.

The next occupant of the upper mill appears to have been James Holmes & Sons who were woollen manufacturers and fulling and scribbling millers. Mr. Holmes kept a Muscovy duck and drake that both swam on the mill dam. A neighbour called Lindley kept a game cock in a field that abutted the dam; the drake would sometimes go from the dam into the field where the game cock lived; the cock would challenge the drake, which would then return to the water. On Monday 31 January 1859 the drake went about 20 yards into the field and was attacked by the game cock. The drake gradually retreated until it reached the dam bank, when it flew at the game cock grabbing it by the neck with its claws and flew to the middle of the dam, where it landed in the water. It then swam to the end of the dam holding the game cock under water drowning it. The report claimed that this was not the first time that this had happened.

A fire was discovered in the stove used by Holmes' at 6.30pm on 20 February 1861, flames spread quickly to the roof which was partly destroyed. The Unity brigade arrived and rapidly brought the fire under control. Damage was estimated at £30.

Heavy rain during the night of November 15 to 16 1866, caused some damage at both mills; the dam walls at the upper mill were damaged with some of the stones being washed away, the trunk or tunnel that carried water from the upper mill to the lower was 'blown up' and rendered useless, and about 30 feet of walling was also washed away.

The partnership between James Francis and Henry Holmes trading as James Holmes & Sons, and also as farmers at Larch House Cartworth, was dissolved in June 1862; a new partnership between James Holmes, Henry Holmes and John Marsh was formed using the same business title of James Holmes & Sons. John Marsh was using part of the mill in 1871 apparently trading on his own, but

Lower mill c.1950 Viewed from Hollow Gate — Reproduced from Centenary Booklet

does not seem to have been doing very well as a sale of wool, mungo, rags, waste, healds and sleys was held on November 15th, when it was said he 'was declining business'. In 1872, Henry Holmes was given permission by Upperthong Local Board to summon and dismiss his workers by sounding the steam whistle at Upper mill, and John Bower & Sons were given similar permission for Lower mill. Although virtually every mill that had a steam boiler would have a whistle, it was generally considered amongst Local Authorities that to allow every mill to sound their whistle would be confusing, distracting, and too noisy; therefore they restricted the privilege to mills that were usually some distance apart, allowing the sound to overlap, alerting workers at every mill.

Bower's were in the process of moving from Lower mill to Dover mill in 1880, when Lower mill was advertised as being to let in May of that year, along with upwards of five acres of land, plus a barn and stable.

H. & S. Butterworth bought Lower mill in 1882 and moved their machinery and production from Hinchliffe mill and Bottoms mill. Henry Butterworth had trained with his uncle Joshua Moorhouse, and had begun trading on his own account in 1850 using outworkers. Henry was joined by his brother Samuel two years later when they formed the company of H. & S. Butterworth, and continued to use outworkers. They eventually rented 'room and power' in Hinchliffe mill, where they began scribbling, spinning and weaving. Dyeing and finishing were still done on a commission basis, while burling was done at the family home 'Healdcarr' in Hinchliffe Mill, which was also used for storage. Henry's eldest son William joined the firm in 1873, and took over in 1879, by which time they were using space in Bottoms mill in addition to Hinchliffe mill.

A new finishing shed was built at Lower mill in 1886, and a second hand Tentering machine was bought for £190. There was always great interest in tentering machines at mill sales, as they were relatively new, and were more efficient than a tentering room in a stove, and infinitely more secure than outdoor tenter posts. The price of a new machine from Whiteley's machine makers of Lockwood varied between £350 for one that would hold 70 yards of cloth, and £500 for the largest model that would hold 130yds of cloth.[17] The price of the new machines included installation, whereas the price paid at auction was for that machine as it was and where it stood. The purchaser would also need to pay for it to be dismantled, transported and re-assembled at the new location.

The Upper mill was again advertised 'to let' in 1874, it still had the water wheel, and possibly a new steam engine as it is described as 25hp rather than 20hp. The yarn preparation machinery is virtually the same as in 1854; but 20 broad looms and 32 narrow looms, 2 warp drying and beaming machines, a bobbin winding machine, finishing machinery plus broad and narrow tenters had all been added. The advertisement also lists 3 fulling stocks, although whether they were in working order is not stated. At least part of the mill was still occupied by James Holmes and Sons; the dyehouse was also available, then currently occupied by George Battye.

Mr. Frank Holmes, who was in charge of Jas. Holmes & Sons, died in 1881, the firm closed and their machinery was sold. The water wheel at Upper mill was no longer in use by May 1886, when it was advertised to be sold.

A company called Kaye & Barnfather were using part of Upper mill in 1888, when they gave a treat for 60 people; how long they had been in business is not known, but Mr. Barnfather left this company in 1889, and went into partnership with a Mr. Graham at Bridge mill; the name of the firm at Upper mill becoming C.T. Kaye & Co.

Also using part of the Upper mill in 1890 was Thomas Rhodes, cloth finisher, when he gave his 45 workers a treat. Rhodes had possibly been using part of the mill for a number of years, as he had been trying, unsuccessfully, to get payment for finishing work done for cloth manufacturers in Mytholmbridge Upper mill in 1885. There was a meeting of creditors of the company held in October 1891, the net liability of the firm was £1,400, and the decision of the creditors meeting was that the firm should be wound up. A sale of machinery was advertised a week later, but no details of what was to be sold were given, which implies that there was not much to sell.

In the late 1880s and early 1890s business was extremely difficult, with many firms being unable to find enough business to carry on trading. One of the first options for an employer to remain in business would be to reduce his prices to his customers, which he would hope to achieve by increasing efficiency and possibly by reducing the wages of his workers. In May and June 1890 the weavers at C.T. Kaye & Co had been agitating for a rearrangement of prices paid for their work. The weavers organised a meeting with the Powerloom Weavers Association on 11 June to discuss the best course of action. Their complaint was that weavers on fast looms were being paid one third less than the rate for slow loom weavers, which was already less than the rate paid to slow loom weavers in Huddersfield. The Association was asked to negotiate on behalf of their members. The officials met Mr. Kaye and talked with him for 1½ hours, but no better offer was made, so the weavers took strike action. The strikers met with the Association again on 9 July, but still no progress had been made towards a settlement. Union members were receiving strike pay, while non union strikers were 'receiving assistance from other firms in the district'. This presumably meant that collections were being made amongst the workers at other mills. It was also reported at the meeting that some looms at Kaye's were being woven by untrained people, and that some work was being sent to mills in Bradford and Halifax. It was reported on 10 October that despite meetings between the weavers and Mr. Kaye no progress had been made towards a settlement. Some weavers said that they were determined to find work elsewhere rather than return to Prickleden; the union said they would continue to support them until they found alternative employment. The strike ended in its 22nd week, around the 21 November, when the weavers and Mr. Kaye agreed on a compromise. The union reported that they had paid a total of £150 to the strikers.

C.T. Kaye & Co. ceased trading in October 1891, they do not appear to have been in financial difficulty, but announced that they were 'giving up business'. Their machinery, plus the contents of the Blacksmith's shop, and office furnishings were advertised to be sold by auction on 12 November. Whether the demise of the firms of Thomas Rhodes and C.T. Kaye & Co. were entirely due to the strike, or whether it had merely hastened the inevitable is open to conjecture.

There was also a dispute at H. & S. Butterworth during this period, the weavers of their slow looms felt that they were under-employed, as the weavers of fast looms were working overtime until 8pm every night, whereas weavers of slow looms were on short time. Mr. Gee from the union met Mr. William Butterworth, who explained how the anomalies had occurred and promised to address the problem. In 1891 H. & S. Butterworth were summoned under the Factory Act for permitting two youths, aged 18 and 15 to work longer than the permitted number of hours. The firm were fined 5s plus 11s costs in each case.

Adverts for 'Room and Power' at Prickleden appeared in 1893; and in 1897 a firm called Crosland Marsh were using the mill, but they moved out in 1898 and their machinery was to be sold. The mill then appears to have been empty, as it is marked on the 1906 25inch Ordinance Survey map as 'disused'. R. W. Rankin took space in the mill before January 1919, when they were advertising for Dobcross weavers; this was followed by several adverts during that year for warpers, winders and weavers.[18] How long they remained in the mill is unknown, but they appear to have been its last tenants.

The dyehouse faired rather better; a company called Netherwood were using the dyehouse in 1897; the buildings were renamed Valley Dyeworks at some point, possibly by Sykes & Co. who were using them in 1910. Wright Hinchliffe & Co. moved to Valley Dyeworks from Kirkbridge mill some time between 1915 and 1919, when Council minutes record that complaints were being received about smoke pollution from Hinchliffe's chimney. The problem was not resolved, and the Council eventually threatened court action, which achieved the desired effect, at least temporarily, as complaints continued sporadically until 1957.

The 1944 flood affected the premises by flooding ground-floor rooms and leaving a thick covering of mud, but did no structural damage. A company trading as Holme Valley Dyeworks Ltd. were using part of the premises in 1961; there is no other information on them. Wright Hinchliffe & Co. appear to have ceased trading in the late 1960s, as their last advert for staff appeared in 1967.

At Lower mill H. & S. Butterworth recovered from the depression of the 1890s and expanded the premises by building a new weaving shed in 1896, which was added to in 1902 and 1903, with a further extension being built in 1907. The Yorkshire Textile Directory of 1910 shows that the company made cloth for coats, that the spinning section had 2,000 spindles, and there were 80 looms. Lighting in the mill was from Selas incandescent gas lights. There were extensions to the finishing shed in 1913, and an addition to the spinning mill in 1914; Butterworth's also submitted plans for a new mill to be built to house the scribbling and spinning sections in 1914, which were approved, and the building was ready for use in the following year. Additions to the weaving sheds were made in 1918 and '19; a dynamo was installed in 1920, which would provide more electrical power for machines at a competitive rate.

More alterations took place during the 1930s and early 1940s, but the flood in 1944 did considerable damage by destroying some of the weaving sheds that were built over the river, flooding others to a depth of fifteen feet, also washing away some machines and damaging others. The Holmfirth Express reported that Lower mill was probably the most severely damaged mill in the valley, and it would be some considerable time before full production could be resumed. Many of the staff at H. & S. Butterworth transferred to Washpit mill, where there was spare capacity, to allow Butterworth's to continue production.

An alarm bell sounded at the mill on the afternoon of Sunday February 3rd 1946, and the sprinkler system came on in the scribbling department. Holmfirth fire brigade attended and found that there was a fire in one of the carding machines, damaging some of the rollers and a quantity of wool. There was also a small fire in a teazing machine in July 1950, when damage was limited to the wool in the machine and on the floor nearby. Production continued until late 1963, when the company announced that 'due to a change in circumstances the company would be closing towards the end of the year'.

An advertisement appeared in the Holmfirth Express in April 1966, offering part time and temporary employment for doublers and cone winders in a new spinning plant in the centre of Holmfirth. Applicants should apply in person to The Spinning Manager, Lower Mill, but no company name was given. In 1968 similar advertisements appeared, applications to Mr. J. Corfield; later in the year prospective employees were told to apply to W. Fein & Sons Ltd. at Lower Mill. Fein's had been in Deanhouse mill for some years, and continued in business at both mills until the late 1970s. Use of welding equipment in the mill caused a small fire in 1971, two appliances from Holmfirth and one from Huddersfield attended only to find that workpeople had extinguished the flames before the fire engines arrived. There was a break-in at the mill in 1983 when tools worth £100 were stolen. Fein's became members of Elders International Wool (UK) Ltd. in 1987; all 50 employees retained their jobs.

The company announced that they were looking for more modern premises in 1992, and submitted redevelopment plans to the council, which were apparently not accepted, as a different plan was submitted in 1995 to convert the old mill to offices and shops, or flats, plus 24 sheltered homes and 22 new houses; the Chimney was to be retained. This plan was approved by the planners,

Lower mill Holmfirth. © A.J. Brooke

but as work had not started by 1998, the approval lapsed. A new plan which included the preservation of the 5 storey mill and the mill chimney, plus 50 new homes ranging from 2 bedroom apartments to 4 bedroom town houses was submitted, Holmfirth Parish Council rejected it, but Kirklees planning department approved it in November 1998. In 2000 it was announced that the original developer had withdrawn, but the architects were in talks with another developer and were submitting yet another plan to Kirklees. The *Express* announced in July 2000 that buildings on the site were being damaged by vandals due to the delay in its development.[19] The site has subsequently been converted to housing.

New Fold mill

This mill was in the area of Goose Green, close to the Elephant and Castle Inn, on the opposite side of Hollowgate from the river. In 1782 it was a dyehouse, when John Beaumont of Upperthong paid £130 to John Haigh, Thomas Haigh, John Bray and John Shackleton for 2 messuages or dwelling houses and one dyehouse in New Fold. The houses were occupied by John Marsden and John Booth. In 1784 John and Ann Beaumont raised a mortgage from Elizabeth Rimington of Sheffield, which was repaid by James Hinchliffe of Upper Bridge in 1788, when he paid £145 to Elizabeth Rimington and £5 to John Beaumont of Upper Bridge, for the two dwelling houses and the dyehouse occupied by Jonas Marsden, Benjamin Priest and John Booth; plus a garden and a barn belonging to the said James Hinchliffe, and a half share in a gable end wall dividing a dwelling house occupied by Jonathon Ackroyd; along with other barns and outbuildings.

James Hinchliffe and his family worked hard over the ensuing years, and when his wife Mary Hinchliffe died in 1825 she left to her two sons Joseph and George a piece of land called the Croft, and the Mill or building with the drying stove built on the land. In addition, she left to her daughter Sarah, who was married to George Farrar, a house, shop and warehouse at Upper Bridge, which were occupied by Joshua Earnshaw and Ely Roberts.

Unfortunately, the number of employees at the mill is unknown, but in 1832 Peter Beardsell recorded in his diary on 11 June: 'Hinchliffe's of New Fold have notice to advance the wages of their workpeople or else a strike is anticipated'. The mill remained in the Hinchliffe family, and by 1841 is shown as having a boiler and steam engine, scribbling and carding engines, in addition to the stove. In the same year George Hinchliffe also took over two dwelling houses, a cottage, press shop, with stable, outbuildings, conveniences and a yard, all in New Fold, also a building nearby that was used as a warehouse, and half of Mod Barn.

William Sandford, a cousin of Jonathon Sandford who had drowned in the flood at Dyson's mill, started his business at New Fold mill in 1852; the firm moved from here to Underbank mill some two years later. There was an incident at the mill in 1857, shortly before the factory was due to close on Monday 30 March, two powerloom weavers working inside the mill were injured by someone shooting through a window into the mill. A workman said that he was attempting to shoot a rat, but the sun was low in the sky and the light so strong that he was unable to aim the gun accurately. One of the weavers sustained serious injuries. A similar incident had previously occurred at Washpit mill.

In 1861 George Thorpe, who had been using at least part of the mill, was bankrupt. It is possible that Thorpe had not been in business very long, as the notice of sale of his machinery lists only 6 power looms with healds, slays, shuttles etc, 1 piecing machine (almost new), warping woofs and creels, burling tables, weigh scales and weights, 4 bags of wool and 4,000lbs of slubbings. The scribbling carding and spinning machinery, on which Thorpe used his piecing machine, were probably part of the mill's fixtures. This assumption is, to some extent, bourn out in June 1869 when 'Room & Power' was advertised as being to let along with scribbling machinery.

Ten years later, the *Huddersfield Chronicle* reported what it described as 'a rather amusing incident' that occurred on the afternoon of Whit Monday:

> *"Some witty wags bent on mischief, gathered a lot of old rubbish and piled it behind New Fold mill. After igniting, it sent up a cloud of smoke and appeared as though the mill was on fire. The fire bell was rung and a buzzer blown, but fortunately it was found to be a joke, and was evidently perpetrated for the purpose of testing the abilities of the various brigades, but it was rather too bad to raise the alarm while the members of the brigades were in the middle of a jolly good dinner".*

The term 'witty wags' suggest that the fire raisers were a group of young people trying to create a spectacle for their amusement; would the attitude of 'the authorities' of today portray the same tolerance?

By 1873 Charles and William Bashforth were using the mill, having moved from Bottoms mill, they had about 30 employees; a fire was discovered around midnight in the stove on Friday November 14th, where some scoured wool was burning. Attempts to extinguish the flames with buckets of water failed, and the alarm was raised. The Unity brigade arrived and put out the fire; Bridge mill brigade also turned out, but were not needed. Damage was estimated at between £40 and £50.

A serious accident occurred at the mill around Christmas 1854:

> *Fanny Hinchliffe, a feeder working for Bashforth Bros. was found 'quite dead' with her head trapped between the fast pulley and the frame of the scribbling engine. It was thought that she had gone to disengage the drive to the machine when the mill engine stopped at 12.30pm and had tripped, hitting her head and dislocating her neck as she fell. She was found by John Shore the engine tenter about 1pm, who lifted her away from the machine and sent for Mr. Berry the surgeon, who was unable to revive her. Her husband James Hinchliffe of Hey Gap also worked at the mill as a fettler, he was so overcome with grief that he had to be assisted home. The inquest jury returned a verdict of 'accidentally injured by falling with her head between the frame and main pulley of the machine'.*

Bashforth's had another fire in a teazing shed on 26 March 1883, which started by spontaneous combustion. The Unity brigade and the brigade from Turner's of Bridge mill both attended and put out the fire. Damage was estimated at about £400. The Bashforth brothers were still occupying the mill in 1884, when the buildings were offered for sale, which were described as:

> *Lot 1: 4 and 5 storey mills, with a boiler house, chimney, engine house, smithy, teazing house, and a warehouse over the warp-drying room. A 3 storey building adjoining the road to Damhouse used for warehousing and spinning. Together with steam engine, steam boiler, 2 reservoirs, main shafting and gearing; steam, water and gas piping; also 2 cottages with wool room over. Lot 2, 3 storey building adjacent to the mill, formerly 3 cottages, now occupied as a paint shop, wagon place and store room. 2 cottages in the mill yard plus a reservoir.*

C. & W. Bashforth appear to have left the mill before 1891, when George Lawton Son & Hoyle were using the premises, they gave their 50 workers a treat at the Elephant & Castle Inn in December, to celebrate the marriage of Mr. Fred Lawton. Lawton, Son & Hoyle were bankrupt in 1896, they had debts of £3,688 8s 4d, and assets of £2,660 2s 8d, leaving a deficit of £1,028 3s 8d. Creditors agreed to accept 12s 6d in the £.

The premises do not appear to have been used for manufacturing cloth from that time, as both the 1906 and 1931 Ordinance Survey maps mark the buildings as 'disused'. Mr. William Butterworth was the owner of the mill in 1904, when he applied to Holmfirth Council to convert part of the mill into 4 houses, which was passed. He made another application in 1906 to convert another part of the mill into 8 cottages, which was refused on three counts, one of which was that there was no damp proof course.

The body of an unknown man was found floating in the mill dam on Sunday 14 July 1907. The police discovered that a man calling himself Fred Brierley had registered and paid for a bed eleven days earlier at Mr. Gibson's lodging house in New Fold; he had then gone out and had not returned. Descriptions of the man were circulated in newspapers, and two women from Halifax identified him as their brother and brother-in-law Fred Brierley an iron fettler, who had led a rambling life for some time. The inquest jury returned a verdict of 'found drowned'.

In July 1915 the *Holmfirth Express* reported that Messrs Batley, Mettrick and Wakefield, a firm of Joiners, had moved premises from Ribbleden Road to New Fold Mill, this should have read Bailey Mettrick and Wakefield, who were moving from Ribbleden mill as the buildings there were all up for auction. In 1928, Messrs. Bailey and Wakefield were dissolving their partnership, and the premises were being offered for sale. The property included the mill building, office, garage, outbuildings, vacant land and a small dam, and was sold for £505. The joinery plant was sold one month later.[20] They were possibly bought by Mr. Bailey, who, in addition to his joinery business also built Holmfirth's first swimming pool, the Lido, on the site.

Small buildings in the area used for textiles

The Wakefield Court Roll of 7 November 1767 records that David and Matthew Hampshire borrowed £250 from James Thornton, corn miller of Honley on the Dwelling House and cottage at Upperthong with the **dyehouse,** barn, outhouses and garden, plus some 20 acres of land; at 4½ per cent interest per year. They repaid the £250 in February 1772 to James Thornton's executor Benjamin Thornton.

James Horncastle's Weaving shop and Warehouse is recorded in the Upperthong Rate Valuation list of 1843. It was in Upperthong Lane close to Chapel Lane, and was possibly the building that now houses numbers 54 to 58 Upperthong Lane. This was presumably the same James Horncastle who was in partnership with Hinchliffe's at Swan Bank mill.

Parkhead Textiles were at 2a Woodhead Road, Holmfirth, in the 1950s and, at least the early 1960s. This is a brick-built single storey building between Woodhead road and Parkhead road. The company were commission weavers, and from the information in the 1962 Yorkshire Textile Trade directory they had six Dobcross WP 4 x 4 looms.

Benjamin Butterworth's Dyehouse and Warehouse: An entry in the Wakefield Court Roll dated 19 November 1736 shows that there was a Messuage with a dyehouse at 'Over Bridge' in Holmfirth, that was sold by James Holesworth of Woolley to Abraham Wood head of Nether Thongue for £160. A dyehouse and warehouse is also recorded in the Upperthong Rate Valuation of 1843, and was in the Upper Bridge area. There was a dyehouse, house, cottage, and possibly a second house where Benjamin's son Joseph lived; also a separate warehouse and barn. They stood between Huddersfield Road and what is now Victoria Park, around where numbers 33 and 33a Huddersfield Road now stand. Most, if not all, of the original buildings have disappeared, but there is one building that was possibly the warehouse or barn still standing behind and to the left of number 33. George Sykes, who recorded his memories at various times in the *Holmfirth Express* started work there in 1849 at the age of ten. He wrote that Butterworth's had wool carded and spun at Hinchliffe Mill mill, which was then presumably woven by handloom weavers working at home. The Wakefield Court Roll suggests, in June 1825, that these properties contained a former brew-house.

Benjamin Earnshaw had a **Raising Shop** and cowhouse at Goose Green in October 1826. Twenty years later, after Benjamin's death, the Court Roll recorded that the building at Goose Green used as a raising shop and cowhouse with 668sq.yds, of land and a close of land called the Croft, also the newly erected dwelling house built by Benjamin and his eldest son John, were passed to John Earnshaw.

Cooper Lane Dyehouse, was also listed in the 1843 Upperthong Rate Valuation. It was about mid-way up Cooper Lane on the right hand side. The plan that accompanies the valuation shows a building beside the road, with a collection of buildings behind. There was a house, a stove and a barn in addition to the dyehouse, all of which were owned and occupied by Ely Wimpenny. The *Wakefield Court Roll* dated 6 August 1847 records that Ely Wimpenny passed the dwelling house, warehouse, dyehouse, stove, barn, stable, garden and yard at Hill, to Joseph Battye of Armitage [Bridge?], Robert Butterworth of Huddersfield, Thomas Iveson of Holmfirth and John Carter of Upperthong.

Also in 1843 at **Hill** there was a house, warehouse, dressing shop and barn, which were owned by Moses Hadfield, but were occupied and used by Sarah Hoyle.

Nab Dyehouse, The Wakefield Court Roll for 1836 records that on 1 June in that year, George Haigh merchant, of Nab, bought from Joseph Moorhouse a bankrupt of Cartworth, via Thomas Motley a woolstapler of Leeds, to whom Moorhouse probably owed money, a dwelling house with barn and stable, and a cottage lately used as a dyehouse. The entry does not record how much Haigh actually paid. An advertisement appeared in the *Huddersfield Examiner* in July 1889, advertising the dyehouse 'to let'; there were also several advertisements for the property in the *Holmfirth Express* between August and October of that year, anyone interested in renting the dyehouse should contact Arthur Preston of Holmfirth. The location of the dyehouse was in the fields below the school at Nab, it is possible to see the area in the field where it formerly stood.

The Wakefield Court Roll for 1824 records a **Dyehouse** on Norwith [Norridge] or Cuttell Bottom in Holmfirth on 409sq.yds. of land next to 6 dwelling houses. The dyehouse was occupied by William Dickinson and Andrew Sanderson; Sanderson bought two one-third shares in the property at £180 each, Dickinson presumably held the other share.

Holmfirth Mending Co. occupied premises at Lane End in the 1950s employing menders in the premises as well as out-menders; they were there until 1969, when the name was changed to Riverside Mending Co. who also had premises in Brockholes in 1966-7; subsequently the name changed to Scarwood Mending Co; whose headquarters were in Milnsbridge.

Notes

1   Bottoms mill
    W.C.R. 4 June, 1828; Diary of Peter Beardsell of Holme, 20 June, 1832; Supplementary Report into the Employment of Children in Factories and as to the Propriety and Means of Curtailing the Hours of their Labour, Part 1; (25 March 1834); W.C.R. 1 June, 1836; Holmfirth Express, 30 April, 1892; Kirklees Archive, T/H/F/36 claims nos. 275, 285, and 296, KC6/1/33; Huddersfield Chronicle, 18 April, 1857; 23 July, 13 Aug. 1859; 12 Jan. 1861; 12 May, 1866.

2   Huddersfield Examiner, 25 July, 1878; Census material supplied by Mr. P. Sandford; Huddersfield Examiner, 20 Dec. 1873, 3 Jan. 1874; J. Mayhall, History of Yorkshire, Vol. 3, p.604, also Huddersfield Examiner, 10 Jan. 1874; Kirklees Archive, KMT2/1/1, 31 Oct. 1876; Huddersfield Examiner, 26 Oct.1878; Holmfirth Express, 31 Dec. 1887, 9 Feb. 1889, Jan. 1891; Hudds Ex.10 Oct. 1891, 23 Jan. 1892; Textile Manufacturer, 30 Jan. 1892; H'firth Exp.6 Feb. 1892; 27 Feb. 1892; Kirklees Archive KC6/8/46; Hudds. Ex. 21 Oct. 1899; Kirklees Archive, KC6/8/43.

3   Holmfirth Express, 11 Feb. 1911, 1 Nov. 1913, also 16 Nov. 1929; Hudds. Ex. 15 Nov. 1913; 3 Sept.1938; H'firth Exp. 10 and 17 June, 1944; , 26 July 1958; Feb. 1959; 27 June, 1959; 23 Oct. 1981.

4   Black Sike mill
    W.C.R. 23 May 1792; 6 Nov. 1795; 5 Oct. 1796; Deeds Registry, R.D.E. 623:943 dated 1800; H'firth Exp. 14 May 1932; Hudds. Ex. 25 Feb, 1 Apr. 1854; Hudds. Chron. 15 Oct. 1864; Hudds. Ex.8 Jan. 1870; 27 May 1871; 6 Jan 1872; Textile Manfr. June 1894, London Gazette, 23 May 1894; Hudds Ex. 12 July 1873, 24 Jan. 1874.

5   Burnlee/Bottoms Dyehouse
    Leeds Mercury 21 Oct. 1848, Hudds. Chron. 17 May 1851; Hudds. Ex. 24 Dec. 1887; W.C.R. 28 Jan. 1842.

6   Spring Lane Mill
    Kirklees Archive, WYK1103/11/1/1; W.C.R. 15 March 1839; Hudds. Ex. 5 Feb, 5 Mar, 30 April 1853; 11 Nov. 1854; Hudds. Chron. 7 Oct. 1854; 12 Jan. 1856; 4 Oct. 1856; 28 Aug. 1857; 4 Sept. 1858; 29 Aug. 1863; 30 Jan. 1864; 19 Nov. 1864; Hudds. Ex.11 Nov. 1865; 7 April, 7 July 1866; 6 Oct. 1866; 13 Mar. 1869; 10 Sept.1870; Hudds. Chron. 19 Nov. 1870; Upperthong Local Board minutes, 18 Oct. 1872.

7   Hudds. Ex. 7 Aug. 1875; 29 Jan. 1876; 20 July 1878; and copy of sale catalogue from Roberts family papers; Upperthong Local Board, 9 Dec. 1881; Hudds. Ex.10 Oct. 1885; Kirklees Archive, KMT/4, 19 October, 1885; Hudds. Ex.5 Feb, 24 Dec. 1887; H'firth Exp.5 Apr. 1890; Hudds. Ex. 16 May, 1891; 19 Nov. 1892; H'firth Exp.29 Jan. 1911; Kirklees Archive, UHO 7 March 1924, and 1 April 1925.

8   Information gathered from Holmfirth Express, Council minutes, etc throughout the period.

9   Hudds. Ex.4 May 1935; Kirklees Archive, UHO 15 Apr. 1959; Information gathered from 'Situations Vacant' columns in the Holmfirth Express; Anecdotal evidence from Mr. Sylvester; H'firth Exp. 25 Oct. 1991.

10 Round Bottom/Riverside Mill
    Hudds. Chron. 12 Oct. 1867; Hudds. Ex. 22 June 1878, 15 July 1879; 5 Feb. 1881; 18 March 1882; 1 May, 1886; also 28 July 1888; also 18 Aug. 1888, and 27 July, 1889; H'firth Exp. 9 Dec. 1889; Hudds. Ex.21 Nov. 1891; 20 Feb 1892; Textile Manufacturer, 26 Feb. 1892; Holmfirth Express, 19 March 1892; 5 Mar, 1894; 11 Dec. 1897

11 Textile Manufacturer, July 1898; H'firth Exp.29 April 1899; 9 Sept. 1899; 4 July 1900; Holmfirth UDC minutes 1907, Yorks. Textile Diry 1910; also 1941, Kirklees Archive, KMT4 Holmfirth, 1940-43, Holmfirth Express 10 June 1944; Anecdotal evidence from Mr. P. Dixon of Wm. Sykes & Co.

12 Parkhead Dyehouse/Mill
    W.C.R. 8 Nov. 1826; 1 June 1831; Kirklees Archive, WYK1103/11/1/1; W.C.R. 11 Oct. 1844; Kirklees Archive, UHO Upperthong, 29 November 1867; Hudds.Ex.9 and 16 March, 1878.

13 Victoria Mill, Holmfirth
    J.M. Hinchliffe 1973, also NMRC documents 1985; Leeds Mercury, 21 Oct. 1848; Hudds. Chron. 17 May 1851; 7 Feb. 1852; Kirklees Archive, T/H/F/36 claims no's 12 and 346; Textile Manufacturer, Feb. 1878; Hudds. Ex. 9 Mar. 1878; H'firth Exp. 16 April 1892; 21 Oct. 1893; 22 Oct. 2 May 1920; 4 Oct. 1924; 1 April 1933; Kirklees Archive, Holmfirth Council records of flood, June 1944; UHO 16 Dec. 1959; 18 Feb. 1961; 16 Nov. 1966; H'firth Exp. 6 Dec. 1969; 25 May 1974, and 14 Oct. 1994.

14 Dyson's/Perseverance mill
    W.C.R. 20 Sept. 1751; 28 May 1788; 7 Oct. 1795; 15 March 1816; 4 Jan. 1822, 15 Feb. 1822; 5 Oct. 1827; Kirklees Archive KC6/8/7 7 July 1827; Supplementary Report into the Employment of Children in Factories and as to the Propriety and Means of Curtailing the Hours of their Labour, Part 1; (25 March 1834); Leeds Times, 27 July 1844; Hudds.Chron.7 Feb. 1852, Kirklees Archive T/H/F/36 claim no. 345; Kirklees Archive, KC6/1/33; also Roberts' family papers, 28 June, 1853; J.M. Hinchliffe,1973; Hudds.Ex. 28 Aug. and 4 Sept. 1886.

15   H'firth Exp.21 June, 1893, Kirklees Archive, KC6/8/7 1895; KC6/8/7 also UHO 13 Sept. 1906; H'firth Exp. 8 May, 1913; Yorks. Fact. Times, 19 Feb. 1914; H'firth Exp.10 June, 1944; 12 Feb. 1949, and 1966; Kirklees Archive, UHO H'firth Council minutes 1951 to 1966; H'firth Exp. 4 Jan. 1964; 16 Jan. 1976; 21 Dec. 1979, 11 April 1980; 24 Sept. 1982, 10 Oct. 1984, 11 Jan. 1985, 21 Feb. 1986, 15 Aug. and 29 Aug. 1986; 14 Aug 1987, and 24 July 1992; 29 April 1995.

16   Batty's/Farrars Upper and Lower mills.
      W.C.R. 19 April, 1665; 1 June 1739; 9 Oct. 1745; 20 Sept. 1751; H.J. Morehouse, pp. 228-9; W.C.R. 23May 1792; 7 Oct. 1795; 5 Sept. 1800; 18 Oct. 1805; 29 Oct. 1806; 11 Sept. 1807; 2 June 1809; 20 Sept. 1811; 2 June 1813; 10 April 1818; 3 June 1829; 20 Aug. 1830; 27 May 1831; Kirklees Archive, WYK1103/11/1/1, 1831; Supplementary Report into the Employment of Children in Factories, Part 1; (25 March 1834); W.C.R. 21 May 1837; 26 Aug. 1842; Leeds Mercury, 4 Feb. 1843; Kirklees Archive, KC6/1/33.

17   Kirklees Archive T/H/F/36 claims no 258 and 341; T/H/F/45 claims no 104 and 144; KC6/1/33; Hudds.Chron, 24 June, 5 Aug. 1854; 8 Sept. 1855; 24 Jan. 31 Oct. 1857; 31 July 1858; 1 Oct. 1859; 23 Sept 1865; 24 Apr. 1869; 5 Feb. 1859; Hudds.Ex. 23 Feb. 1861; 17 Nov. 1866; Hudds. Chron. 24 Nov. 1866; Hand bill in Roberts family papers; Upperthong Local Board minutes, 18 Oct. 1872; Hudds. Ex. 1 May 1880; H & S Butterworth Centenary booklet. 1952; Wm. Whiteley & Sons 1877 price list in Roberts family papers;

18   Hudds. Ex. 21 March 1874; 24 Sept. 1881; 29 May, 1886; H'firth Exp. Jan. 1888, and 5 July 1890; 25 Jan. 1890; Hudds. Ex.3 and 10 Oct. 1891; Yorks. Fact. Times, 20 June, 11 July, 10 Oct., 21 Nov. 1890; H'firth Exp. 5 July 1890; 7 Feb. 31 Oct.1891; Hudds. Ex.7 Jan. 1893; 11 June 1898; H'firth Exp. 25 Jan.1919.

19   Kirklees Archive, KMT4 6 Dec. 1897, UHO 1919; 10 July 1957, 10 May 1961; H'firth Exp. 15 Jan. 1910; Holmfirth UDC Flood report, 1944; H'firth Exp. 1967; 17 June, 1944; 9 Feb. 1946; 22 July 1950; 19 Oct. 1963; 15 April 1966, and 1968 passim; 19 June 1971, and 22 April 1983; 13 Feb. 1987, Apr/May 1992, 5 May 1995, 17 Apr. 1998; 14 Aug. 1998, also 19 May, 2000; 21 July 2000.

20   New Fold Mill
      W.C.R. 6 March 1784; 18 Jan. 1782; 29 Aug. 1788; 2 Nov. 1825; 15 Jan. also 9 April, 1841; Wm. Sandford & Son Ltd. centenary booklet 1954; Hudds. Chron. 4 April 1857; 19 Oct. 1861; 5 June 1869; 3 June 1871; Hudds. Ex. 5 Feb. also 22 Nov. 1873; 2 Jan. 1875; 21 June 1884; H'firth Exp. 5 Dec. 1891; 8 Feb. 1896; Kirklees Archive, KMT4/UHO 18 Feb. 1904, 18 Jan. 1906; H'firth Exp. 20 July 1907; 31 July 1915; 20 Oct. 1928

CHAPTER 10

Holme Styes to Holmfirth

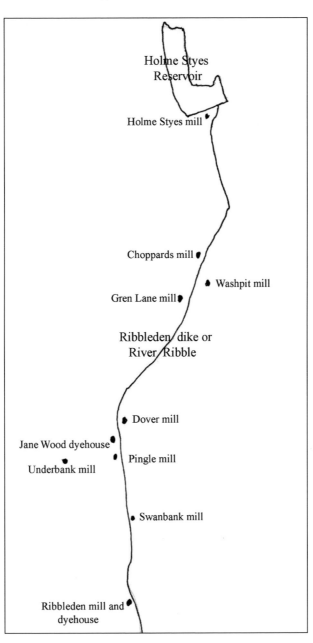

Holme Styes Reservoir

Holme Styes mill

Choppards mill

Washpit mill

Gren Lane mill

Ribbleden dike or
River Ribble

Dover mill

Jane Wood dyehouse

Pingle mill

Underbank mill

Swanbank mill

Ribbleden mill and
dyehouse

Holme Styes Mill

In January 1791 the Wakefield Court Roll recorded that:

> John Greensmith clothier of Copthurst, John Batty fulling miller of Hinchliffe mill, Ely Hinchliffe clothier of Arrunden and Joseph Marsden clothier of Cartworth, took from Humphrey Kaye clothier and Elizabeth his wife, of Copthurst, and Thomas Littlewood yeoman of Damhouse, firstly, the Little Close in Wooldale by estimation 1 rood, now in the occupation of the purchasers; secondly, a parcel of land by estimation 1 acre, marked and staked out at the bottom of Round Close Wood in Cartworth, now in the occupation of the purchasers; thirdly, a stream of water dividing the said close and parcel of land; fourthly, liberties for the purchasers to get stone and other materials in a close owned by Kaye called Round Close; to take, lead and carry the same in the winter season only, with wagons, wains, carts or other carriages to the premises, to build a mill and dwelling house without making satisfaction, and also to take into the stream another stream known as Holme Styes Dike in such a manner as they see fit.

The mill was built that year, whether the four men who built it all worked there is not known, but in 1808 Ely Hinchliffe left his quarter share in the mill to his trustees who were Ely Hobson of Holme Roy Nook Honley, Joseph Mellor of Holmfirth, and John Batty of Hincliffe mill, with instructions to sell his interest in the mill as soon as possible after his death; Ely Hinchliffe possibly saw the mill as a bad investment. The next information on the mill comes in 1828, when it is described as a former Scribbling mill. This was just before the time that the three reservoirs Bilberry, Bowshaw and Holme Styes were being constructed; and as the mill was on the small area of flat land in front of what became the Holme Styes embankment, virtually where the former filter house now stands; working the mill while the reservoir was being built immediately behind it would have been almost impossible.

Isaac Parker Newton paid £48 to Ely Hobson, trustee of Ely Hinchliffe, for Hinchliffe's quarter share in the former scribbling mill in September 1828, which he sold one month later to Jonathon, George and William Battye of Brown Hill, along with a quantity of land at Brown Hill, for a total of £293 5s. The person who would benefit from the transaction was James Battye.

In 1851, Arthur Blencoe Newton of Stagwood Hill sold the mill to Joshua Barber of Cartworth Moor for the sum of £100. It was described as being in the townships of Wooldale and Cartworth, and was a former scribbling mill, implying that it was disused at the time. The mill had a wheel-race, and in addition, in order to increase the amount of water getting to the wheel, a goit had been marked out from the bottom of the reservoir by-wash to the mill.[1] The mill is shown on the 6 inch O.S. map of 1853 as an 'L'-shaped building at the foot of the reservoir embankment, but is not marked being as a mill. The majority of Joshua Barber's manufacturing was carried out at Bottoms mill, where he also had a warehouse that was destroyed by fire in 1868; the firm was found to be insolvent in 1873 and was wound up. The mill was offered for sale in December 1873, but there is no indication that it was ever used again.

Choppards Mill

Built on the outskirts of the hamlet of Choppards, probably in the first decade of the nineteenth century, the owners of the mill in 1811 were the Brook and Moorhouse families; James Brook, eldest son of Jonathon Brook deceased, passed 4 shares in the Fulling and Scribbling mill with the water wheel, dyehouse, stove, reservoir, mill dam, mill race and mill race bank at Choppards to Joshua Brook. James also passed 2 shares each to the other occupants of the mill, Thomas and John Moorhouse. The number of owner occupiers of the property had increased to six in 1818, with John, James and Joshua Brook, also Thomas, James and John Moorhouse, all holding equal shares in the mill.

James Brook was short of money in 1824, he pledged a one-sixth share of the mill to Thomas, James and Joseph Motley, woolstaplers of Leeds for £350, and a second one-sixth share of the mill to Thomas Motley for the same amount. The Brook's also sold their house in Choppards for £800. James Brook was declared bankrupt in June 1825, which had a disastrous effect on the value of the mill; in September 1828 Henry Tudor of Huddersfield sold a fifteenth part of the mill to Thomas Moorhouse of Hebson House Fulstone for just 10 shillings, which effectively valued the whole property at £7 10s. The occupants of the mill at that time were Thomas, George and John Moorhouse, and the assignees of the bankrupt James Brook. The value of the mill and business had started to recover by 1830 when Mary Moorhouse bought a sixteenth part in the mill for £20, which valued the whole at £320. The James Brook who had become bankrupt had died by 1834; the three Motley brothers of Leeds who had bought one third of the mill in 1824 for a total of £700, sold their holding for a mere £300 to a Thomas [blank] from Barnsley in 1835.

The main part of the mill building was about 45 feet long by 15 feet wide, and three storeys high; the Moorhouse family were still occupying the premises in 1838, when they decided that more space was needed and were in the process of adding an extra storey when, due to the weight of stone placed on the upper floor by the builders, it gave way depositing stone and wood on the floor below. Fortunately, this floor was stronger and held in place, otherwise the whole lot would have fallen onto the mill engine on the ground floor. A man who was working on the upper floor when it collapsed managed to avoid injury by clinging to the wall until he could be rescued.

Tom Moorhouse & Co. continued to occupy the mill until Tom Moorhouse's death around 1850, when the Haigh family took over. In 1853 the Holme Reservoir Commissioners list the owners of Choppards mill as: Thomas Haigh, Samuel Haigh, and Jonathon Moorhouse, trustees of Thomas Moorhouse deceased; [blank] Moorhouse and Jonathon Saxton, trustees of Daniel Moorhouse deceased; John Moorhouse; Joshua Brook and his wife Lydia; Abraham Taylor and his wife Martha; Jonathon Mellor and his wife Catherine; Elizabeth Thorpe; Thomas Whitehead and Elizabeth Whitehead, children of Sarah Whitehead deceased. The occupier of the mill was Benjamin Haigh. The mill along with a dyehouse, stove and warehouse, were advertised to let in December 1855, complete with machinery for scribbling, carding and spinning wool, also fulling stocks. The occupant was still Benjamin Haigh. By 1857 Haigh had decided to leave the district and consequently advertised his furniture and farm stock at Arrunden, and the machinery in Choppards mill to be sold by auction on February 4th and 5th. Much of the machinery in the mill belonged to the owners of the building and was leased to the occupier at an annual rent, the machinery that was for sale consisted of: 5 broad looms and gearing, 2 warping woofs with creels and broitches, an iron stove and piping, winding-on and sizing raddles, skeps, shuttles, healds, dyewares and other sundries.

The mill was taken over towards the end of 1856 by the Choppards Mill Company, which was possibly Ely Wimpenny of Burnlee. At the quarterly meeting of the Reservoir Commissioners in December 1856 the Choppards Mill Company asked for an abatement of the water rate for the period 29 September to 27 November when the water wheel had not been in use; suggesting that Benjamin Haigh had ceased production in late September, and the new occupants moved into the mill in late November. The Commissioners agreed to allow a reduction of one sixth of the annual rate.

A fire was discovered at the mill about 7am on Wednesday the 27th of May 1857, when a bale containing about 100lbs of cotton fibre caught fire. The bale was quickly dragged outside by workpeople, and the fire put out. Business does not appear to have gone well for Mr. Wimpenny, as the mill was advertised 'to let' for a term of years or from year to year in December 1861, and would be ready for the new tenant in 'a few weeks'. It was described as a Fulling and Scribbling mill, with a 42ft diameter water wheel 6ft wide, steam engine and boiler, 4 fulling stocks, a washing machine, 5 scribblers, 4 carders, 4 billies, willey, 3 prs. of mules, together with the dyehouse and fittings, stoves, cottages and other connected buildings. There is no mention of the amount of rent required; prospective tenants had to apply to George Tinker & Son, Auctioneers, for those details. The mill does not appear to have been let, as it was advertised again in December 1862.

The next tenant was Charles Cromack, who was using at least part of the mill by July 1863;

another tenant was B. Bray & Son, who had assigned their goods to creditors in March 1865, when their machinery was advertised for sale by auction. The property was advertised for sale by private treaty, rather than by auction, in June 1866, when the tenant was still Charles Cromack; and was advertised to let in December of that year.

A sale of machinery was advertised to take place on 9 June 1869, under distraint for rent, but the owner of the machinery is not given. This was followed by an advertisement for a much larger sale of machinery in February 1872, when again, the vendor is not given. William Sykes & Son auctioned the mill on 6 May 1896, when it was described as the mill, dyehouse, cottage and land, with engine, boilers, shafting, gearing, and water wheel; and the first mill below Holme Styes reservoir. It was sold for the sum of £500; the buyer was Mr. H. B. Sykes from the auctioneers, who was acting as the agent for an unnamed buyer.[2] It is possible that the unnamed buyer was Jas. Watkinson & Son, who eventually acquired the mill and demolished it. They used the place where it formerly stood for depositing ashes from the boilers at Washpit.

In addition to the mill, there were two other sets of premises in Choppards that were used for textiles, both of them had connections to the Brook family; the first was a **Raising and Dressing shop** which, in 1826, was occupied by Joshua and Jonathon Brook, there were also at least 3 cottages with a garden and outbuildings, where Joshua and Jonathon, along with their brother Benjamin all lived; also two former cottages that were being used as a warehouse. The raising and dressing shop is described as 'newly erected', along with a barn, mistal and outbuildings, and a cottage that was attached to the barn. There were also several closes of land. Samuel Walker of Golcar paid £1,000 to Jonathon Brook and Elizabeth his wife in 1827 for all the land and buildings mentioned here; whether he was buying the property or providing Jonathon with a mortgage is not stated.

The second premises are two buildings in Choppards used as a **Pressing shop and a Dressing shop**. These had formerly been in the possession of James Brook, but in 1826 were being used by Benjamin Brook, when George Charlesworth of Gully, William Boothroyd of Goose Green, and George Hinchliffe of Cartworth, who were masters and wardens of The Old Sick Club in Holmfirth provided a mortgage of £200 on the two buildings used as a pressing shop and a dressing shop and warehouse, with a small building adjoining used as a coal-place; there were also 2 parcels of land included. John Brook of Lindley and William Shaw of Botham Hall, repaid the mortgage to the Holmfirth Old Sick Club in 1829, and also paid £30 to Benjamin Brook for the land and premises previously mentioned.[3] The precise location of either of these properties is not known.

Washpit Mill

Joseph and George Hinchliff told the Factory Commission Enquiry in 1833 that the mill had been built in July and August 1822, with an additional part being added in 1827. The original mill was built on the right bank of the stream, in Wooldale township, but later in its development buildings were erected in Cartworth township as well. Although there was a plentiful supply of water from Higgin dike or the River Ribble as it became known, it seems that the original mill did not have a water wheel as the Hinchliff's told the enquiry that the mill had only steam power supplied by a 6hp steam engine. They also said that the mill was engaged in 'making woollen in all its branches', which meant that they were taking raw wool and processing it into spun yarn, as, at the time, they had neither looms nor fulling stocks at the mill. In common with many other mills at that time they were possibly engaged in what was known as 'country work', that is processing loose wool into yarn on behalf of the local self-employed weavers. They employed 72 people; there were 2 boys and 2 girls under 10, each earning 4s per week; 5 boys and 3 girls under 12, each earning 6s; 3 boys and 3 girls under 14 earning 7s; 4 boys under 16 earning 8s; 4 boys under 18 earning 10s; 2 males under 21 earning 16s; and 44 men over 21 each earning £1 per week. About twenty of the children were reliant on the person for whom they worked for their wages. The working day was from 6am to 8pm throughout the year, with a total of 2 hours allowed for the three mealtimes, when the scribbling machines did not stop, but were attended by 14 year old boys who took it in turns to get their meals. The mill worked two hours less on Saturdays. In response to the question 'had they ever considered employing more than one set of children', they answered: "No, nor do we think it necessary for the hours of these children we employ, as they are all quite healthy and not distressed in doing it". Their answer to the question on having working hours regulated by Act of Parliament was: "If all the mills in the same business worked the same time as within stated, there could be no great evil in them; but have no objections to less time for the labour of children".

A four storey mill was added by 1840, which was approximately 70ft long by 54ft wide, it was described in the Wakefield Court Roll as: 'all that capital mill with water wheels, goits, dams etc. lately erected by Joseph Marsden and used as a fulling mill'. John Hinchliff manufacturer, of Cross, paid £2,000 to James Brook merchant, of Huddersfield for the whole mill. A second entry in the court roll some 3 months later records that Joseph Brook, Charles Brook, Benjamin Wilson and John Wilson paid £2,000 to John Hinchliff of Cross for some land and Washpit mill, which Hinchliff had enlarged, and was now used for scribbling and fulling.

The firm received royal recognition in 1846, when the mill foreman, James Hirst presented a three yard length of cloth to HRH Prince Albert; the Prince later wrote to thank the firm for the gift saying that he would wear it.

A fire broke out in the drying stove on 12 August 1848, when a 'considerable quantity' of wool was burned and some damage was done to the building. The fire was caused by the overheating of the flues from the boiler. The *Leeds Intelligencer* commented on the lack of a fire engine for the Holmfirth district.

In 1853 the Holme Reservoir Commissioners recorded that David Hinchliff, William Hinchliff and John Hichliff were the owners and occupiers of the mill. The partnership ended in 1854, when William and John Hinchliff left the firm, leaving David to single-handedly run the business. In common with many other manufacturers, W. & J. Hinchliff gave their workers a treat after the end of the Crimean war in 1856. The standard fare for men on these occasions was roast beef and plum pudding; whereas most reports say that the women 'had an excellent tea'; there is no indication of what they got, but obviously not roast beef and plum pudding.

The Hinchliff's were only using part of the mill in 1857, when they advertised that two third parts of the premises were available to rent; consisting of the four storey mill plus its attic, 22yds long by 16yds wide. A detached 2 storey willow house, dyehouse, wool and tenter stoves, warehouse, stables and sheds etc; and a dwelling house, cottages and 5 acres of land. The mill contained fulling stocks, carding and spinning machinery, with room for more machinery and power looms. Applications to be made to W. & J. Hinchliff at the mill; the advertisement gave no indication of the rent required. Confirmation that the Hinchliffe's were experiencing problems came in October 1857, when John Hinchliff, along with his family, emigrated to Australia. They were seen off at Holmfirth station by friends and former workers at the mill. William Hinchliff with his family followed John to Australia in February 1858.

The Hinchliff brothers appear to have mortgaged the mill with Mr. Charles Brooke of Healey House, who, in 1861 leased it to David and Sarah Ann Hinchliff of Marble Hall, but business was still difficult, as in 1863 the Reservoir Commissioners issued a warrant of distress against David and Sarah Ann for £22 7s of unpaid water rates for the mill.

A document in the archive of the West Yorkshire Archaeology Advisory Service in Wakefield, relating to Holmbridge mill, suggests that James Watkinson & Sons were using Washpit mill from 1862, but there seems to be no other substantiation of this. A sale of machinery was advertised in November 1865, but the vendor is not named. The reason given for the sale is that the mill had been let, and the machinery had to be cleared out.

In October 1866, Jonathon Charlesworth a slubber, charged John Howard engineer, with Assault. Howard had been dissatisfied with Charlesworth's work, ordered Charlesworth out of the mill and kicked him, which gave rise to the complaint. Mrs Charlesworth was in court and made some 'unbecoming remarks' to Howard; who replied in still more uncomplimentary language. Howard was fined 1s plus 16s 6d expenses.

Lumb and Thompson took space in the mill, but seem to have fared no better than the Hinchliffe's, as they also were in financial difficulties by 1868. Having assigned their assets, the creditors decided that they should be sold and a sale of machinery took place on 1 April, consisting of scribblers, carders, piecing machines, billies, spinning mules, warp drying balloon, 20 narrow power looms, 6 broad power looms, fulling stocks, and 7,000lbs of Mungo, waste and wool.

The mill was offered for sale in 1869, the description remaining identical to the previous one, except that a new water wheel had been fitted in 1868. It was also offered for sale in 1871, when it was possibly bought by James Watkinson, who were definitely in the mill by 1873. Day and Watkinson came into being in 1859, therefore it is possible that they were using this mill by 1862, but their place of business is not known; by 1864 the firm was known as Day, Watkinson & Company, but by 1875 the Day connection had ceased, and the firm became James Watkinson & Son.[4]

In March 1872 Watkinson's invited tenders for building a weaving shed, engine house, boiler house, willow house, tenter stove, and a long chimney. John Radcliffe & Sons, builders, appear to have submitted the successful estimate, and were in the process of building the mill chimney in August, John Pogson of Honley was using a rope and pulley to hoist stone up for his workmates when his left hand became caught between the rope and pulley severing two of his fingers at the middle joint. He was treated at Huddersfield Infirmary.

Forty of James Watkinson's power loom weavers went on strike on 14 April 1875, in protest at a woman being employed to weave one of the broad power looms. They refused to return to work until a man had been appointed to weave the loom; the problem was resolved and the weavers returned to work on the 22nd. A rather more serious strike by the weavers began in May 1876; Watkinson's had introduced a new cloth to their range with fewer picks per inch. Based on the weaving rates agreed between weavers and manufacturers in the district in 1874 the weavers of this cloth would have made a very good living from it. The firm suggested that the rate for weaving that cloth should be fixed at 27s per week, to which the weavers, supported by the Powerloom Weavers Association, would not agree and came out on strike. The *Huddersfield Weekly News* described it as 'a wealth wasting event'. After several weeks Watkinson's began employing other weavers, for which they were applauded by some and chided by others. The strike came to an end on 19 June, when Watkinson's agreed to the striker's demands that the new weavers should be laid off.

The firm gave a treat to their 140 workers in January 1878 at the Druids Hall in Holmfirth; Mr. T. B. Watkinson congratulated the workers on their prosperity throughout the past year, despite the bad state of trade prevalent at the time. Business continued to go well for Watkinson's, as they made several additions to the mill in the 1880s and 90s with a new dyehouse, a new boiler house and additional warehousing. The additional business meant that the workforce also increased to around 250 by 1888, and 300 or so by 1893. Watkinson's continued to expand and update the premises throughout their tenure.

Brook Hollingworth was working at the top of a building in August 1880, steadying a piece of timber that was being lifted into position by a crane, when he lost his balance and fell to the ground inside the building. He was badly injured, and was taken to his home in Cumberworth.

A fire started in one of the new warehouses on Sunday 30 January 1898, which was spotted by the engine tenter's wife. Her husband sounded the mill buzzer and then fixed the fire hydrants in position and connected the hoses ready for the mill's own fire brigade. The fire bell in Holmfirth church tower was rung and the Unity fire brigade arrived at the mill about 30 minutes later. The new warehouse was by now well ablaze, so efforts were concentrated on saving the old mill nearby, which was successful as only some of the windows in that building were damaged by the heat. After the collapse of the roof and floors of the new warehouse, the fire was brought under control; damage was estimated to be about £2,000. There was also a fire in one of the drying stoves on 27

March 1902, which was put out by the firm's own fire brigade; damage to the contents of the stove was estimated at £100.

The *Yorkshire Trade Directory* for 1910 lists James Watkinson & Sons Ltd. as having 5,700 spindles, and 140 looms, and points out that the company also had production space in Bridge Mills. It gives their production as 'mixed goods'; throughout the life of the company they produced woollen cloth, being one of the few companies in our district not to move almost entirely into worsteds. One of their principle areas of production was serges for military uniforms stemming from their production, in 1900, of the first wool-dyed khaki serge used by the British government. It was possibly increased business in this area, due to the First World War, that prompted the company to advertise for commission weavers in the *Holmfirth Express* in 1915. Mr. James Brook Watkinson died on 17 January 1922 at the age of 58, having been connected with the mill throughout his life.

Production continued to increase; by the early 1940s the spinning capacity had increased to 7,800 spindles, but the number of looms had fallen slightly to 130, probably due to the installation of modern faster looms that would produce more cloth in a shorter space of time.

Mr. Jeremy Kilner, a former Managing Director of the company, told me that the workforce prior to the Second World War was between 500 and 600, whereas when he joined the company in 1952 they employed 340 people; this was not due to a reduction in output, but was entirely due to improvements in machinery. Everything appeared to be going well until the 1970s when all mills were experiencing difficulties.

Early in 1980, James Watkinson & Sons Ltd. went into receivership; it was announced in May that the workforce was to be reduced from 230 to 102; and in early October it was announced that the company would close before Christmas, but that part of the mill had been bought by a 'secret buyer'. Two members of Watkinson's staff bought some assets from the receivers and started a new company called Beaumont & Coldwell, which used part of the mill for a number of years before moving to a unit in Armitage Bridge mills.

Westwood Yarns carpet yarn spinners, a division of Victoria Carpet Co. of Kidderminster, were

Washpit and Green Lane mills. © A.J. Brooke. – Green Lane mill is on the bottom right.

using part of the mill by 1988, they have since made alterations to the buildings, demolishing some of the older parts of the mill. There was a serious accident in 1989 when 33 year old Charles Kevin Allsop was removing an electric motor from a cloth tentering machine. He lost his balance and fell backwards onto the concrete floor. The electric motor that he was holding injured his chest. He was taken to the Huddersfield Infirmary, where he later died; the impact of the motor had ruptured his heart muscle. The inquest jury returned a verdict of accidental death.[5] Westwood Yarns made additions to the buildings in the 1990s, and were still in production in 2010.

Green Lane Mill

Built downsteam, and within a few hundred yards of Washpit mill, Green Lane predates Washpit, having been built in 1809 by James Haigh. In March 1822 James Haigh's sons Thomas, John and Webster, all of Dunsley in Cartworth, who worked at the mill, raised a mortgage of £800 on the mill and about 6¼ acres of land from John Scholefield of Horbury. This mortgage appears to have been taken over later in 1822 by Thomas Motley and Thomas Jowitt, both of Leeds who were both woolstaplers, plus George Farrar dyer, of Prickleden, and John Taylor clothier of Ward Place. In this entry in the court rolls the mill is referred to as Green Lane Bridge mill.

The mortgage was repaid with interest in 1839, when the shareholders in the mill were Mary Newton widow, of Woodhead Cheshire, Thomas Martin surgeon and Mary his wife of Holmfirth, James Brook and Elizabeth his wife of Choppards, Ann and Martha Haigh spinsters formerly of Dunsley but now of Holmfirth, and Thomas Haigh Martin surgeon of Holmfirth. Later in the year Thomas Haigh Martin bought a fifth part of the mill from James and Elizabeth Brook for £88.

The occupants of the mill in 1833 were Messrs Hinchliffe & Taylor, who told the Factory Commissioners that the mill was used for Scribbling, Carding and Slubbing, and had both steam and water power. The steam engine delivered 10hp whereas the water wheel delivered a maximum of 8hp; unlike the majority of mills in the area, they relied on steam power for 9 months of the year. They employed a total of 20 people, 4 boys and 1 girl under 12 earning 4s per week, 3 boys and 4 girls under 14 earning between 4s and 4s 6d, 2 girls under 16 earning 6s, 2 men over 21 earning 16s. They also employed 2 boys under 18, 1 boy under 21 and 1 man over 21 who were paid on piece rate, they each earned on average 18s per week. The exception was the mill manager who, for a 70 hour week earned between £2 and £2 5s. The hours of work were 6am to 8pm in summer, and 8am to 9pm in winter, on Saturdays they worked 2 hours less. Workers were allowed a total of two hours for meals, during which time the machinery was stopped.

In 1839 Richard Bower of Upperbridge, George Thewlis of Binns, and Robert Ramsden of Upperbridge all clothiers, trading as Bower & Co, leased Green Lane Bridge mill for a term of 13 years. The engineer at the mill in 1843 was Joseph Roebuck, a 14 year old boy named Edward Battye had gone to Roebuck on trial for an apprenticeship. Roebuck was convicted of repeatedly working the boy from 4am to 9.30pm without meal breaks; for which he was fined £6 11s.

The Reservoir Commissioners listed the owners of the mill in 1853 as Mary Newton, Ann Haigh, Martha Haigh, also William Day Martin and John Wiley who were trustees of Thomas Haigh Martin deceased. The occupants of the mill were Richard Bower, George Thewlis and Robert Ramsden.

Along with many of the other mills in the district Richard Bower & Co. gave their workers a treat after the declaration of peace in 1856. A 'Yarn Ready Reckoner' developed by John Bower was described in the *Huddersfield Examiner* as showing 'the length and weight of yarn required to run equally together for twisting, or any other purpose in every department of manufacturing'. There does not appear to be any information available to show how successful the ready reckoner was.

William Lockwood was putting a strap onto a machine on 6 September 1866, when his clothing became caught and he was drawn several times around the drum breaking one arm and injuring his leg, he also had internal injuries. He was taken to the Infirmary for treatment. A man named Brook, who was married with six children, was working as a beamer and sizer at the mill in 1867, he tripped over a rope that was laid on the floor and fell and broke his leg. He too was taken to Huddersfield Infirmary for treatment.

Richard Bower & Co. were still occupants of part of the mill throughout the 1860s, but were not finding business easy, as a liquidation sale of cloth was held on 3 February 1871, followed by the sale of wool, yarn and other items also in February.

Later in the year the mill, spinning factory and other buildings, along with the machinery was advertised as being to let for a maximum of 7 years, with or without the house and land. Application to be made to Mr. Kidd solicitor, of Holmfirth. The premises were advertised as being to let several times during the following year, until in September 1872 the mill was put up for auction as a fulling and scribbling mill, with the plantation, dam, weirs, goits and fall of water. It consisted of the Spinning mill 4 storeys high, boiler house with drying stove over, engine house, chimney, willey house with store room over, 2 storey warping place, with warehouse and other outbuildings. Machinery: water wheel, steam boiler, 14hp beam engine, shafting and going gear, willey, condenser sets, scribbler, carder and billey, 3prs mules, balloon and beaming frame, 6 broad power looms, 2 double fulling stocks, and other mill furnishings. Also dwelling house, outbuildings and stables, and several closes of land.

The mill appears to have been bought by Broadhead Bros. who were described as the owners and occupiers in 1874, when a fire broke out about 2am on Friday 18th September. It was not discovered until about one hour later, by which time it had taken a good hold. Neighbours began moving stock from the burning premises, but about 30 minutes after discovery of the fire the roof of the building collapsed; minutes later the Unity fire brigade arrived and concentrated on confining the fire to the old part of the building. The brigade from Bridge Mill arrived about 4am, and the combination of the two engines stopped the fire from spreading, but the old mill was completely burned out and the stock and machinery ruined. Damage was estimated at £2,000. The report of the fire said that patent 'extincteurs' kept on the premises had been used but 'were of little use'. This prompted a letter from Mr. T.B. Watkinson of Washpit mill, who pointed out that men from his mill had taken the extincteurs to Green Lane mill before the fire engines arrived and had succeeded in stopping the fire from spreading further. He wrote 'It is the opinion of those who were there that nothing would have saved the new part of the mill if the extincteurs had not been used'.

The mill was advertised for sale again in May 1875, by which time the damaged part had been rebuilt. There was another fire at the mill in November 1889, when the occupier was Joseph B. Wood, spinner; the fire started in a 'Fearnought' machine, the alarm at Washpit mill was sounded, and Watkinson's sent men to assist. Bales of yarn stored near the machine were removed, and hand hoses and buckets were used to quench the flames. The fire was put out in about twenty minutes. It was also reported that 'a few fire engines from Holmfirth were despatched and were on their way to the fire, but were not needed'. Joseph Wood died in 1891, his executors offered the mill and machinery, plus the house and land for sale as one lot in July of that year, but it was withdrawn due to lack of interest. Alfred Wood, possibly Joseph's son, had continued trading as J. Wood, but in November 1894 was declared bankrupt, and the mill and machinery were again advertised for sale by auction.

The mill was possibly bought by Jas. Watkinson & Sons in 1894 or 1895, as subsequent advertisements for the premises direct interested parties to apply to them for details. An example of this is an advertisement in the *Holmfirth Express* on 26 January 1895 describing the mill as: comparatively new, substantially built and well lighted. It will hold at least four sets of Scribbling and Carding machinery and Mules to follow, and has been run for the greater part of the year entirely by the water wheel, which is in very good condition. There is a good steam engine...and a first rate boiler will shortly be put in to replace the present one. There is now a Teazer, three sets of 60in. machines and mules to follow in the mill, and arrangements could be made respecting them. Plentiful supply of water. For further particulars apply to James Watkinson & Sons, next mill'.

There does not seem to have been a response to the advertisement, as more adverts appeared, particularly in 1898 and 1899. The *Yorkshire Textile Directory* for 1910 noted that J. Bower and Sons Ltd, who were also in Dover mill, were using the premises.

There is a suggestion that before the First World War, the mill's boiler exploded; the cost of repairing the damage was considered to be too great, and the mill was left empty; although there does not appear to be any documentary evidence to substantiate this. After it became empty, it was used by James Watkinson & Sons for storage of raw wool until 1979, when it was bought by Rowan Weavers, who made flat-weave floor rugs from surplus yarns bought from Upholstery cloth manufacturers; and also supplied weaving kits for craft enthusiasts to weave at home. In 1983 Rowan Weavers was renamed Rowan Yarns, when they began supplying yarns to British Designer Knitters, individual designers who then employed hand knitters to make garments for the worldwide bespoke market. Coats Crafts, whose headquarters were in Darlington, bought Rowan Yarns in 1995. In 2009, Coats Crafts moved their world headquarters from Darlington to Green Lane mill.[6]

Dover Mill

This mill was downstream from Green Lane mill, on the Cartworth side of the river. The date of its building is not known, but was possibly in the 1790s, or the very early years of the nineteenth Century. In 1815 Ruth Brook of Dover Mill paid £1,100 to Bethel Earnshaw Stag of Ramsgate Lodge Cumberland, for the dwelling house, fulling mill, barns and outbuildings, along with several closes of land called the Ing, the Round Brow, the Low Bottom, the first, second and third Mill Banks, the Potato Piece and the Wood. In the following year Ruth Brook raised a mortgage of £500 on the property from Cuthbert Metcalfe of Keighley.

In 1825 Emor Brook raised a second mortgage of £250 on the property from Richard Boothroyd innkeeper of Holmfirth. The second mortgage was taken over by Leonard Metcalfe of Keighley, Richard Metcalfe of Hawes, and John Clapham of Uttley near Keighley in 1828; the original mortgage of £500 was still held by Cuthbert Metcalfe; the occupants of the mill were at that time Emor Brook and Joseph Crosland. The premises became the subject of a dispute in the Chancery Court in 1836; the court ruled that the premises, now consisting of the fulling mill with 3 dwelling houses plus outbuildings and 8 acres of land, should be sold. The occupants of the mill were then Emor and James Brook. The mortgagee Cuthbert Metcalfe died in late 1836 or early 1837, after which his two daughters applied for a licence of heriot on the property to establish their claim.

The land and property were bought by Ebenezer Tinker of Bank House Meltham, and Thomas Dawson of Keighley, for a total of £1,180 2s in 1838; two years later it was sold to George Hinchliffe of Nabb for £1,410.

The Reservoir Commissioners recorded that the owner of the mill in 1853 was George Hinchliffe, and that the occupiers were George Hinchliffe and John Thorpe Taylor. J.T. Taylor had used part of the mill since 1851; he gave several 'treats' to his workers over a period of years. The first was a substantial supper to around 100 workpeople and friends on 4 March 1851; after the meal Mr. Taylor gave an eloquent speech in which he 'inculcated on all present the advantage of moral, mental and religious culture'. On 24 June 1854 Mr. Taylor gave a treat to 250 people at the mill to celebrate his recent marriage. After the meal everyone went to a specially erected marquee for an evening of 'mirth and merriment'. He also gave a treat to his workers on 31 May 1856, to celebrate peace having been declared in the Crimea.

The mill was offered for sale on 4 July 1866, when it was described as 'All that capacious and excellent Fulling and Scribbling mill situate at Dover; 4 storeys and attic 52' x 40' inside measure; water wheel house, miller's cottage, boiler and engine houses with drying stove over them, willow house, offices, warehouse, dyehouse 42' x 28' supplied by a never failing stream of pure water: together with the water wheel 34' diameter by 8'3" wide; 16hp steam engine and steam boiler, shafting, going gear and fixings. Also an excellent dwelling house currently occupied by Mr. Abraham Taylor; and 10 cottages in the mill yard. The mill does not appear to have been sold, as Mr. George Hinchliffe was still listed as the owner in 1868.

The mill was advertised 'to let' in November 1867 due to J.T. Taylor having moved to Ribbleden mill earlier in the year, the premises were as previously described, and had some machinery inside, which would be let with the mill. The advertisement emphasizes the purity of the water supply for dyeing and finishing, which suggests that this came from a separate stream than the river, which would be partially polluted by mills upstream. This is possibly the time when Bower's moved their operation from Green Lane mill to Dover.

The Cartworth land valuation book from 1859 to 1873 shows that in 1868 the mill was still owned by George Hinchliffe, also that another storey had been added and the attic improved; also a new warehouse had been recently built. The mill was advertised to let between June 1869 and March 1871, apparently without success, as it was then advertised to be sold by auction on 5 June 1872, along with the mill house which is described as being 'newly erected', and the ten nearby cottages. A spinner named John Beaumont was using part of the mill in 1873 when, in August, he filed a petition for bankruptcy with liabilities of £400. Some two months later his trustees advertised his machinery and other goods for sale, which was one pair of spinning mules with 440 spindles, and one mule with 220 spindles plus a quantity of waste yarn.

In 1885 Bower's were having some new machinery delivered made by Charles Lockwood of Penistone. The machines were transported in two trucks pulled by a Traction Engine; Joseph Wood, a 25 year old unmarried man was the stoker of the engine. After arriving at Dover mill, Wood was in the process of uncoupling the engine from the trucks to allow two horses to be attached to one of the trucks to pull it into position for unloading. Wood was attempting to keep the truck away from the engine when he became trapped and crushed between them, killing him instantly. At the subsequent inquest the jury returned a verdict of 'accidental death'.

J. Bower & Sons were sued in 1886 by Sarah Thorp of Cliffe for £2 16s, made up of £1.8s for wages due, and £1 8s for wages in lieu of notice. Miss Thorp had worked for John Bower for seven or eight years as a healder, and for many years prior to that for John Bower's father. She wished to go to a wedding one Saturday in March, and had asked John Bower the day before for permission to go. He told her that she could go to the church ceremony and to the wedding breakfast, but must then go to work. Sarah Thorp said that the ceremony and wedding breakfast took up more time than she had anticipated, consequently, as the firm closed at 1pm on Saturdays she thought that it was not worth her going to work. On Monday morning John Bower refused to allow her to resume work and sent her home. Bower said in evidence that the wedding took place at 8am and was over by quarter to nine, when she should have returned to work. The judge asked Bower if he would agree to pay a total of £1 to Thorp, which Bower agreed to do.[7]

The firm were employing around 170 workers in January 1887 who were given a treat at Holmfirth Town Hall. A fire was discovered in the stove at 3am on the morning of Saturday 11 August 1888. The alarm was raised, which brought workers from the night shift at James Watkinson's to help. Hoses, kept on the premises, were used to put out the fire. The contents of the stove, which were not insured, were completely destroyed. The damage was estimated to be over £300. There was also a small fire in a condenser set in February of the following year, which was put out by workpeople, with only a small amount of damage.

The Factory Inspector visited Dover Mill at 5.40pm one day in November 1890, and found that all the staff were still working, when the regulation time for finishing was 5.30pm. He had gone at that time deliberately, as he had heard that due to a holiday in September, instead of the regulation 10 hour day, the firm were working 10¼ hours a day to make up the lost time. The inspector had managed to get the names of eight people, but the rest had escaped by using other doors. Bowers were fined 5s plus costs for each of the eight cases.

William Wimpenny was a teenage lad working at Dover mill, as did his father Joseph, who was a cloth miller. When William arrived at work on 27 January 1894 he went looking for his father who should have arrived first, but could not find him. William's grandmother told the lad that his father might be 'in another 'ole in t'mill'. Still unable to find his father, William went looking for him and eventually found his cap lying on the dam bank at Bottoms mill. His father's body was found in the dam soon afterwards. The inquest was told that Joseph's wife had got into debt, and had then run away. The jury returned a verdict of 'Suicide by drowning while temporarily insane'.

The firm's Managing Director John Bower, appeared at Holmfirth Police Court in September 1900, charged with aggravated assault on a 15 year old employee Nellie Charlesworth. He had pushed Nellie into the dam and held her there for five minutes; the following morning one of her legs was badly swollen. Bower was fined £10 plus costs. In evidence, he said that he had done it because she threw a stick into the dam. Lucy Beaumont of Scholes, a knotter and burler, sued Bowers for 17s in 1901, being two weeks wages at 8s 6d per week, in lieu of notice. She had been dismissed on returning to work after being off 'badly'. She was awarded the money.

Bower's enlarged the premises by building a new woollen shed in 1902. Emma Turton, a Twister, of Bankend, caught her right hand in the twisting machine in 1907. She was taken to Dr. Thorp's surgery where she was found to have badly lacerated her middle finger and damaged the other fingers on that hand. After being treated by Dr. Thorp, she was taken to Huddersfield Infirmary.

A Textile Directory of 1910 records J. Bower & Sons as being manufacturers of fancy woollens and Bedford cords. Bowers were still in the mill in 1920 when they had plans for a new weaving shed passed; but by 1948 had been replaced by Britton Rugs, who built a new storage shed and also a new boiler house.

In 1959 the premises were being used by Britton Rugs Ltd; Dover Woollens Ltd. and H.G. Turner & Co. Ltd, Dyers. A fire was reported at 8.22pm on 7 July, six appliances attended, two from Holmfirth, two from Huddersfield, one from Slaithwaite, and one from Skelmanthorpe. The Meltham engine was also on stand-by at Holmfirth fire station. The premises of Dover Woollens and Britton Rugs were completely destroyed, but the premises used by H.G. Turner & Co were only slightly damaged. Their 22 employees would be able to return to work fairly quickly.

Britton Rugs Ltd. transferred their business to Spring Lane mills at Bottoms, where they last advertised for staff in 1961. The fire seems to have put Dover Woollens Ltd. out of business, as there is no further record of them at Dover, or at any other mill in the district. H.G. Turner & Co were using Dover mill until 1962, which was the year that they last advertised for staff. A company called Binswell Ltd. who were part of the Readicut group of companies, and were principally dyers of rugs for L.R. Davies of Castleford another member of the group, were using the mill from 1966 until they moved to Brookfield mills, Penistone Rd. Kirkburton, where they were advertising for staff in 1988. Plans were submitted to Kirklees Council in 1984 to turn a derelict building at the mill into 6 houses, which was presumably rejected as it was followed by a plan for one house. This was also rejected. A plan to convert the whole site to housing was submitted in 1989 and approved by the Council, but little development took place.[8]

Jane Wood Dyehouse

The site of this dyehouse was only about two hundred yards below Dover mill. It was probably built in the early years of the nineteenth century; the earliest information that I have found dates from 1826, when the Wakefield Court Roll records that Thomas Webster of Morley, a gentleman, paid £500 to Sir Peter Pole, Baronet, Charles Pole and John Price merchants and co-partners, of London, in repayment of a mortgage taken from them by Jonathon Turner Innkeeper, of Upperbridge, for the Great Spring Wood and an adjoining close of land known as the Old Jane, formerly in the possession of Thomas Littlewood, then John Littlewood and Hannah Hinchliffe, now of Jonathon Turner, with the dyehouse, its vats, pans, water wheels and other fixtures; also all other buildings lately erected by Jonathon Turner. The mortgage had also covered some land and property in the Upperbridge area of Holmfirth. The money to repay the mortgage had come from Turner taking another mortgage from Hannah Webster of Morley and Christopher Topham of Wortley, for £700. The Holme Reservoir Commissions did not include this property in the Voting Register of 1853, but in the following year they recorded the owners of the dyehouse as John, Joseph, James and William Turner, and the occupier of the premises as Joseph Preston.

The property was the subject of a case in the Chancery Court in 1861, of Turner v. Turner, when the court ordered that the property should be auctioned. The auction was held on 21 August at the George Inn at Upperbridge, which was also Lot 1 of the auction; the house and dyehouse at Jane Wood were Lot 6. At that time, the dwelling house with the outbuildings and gardens was occupied by Joseph Preston; and the dyehouse with its water wheel, dams, weirs, goits and fall of water, is described as having 6 dye vats and brickwork, scour pans, wash cisterns, pipes, taps and valves, indigo rocker and gearing etc. along with a cottage, stable, outbuildings and a close of land, which was occupied by Edward Fozzard. The names of the buyers of the properties are not known.

The dyehouse and dwelling house were again offered for sale in the *Huddersfield Examiner* in August 1887, when the dyehouse was described as being 'lately occupied by George Greenwood', indicating that it was currently empty; the tenant of the dwelling house was a Mr. Bower. A note in the *Examiner* of the following week states that the property had been withdrawn from the auction and later sold privately.

Jill Hinchliffe, in her dissertation for her degree in 1973, when the buildings were still standing, wrote that it was then in a ruined state, but that the main features were still discernable. She described it as being about the size of a large cottage, two storeys high with regularly spaced square windows, and walls of randomly laid stone. Power was supplied by the water wheel, which was in use up to 1889, but was broken by 1896. The dyehouse fell into disuse during the following year.[9] The site of the former dyehouse is now occupied by a good sized bungalow.

Pingle mill / Lower Dover mill

The site of this mill was on the inside curve of Higgin dike by a waterfall and opposite Underbank mill; although it was on the right bank of the stream, it was still classed as being in Cartworth rather than Wooldale as the township boundary leaves the stream just above Pingle mill to deviate slightly eastwards, travelling north until reaching Ribbleden mill where it reverts to the stream. The lease for the land on which the mill was built was given for a period of 63 years and dates from 14 July 1783. The owner of the land was Joshua Littlewood of Damhouse, he passed the 1 rood of land known as the Pingle to John Hudson of Holmfirth with permission to build a mill and fix 'engines' therein. Also included was permission to build a dam across Higgin Dike at or near a place called Jack Lane End, and also to dig a goit to the north of the Pingle to a spring or fountain at Intake Lane End to convey more water to the dam; then to build a tail goit from the mill back to Higgin dike.

The mill was advertised for sale in 1788 as: 'All that Scribbling mill with the appurtenances, together with the machines, cards and engines…situate, standing and being at Underbank in Holmfirth, now in the possession of John Hudson'. The Court Roll of 1790, records that Jonathon Shaw gentleman, of Shaleys in Upperthong, John Hudson shopkeeper, of Holmfirth, and John Fallas clothier, of Wood Upperthong, passed to Michael Normington Yeoman, of White Gate Head in Soyland, a close or parcel of land in Cartworth called the Pingle, containing 1 rood, with a mill and other buildings erected there, and all wheels, engines and machines fixed in the mill; also the liberty for Normington or his servants or agents, to erect a dam near to a rivulet called Higgin Dike running through or near the Pingle and near a place called Jack Lane End, intended to serve the mill or engines with water, and to make a goit to Higgin Dike to feed water to the dam, and a second goit to take water from the mill back to Higgin Dike, which suggests that although these permissions had been given previously they had not been carried out.

In 1793 Joseph Bray of Holmfirth paid £142 to John Fallas for a moiety in the close of land known as the Pingle with the scribbling mill. Joseph Bray bought the other half share in the mill in 1797 from Michael Normington's executors by raising a mortgage from John Scholefield of Horbury; the occupant of the mill at that time was Ely Hoyle. Abraham Littlewood of Damhouse also raised a mortgage on a Messuage in Underbank with six acres of land including the Pingle, with the Scribbling mill and other buildings occupied by Ely Hoyle and Abraham Littlewood, from James West of Rastrick for £300 in 1804.

John Bray of Holmfirth appears to have raised two mortgages on the mill; the first was in 1807 from John Scholefield of Horbury, and the second was two years later from Joseph Knowles, also of Horbury. On both occasions the occupants of the mill were Eli Wimpenny, Ebenezer Wimpenny and Richard Woofenden. Joseph Bray also mortgaged part of the mill with John Irving of Halifax in 1812, when the occupants were still Eli and Ebenezer Wimpenny, and Richard Woofenden.

The scribbling mill was being used by Eli Wimpenny of Newhouse Upperthong, Ebenezer Wimpenny of Burnlee, Benjamin Butterworth of Upperbridge, and Richard Hargreaves of Hill, from 1 May 1820; later in that year Joseph Bray repaid £220 to John Scholefield of Horbury for the mill plus a dwelling house and stable at Mill Hill in Holmfirth, which presumably cleared his debt to Scholefield. He also repaid £125 16s to John Irving of Halifax, to clear that mortgage.

Eli Wimpenny and Benjamin Butterworth paid £520 to Joseph Bray for a moiety in the field called the Pingle with the scribbling mill in 1821. The Rev. James West passed his interest in the field and mill to John and Sarah Senior of Lower Damhouse, also Elizabeth, Hannah and Mary Littlewood of Upper Damhouse, in 1824. Ebenezer Wimpenny and Richard Hargreaves paid £480 to Joseph Bray in 1827, who by then had moved from Holmfirth to Nabb, for the second moiety on the land called the Pingle; the entry makes no mention of the mill, but it must still have been standing at that time.

The original 63 year lease should have expired in 1846. The Cartworth Rate Valuation record of 1859, gives the owners of the mill as 'Hannah Littlewood and others', and names the mill as Lower Dover Mill, which was by then 'in ruins'.

In 1872 the land was offered for sale by auction, when the auctioneer made every effort to make it seem an attractive proposition by describing it as 'All that valuable parcel of land being the site of the ancient Pingle mill, situate on the bank of the Ribbleden rivulet, with the capital weir and goits thereto belonging, having 36ft of fall, and the whole volume of the waters of the stream for motive power supplemented by the Holme Styes reservoir, the area being 1,100sq.yds. The site of Pingle mill with its large water power may be turned to very profitable use at no great cost'. Whether it was sold is not known. The site was again offered for sale as 'land where Pingle or Lower Dover mill once stood' in August 1887, but was withdrawn at the auction.[10] The site of the former mill is now much overgrown, there are concrete foundations for a building on the land, which appear to be of a much later date than the mill.

Underbank mill

The earliest record for this mill, which stands on the rising ground on the eastern side of Dunford Road, comes from the *Leeds Intelligencer* in 1796, when it was advertised for sale as 'the lately erected Scribbling mill on part of a close called Far Underbank'. It appears that the mill never had a water wheel, but always relied on steam power. Two documents in the Wakefield Court Roll, both bearing the same date 3 May 1805, record that the mill was passed to Thomas Bedford of Emley, and secondly, that he then sold it to Hannah Gartside of Holmfirth; the mill is again described as being 'lately erected'. Baines' Directory of 1822 records that John and Joseph Bray were cloth manufacturers in Underbank, but do not give an address; however, the Land Tax Returns for Wooldale in that year give John Bray as the owner of Underbank mill, and Ellis & Co. as the occupants.

Joshua, Joseph and Abel Cuttell were using the mill in 1829, which they named 'Cuttell mill', where they were trading as Joshua Cuttell and Brothers. It is possible that they had altered the original building in 1825, as in their answers to the Factory Commissioners in 1834 they said that the mill was used for 'preparing and finishing woollen cloth'; and also that the mill had been built in 1825 with power being supplied by a 10hp steam engine. The Cuttell's were one of the first manufacturers in the district to carry out the finishing processes of their cloth in their own mill rather than putting it out to a Dressing Shop. In 1834 they employed a total of 34 people, only one of which was a girl; 4 boys under 10 earned 3s 6d each, 2 boys under 12 earned 4s each, 6 boys under 14 earned 4s 6d and the 1 girl under 14 earned 4s, 2 boys under 16 earned 5s 6d, 3 boys under 18 earned 9s, 3 males under 21 earned 13s 6d, and 13 men over 21 earned 18s 6d. None of the children were reliant on the person for whom they worked for their wages, Cuttell's paid everyone direct. Hours of work were 6am to 8pm in summer, but 7am to 8 pm in winter 'because in winter we think it a pity to call them from their warm comfortable beds so soon'. They worked an average of two hours less on Saturdays all year round. Workers were allowed half an hour for Breakfast, 1 hour in summer for dinner, but only half an hour in winter, and half an hour at Drinking; the machinery was stopped for breakfast and dinner, but not at drinking, when 3 boys would work 'serving a moving feeder'. They allowed 3 days holiday at Christmas and at Easter, plus half a day in March and October, 'which, with the other occasional half days by accidents in the moving power, make about ten days a year; of course not paid for'. They thought that the possibility of getting two sets of children to allow part-time education would not be possible due to the lack of numbers, and that if implemented, their work would suffer as being off for half a day would 'unsettle their minds'. Cuttell's also said that if part-time working was introduced, 'machinery would be adapted to supersede them, which would be very injurious to many families, and cause a great deal of distress'. They also thought that parliament could legislate for 12 hours a day, or even eleven without much risk, but to go further than that would, in their opinion, be injurious to all parties.

The three brothers ended their partnership with a document dated 26 January 1838. After the dissolution of the partnership the name of the company was changed to Joshua Cuttell & Sons; no reason for the dissolution is given, but in the 1841 census Joseph is shown as being a Woollen manufacturer; and Abel is shown as a Clothier. Joshua Cuttell was in financial difficulties in June 1842 when his assets were assigned to his creditors. His bankruptcy was confirmed on 1 October 1844, and notice of a first and final dividend of 2¼d in the £ that would be paid on or after 25 February 1845 was posted in the *London Gazette* around 22 February 1845. Abel Cuttell junior's Obituary in

Underbank mill, main building. © the Author.

1875 records that the firm in which his father had been involved went out of business while Abel junior was still 'quite a youth', and gives the reason for their demise as difficult trading conditions brought about by the strictures created due to the Government's imposition of the Corn Laws.

In 1844, George Hinchliffe redeemed a mortgage of £440 on 2 closes of land and Cuttell's mill at Underbank from the Huddersfield Banking Company, and occupied them. The *Huddersfield Chronicle* lists a sale of machinery at Underbank mill in 1852, which, it says is 'due to the owner declining business' but does not give a name. The machinery consisted of 2prs of spinning mules, 7 narrow power looms, a beaming frame, a balloon or warp drying machine, and various sundries.

A man called Joseph Woodhead was adjusting the strap on a machine in April 1855, when his clothing became caught up and was carried round the drive wheel, receiving serious injuries.

G. Thewlis & Sons were occupying part of the mill in 1861; placards posted on walls in Holmfirth in June declared that their weavers had been on strike since late February against wage reductions imposed by the company. Thewlis's employed a non union weaver called Bilcliffe on 10 May to try to break the strike; when he left work in the evening, *'hundreds, if not thousands of people including many women and girls hooted him from the mill home'*. The same thing happened on the following night, but that evening, the young man was taken ill and was unable to work for the rest of the week. The striking weavers dissociated themselves from the mob by issuing placards saying that they were 'disgraceful proceedings, wrong in themselves, and particularly injurious to the people they were intended to help'. Three weavers, John Cartwright, Jessie Sanderson and Joshua Moorhouse appeared in court on 15 June charged with intimidating Thomas Bilcliff, and calling him foul names. Bilcliff said that he had been pushed down and his clothes torn; and a crowd of 300 to 400 stopped him from taking shelter anywhere as he walked from the mill to his father's house at Hill. Other witnesses supported Bilcliff's account, and the three were given the maximum sentence of three months imprisonment, but without hard labour. Abel Thewlis charged Ben Lockwood a weaver, for leaving work without notice. Lockwood, in his defence, said that when he took the job 'a kind of strike was on foot amongst the weavers', and he didn't realise that they were still out; he had left because he did not wish to be branded a 'black sheep'. He was given the choice of a month on the Treadmill; or going back to work, which he chose. Three other weavers in court on the same day on similar charges and given the same options also agreed to resume work. In September, the three strikers who had been convicted of intimidating Bilcliff were released from Wakefield prison. They were met at Holmfirth Station by friends and the Temperance Band, and marched to a meeting of the Weavers Association at the White Hart to welcome them back.[11]

William Sandford moved from New Fold mill to Underbank mill in the late 1850s or early 1860s, when he told the River Pollution enquiry that at that time he employed 40 people scribbling and carding wool; power of 20hp was supplied by a steam engine; they produced 35,208lbs of goods per year, valued at £3,600; and neither dyes nor bleach were used in their processes. Abel Cuttell junior was also using part of the mill around this time in addition to Swanbank mill as, at the time of his Bankruptcy in 1873, he had 1 carder, 1pr mules, 5 powerlooms and sundries in Underbank mill that were auctioned on 19 May.

The mill was offered for sale in 1882, when Wm. Sandford's are shown as tenants, it was described as a 4 storey mill 78ft by 33ft with an attic and basement, a 3 storey warehouse, a steam powered beam engine with a 19inch cylinder and 4ft stroke, and a boiler fitted with Galloway tubes. The mill was bought by William Sandford. The 1881 census records that Sandford's employed 74 people, made up of 41 men, 23 women and 10 boys.

Thirty employees of Sandford's were given a treat at the Masons Arms Underbank in January 1887, which was possibly just for the male employees. Joe Beaumont, aged 17, was working as a piercer at the mill in 1888 when his left arm was drawn into the machine and torn off. He was taken to Huddersfield Infirmary for treatment. The Factory Inspector took Sandford's to court in 1890 for permitting a girl to work outside the legal hours of 6.30am to 5.30pm. Sandford's admitted the offence, but pointed out that their actual hours of work were 6.45am to 5.45pm. The Factory Inspector said that the mill should have sought permission from the Inspectorate to vary their hours of work. The bench imposed a fine of 5s plus costs.

The mill had been using water from the Council water mains to provide steam and for other uses, but in 1894 they requested that this supply should be disconnected as they had built storage reservoirs at Bank End. William Sandford took his son Jonathon, named after William's cousin Jonathon who died in the 1852 flood, into partnership in 1895, when the firm became Wm. Sandford & Son. William Sandford died in 1896.[12]

In 1907 William Sandford & Son were employing 7 women and 12 men; the firm of J.S. & J. Bates was also using part of the mill, and employed 4 women and 6 men. The *Yorkshire Trade Directory* of 1910 records that Sandford's had 1,400 spindles and 22 looms and were making fancy cloths; by which time their workforce had presumably increased. A fire broke out under a condenser hopper used by J.S, & J. Bates at 7.30pm on 3 Feb. 1911, workpeople immediately began using hand held extinguishers and buckets of water, while Mr. J. Sandford and others attached a hose to the hydrant in the mill yard. The fire was extinguished before the council's hose cart, the Ribbleden mill brigade and the Unity brigade arrived.

Sandford's became a limited company in 1919; Mr. Jonathon Sandford died three years later in 1922, and was succeeded by his sons. The *Yorkshire Textile Directory* of 1942-3 records that Sandford's then had 39 looms, and that Levi Kaye & Co. yarn spinners, were also using part of the mill. After the Second World War the premises were extended by adding a yarn store in 1947, additional office space in 1949, and a new weaving shed in 1954.

The company wrote in the Centenary Booklet that after the end of the war the export trade had increased considerably, 'and Sandford's Worsteds are now being sold in many parts of the world'. However, in common with the majority of wool textile manufacturers, trade became more difficult over the next 20 years, to the point where, in 1978, the company announced that 25 members of staff would be made redundant, but the firm was not closing down. However, one year later the company was out of business and the mill was advertised for sale by auction, with the plant and machinery being auctioned at a later date. The mill was bought by Mr. Selwyn Smith, who used it to store machinery prior to it being sold to buyers in second and third world countries.

In 1985 the mill was bought by Rowan Weavers of Green Lane mill, who used it for storage and despatch until 1994, when the building nearer to Holmfirth was sold to the Crag Rats Theatre Company; and the original mill was bought by Mr. Robert Hall, who intended to covert it into living accommodation. Plans to convert at least part of the mill to a health studio, offices and a meeting room for hire were put forward in 1996, and were accepted by Kirklees.[13]

In October 1830, William Stephenson of Sands Holmfirth bought land and property including a **Dyehouse** previously in the possession of John Bray, then Joseph Bray, followed by John Brooke, currently of Joseph Cuttell, near to Underbank Mill.[14] The exact location and how long it remained in use is unknown.

Swanbank mill

The mill stood on the Cartworth side of the stream, about 300 yards downstream from the site of Pingle mill. Hinchliffe and Horncastle told the Factory Commissioners in 1833 that the mill had been built in 1825, which corresponds with the Wakefield Court Roll entry in recording that Joshua Littlewood of Lower Damhouse surrendered the new Scribbling and Fulling mill at the bottom or East side of Swan Bank Wood, called Swan Bank mill, to the use of John Hinchliffe the elder of Barnside Hepworth, John Hinchliffe the younger of Scholes, and James Horncastle of Lane Upperthong, for 21 years from 16 June 1827. Joshua Littlewood had presumably borrowed the money to build the mill from Sarah Ibbotson, a spinster of Scarborough, as, in 1827 George Jessop a drysalter of Honley, took over the mortgage by paying £2,200 to Sarah Ibbotson and Joshua Littlewood gentleman of

Drawing of the Original Swanbank mill. Collection of A.J. Brooke

Lower Damhouse, for a dwelling house, barn, stable and cowhouse, at Damhouse occupied by Jonathon Turner, 4 cottages a barn and cowhouse also at Damhouse and ten closes of land plus 2 woods, totalling 22 acres 3 roods 19 perches, with the newly erected Fulling and Scribbling mill built by Joshua Littlewood and called Swan Bank mill.

Hinchliffe & Horncastle told the Factory Commissioners that the mill was used for scribbling, spinning, fulling and finishing of woollen cloth. Power was from either a water wheel or a steam engine, both of which delivered 12hp. They had 35 employees, 2 girls under 10 earned 3s 6d; 2 boys and 1 girl under 12 also earned 3s 6d, and 2 boys under 12 earned 4s; 1 boy under 14 earned 5s, while 2 girls under 14 earned 3s 9d; 5 boys under 16 earned 5s 4d; 1 boy under 18 earned 10s; of the 2 girls under 21, one earned 6s and the other earned 16s; of the 17 men over 21, 13 earned 18s while the other four earned 25s. Six billy-piecers, one mule piecer and 2 carder layers-on were reliant on the person for whom they worked for their wages, the others were paid by the management. Hours of work were 6am to 8pm, with two hours less on Saturdays. There was a total of 2 hours per day allowed for meals, but the water wheel or steam engine continued running as the fulling stocks and scribbling engines did not stop; staff had to supervise the running of these machines during meal breaks. Four whole days per year, in addition to Sundays, were allowed for holidays. In answer to the question about possibly employing two sets of children to allow for part-time education Hinchliffe and Horncastle said:

> "We have never found it necessary to employ two sets of children, as ours work cheerfully the full time. The children's health and appearance will bear a comparison with those who never work in mills. We find the billy-spinner (or slubber) will earn 31s in a week of 72 hours, out of it he pays his piecers and layer-on 11s for the week. Now, in case such slubber is necessitated to employ two sets of children, we think he must, on a fair calculation, pay 9s per week to each set, or 7s per week more than his present payment; and to make up this extra outgo, he must work fifteen hours and three-quarters extra time each week, or something more than two hours and a half per day."

On the question about regulating the hours of work by Act of Parliament, they submitted the following:

> *"We consider all legislation injurious, unless parliament could legislate for the whole world. If they prohibit young children from working in mills and factories, they deprive the poor widow in numberless instances of all her dependence, except the usual parish allowance, which will amount to taking away one half or upwards of her own and her fatherless children's bread. If they restrict children to ten hours per day, they might as well diminish the time to seven or eight hours, for it will compel the use of two sets of children; and, in order to meet the increased payment, the adult (who works by the pound or piece work, and pays the children,) will be necessitated to work two hours and a half or three hours per day extra. If they stop the moving power after it has run ten or eleven hours, they must either compensate us, or we shall be immense losers, as we stand upon a very high rental, and a long lease."*

These answers are largely typical of the thoughts of most manufacturers throughout the north of England, and of many throughout the entire country, in 1833. They seemed unable to comprehend the need for change; fortunately this attitude altered, albeit gradually, over the next sixty or so years.

The mortgage changed hands again when Anne Hudswell spinster of Leeds, paid £3,000 for the land and property previously outlined including Swanbank mill in 1834; it was subsequently bought by Nathaniel Dickson in 1842 for £3,500, who sold it to John Roberts of Hinchliffe Mill for the same amount in 1846.

There had been a fire at the mill on Friday 29 January 1841, which destroyed several woven pieces. The fire was thought to have been caused by the stove overheating. Damage was estimated at about £200, which was not covered by insurance. This fire came only about six weeks after a similar fire at Ribbleden mill, which is only a few hundred yards downstream from Swanbank. Having reported both fires, the *Leeds Intelligencer* asked: 'when will Holmfirth get a fire engine?' Hinchliffe & Horncastle's lease came to an end in June 1847, when their machinery was advertised for sale by auction. It consisted of a large quantity of machinery for producing yarn, weaving it into cloth, and finishing it.

Abel Cuttell (junior) was occupying the mill in March 1852, when he took John Hargreaves of Victoria Street Holmfirth, described as a shoemaker and cloth manufacturer, to court to recover £14 15s 7d for work done. The dispute arose due to the methods used to calculate the amount of cloth processed. Hargreaves calculated it by the number of individual pieces regardless of length; whereas Cuttell calculated it by yardage. The discrepancy was due to weavers having increased the length of pieces. The court found in favour of Abel Cuttell and ordered John Hargreaves to pay Cuttell £14 10s.

The Holme Reservoir Commissioners list the owner of the mill in 1853 as Joshua Littlewood, and the occupier as Abel Cuttell A girl called Wadsworth got her arm caught while she was oiling a moving machine on Thursday 5 March 1857, two days later the *Huddersfield Chronicle* reported that she was 'progressing favourably'. Abel Cuttell treated his 40 employees to a substantial supper at the Masons Arms in January 1860; and later in the week he hosted a tea for the wives and sweethearts of the men, when 60 were present.

In February of that year the Unity Fire Office had decided to dispose of some of their engines and offered to sell the one at Holmfirth to the town. A meeting held at the Elephant & Castle Inn was chaired by Abel Cuttell, where it was decided to buy the engine for the district. A subscription list was opened with the required amount soon being reached, and the engine purchased. The Unity engine gave many years of service and was manned by an enthusiastic crew who were invariably the first to arrive at every fire.

John Ellis, a weaver for Cuttells, presumably had a disagreement with the company, as he left a part woven piece in the loom and went to work elsewhere. Abel Cuttell brought a case against Ellis, saying that he did not wish to be vindictive, but wanted to show weavers that they could not behave this way with impunity. [The accepted course of action was that the weaver finished his piece (downed) before leaving]. The magistrate did not impose a fine, but ordered that Ellis should pay 8s costs.[15]

Abel Cuttell renewed his lease on the mill, dyehouse, press shop and other buildings in 1864 for a period of 21 years at a rent of £234 13s 4d per year, from George and Joseph Roberts of Hinchliffe Mill and Joshua Littlewood of Damhouse. Business appears to have been difficult for the firm in the later 1860s, as his assets were assigned to creditors in April 1867; the appointed Trustees were Richard Porritt and Henry William Anders, both woolstaplers of Huddersfield, also Benjamin Mellor cloth finisher of Albert mill Holmfirth.

Swan Bank mill was offered for sale by auction on 3 March 1869, when it was described as:

> *"All that valuable stone built woollen mill, 4 storeys and attic called Swan Bank mill, occupied by John Brook & Sons; with the engine and boiler houses, stove, teazing room, dyehouse, warehouse, water wheel, steam engine, boiler, fulling stocks, shafting, going gear, and the other machinery and effects belonging to the vendors. Mill dam, waterfall, weir, dam banks, yards and various land thereto belonging; also Swan Bank Wood, and Hammond Royd Wood".*

The vendor is not named, but it could have been the executors of Joshua Littlewood, and the Roberts's of Hinchliffe Mill, as Lot 2 was the dwelling house lately occupied by the late Mr. Joshua Littlewood. The mill may not have sold, as the owner in 1874 is given as Mr. John Littlewood. Although his name is not mentioned, it seems that Abel Cuttell was still occupying part of the mill. A policeman, who was passing the mill at about 2.30am on the morning of Saturday October 9th 1869, noticed that smoke was issuing from a window in the stove and raised the alarm. The fire was extinguished by neighbours with buckets of water; damage to materials in the stove belonging to John Brook & Sons was estimated at £16.

A carrier was transporting a cast iron dyepan in a horse-drawn lurry along icy roads from Wakefield to Swanbank mill in February 1871. Having fitted chains to the wheels of the lurry he had successfully negotiated the various hills and valleys until arriving at Pog Ing and beginning the descent to Holmfirth, where there was a particularly large patch of ice. The lurry skidded diagonally across the road and collided with the kerb close to Holmfirth Railway Station dislodging the dyepan, which fell to the ground and broke into several pieces. The broken pieces were reloaded onto the lurry and the party returned from whence they came.

An entry in the *London Gazette* of 25 April 1873 announced the bankruptcy of Abel Cuttell, and that the first creditors meeting would be held on 7 May. This was followed by the sale of machinery on 19 May, including: 1 carder; 1pr Mules; 5 powerlooms with jacquards and gearing; a broad warping balloon, sizing machine, bobbin winding machine; mill furnishings etc. There was also a small amount of machinery in Underbank mill belonging to Mr. Cuttell. After his bankruptcy Abel Cuttell became the Sanitary Inspector for Austonley, Cartworth, Holme, Netherthong and Upperthong local boards in August 1873. He died on 2 Nov. 1875 while giving his report to a meeting of the Cartworth Board.

A fire in the stove was discovered at 7.30pm on Monday September 14th 1874, neighbours armed with buckets of water managed to stop the fire spreading until the Unity brigade arrived. Due to the number of onlookers the fire fighters were delayed for some minutes as they were unable to manoeuvre the engine into position. There were so many sightseers that two children who were at the back of the crowd lost their footing and fell into the river; fortunately they were not hurt. The fire was put out about one hour after it had been discovered, by which time the roof had collapsed. Damage to materials in the stove, which belonged to John Brook & Sons, was calculated at about £100; the report omits to estimate the cost of repairing the building.

The mill was again advertised for sale in June 1876, when it was described as being 4 storeys high, 99ft long by 46ft 6in wide inside, engine and boiler houses, stove, teazing room, dyehouse, warehouse; plus a 40ft diameter water wheel, steam engine, boiler, fulling stocks shafting and going gear; also machinery in the premises that was the property of the vendors (not specified). Swan Bank Wood and Hammond Royd Wood were also included, a total of 3 acres 14 perches. John Brook & Sons ran into financial difficulties and filed a petition for bankruptcy in December 1878, with debts estimated at £14,000; the creditors agreed on liquidation by arrangement, and their machinery was advertised for sale by auction on January 30th. The winding up procedure continued throughout that year and into 1879.

The Holmfirth Prosecution Society brought a case at Holmfirth Police Court against Henry Armitage a millhand for damaging a sluice gate or shuttle, belonging to Mr. John Littlewood of Manchester, who had probably bought the mill in 1876; his local agent was Mr. G.H. Hinchliffe of Nabb House. A Mr. Castle who looked after the property saw Armitage pull the shuttle up and throw it in the goit. The bench observed that a lot of damage was being done to property by lads, and levied a fine of 1s 6d plus costs.

As discussed elsewhere, the 1880s and '90s were difficult times for textile manufacturers. Despite alterations and improvements being carried out at the mill in the early 1880s, there were several attempts to either sell or let the mill during that period without much success. The mill was offered for sale in July 1890, but was withdrawn at the auction when the bidding failed to exceed £1,100. The mill had been empty for many years before being bought privately by Mr. John Beever, who had been brought up at Well Hill, Underbank, and as a youth had worked at both Ribbleden and Swan Bank mills; but had moved to Huddersfield where he started his own business.

An advertisement appeared in the *Holmfirth Express* in October 1895 for 'a few rug weavers', those people who were interested should apply to Friend Mellor at Swan Bank Mill; he was, presumably, the manager of Swan Bank for John Beever. Mr. Mellor advertised on a regular basis for weavers well into 1896; but in 1897 John Beever began advertising under his own name for rug weavers to work at Swan Bank mill. The type of rugs that were being made were known locally as 'pegged' rugs. The pile was made from strips of fabric about 4 inches long and 1 to 1½ inches wide, which, in the hand made version, were pushed through a piece of canvas, so that when the canvas was laid flat, each strip stood in a U shape to form the pile. The best fabric to use for the pile was fulled or milled woollen overcoating, as its density gave it strength and resilience. The manufacture of these rugs was, for many years, very much a cottage industry; when making these rugs in the home, design and colour was often determined by the fabric that was available rather than what was most desired, as the usual source was cast-off clothing. John Beever, however, developed a method of weaving these rugs on a handloom, which was much quicker, enabling them to be sold for around 5s each. John Beever had factories in Alfred Street and Brook Street Huddersfield where, in addition to rugs he also made cloth for military and brass band uniforms, which would give him a range of bright plain colours in the correct type of fabric from which to make the rugs. He also started a tailoring business for uniforms, giving him a supply of free off-cuts. He maintained that he was receiving orders for 2,000 rugs per week, although whether he could ever supply that quantity is questionable as, in common with other rug manufacturers in the district, he appeared to be almost permanently short staffed, having a virtually permanent advertisement for weavers to work at Swan Bank mill, in the Holmfirth Express, and frequent adverts for weavers in the Huddersfield papers. John Beever died on 31 January 1913 at the age of 71, but the business continued to be run by the family, trading as John Beever & Sons.

A fire was discovered at 6pm on 24 October 1924, and in 15 minutes all 4 storeys were ablaze, completely gutting the mill. The Holmfirth Fire Brigade attended and sustained some damage to the fire engine, but, due to the intensity of the blaze, their efforts on this occasion were somewhat ineffectual. The majority of the space in the mill was being used by Mr. R. C. Waller, a woollen manufacturer; John Beever & Sons still occupied part of the mill, after the fire they moved to their premises in Brook Street, Huddersfield. The fate of Mr. Waller's business is not known, but he does not appear to have restarted in Holme Valley.

Replacement buildings on mill site, since converted to apartments. © the Author

This incident brought an end to textile production on this site; it was eventually taken over by Hinchliffe Mill Co-operative Society Ltd, who built a bake-house and slaughter house here. By comparing the area covered by the mill against the size of the new building, as shown on the 25inch Ordinance Survey maps of the 1890s and 1930s, the co-op building covered the greater floor area, but did not have as many floors as the mill. In 1967 Messrs. G.W. Castle, Motor Engineers, whose main office, showroom and workshop were on Woodhead Road in what is currently the 'Holmfirth Mills' shop, applied for change of use of the Swan Bank premises from a Bake-House and Slaughter House to motor vehicle repair, spray painting and storage, which was approved by Holmfirth Council. Castle's applied to Kirklees Council in the 1990s to change the use of the premises to 11 apartments, and to build one house, but this was refused. A plan for 7 apartments and one house was also rejected.[16] In 1996 the plan for 7 homes in the mill building had been approved; the developers then submitted a revised plan for 5 homes, which the Parish Council approved, but was rejected by Kirklees. The former workshop buildings currently contain 11 apartments.

Ribbleden mill and Dyeworks

This mill and dyeworks are on the west side of Dunford Road, about 100 yards or so from Victoria Square, between the road and Rivelin Dike. The mill was built in 1808 by Joshua Moorhouse a clothier, and John Dickinson who was a butcher, they each owned a one-third share in the property, with the remaining third being owned by Joshua's eldest son Matthew Moorhouse. In addition to the mill, the transaction included several closes of land in Cartworth known as the Rippledens, along with barns and stables. John Dickinson died in 1819, leaving his one third share in the mill, which had both a water wheel and a steam engine, and land to his two sons William and John. Joshua Moorhouse left his one third share in the mill and land to his second son Joseph.

William Dickinson sold his one sixth share of the land, the mill which is described as a newly erected Scribbling mill, plus 2 cottages in Cuttell Bottom, to William Sykes of Clough House Slaithwaite, for the sum of £300 in September 1823. An advertisement in the *Wakefield and Halifax Journal* of 10 October 1828, offered a one third share in the fulling and scribbling mill called Ribbleden mill, with its water wheel, reservoir and dam. This was possibly bought by Joseph Moorhouse the younger and George Moorhouse; the mill is described as also having a stove, 3 cottages and several closes of land, for which they paid £1,600.

In 1833 Moorhouse and Dickinson told the Factory Commissioners that both the water wheel and the engine delivered 10hp; they employed 23 people, 1 boy under 10, 2 boys and 2 girls under 12, 2 boys and 2 girls under 14, 1 boy and 2 girls under 16, 2 boys under 18, 1 man under 21, 7 men and 1 woman over 21. The information given on wages is very limited, piecers were paid 3s 6d per week; layers on 4s to 5s; 6 males were paid by piece rates, earning 18s 6d for a 72 hour week; 15 people relied on the people for whom they worked for their wages. There was no payment for overtime. Hours of work were 6am to 8pm all year round, except on Saturdays when they were less; workers were allowed a total of two hours for mealtimes, but the machinery was not stopped at dinner time, which meant that a layer-on worked through. There were three days holiday at Christmas, and 3 days about the time of Holy Thursday, with occasional half days, all of which were unpaid. On the question of reducing working hours the answer was: 'The men who are employed in this mill are desirous of working longer than ten hours; and individuals who have been employed here for the last 25 years, are of opinion, that it would not be injurious to the health of themselves or their children to work twelve hours per day'.

William Dickinson died in 1834, his son Frank paid 2s 4½d to the court for licence of Herioting his father's share in various parcels of land and buildings in Holmfirth including Ribbleden mill. Two years later, James Horncastle of Lane, Upperthong, took two undivided one-third shares in the mill, 3 nearby cottages and the land; the occupants of the mill at that time are given as James Horncastle, James Buckley, John Dickinson and Frank Dickinson. Also in 1836, on 26 October, George Gartside, Joshua Cuttell, John Dickinson and Joshua Moorhouse, took a one-sixth share in the mill, cottages and land, from the estate of William Dickinson (deceased).

In May 1840, Horncastle, Buckley & Co. was summoned to the court of petty sessions held at the White Hart Inn Holmfirth, to answer four charges brought by Mr. James Bates Superintendent of Factories. The charges were: firstly not making a proper entry in the time register book; secondly, not allowing two children proper meal breaks; third and fourthly, employing two children under 18 years of age without their Christian and Surnames being entered in the register of workers. Mr. Bates had visited the mill with Mr. J Sanders, Factory Inspector, on May 7th, when they discovered two children secreted beneath the feeder of one of the engines, and covered with wool; and that the slubbers were "very evasive in their answers to the interrogatories of the inspectors, to whom they behaved very disrespectfully". Mr. Bates said that these were the worst cases that had come to his attention in this area, and he urged the bench to inflict the full penalties. Mr. Buckley appeared for the mill, but was unable to disprove any of the complaints. The magistrate, Mr. John Harpin of Burnlee, (a millowner), said that despite the seriousness of the cases, it was the first time that the company had been brought before the court, and he felt that the fine should be mitigated to £1 plus costs for each offence. Mr. Bates made it plain that he was very dissatisfied with the large reduction of the fines.

In 1841, George Gartside of Holmfirth, Joshua Cuttell of Shaleys Upperthong, Joseph Dickinson of Holmfirth, and Joshua Moorhouse of Cuttell Bottom Holmfirth, sold their one-sixth share in the mill, cottages and land, to Joseph Butterworth for the sum of £440, which Butterworth appears to have raised on a mortgage from John Richardson of Wakefield.

The Holme Reservoir Commissioners give the owners of the mill in 1853 as Joshua, George and Joseph Moorhouse, Frank Dickinson and Joseph Butterworth; the occupiers were Joshua Moorhouse, Joseph Moorhouse, and James Buckley. In September 1853 a girl called Wagstaff, who was about 16 years old, was sweeping the floor in the mill near to an engine, when her clothing became entangled with machinery. Medical aid was immediately procured. She was badly bruised about the head and legs, but was said to be recovering. The writer of the report observed that it was an accident that could easily have proved fatal.

One month later Walter Buckley, mill engineer, gave a treat to his colleagues at the mill to celebrate his recent marriage. A one third share in the mill was offered for sale by Auction on 24 April 1856; the mill was described as: a 3 storey high fulling and scribbling mill, and the newly erected 4 storey high spinning mill, also the dam, goit, yard and outbuildings, tentering house; along with the fulling stocks, water wheel, steam engine and boiler, shafting, going gear, scribbling and fulling machinery; now in the tenure of Mr. Joseph Butterworth and others. Also the wool stove near the mill, 3 cottages, and 3 closes of land. Mr. J. Butterworth gave a treat for his workers on 31 May 1856, to celebrate the declaration of peace on the Crimea.

During the first week of August 1864 a girl named Battye tried to drown herself by jumping into the mill dam. Her action was seen by a Mr. Hellawell who jumped in to rescue her which, despite her reluctance, he managed to do. In court it was reported that a number of circumstances had preyed on her mind, but none was serious enough to make her attempt suicide. The magistrate gave her a 'suitable reprimand' and dismissed her.

An advertisement inviting builders to tender for the erection of a mill, engine house, boiler house, dyehouse, teazing room and long chimney appeared in the *Huddersfield Chronicle* on 2 February 1867. John Thorpe Taylor moved from Dover mill to Ribbleden mill in late 1866 or early 1867. A sale of machinery took place at the mill in March 1867, authorised by Mr. Taylor, consisting of a quantity of machinery necessary for converting wool into yarn, plus fulling stocks and a steam engine and boiler. This was presumably unwanted machinery that was in Ribbleden mill, rather than machinery that had been brought from Dover mill but was not required.

Two accidents occurred at the mill in 1873, in late January John Crossley, a piece dyer, got his fingers caught while he was cleaning the friction pulleys of a machine. Dr. Trotter had to amputate one finger at the second joint. On 4 April a young man called Walter Bray of Town End got his right hand caught in the machine that he was operating. Dr. Totter was again obliged to remove one finger at the second joint.

Mr. Taylor gave a treat to about 200 people, made up of workpeople and family friends, in October 1873 to celebrate the coming-of-age of his nephew Walter Preston. A gathering of all the workers was held at the mill on 27th August 1877, when a Dining Room clock of marble and gold was presented to Mr. Walter Preston by the workpeople to celebrate his marriage two days later to Julia Ann Butterworth of West View Holmfirth. Mr. James Brook, who was the firm's longest serving employee, having worked for the firm for between 30 and 40 years, spoke. About 100 employees enjoyed a treat in the new Lecture Hall in Holmfirth January 1880; the meal was in the low room, but the speeches, toasts, games and dancing to music provided by Wooldale Brass Band was in the large room. Mr. Arthur Preston was absent, on business in New Zealand. The firm also gave their 120 workers a treat at Holmfirth Town Hall in January 1885, at which J.T. Taylor was present, despite having retired from the firm some time previously. He said that he was always glad to visit them and give them the benefit of his knowledge and experience.

Joseph Wimpenny a 48 year old weaver with 8 children, living at Newdoorstones Holmfirth, had left home on the morning of Thursday 27 January 1898, and did not return. On Saturday morning Joseph W. Moxon engine tenter at Taylor's saw the body of a man in the river near the dyehouse, with the face and one shoulder in the water; he informed the police. At the inquest several people said that they had seen Wimpenny on the Thursday evening in a 'jovial mood', and had directed him towards his home on two occasions. But he had 'got lost', and fell into the river where he died. There were marks on the wall near the body that appeared to have been made by clogs, indicating that Wimpenny had tried to save himself, but failed.

W. Preston, F. Holroyd and A.L. Tyas, who had been trading as J.T. Taylor & Co. for some years dissolved their partnership in March 1899. This was followed by an advertisement in June 1901 that the mill and machinery were available to let, which was unsuccessful, as the mill and machinery were offered for sale on 23 July, because the firm of J.T. Taylor & Co was retiring from business. The buildings were described as:

Lot 1, Main Mill, 70ft x 54ft. 4 storeys high, used for scribbling, spinning, weaving, milling and scouring; 5 storey mill 84ft x 28ft, used for weaving, spinning, twisting and winding; 3 storey plus attic 82ft x 36ft used for weaving, finishing, offices and warehouse. Teazing place and perching room 45ft x 27ft; tentering room 48ft x 15ft; brick and stone warping and store rooms. Boiler house with

Ribbleden mill. © the Author

stove over; smith's shop and store room with winding room over; engine house; octagonal stone-built chimney 40yds high. Steam engine, 2 boilers, shafting and gearing, gas, steam and water pipes.

Lot 2, Dyeworks 72ft x 52ft, divided for piece and wool dyeing, with fixed plant.

Lot 3, 5 Cottages/dwelling houses known as Ribbleden Hill.

The sale of machinery took place 8 days after the mill sale, on 31 July, and included machinery covering every process of cloth production, and also office, warehouse and mill furnishings. The *Holmfirth Express* reported, after the date of the auction of the premises, that all three lots were withdrawn as no bids were received.[17] The fate of the machinery is not known, as the outcome of machinery sales were never reported.

Tom Scott Brierley and John Chester took possession of the dyehouse in 1903, trading as Brierley, Chester & Co. Their partnership was dissolved in April of the following year, with Tom Scott Brierley continuing to trade as Brierley & Co. He was examined for bankruptcy on 18 June 1906, when he was found to have liabilities of £393 0s 4d, but his assets amounted to only £3 15s.

Lawton & Co, formerly of New Fold mill, were using the mill by 1905, when they applied to the council to be supplied with mains water for drinking. The council also gave Lawton's permission to use some mains water in training the firm's fire brigade. In 1907, Lawton's weavers were dissatisfied with the rates of pay that they were receiving, which were lower than the rates set by the Huddersfield Masters Association in 1883. Over 40 of them met with Mr. Gee, Secretary of the Powerloom Weavers Association and Mr. Ben Turner, who was also an official of the union, on Monday 24 November, to discuss the possibility of strike action. The union authorised members to withdraw their labour from Wednesday 26th after downing their current warp. The strike was still in progress in early January, with Lawton's still refusing to increase their rates of pay, saying that they would prefer to move the looms to Halifax. Some agreement must have been reached, as the *Yorkshire Textile Directory* for 1910 showed that Lawton's were still using the mill, and had 2,500 spindles and 60 looms in there, and that they also had premises in Halifax.

In February 1909 William Rollinson was badly injured when he came into contact with a projecting part of a beaming machine, sustaining cuts to his head and bruises on his arms. Mr. Fisher Dispensing

Chemist, rendered first aid, and then Rollinson was seen by Dr. Wathews before being taken home. The report points out that Mr. Rollinson was wearing a new smock made from material that did not tear, had he worn one of thinner fabric, he may have only suffered a torn smock. The mill was offered for sale in June 1913, and again in May 1915, by which time Lawton & Co were no longer using the mill, as all the mill buildings with the exception of the dyehouse were vacant. The dyehouse was occupied by John Davis & Co. Lot 2 was a builders yard occupied by Wagstaff & Turner; Lot 3 was a 2 storey joiner's shop occupied by Bailey, Mettrick & Wakefield; there was also building land, cottages and a house known as 'Oaklands' Holmfirth; also a house known as 'Wood Leigh' Ribbleden Hill, occupied by John Davis. The vendors of the property were Julia Ann Preston, Arthur Preston and Herbert Butterworth, who were the executors of the late Walter Preston. The mill and dyehouse were sold for £2,000; lot 2, the builder's yard, sold for £200; and lot 3 the joinery shop sold for £300. The buyer of the mill was presumably James Lumb who carried out several improvements. Among them were a combined staircase, lift well and sprinkler tower; and new boiler house and engine house, in 1916.

A company called Brierley & Wall were using part of the mill in 1916, whether this was the same Brierley who had been using the dyehouse ten years previously is not known, but the new company were advertising for Fettlers, so were in scribbling and carding, not dyeing. The council complained to all the occupants of the mill, in May 1917, about the pollution caused by high emissions of thick black smoke from the chimney, which was causing problems for residents in the area and the staff and pupils at the nearby National School, which at that time was just next door. Later in the year the emissions reduced after the council threatened to take court action. Complaints to the council from residents continued until 1920, when, apart from commencing court action against J. Davis & Co. and Brierley & Wall, they also decided to carry out daily observations on smoke emissions both here and at Valley Dyeworks, where residents in the Prickleden area had also been complaining.

Brierley & Wall, who were woollen spinners, and also had premises in Lepton, bought the Picturedrome Cinema, which was almost straight across the road from the mill in Dunford Road, in September 1920 for £1,000, while it was still showing films. It appears to have closed as a cinema on Christmas Day that year, after which, Brierley & Wall moved their production from the mill. The Picturedrome was the first cinema in Holmfirth, having been converted from a former Roller Skating Rink and opening on 9th September 1912. The electricity to run the projector was provided by an engine driving a dynamo. Unfortunately, the further fortunes of Messrs. Brierley & Wall in Holmfirth are not documented. The 'Holme Valley Theatre', off Victoria Street, which later became the 'Valley Theatre', opened on Easter Monday 24 March 1913.

J. Davis & Co. went into receivership in February 1931, but remained in business. The company name was changed to Davis Dyers Ltd, for whom a receiver was appointed in September 1939; but again they continued in business. An advertisement appeared in the Holmfirth Express on 14 October 1939, which read: H. Helm, youth 16-17 required for Poultry Farming; which suggests that, at that time, part of the mill was being used for rearing chickens.

A note in the minutes of Holmfirth Council in April 1947 records that a 'Huddersfield firm' were to take over part of the mill for woollen spinning, but does not record the company's name. In January 1950 Roland M. Greaves advertised in the Holmfirth Express for Twisters and Reelers to work daytime or evenings; this is the only reference found for this company. Holmfirth council recorded that steam emitting from the premises of Davis Dyers Ltd. was causing a danger for traffic in January 1955. Eric Hadfield Ltd. was in part of the mill from at least September 1956, when they were advertising for staff. They were listed in the Yorkshire Textile Industry Directory of 1962 as Eric Hadfield (Yarns) Ltd. Yarn Doublers, Reelers and Winders.

Davis Dyers Ltd. continued in business throughout the 1960s, and in 1972 were fined the maximum of £100 for discharging untreated effluent into the River Ribble. They were said to be one of fifteen firms in the Holme Valley guilty of this offence. The rate of flow from the outlet pipe was between 150 and 200 gallons a minute, a total of 500,000 gallons per day. The five storey mill, and a chimney that had been built mid nineteenth century, were demolished in July 1974, leaving a second chimney bearing a date stone of 1858 still standing. The mill was owned at that time by Baddeley Bros. who had busses and taxis. Steam escaping from a pipe had brought down part of the dyehouse roof, which was still being used by Davis Dyers Ltd., on 3 Aug. 1977; fortunately no-one was injured. Davis Dyers Ltd. again went into receivership in early 1986, the Managing Director Mr. Brian Duckett had agreed to buy the company from the receivers, and had registered a new name of Holmfirth Dyers Ltd. The new company began trading on 1 May 1986, at which time it had 14 employees. By July 2010, the company had become dyers and finishers, and the number of employees had increased to around 60.[18]

Notes

1 Holme Styes Mill
   W.C.R. 28 Jan. 1791; 15 Feb. 1808; 26 Sept. and 29 Oct. 1828; Kirklees Archive, KC6/8/21 9 Aug. 1851.
2 Choppards Mill
   W.C.R. 29 May, 1811; 1 May 1818; 2 June, 1824; 8 June 1825; 5 Sept. 1828; 7 May 1830; 15 Jan. 1836; Leeds Mercury, 22 Sept. 1838; Kirklees Archive, KC6/1/33; KC6/1/5; Huddd. Chron. 22 Dec. 1855; 31 Jan. 1857; 30 May 1857; 7 Dec. 1861; 27 Dec. 1862; 25 Mar, 1865; 16 June, 1Dec. 1866; 5 June 1869; Hudds. Ex. 10 Feb. 1872; H'firth Exp. 25 April, 9 May 1896; W.C.R. 8 Nov. 1826, also 11 May 1827; 27 Oct. 1826, and 30 Oct. 1829
3 W.C.R. 8 Nov. 1826, also 11 May 1827; 27 Oct. 1826, and 30 Oct. 1829
4 Washpit Mill
   Supplementary Report into the Employment of Children in Factories and as to the Propriety and Means of Curtailing the Hours of their Labour, Part 1; (25 March 1834); W.C.R. 30 April, 2 July 1841; Leeds Mercury, 30 Oct, 1846; Leeds Intelligencer, 19 Aug. 1848; Hudds. Chron. 7 June 1856; 25 April 1857; 27 Feb. 1858; 27 July 1861, 14 Nov. 1863; 4 Nov. 1865; 3 Nov. 1866; Hudds. Ex.31 Oct. 1857; 21 Mar. 1868; 15 May 1869, 21 Oct. 1871; National Monuments Record Centre, Swindon, information on Washpit Mill, February 1986.
5 Hudds. Ex. 2 March, 10 Aug. 1872; 17 April 1875; 17 June 1876; 12 Jan 1878; 14 Aug. 1880; 5 Feb. 1898; 21 Jan. 1922; Hudds. Chron. 24 June, 1876; Hudds. Weekly News, 6 May 1876; Cartworth and Wooldale Local Board Minutes 1888 & 1893; H'firth Exp. 29 March 1902; 23 Jan. 1915; 14 March 1980; 9 May 1980; 3 Oct. 1980; J. M. Hinchliffe, Unpublished dissertation 1973.
6 Green Lane Mill
   W.C.R. 29 March, 30 Oct. 1822; 17 May, 5 June 1839; Supplementary Report into the Employment of Children in Factories and as to the Propriety and Means of Curtailing the Hours of their Labour, Part 1; (25 March 1834); W.C.R. 4 Jan. 1840; Leeds Times, 18 Nov. 1843; Kirklees Archive KC6/1/33; Hudds Chron. 31 April 1856; 22 July 1871; Hudds. Ex. 21 July 1866; 8 Sept. 1866; 19 Jan. 1867; 28 Jan. 11 Feb. 1871; 19 Sept. 1874; 26 Sept. 1874; 17 Apr. & 15 May 1875; H'firth Exp. 30 Nov. 1889; 25 July 1891; 24 Nov. 1894; Textile Manufacturer, Nov. 1894; Anecdotal evidence from Mr. S. Sheard, cofounder of Rowan Weavers, May 2011.
7 Dover Mill
   W.C.R. 20 Jan. 1791; 1 Dec. 1815; 2 Feb 1816; 8 June 1825; 28 Sept. 1838; 8 May 1840; Leeds Mercury, 2 July 1836; Kirklees Archive, KC6/1/33; Hudds. Chron. 8 Mar. 1851; 1 July 1854; 16 June 1866; 30 Nov. 1867; Hudds. Ex. 7 June 1856; 1 June 1872; 30 Aug. 18 Oct. 1873; 21 March 1885; 17Apr. 1886; Kirklees Archive, KMT16/Cartworth Valuation 1859.
8 H'firth Exp. 22 Jan 1887; 2 Aug. 1888; 2 March 1889; 15 Nov. 1890; 15 Sept. 1900; 10 Aug 1901; 27 July 1907; Hudds. Ex. 3 Feb. 1894; Kirklees Archive, KMT4 21 Aug. 1902; UHO Holmfirth 7 April 1920; 2 April and 6 Dec. 1948; 17 Jan 1962; H'firth Exp. 25 May, 20 July 1984; 28 July 1989.
9 Jane Wood Dyehouse
   W.C.R. 15 Dec. 1826; also 28 Sept. 1838; Kirklees Archive, KC6/1/33 1854; Hudds. Ex. 17 Aug. 1861; 20 Aug, 5 Sept. 1887; J. M. Hinchliffe, Unpublished dissertation 1973.
10 Pingle mill/Lower Dover mill
   W.C.R. 22 Oct 1783; 4 Feb. 1785; 28 Jan. 1791; 9 Oct. 1793; 1 Nov. 1797; 5 Oct. 1804; 6 Mar. 1807; 15Sept. 1809; 29 May 1812; 31 May 1820; 10 Nov. 1820; 18 May 1821; 14 May 1824; 30 May 1827Leeds Intelligencer, 7 Oct. 1788; Kirklees Archive, Cartworth Rate Valuation 1859; Hudds. Ex. 6 July 1872; 20 Aug. 1887.
11 Underbank mill
   Leeds Intelligencer, 11 April 1796; WYCRO QE13/2/39, 1822 Wooldale township; Huddersfield Examiner, 6 Nov. 1875; Supplementary Report into the Employment of Children in Factories and as to the Propriety and Means of Curtailing the Hours of their Labour, Part 1; (25 March 1834); London Gazette, 14 April 1838; W.C.R. 6 April, 1844; Huddersfield Chronicle, 3 April, 1852; 28 Apr. 1855; 8, 15 and 22 June, 21 Sept. 1861
12 Hudds. Ex. 10 May 1873, 8 July 1882; Census Returns 1881; Holmfirth Express, 30 June, 1888; 29 Nov. 1890; Kirklees Archive, KMT4 Holmfirth, 4 Jan. 1894; Text. Manufacturer, July 1895; Sandford's Centenary Booklet published 1954.
13 Kirklees Archive, UHO Holmfirth 4 July 1907; H'firth Exp. 4 Feb. 1911; 13 Jan. 1978; 3 May 1996; Centenary Booklet 1954; Kirklees Archive, UHO Holmfirth 12 May 1947, 11 July 1949, 8 Feb. 1954; Anecdotal evidence from Mr. S. Sheard, formerly Rowan Weavers, 2011.
14 W.C.R. 27 October 1830.
15 Swanbank mill
   W.C.R. 27 Oct. 1826; 26 Jan 1827; 12 Dec. 1834; 28 Jan. 1842; 24 July 1846; Supplementary Report into the Employment of Children in Factories and as to the Propriety and Means of Curtailing the Hours of their Labour, Part 1; (25 March 1834); Leeds Intelligencer, 6 Feb. 1841; Leeds Mercury, 22 May 1847; Huddersfield Chronicle, 20 Mar. 1852; 7 Mar. 1857; 21 Jan. 1860; 4 Feb. 1860; 24 Nov. 1860; Kirklees Archive, KC6/1/33.
16 London Gazette, May 1867, 11 Dec. 1877; 12 Feb. 15 Nov. 1878; Hudds. Chron. 6 Feb. 1869; 16 Oct. 1869; Hudds. Ex. 19 Sept 1874; 11 Feb. 1871; 10 May 1873; 6 Nov. 1875; 19 Sept 1874; 10 June 1876; 8 Dec. 1877; 5 Jan 1878; 24 July 1881, 2 Aug. 1884; 26 May 1888, 19 July 1890; H'firth Exp. 2 Aug. 1890; 28 November, 1891; J. Beever's Obituary 3 May 1913; 25 Oct.1924; 25 Nov. 1994; 1 Mar. 1996; Kirklees Archive, UHO Holmfirth, 15 Feb. 1967.
17 Ribbleden mill and dyeworks
   W.C.R. 19 Nov. 1819; 29 June 1821; 26 Sept. 1823; 28 Oct. 1829; 10 Oct. 1834; 26 Oct. 1836; 3 Sept. 1841; Supplementary Report into the Employment of Children in Factories and as to the Propriety and Means of Curtailing the Hours of their Labour, Part 1; (25 March 1834); Leeds Mercury, 16 May 1840; Kirklees Archive, KC6/1/33 1853; Hudds. Ex. 24 Sept. 1853; 7 June 1856; 16 Mar. 1867; 12 Apr; 18 Oct. 1873; 10 Jan. 1880; 1 Sept. 1877; 10 Jan. 1885; 5 Feb. 1898; 15 June 1901; Hudds. Chron. 15 Oct. 1853; 19 Apr. 1856; , 6 Aug. 1864; 20 July 1901; Textile Manufacturer, March 1899; H'firth Exp. 27 July 1901.
18 Textile Manufacturer, April 1904; H'firth Exp. 23 June 1906; 11 Nov. 1916; 4 Sept. and 25 Dec. 1920; 7 Sept. 1912; 22 Mar. 1913; 26 Feb. 1972; 20 July 1974; 5 Aug 1977; 9 May 1986; Kirklees Archive, KMT4/UHO Holmfirth, 3 Aug. 1905, 20 June 1907; 9 Dec. 1915, 17 Feb, 6 Dec. 1916; 9 May, 1917; 6 Oct. 1919, 5 July, 13 Sept. 1920; 16 Mar. 1931, also 18 Sept. 1939; KC6/8/35-36 1915; Yorks. Fact. Times, 29 Nov. 1907; 3 Jan. 1908; Worker, 20 Feb. 1909; also Anecdotal evidence gained on a visit to the premises, 6 July 2010.

CHAPTER 11

Holmfirth to Mytholmbridge

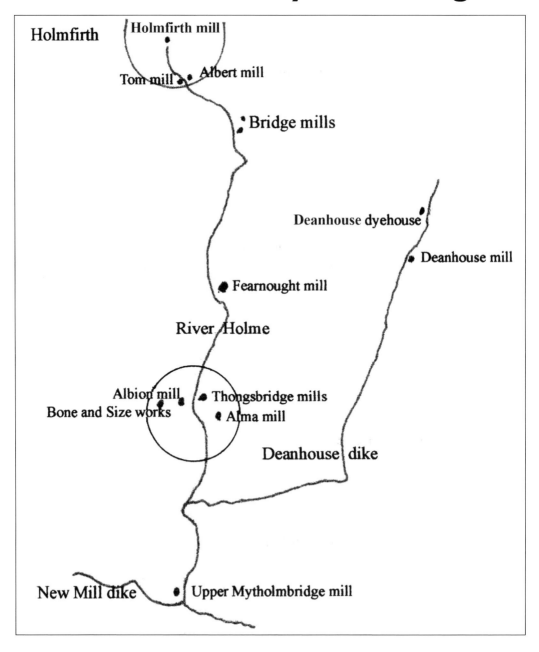

Holmfirth mill

Henry James Morehouse maintained that the corn mill known as Cartworth mill was built in what eventually became the township of Holmfirth. If he was correct in that assumption the mill was already in existence in the year 1274. Even if he was wrong, there was a corn mill built here on the land between what became Towngate and the river Holme by 1316, when the Wakefield Court Roll for that year recorded that:

> *Cartworth mill and the new mill at Holnefrith are demised this year to William the Forester of Holnefrith for 41 marks [£27 6s 8d] payable at the usual terms. Pledges: William Wolf of Thwong, John the Couper of Wlvedale, Richard del Bothe, William del Bothe, Jordan the Milner, Richard Michel of Foghleston, Robert son of Sarah of the same place, Thomas the Couper, Adam Kenward, Robert son of Matthew of Foghleston, Robert of Wades, John of Loukes of Wlvedale, and Thomas son of Simon.*

The reason for the pledges was that should the fee farmer fail to pay the rent for whatever reason, the court would call on the pledgers to make up the shortfall. The mill was let on an annual fee to various fee farmers for around the next 200 years until, in the sixteenth century it was let by deed to the Allott family of Bentley Grange. A Survey of the Graveship carried out in the 16th century, but not dated, records that in addition to the mills, Robert Allott had the water rights on the River Holme between the Queen's mill in Holnefrith and Mytholmbridge. The mention of the 'Queen's mill' denotes that the survey was carried out some time between 1553 and 1601, during the reign of either Queen Mary, or of Queen Elizabeth I.

As mentioned in Chapter 5, the mills were hit by flood waters in 1777, the corn mill was completely gutted, with all the windows and doors being washed away, but the walls remained standing; the fulling mill was totally destroyed. At this time the mills were owned by Mr. Bryan Allott junior, rector of Burnham in Norfolk, who was in great financial difficulty and was in prison for debt. The mills were offered for sale in 1784, an advertisement in the *Leeds Mercury* described them as:

> *'CROWN MILLS at Holmfirth, to be sold together or in lots, on 1 June. An ancient and well-accustomed Corn Mill and Fulling Mill, with a dwelling house, now in two tenements; with a close adjoining the mill dam containing near 3 acres of rich meadow land extremely well situated for building and lying in length against the Turnpike road leading from Huddersfield to Woodhead.*
>
> *The situation of the mill is remarkably advantageous for carrying on a most extensive trade, as erection of any other works which the purchaser may choose in the Woollen, Cotton or other manufactures, having a good command of water, and being situated in the midst of a populous trading country. The fulling mill and one tenement may be entered immediately, the corn mill and second tenement on 28 August, and the close in February next. David Hinchliffe of Holmfirth will show the premises.'*

It appears that after the flood, the mills had been restored and repaired before 1784, but the fulling mill was not being used. The 3 acres of rich meadow land were across the river, and eventually became part of the areas known as Norridge and Newtown. The mills were probably bought by John Fallas of Wood in Upperthong, who carried out some rebuilding or renovation in 1786. John's Widow Elizabeth along with their son James sold the mills to William Gartside of Holmfirth in 1804. William Gartside died childless, in his will he passed the mills to his two brothers John and George, who were admitted as owners of the mills in February 1813.

The Gartside's increased their landholding in 1821 by buying 2 cottages, a stable and 4 yards of land at Mill Hill, which was where the fulling mill stood, for the sum of £225 from Joseph and Lydia Bray of Holmfirth. The brothers replied to the enquiry by the Factory Commissioners in 1833: the premises were used for scribbling, carding and slubbing wool, and for fulling cloth; the buildings had been applied to their present purpose in 1786, and enlarged in 1819. Machinery was driven by either a water wheel or steam engine, both of which delivered 14hp, with part of the power being used for cloth finishing by J. Charlesworth & Sons, who, in addition to using part of Holmfirth mill also had premises in Holmbridge Mill. Gartside's employed 23 people, I boy and 2 girls under 10, 3 boys and 4 girls under 12, 3 boys and 3 girls under 14, I boy under 16, and 6 men over 21. The only information they provide on wages is that regular wages, when in full work, were 4s per week; but as they did not keep a book it was impossible to obtain a figure for average earnings. The 4s per week presumably applied to the under 12s. The Gartside's paid all employees direct. Hours of work when fully employed were 5am to 9pm including Saturday, with no payment for overtime; as regards meal breaks they said "No time allowed but by exchanging hands one for another; but most of the hands have to eat and work, and this is a general practice in this neighbourhood". Children were not allowed any time for meals. Employees were allowed 3 days holiday at Christmas, I day at Easter and 3 days at Holy Thursday, all unpaid. To the question about employing more than one set of children they answered: "Never; objection first, it is not possible to obtain two sets of children in this part of the country in every mill. Second, if it was practicable, it would be a cruel system, the adults would be almost worked to death. Third, if one mill should be able to obtain two sets, and not another, they who had two sets would run those who had only one; for by working for less wages, they would monopolise the work of two mills." On the subject of corporal punishment they answered: "Corporal punishments are inflicted on all the children employed in the mill; and it is necessary to punish them in that way, so long as they work so many hours per day, otherwise their work would be ill-performed." It was necessary to employ children less than twelve years of age to piece cardings for the slubbers. In view of the answers to the foregoing questions, the Gartside's answer to question 27 about parliament regulating factory hours is, to say the least, surprising: "We beg to remark, that we think it is high time the legislature interfere on this subject. The system of working, as at present conducted, is one of cruelty and degradation; it is even disgusting to any man in humanity, whether he be a mill proprietor or not; but the humane are bound to practice it so long as it is the general practice." The return is signed 'John and George Gartside'.

It is worth comparing the answers given to the Factory Commissioners by the Gartside's with those given by Charlesworth's, who were also using part of the same mill. They were occupied in the Dressing and Finishing of Woollen cloth, with an all male workforce of 21, made up of I boy under 12 earning 4s, 3 under 14 and I under 16 all earning 6s, 2 under 18 earning 7s, 2 under 21 earning 13s 6d, and 12 over 21 earning 21s. Overtime was paid at the same rate as normal working. Their hours of work were from 6am to 8pm, with two hours less on Saturdays. Meal breaks were 30 minutes at 8.30am for Breakfast, I hour at 12.30 for Dinner, and 30 minutes at 4.30pm for Drinking; during these times the machinery was stopped allowing all to have their meals together. They did not give details of holidays, just 'various holidays at wakes etc.', which were unpaid. They had not tried to recruit a second set of children, nor did they permit the use of Corporal Punishment. In answer to the question of Parliamentary legislation they said "We advocate some restriction as to the labour of children. Our scribbling carding and fulling mill is at Holmbridge in the township of Austonley. See return Barber & Co. Our system of manufacture is chiefly on the old system of the cottage or domestic kind; viz. by the weavers, spinners, etc. at their own cottages.' The return is signed Joseph Charlesworth & Sons. In 1840 Charlesworth's were still using the fulling mill on Mill Hill for dressing and finishing; George Gartside had bought his brother's share in the mills, which he would pass to his sons Joseph and William on his death. They also owned a sizing shop at Bridge, which was occupied by George Exley. George Gartside died in December 1844, when the mill was being considerably enlarged.

Isaac and Charles Beardsell of Holme went to look at it while the alterations were in progress, and Isaac gives an account in his diary of what he saw:

> 'It was rather late when we got to Holmfirth, I called of Joshua Moorhouse, we Look'd the mill etc. through, he explained to us how they intended to rebuild it. The part which they intend rebuilding will be about 28yds long and 18yds of it 13yds wide, and the remainder about 10yds wide; there will be the ground floor occupied with Stocks etc. 3 rooms [floors] above and the Attic. The other part of the mill is about 18yds long by 8yds wide, the ground floor is divided into several rooms, 3 rooms [floors] above

and the Attic. The Machinery etc. which they say is valued at about £1,000 looks very poor, there is a Tenter Stove heated by Steam 26½yds long; a dyehouse very small, with 2 pans in it, and they propose to rebuild the mill, put a new steam boiler in of 30 horse power, put two new water wheels in 19ft diameter, 8ft broad, there is about 17 feet of fall and the Reservoir rates about £55 a year. They want a Rent of £450 when they have repaired and made the alterations etc.

The underlining of the amount of rent would indicate that Isaac thought it too high. He and Charles made an offer of £400 a year, which they refused to increase even though they were told that someone else was interested, but were subsequently very put out when they were unsuccessful. The new tenant of the mill was Mr. Nathan Thewlis, who had been using part of the mill prior to the rebuilding.

The flood of 1852 caused considerable damage in Holmfirth, the *Huddersfield Chronicle* reported that:

'At the Holmfirth Mill in the occupation of N. Thewlis & Co. the destruction is very great. The dam stones are washed down and the dam destroyed, together with two dyehouses, tenter stove, and the warehouse belonging to Mr. R. Bower. The loss sustained by Mr. Bower is supposed to be about £100. The number of hands employed was about 80 or 90. ....A blue dyehouse belonging to Messrs. Roberts & Son, together with a wool stove in the occupation of the Holmfirth Mill Company is destroyed, and one corner of the dwelling house of Mr. Roberts is carried away.'

The sizing shop referred to earlier that was owned by the Gartsides and tenanted by George Exley, was located below the County bridge and was also destroyed by the flood. The house in which the Exley family lived was next door to the sizing shop, and was extensively damaged. The family managed to escape by climbing through a rear window. There is no mention of any damage to either of the four storey mills, but it is hard to believe that such a large volume of flood water did not enter the buildings through doors and windows causing at least some damage to machinery. J. Mayhall writes: 'The Holmfirth mill sustained very serious damage', but does not elaborate. Nathan Thewlis submitted a claim for damage to buildings, machinery and stock, totalling £2,079 5s 5d, which was reduced to £1,754 11s 5d by the flood committee. He appears to have been paid £862 16s 11d in settlement. George Exley submitted a claim for buildings, machinery, stock and furnishings, amounting to £230 0s 6d, this was reduced to £146 8s, and he was paid £100.[1] Despite the reported loss by Mr. Bower in the *Huddersfield* Chronicle, there is no record of a claim having been made by him.

A small fire started in a box of woollen waste stored in an outbuilding belonging to Nathan Thewlis in July 1852. No serious damage was done, but the report pointed out that this was either the fourth or fifth time that this had occurred in just a few weeks. The Reservoir Commissioners give the owners of Holmfirth mills in 1853 as Mary Gartside, Nathan Thewlis and Joshua Morehouse, who were trustees of George Gartside deceased; the occupants of the buildings were Nathan Thewlis, George Thewlis, Joshua Hoyle, Robert Ramsden, John Bower and Richard Bower. All the employers combined to give a treat to their 70 workers on 21 April 1855, marking the 'footings' of several new workmen, and the inauguration of new tenants in part of the mill. The meal was followed by a 'free and easy'. Fire broke out in the engine house and stove used by Nathan Thewlis in early December 1855. The fire bell in the church tower was rung and the Unity brigade soon arrived at the mill. The lack of wind helped in controlling the fire and damage was kept to a minimum.

Thursday 29 May 1856 was the day chosen by Holmfirth to celebrate the end of the Crimean War. A large procession walked around the district, from Holmfirth to Holmbridge then via Dobb back through Holmfirth, on to Thongsbridge, Wooldale, Totties, Scholes Moor, Cross, Underbank and Lane End back to Holmfirth, finishing at the Town Hall. There was a Grand Firework Display in the evening, and some public buildings were illuminated.

George and Nathan Thewlis, Robert Ramsden, Joshua Hoyle, Richard Bower, also Henry,

James, William, Jonathon and Jonas Bower, all partners of Thewlis & Co. ended their partnership in December 1859. The reason given for the dissolution was 'the effluxion of time'.

A fire was discovered at the mill about 4pm on Sunday 5 June 1864; there had been a smell of burning in the area for about four hours prior to its discovery, but no-one had taken much notice until smoke and flames began issuing from the upper floors of the mill. The tenant was Mr. Jonathon Thorp, but he had sub-let some of the rooms to John Hinchliffe of Netherthong. The Unity brigade were quickly on the scene, and had the fire under control before the brigade from John Brooke & Sons of Armitage Bridge arrived. The floor of the room affected was saturated in oil, and had burned through in several places; there were 6 scribblers and 3 or 4 billies in the room, most of which were damaged, along with large heaps of slubbings that were ruined. The flames had also burned through to the floor above. The building and machinery were owned by Mr. Thorp; the materials were the property of Mr. Hinchliffe. No estimates of the damage were given. Within days of this fire, a meeting of manufacturers was held at the Elephant & Castle Inn. Concern was being expressed about the cost of Fire Insurance for mills, and that the only engine available to cover all the Holmfirth and New Mill area was the small Unity engine. Enquiries showed that a total of £2,000 a year was being spent by manufacturers on fire insurance. One of the number pointed out that if there was no claim in five years, £10,000 would have been unnecessarily expended, which was enough to build and equip a large mill. The problem was discussed for a week or so, until someone suggested that every manufacturer in the area should contribute £1 for every slubbing billy they possessed, which would yield enough money for the district to buy a second engine. Those present at the meeting approved and adopted the idea, but the funds failed to materialise; leading to Barber's at Holmbridge and Turner's at Bridge mill designing and building their own engines.

Another fire was discovered in the teazing room at the mill in early August 1868, but was extinguished before much damage was done. A more serious event occurred on Tuesday 23 November 1868 while George Morton aged 63 and a man called Jessop, both Fettlers working for Jonathon Thorp, were cleaning a machine when the drive belt came off. The machine was presumably stopped at the time. While attempting to put the belt back on, Morton's foot became caught between the belt and the drum and he was carried round the shafting which revolved 80 times per minute. He was badly mutilated, and death was almost instantaneous. While attempting to extricate his work colleague, Jessop's hand also became caught and he was drawn up to the shafting, but he fell and escaped without injury. As was usual, the inquest jury returned a verdict of 'accidental death'. A 3 year old girl called Sarah Jane Battye daughter of Mr. J, Battye a tailor of Lane End, went with two friends to play in a field adjoining Holmfirth mill where there were some 'Seak' pits about six feet deep containing waste liquids, including Vitriol and other compounds from the mill, in early May 1872. The girl fell into a pit that was more than half full, fortunately she was seen by a workman who quickly pulled her out. After being taken home she was seen by the surgeon Mr. Berry, who directed that emetics should be administered to clear her system of any Vitriol or other poisons that she may have swallowed. She was said to be in a precarious state.

Ownership of the mills had passed to Miss Gartside by 1873, who was the daughter of George Gartside. There was possibly a growing awareness of public safety in Local Authorities at this time, as Wooldale Local Board asked Miss Gartside that the mill dam, which was alongside the mill between Towngate and the river, should be fenced round. The river is considerably lower than where the mill stood in the area that eventually became known as 'The Gartside Estate', which poses a question as to how water was got from the river to the mill dam. The 25in Ordinance Survey map of 1893 shows a substantial weir existing across the river just downstream of Victoria Bridge, running from in front of the cinema building to the entrance to the dam, which would raise the upstream water level to that of the dam, this has since disappeared. The mill was advertised as being to let in July 1874, and again in September when it was described as:

'All those extensive woollen mills called Holmfirth Mills, well furnished with modern machinery,

water and steam power; with dyehouse, stove, warehouse, offices and other conveniences. The mill is situated at Holmfirth about 150 yards from the Railway Station, and has a good supply of water for dyeing, scouring, fulling and finishing purposes. Particulars from S. Wimpenny, Auctioneers and Valuers, Huddersfield and Holmfirth; or to the present occupants Jonathon Thorp & Sons who will show the premises.

While Thorp's were moving their machinery out of the mill in December 1874, to transfer it to their new premises at Dobroyd, New Mill, a rope that was being used to lift a willow machine onto a lurry broke, and the machine fell onto Mr. Thorp's foot. He was attended by the surgeon Mr. Trotter, but was not seriously injured, and was taken home.

Upperthong Local Board recorded in 1877 that Gledhill & Brook had submitted plans for a new corn mill to be built on Crown Bottom, which they passed; but this was probably never built as a sale of finishing and spinning machinery was advertised to take place at Holmfirth mill in October 1877, because the space had been let for use as a corn mill. Gledhill and Brook continued to use the corn mill in Holmfirth mill until after 1934. A company called the Holmfirth Patent Wool Company were using part of the mill by 1879, fire was discovered in the drying stove on 22 Jan. 1880, about 11.15pm; the alarm was raised and a hose connected to the water main, which had only recently been installed. This hose was 'very efficient in assisting to extinguish the fire and in checking the spread of flames to the rest of the mill, which is one of the oldest in the neighbourhood'. The Unity brigade and the brigade from Messrs J.T. Taylor & Co both attended and assisted in extinguishing the flames. Damage to the stove building which was not insured, was estimated at £40; damage to the contents of the stove, which were insured, was estimated at £100. Wooldale Local Board sent the Patent Wool Company an invoice for £2 2s in January 1880 for using mains water to extinguish the fire, which was not paid, resulting in the Board deciding to sue the Patent Wool Company to recover the money in September of that year.

Four youths were charged with stealing 6lbs of Brass valued at 9s from the mill on 26 January 1885, the property of Miss Gartside. They were Ben Bower aged 13 of Towngate, George Bramall aged 17 of Church Terrace, William Beardsell aged 16 of Towngate, and Fred Beaumont aged 14 of Churchyard. After hearing the evidence, the bench fined Beardsell and Bramall 20s each plus costs, and Beaumont and Bower 10s each plus costs. About 8pm on Monday 11 May 1885, a fourteen year old lad called Bower, son of Henry Bower of Towngate met with an accident at the mill. He kept pigeons in a room over the old dyehouse at the mill, and had climbed a ladder to reach them when he fell to the bottom; which was where his mother later found him unconscious. He was taken home where he was visited by a doctor who found that he had no serious injuries, and could be expected to recover. Could this be the same Bower who was implicated in the theft of Brass?

James Watkinson & Son were using at least part of the mill in 1888, when they gave a treat to all their workers, totalling about 250 between Washpit and Holmfirth mills, in January. They subsequently moved all their operation to Washpit, as part of Holmfirth mill was advertised as being to let in June of the same year, and Watkinson's name does not occur again as an occupant of this mill.[2] Machinery that had belonged to the late George Gartside was offered for sale on 22 November, consisting of: 4 condenser sets, 2½ prs self-acting mules; 3 power looms by Schofield & Kirk, hydro extractor, spike willey, wringing machine, weighing machine, iron cistern, hand cart etc. Also yarn and waste.

Armitage & Clelland of Huddersfield moved into part of the mills in 1889, and gave their 50 workers a treat in January 1890. Peace and harmony was short-lived in their mending room when it became known that all were not receiving the same rates of pay, and on 4 February the menders came out on strike. The firm rectified the problem by dismissing the two women who were receiving more than the rest, and the other menders went back to work. A sale of equipment that had presumably been in the corn mill was advertised to take place on 25 June 1891, on the instructions of Mr. Charles Haigh, but no company name is given. Items included 1 pair 32inch diameter grinding stones, suitable for Corn grinding on an iron frame with under gear; an iron crusher on a strong iron frame; 8 inch sugar grinding mill; 2 iron cooling slabs; 2 corn bins, various sundries, and 20 tins of biscuits.

A case began in the West Riding Assize Court in Holmfirth in August 1892, which suggested that Holmfirth mill was in a dilapidated state. The court's time on this occasion was spent in listening to Counsel present arguments to determine ownership of the mills which were not resolved, and the case was adjourned to a future date. The condition of the buildings was no doubt deteriorating, as they had stood for a good number of years, with a succession of occupants, and without renovation.

The woollen and worsted manufacturers seem to have moved to other premises and during the 1890s were replaced by rug makers. An advertisement appeared in the Holmfirth Express in November 1891 for rug weavers and 'putters-in' to work at Holmfirth mill, but gives no company name. The need for 'putters-in' suggests that the firm were in competition with Beever's at Swanbank mill, making pegged rugs. Another nameless firm advertised for 30 girls to train as velvet cutters in 1897. John Thornton was advertising for rug weavers in 1902; there was also a firm called Armitage using part of the mill in 1900, when Edgar Armitage was ordered by Holmfirth Council to remove refuse from the mill yard as it 'gave off offensive effluvia'; and George Armitage, who also had premises in Spring Lane mill was advertising for rug weavers at Holmfirth mill in 1905. This advertisement appeared regularly until the end of April 1906. James Holmes, who was possibly a member of the Holmes family who had the rope works at Kirkbridge and rug manufactory at Tenter Hill mill in Wooldale, was also using part of Holmfirth mill for rug making in 1906, when the council agreed to supply the firm with drinking water from the mains for 5s per year, unless the number of employees rose to more than 15, when they would have to pay an additional 4d per person.

The Smithy was being used by George Bullock in 1906; but the mill was not fully tenanted. The old mill, plus the dyehouse and 1 room in the new mill were advertised to let from 12 October 1907, to the middle of January 1908. The new part of the mill began being advertised to let in early October 1908, the advert appeared weekly throughout 1909 and continued until April 1910, when it changed to: 'To let – the large mill and dyehouse; also 2 rooms in the new end of Holmfirth Mill. Apply Wm. Sykes & Son, or Wm. Brown Architect, Holmfirth.' This advert ran until the end of 1911.

The owner of the mill in the early 20th Century appears to have been Mr. Henry Thorp, who lived in Harrogate. He wrote to the council in 1910 offering to supply electricity for street lighting, indicating that the mill possibly had a generator installed. He wrote again in 1911 complaining that rubbish and street sweepings from Towngate were being left in a place where they were blowing into the mill dam. In 1915, the Inspector of Nuisances reported to the council that the mills were occupied by several tenants who had to share two midden privies. There were a total of 29 employees: the Smiths shop employed 2 men; a Joiner's shop employed 1 man; the Mechanics shop/Motor garage, Coldwell Bros. employed 2 men; the corn mill, Gledhill & Brook's, employed 3 men; there were two weaving rooms, one of which was Albert Mallinson & Son; one weaving room employed 3 men and 3 women, the other employed 4 men and 5 women; There was also a mending room employing 6 women. The council directed that the two midden privies should be altered to two Water Closets for the women, and one Water Closet and one Urinal for the men.

The second phase of the scheme to widen Towngate was under way in January 1922, when an article in the *Huddersfield Examiner* of 14 January remarked: 'The old buildings revealed by the demolition of the shops opposite the White Hart Hotel have a decidedly picturesque appearance'. The new road cut across one corner of the mill dam.

The mill continued in use, and was included in the auction of the Gartside Estate in June 1928:

> *Lot 1, included the Friendship Inn, which stood on Towngate more or less opposite the White Hart, one shop, a storeroom with stable under, one 4-storey mill plus attic, 83ft 3in long, 36ft 3in average width, occupied by H. Mettrick, joiners, and part unoccupied.* This sold for £2,000.

> *Lot 2, was the 3 storey mill, 78ft 6in long by 28ft wide, occupied by Holmfirth Motor Co. on the ground floor, and W.H. Lockwood, commission weavers on the two upper floors. Also part of the Joiner's shop,*

a stone built garage occupied by Mr. P.N. Brown, and the conveniences; plus a plot of land between the mill and the river containing the remains of the dam and weir. This sold for £2,800.

Lot 3, was the four storey corn mill plus attic, 56ft 3in by 25ft 9in, occupied by Gledhill & Brook; also the remaining part of the joiner's shop 56ft by 8ft 6in, occupied by H. Beever, the disused dyehouse occupied by E. England & Sons, and the long chimney; also some vacant land behind the dyehouse, next to the old burial ground. These sold for £700. Lots 4, 5, and 6 were properties further up Station Road. It was recorded in the minutes of the council meeting held on 20 June that the three lots comprising Holmfirth mill had been bought by the council, with the intention of demolishing the buildings. The first of the tenants to move out were the commission weavers W.H. Lockwood, who left one year after the sale, in June 1829.

It was announced at a council meeting in December 1931 that at least one floor in the mill was very weak, and that the water wheel was in danger of collapse. Although the council were supposedly clearing the occupants of the mill, they gave permission for the 1st Holme Valley Scout group to use part of the top floor of the new mill for meetings on a temporary basis. Tenancy of the dyehouse was due to terminate on 30 June 1932, G. W England finally left on September 30th. The council minutes for November 1932 show that a Mr. Hinchliffe would be the tenant of the dyehouse from 1 December. That building was finally demolished in 1935. From January 1934, Gledhill & Brook rented the 2nd 3rd and 4th floors of the corn mill on an annual basis for £35 a year. The demolition of the chimney that was attached to the dyehouse, and stood next to the mill took place on 29 July 1936, using the 'pit prop' method. The masonry on two adjacent sides of the chimney is removed at the base and replaced with wooden supports. A large fire is lit in the base of the chimney giving it a final appearance of being used; when the timbers burn through the chimney falls in that direction.[3] H. Mettrick, the joiner, appears to have continued his tenancy until 1954, when the *Holmfirth Express* announced on 20 March, that a sale of joinery equipment and wood belonging to Mr. Mettrick would take place at the mill. One of the earliest modern buildings to be built on the site was that of the Post Office, which still remains; the major part of the site is now being used as a car park.

Newtown Mill

The date for building this mill, which stood at the junction of School Street and Market Street in Newtown, is not known. The earliest information on the premises comes from the minutes of Upperthong Local Board, who recorded that an application had been received from John Batley & Sons manufacturers of Shoddy and Mungo, for a supply of mains water to the steam boiler at the mill in February 1883, which they agreed to. The premises were offered for sale in 1896 and were described as: the 3 storey mill, with boiler house, engine house, stable and outbuildings, including engine, boiler and shafting, occupied by John Batley & Sons, Mungo manufacturers. Plus a cottage and four storey warehouse, (unoccupied); also 2 dwelling houses fronting onto Huddersfield Road. The press reported that the property was bought by Mr. W. Bailey [or should that have read Mr. W. Batley], for £810.

John Batley & Sons continued to occupy the premises, and by 1909 ownership of the company had passed to Mr. William Batley, who unfortunately died on September 27th from a heart complaint while on holiday in Colwyn Bay. The business was advertised for sale by auction on October 9th as a 'going concern'. Whether ownership of the company changed hands is not known, but the firm continued trading as John Batley & Sons, and is recorded in the *Textile Industry Directory* of 1942-3 as still being Shoddy and Mungo manufacturers. A garage at the mill had been advertised as being to let in January 1938, applications to C. Lawton, Prickleden House, Holmfirth.

The date when John Batley & Sons ceased trading is not known, but the buildings were advertised for sale by private treaty, with vacant possession, in July 1958, when they were described as: Ground floor: warehouse 35ft by 19ft 10in; drying room 17ft by 17ft; boiler house 29ft 6in by 11ft with Lancashire boiler; engine house 19ft 5in by 20ft with Lancashire steam boiler. First floor: warehouse

35ft by 19ft 10in. Second floor, Warehouse 53ft 9in by 19ft 10in. Sorting room 20ft by 19ft 6in. Also cottage adjoining occupied by Messrs. Carters; and Garage in the occupation of D. Howard Esq. As it was a private sale, there is no indication of whether anyone bought it. The premises were advertised again as Lot 1 in a sale with other properties to be auctioned on 13 April 1960.[4] The report of the auction gives details of two lots, but makes no mention of the mill, or of a house at 28 Paris, Scholes, which suggests that they were either sold privately prior to the auction, or were withdrawn.

The property ultimately became owned by the local authority, and was demolished to allow School Street to be widened.

Tom mill

Standing on the right bank of the River Holme, below Holmfirth mill, close to the County Bridge, was a mill that was marked as Tom mill on the 6 inch Ordinance Survey map of 1853, but which had actually disappeared before the map was published. The earliest information I have found is in the Wakefield Court Roll of 1796, when James Hirst of Bottoms relinquished his claim to 130sq.yds. of land in the north-west corner of a close of land called Lumb Bank in Wooldale, in favour of Thomas Charlesworth clothier of Holmfirth with permission to 'dam the water flowing in the watercourse alongside the close called Lumb Bank for the purpose of working any mill or machinery Thomas Charlesworth his heirs or assigns may erect'. The agreement also gives permission for Charlesworth 'to make a goit or drain through a close called Low Fold into the said watercourse'.

In the following year Thomas Charlesworth of Cuttell Bottom Holmfirth, raised a mortgage of £80, from Joshua Woodhead of Bridge mill, on the land and partly erected Scribbling mill. Charlesworth raised a second mortgage on the land and mill from Woodhead twelve years later, this time for £220. Charlesworth was still the occupant of the mill in 1815, when his address is given as Norwich Upperthong, which was presumably on part of the '3 acres of rich meadow land' opposite Holmfirth mill, when he appears to have taken a further mortgage of £200 on the mill from John Allison of Huddersfield. The mill is described as a scribbling, carding and slubbing mill, plus the machinery, engines and utensils, situated at Brigg in that part of Holmfirth that lies in Wooldale.

Ownership of the mill changed in 1847, when Joseph Broadbent of Longwood and John Roberts Haigh of Marsden paid Thomas Charlesworth £375 for the 130sq.yds. of land and the scribbling mill on Lumb Bank Wooldale. The mill was still being described as 'lately erected' even though it had been built 50 years earlier. Broadbent and Haigh also paid £350 to Richard Woodhead of Stalybridge, presumably the son and heir of Joshua Woodhead of Bridge mill, for his share of the mill at Lumb Bank.

The *Huddersfield Chronicle* gives two accounts of the 1852 flood; the first account says 'the old mill being used as a wool warehouse by Mr. Wood is washed away'. Mr. Robert Wood submitted a claim for stock destroyed and damaged totalling £322 14s 3d, which the committee reduced to £300, but there is no record of any money being paid. The second account of the flood maintains that the mill dam, which had been the subject of a much earlier court case resulting in the mill-owner being imprisoned for 29 years, was washed away, causing £6,000 damage.[5] However, there does not appear to have been a claim for damage arising from this. Whichever account is correct; the mill had disappeared with the flood and was not rebuilt.

Albert mill

This mill stood on the left bank of the river just upstream of the County Bridge, virtually across the river from the former Tom mill. A Memorandum of Agreement between Benjamin Mellor, cloth finisher, of Newgate Wooldale, and George Roberts Haigh farmer, of Marsden dated 1865, records that Mellor bought 1,402sq.yds. of land at Bridge Mill Bottom in the township of Upperthong from Haigh for £219 1s 3d, which is 3s 1½d per sq.yd. The date of construction was also commemorated by a date stone for 1865 in the mill wall. When the building was complete, Benjamin Mellor & Sons moved their dyeing and finishing business from Lower mill into Albert mill, which they appear to have shared with another manufacturer for a time, as an advertisement for carding, spinning and weaving machinery that belonged to a tenant whose lease had expired, appeared in the *Huddersfield Examiner* of March 1872, but does not name them. It consisted of: 3 condenser sets, 1pr self-acting mules 650 spindles, 6 12quarter 3box power looms with Jacquards, 1 narrow 2box loom, heals slays and gearing, warp drying balloon, 1 50in Willey. All of which would have been of no use at all to a firm of dyers and finishers.

Although the mill was recently built, it was not long before more space was needed, Mellor's submitted plans to Upperthong Local Board in 1872 to build a new warehouse, which were passed. A fire was discovered in the drying stove on the night of Friday 24 July 1874, yarn belonging to John Seddon, who was using part of the mill, was smouldering; it was extinguished using patent Extincteurs that were kept on the premises. Only slight damage occurred, estimated at £4 to £5. Upperthong Local Board also passed plans submitted by Mellor's to build a new finishing room and two new sheds in 1881.

Benjamin Mellor & Sons were in the habit of giving their workers a treat in January each year, as did a number of other manufacturers, some 200 people attended the one in January 1891, which marked their fiftieth year. Mr. Benjamin Mellor, Mr. A.P. Mellor, and Joseph R. Mellor who was Benjamin's son and the current head of the firm, were all in attendance. Mr. Benjamin Mellor died aged 86 on 8 September, 1897, only some seven weeks before Mr. Thomas Mellor Haigh, who was also connected with the firm, married Miss Mellor the daughter of Joseph R. Mellor on 27 October. As both the bride and groom were connected with the company, the mill was closed for the day in honour of the occasion.

In 1900 the firm was registered as a limited liability company, and became known as B. Mellor &

Albert mill. © A.J. Brooke

Sons Ltd. Several alterations were made to the premises around the turn of the century, including a new shed in 1898; a finishing room and warehouse over the river in 1902; and various unspecified extensions to the mill in 1908, all of which the council passed. One application that the Council refused to allow came in 1903, when Mellor's applied for permission to turn their effluent into the new sewer that was being built, rather than into the river. The council, in common with other local authorities, said that they could not accept industrial effluent. Council's throughout the area adhered to this policy until directed by government, through the West Riding County Council, to accept effluent from mills and factories and find ways of treating it, rather than to allow it to continue to be discharged untreated into rivers.

The *Yorkshire Trade Directory* of 1910 lists Benjamin Mellor & Sons Ltd. as dyers, fullers, finishers, waterproofers and shrinkers. Although Mellor's, and many other mills, had employed, in some cases, literally hundreds of workers every day for years, it was not until the early twentieth century that government decreed through the Factory Acts that companies employing more than 40 people in their premises must provide a fire escape. Mellor's were one of the firms to be advised of this in July 1911.

During the Second World War many women were employed in mills to take the place of men who had been drafted into the forces. In 1940, two women were operating the steaming and brushing mill in the dry finishing department, which, even in the mid 1950s, was still very much a male preserve. The National Union of Textile Workers; and Mr. T. Beattie, were said to be "keeping a careful watch on the situation!"

The flood on the afternoon of Whit Sunday, 29 May 1944, caused much damage in the district. Due to the reporting restrictions in force at the time, brought about by the War, it is difficult to obtain an accurate assessment of the damage suffered by many of the mills. The official report by Holmfirth Urban District Council says simply that Albert mill was flooded, but gives no indication of depth of flooding, damage suffered, or even the number of days, if any, of lost production. A fire was discovered on the premises at 10.30pm on 21 January 1957, fire appliances from Holmfirth, which was literally across the road from the mill, also from Meltham and Huddersfield attended, the fire was under control by 11pm. A wooden office on the first floor was destroyed, and several pieces of cloth were damaged.

In 1968, it was announced that B. Mellor & Sons Ltd. had become part of the Allied Textiles group of companies, whose headquarters at that time were in Clayton West. Other members of the group included James Haigh Ltd. and T. Birkhead & Sons Ltd, both of whom were also dyers and finishers. There were expansion plans in December 1979, when Mellor's announced that they were also going to take some of the work that had formerly been done by James Haigh Ltd. Colne Road, Huddersfield. This was followed in October 1983, by the announcement that Mellor's would be renamed James Haigh Ltd.

In November 1987, James Haigh Ltd. announced that they would be closing, probably before Christmas, and that the final 20 employees would lose their jobs. Less than two years later it was reported that the mill would be demolished and a new Cooperative supermarket would take its place.[6]

Bridge mills

These mills formerly stood either side of the Huddersfield to Woodhead Turnpike road at the junction with New Road. The earliest mills were between the road and the river, and were recorded in a late 16th Century survey of the Graveship of Holme, and are referred to in the section on Holmfirth mill. The entry reads:

> *Edward Booth holdeth by copy two messuages one fulling milne and xxiij acres and j rood and payeth by year 7s 1d ob. [7s 1½d].*

An entry in the *Wakefield Court Roll* of 2 May 1739 records that on 4 November 1738, George

Castle and Mary his wife took a mortgage on Brigg mill with the house and several closes of land for £600 at 4¼ percent per year from Thomas Wagstaffe of Woolley near Mottram, Cheshire. George Castle died on 11 April 1739, leaving his wife Mary and his son John as his heirs. John Castle took a mortgage of £700 from Margaret Wentworth spinster of York in October 1740, which he paid to Thomas Wagstaffe for the house, mill and land which were described as:

> *All that one messuage called Brigg with several closes of land called the Nether Bottom, the Upper Cornfield, the Nether Cornfield, the Nether Wood, the Little and Great Bosks, the Stone Royd, the Clay Close, the High Close, the Kiln Croft, the Lumbank, the Upper and Nether Bottoms, the Wood, and the three Rockley Royds; also the fulling or cloth mill erected on part of the Clay Close.*

In March 1742, the description of the property alters. After the description given above is added: *and the Corn mill or mills with outbuildings, stables yards, gardens water ways etc.*

An entry in the Court Roll on 27 April 1743 slightly clarifies the position of some of the land, as it records the Lumbank, the High Close, the Stone Royd, the Great and Little Birks, the Nether Wood and the Kirkby Royd as all being in the township of Wooldale when they were passed to William Shackleton of Holmfirth, and therefore on the right bank of the river; in fact Tom mill was built on the Lumbank. All the others were presumably on the opposite side of the river in Upperthong Township.

The mortgages on the house, mill and remaining land, were taken over by William Radcliffe of Milnsbridge in June 1745; one year later in June 1746, the property was taken over by Samuel Haigh of Marsden when he paid £795 to William Radcliffe, and £55 to John Castle. The site still had a fulling mill and a corn mill in 1756; but in 1782 the description states that the messuage now comprises two houses rather than one, and the two mills are both water corn mills, one for the making of oats or meal and the other one for grinding flour. Later entries describe them as 'a making mill and a corn mill'. There was also a drying kiln, and the occupant of the mill at that time was Joseph Woodhead.

Samuel Haigh died in 1787; the mill then passed to his great nephew Daniel Haigh a drysalter

Bridge mills. © A.J. Brooke

of Marsden. In 1793 there were three mills on the site, the corn mill and the making mill, plus the newly erected Engine mill, which adjoined one of the others and was used for the scribbling and carding of wool. All three mills, plus the drying kiln and the two dwelling houses, and also the land were in the possession of Matthew and Joshua Woodhead. Joshua Woodhead appears to have been accumulating some wealth, as he bought Lower Wickens in Upperthong in 1798.

Water for the mill was initially taken from the River Holme on a bend upstream from the mill by means of a weir built across the river, and stored in a long narrow dam. One of the mills was advertised for sale in the *Leeds Mercury* of 5 January 1811, when it was described as a 'Large commodious building, now used as a scribbling mill at Bridge Mills Netherthong, with water wheel, machinery and large reservoir, also a wood, and two cottages in the possession of Jonas Roberts and William Cuttell'. There must have been an increased need for water at the mill, as the Wakefield Court Roll recorded in May 1811 that Benjamin Bradshaw of Huddersfield had passed to Jonas Roberts of Bridge mill 900sq.yds. of woody ground in Mark Bottoms wood to build a reservoir for the mill. The attempt to sell the mill in 1811 appears to have failed, as it was re-advertised in two Leeds newspapers, the *Leeds Mercury* and the *Leeds Intelligencer* in January 1813.

George Roberts of Height, Linthwaite, died in 1824, he gave his claim on the estate at Bridge mills to David Haigh and Sarah his wife (nee Roberts), with the proviso that after their deaths they would pass it to David Haigh the younger and George Roberts Haigh as tenants in common. The occupants of the mills in 1833 were William, Richard and John Woodhead who were scribbling millers, and traded as William Woodhead & Sons. They also had tenancy of the corn mill, plus 2 water wheels, drying kiln and stove, and the two dwellings with the barn, stable and mistal, also several closes of land. Later in the year, Joseph Broadbent of Longwood became the tenant of part of the woollen mill; he occupied the top floor of that mill, the room on the north side of the mill on the second storey, and also half the room on the ground floor, along with half the power from the water wheel.

William Woodhead & Sons were bankrupt in early 1838, the Fiat in Bankruptcy dates from 22 February; they are described as scribbling millers, dealers and chapmen. Their assets were assigned to Joshua Hammond a surveyor of Birmingham, and Robert Hargreaves auctioneer, of Holmfirth, who surrendered the unexpired portion of a 21 year lease on the mills dating from 1 August 1833, back to the owners of the mills who were still the Haigh family of Marsden; Joseph Broadbent of Longwood was then the sole tenant. William Woodhead died while the negotiations with their creditors were going on, but they seem to have been completed by mid July 1838, when Richard and John Woodhead were issued with certificates to say that 'they had conformed themselves in all things to the Act of Parliament concerning bankrupts'.

In August 1838, Joseph Broadbent leased the two mills with the houses and land from the Haigh family for 22 years. The mills were offered for sale by auction on 31 October 1849, and were described as: 'All that capital freehold woollen mill called Bridge Mill, with the steam engine and boiler, shafting, gearing and mill extras; also the reservoir or dam on the west side of the turnpike road there; and also the large reservoir in Mark Bottoms wood, with the privileges of taking the waters of the Hebble Dike for the use of the mill. A large portion of the mill, which is five storeys, is of recent erection; the remaining portion is four storeys. The purchaser may have the option of taking the mill machinery at valuation.' The houses and land were available as other lots.[7]

It is probable that Joseph Broadbent became the owner of half the mills at this time, along with George Roberts Haigh who had the other half. James Brook & Sons had taken premises in the mill prior to 1852, after the flood they submitted a claim to the Relief Committee for damage to buildings, machinery and stock for £153 2s 6d, which was reduced to £137 7s 6d. The page in the Ledger is marked 'disallowed', but no explanation is given and nothing was paid. Joseph Broadbent & Sons also submitted a claim for buildings, machinery and stock totalling £995, this was reduced to £762 17s 6d, and a total of £363 16s 7d was paid. The number of people put out of work at this mill by the flood was fifty.

Mrs. Senior the wife of the engineer at the mill discovered a fire in the stove at 2.30am on Thursday 13 July 1852, she immediately raised the alarm, and the fire was contained within the stove building which held about 500lbs of wool belonging to James Brook, valued at £26 to £27. Damage to the building was estimated at £40; the origin of the fire was unknown. The *Huddersfield Chronicle* reports on a treat given by James Brook & Sons to all their workpeople, including out-weavers, burlers and piecers, on Good Friday 1853. About 300 workers attended the event at Holmfirth Town Hall. The report reads: 'the provisions comprised good old English fare of Roast Beef and Plum Pudding. A cow had been slaughtered to provide the meal, and after it was over there were several large quantities of meat and fifteen puddings which had not been opened. The Holmfirth Temperance Band was in attendance to provide entertainment, which was also interspersed with songs and dancing'.

On 28 February 1854, an unnamed girl was working in the mill when her hand became entangled with machinery, fortunately she only suffered bruising. Charles 'Ancient' Fitton and two other men were found by Constable Earnshaw fishing illegally in a stream between the mill and Marks Bottoms, belonging to James Brook, on Sunday 11 June 1854. Fitton was given a severe reprimand by the bench, and after promising never to fish that stream again was fined 9s including costs and given two weeks grace in which to pay. In September of the same year someone placed a quantity of wool on top of a steam boiler to dry it. Later it was realised that the boiler was becoming overheated, and on inspection it was realised that the boiler was dry. The fire was withdrawn and the wool removed, avoiding a fire and possible explosion.

James Brook attended a public meeting in Holmfirth Town Hall on 5 March 1856, and became embroiled in an argument with Abraham Hinchliffe, a weaver, of Gulley. Brook struck Hinchliffe drawing blood, and appeared in court on 8 March, charged with assault. He was found guilty and ordered to pay a fine of £2 plus 16s costs. A meeting of manufacturers was held at the Elephant & Castle in May 1856, with James Brook in the chair. It had been called to discuss whether manufacturers in Holmfirth and District should join those in Huddersfield to recommend Parliament to accept birth certificates issued by the Registrar as proof of age for children, rather than those issued by Surgeon's; the motion was adopted. If this became law manufacturers would avoid paying surgeons for the certificates. A few months later James Brook & Sons left Bridge mill and moved to Bradley mills in Huddersfield, where a sister company, James Brooke & Bros. appears to have also been founded about 1852.

A fire was discovered in the stove belonging to Joseph Broadbent & Sons about 2.45pm on 6 June 1857. The Unity brigade attended and the fire was extinguished by 3.30pm. Damage was estimated to be around £20. About 10pm on the same day another fire was discovered at the mill, this time on the top floor, which was also being used by Broadbent's, and which, at one time, appeared to threaten the entire building. The Unity brigade worked hard for two hours to bring the blaze under control. Despite earlier appearances, damage was estimated to be only between £100 and £120. The cause of the fire was not known. A large crowd had gathered during the fire, some to help and others to watch the proceedings outside the mill. The auctioneer George Tinker was in charge of two lines of men passing buckets and cans of water across Huddersfield Road between the reservoir and the fire. Mr. Tinker was stopping people from breaking the line, and keeping the crowd back; he did not know Inspector Parkin of the police, who was in plain clothes, and did not say who he was, but was trying to get through the line. An altercation ensued, which ended in the Magistrates Court. The bench attempted to get the two men to settle their differences amicably, but as this did not happen, the charge was withdrawn. Another fire was discovered in Broadbent's stove on the evening of 6th July 1857; the Unity brigade was quickly on the scene and extinguished the flames. No suggestion as to the cause of the fire was given; damage was estimated at £80. Joseph Broadbent & Son ceased trading before 6 February 1858, and a creditor's meeting was called for 10 February. They had debts totalling £7,048, and their assets amounted to £3,081; their creditors agreed to accept 8s 6d in the £ to be paid in four instalments, which allowed them to stay in business.

A teazing machine belonging to Broadbent's that was processing cotton caught fire in September 1859. The cause was thought to be a nail mixed with the fibres that had come into contact with the teeth of the machine causing a spark. The boy who was operating it opened the door allowing burning cotton to spill out and ignite more cotton that was on the floor. Other workpeople were able to put out the fire using buckets of water; the boy suffered slight burning to his face, and his hair was singed.

Joseph Turner & Sons were using part of the mill by 1860; they gave a treat to 70 workers at the Royal Oak Inn, Thongsbridge on 27 January of that year. The mill was offered for sale in September 1861, but the Vendor is not named; it is described as:

> Lot 1 the two mills called Bridge Mill: the 'Old Mill' is 4 storeys high and attic with the willey room adjoining; the other is the 'Spinning Factory' 3 storeys high and attic; the boiler house with stove over, warehouse old building formerly used as a foundry, with stables cowhouses, yard and other conveniences, well suited to woollen, cotton or corn mill. Two cottages, water wheel 19ft 2in diam. by 8ft 10in wide, 16hp steam engine and 37hp boiler with pipes, shafting and going gear. Now occupied by Joseph Senior. Machinery available at valuation if required.

> Lot 2 Close of land opposite the mill, having 80yds frontage to the Huddersfield to Woodhead turnpike road, containing 1,240sq.yds. Purchaser can have immediate occupation of the premises if required.

The purchaser was probably Joseph Turner, as he certainly owned the property in May 1865. The building that now stands across Huddersfield Road from the original mills, on what was described as Lot 2 in the sale, was intended as a warehouse. This was being built in April 1865 when John Quinn, a builders labourer, was carrying either stone or mortar to the fourth storey; he fell backwards and landed with his neck across a joist, dislocating it. A fellow workman called Hudson had the presence of mind to 'pull it in'; Quinn was said to be making a slow recovery. In May, Turners gave a 'rearing supper' at the Kings Head [White Door] Inn Holmfirth, for the 53 men employed in building the new warehouse, Joseph Barrowclough & Sons were the Architects; W. Wadsworth & Co. were the Contractors. After the supper the various groups congratulated one another on 'the most stately warehouse in the neighbourhood of Holmfirth'. In July 1866 Joseph Turner passed the freehold of the mill, with the warehouse, dwelling house, dam, boiler, steam engine and machinery to his two sons John and Thomas Turner, in equal shares. The mill dam and the tail goits from the water wheels were damaged by flood waters on 16 Nov. 1866. It was thought that it would be anything up to two months before the mill could again be run on water power.[8]

George Greenwood, who had previously had premises in Thongsbridge mill and was a cloth finisher, was using part of the mill by 1870 when he gave his workpeople a treat at the Royal Oak on January 8th. Joseph Turner & Sons were one of the few companies in the district granted the privilege of summoning workers by blowing the mill whistle in October 1872. A fire was discovered in the stove belonging to Turner & Sons about 10pm on Wednesday October 7th 1874, which was put out by the firm's own fire brigade; damage amounted to 'a few pounds'

About 1am on Boxing Day (26 Dec.) 1876, George Greenwood's workers discovered that a number of pieces of cloth were smouldering. All the affected pieces were taken into the mill yard and the fires extinguished. The cause of the fire was not determined, the value of the pieces was estimated to be between £600 and £700; no damage was caused to the buildings. A firm that were using part of the mill in February 1881, but possibly had not been in business very long was that of James Hinchliffe & Sons, who were in liquidation, their machinery, consisting of 2 condenser sets, 1pr. self-acting mules, a new twisting frame, 8 broad and 2 narrow power looms, warping balloon plus beaming frame and a bobbin winding frame, was advertised to be sold on 10 March 1881, although they may not have gone out of business then, as their name occurs again in 1890, when they were again in liquidation, and had a greater quantity of machinery. A firm named S. Boothroyd was 'declining business' in May 1886, when his machinery consisting primarily of 9 power looms plus some other pieces were advertised to be sold on 17 May 1886. How long they had been in business is not known, as this is the only reference found.

George Greenwood's company had expanded by 1888, and had become Greenwood, Senior and Greenwood; they gave a treat to their 80 workers at Holmfirth Town Hall on 14 January. Arthur Tinker, who was trading as George Tinker & Son, had moved from Bankend mill in late 1889; he filed a petition for Bankruptcy on 14 April 1890, and was put into receivership. The first Creditors Meeting was held on 23 April, when it was revealed that he had liabilities of £1,378 7s 6d, his assets amounted to £421 12s 3d, leaving a deficit of £956 15s 3d. Mr. Arthur Tinker had started the business at Bankend mill in 1874 with his brother Ben; Arthur had introduced £600 capital and Ben £40. The partnership ended on 16 November 1888, when Ben left the firm. Mr. Tinker attributed his failure to 'long continued ill health, and very strong competition in his chosen sector of the industry', which was manufacturing Stockinet. A Winding-up order was issued on 28 April; at his public examination on 12 May it was decided that a first dividend of 4s 6d in the £ would be paid in September 1890; which was followed by a second and final dividend of 6¾d in the £ payable on 19 October 1892.

Barnes & Taylor were using part of the mill by 1891, when they gave their 50 workers a treat on 24 January. Their business had been started in 1877 at Moll Springs mill in Honley, the date that they moved to Bridge mill is not known. They ran into financial difficulties in 1891-2, and a creditors meeting was held on 22 January 1892, when it was announced that the firm had liabilities of £12,078 7s 3d, their assets amounted to £7,209 12s 5d, leaving a deficit of £4,868 16s 10d. A Deed of Assignment was issued, with Mr. W.H. Armitage of Armitage & Norton Accountants, being named as the Assignee, and a Committee of Inspection made up of the five largest creditors being appointed. A sale of machinery was held on 25 February 1892, which included condenser sets, mules, warping machines; fast power looms; pattern loom with jacquard; hydraulic presses; tentering machine; Fulling stocks; milling machine; washing machine; office furnishings, and many sundries; also a large quantity of yarn. The mills were then possibly largely empty for some years, although Greenwood, Senior & Greenwood's tenancy continued.

The *Yorkshire Factory Times* reported in August 1896 that Bridge mill would soon be partially occupied, and some much needed improvements were to be carried out. One company that began their business in Bridge mill in 1896 was Bower, Roebuck & Firth, who then moved to Glendale mill New Mill within two years. T. Birkhead, who established their business in 1883 had taken premises in Bridge mill prior to 1899, when they were advertising for menders to work at home, this was the earliest advertisement for out-menders that I have found. Mr. Prior the factory sub-inspector visited the mill in August 1901, and charged Greenwood, Senior & Greenwood, and also Thomas Birkhead's with failing to lime wash the interior walls of their premises. The Factory Act stated that interior walls must be lime washed within 14 months, regardless of their appearance. Both companies pleaded guilty to the charge and were each fined 10s plus 2s 6d costs.

Mr. George Greenwood, of Greenwood Senior and Greenwood suffered a slight accident at the mill in 1904. He was walking through the mill on the morning of 19th October when, due to an eye condition, he came into contact with one of the machines and sustained a broken arm and some bruising. He was taken home where he was said to be 'recovering'. The company left Bridge mill in 1906 and moved to Perseverance mill, where they traded as Walter Greenwood & Sons.

James Watkinson & Sons, who were at Washpit mill, also had premises in Bridge mill between 1907 and 1910, and possibly longer; when they were recorded as manufacturing 'mixed goods'. Also listed at Bridge mills were Fred Lawton & Sons having moved from Ribbleden mill, who were making 'fancy cloths'. Lockwood Bros. moved here from Lee mill in Scholes during 1912, and were here until 1914 when they appear to have given up business. Thomas Birkhead & Sons were employing 30 to 40 people in May 1913 when they asked Holmfirth Council to supply them with drinking water. A Factory Inspector made a report about Bridge mill to the Council in the following year, in which he said that, the privies at the mill 'were so foul as to be a nuisance'; the remedy appears to have been left to the owner of the property, who was Thomas Turner.[9]

The mills and Bridge Mill Wood were offered for sale by auction in May 1916, the vendors were Thomas Turner's executors. Lot 1 was the mills, which had a floor area of over 8,000sq.yds; along with the land known as Bridge Mill Wood and plots of land adjoining the Holme and Hebble rivers. They were bought for £6,100 by an anonymous buyer, which was possibly Walter Gledhill & Son, as they appear to have moved into the mill in that year. Lot 2 was the six cottages, numbers 156 to 166 on Huddersfield Road, which were withdrawn at the sale, presumably because they failed to reach the reserve price. Later in the year a company called Cartwright & Co. were also using part of the mill, and advertised for weavers.

In 1917 the *Yorkshire Textile* Directory listed Walter Gledhill & Son as having 3,150 spindles and 61 looms, manufacturing woollens and worsteds. Fred Lawton & Sons were still occupying part of Bridge mill in 1919, when they were listed as being plain and fancy worsted manufacturers; but they moved to Sudehill mill at New Mill, either in late 1919 or early 1920. Thomas Birkhead & Son moved from Bridge mill to Lee mill at Scholes about 1921, when they also became a Limited company.

Walter Gledhill is credited with developing a shuttle-less loom. Instead of shuttles the loom used a rapier with a small gripper to seize the weft and carry it to the centre of the loom and another gripper then takes the weft and draws it to the opposite selvedge. The article claimed that the yarn did not need to be as strong as that in a conventional loom, as the warp did not need to open as wide to allow the passage of the rapier, neither was the weft jerked as when weaving with a fly shuttle. Each colour in the weft had its own gripper that attached to the rapier when required; enabling the loom to weave many designs including checks; looms then currently in use could weave designs using up to seven colours, although the makers claimed that they could readily be adapted to take more if necessary. Some looms were already installed in mills in the Huddersfield district.

During their tenure of the mill Gledhill's added various extensions to the premises: a new weaving shed was built in 1920, with an additional one being built in 1934; a new weft room in 1940, and another additional shed in 1949. The firm's weavers had formed a closed shop prior to October 1941, when one of them decided that he or she wanted to leave the union; the shop steward contacted the union secretary for advice, and was told that if the weaver left the union they would also have to leave the company. The union's minutes do not record the outcome. Gledhill's went into receivership in 1965, the receiver decided that the company should be wound up and the machinery sold. The sale took place over two days on the 2nd and 3rd of June, 1965. Some 200 workers lost their jobs; bringing textile production at this mill, which had spanned some 400 years, to an end.

The mills were bought by Hepworth Iron Company's Engineering division, to house their non Ceramic interests. There was a small mill dam on the corner of Huddersfield Road and New Road that was no longer required by the 1980s, so it was decided that it should be dismantled, filled in, and made into a car park. While workmen were excavating the dam they found 2 bones that were possibly human, shoes, a thimble, buttons from a Lancashire and Yorkshire Railways uniform, and a ring inscribed 'Annie' on the inside. A report in November 1987 said that based on the artefacts found with the bones, they came from a woman, one bone came from the arm and the other from the leg; it was thought that the bones were between 50 and 200 years old, possibly from a victim of the 1852 flood. The remains of the unknown woman were buried in the Garden of Remembrance in Cemetery Road Holmfirth in December of that year.[10]

Fearnought / Pickwick mill

In a complete contrast from Bridge mill which is one of the oldest mills in the district, to the newest. Fearnought mill is a single storey building, built from red brick, originally with steel-framed windows, probably around 1930; as it does not appear on the 1930s edition of the 25inch map of the area, which would have been surveyed in the late 1920s, and no record of the plans exist in the Kirklees Archive. Plans for the former Holmfirth Urban District have only been retained by Kirklees from 1931 onwards. The first tenants of the mill were the North British Rayon Co. who also had premises in part of Spring Lane mill at Bottoms. They submitted plans for two small extensions to be built on to the building in June 1949, but later in the year submitted amended plans for larger extensions, presumably because they had decided to leave Spring Lane mill and consolidate production at Fearnought. These plans were approved by Holmfirth Council in January 1950; the company moved all production to Fearnought towards the end of that year.[11]

North British Rayon left Holme Valley in 1957; the mill was then bought by Sam Weller & Sons Ltd of Bradford, who, understandably, changed the name of the building from Fearnought to Pickwick mill. They had begun their business as wholesalers in Bradford in 1911; and later diversified by manufacturing woven cotton cloth, including blowing wrapper, in Liverpool from 1952; moving back into West Yorkshire into the single storey premises at Fearnought mill, which ideally suited their requirements, in 1957. Their entry in the *Yorkshire Textile Directory* for 1957 says that they were making decatising and other textile machinery cloths used by dyers and finishers, linen shrinking wrappers, warp beam wrappers, wool sheets etc. Their main offices at that time were at Pickwick Works, Peckover St. Bradford. They are one of the few textile manufacturers in our area to continue production into the twenty-first century.

Dean Brook – Deanhouse mills

Not on the River Holme, but in the village of Deanhouse, the mill stood alongside Dean Brook mainly on the Honley side of the stream and was already in existence by 1791, when it was owned and occupied by Nathaniel and Godfrey Berry. They were in financial difficulties in 1798, when their assignees ordered that the mill should be sold. The property was described as: 'All that large fulling and scribbling mill, together with the dyehouse and several other buildings standing in Dean Clough Honley. Lot 2 was the house, outbuildings and gardens, plus a small dyehouse; lot 3 was a 3 storey drying house with outbuildings; lot 4 comprised land, and lot 5 was a brick warehouse and a small building. The mill premises were described as being lately built and in good condition, they were

Deanhouse mill. © A.J. Brooke

also freehold. The building contained some machinery, which is described as engines, stocks, wheels etc. It seems likely that the premises were not sold, as in 1800 the Berry's assignees conveyed the premises to John Waterhouse, a merchant of Halifax. The property was offered for sale again in 1803, by which time a steam engine had also been fitted. The main mill was 36 yards long, 15 yards of it was 9 yards wide, the other 21 yards was 7½ yards wide. In 1837 ownership of the property passed to Joseph Firth of Shepley Lane Head, and Walter Walker of Thurstonland.

The mill was visited by the Plug Rioters in August 1842, when they probably drew the boiler plug to stop the mill from working, and possibly also drained the dam to delay the resumption of work as long as possible. Hiram and Abraham Littlewood were using the mill in 1848, when adverse financial circumstances forced them to assign all their personal effects and estate to Abraham Hirst wool merchant, Edmund Eastwood dyer and John Armitage wool merchant, all of Huddersfield.

In 1852 the mill was occupied by William Haigh, he had previously let the top floor of the mill to John Heap & Sons of New Hagg who, when installing their machinery had taken it in by climbing onto the roof of a single storey building, then putting the machine parts through a window into the room where it was to be used. Heap's were moving to Smithy Place Mill in late June 1842 and wanted to take the machinery out by the same route. Haigh said that the roof of the lower building was unsafe, and wanted Heap's to use the window at the other end of the mill which, due to the slope on which the mill was built, was much higher. Heap's said that they would pay for any damage caused by removing the machinery by their preferred route, but Haigh was adamant and ordered his men to stop them. Haigh's men climbed onto the roof armed with sticks and iron bars. Mark Heap led his men onto the roof at the charge. The fight that followed was termed by the Press as a 'Serious Riot'; Mark Heap received a blow on the head and fell over 12 feet to the ground, others also had bloody heads; a second attack on those on the roof was driven off, and Tom Dyson threw Mark Heap in the mill dam. Edward Heap who had been pushed into the dam by a woman, climbed out and shouted 'Brick 'em lads, brick 'em', and a shower of stones and other missiles drove down the defenders at the second volley, and a number were thrown in the dam. Heap's then removed their machinery by their preferred route. John, Edward and Mark Heap later appeared in court accused of assault; Mark Heap had assaulted William Haigh the day after the fracas, he was bound over to keep the peace for one month.

Hiram Littlewood's son Henry aged 14, was working as a piecer to the spinner Henry Crooks, who was a few minutes late for work on the morning of Monday 10 January 1853. Henry decided to fit the machine's drive belt over the pulley on the shafting. Instead of getting the ladder he climbed on top of the spinning frame and managed to put the strap over the pulley. He then put his apron over the revolving shaft and gripped it with his hands intending to swing off the frame and land in the 'mule-gate'. The shafting took the apron and the boy round with it, knocking him against the joists of the ceiling/floor above, breaking both his arms and crushing his body. After being seen by a doctor he was taken to Huddersfield Infirmary, he died on the 16th.

William Haigh occupied only part of the mill in February 1859, with Thomas Dyson occupying another part. Haigh was attempting to recover upwards of £6 from Dyson for work done at the mill; Dyson was claiming more than that amount in counter damages for keeping scribbling engines in good order. The judge allowed Dyson £4.

William Haigh was the trustee for the creditors of James and Benjamin Eastwood who were also using part of the mill. Haigh went to the mill on 19 May 1859 to find out why the mill was stopped. On entering the yard, he was met by James Eastwood who abused him and followed him wherever he went. When Haigh entered the mill both Eastwood brothers followed and abused him, swearing that 'they would knock his soul out'; back in the yard they attempted to push him into a pig sty. Haigh said that he believed his life to be in danger, and that he dare not go back to the mill to look after the creditors' interests. The Eastwood's were bound over in the amount of £20 each to keep the peace for six months.

The mill was advertised for sale in December 1859, by which time the only tenant appears to have been Thomas Dyson, with part untenanted. It was described as having 2 mills, engine and boiler houses; dyehouse and dam; willey room and buildings; various cottages, gardens and outbuildings; 3 dwellings, a joiner's shop with the upper part now a dwelling, formerly a weaving shop. There was a steam engine and two boilers, the mills contained machinery for processing raw wool into yarn. A document in Wakefield Record Office dated 26 May 1860 shows the owners of the mills as being Mary Taylor Fairburn widow of Mirfield, William Crowther bookkeeper of Armley Mills, Benjamin Chadwick gentleman of Dewsbury, and Thomas Dyson manufacturer, of Elm Wood Netherthong.

A Gasworks was being built in Deanhouse in 1861, which would supply all the premises in Netherthong and Deanhouse, including the mill and the new workhouse that was also in the course of construction. Thomas Dyson lived at Elmwood Villa, Holmfirth, he gave his workers a treat in the large warehouse at the mill in January 1862. The account does not give the number of people employed, but describes them as the 'numerous workforce'.

In September 1866 a new chimney was being built at the mill, on Sunday 16th some young men were using the windlass to crane one another up the inside of the chimney to the top, a distance of about 20 yards. While three of them were at the top someone removed the handle from the windlass, allowing it to descend rapidly, with its passengers, to the ground. The leg of one of them, named Hollingworth, came into contact with stonework inside the chimney and was fractured. He was taken to Huddersfield Infirmary for treatment, and was later said to be recovering slowly.

A fire was discovered in the stove by Absolom and Daniel Woodhead about 4.30pm on Saturday 23 July, 1870. Neighbours tried to extinguish the blaze with buckets and cans of water, and were eventually joined by the fire engine from Josh Mellor & Sons, Thongsbridge mills. Damage, which was mainly to the building, was estimated at £50. Several other brigades, including that of John Brooke & Sons, Armitage Bridge, also attended, but were not needed. The cause of the fire was attributed to spontaneous combustion.

Dyson's were charged with three offences of using unjust weights in December 1881. Some of the weights used in the mill to weigh quantities of wool or yarn were found by inspectors to be incorrect; for example, of two 7lb weights one was light by ¼ oz, the other by ½ oz; a 14lb weight was found to be 2½ozs light. Defence counsel pointed out that the weights were used for weighing yarn given to the weavers, who were paid by the yardage of the pieces, not by weight. The bench fixed a nominal fine of 1s for each offence.

A large number of alterations and extensions took place at the mills over a period of years, and the number of workers also increased, from 170 in 1883, to 200 in 1898. In April 1905 George Henry Senior, the foreman scourer at the mill, gave one week's notice and was asked to leave the key to the Milling Room in the Boiler House when he went home that evening, which he failed to do. Arriving for work the following morning Senior was told that he would not be paid as he had broken his contract. Senior sued Dyson's for £1 16s unpaid wages. After hearing evidence from both sides, the bench dismissed the case.

The *Yorkshire Textile Directory* of 1910 lists Dyson's as manufacturers of fancy cloths, with 5,500 spindles and 50 looms; they also had an Office and Warehouse in Lion Arcade Chambers in Huddersfield. Alterations and extensions to the mill continued to take place throughout the period to the end of the 1940s.

A fire broke out at the mill early on the morning of 19 July 1946. The fire was in a wool warehouse, but also affected the finishing department that was next to the warehouse. The building was reduced to a shell, with 70 bales of wool and a large number of pieces of cloth being destroyed. Only six or seven men working in the finishing room would be out of work due to the fire, and only until the damage to machinery had been repaired. Thieves stole 14 pieces of cloth during the Whitsuntide weekend in 1948, valued at between £700 and £800.

During the late 1940s or early 1950s Dyson's were taken over by Edwin Walker & Co. of Field mills, Leeds Road, Huddersfield; production at Deanhouse appears to have ceased in 1953, or possibly 1954.

The *Yorkshire Textile Directory* records that W. Fein & Sons, who were processors, blenders and carders of Rabbit Hair, Angora, Hares Fur, Cashmere and Camel fibres, were using part of the mill in 1955. They advertised for a skilled fitter to erect machines in August of that year, and production was expected to start in September. Heywood Yarns Ltd. also moved into part of the mill in 1955, they were taken over by Rennard and Garside of Taylor Hill Mill, Huddersfield, but continued to use Deanhouse into the 1970s. Fein's moved production to Lower Mill around 1970, but continued to use Deanhouse mill as a warehouse.

A company named Century Steel were using part of the premises in June 1983. A fire broke out on 5 June, which the fire brigade subsequently attributed to arson. Firemen from Holmfirth and Huddersfield arrived at the premises about 2.30am to find the building engulfed in flames, an office and workshop were destroyed. The damage was estimated to be around £70,000. Much of the mill was demolished by 1985, with only 1 building being left in use. A plan to build houses on the site was approved by Kirklees Council in 1988, and the final building was demolished the following year.[12]

Deanhouse Dyehouse

The date of construction of this dyehouse, and its precise location are not known; from the description of the contents it was of a reasonable size. The map that accompanies the Honley Rentals book marks a dyehouse on Dean Brook upstream from Deanhouse mill, but whether this is the site is unclear. The only reference to it is contained in a file in Kirklees Archive, and is dated 5 November 1819. The document records the transfer of the property from James Kenworthy dyer of Netherthong, to Joshua Eastwood clothier of Meltham, for the sum of £250, which included the fixtures and fittings, also the stock-in-trade. The dyehouse was equipped with 4 vats with lids and grates; 3 pans with grates; 1 cradle for grinding Indigo; 1 cistern for washing wool; 3 troughs to carry the water to the utensils, various barrows and scrays for wool, woad rakes, 1 Indigo tub, 2 barrels, 3 kits, and 1 pigin dish. Unfortunately, this represents the sum total of knowledge on this dyehouse.

River Holme – Thongsbridge mills

These mills stood between the Huddersfield to Woodhead Turnpike road and the river Holme; beginning as a single building, but expanding considerably over the many years of their existence. The earliest information on the mill is to be found in a Deed held by the Yorkshire Archaeological Service in Wakefield, dated 1586:

> *John Beaumont, Thomas Wodehede, and Henry Boythe of Neytherthwong, together with Anthonye Wylson lately have purchased of Thomas Wentworth of Northelmsalby certain messuages, cottages, lands and tenements of Thomas Wentworth in Nytherthwong as by a dede of ye same Thomas Wentworth bearing date 14 June, 15 Elizabeth (1573). We John Beaumont, Thomas Wodehede and Henry Boythe have realeased to Anthonye Wylson all that Fulling or Walk Mylne, one house, garden to the same fulling mylne adjoining, together with the dams, goat [goit] and water course.*

The mill is shown on Jeffries map of the 1770s, which is also the time when the next information appears, recording the death of Hannah, the wife of John Cooks of Thongsbridge mill in 1777. In addition to the fulling mill there was also a corn mill by 1796, when it was offered for sale on February 17th. The advertisement reads: 'all that bankrupt's real estate situate at Thongsbridge consisting of a messuage, barn and other outbuildings, together with a Corn mill, Fulling mills, cottage and other housing and land thereto belonging containing about 55 days work'. The amount of land would be in the region of 55 acres.

Ownership of the mill at this time is unclear, but the occupants of the mill in 1802 appear to have been named Earnshaw, Walker, Ainley and Woodhead, who were described as Scribblers, and were responsible for insuring the premises. There is also mention of Cook's mill at Springbottom, but no other details. It was offered for sale again in October 1809, when the owner was William Newton of Stagwood Hill. The mills were described as:

Thongsbridge mills. © A.J. Brooke

Lot 1. Corn Mill.

Lot 2. Fulling mill with 2 double and 2 single fulling stocks. 4 scribbling engines with 4ft wire each; 2 carders, 2 slubbing billies with willow.

Lot 3. Fulling mill adjoining above, 16ft water wheel with 16ft of fall; 2 double 2 single fulling stocks, 2 driving stocks.

Lot 4. Cook's mill, consisting of water wheel, 2 carding machines, 2 billies. Messuage etc.

Premises adjoining Huddersfield to Holmfirth turnpike. Excellent repair, good water supply.

Ownership of the mills had passed to Joshua Robinson by the 1830s, whose family were also using Lower Mytholmbridge and Smithy Place mills at that time. A lease dated 1 October 1839 records that Godfrey Mellor and Thomas Mellor took part of Thongsbridge mills for a term of 14 years. The premises that they occupied consisted of a scribbling mill, the stove on the south side of the scribbling mill, and the nearby dyehouse which the Mellor's were already using. Also a cottage occupied by Thomas Spivey. Machinery in the mill included 4 billies, scribbling and carding engines, a Fearnought teazer, wheels, drums, shafts, straps, going gear and machinery. The rent for the whole was £350 per year.

A 14 year old boy named Joseph Chambers was working for Mellor's in November 1848. On Saturday the 11th a strap had been taken off a machine to allow men to work on it safely, but was still round the pulley on the shafting. Joseph began playing with the strap which became wrapped around his arm, drawing him up and around the shafting that was revolving about 60 times per minute. The water wheel was stopped and the boy taken down; his skull, left arm and thigh were all badly broken. He was taken to Huddersfield Infirmary where he died about an hour after admission. The inquest jury returned a verdict of accidental death.

The 1852 flood caused substantial damage, the report reads:

'The mill belonging to Messrs. Robinson at Thongsbridge is situated on the left hand and abuts onto the river. The scribbling mill stands a short distance off the stream, and between the two was the fulling mill, one storey high. About two-thirds of the latter building is carried away, and the stocks are

removed from their places and are much broken. In the bottom of the scribbling mill there is slight damage to a pair of billies in the take of Messrs. Mellor. The boiler is washed from its fixings and has been rolled for several hundred yards, and the wool-stove is completely destroyed together with one of the stables from which a valuable cow was also lost. The goits are much damaged. A number of cottages adjoining the premises are more or less damaged, but no lives were lost.

A joint claim was submitted to the Flood Relief Committee by James and George Robinson, and Joseph Mellor, for damage to buildings, machinery, dams, goits and stock for a total of £803, reduced by the inspectors to £463. This claim was added, by the committee, to those from Robinson's at Lower Mytholmbridge and Smithy Place. The reduced amounts for the three mills total £982 7s; the total amount paid was £623 8s 9d, which is about two-thirds, making Thongsbridge mills share around £308.

In June 1852, John Bates the Factory Inspector summoned D. Sykes of Netherthong, a mule spinner working at Mellor's, for working his 12 year old son John Sykes after 1pm when he had also worked in the morning; and for not allowing his son to attend school. Sykes pleaded guilty to both charges. Mr. Bates asked the bench to impose the minimum fine, as he felt that this would have the desired effect. The bench imposed a fine of 5s plus costs on each charge, a total of £1 8s.

The Reservoir Commissioners, in 1853, record the owners of Thongsbridge mill as being James and George Robinson, trustees of Joshua Robinson deceased; the occupants were James Robinson, George Robinson, Godfrey Mellor and Thomas Mellor.

John Mellor of Godfrey Mellor & Sons was summoned by John Woodhouse of Netherthong for withholding 16s 6d of wages, which Woodhouse maintained were due to him for weaving a piece of cloth; the case was heard in January 1855. A warp had been given to Woodhouse six weeks previously, but no pattern had been supplied; Mellor's maintained that Woodhouse had been given instructions about the pattern, but had subsequently woven it wrongly, which was why they withheld the money. The case was adjourned to permit Mellor's to produce their books to determine who was correct, but no subsequent report was given.

In May 1856 George Greenwood, who rented room and power in the mill, was walking through a room used by Robinsons on May 17th, where John William Bower aged 14 was working at a rag machine. Greenwood approached him and after promising 'to kick his soul out' he knocked Bower down and throttled him. Greenwood said to Bower that he 'would have th'oile a'fire'. James Bower, the boy's father, who also worked for Robinsons, said that his son was feeding the rag machine, there was no fear of the place catching fire; he went into the room where his son was working and saw that Greenwood had his son by the throat. He had taken hold of Greenwood's coat and asked him what he was doing. Greenwood then offered to hit James Bower, who made no verbal response but walked away. Greenwood followed him and pushed him into a washer. Each time Bower tried to get out, Greenwood pushed him back in. At the trial on May 27th James Bower's account was corroborated by Joseph Earnshaw. Greenwood said that he had taken room and power from Mr. George Robinson, and had been annoyed for three months by the boy's management of the rag machine. Greenwood had remonstrated with George Robinson who had assured Greenwood that he would not be annoyed again. Greenwood said the boy had continued his mismanagement of the machine, which was why he had acted in the way he did. The bench imposed fines and costs against Greenwood totalling £1 15s. Although George Greenwood's trade is not mentioned in the account, it is possible that he was the same George Greenwood cloth finisher, who was using part of Bridge Mill by 1870.

On 17 February 1858, George Sanderson aged 14, who was working for Mellor's, was putting a strap on a condenser when his clothing became caught and he was drawn into the mechanism. After being released it was discovered that he had a broken thigh, and he remained unconscious for about two hours. He was taken to Huddersfield Infirmary where he was later said to be recovering. A fire was discovered in a drying stove belonging to George Robinson, about midday on Saturday 23 October 1858. Despite there being workers on the premises who were quickly on the scene, several pieces of cloth were destroyed. Damage was estimated at about £70. Another fire broke out in the boiler house used by Godfrey Mellor at around 10pm on Wednesday 19 January 1859, which was extinguished by neighbours. The cause of the fire was attributed to overheating of the flues; damage was described as 'trifling'. On the evening of Monday 18 July 1859 a violent thunderstorm with large hailstones caused considerable damage to the roof lights at the mill, smashing around 2,000 panes of glass.[13]

A notice was posted on a wall in Godfrey Mellor's mill on 22 February 1860 saying that all employees had to give two weeks notice of their intention to leave the firm. After reading the notice all the weavers walked out, while the rest of the employees returned to work. [Up to this point it had been the general practice that weavers could terminate their employment without giving prior notice, if they wished to do so, each time they reached the end of a warp.] The weavers were also aggrieved that they were being penalised for bad work or mistakes being made by menders when repairing knots in warp threads. On March 1st the striking weavers sent a note to Godfrey Mellor saying that they would not return to work until the offending notice was 'pulled down', neither would they pay fines for knotting mistakes. Three of the weavers, Joseph Hudson, Henry Lawson and Joshua Woodhead, appeared in court on March 6th charged with unlawfully neglecting their work for 8 days. Godfrey Mellor said that he was not bringing the case simply to obtain a conviction, the penalty was three months imprisonment; but to show the men that they could not walk out leaving unfinished warps in their looms. The weavers said that they had tried to negotiate with Mr. Mellor, who had 'laughed at them, called them babies and walked away'. The magistrates said that they respected the rights of both men and masters, but they had no option but to convict and sentenced each of the three weavers to one month in prison. This judgement appears to have subsequently been set aside.

Godfrey Mellor met some of the weavers on March 14th, when he then said that the notice would not apply to weavers, who would still be at liberty to leave each time they finished a warp. He hoped that the weavers would accept that and return to work the following day and finish the warps already in the looms. The weavers sent the three men who had been sentenced, whom Mellor could not employ while the case was still pending. The case was heard on 20 March; the weavers were represented by Mr. Roberts of Manchester who was known as 'The Miners' Attorney General'. The bench was made up of three manufacturers: John Brooke, T.P. Crosland and S. Haigh, Mr. Brooke asked whether anyone had any objection to them hearing the case, which no-one had. The hearing lasted two hours, after which the magistrates gave their findings in writing. They recommended that all the weavers should return and finish the work already started; the masters and weavers should then enter into discussions and make arrangements giving them mutual agreement and satisfaction. All parties appear to have accepted this and returned to work.

Tom Mellor gave a treat for his workers to celebrate his son's Coming-of-Age on Wednesday 2 April 1862. The women sat down to 'a good knife and fork tea', and the men had 'a good English supper'. Afterwards they were joined by friends and family. Joseph Mellor was in financial difficulty in 1865, on 20 May he covenanted to pay a dividend of 10s in the £ to his creditors in three equal instalments of 3s 4d each, in 4, 8, and 12 months time.

Mr. Tom Mellor was a member of the Netherthong Local Board; a proposal was made in the mid 1660s to construct a road from Netherthong, following an established footpath, to join the Huddersfield to Woodhead Turnpike road by Bridge mill. The only road to Netherthong at that time ran from Thongsbridge via Crodingley. The argument in favour of the new road was that it would be less steep than the existing road making transporting goods easier, and was a shorter route between Netherthong and Holmfirth than the existing road. Thomas Mellor, who said he was the largest ratepayer in the township, was against it, saying that he and 62 other occupiers and millowners who paid rates would derive no benefit from it. Eventually, New Road was built.

A 19 year old weaver named Alfred Castle was working for Godfrey Mellor in February and March 1866, and had told his mother that 'his loom would kill him'. Castle had gone home at dinner time on Monday 5 March and had not returned; he had hung himself at his mother's house at Wooldale Townend. At the Inquest the tuner at Mellor's said that Castle had only worked there 'a week or two', Castle had asked him to fit new pickers on his loom on that morning, which Booth had said he would do in the afternoon; apart from that he knew of no other problem with the loom. Mary Castle, Alfred's mother, said that her son had been low in mind for some time, and had said that he should not live long and would never ask for another loom. Mary Ann Beever, a neighbour, said that Alfred had come into her house on the Monday, he had not complained of being poorly, but was red in the face and looked wild and strange, and had said he felt cold. Castle then went home, some time later Beever went into the Castle's house and found Alfred hanging from a beam in the garret. The jury returned a verdict of Temporary Insanity.

Thomas Mellor celebrated two weddings in the family in 1866, the first was the marriage of his only son Charles Alfred to Miss Alice Jane Marsden of Mirfield, in July, when the mill and the family home were decorated with flags. The second was the marriage of Mr. Mellor's third daughter to Mr. Buchanan, a London merchant, on 27 October. Both occasions were marked by treats to the workforce held at the Royal Oak for the men, and in the large warehouse at the mill for the women. The men had a dinner, while the women had a Tea; the liquid tea 'being well laced with Brown Cream [Rum], they were soon in motion and dancing became the order of the evening'.

Four fire brigades from the district held a contest at Prickleden mill dam during the first week in June 1867. They came from Mellor's at Thongsbridge, Turner's at Bridge mills, the Unity brigade, and Barber's of Holmbridge. The first test was to see, after a simultaneous start, who could be first to pump water from their hose; Mellor's were first, Barber's second, Turner's third and Unity fourth. There was also a 'junior brigade' with a smaller engine from Barber's, which pumped water through before any of its larger rivals. The second contest was to find which brigade could throw the water highest, John Harpin from Bottoms mill was the judge for this event, he gave his decision to Turner's. After the contest all the teams went to the Elephant and Castle Inn for a meal and a convivial evening.

In the same month someone put a piece of timber between a segment of the water wheel and the spur wheel of Thomas Mellor's mill in an attempt to damage them. The Holmfirth Prosecution Society offered a £20 reward to any one who would supply information leading to a prosecution of whoever had been responsible. They also offered a £10 reward for information leading to a prosecution of whoever had poured 'gas tar' into the filtering reservoir at the mill in July 1868. There is nothing to suggest that information in either case was forthcoming.

John Wormald who worked at T. Mellor & Sons as a cloth presser, appeared in court in Huddersfield on 30 April 1868 charged with stealing 4 yards of cloth from his employer. Witnesses said that Wormald had been seen going into the warehouse in the mill on Saturday 25 April and leaving shortly afterwards carrying a parcel. He had left the mill via a small private entrance rather than by the main gate. William Smith of Elland said that he had bought the cloth from Wormald on the Saturday night for £3 6s, he had then given the cloth to the police. Wormald denied the charge, but was committed for trial at the quarter sessions.

A fire was discovered at the mill in the early hours of Tuesday 23 June 1868, by a man on his way home. He raised the alarm and the mill's fire engine was put to work. Shoddy in a storeroom was found to be burning, but only a small amount of damage was done. The cause was attributed to the boiler flues having become overheated. Engines from Turner's at Bridge mill and the Unity brigade also attended, but were not needed. There was also a small fire in the stove at the mill on 11 November 1871, which was extinguished by getting buckets of water there quickly, with little damage being done. Yet another fire was discovered about 3am on 19 September 1872 by a man who worked for Balmforth's. It appeared to be either in the boiler house or the stove belonging to Thos. Mellor & Sons. The mill's own fire engine, helped by the one from Bridge mill, soon had the blaze under control. Some pieces were saved, but damage amounted to between £500 and £600; had the wind been blowing from a different direction the outcome could have been much worse. The cause was not known, but was thought to have been brought about by 'overheating'. An advertisement for an experienced Engine Tenter and Blacksmith appeared in October of the same year; there is no indication of whether this was a direct result of the fires or not.

Jonathon Buckley was a spinner working for T. Mellor & Sons, who got one hand caught in his machine on Monday 27 January 1873. One finger was so badly damaged that it had to be amputated. An advertisement for machinery to be sold appeared in February 1875, stating that the part of the mill housing the machines had been leased for a different purpose, but no company name is given. The machinery consisted of 3 condenser sets, 4prs hand mules, and 3 power looms. What the different purpose was is not clear as subsequent events give no indication of the change.

C.A. Mellor, Thomas Mellor's son, had given some land near the mill to allow a mission church to be built. The foundation stone was laid on 23 May 1877; for the previous six months services had been held in a warehouse at the mill. The population of Thongsbridge at that time was about 400, and the nearest church was in Netherthong.

A fire was discovered on the second floor of the premises used by Godfrey Mellor & Sons shortly before 4am on Saturday 1 June 1878, by a mill hand called Abraham Barrowclough. The alarm was raised and the mill's fire brigade assisted by Turners from Bridge mill plus neighbours, all combined to get the fire under control. Damage, which was insured, was estimated to be between £600 and £700. The cause of the fire was given as 'overheating'. Thomas Mellor died in 1880, his will was contested, and the Chancery court ordered that the mill should be sold. The mills were again offered for sale or to let in August 1883, when they were described as having steam and water power, with dyeing and fulling plant, 7 closes of land, plus a dwelling house occupied by Mr. Walter Lodge, and a cottage.

George Woodhead & Sons were converting part of the mill to a corn mill in 1886 when they applied to Upperthong Local Board for permission to install a hoist, which was granted. The buildings used by Tom Mellor had not been sold prior to 1887 when they were again advertised for sale pursuant to orders of the Chancery division of the High Court. The main mill was 4 storeys high plus attic, 64yds long by 15yds wide with an external staircase and fitted with closets; boiler house with two drying stoves over with perforated iron floors 46ft 6in by 22ft 2in; an octagonal chimney 120ft high, the spinning mill was 4 storeys high with 814sq.yds of floor space; the fulling mill was 2 storeys high plus attic; there was also a tentering room, dyehouse, warehouse, and blacksmith's shop plus an office.

B. Vickerman & Sons of Taylor Hill mill, Huddersfield, were using premises in Thongsbridge mill from at least November 1887, when they applied for plans for a new drying room to be passed, and in the following year for a new dyehouse, also a smith's shop, and an addition to the boiler house. It is possible that they bought the premises previously owned by Tom Mellor, although the planning applications arguably question that assumption.

J & J Lancaster were using premises at the mills in January 1890, Mr. Prior the Factory sub-inspector saw a bright light in a room at 6.40pm, when all work should have ceased at 5.30pm. He found two women burlers were working on an urgent piece which, Mr. Lancaster told the court, they would have had left on their hands had it not been finished. The firm were fined 10s plus 8s costs for each offence.

Boothroyd Wimpenny had started in business in 1882 with £300 capital, in partnership with a William Eastwood. The partnership was dissolved in 1888, since when Wimpenny had traded on his own as Boothroyd Wimpenny and also as Wm. Boothroyd. In February 1890 he had liabilities amounting to £2,135 0s 6d, his assets amounted to £1,354 15s, leaving a deficit of £780 5s 6d. At the creditors meeting he offered to pay 9s 6d in the £ in three instalments over a nine month period, which was accepted by the majority of creditors. In addition to the premises at Thongsbridge mill, Wimpenny also had a warehouse and showroom at Littlewood Buildings, Upperhead Row, Huddersfield.

George Woodhead & Sons the corn millers were also possibly experiencing liquidity problems in 1890, when they advertised room and power to let for 20 to 25 looms. On 6 February 1892 the Factory sub-inspector Mr. Prior visited B. Vickerman and Sons at 8.45am and found Bridgett Quinn and Harriet Annie Wood cleaning under a scribbling machine. A notice showed that the mill stopped for Breakfast between 8.30am and 9am, Prior questioned the two women who told him that they were allowed to get their breakfast after the others had resumed work. The two were questioned again in court, and said that they were paid for doing the work, that they were allowed a break later, and that they were happy to do the job. The court decided that although technically an offence had been committed, they restricted the fines to 5s plus costs in each case.

In January 1893 Woodhead's were insolvent and a committee of creditors was appointed, they appear to have ordered that the premises and machinery should be sold. In March the 5 storey mill 55ft by 20ft 6in, the 5 storey mill 48ft by 24ft 6in, the grain store, sheds, boiler house, engine house, chimney, smith's shop, stables and other buildings were offered for sale by auction, as were the beam engine, boiler, shafting and gearing, the roller corn milling machinery, 2pairs of French stones, 1pair of Grey stones, the Barley separating machine and cockle separator, the bean splitting machine, oat rollers etc; also the Grocery shop and Post Office with its adjoining cottage, occupied by Mr. George Whiteley. The sale was held on 21 March, but was withdrawn as the highest bid of £900 was unacceptable to the vendors. The steam engine, flour machinery, a bone mill and 4 horses were again advertised to be sold by auction on 23 February 1894.

On 10 August 1895, B. Vickerman and Sons took their 650 employees from their premises at Taylor Hill and Thongsbridge to Blackpool for the day as a treat, in honour of Mr. A. Vickerman Priestley's marriage. The special train left at 5.30am and arrived in Blackpool in time for Breakfast. After spending the day sightseeing in the town, the tower, and along the beaches, the company returned by train arriving back at half-past midnight.

Charles A Mellor was advertising for rug weavers to work at Thongsbridge mill in May 1903; this was a branch of textiles that appears to have been expanding at this time, as the same paper also carried advertisements for rug weavers to work at Holmfirth mill and Swanbank mill. Rug manufacturers seemed to have great difficulty in attracting weavers, as there were frequent advertisements for rug weavers in the papers. The process was very different from weaving cloth, and in an attempt to attract applicants two of the advertisers were offering to subsidise trainee weaver's earnings until they became proficient.

The buildings that had been used by Woodhead's corn millers, along with the Grocery shop and Post Office with the cottage, still occupied by Mr. George Whiteley, were again offered for sale in November 1904. The occupants of the mill buildings at that time were Thornton & Co, John Woodhead, Herbert Batley and Whitfield Preston. The property still did not change hands as it was withdrawn again due to the lack of bids.

The *Yorkshire Trade Directory* for 1910 records Thongsbridge Mills Spinning Co, which was an offshoot of Vickerman's, at the mills with 7 sets of carding machines; and also B. Vickerman & Sons as having 5,000 spindles and 28 looms. On Friday 10 March 1911, Vickerman's gave a treat for their workpeople from Taylor Hill mills and Thongsbridge mills, plus friends, at the Mechanics Hall in Lockwood, when 800 people attended. Mr. A. Vickerman Priestley was now the company chairman. The meal was followed by dancing and entertainment into the early hours of Saturday. The report gave no indication of a reason for the occasion, which had been organised by a committee of 18 people made up of 9 women and 9 men.

The fortunes of the company altered dramatically between 1911 and 1938, when the company announced in late June that it was to close after 170 years of trading. The business had started at Steps mill Honley, and later moved to Taylor Hill mills. The reason for the closure of the firm was not given. Two weeks later it was announced that W.H. & J. Barber of Holmbridge were to buy Vickerman's business, but they would not give a guarantee of employment for all the workers.

A company named R. L. Robinson, who were dyers of loose wool, waste and slubbings were using part of the premises by 1937 when a fire was discovered in their premises just before 4.30am on 21 May. The fire was seen by night workers at Woodhead's of Albion mill, who rang the Holmfirth fire brigade at 4.30am, the fire engine arrived 8 minutes later, and by 5.55am the fire was extinguished. Mr. Robinson contacted Holmfirth Council to thank them for the brigade's prompt attendance, which prevented further damage being done.

Boothroyd Rugs were using part of the mills by 1939, their main business was the production of wool and mohair rugs, but they also wove blankets. In 1943 the firm was in court charged with Purchase Tax evasion. The firm was ordered to pay a fine of £300 for making false returns on Purchase Tax; and the two directors, Jack Irvin Boothroyd of Sands House Holmfirth, and Edward Alfred Batt of Woodleigh Brighouse, were fined £180 each for the same offence. The defendants were also ordered to pay 24 guineas costs. It was alleged that £4,000 of sales had been omitted from the accounts, and that Boothroyd Rugs had asked some customers to suppress their records in the same way. The firm had since sent cheques for £642 2s 4d to cover the unpaid Purchase Tax.

The buildings on the lower part of the site, nearest to the river, were inundated by flood waters in 1944, the report in the *Holmfirth Express* says that considerable [but unspecified] damage was caused on the lower floors of both Boothroyd Rugs and R.L. Robinson, who were yarn spinners. The Holmfirth UDC Report records that R.L. Robinson's lower storey was flooded leaving considerable debris and sludge; and that Boothroyd Rugs was flooded. There does not appear to have been any damage to buildings. Boothroyd Rugs continued in business at Thongsbridge until either late 1965 or early 1966, when they moved to Grove mill Honley; R.L. Robinson continued into the 1970s. They had a small fire in a wool drying machine in July 1972 that was extinguished by workers with only slight damage to the contents of the machine.[14] R.L. Robinson's last advertisement for staff appeared in the *Holmfirth Express* in 1979. Some of the buildings have since gradually disappeared, while those remaining have been put to a variety of uses.

Albion mill

The precise date of building for this mill is not known; however, it was built by Joseph Barber of Kilnhouse Bank Holmbridge, and was in existence before 1848, as in that year Joseph left, in his will, land at Thongsbridge near Miry Lane, measuring 59 yards along the river, and 31 yards wide from the river (1829sq.yds.), with the 'newly erected' mill known as Upper Holme Bottom mill, 3 cottages, stove, stable and other buildings then occupied by his son John and son-in-law George Hirst, (who later owned and occupied, along with his brother John Hirst, Lower Digley mill). To be held in trust for, and rent and profits from the mill paid to Joseph's daughter Sarah who was the wife of Daniel

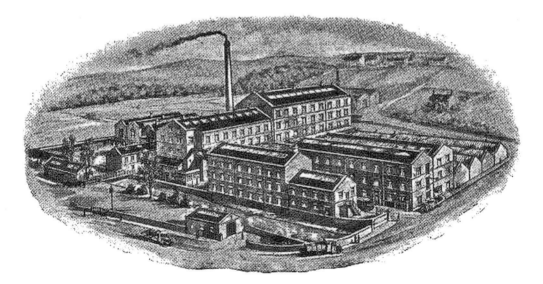

Artist's impression of Albion mill. © the Author.

Woodhead. In 1861 the 4-storey mill with its lofty and well ventilated rooms, was being advertised to let along with the steam engine, boiler, scribbling and carding engines, billies, spinning mules and a willow; prospective tenants should contact Firth Barber at Kilnhouse Bank. The following year the mill was bought by John Woodhead, son of Daniel Woodhead mentioned above, he renamed it Albion mill.

In April 1866 Angela Darnley and Edith Pickering who both worked at Woodhead's, were charged with leaving their employment without giving notice, contrary to the law. Mr. Woodhead had posted a notice on one of the walls in the mill stating that 7 days notice had to be given by anyone who intended to leave, which the women had seen. However, as they were both unable to read they did not know what it was. The magistrates said that Mr. Woodhead should have called his workers together, shown them the notice and explained its implications. The cases against both women were dismissed. Despite Woodhead's carrying out the recommendations of the magistrate, Emma Roebuck left work on 12 May 1866 without giving notice. Tom Whitehead the foreman, confirmed in court that the notice had been read and explained to all the workers. The magistrates said that Roebuck should either return to Woodhead's and work her notice, or go to prison. Her father said that she should elect to go to prison; the report does not record the outcome.

Some machinery was damaged by flood waters due to excessive rain on 16 November 1866. Woodhead's were not using the entire mill, as in 1870 they were advertising room and power for rent, this was advertised again in 1876, when they were also offering a 10hp beam engine for sale. Tenders had been invited for the erection of a new mill on the site in May 1875; Woodhead's must have given the contract to Edward Wadsworth, Paul Coldwell and Alfred Gill, trading as Wadsworth & Co, but then changed their minds and withdrew it. Wadsworth & Co sued Woodhead's for £50 damages in October of that year, the case was adjourned without resolution.

John Woodhead died on 14 November 1891 after a long illness, but the business continued, being run by his only son who was assisted by his uncle. The name of the firm then became John Woodhead & Son. Despite difficult trading conditions in the 1890s, Woodhead's business prospered to the point where additional space was needed. A new warehouse was added in 1895, new offices and other buildings in 1898, a new work-shed in 1901 and an additional mill in 1902; they had also applied to the council for permission to use the piped water supply to work an hydraulic crane in 1900; all of which were granted.

The Yorkshire Trade Directory for 1910 records that Woodhead's were spinners of lambs-wool and merino yarns, and had 10,000 spindles. A visit to the firm in 1910 by a Mr. Butler, Factory Inspector, resulted in Woodhead's being summoned for not having all the drive belts on the condenser sets protected by metal cages. Mr. Butler said that he had visited the company in 1909 and pointed out that all drive belts should be protected, but on his visit in 1910 he found that while some of the belts were behind guards, 79 were not. Mr. Woodhead said that he had asked a Huddersfield firm to supply and fit the guards, but they had only supplied a few when it had been convenient to them. Mr. Woodhead had spoken to the firm and could report that the remaining guards were now partially ready. The bench imposed a fine of £2 plus 6s 6d costs.

The flood of May 29th 1944 damaged the road bridge carrying Miry Lane over the river and tore up the tar macadam surface of the road. The water entered the ground floor of the mill damaging four carding machines and a large quantity of wool, leaving a considerable amount of debris and sludge in its wake.

Woodhead's, which had become a limited company in 1924, was bought by Yorkshire Fine Woollen Spinners Ltd. in 1947. The firm continued production at Albion mill until in 1976 they moved part of their operation to Dobroyd mill at Jackson Bridge; the rest of the company followed in 1978, the reason for the move was given as a need for more modern premises. At Dobroyd they moved into the single storey sheds on the hillside behind the original mill.

Some smaller companies moved into parts of Albion mill during the 1970s, Thornbank Tweeds were advertising for staff in December 1977; they also had a mill shop in Clarence mill Holmbridge in 1982. John Stephen Ltd. and J.R. Shepherd (woollen spinners) were both advertising for staff in January 1978; and a company trading as PJ Textiles complained in January 1982 that despite high unemployment and constant advertising they were unable to attract trained sewing machinists.

The mill was subsequently split into units and let to a variety of businesses, none of which appear to have been in textiles. In September 1983 three fires broke out simultaneously in separate units. The first to be found was in a lean-to shed next to a single storey building, the shed was used as an office and store by Hobson's Choice, who had a shop in Victoria Street Holmfirth. Two firemen received burns to the hands when a drum containing oil caught fire; they were treated at Huddersfield Infirmary and allowed to go home. A search of the premises revealed the second fire, which was in a stable that was being used for storing hay; and the third was in a unit in which plastic bobbins were stored. This unit had a sprinkler system that helped to contain the fire. A police statement said that arson was suspected.[15]

Alma mill

The 6 inch Ordinance Survey map of 1853 suggests that there was a woollen mill alongside the Huddersfield to Woodhead turnpike road, between the road and what is now the bowling club. An inspection of the wall on the bowling club side confirms that there have been buildings there, but it is not possible to identify their use. A hand written note made by Mr. Henry Roberts of Butterworth & Roberts on a sale catalogue of machinery from Alma mill in 1896 suggests that the buildings known as Alma mill were erected in 1854. They stood on the opposite side of Huddersfield Road from the mill marked on the 6 inch map. This information is confirmed by the 25 inch O.S. map of 1893. The mill was built by Joseph Mellor & Sons, who also occupied part of Thongsbridge mill. They held a celebration to mark the opening of the new mill, which was described as 'a substantial commodious building', on 3 November 1855, when they gave a treat for their 300 employees. There was a banner proclaiming 'Success to the Allied Army [who were fighting the Crimean War] and Prosperity to Alma Mill'. Mr. Godfrey Mellor was Chairman of the gathering and made a speech in which he said that "as a child he remembered washing wool in a basket, and that he never thought he would employ the number of people that he did at present".

The firm advertised for someone to look after the mill boiler in February 1858, they were possibly having difficulties with it, as the advertisement stated that it was under inspection by the Engineer of

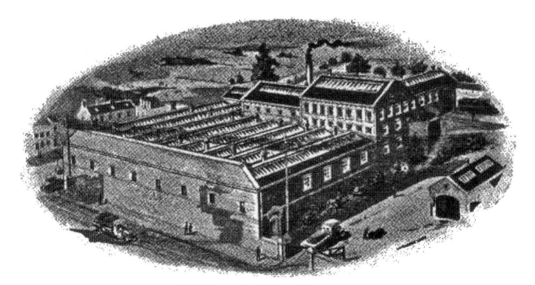

Artist's impression of Alma mill. © the Author.

the Huddersfield Boiler Association, so only competent men need apply. There was a fire at the mill in October 1858; it was discovered about 2am on Saturday 2nd October by a man who was sleeping at the mill. He raised the alarm and neighbours quickly arrived to help; the Unity brigade was sent for, but the fire was extinguished before it arrived. The origin of the fire was uncertain, but was thought to be in a large quantity of waste wool on the second floor. Damage was estimated to be around £200, which was covered by insurance.

On Tuesday 12 June 1860, James Lee aged 18 was sitting in the hoist doorway on the third floor gable end of the mill overlooking the road. A strong gust of wind blew the door shut behind him, throwing him into the road. He managed to land on his feet, but one of his legs was severely fractured and he also received other injuries. He was taken to Huddersfield Infirmary, and on Thursday was said to be as well as could be expected. Mellor's submitted a plan to Netherthong Local Board in August 1885 to enlarge their weaving shed, which was passed. Tenders for building reservoirs and filter beds at the mill were invited by Edward Holroyd & Sons builders, in September 1884.

Benny Senior who was a weaver, and Matt. Haigh who was a millhand, were dismissed for refusing to do work that was the subject of a dispute between other weavers and the mill manager in July 1890. They had been asked to do the work on two occasions; no action was taken on their first refusal, but they were instantly dismissed after refusing a second time. They were dismissed on a Saturday, their solicitor argued that they should have received seven days notice from the next payday, which was the following Friday. The bench withheld judgement for one week, and then awarded the pair one week's wages of £1 2s each, rather than two.

A large sale of machinery was held at the mill on 6 February 1896, neither the advertisements in the press nor the sale catalogue give the name of the vendors, but it was presumably Mellor's, as they appear to have been the sole occupiers. The machinery included: 8 condenser sets; 4prs. self-acting mules; 54 power looms, 5 wooden pattern looms; a large quantity of scouring and finishing machinery; also dyehouse machinery, plus the contents of mechanic's shop and many sundries. This sale was followed in March 1902 by a sale of the motive power equipment: 2 steam boilers, a fuel economiser; and two, or possibly three, beam engines; pumps, shafting, gearing etc, steam, water and gas piping. Plus a 10 ton platform weighing machine. The mill was obviously no longer being used. In November 1920 Netherthong Local Board complained that although the mill had been empty for some time, an amount of £334 for the mill was still included in their rate assessment by the county, which they presumably had to pay.

The next tenant, in part of the mill was Mr. C.W. Sheard, trading as Sheard Bros. Shoddy Waste and Mungo merchants; the other part of the mill was empty. Sam Hollingworth who lived in a cottage adjoining the mill, was awoken at 2.10am on Saturday 12 January 1907 by a dog barking. He found that the mill was ablaze and gave the alarm, rousing neighbours to help fight the flames. The buzzer at Vickerman's in Thongsbridge mill was sounded, arousing more sight-seers, and a hose was attached to the council water main. The brigade from Woodhead's of Albion mill also attached their hose to the council main. A policeman on duty in Victoria Street Holmfirth heard Vickerman's buzzer at 2.25am and roused both the Council brigade and the Unity brigade; one crew attached their hose to the council main, and the other drew water from Thongsbridge mill dam. Two hoses were directed onto the front of the mill, and two onto the rear; the three that were attached to the council water main were not very effective as it was only a three inch pipe. The fire inside the mill was so ferocious that the hoses were redirected onto the adjacent buildings to keep them from bursting into flames. After the floors and roof of the mill had collapsed, the Huddersfield brigade arrived with their steam powered fire engine 'Phyllis' pulled by three horses. They were able to direct two strong jets onto the flames inside the mill and extinguish them; leaving only the four outer walls standing. The mill was three storeys high at the front on to Huddersfield Road, but five storeys high at the rear. The owners of the building were Albert Pearson and Lewis Batley who, like the tenants, were only partially insured. Estimates of the damage varied between £1,500 and £2,000. The report in the *Holmfirth Express* ends with: "Fortunately, but a few hands are thrown out of employment".

Alma Mill after the fire February 1907. © A.J. Brooke

An advertisement appeared in the *'Express'* in June 1907 offering heavy foundation stone for sale from the mill's engine bed. The mill was rebuilt, and C.W. Sheard was still occupying it trading as a Shoddy Merchant in August 1911, when there was another fire discovered at 6.15am on Wednesday 2 August. Workpeople from Woodhead's and Vickerman's attempted to put out the fire, but by 6.25am the flames could be seen from Rotcher in Holmfirth. The Unity brigade pumped water onto the fire and the brigade from Woodhead's were ready to help, but were not needed. The roof collapsed at 6.40am, and one gable end also fell. Brown and Blackburn's chemical works adjoining the mill removed some of their stock for safety. Damage to the five storey building and stock was estimated at £1,200. The mill was again rebuilt, as John Woodhead's were using it during the 1940s in addition to Albion mill.[16]

Thongsbridge Bone and Size Works

The plans for the proposed works were submitted to Wooldale Local Board by Mr. James Batley in July 1873; they were to be sighted off Miry Lane just above Albion mill. The Board refused to pass them and returned the plans to Mr. Batley in August 'as the buildings did not adjoin the road'. The works were obviously built, as the next information on them also comes from the minutes of Wooldale Local Board in 1878, noting that the firm was to be visited by the Nuisance Inspector, as the Board had received complaints from residents of an 'offensive smell'. Batley's applied to the Local Board to erect some outbuildings in September 1879, which were approved. Complaints about the smell and fumes from the plant continued, and in July 1880 the Board gave Batley's notice to remedy the problem within 28 days.

Whatever actions Batley's took were ineffective as the problem continued and in May 1881 residents of Thongsbridge submitted a petition to the Board asking that Batley's should abate the nuisance. In July of that year the district's Medical Officer gave a signed statement to the Board that James Batley's bone boiling works were: 'a serious nuisance, an annoyance to residents in the neighbourhood, and were dangerous to public health'. The Local Government Board in Wakefield was also pressing for the problem to be resolved.

Despite the various resolutions the problem persisted; ownership of the company had passed to George Batley by 1892, when the West Riding Medical Officer conducted an enquiry into the problem and his report was published in April of that year. He found that there was a problem with the effluvia emitted from both the chimney and the buildings, which had been the cause of illnesses; and that there was still much work that needed to be done by Batley's to control and contain the problem. The main problem was that the works had been constructed without planning consent, and were sighted in the bottom of a steep sided valley with population living on the higher ground. Offensive materials were allowed to accumulate, and waste was spread on the surrounding land from time to time. He also said that the Holmfirth authorities had failed to take the necessary action to protect the public despite repeated complaints.

Holmfirth Local Board took Batley's to court later in the year; evidence was given that open truck loads of bones and horns arriving at Thongsbridge railway station on Saturdays were often left until Monday before being unloaded and taken to the works. The board had received numerous complaints over a long period about the smell emanating from the trucks and the works, and also that refuse from them littered the roads. Batley's said that they made large quantities of Agricultural manure, and size for warps, and had been in Thongsbridge for many years. The case was adjourned for six weeks, after which time the court ordered Batley's to abate the nuisance.

The problem continued, with the local authority receiving complaints from residents on a regular basis. In October 1899 the *Holmfirth Express* printed a letter from a property owner in Thongsbridge refuting George Batley's claim that landlords were unable to let their empty houses in the village due to their poor state of repair. The writer said that he had shown his properties to several prospective tenants who would have been happy to live in them, but for the noxious smell from the bone boiling works.

Size was used to coat the warp threads of woollen cloth to minimise breakages. From the 1870s many of the mills in Holme Valley stopped manufacturing woollens and began weaving worsteds, which were becoming more popular. This changeover reduced the demand for size, as worsted threads are both stronger and smoother than woollen. The Batley family appear to have given up the bone boiling business, but retained the works; in 1914 they advertised in the *Holmfirth Express* for girls to sew and pack 'Elbie Dustless Dusters'. The owner of the company at this time was Mr. Lewis Batley.

The next information on the firm comes in an advertisement for James Batley in 1950, who was trading as a seed and fertiliser merchant.[17] The premises were subsequently bought by Mr. Selwyn Smith of Shepley in the 1980s, and having been split into units are let to a variety of tenants.

In 1824 there was a Dwelling house with a **Dyehouse,** buildings and several cottages, plus 10 acres of land at **Hey** near Thongsbridge, which was bought by William John Norris and Edward Wainhouse. The occupier at the time was Joseph Roberts.

In October 1846, George Beaumont of Manchester paid £1,400 to the Venerable Charles Musgrave DD Vicar of Halifax, and John William Norris, of 19 Bedford Place, Russell Square, Middx. for the Dwelling house, weaving shops, warehouses, dry houses, pressing shops, dyehouses, and reservoirs, also the barn, homestead cowhouse and other buildings, yard, gardens, plantations and various other pieces of land at Hey Thongsbridge.[18]

Mytholmbridge Upper mill

The date of origin of this mill is unclear, it is certainly one of the older mills in the district, but just how old is difficult to determine. H.J. Morehouse writes about the existence of an indenture dated 23 March 1541, when John Storthes, Gentleman, of Shittlington, conveyed to John Walker a clothier, of Thurstonland, and John Walker his son, for £100:

> 'one messuage, four score acres of land, sixteene acres of meadow, twenty acres of pasture and four acres of wodd, &c., in Thurstonland, with commons &c'. A stipulation within the deed was: 'that John

Walker and his heirs, at all tymes as they shall have any cloth redy to be mylled, or any corne to be ground, shall exercise and occupy the myll or myllnes within the lordship of Thurstonland, if they be truly well and reasonablye sued and used; and they to pay for the mylning of the seyd cloth and grinding of the seyd corne, according after the maner and custome as other freeholders and tenants ther do'. And that 'John Walker and his heirs in tyme to come, shall never erect, buyld, nor set up, within the seyd lordship, any manner of myll or myllnes'.

The earliest known reference to a fulling mill at Mytholmbridge is contained in the *Wakefield Court Roll* of 1552, when it was already built and working. The owner of the mill was Edward Bilcliff, he passed a moiety in the mill to Richard Charlesworth of Huddersfield; the tenant of the mill at that time was John Armitage. Crump and Ghorbal maintain that this was a Soke mill, but that is obviously not the case. The nearest Manorial/Soke mills at that time were at New Mill.

In 1734 the owner of the mill was John Radcliffe of Almondbury, he let the fulling mill, with a newly erected house or cottage occupied by Nathaniel Shaw, to Thomas Hobson of Hagg, Jonathon Hobson of Wooldale and Francis Tinker of Hepworth. In 1756 John Radcliffe surrendered a close of land called the Lower End Royd near the mill, containing a house occupied by Jonas Hobson, to William Horsfall of Storths Hall, to enable the building of a weir in the river that would turn water into a goit for the mill.

In the 1780s, there was a fulling mill and a corn mill at Mytholmbridge; the fulling mill took its water supply from the River Holme; whereas the corn mill took its water from New Mill dike. The tenant of the fulling mill in the late 1780s was John Hobson who was also responsible for insuring the mill; the owner by then was Thomas Radcliffe Esquire, who lived in Charleston, South Carolina. There was also a second fulling mill just downstream from the upper mill, known as Mytholmbridge Lower mill. John Hobson, along with Jonas Hobson of Thurstonland and Thomas Dransfield of Wooldale, had a 25 year lease on the upper mill; the lower mill was owned and operated at that time, by John Armitage of Kettlethorpe near Sandal Magna. The land between the sites of the two mills is fairly flat, which caused some problems in the late eighteenth century when the mills relied on water power. Water for the upper mill was taken from a bend in the river about 250 yards upstream from the mill and carried via a goit into a small dam behind the mill buildings; water for the lower mill was taken from behind a weir in the river about half-way between the two mills and carried via a goit to a somewhat larger dam behind that mill. In order to increase the flow of water into their dam the tenants of the lower mill raised the height of the weir a few inches, raising the water level in that section of the river sufficiently to stop the upper mill's wheel from turning. A court case ensued which, in 1794, was referred to three independent assessors to be resolved. They considered the problem and in 1796 decreed that a stone marked 'Level' should be set into the ground beside, and at the height of, the weir for the lower mill; with a similar stone set at the height of the same weir, 9 feet from the house attached to the upper mill. When these stones were in position they were below ground level, and would be covered. To provide visible reminders of the correct level, a one inch hole was to be drilled in the upright of the lower mill's door frame 2 feet 10 inches above the door sill, which would be level with the weir; with a one inch hole being drilled in the doorframe of the upper mill that would be 11 feet above the 'level' stones. The old weir was to be kept at the correct height. In addition an aqueduct six feet wide and fourteen inches deep was to be constructed to carry water from the outfall of the upper mill's waterwheel across the river where it would then enter a tunnel ten feet wide by seven feet high with an arched roof that was to be dug, built and covered at Thomas Radcliffe's expense, to carry this extra water to the lower mill's dam. This, they felt, would prevent any recurrence of the problem.

In 1794 Thomas Radcliffe of Charlestown South Carolina had passed the use of the house, 4 cottages, barn, stable, dyehouse, drying house and other outbuildings, along with the garden, orchard and 25 acres of land to John Hobson. He also passed the use of another house, the fulling mill and a covered shed opposite the fulling mill used for Burling, to John and Jonas Hobson and

Thomas Dransfield. Radcliffe reserved the right to take away from the premises all the ashes and manure 'raised bred or made' within the site.

In his will dated 12 September 1806, Radcliffe left his estate in Yorkshire to the use and enjoyment of his widow Lucretia Constance Radcliffe for the term of her natural life. After her death, which occurred in late 1811 or early 1812, it was to be divided between Mr. Charles Radcliffe, of Halifax; Mrs. Elizabeth Atkinson, wife of Richard Atkinson frizer [leather dresser] of Aspley Huddersfield; and Mrs. Mary Beeston who lived in Manchester, as tenants in common. The estate included the fulling, scribbling and carding mill, stocks, going gear etc. at Mytholmbridge, late in occupation of John Hobson deceased, now of his assignees Jonas and George Hobson, and Thos. Dransfield, Wm. Leigh, and Thomas Marshall. The rasping and grinding mill at Kirkbridge, New Mill; houses and cottages at Mytholmbridge, Kirkbridge, Wooldale, Wooldale Townend and Knowles, and land totalling 109 acres 3 roods 1 perch spread throughout the district. During the next thirty years these three portions of the estate each became divided and sub divided, making a total of ninety portions that were bought and sold many times.

An entry in Isaac Beardsell's journal dated 18 January 1844, suggests that Joshua Mellor, possibly with Samuel, had recently taken the tenancy of Mytholmbridge mill, either in late 1843, or at the beginning of January. The mill, which could run three billeys, and had stocks to run five or six pieces, was 'only in a poor state of repair', but the rent was only £80 per year. The flood of 1852 damaged the mill; the report in the *Huddersfield Chronicle* of February 7th indicates that two firms who were using the mill submitted damage claims: Joseph & Samuel Mellor claimed £107 19s 4d for damage to mill buildings, the mill dam and the fulling stocks. This was reduced to £77 14s 4d by the inspectors, and a total of £40 was paid. Ann Armitage & Son, who were dyers, claimed £111 for stock destroyed and damaged. This was reduced to £106 by the inspectors, but there is no evidence to suggest that any payment was made.

The Reservoir Commissioners recorded the owners of Mytholmbridge mill in 1853 as 'The trustees of Charles Radcliffe Esq. deceased, and others'; and the occupiers as Joseph and Samuel Mellor; it appears that Ann Armitage & Son were unable to continue trading after the flood. The owner of the Corn mill is recorded as Charles Horsfall Bill Esq., and the occupant was Mary Knutton.

The partnership between Joseph and Samuel Mellor was dissolved by mutual consent on 9 October 1856. Joseph Mellor had given a treat to his workers at the Royal Oak, Thongsbridge on October 4th to celebrate the marriage of his son Edwin; Beaumont's Brass Band provided music for the evening entertainment. He also gave a treat to 50 workers on 7 January 1859. In early January 1861, the 90 women workers at the mill enjoyed a treat at the Royal Oak, where they were joined by the women who worked for George Greenwood at Thongsbridge mill, bringing the total to well over 100. The 60 men at Mellor's enjoyed a Tea with roast Beef and Ham, also at the Royal Oak, on Tuesday 15 January, 1861; after the meal the company were joined by two of Mr. Mellor's sons.

By 1865 Joseph Mellor was experiencing financial difficulties, in March he assigned all his goods to the benefit of his creditors; the assignees were Matthew William Cliffe wool merchant of Huddersfield, George Greenwood finisher Thongsbridge, and Frederick Shaw card maker Huddersfield. At a meeting with his creditors in May of that year he promised to pay them a total of 10s in the pound in three instalments of 3s 4d, to be paid in four, eight and twelve months time, which they accepted.[19] A fire was discovered in the drying stove at the mill, which belonged to Mr. Mellor, at 4am on Sunday 25 November 1866. The stove was built over the boiler house, and was in a separate building from the main mill. When the alarm was raised a number of people ran to the mill, but the fire had such a good hold that it was not possible to extinguish it; so efforts were concentrated on stopping it from spreading to the main mill, which, due to the efforts of the people, who were also helped by a favourable wind, succeeded. The Unity brigade had been alerted, but when they arrived the stove had been destroyed and the boiler house below was in flames, which they were able to put out; only the outer walls of the boiler house were left standing. Mr. Mellor estimated the cloth and wool destroyed was valued around £130; the stock and the buildings were covered by insurance.

In June 1867 Joseph Mellor was again in debt, in a Deed of Assignment he assigned all his assets to his creditors, who ordered that a sale of machinery and wool should be held at the mill on 4 September 1867. By February 1868 Joseph Mellor had ceased to occupy the mill, as it was advertised 'To be let, (late in the occupation of Mr. Joseph Mellor), within 5 minutes walk of Thongsbridge Railway Station'. Anyone interested should apply to Mr. Edmund Eastwood dyer, Huddersfield.

The 1871 census records that John Newsome, a fulling miller, employed 19 people at the mill. The dyehouse was advertised to let in July 1871, capable of dyeing wool or cloth, with 4 Woad or Indigo vats, an Indigo mill, a steam boiler, 2 Iron dyepans, a wooden scouring pan, a cistern, and a good water supply. Again, application should be made to Mr. Edmund Eastwood, Engine Bridge, Huddersfield.

Between 6am and 6.30am on the morning of Saturday 7 November 1877, a boy called Fred Turner, and a boy called Hemmingway [their ages are not given] were waiting at the mill for the arrival of Fred's uncle, so that they could start work. They decided to go into the mill and put the drive belt for the machine over the pulley on the shafting, so that when the uncle arrived they would be all ready to start. They got a ladder and put it into position; Fred climbed the ladder whilst Hemmingway held it steady. As Fred attempted to put the drive belt over the pulley his smock got caught up and he was whirled around the shafting. A spinner who was standing outside heard the boy cry out and ran into the mill, while Hemmingway ran to the engine house to get the shafting stopped. Fred was released and taken to Huddersfield Infirmary where he died on Sunday morning. The inquest jury returned a verdict of 'accidental death'.

Although there had been a corn mill at Upper Mytholmbridge for many years, possibly for longer than the fulling mill, there is little information available. One incident that is recorded is the fire that was discovered by one of the miller John Knutton's daughters at 9.30pm on the evening of January 15th 1880. John Knutton had locked the mill at 9pm and gone home, half an hour later his daughter noticed a light in the mill and told her father who quickly returned and found the mill on fire. News of the fire soon spread, and engines from Batley's Thongsbridge, and Robinsons of Smithy Place mill soon arrived, but despite their efforts, they were unable to save the building. The mill contained 400 to 500 packs of Beans, Indian Corn etc all waiting to be ground, belonging to James Hoyle of Holmfirth, S. Drake & Sons Honley, and D. Earnshaw of Netherton, most of which were burned. Damage to the mill and its contents were estimated at £700, none of which was insured. The corn mill does not appear to have been rebuilt, as there is no mention of it on the 25 inch O.S. map of 1893.

Joshua Hoyle was using the fulling mill during the 1870s, he decided in 1881 to give up his business as his health was declining; his machinery was advertised for sale by private treaty in May of that year, consisting of 5 condenser sets, 2prs of self-acting mules, 2prs of hand mules, balloon and winding frame, 26 power looms, twisting machine, bobbin winding frame, burring machine, waste cleaner, milling machine and 1 washing machine. The advertisement also said that the mill was available at a reasonable rent from the owner of the mill, who was still Edmund Eastwood who lived in New North Road Huddersfield.

It is probable that the purchasers of much of the machinery were the next tenants of the mill, James Bowes and Henry Silverwood. The two men formed a partnership and traded as Bowes & Silverwood, manufacturers and merchants, with premises at Mytholmbridge mill, and at Lion Arcade in Huddersfield. They took up their tenancy of the mill in 1881, and in January 1882 submitted plans to Wooldale Council for extensions to the mill and new sheds, which were passed. They gave a treat for their 127 employees at the Duke of Leeds Hotel, New Mill, in February 1882. After an excellent dinner, James Bowes said that trade in the area was good, and when it was good for the masters, it was also good for the workpeople. Henry Silverwood said that he hoped that the workers would all unite and help each other, and that he had no desire to get rich; if he and his partner could get an honest living and carry on a respectable trade, that was all they had in view at present. There was dancing, interspersed with songs, recitations and speeches, during which nuts, figs and brandy-snaps were 'handed round in abundance'.

Two years later, in March 1884, the public examination of Bowes and Silverwood took place in Huddersfield because they were bankrupt. James Bowes said that Silverwood was responsible for the purchase of their machinery, which had cost £2,300. Their Balance Sheet for 1882 showed a surplus of £415 with the machinery valued at £2,000. In January 1883 another Balance Sheet was prepared showing a surplus of £312. Although, as far as Bowes was aware, no new machinery had been bought that year, the machinery had increase in value on the Balance Sheet to £4,647. Had it been shown at its cost price the balance sheet would have shown a deficiency of £1,800. 55 looms costing between £5 and £6 each were shown on the balance sheet at £30 each. A Balance Sheet prepared in 1884 was showing a deficiency of £2,140 with the machinery valued at £4,883 which, Mr. Bowes thought, should not be more than £2,000. This would have given a deficiency in excess of £3,000.

Bowes also said that he never ascertained the cost of making pieces before selling them, the selling price was given to him by Silverwood, and he had never queried it. He believed that he had always sold their pieces at a profit; he knew nothing about manufacturing and only attended to the selling. When he found that the value of their machinery had been inflated, he did nothing to correct it as he believed at the time that his partner was honest.

Mr. Silverwood said that it was not correct that he had denied the cost of pieces to Bowes; they had pieces at 4s 6d a yard that they had sold at 4s 3d, but only during the last year. He said that this was not with his consent, his partner had done it and he did not know why. Silverwood did admit that he had fixed the selling prices and given them to Bowes; he also said that he had no record, in any way, of the cost of making the pieces.

The examination was adjourned to allow Bowes and Silverwood to submit statements showing what had been paid for machinery in 1882, and showing the profit or loss made on pieces. A Committee of Inspection had been set up and ordered that the firm's machinery should be sold. The London Gazette gives notice that Bowes and Silverwood would pay a first dividend of 3s in the £ to creditors on 25 June 1884; their second and final dividend of 1s 5¼d in the £ would be paid on 27 March 1885, along with a payment of 3s 4d in the £ levied on the personal estate of James Bowes, and a payment of 4s 9d in the £ from the personal estate of Henry Silverwood. Giving creditors a total repayment of 12s 6¼d in the £. Silverwood was discharged from bankruptcy on 1 January 1887.[20]

Thomas Rhodes cloth finisher, who had premises in Prickleden mill, made a claim against the widow of Joseph Boothroyd, who was the administrator of her husband's estate, for £22 0s 1d for swinging and drying a large number of pieces of cloth. He had asked Boothroyd for payment in the presence of John William Horsfall, who also owed Rhodes money for the same service. Boothroyd, whose premises were in Upper Mytholmbridge, had previously made a claim against Rhodes for dyeing done; but had died two days before Rhodes' counter claim by falling into a vat full of scalding water. Horsfall had since gone out of business. The case was adjourned and does not seem to have been resumed.

The mill was offered for sale by auction on 18 June 1885 as Lot 21 in the sale of the total estate that had belonged to Thomas Radcliffe of Charlestown South Carolina, when it was described as having a dyehouse, stove, warehouse, joiner's shop, yards, water wheels, goit, water privileges, boiler, steam engine and going gear. Also two closes of land called the Cinder Hill and the Holme, and a small wood on the opposite side of the river. It was withdrawn at the auction as bidding stopped at £1,900; and was later bought privately by John Tinker of T. & J. Tinker, who moved their business here from Bankend mill at Holmbridge.

In February 1892 Tinker's told three of their male weavers from a total of around twenty, that they were going to reduce the rate paid for weaving serge's by Id per string. The weavers argued that this would reduce their wages by 4s per week, taking them below the rate agreed for women weavers, and walked out as they downed their warps; half the men affected were union members and were supported by them, the others applied to join the union but would not necessarily receive immediate support. The dispute was still ongoing in early March, when the *Yorkshire Factory Times* reported that Tinker's had said that if it was not resolved they would contract to have the cloth woven in Bradford. There are no further reports on the disagreement, suggesting that the problem was resolved by some means.

Tinker's made various alterations to existing buildings, and in 1901 applied to build a new warehouse across Luke Lane, which would be joined to the main mill by a bridge. In July 1902, Factory Inspector A.F.J. Donnolly visited the mill at 6.15pm and found six women working in the new building sewing Puttees and affixing tapes to them. He charged Tinker's with employing Emily Brook, Alice Turner, Mary E. Tinker, Lydia Marshall, Ellen Biltcliffe and Mary Newton at night. In their defence Tinker's said that the women were working on an Army contract that had to be completed; and that they were not employed on industrial premises as that building was separate from the mill and contained no motive power or shafting. The inspector said that as it was attached to the mill by the bridge it was part of the industrial premises, and there were also mending tables in the room in which the women worked, which was a recognised industrial process. The bench found that the case was proven, and fined Tinkers £1 plus costs in each case, a total of £9 15s

Alfred Marsden, a dyer's labourer who worked at the mill, was walking along the goit between the mill and the river about 12.40pm on Wednesday 16 January 1907, when he found the body of a woman in the water of the goit. It was a 25 year old woman called Janet Smith, the daughter of James Smith, landlord of the Sycamore Inn Wooldale. She was employed as a weaver at Rock mill in Brockholes. Her boots and stockings were found neatly folded on the bank of the goit at a point where the water was about two feet deep. She had left work at 5.30pm as usual the night before, and had been seen by her sister about 6pm who had wished her 'good night'. She was said to have recently been depressed. The jury returned a verdict of 'Suicide by drowning while of unsound mind'.

Finishers at T & J Tinker went on strike in late February 1907; they had been on strike about one year previously for a day and a half, complaining that overtime and short time were not being shared equally between all the men in the department. They had resumed work on the understanding that, as far as possible, all the men would be treated equally, which had not happened. They also complained about the use of 'rushing tactics' by the firm, and they wanted a dismissed colleague to be reinstated. The men also complained that girls were being employed as tail-enders [assistants] on some machines instead of boys. One of the partners met with the men and said that the company were taking a firm stand; he told the men that they had all "done", but if any of them wanted to apply to work they would be seen 'separately and privately'. The firm advertised in the local papers for labourers, the men who had been laid off submitted an advertisement explaining the dispute to one of the papers, but the paper refused to print it. The Rev. W.H. Heap announced to his congregation during the evening service at Queen Street Mission in Huddersfield that there were vacancies in the finishing department at Upper Mytholmbridge mill. On the Monday morning about a dozen men arrived at the mill, all bearing a ticket with Queen Street Mission written on one side and T & J Tinker written on the other, hoping for interview. They were stopped by pickets who explained the dispute, and all the men turned back. '*The Worker*' contacted the Rev. Heap to tell him how his church had been used; he said that he was not aware of the dispute, but had been told by a lady in his congregation that Tinker's wanted men. The firm said that they would not employ union members in future, but the original staff were re-employed on the original terms and were allowed to retain their union membership.

Tinker's were the subject of an investigation by the Rivers Board in 1909 into possible pollution of the river due to mills discharging manufacturing effluent into it, in contravention of the Rivers

Pollution Act of 1876. The processes that caused the offending pollution were scouring and dyeing. The majority of the scour was discharged into a goit that then flowed into the river Holme, and some of the refuse from the dyehouse was also discharged into the river. Correspondence between Tinker's and the Rivers Board dated from 1897, when Tinker's had said that they were hopeful of being able to direct the effluent into the Council sewers, but the Council had said, on the completion of outfall works in 1904, that the plant could not cope with industrial effluent and would consequently not accept waste from mills. Dr. Wilson, chief inspector for the rivers board, pointed out that the mills immediately above and below Upper Mytholmbridge each had water purification plant, but Lower Mytholmbridge had to use the polluted water from Tinker's mill. The inquiry closed without a resolution to the problem.

Production stopped at the mill in February 1913 when the shaft connecting the mill engine to the fly-wheel broke. The damaged engine was removed and replaced in seven days with one that was at Bottoms mill but was not being used, allowing production to restart at 6.30am on Monday 24 February. In November 1913 John Tinker presented every member of the workforce with 10s to mark the Golden Jubilee of his brother Tedbur and himself starting the business at Upper Digley mill, and moving to Brownhill mill in 1863 with 12 employees; they currently had a workforce of over 300 spread between Bottoms and Upper Mytholmbridge mills. They had originally produced mixed tweeds, and later Stockinet, but when this went out of fashion they turned to producing serges, woollens and worsteds.

Tinker's had left Upper Mytholmbridge by August 1922, concentrating all their production at Bottoms mill. The premises at Upper Mytholmbridge were advertised for sale by Auction on the 23rd of that month, comprising the:

> Stone built main mill, 3 storeys and attic, 99'6" x 44'9", with basement under part, large cistern on roof. 4 storey mill 61' x 24'8; tentering place 45'7 x 21'2 with basement under; office 35'x 21' with open store place under; old engine house, 2 storey building 42' x 20'8 average. Long range of building forming 4 dyehouses, storeplaces, mechanic's shop and stable; 2 storey warehouse 100'6 x 27'; boiler house with stove over; chimney shaft; stone built cottage and conveniences. Together with horizontal condensing steam engine, Lancashire boiler with mechanical stoker, Green's fuel economiser, main shafting and gearing, wagon weighing machine, electric lighting installation, steam and water piping throughout. Also vacant land and water rights.

The mill was bought for £2,100 by an unnamed buyer.

Seedhill Schofield Finishing Company Ltd. was using part of the mill by April 1923, when they were advertising for menders. From their entries in the *Yorkshire Textile Directory* they were tenants until at least 1931. They were joined, for at least part of the time, by a company called Littlewood's Ltd. who gave three months notice to Holmfirth UDC in November 1930 that they would be vacating the premises and would no longer need their electricity supply.

Victoria Textiles Ltd, whose main production was in Victoria mill in Honley, were using part of Upper Mytholmbridge mill in September 1945, when they applied to Holmfirth Council to erect a new shed, which was approved. They continued to occupy part of the mill during the late 1940s, throughout the 1950s and early '60s. The name of the company at Mytholmbridge changed to W.O Shaw Ltd in 1959, although they continued to trade as Victoria Textiles in Honley. The last advertisement for staff for Mytholmbridge appeared in 1963.

During the 1940s Leonard Hobson began manufacturing hearth rugs in part of the mill, trading as L. Hobson (Rugs) Ltd., his first entry in the *Yorkshire Textile Directory* was in 1948, and he continued in business until the late 1960s, or possibly the 1970s, although he had ceased to make hearth rugs and was making horse blankets, which he sold through a shop called Turf Horse Clothing that had premises on Huddersfield Road in Thongsbridge. Mark Gledhill & Sons Ltd. manufacturers of Hi-Pylon rugs had moved from Ribbledon mill Holmfirth to Upper Mytholmbridge by 1969 and, according to the *Yorkshire Textile Directory,* were in the mill until at least 1971. There was a fire on the top floor of the part of the mill used by L. Hobson (Rugs) Ltd. in 1978, by which time the premises had been taken over by O. Tiltscher & Sons, who were making rugs, curtains and cushion covers, employing 15 people. Although the premises were damaged, Tiltscher's said that they were certain of being able to continue by moving to a different part of the mill. The firm were still there in 1997, when they were given permission to work 24 hour days in three shifts.[21]

The buildings of the main mill that still remain have been converted into living accommodation; there is a building across Luke Lane that was originally connected to the main mill by a bridge which has since been removed, and the building is now empty; also new houses have been built on land that originally contained mill buildings.

Notes

1   Holmfirth mill
     W.C.R. 6 Nov. 1316; Kirklees Archive, KX175/3; H.J. Morehouse, History of Kirkburton and the Graveship of Holme, p. 148; Leeds Mercury, 20 Apr, 13 May 1784; H.J. Morehouse, p.148; W.C.R. 26 Feb. 1813; 23 Feb. 1821; Supplementary Report into the Employment of Children in Factories and as to the Propriety and Means of Curtailing the Hours of their Labour, Part 1; (25 March 1834); W.C.R. 4 Dec. 1840; Isaac Beardsell's Diary 1844-46; 28 Dec. 1844; Huddersfield Chronicle, 7 Feb. 1852; J. Mayhall, Annals of Yorkshire; Vol. 1, p.606; Kirklees Archive, T/H/F/36 claim no. 234; also claim no. 139.

2   Huddersfield Chronicle, 17 July 1852; Kirklees Archive, KC6/1/33; Huddersfield Chronicle, 28 Apr. and 5 Dec. 1855; 31 May 1856; 24 Dec. 1859; 11, 18, 25 June, and 2 July, 1864; Huddersfield Examiner, 8 Aug. and 28 Nov. 1868; Huddersfield Chronicle, 4 May 1872; Huddersfield Examiner 11 July and 12 Sept 1874; 2 Jan. 1875; 13 Oct. 1877; Huddersfield Chronicle, 24 Jan. 1880; Kirklees Archive, UHO Wooldale, 29 Jan. also 9 Sept. 1880; Huddersfield Examiner, 31 Jan. and 16 May 1885; Holmfirth Express, Jan. 1888, also Huddersfield Examiner, 2 June 1888;

3   Huddersfield Examiner,. 17 Nov. 1888; Holmfirth Express, 25 Jan. 8 Feb. 1890; 20 June 1891; 6 Aug. 1892; 21 Nov. 1891; 2 Jan. 1897; 29 Nov. 1902; 7 Jan. 1905; also Kirklees Archive, KMT4 Holmfirth 17 May 1900; Kirklees Archive, KMT4 Holmfirth, 12 Nov. 1906; UHO Holmfirth, 21 Nov. 1910, also 18 Dec. 1911; 22 July 1915; 20 June 1928, 5 Feb. 1929, and 14 Dec. 1931; 1 Oct 1931, 3 Feb. 1932, 7 Oct. 1935, 8 Jan. 1934; Huddersfield Examiner, 1 Aug. 1936.

4   Newtown Mill
     Kirklees Archive, UHO Upperthong 23 Feb. 1883. Holmfirth Express, 5 Feb. 1896; Ibid, 2 Oc. 1909; 1 Jan. 1938; 26 July 1958; 19 Mar. 1960

5   Tom mill
     W.C.R. 5 Oct. 1796; 1 Nov. 1797; 7 June, 1809; 2 Mar. and 12 Apr. 1847; Huddersfield Chronicle, 7 Feb. 1852; also Kirklees Archive, T/H/F/45 claim no. 44. 1852.

6   Albert mill
     Kirklees Archive, KC/6/8/35 April, 1865; Huddersfield Examiner, 16 Mar. 1872; Kirklees Archive, UHO Upperthong, 18 Oct. 1872; Huddersfield Examiner, 1 Aug. 1874; Kirklees Archive, UHO Upperthong, 11 Feb. 1881; Holmfirth Express, Jan. 1891; 18 Sept. also 30 Oct. 1897; Textile Manufacturer, 22 Dec. 1900; Kirklees Archive, KMT4 Holmfirth, 8 Sept 1898, 16 Oct. 1902, 2 & 16 March 1908; 9 March 1903; 13 July 1911; KC28/3, 4 Oct. 1940; Holmfirth Express, 26 January 1957; 29 June 1968; 14 Dec. 1979, also 20 Oct. 1983; 13 Nov. 1987, 20 July 1989.

7   Bridge mills
     W.C.R. 2 May 1739; 3 May and 22 Oct. 1740; 26 Mar 1742; 17 Apr and 10 Jun 1743; 22 Mar. 3 May 14 June 1745; 16 June 1746; 1 June 1756; 22 Mar. 1782; 23 May 1797; 18 Nov. 1791; 11 Jan 1793; 17 Oct. 1798; 8 June 1803; Leeds Mercury, 5 Jan. 1811; also W.C.R. 29 May 1811; W.C.R. 10 Dec. 1824; 15 Aug. and 30 Oct. 1833; 15 June, 17 Aug. 1838; London Gazette, 29 May, 13 July, 1838; Leeds Mercury, 20 Oct. 1849.

8   Kirklees Archive, T/H/F/36, claim no's 57 and 220; Huddersfield Chronicle, 7 Feb. also 17 July 1852; 2 Apr. 1853; 4 Mar, 24 Jun, 16 Sept. 1854; Huddersfield Examiner, 15 Mar. 1856; Chronicle, 24 May 1856; Examiner, 17 Nov. 1883; 13 June 1857; Chronicle, 27 Jun. and 11 July 1857; 6 and 13 Feb. 1858; 10 Sept. 1859; 4 Feb. 1860; 7 Sept. 1861; 27 Jun. and 11 July 1857; 6 and 13 Feb. 1858; 10 Sept. 1859; 4 Feb. 1860; 7 Sept. 1861; 15 Apr. and 6 May 1865; Kirklees Archive, KC315/Turner; also Registry of Deeds Wakefield, Ref. ZF, 10 July, 1866. Chronicle, 24 Nov. 1866

9   Kirklees Archive, UHO Upperthong, 18 Oct. 1872; Hudds Ex.10 Oct. 1874; also 12 Jun 1875; 30 Dec. 1876; 26 Feb 1881; 1 Mar. 1890; 15 May 1886; H'firth Exp. 21 January 1888; London Gazette, 18 April 1890, also late April 1890; H'firth Exp. 19 April, and 3 May, 1890; 31 Jan. 1891; Hudds Ex.23 Jan. and 20 Feb. 1892; H'firth Exp. 26 Apr. 1924; 9 Sept. 1899; Hudds Ex. 24 Aug. 1901, 22 Oct. 1904; Kirklees Archive, UHO Holmfirth, 13 Sept. 1906; 23 May 1907; Yorkshire Textile Directory, 1910; 1913 and 1914. Kirklees Archive, UHO Holmfirth, 1 May 1913; also 23 July 1914

10   H'firth Exp. 1 and 15 April 1916; 25 Nov. 1916; also Yorks. Text. Diry, 1916, and 1917; Deeds RegistryWakefield, Deeds vol.26 p.1269 no.485; Kirklees Archive, KC6/5/5-6; H'firth Exp.14 May 1932; Kirklees Archive, UHO Holmfirth, 14 Jun. 1920, 26 Feb. 1934, 24 Jun. 1940, 10 Oct. 1949; KC28/1-6; Hudds Ex.5 June 1965; H'firth Exp. 29 May, 6 Nov. 18 Dec. 1987.

11   Fearnought/Pickwick mill
     Kirklees Archive, UHO Holmfirth, 13 June 1949, 16 Jan. 1950.

12   Deanhouse mill
     Leeds Mercury, 29 Sept. 1798; 20 Dec. 1800; 22 Jan. 1803; Kirklees Archive, KC165/385; Leeds Merc. 20 Aug 1842, 12 Feb. 1848; Hudds Ex. also Chron.3 and 17 July 1852; 15 Jan. 1853. Hudds Chron. 26 Feb, 4 Jun. 1859; Examiner, 10 Dec. 1859; NMRC docs. 26 May 1860; Hudds. Chron. 23 Mar. 1861; , 11 Jan. 1862; Hudds. Ex. 22 Sept. 1866; Hudds Chron. 30 July 1870; 10 Dec. 1881; Holmfirth Express, 20 July 1946; 22 May 1948; 6 Aug. 1955; NMRC survey 1985; H'firth Exp. 10 June 1983, 19 Feb. 1988.

13   Thongsbridge mills
     Yorks. Arch. Serv. Wakefield, MD28/1 1586; Almondbury Parish Records 1777; Leeds Mercury, 13 Feb. 1796; Dartmouth Terrier, 193, 1802;

Leeds Intelligencer, 30 Oct. 1809; The lease is the property of Mrs. P. Beardsell of Knaresborough, Leeds Intelligencer, 18 Nov. 1848; Hudds Chron. 7th Feb. 1852; Kirklees Archive, T/H/F/36, claim no. 300; Hudds Ex. 26 June 1852; Kirk. Archive, KC6/1/33, 1853; Hudds Ex., 27 Jan. 1855; 31 May 1856; 20 Feb. 1858; Hudds Chron. 30 Oct. 1858; Hudds. Ex. 22 Jan., 23 July, 1859.

14   Hudds Chron. 25 Feb. to 24 March 1860; Hudds Ex. 24 March 1860; Hudds Chron. 5 April 1862; 3 and 10 Mar. 9 July, 10 Nov. 1866; 9 June 1867; H'firth Exp. 3 Nov. 1955; Hudds Ex. 2 May, 20 June 1868; Hudds Chron. 24 Nov. 1871; Hudds Ex. 21 Sept 1872; 1 Feb. 1873; 6 Feb. 1875; 26 May 1877; 8 June 1878; 7 Aug. 1880; 11 Aug. 1883; Kirklees Archive, UHO Netherthong, 22 April 1886; Hudds Ex. 9 July 1887; Kirk. Arch. UHO Netherthong, 24 Nov. 1887, also 10 May 1888; Hudds. Ex.1 March , 17 May 1890; 18 March 1893; H'firth Exp. 17 Feb. 1894; 10 Aug. 1895; 23 May 1903; 20 Oct. and 12 Nov. 1904; 18 Mar. 1911; Hudds. Ex. 2 and 16 July 1938; 22 May 1937; Kirk. Arch. UHO Holmfirth 24 May 1937; H'firth Exp. 3 April 1943; 10 June 1944; Also Kirk. Arch. Holmfirth UDC Report of Cloudburst May 29 1944; H'firth Exp. 15 July 1972.

15   Albion mill
Hudds Ex. 24 Aug. 1861; H'firth Exp. 21 Nov. 1891; Hudds Ex.21 April 1866; Hudds. Chron. 2 June, 24 Nov. 1866; Hudds Ex. 15 Jan. 1870; 1 May, 30 Oct. 1875p; 15 Apr. 1876; H'firth Ex. 21 Nov. 1891; Kirk. Arch. KMT4 Wooldale, 1 Mar. 1895, 5 May 1898, 14 June 1900, 31 Oct. 1901, 7 Aug. 1902; H'firth Exp. 5 Nov. 1910; 10 June 1944; Kirk. Arch. Holmfirth UDC Report of the Cloudburst on May 29 1944; 13 Dec. 1947; 25 June1976; and 1978; See H'firth Exp. on relevant dates; Hudds. Ex. 17 Sept. 1983; also H'firth Exp. 23 Sept. 1983.

16   Alma mill
Hudds Ex. 10 Nov. 1855; 27 Feb, 9 Oct. 1858; Hudds. Chron. 16 June 1860. Hudds Ex. 20 Sept. 1884; Kirk. Arch. UHO Netherthong 27 Aug. 1885; H'firth Exp. 26 July 1890; Hudds Ex. 9 Aug. 1890; Hudds Ex. 18 Jan. 1896; Catalogue in Roberts family papers; Hudds Ex.15 Mar. 1902; Kirk. Arch. UHO Netherthong, 10 November, 1902; The Worker and H'firth Exp. 19 January 1907; 5 Aug 1911

17   Thongsbridge Size and Bone Works
Kirk. Arch. UHO Wooldale, 7 Aug. 1873, 25 April 1878; 11 Sept. 1879, 15 July 1880, 19 May 1881, and14 July 1881; Hudds Ex. 25 April 1892; H'firth Exp. 3 Sept. and 15 Oct. 1892; 14 Oct. 1899; 7 Mar. 1914; 11 Mar. 1950.

18   Property at Hey
W.C.R. 2 June 1824; 16 Oct 1846.

19   Mytholmbridge Upper mill
H.J. Morehouse, Kirkburton and the Graveship of Holme; pp. 122-3; W.C.R. 1552; W.B. Crump, G. Ghorbal, History of the Huddersfield Woollen Industry; p. 44; Deeds Registry Wakefield, QE13/2/39; Kirk. Arch. KC485; also KC1061 Box 8. 1796; W.C.R. 1 May 1795 2 entries; Kirk. Arch. KC165/39, 1812; W.C.R. 1 May 1818, 26 Oct. 1820, 14 Dec.1821, 17 Jan 1823, 8 Feb. 1833, 21 Nov. 1834, 28 Jan. 1842, 28 July 1843, 9 Sept. 1843; Kirk. Arch. T/H/F/36 claim no 117; T/H/F/45 claim no. 43; KC6/1/33 1853; Hudds Chron. 11 Oct. 1856; 8 Jan 1859; 5 and 19 Jan. 1861; London Gazette, 20 May 1865.

20   Hudds Chron. 1 Dec. 1866; London Gazette, 9 July 1867; Hudds. Chron, 24 Aug, 1867; also Poster held in Roberts family papers; Hudds. Ex, 1 Feb. 1868; Hudds Chron. 22 July 1871; Hudds Ex. 14 Nov. 1874; Hudds Chron. 17 Jan. 1880; Hudds Ex. 28 May, 1881; Kirk. Arch. UHO Wooldale, 26 January 1882; Hudds Ex. 11 Feb. 1882; 15 Mar, 26 Apr. 1844; London Gazette, 27 May, 27 June 1884; 3, 10 Feb, 20 March 1885; Textile Manufacturer, Feb. 1887

21   Hudd.s Ex. 18 April, 30 May 1885; H'firth Exp. 13 Feb. 1892; Yorks. Fact. Times, 12 Feb, 4 March 1892; Hudds Ex. 4 Oct. 1902; H'firth Exp. 19 Jan. 1907; The Worker, 2 March 1907; Hudds Ex. 2 Oct. 1909; H'firth Exp. 1 Mar. 1913; Hudds. Ex. 13 Nov. 1913; H'firth Exp. 12 Aug. and 26 Aug. 1922; Kirk. Arch. UHO Holmfirth UDC, 14 May, 1923; 4 Feb. 1929; 17 Nov. 1930; 1 Oct. 1945, 12 Sept 1949, 8 June 1955, 13 Feb 1963; H'firth Exp. 14 April 1923; 24 Oct. 1959; 3 Feb 1978, 19 Sept. 1997.

CHAPTER 12

Upper House to New Mill

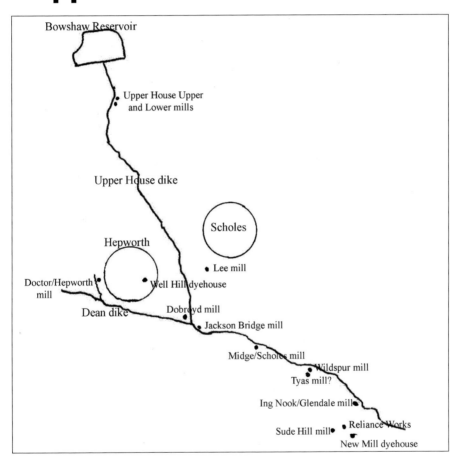

Upper House Dike – Upper House / Over House mills

There were two small mills in the hamlet of Upper House, which was sometimes also referred to as Upper Wickleden or alternatively Over House, and lies downstream from Bowshaw reservoir. Built in the early 1790s, the earliest reference to them comes from the Wakefield Court Rolls, which record that:

> Samuel Walker of Lascelles Hall, William Moorhouse of Upper House, John Hinchliffe of ? and Christopher Moorhouse of Sandygate surrendered 'The intirity of the Rough Ing' to the use of Benjamin Moorhouse of Hepworth and his heirs on 18 May 1791. Benjamin Moorhouse was admitted as tenant on 24 June 1791.

They built one fulling and one carding mill on the Rough Ing, with a dam between the two mills; there were also two dams on the higher ground behind the mills, which are now in the garden of the house just upstream from the sight of the mills. The mills were assessed for rates by the Holme Reservoir Commissioners; therefore water must have been taken from the dike that now comes from Bowshaw reservoir, somewhere upstream of Upper House and brought via a goit or pipeline to the dams, although there is no sign of a goit's existence today. One moiety [half share] in the land and property was granted to John Hinchliffe, and the other was granted to William Moorhouse and Christopher Moorhouse as tenants in common. The property is described as approximately 1 acre of land, with fulling and scribbling mills plus other buildings, with the engines, cards, machinery, fulling stocks and going gear therein. Both mills were occupied by John Hinchliffe.

William Moorhouse of Upper House sold half of his share in the mills, which was one-eighth of the total, to Benjamin Moorhouse of Hepworth for £24 in 1794. Christopher Moorhouse subsequently died, leaving his quarter share in the mill to his son William Moorhouse who also lived at Sandygate; he applied for a licence of herioting his father's estate in July 1818, and then contracted to sell the quarter share in the mill to John Hinchliffe for £250. William Moorhouse of Upper House appears to have sold half his quarter share in the mills to one William Holdam, as mentioned in his will of July 1796, leaving his now one-eighth share in the mills to his son Benjamin. Benjamin, who lived at Ox Lee, passed this one-eighth share to his eldest son John Moorhouse in October 1807.

John Hinchliffe the elder lived at Moorside Farm above Hade Edge, which carries a date stone bearing his initials along with that of his wife Ann and the date 1791. They appear to have moved to Bent in Wooldale by 1820, when his will was registered in the Manor Court. His son John had taken over the property at Moorside, and probably the mills as well, when in May 1821 Joseph Roberts of Overhouse paid £100 to John Hinchliffe for a quarter share in the Rough Ing and the two mills occupied by John Hinchliffe.

John Hinchliffe (the elder) and his wife Ann were possibly owing money, or could have been raising a mortgage in October 1822, when they surrendered two closes of land near Daisy Lee in Scholes with a house built by John Hinchliffe on one of the closes; plus the undivided moiety in the Rough Ing and the two mills with the outbuildings, engines etc. then occupied by William Moorhouse; to the use of John Hirst, Woolstapler, of Huddersfield; but the amount of money involved is not recorded.

John Moorhouse of Ox Lee and Elizabeth his wife, passed his one-eighth share in the mills to Thomas Hardy of Black Syke in 1839, but the court roll fails to record the price. In 1842, Joshua Walker of Oakwell House Birstall, paid £250 for a quarter share in the Rough Ing and the fulling and scribbling mills to John Hinchliffe (junior) and his wife Lydia. The mills were then occupied by John Hinchliffe & Co.

The mills were quite small, consequently the volume of production was low and was probably limited to producing slubbings and fulling cloth for the self employed clothiers of the immediate area. By the mid nineteenth century larger mills were scribbling wool and then spinning yarn, and some were installing power looms in weaving sheds, rather than providing slubbings or yarn for handloom weavers.

In 1853 the Holme Reservoir Commissioners record the owners of the Upper mill as Joshua Walker and Thomas Hardy; the owner of the Lower mill was Charles Gleadall. The occupant of both mills was William Vautry. The mills were owned by the same people in 1854, but were, by then, unoccupied. There is a note in the Minute Book of the Commissioners in 1854, saying that the mills would never use enough water to raise the annual charge to £100, therefore they were to be de-registered.

The fate of the mills after the mid 1850s is unclear, but it seems that they were not used for textiles as an advertisement for Dobroyd mill in 1861 claimed that it was the first mill on the stream below Bowshaw reservoir; there is however some indication that they were possibly used for rearing

Chickens. An advertisement appeared in 1862 offering an interest in the mills for sale by order of the Trustees of the late Joshua Walker Esquire. It offered a house and two cottages in Hepworth, plus land in Hepworth and in Cartworth; also 3 undivided eighth parts in sites and materials of two fulling and scribbling mills, now in ruins, with the land, dams, goits and roads belonging, situate at Upper House and now unoccupied.[1] The outcome of the sale is not known.

There is a suggestion that stone from the mills was used by John Hinchliffe (junior) to construct a barn at Moorside Farm that carries a date-stone for 1901. The remains of the mills with the dam between them can still be found close to the stream just below Upper House, although they are much overgrown with vegetation. The most prominent feature is the walling behind the dam, constructed to stop debris from the hillside falling into the water.

Dean Dike – Hepworth / Doctor Mill / Dyehouse

This mill stood in Main Gate Hepworth, a few yards higher up the road than the school; the water supply came from a tributary of Rakes dike that ran close to the mill. A deed held in the Deeds Registry in Wakefield dated 1791 gives the owners of the property as Josiah Wordsworth, Apothecary, also William Marshall, John Heap, Joshua Brook, Joshua Swallow, Christopher Gudgeon, John Oldham senior and John Oldham junior. Could it be due to Josiah Wordsworth's profession that the mill became known as Doctor Mill? An entry in the Wakefield Court Roll of 1794 says: 'the mill at Hepworth now erected with the dams, goits, weirs, appendages and appurtenances', with the same occupants as in 1791, was mortgaged by John Milnes of Wakefield, who passed his interest in the property to Robert Parker of Halifax.

The Court Roll of 1807 records that John Pemberton Heywood of Wakefield, William. Norris of Halifax, Jane Lord of Rochdale and John Sturgis of Bolling Hall Bradford, surrendered their interest in the land and the mill, which is again described as 'newly erected', to Joseph and William Heap of Barnside. The Heap's raised a mortgage on the land and scribbling mill, with a nearby cottage that had recently been used as an engine house, from Mary Charlesworth of Honley in February 1808.

The mill, engine house and land became part of a large land transaction in the 1820s, initially valued at £7,000 in 1822, but rising to over £8,000 by 1824. By 1824 the sole occupier of the mill was William Heap. William Heap was still the occupant of the mill in 1843, when William Adams surrendered to his son also called William, and Joseph Jowitt and Thomas Peace, the land and mill with the cottage used as an engine house, and 2 other closes of land near the mill.

The *Leeds Mercury* carried an advertisement for the sale of machinery at the mill in 1850. Henry Hinchliff had been using the mill but was not doing very well as his assets had been assigned to creditors. The advertisement read: '*Machinery for sale by auction on the morning of 9 May belonging to Henry Hinchliff at Doctor Mill Hepworth, under a deed of assignment. 3 billies, 3 60in scribblers, 3 32in carders, 1 spike willow, about 200lbs of Black warp, 50lbs of Blue warp, plus sundries. At 1pm in the afternoon at the house of Henry Hinchliff at Scholes, household furniture, farming stock, dyewares and stock in trade will be auctioned.*'

A fire was discovered in the drying stove at the mill on the 9th of April 1857, which was quickly put out by nearby residents; a building next to the stove was destroyed. The owners of the mill were given as Messrs. Shaw. Charles Hinchliff was using the mill during the 1860s, but was obviously finding business difficult as his assets had been assigned to creditors in 1865, who ordered that his goods should be auctioned on 24 August. They consisted of 4 almost new broad power looms, 3 boxes each end, with a 7ft reed space, complete with gearing; a warp drying balloon with beaming frame, a warping woof and creels, a bobbin winding machine, cops of yarn, and dyewares. It is possible, although not certain, that the two Hinchliff's were related.

The mill was possibly empty throughout the later 1860s as it was advertised several times. The advertisement in the *Huddersfield Examiner* of 18 January 1868 reads: *To be Let, Hepworth mill near Holmfirth, either from year to year or for a term of years, containing 4 scribblers, 4 carders, 4 billies, and 4prs of mules, with a large quantity of spare room suitable for looms or warehousing. Immediate possession may be had. Apply Wm. Shaw, Hepworth.* This was followed in July of the same year by an advertisement offering for sale by auction 4 9quarter power looms 3 boxes each end by Schofield & Co, which were possibly the same looms that had been advertised in 1865; also 4 9quarter power looms 3 boxes each end by Hutchinson & Hollingworth, plus a warp drying machine with winding-on frame, and a 30 spindle bobbin winder; but did not give the name of the vendor.

William Brook & Sons dyers, began their business at Hepworth mill, which they renamed Hepworth Dyehouse, although the precise date is unknown. A report in the *Holmfirth Express* dated 1 January 1887 records that in recent weeks workmen had been engaged in raising the height of the mill's chimney to 21 yards. It had reached a height of 20 yards when work had to stop due to severe frost. On resuming work, during the morning of 28 December it was noticed that the flues had closed in and that the foundations had, to some extent, given way. The chimney was no longer perpendicular, and as it was expected to fall the workers left the site. A few minutes later the chimney fell across the newest part of the mill only erected about two years previously, after a fire. The chimney also pushed part of the mill into the highway and damaged the boiler. No-one was injured. Brook's were tenants at the mill, they moved their business to Slaithwaite, and their unwanted machinery, consisting of 2 vertical high pressure steam engines, 2 steam boilers 1 24ft x 7ft, 1 18ft x 6ft; 1 hydro extractor with steam engine, a Siemens electric machine 1,200 candle power, platform weighing machine up to 5 tons, plus various sundries, were offered for sale by auction on Wednesday 8 June, 1887.[2]

Some rebuilding took place as the mill was advertised as being 'to let' throughout June, July and August 1888; although there is no evidence to suggest that it ever attracted a tenant. The 25inch Ordinance Survey Map of 1893 marks the building as a 'woollen mill', but subsequent maps published in 1905 and 1932 show it as 'disused'. The site of the mill has recently been used for housing, but records its former use in the name: Old Mill Court.

Other premises in the Hepworth area

Joshua Heap, son of Joshua Heap deceased, applied for a licence of heriot for a **dyehouse** in Hepworth, occupied by his mother Sarah Heap, in April 1733.

John Tinker of Hepworth obtained a licence of heriot for several cottages, **2 dyehouses and 1 press shop** all in Hepworth, along with several closes of land, in the tenancies of Matthew Moorhouse, Joseph Heap, George Roebuck, widow Roebuck, John Shaw, Joshua Booth and Francis Tinker, in 1778. The property would have been previously owned by his father.[3]

There is also evidence of a **Dyehouse in Hepworth**, in 1822, James Moorhouse, son of the late Matthew Moorhouse of Hepworth, late of Scholes, paid 1d for a licence of herioting a Dwelling house with a little croft in Hepworth, formerly tenanted by Christopher Moorhouse and James Booth, with a Dyehouse. An advertisement appeared in 1853 for the sale of Dyehouse equipment by A.T. & S. Tinker, at **Well Hill** Hepworth consisting of a dyepan that would take 340lbs of wool plus its brickwork and fittings, and an almost new scouring pan with brickwork and fittings.[4]

The sale in 1821 of a house and land at **Barnside** Hepworth to Charles Gleadall, William Carr and John Halliday, had an exception clause, namely 'the **dyehouse** and **stove** and land whereon they stand, and all the land lying between the Penistone Road and the Little Lee now or late in the possession of John Hinchliffe, which is the property of John Marsh'.[5]

The *Wakefield Court Roll* of 1828 mentions 2 Dwelling Houses at **Snowgate Head**, with a barn, stable, mistal, **dyehouse, press shop** and other outbuildings. In 1830 John Tinker of Carr in Shepley bought land and property at Snowgate Head including the dyehouse and press shop occupied by George Smith. The following year Joseph Marsden of Snowgate Head bought some property including the dyehouse in May from John Tinker, who had, by then, moved to Cumberworth. Tinker and Marsden then sold the 2 dwelling houses, barn, stable, mistal, press shop and dyehouse and outbuildings, still occupied by George Smith, in August of that year to John Dyson of Wood Nook.[6]

Rakes Dike – Dobroyd mill

Situated about three hundred yards upstream from Jackson Bridge close to the confluence of Dean dike and Rakes dike, the earliest mention of this mill comes from the *Wakefield Court Roll* of 1799, when Matthew Moorhouse bought from Jonathon Goddard 'All that wood known as Dob Royd wood and Little Dobroyd in Scholes'. This was followed in 1814, when Matthew Moorhouse passed 'All that Fulling and Scribbling mill with machinery, cards, engines etc. at Dobroyd mill with Dobroyd wood, also two cottages near the mill, with Kemphouse wood' to his sons James and William Moorhouse; suggesting that the mill was probably built around 1800. In 1853 the Holme Reservoir Commissioners give the owners of the mill as James and William Moorhouse, executors of Matthew Moorhouse deceased; James and William were also the tenants of the mill. John Holroyd was employed by the Moorhouses to collect 'wash' [urine] from local houses. He was charged by P.C. White with leaving his horse and wash barrel unattended for more than one hour and being more than 100 yards away from his horse. Holroyd denied both charges and said that he had left his horse and cart in the road running between the church at Sude Hill and the Shepley turnpike road while he collected wash from nearby houses which, he argued, was usual practice. He also said that he had not been more than twenty yards away from his horse. Holroyd also produced 'respectable witnesses' to substantiate his claims. The bench found that that the law was at variance with practice, but pointed out that they were bound to administer the law. They imposed a fine of 1s. plus costs, which Holroyd refused to pay; he was committed to Wakefield prison for one week.

Jonathon Moorhouse was bankrupt by 1860, when his machinery and stock-in-trade were advertised in May, including logwood, camwood, fustic, alum, sanders and peachwood, which were all materials for making colours used in dyeing; also dyeing utensils, a box of new cards for carding machines, nine bags of Botany wool, yarn for warps and weft, shoddy, mungo, thrums and nippings. The mill was advertised to be let or sold in November of the same year, along with the stove, dyehouse, willow house, four cottages, and 8 acres 1 rood 32 perches of land including the wood and a reservoir; a quantity of yarn preparation machinery, the fulling mill with 7 double fullers and 1 driver, 2 washing machines; together with a 25hp steam engine, and a 42ft diameter water wheel with 32 feet of fall. Anyone who was interested should apply to Moorhouse Bros. New Chapel, Penistone. It appears that no-one bought the mill, as it was advertised again in March 1861, when the advertisement stressed that it was the first mill on the stream below Bowshaw reservoir, confirming that the mills at Upper House were no longer operating.

The mill was also offered for sale in March 1869 but, again, it does not appear to have sold. In May of that year a 22 year old woman called Mary Webster committed suicide by drowning herself in the mill dam along with her 15 month old son, whom she had tied to her waste before entering the water. She was possibly unmarried, as the report said that at the time of her pregnancy she had had 'some unpleasantness' with her parents who turned her out of the house, and she had subsequently lived at the house of a neighbour called Mitchell. It was reported to the Coroner that the family dispute had played on her mind, and had probably contributed to her actions. The jury returned a verdict of 'Found drowned without marks of violence'.

The mill was again advertised for sale in December 1872, when John Kilburn was the tenant. It appears to have been bought by Jonathon Thorp & Sons, who were occupying part of Holmfirth mill at the time. The mill as it stood was not to Thorp's liking, as they commissioned a second mill to be built. In September 1873 a temporary hoist had been erected to permit building materials to be raised to the upper level of the new mill. On the afternoon of the 8th, James Turner who was a contractor was in the hoist with two wheelbarrows loaded with stone. As he approached the top level one of the chains holding the cradle broke, causing the cradle with its load to fall about fifty feet to the ground. Mr. Turner was taken to his home where he was examined by Dr. Trotter, who found that Turner had a broken ankle but no other serious injuries. The impact of the cradle hitting the ground was so great that both wheelbarrows were smashed and their feet had been driven through the cradle floor. One of the reasons for Thorp's moving to Dobroyd mill was that it was then the

Dobroyd mill, taken Feb. 2013. © the Author

first mill on the stream, which would give them a constant supply of clean water to enable them to dye the bright colours that they needed for their designs.

Thorp's organised visits to the seaside for their workpeople, taking them to Scarborough in 1883 and Blackpool in 1886. In 1888 they put a notice in the *Holmfirth Express* that they were running a special train to Blackpool in July for their workers, and if any members of the public would like to accompany them they could do so at a cost of 2s 9d or 1s 4½d, which would be the return fares for adults and children. The special train left Holmfirth at 5.30am on Saturday 14th July, with all the 350 or so workpeople and in excess of 100 members of the public, a total of between 500 and 600, arriving in Blackpool at 9.30am. The weather stayed fine until 6.45pm, and the train left at 7pm arriving in Holmfirth at 11.30pm.

Fire broke out at the mill on Saturday 25th August 1888. It started in the condenser room about 3.35 a.m. and spread quickly. Thorp's were manufacturers of woollens, worsteds, and stockinet's; the men working in the mill tried to quench the flames with buckets of water, but without success. Some stocks of pieces were saved by being carried out and laid in a nearby field, and some bales of wool were taken to the bottom of the mill yard. One man left on horseback shortly after the outbreak of the fire to raise the alarm in Holmfirth by ringing the bell in the church tower, arriving there about 4.20 a.m. The Unity fire brigade arrived at the mill around 5.30am, followed some 15 minutes later by the brigade from Joseph Turner & Sons, Bridge Mill. They were too late to save the big mill, which was 54 yards long, 18 yards wide and five storeys high, the roof and part of the front wall having collapsed at 4.30 a.m., but they were able to stop the fire spreading to other buildings. The ground floor of the main mill contained the teasing room, with teasing and burring machines, fearnought, waste grinding machines, and a dynamo that supplied the dyehouse

and other rooms with electricity. A passage divided this part from the fulling mill, containing milling and scouring machines, the water wheel, and the dye-wares store. On the first floor of the main mill were 8 condenser sets, 2 sets of combing and gilling machines, 3 raising gigs, 1 Moser patent gig, and 1 Whiteley's tentering machine. The second floor had 3 pairs of self-acting mules, 2 curling machines, and 30 to 40 bales of 'tops' wool, plus a large stock of woollen and worsted yarns. The third floor contained a complete set of worsted drawing and spinning machinery, 48 stockinet machines, 2 twisting machines, and 6 winding machines. On the top floor were 33 power looms, 2 fast looms, a German patent knitting machine, hank winding machinery, pattern and jacquard looms, balloons and winding off frames, warping, woof, and creels etc. Both fire brigades were engaged in damping down operations until Saturday evening, at which time Turner's brigade returned to Bridge Mill; the Unity brigade staying until Sunday morning. Apart from destroying the mill, heat from the blaze had scorched grass in nearby fields and had melted the coverings on telephone cables. The mill employed between 300 and 400 people, damage was estimated to be between £25,000 and £35,000, insurance cover totalled £19,000.

Mr. Henry Thorp one of the partners, was also co-owner of Holme Bottom mill, the tenants were Beaumont, Son, & Co. who offered to carry out work for Thorp's, as did Pitt, Booth & Co. of Sudehill Mills. Various other manufacturers in the district manufactured yarn for the stricken company. The main 5 storey mill was rebuilt, and the mill, complete with all its machinery was advertised for sale on 25 July 1889; but it seems that the sale did not take place as, on Friday 11 January 1895, the Thorp family entertained some 200 people made up of relatives, friends of the family and some employees at Hepworth Endowed School, to a dinner to celebrate the marriage of Mr. Hubert Thorp to Miss Charlesworth of Birdsedge, which had taken place on 31 December.

The meal was followed by speeches, the presentation of gifts to the couple, also entertainment and dancing until 2.30am on Saturday morning.

In 1897 a dispute arose between Thorp's and Edward Hirst & Sons of Wildspur mill, which is some way downstream from Dobroyd. Thorp's complained that Hirst's had trespassed on their land and were illegally directing water away from Dobroyd towards their own mill. The problem seems to have arisen because the water in Rakes dike was polluted with Iron Oxide coming from old coal workings, whereas the water from Dean dike was clear. Hirst's had built a barrier of stones gathered from the river bed to channel clear water into a culvert that carried it to their dam, which Thorp's objected to as the polluted water was being directed towards their mill. Hirst's said that they had bought Jackson Bridge mill, not to use, but solely to give them access to clear water. The court case was adjourned and does not appear to have been resumed.[7]

Whether this dispute was a factor, or whether it was due to trading conditions is unknown, but both mills were advertised for sale during 1899. Dobroyd mill was advertised for sale by auction on 25 July, and described as having a 'nearly new' 4 storey mill 54yds by 18yds; a 4 storey finishing mill 569sq.yds of floor area, plus tentering room, dyehouse, detached willey room and other buildings, plus an engine room, boiler house and chimney. Along with 2 cottages, 2 reservoirs and woody land, a total of approximately 8 acres 3 roods. A water wheel 30ft diameter 4ft 6in wide, 2 steam boilers, tandem steam engine, shafting, going gear and piping. A dynamo for 300 lights, with 100 lights currently in use. The machinery was available at valuation if required. The highest bid at the auction was £3,400 which was not acceptable to the vendors, and the lot was withdrawn. The machinery, which ran to a considerable amount, was advertised to be sold on the 9th of August but may not have sold. Also advertised for the two weeks prior to the sale of Dobroyd were the mill and machinery at Wildspur, and New Mill mill. In each case the Auctioneer was George Tinker; the two advertisements for Dobroyd, one for the mill the second for machinery, plus two advertisements for Wildspur mill and machinery, and the one for New Mill mill, plus an entry by Mr. Tinker extolling the virtues of the clear water that supplied the mills but with no mention of the dispute, took up an entire column each week in the Huddersfield Examiner. It was a very difficult time for business, with many bankruptcies and much property for sale, but George Tinker certainly seemed to be trying hard to attract interest. For some weeks after the sale date of Dobroyd mill a box in Tinker's section of the 'Sales by Auction' column reminded manufacturers that the premises at Dobroyd were available to buy, or to rent.

A company called Barker & Moody were using the mill in 1905, when they were advertising for 'good weavers'; but the partnership did not last, as in January 1907 the firm was trading as J.H. Barker & Co. when they advertised for a pattern weaver capable of weaving a hand loom. Barkers were still the occupants of the mill when it was again advertised for sale along with the machinery in May 1907 and also in July of that year. The advertisements again stressed that it was the first mill on the stream; and that a water rate of £30 12s 7½d was payable annually to the Holme Reservoir Commissioners.

The Yorkshire Textile Directory for 1910 lists the occupants of the mill as Dennison & Sharman, who were manufacturing fancy woollens, tweeds, mantles and costume cloths; they had 2,800 spindles and 70 looms. They were trading under the same title in 1916, but in 1917 the name had changed to C.J. Sharman & Co. This name continued until June 1919 when the firm was taken over by a Mr. William Haigh, who changed the company's name to Dobroyd Mills Co. with himself as Managing Director. The company appears to have been successful from the outset, making many alterations and extensions to the premises over a number of years. They had one brush with authority in 1929 when the Factory Inspector brought an action against them for not white washing the interior walls of the mill for over 2 years; the Factory Act stated that they should be done at least every 14 months. They were fined £10 for the offence.

The dyehouse at Dobroyd was used by Tom Lees & Co. from at least 1923 until 1928 when they moved to Thirstin Dyeworks in Honley. They dyed woollen and worsted cloths in indigo, alizarin (which is the red obtained from Madder), and other colours. Dobroyd Mills Co. eventually acquired the share capital of Eastwood Bros. of Thirstin mill Honley, although the Eastwood name continued at Thirstin for several years after the takeover. Increased business during the late 1930s and '40s also allowed Dobroyd Mills Co. to buy Holme Bottom mill in New Mill, which they used for storing wool. There were a considerable number of additional buildings erected at Dobroyd from the late 1930s to the mid 1950s, which were used as weaving sheds, warehouses, and additional offices. A fire in the mill was spotted by an employee who was walking home at 1.45am on Saturday 14 December 1957. Damage was restricted to the room in which the fire had started that was used for storing wool, although there was also water damage to teazing machines on the floor below. In addition to the mill's own fire brigade, appliances from Holmfirth, Huddersfield, Slaithwaite, Meltham and Marsden also attended.

William Haigh had died in 1956, and was succeeded as Managing Director by his son Keith; in 1968 the mill extended to over 70 acres, and was awarded the Queen's Award to Industry in that year for increases in their exports between 1964 and 1967. At that time the company employed around 600 people. Production at Thirstin mill ceased in either late 1969 or early 1970; a fire broke out in a room at Dobroyd mill in July 1971, which was contained by the sprinkler system until fire brigades from Holmfirth and Skelmanthorpe, along with a turntable ladder from Huddersfield attended. Only a small amount of mechanical damage was done, estimated at £1,000.

It was reported in April 1974 that Dobroyd was to close later in the year with the loss of 200 jobs, even though they reportedly had a full order book. The reason for closure was given as 'a shortage of skilled operatives'. A sale of plant and machinery was held at the mill over 3 days in October 1974, when virtually all the machinery would go to foreign buyers.

There was a report in 1974 that Yorkshire Fine Woollen Spinners would be taking over the mill, although this did not happen for some time. The *Holmfirth Express* reported on 30 April 1976 that the mill had been targeted by vandals, and numerous windows had been broken. This was followed in June of that year by an article saying that John Woodhead's of Albion mill Thongsbridge, who were members of the Yorkshire Fine Woollen Spinners group, would be moving into the mill, which they did in 1978. A fire was discovered at the mill on Sunday 9 December 1979 by a man who had been installing new machinery at the mill. Fire crews from Holmfirth, Huddersfield and Skelmanthorpe attended; no details of the damage were given, except to say that it included part of a glass and tiled roof. In June 1980 it was reported that Woodhead's had replaced 3 pairs of spinning mules with 6 new spinning frames at a cost of £400,000.

Two years later the group went into receivership, the receivers saying that they were hopeful of a takeover; the OCM Group of Liversedge took over the premises in January 1983, re-employing 60 people who had previously worked for Woodhead's, but making 45 others redundant. The name of this branch of OCM was changed to Dobroyd Mills Ltd. The group opened a mill shop at Dobroyd in 1991 under the John Woodhead name.[8]

Other companies using the premises were Cottage Knitwear Ltd. who was advertising for experienced Burlers in May 1987; Jonathon Thorp (successors) Ltd. moved from Valley mills into part of Dobroyd in an attempt to reduce overheads during January or February 1988, but went into receivership later in the same year. The business was bought from the Receiver by Mr. Geoff Metcalfe and Mr. John Dempsey in 1989, and renamed JT Knitting Ltd. The Woodhead's spinning business, and the mill, was bought from OCM by Z. Hinchliffe & Sons Ltd. woollen spinners, of Denby Dale who still use part of the mill for warehousing, along with JT Knitting Ltd.

Lee mill Scholes

Already in existence before March 1822, this mill stood on the sharp left-hand bend on the Scholes to Jackson Bridge road, the butcher John Goddard of Scholes paid £300 to Cookson Stephenson of Holmfirth; and £327 to John Tackherd Townend of Edwardthorpe Darfield, for several buildings and

Lee mill. © A.J. Brooke

parcels of land including '*All that mill situate in Scholes used for the scribbling and carding of wool known as Lee mill, and occupied by John Battye, Thomas Hardy, Joseph Heap and William Senior*'. Goddard sold the mill, along with the four closes of land, a dwelling house and seven cottages plus a mistal to Thomas Farrar of Prickleden in May 1822 for a mere £550, giving him a loss of £77. Farrar had possibly taken a mortgage to buy the mill and make alterations or renewals, as in March 1828 he paid £1,000 to David Haigh of Southowram and Isaac Thwaite, who were the executors of George Haigh deceased, for land and premises including Lee mill, which is described as 'lately built'; it also included the seven cottages which were occupied at that time by Joseph Wagstaff, Jonas Sandy, Jonas Holmes, Joseph Taylor, William Marston, Jonas Hampshire and Nathaniel Roberts.

Richard Battye, a drysalter of Newtown Upperthong, paid £3,500 for the mill, dyehouse, warehouse, stable etc. plus over ten acres of land in February 1837. Reflecting the amount of development of the site carried out by Thomas Farrar.

A man was oiling a machine on the afternoon of Friday 16 December 1853, when his hand caught in some cogwheels and was crushed by them. Two fingers were so badly damaged that they needed to be amputated; the others, although injured, were expected to heal. The mill was offered for sale by auction on 24 April 1856, when it was described as:

> *All that substantially built and commodious woollen mill situate at and called Lee Mill in the hamlet of Scholes…with the dam, spacious dyehouse, dwelling house, cottages, warehouse, stove, gas works, outbuildings and appurtenances thereto belonging; also the several closes and allotments of land thereto belonging, and now in the occupation of Mr. John Stocks Battye and Mr. George Farrar and their undertenants.*

The reason for the sale was probably Richard Battye's death, as the machinery in the mill was also offered for sale in August 1857, due to a Chancery suit of Battye v. Battye and consisted of: 7 scribbling engines, 6 carding engines, 2 piecing machines, 6 billies, 1 willey; 4prs spinning mules, 2 bobbin winding machines; 4 broad power looms, 4 narrow power looms, beaming machine, plus sundries.

The mill was bought by the Lockwood family, who also had a business in New Mill mill. Ben Taylor was a cloth dresser at Lee mill when, in September 1862, he was charged with stealing ten £5 notes two sovereigns, three half-crowns, one shilling and two pennies from John Bower of Wooldale who was a shopkeeper. Bower had got the money that afternoon from Kidd & Jessop Solicitors in Holmfirth, wrapped it in his handkerchief and put it in his pocket. On his way home he called at Bray's beershop at Cinderhills where he stayed until between 10 and 11 o'clock. Bower was intoxicated when he left, and remembered nothing until 3.30am the following morning when he found himself at the door of George Exley butcher of Totties. Exley got up and found Booth on his doorstep without coat, hat or boots. He let Bower in who, after becoming more sober, went home minus the missing articles of clothing and the money. After a few hours sleep Bower went to Lee mill where he heard William Tattersall say to another man "That is the man that Ben Taylor and me lifted up at Paris last night". Bower went to the police who found that Taylor had been spending money freely in Huddersfield; he had also given a man named Starkey a £5 note to cash for him. Taylor, Tattersall and Starkey were charged jointly with being implicated in the robbery. Tattersall told the police that he and Taylor had found Bower lying in the road at Paris, they helped him up and walked with him until they got near Taylor's house, where Tattersall left them. Starkey admitted that he had got the £5 note changed by Henry Brook of Union St. Huddersfield. Taylor went to collect the money and Brook told him that two policemen had been enquiring about the note. Brook asked where the money had come from; Taylor said that it had come from the pocket of a man near Scholes, and that there were ten £5 notes. Other evidence showed that Taylor had been spending money extravagantly, which was suspicious as he was married with four children and earning 15s per week. Taylor was committed to the Assizes at York.

Lockwood's were having a new mill built in 1862, which in November had reached the point where the roof was being constructed. On Monday 3 November William Shore was working on one of the main support beams when it gave way and broke through the joists of the lower floor taking Shore with it. During its descent the beam hit Thomas Barrowclough and also took him to the bottom. The two men were taken to their respective homes and medical help was called. Shore had a fractured arm and other injuries to various parts of his body, and on the 7th was said to be progressing favourably; Barrowclough had suffered both internal and external injuries, his recovery was said to be doubtful. Lockwood's gave a treat to 300 workpeople, presumably from both mills, in December 1867 at the Shoulder of Mutton Inn New Mill, to celebrate the marriage of James Lockwood. Entertainment was provided by Beever's Overture Band from Hepworth, which played Overtures, and also music for dancing. Lockwood Bros. gave a treat to 250 workpeople in January 1890 to celebrate the coming-of-age of Kenyon Lockwood; the workers presented Kenyon with a gold Albert and seal that had been suitably inscribed.

There was a strike of weavers at the mill in October 1890; the accepted method of allocating warps to weavers was that any weaver who downed added their name to the bottom of a list of people waiting for warps; when a warp became available it was given to the weaver whose name was first on the list. On the 28th a new warp was twisted in to a loom immediately after the weaver had downed, annoying all those who were already waiting. They complained to the management who refused to allow the warp to be moved to another loom, but did say that the weaver who was at the top of the list could weave it in the loom that it was already in. The weavers would not accept this saying that it would disrupt the system, and came out on strike. Lockwood's advertised for more weavers, the striking weavers countered this by issuing hand bills to weavers in all the surrounding mills explaining the dispute and asking them not to respond to the advertisements. The Weavers Association became involved and wrote to Lockwood's asking them to agree to meet union representatives, which Lockwood's refused to do but did say that they would meet another deputation from the workers, but still no settlement was reached. The YFT reported on November 21st that the strike had ended; Lockwood's had agreed to dismiss the girl who had been weaving the loom and allow the usual weaver to take it over again.

Hirst Charlesworth aged 30 of Paris Scholes normally worked in the finishing department; on 23 August 1909 he was helping mechanics to install a new drive system in the mill, while the old system was still running. While helping to lift a new drive shaft through a hole in a wall his clothing became caught in a moving cogwheel of the old system and he was twisted around shafting. After being released he was seen by a Doctor who gave what help he could, and recommended that Charlesworth should be taken to the Infirmary. Their diagnosis was that his spine was badly injured, possibly broken. He was presumably kept as an in patient, but no further information seems to have been given.

Lockwood Bros. put the mill, plant and machinery plus yarn, up for sale in August 1912, when they said that they were giving up business. The premises were, by then, somewhat larger than when they had bought them. Lot 1 consisted of:

> *Main mill 5 storeys plus attic, 81ft 9in by 44ft 9in used for scribbling, spinning and finishing, with engine house on ground floor. Spinning and finishing mill, 5 storeys plus attic, 65ft by 27ft 3in; 2 storey offices and burling rooms, 88ft 9in x 17ft 9in; 2 storey piece warehouse and wool store, 58ft 3in x 30ft 3in; 2 storey boiler house with stove and dining room over, 53ft x 28ft 10in; fire engine house and stores, 38ft 6in x 17ft 6in; worsted combing spinning and willeying mill, 4 storeys plus attic 103ft 5in x 43ft; engine house 30ft x 10ft; weaving shed 142ft x 84ft 4in; oil extracting shed 27ft 4in x 21ft; mungo shed 36ft 3in x 21ft; 2 storey pattern weaving and yarn warehouse, 36ft x 23ft 6in; Wool store 30ft 5in x 22ft; dyehouse, tentering place, office and stores 70ft 8in x 43ft 6in and 36ft x 10ft 5in; plus other sundry buildings. Steam boilers, steam engine, going gear, and reservoirs.*

> *Lot 2: 4 cottages.*

The machinery was advertised to be sold over two days, 28 and 29 August, and consisted of all the machinery necessary for scribbling, spinning, weaving, dyeing and finishing; plus contents of offices, warehouses and mechanics shop also 65,000lbs of woollen and worsted yarns.[9] The mill and the cottages were withdrawn at the auction, probably because they did not reach the reserve price. The results of machinery sales were never published, therefore it is not possible to say whether it sold or not.

The eventual buyer of the mill was probably E.H. Sellers & Sons Ltd. who were yarn spinners and manufacturers, and were definitely using the mill in 1915, when they were advertising for piecers. By 1918 they had provided a Dining Room, Bowling Green and ornamental gardens for their workpeople to enjoy, which were opened on July 27th. The *Yorkshire Textile Directory* lists Sellers as having 5000 spindles and 60 looms in 1923, when John Moorhouse & Sons, commission weavers with 18 looms were also using part of the mill, as were Thomas Birkhead & Son Ltd. who were dyers and finishers, and had moved from Bridge mill Holmfirth. John Moorhouse & Sons had increased their number of looms to 26 by 1925. Public concern for air pollution was growing during the 1920s, New Mill council wrote to E.H. Sellers & Sons Ltd. in 1929 warning them that if they persisted in producing the amount of smoke that they had been doing, the council would be forced to take legal action. The warning seems to have the desired effect, as no further complaints were listed.

Sellers operated a night shift during the 1930s; over 20 men were working on the night of 20-21 November 1934, when they discovered a fire had broken out at 2am. They rang the Holmfirth brigade first, to be told that the council had told them that they must not attend fires in New Mill district, which was covered by Huddersfield. The brigade from Huddersfield arrived at 2.30am, but decided that they would need help, so Holmfirth was telephoned again at 2.35am, they turned out at 2.40am and arrived at the mill at 2.50am. [It is interesting to compare these response times to those from the fire at Dobroyd mill in 1888]. One wall of the 4 storey mill had collapsed at 2.40am, with some stones and mortar falling into the mill dam; the weaving shed, carding and spinning shed, and weft room were all gutted. The engine room and a 2storey building next to the 4 storey mill were both partially wrecked. Damaged machinery included 4 warping frames, a sizing machine, 4 sets of condensers and 3 pairs of mules. 100 people were put out of work. No estimated cost of the damage was given, but the mill and contents were fully covered by insurance. In April 1935 New Mill council sent a bill to E.H. Sellers for the cost of the Huddersfield fire engine attending the fire.

Thomas Birkhead & Sons installed their own electricity generating plant in late 1935 because they were finding that the supply from the mains was unreliable, and terminated the agreement for supply that they had with the local council in January 1936; although later in the year they asked that a supply should be available in case of emergency. E.H. Sellers continued production at the mill until 1950 when they were bought by the Ocean Trust Company, and production was transferred elsewhere; although they did employ around 20 menders in other premises in Scholes for a time. Birkheads continued their dyeing and finishing business at the mill until the 1980s, when they were bought by Gamma Beta Holdings, and the business transferred to High Burton where they had possibly had a branch since the late 1930s. The business was subsequently transferred to Yew Tree mill Holmbridge in 2000.

The David Brown Corporation bought Lee mills in 1951 for £13,000, for use by their electrical division, and began production in October of that year. Over the next fifteen years they carried out a variety of alterations to the premises, but then activity seems to have ceased.. Broomfield Engineering Co. was using the mill from at least August 1973 when they were advertising for staff, until they closed in September 1975 making 55 people redundant. The DAC (Yorkshire) Co. Ltd was using the mill from September 1976 when they were advertising for a press setter, however, they went into receivership in 1980 and ceased trading in November of that year.

A large fire broke out in the mill on 1 February 1981 causing £100,000 of damage, which was assumed to be deliberate, as quantities of petrol, oil and paraffin had been used. This was not quite the end of industrial use of the mill as a company called Vactor Ltd. making road-sweeping vehicles had 16 employees working there in September 1996.[10]

New Mill Dike – Jackson Bridge mill

The early history of this mill comes, once again, from the *Wakefield Court Rolls*, which principally covers changes of ownership of the property. Standing on the left bank of the river a few yards downstream from the bridge, this mill was already in existence as a corn mill in 1759, the miller was John Booth who, along with his wife Ruth, had raised a mortgage from Benjamin North of Fenay in Almondbury. The property is described as:

> *a Messuage or dwelling house with the water corn mill and drying kiln situated at Jackson Bridge with a small croft called Holt Holm adjoining the mill and the ground contiguous to the said house mill and kiln beginning at the end of the bridge next to the house alongside the rivulet down to the mill then turning to the brow next behind the Swine hull mistle and stable all occupied by John Booth.*

The mortgagee became William Shackleton of Wakefield by February 1777. John Booth had died by May 1874, when his son also called John Booth paid 3d to the court for a licence of Heriot for his father's property including the mill and its appurtenances. John Milnes of Wakefield became the mortgagee in 1789; the court roll does not record the amount of the mortgage. In 1791 John Booth also borrowed £48 at 5 percent a year interest, from Cookson Stephenson gentleman of Holmfirth, (who was actually a solicitor). The property was described as a Messuage with brewhouse and half the garden, with adjoining corn mill and scribbling mill, drying kiln, croft and appurtenances, now in the occupation of Jonathon and Robert Kershaw. There were also six cottages at Jackson Bridge belonging to the mill. This is the first mention of the scribbling mill, which, at that time, was presumably in part of the corn mill; but became the main business, as subsequent entries omit any reference to corn milling. John Booth let the scribbling mill to Matthew and James Moorhouse, and Joseph Tinker, all clothiers and all from Scholes; also Isaac Holmes and Joseph Broadhead both clothiers from Hepworth. They rented the scribbling and carding mill with the house and drying kiln and a close of land called the Holme measuring 1½ roods, from 21 May 1801 for a term of 40 years at a rent of £36 a year, with an additional rent of £20 per year payable in the first four years.

John Booth repaid both mortgages on the mill in September 1806, by paying £300 to the executors of James Milnes deceased, of Wakefield, and £48 plus accrued interest to Cookson Stephenson of Holmfirth. In October of the same year, James Booth, John's son, and his wife Martha passed the

Jackson Bridge mill. Collection of A.J. Brooke

property to Matthew Moorhouse of Scholes, Joseph Tinker who had since moved to Hepworth, Isaac Holmes who had since moved to Holmfirth, and Joseph Broadhead of Hepworth. Joseph Broadhead sold or mortgaged his share in the property to Matthew Moorhouse in September 1809, but continued as one of the occupants; similarly Isaac Holmes sold or mortgaged his quarter share in the property to Aaron Floyd of Whitley for £140 in March 1816.

James and William Moorhouse of Sandygate Scholes paid £600 to Joseph Broadhead for his interest in the mill in February 1822. Joseph Tinker died in 1834, via his will he passed his share of the mill to his wife and sons; Mary his wife sold or mortgaged a quarter share in the mill to William Stephenson for £250 in December of the same year. She also passed a quarter share in the mill, house and land to George Tinker of Scholes in 1835.

The mill was advertised to be sold by auction on 26 October 1836, when it was described as:

> *All that substantial scribbling mill, 4 storeys high besides attics, with the engine house and requisite outbuildings, in the possession of Mr. Thomas Farrar deceased; and the Corn mill connected therewith now in the occupation of Mr. John Haigh; and also the extensive blue dyehouse, with counting house, warehouse, stables, gig house and cart sheds; with the water wheel, reservoir, dams, yard and other conveniences, plus 2 closes of land.*

All the property was copyhold to the Manor of Wakefield. Isaac Holmes left his share of the mill to his four sons Joseph, Jonathon, Isaac the younger, and William Holmes; and to his daughter Mary wife of Thomas Makin of Gainsborough for the term of her natural life. They were to receive equal half yearly shares in the revenue from the mill. Isaac paid £100 to his brothers Joseph and Jonathon for their shares in the mill, house and land in March 1838.

The mill apparently had a steam engine when John Harpin of Birks House Burnlee, paid £240 to Christopher Moorhouse of Shaley for a quarter share in the property in October 1847. It is possible that this was also a mortgage, as the register of voters compiled by the Holme Reservoir Commissioners in 1853 list the owners of the mill as Christopher and William Moorhouse, and Benjamin Stanley with his wife Mary; the occupants of the mill were Francis, Henry, James and Thomas Holmes. In May 1861 James Holmes & Sons placed an advertisement in the 'Sales by Private

Contract' column of the *Huddersfield Chronicle*, for 4½ pairs of Spinning mules with a total of 2,200 spindles that were to be sold 'cheap', but no prices were quoted. The mules would be available on the expiry of their lease in October. Another advertisement appeared in October for 7 spinning mules with a total of 1,800 spindles that were still available, the only pair that had been sold were the smallest ones with 200 spindles each. The premises were also advertised as being available to rent in October and were described as: 'Two adjoining mills, the old mill 45ft by 33ft, 4 storeys plus attic; the new mill 60ft by 21ft with 4 storeys. Both mills had steam and water power, with a never failing supply of soft spring water'. There were also 4 billies with engines and 6 double fulling stocks, which were fixtures. Anyone interested should apply to Chris. Moorhouse & Co. of Scholes. Two quarter shares in the mill and fixed machinery were offered for sale in October 1863, but there is no indication of the identity of the vendor.

The mill was advertised to let in January 1864; there were two 4 storey mills plus a steam engine and water wheel, and also machinery. An advertisement in July said that due to the mill being re-let, some of the machinery was for sale. A number of alterations were carried out prior to James Moorhouse taking up tenancy of the mill in the following year. Uriah Tinker of Meal Hill and Hepworth Iron Company were jointly interested in constructing a drift or canal from the mill's water way that would give them access to the coal and minerals in the area. It was claimed that the workings would convey 'a considerable stream of water' that could be advantageous to the mill.

In November 1866 James Moorhouse summoned a weaver, James England, for leaving work without notice. The clerk to the court objected to the wording of the charge as it did not specify the length of notice required; the charge was amended to one of neglecting work for more than 7 days. England said that he had woven half the piece when the foreman discharged him, telling him that he would not be paid for any more work he did there; he had then got work elsewhere. Mr. Moorhouse said that the foreman did not have the authority to sack someone without consulting him first, and that he had seen England several times since he had left and had asked England to return and finish the warp, but England had not done so. The magistrate told England that he must return and finish the piece or go to work in Wakefield for seven days. England chose to go to Wakefield.

A company by the name of Allison and Exley had been occupying the mill during the 1870s, and were given as the current occupiers when the mill was advertised as being 'To Let' in July 1879, along with 3 sets of scribbling machinery, self-acting mules, looms, fulling and scouring machinery to follow; convenient dyehouse and warehouse, water power, steam engine, boiler and the necessary gearing. Situated near local collieries. The mill does not appear to have attracted a tenant, as the machinery was advertised for sale in November of the same year.

It is possible that the mill remained empty until 1888 when it was advertised for sale by auction on 6 June; at that time it was described as having a well fitted dyehouse, land, useful sheds and other outbuildings, 2 reservoirs, one supplied by a never failing artesian well. It was the purity of the water from this artesian well that was the primary reason for Edward Hirst & Son of Wildspur mill buying this mill in 1888 for the sum of £780.

Hirst's subsequently let the mill; the *Yorkshire Textile* Directory shows that the mill was being used by Herbert Hinchliffe, waste dealers, from at least 1912 until 1931. There was a fire at the mill in October 1919; Councillor Hinchliffe had left the mill at 12.30 to go home for lunch, he had not been sat down more than five minutes when someone arrived to tell him that the mill was on fire. The cause was attributed to 'spontaneous combustion', and damage was estimated to be around £1,000.[11] The 25inch Ordinance Survey map published in the 1930s shows no signs of buildings on the site, only the dam; which is how it has remained.

Midge / Scholes / Valley mills.

Shown on the 1853 6inch Ordinance Survey map as Midge in the Wood mill, this mill stands a few hundred yards downstream from Jackson Bridge and was surrounded by woodland. The earliest information that is available comes in 1805, when John Goddard a butcher living in Scholes, let the

Scholes/Midge/Valley mill 2012. © the Author

scribbling and carding mill for 11 years to William Taylor, Thomas Hardy and Joseph Heap from 4 October. An Insurance document dated February 1813 shows that Joseph Heap, John Battye, William, John and Thomas Senior, all wool scribblers, were using the mill at that time. John Goddard next let the mill for a period of 20 years to John Battye, Thomas Hardy, William and John Senior from 7 April 1817. The Enclosure Awards for the Graveship of Holme compiled in 1834 refer to the mill as Midgeley mill.

The owner of the property in 1853 was Mr. John Moorhouse, he also occupied the mill along with Mr. John Lockwood. Moorhouse and Lockwood applied to the Reservoir Commissioners in June 1856 for a reduction in water rates for the year, as they had dismantled their water wheel. The Directors, who list the mill as Midge mill, ordered that the rate should be reduced by £7 14s 10½d, leaving a balance of £10 13s 11d to be paid. Moorhouse and Lockwood later replaced the water wheel, as it was listed as part of the mill's accoutrements when the mill was advertised 'to let' in 1871.

Jonathon Mitchell the 21 year old son of John Mitchell of Midge Mill, had become intoxicated at the Shoulder of Mutton Inn Holmfirth on Monday 23 May 1858. As he stood up to leave, he caught his foot on a chair leg and fell, banging his head on the fender. He was carried from there to his uncle's house in New Fold, where a doctor saw him on the Tuesday morning; Jonathon died on the Wednesday. The inquest jury returned a verdict of 'dying from injuries received in a fall'. John Lockwood seems to have been finding business difficult in the 1850s and '60s, as he advertised his machinery for sale due to declining business in March 1869. He had 10 power looms, 6 narrow doeskin looms, a sizing machine, warp drying balloon, and sundries.

The mill was advertised as being 'To Let', during 1870 and 1871, until in March 1871 an advertisement for a machinery sale announced that all the machinery had to be sold as the mill had been let. The new tenant was Amos Senior, who ran into financial difficulties in 1873, with his yarn being auctioned in May, and his machinery in December. T. Mellor had been using the mill presumably during the late 1870s and until his lease expired in 1881, when the premises were again advertised to let. An auction sale of machinery was held at the mill on 29 November 1884, when 2 condenser sets, 1 pair of self-acting mules with 660 spindles, 1 self-acting mule with 360 spindles, 1 milling machine, 2 wringing machines and 1 willow were available, but there is no indication of who owned the machinery.

The property was advertised for sale by auction on 7 September 1886 consisting of the mill, boiler house, engine house, warehouse, dyehouse and other buildings, yards and reservoirs. With the steam engine and boiler, water wheel, fulling stocks, dyepans etc. Also 4 cottages at Mearhouse Bank. All the lots were withdrawn at the auction due to the lack of interest. The mill and the cottages, plus 3 acres 2 roods 25 perches of land were advertised for sale again in May and June 1888.

This mill was also bought by William Hirst of Edward Hirst & Sons, principally for the water rights, for £700. The Ordinance Survey map of 1893 shows 2 buildings, with a possible third building to the north of the others, and the mill dam, marked as Midge mill; whereas on the 1906 and 1932 maps the buildings are marked as Scholes mill.

Jonathon Thorp & Sons had ceased trading and left Dobroyd mill in 1899; but in 1910 they were established in part of Scholes mill, which they renamed Valley mill, making stockinets, tweeds, mantle and costume cloths. Thorp's added the word Successors to their title around 1911. William Hirst was using the other part of the mill; by 1916 he had been replaced by John Moorhouse who was using part of the mill into the 1920s. Thorp's continued to use the mill through both World Wars, making a series of alterations to the premises in the 1950s and '60s. An article in the *Holmfirth Express* on 16 May 1975 said that they were making knitted fabrics, and had booked £100,000 of orders at an exhibition that year. However, business was on the decline, and in 1988 Thorp's sold Valley mill and moved into part of Dobroyd mill, but failed to avoid receivership late in 1988.[12] The buildings at Scholes/Valley mills have since been converted into living accommodation.

Tyas mill

The whereabouts of this mill is something of a mystery; with all the information for Tyas mill coming once again from the Wakefield Court Rolls. Originally, John Rowley of Cawthorne Lanes surrendered 1 acre of land known as Mill Wood lying in Scholes with water descending to a place called the New mill, plus all the timber etc. growing there, to the use of John Tyas of Long Ing from 8 April 1742. This description suggests that the land was between Scholes mill and New Mill mill, possibly where Wildspur mill subsequently stands. In June 1756 Christian Tyas, only son of John Tyas deceased applied for a licence of Heriot for various properties in the Scholes area that had been owned by his father. Christian passed the use of the fulling mill known as Tyas mill, along with a cottage and land known as the Park, Rye Bank wood and Mill wood, to Luke Bower of Totties in April 1785. The occupant of the mill was Peter Haigh, while the cottage was tenanted by Joseph Mitchell.

Luke and Elizabeth Bower immediately took a mortgage on the 'Fulling mill near Scholes commonly known as Tyas mill with the cottage adjoining occupied by Joseph Mitchell, also the land known as Park and two areas of woodland called Rye Bank wood and Mill wood', from Joseph Shaw of Farnley Tyas; possibly as a means of paying Christian Tyas. This entry in the court roll also mentions Moorhouse Bank being above the fence at the top of Rye Bank wood.

In June 1817, Ann Brown, the daughter of Luke Bower (now deceased) and wife of Richard Brown, paid 1s 1½d for a licence of Heriot for 'all that Fulling mill at Scholes commonly called Tyas mill late in the possession of Peter Haigh, but now of Richard Brown, with the dwelling house late in the possession of John Battye as undertenant to Peter Haigh, but now of Jonathon Battye or his undertenants, plus a piece of land known as the Park and several pieces of woody ground and woodland; also 4 cottages at Wooldale Cliffe. An entry in the following year shows that, in addition to the property already mentioned, three cottages were newly erected near the mill, and were occupied by John Goodman, Betty Bower (widow), and Richard and Ann Brown.

In 1831 Samuel Wood of Slaithwaite paid £600 to Richard Brown and the executors of Joseph

Shaw of Farnley Tyas for Tyas mill near Scholes, and the newly erected cottages near the mill in the tenure of John Battye, John Goodman, Betty Bower (widow), and Joseph Robertshaw, with the land and the 4 cottages at Wooldale Cliffe tenanted by Joseph Fallas, Benjamin Fitton, George Morton and John Johnson.[13]

The information on Tyas mill ends here; whether the mill was destroyed by fire or suffered some other catastrophe in unclear, or perhaps the people operating the mill went out of business.

Wildspur mill

Sydney Morehouse, acquired some land between Jackson Bridge and New Mill, possibly the site of the former Tyas mill, and either built a new mill or renovated the old one, giving it the name of Wildspur mill. Isaac Beardsell writes in his Journal of 1844, that he discussed with Sydney Morehouse the possibility of renting the mill, but the matter was not pursued.

In 1847 a serious fire broke out on the third floor of the mill on 23 October, which virtually destroyed the main building. Jonathon Hinchliffe was the tenant of the third floor of the mill, his losses were calculated at £500; James Hoyle occupied the first and second storeys, his losses amounted to about £1,000. Sydney Morehouse had the building insured for £750, but his mules on the fourth floor and in the attic were not covered. The brigade from David Shaw's Crossley mill in Honley managed to stop the fire spreading to the engine house, willeying house and other outbuildings, but the main mill was beyond saving when they arrived.

James Wood was occupying part of the mill in February 1851, when it was visited after 6pm one evening by the Factory Inspector James Bates. He found three people named Oxley, Kaye and Littlewood, who he said were operating a spinning mule in the mill. Mr. Wood made it clear to the court that Oxley did not work for him, but was merely waiting for one of the other two, but that the others were working for him. Mr. Bates said that he would be satisfied with only expenses in the case

Wildspur mill 2012. © of the Author

of Oxley. The bench imposed fines of 40s each on the two cases, which, with expenses on all three came to a total of £5 6s. This was the first case to be brought in the district under the new regulations.

The Holme Reservoir Commission gives the owner of the mill as Sydney Morehouse in 1853, and lists the occupants as Sydney Morehouse, James Lockwood, James and Charles Wood. A new weaving shed was built by 1857, measuring 22 yards by 18 yards. An advertisement in July said that room and power was available with three rows of shafting capable of running 30 pairs of broad power looms. This was followed in October of the same year by an advertisement offering the five storey 'almost newly erected' mill, weaving shed, dyehouse, stove, willow room, 4 cottages and 4 acres of land 'To Let'. The mill was advertised for sale again in 1859, when Eli Moorhouse was the tenant, with an almost identical specification to that of 1857, except that a Reservoir of 1 acre is added, plus water from 3 other dams being piped to the mill; and still claiming that the mill was 'recently built by the owner Sydney Morehouse'.

Charles Hirst of Birdsedge had been using premises in the mill from about 1852, but had not signed a lease until some 18 months later, when he committed himself to a ten year tenancy. After the death of Sydney Morehouse senior in May 1855, Hirst realised that neither Mrs. Morehouse nor her son were aware of the document, and made out that he was on a yearly tenancy, giving notice to quit on 1 July 1856. Hirst had also approached the Morehouse's farm servant, asking him to find the document and give it to Hirst, promising him £5 if he could find it. Mrs. Morehouse found the document in February 1858, and insisted through her solicitors that Hirst should honour the agreement by paying past rent and taking out a new contract for the remainder of the term; which Hirst was not inclined to do. The case was heard in the Chancery Court in July 1859, when the judge found in favour of the Morehouses, but recommended that in order to avoid prolonged litigation they should accept £600 plus costs in settlement.

The mill appears to have been unoccupied between 1860 and 1865, after which it was bought and occupied by Edward Hirst & Son. About 11am on Wednesday 3 March 1869 the governor on the mill engine broke, causing the flywheel 'to revolve with frightful velocity'. It eventually broke and pieces flew in all directions, some being found twenty to thirty yards away. No-one was injured, but some workers were laid off for around two weeks until the engine was repaired and the flywheel replaced. A fire was discovered in the drying stove on 10 May 1871, which was put out by neighbours and workers using buckets and the mill's hose pipe. Damage to the contents of the stove and its floor was estimated at £60.

William Castle, a weaver of New Mill, was charged on Wednesday 7th August 1872 with 'wandering about in an unlawful manner and being found lodging in a boiler house without being able to give a good account of himself'. The firer at Wildspur mill said that he found Castle in the boiler house about 5am on Tuesday morning and, as he could not give a satisfactory account for being there, the firer fetched Police-constable Settle who took him at once to Holmfirth police office. Soon after arriving there Castle was taken ill and had to be taken by cab to Deanhouse Workhouse, where he was seen by Dr, Trotter who certified that Castle was fit enough to appear for trial on Wednesday. Castle could give no defence to the charge and, as he had been convicted twice before on similar charges, he was committed to prison for two months as a rogue and vagabond.

A fire was discovered shortly after midnight in the waste room at the mill on 3 November 1883, by Mr. Jonathon Moorhouse of Greenhill Lane New Mill. He raised the alarm, and the mill's fire hose was used along with buckets of water to douse the flames. The cause of the outbreak was not identified, but damage amounted to between £300 and £400. Another fire broke out in the piece stove at the mill between 3.30 and 3.45am on 2nd January 1884. It was first seen by P.C. Ambler at 3.40am when he was near Muslin Hall, he arrived at the mill at 4.05am. Walter Sykes, who lived on the premises, saw the fire at 3.45am and raised the alarm. A hose pipe was used to get water from the reservoir, plus buckets of water; the fire was put out by 5.30am. A quantity of cloth and some wool were burned, and part of the roof of the building was destroyed. Damage was estimated at £200, which was partly covered by insurance.

Abram Taylor had been head finisher for the firm for 37 years in October 1886, when Jonathon Mettrick one of the oldest employees, presented Mr. & Mrs. Taylor with a 'Testimonial of Esteem and Affection' from Hirst's employees, to mark their Golden Wedding. The number of people employed by Edward Hirst & Sons was between 80 and 90 during the late 1880s.

The Factory Inspectorate took Hirst's to court in October 1888, for breaching the Factory Act by employing five young people more than ten hours a day. Mr. Crawshaw, the mill manager, admitted the offence and explained that the young people had been allowed half a day off during the previous week without loss of pay, to attend an Agricultural Show in Huddersfield, on the understanding that they would make up the time by working an extra 30 minutes per day during the following week. The court did not impose a fine, but Hirst's were asked to pay costs.

The dispute with Jonathon Thorp & Co. about water rights came to court in 1897, and the Factory Inspector reported to the Council that the means of escape from the upper floors at the mill was inadequate in the same year. Whether these factors, along with the difficult trading conditions of the era were instrumental in Hirst's deciding that they would give up the business is unknown, but they advertised a sale of materials and yarns, with a total of 54,000lbs (over 24 tons) of yarns, and 3 tons of rags to take place on 27 July 1899, followed by the sale of a considerable quantity of machinery on 2 August.

Copley Marshall & Co. Ltd. became tenants during the early years of the 20th century; they were certainly there in August 1909 when they applied to New Mill council for permission to install water closets at the mill. The *Yorkshire Textile Directory* of 1910 records Copley Marshall as being 'hank and warp mercerises, dyers and bleachers, sizers, winders and dressers, specialists in all kinds of mercerised yarns for art needlework, and makers of Wildspur sewing and machine threads'. The company were using the mill until at least 1988, and during their tenure they carried out a number of enlargements and alterations including a new tentering room, additional offices, and the installation of an electricity sub-station.

In 1941 the firm were also involved in the survey undertaken by the wartime Government enquiring about the number of employees, amount of spare room etc. in order to formulate plans for the concentration of industry, to improve productivity and economise on the use of fuel and power.

The company had ordered a large quantity of Egyptian cotton to the value of £40,000 in 1987. When it arrived in London it was impounded by Customs who, due to the political climate at the time, refused to allow it into the country unless Copley Marshall guaranteed that after it was processed it would all be sold outside the EEC. Copley Marshall were unfortunately not able to guarantee that, and were forced to pay the Customs Authority £500 per week for storage in a Bonded Warehouse, until they could find someone outside the EEC who would take it.[14] The firm subsequently closed, and the buildings have since been converted to living accommodation.

Ing Nook / Glendale mill

This was the first fulling mill in the Fulstone/Scholes/Hepworth area, the earliest date for its existence is in the *Wakefield Court Roll* of 1539, which states that John Rowley surrendered to his son Stephen Rowley, one rood of land and water in the water called Newmillwater with a certain pond for a fulling mill built and established there with appurtenances. H.J. Morehouse maintains that the first Scribbling engine in the area was installed here about 1780, this is confirmed by John Earnshaw fulling miller of Thongsbridge applying, in 1805, for a licence of heriot for:

> *'All that scribbling mill together with the machines cards and engines, situate at New Mill in Fulstone, late in the possession of Abraham Earnshaw but now of Joseph Roberts and others. Together with a*

Ing Nook/Glendale mill, 2013. © the Author.

dwelling house with a garden and orchard situated between the house and the scribbling mill, and a parcel of land to the west of the mill 10yds by 10yds with two houses erected on it in the occupation of Joseph Hatfield and John Wadsworth'.

The following year Earnshaw raised a mortgage on the property from Joseph Roberts of Thongsbridge, James Turner clothier of Ridings Wooldale, and Richard Woodhead clothier of Thongsbridge for the sum of £330. Earnshaw surrendered the property to the three mortgagees in October 1808.

By 1822 the buildings appear to have lost their textile usage, as they are described as

'the building previously used as a scribbling mill, but recently converted into two cottages occupied by John Booth and William Bedford; also a cottage occupied by William Dawson with the garden, and the land to the west of the mill 10yds by 10yds with 3 cottages occupied by Joseph Bray, John Hadfield and John Marsden'.

The building that had been made into two cottages was converted back to its original use by 1830, when Hezekiah Tinker bought the dwelling house, barn, stable, cowshed and shop, called Green Hill Bank, and the fulling and scribbling mill called Ing Nook occupied by Thomas Hinchliffe. Hinchliffe and John Booth took over the mill in August of the same year.

In 1834 John Hinchliffe of Scholes, Jonas Beardsell and Ben Roberts both of Greenhill Bank, took the mill with the machinery, dam and goit, plus dwelling house with the barn, stable etc. and the two cottages on a 21 year lease from Thomas Hinchliffe of Ing Nook and Hezekiah Tinker of Silkstone. In March 1837, William Chadwick got his leg entangled with the drive belt of a machine, which took him round the shafting, forcing him between the drum and the wooden beams above, he was fatally injured. The mill was visited by the 'Plug Rioters' in August 1842, when they probably drew the boiler plug to allow the water and steam to escape; and possibly drained the mill dam to stop the firm from refilling the boiler.

In the following year Jonas Beardsell borrowed £500 for the remainder of the 21 year lease from

George Armitage of Edgerton, John Armitage and Edward Armitage both of Milnsbridge, surrendering a one-third share in the mill, land and other property as security. Abel Cuttell of Wooldale paid £300 to Ben Roberts of Greenhill Bank for a quarter share in the remainder of the 21 year lease on the mill in 1845. An advertisement appeared in the *Leeds Mercury* on the 6 January 1849, to sell the remaining 5/12ths of the mill's lease. The total rent for the premises was £150 a year.

The Holme Reservoir Commission records show that in 1853 the owner of the property was Hezekiah Tinker, and the occupier was John Hinchliffe & Sons; this was confirmed in the following year when the fulling and scribbling mill along with the dyehouse and stove was advertised to be let; presumably because John Hinchliffe's tenancy was coming to its end. The premises were advertised 'to let' again in 1857, when the mill was described as having 3 scribblers, 3 carders, 3 billies, 3 pairs of mules and 5 fulling stocks. Applications still had to be made to Hezekiah Tinker of New Mill, nr. Holmfirth.

The next tenant appears to have been Eli Moorhouse. John Day was the engineer at the mill in January 1859 when a young child of his fell into a plug hole in the dyehouse while boiling water was being released from the dyepan. Prompt action by the staff in the dyehouse prevented serious injury to the child.

A fire was discovered in the stove in August 1868, which was put out by workpeople before much damage had been done. A fire was discovered in the third storey of the mill at 2.15am on Wednesday 12 October 1870, which did considerable damage to the warps in the looms. The Unity and Bridge mill brigades attended and put out the fire; the original estimate of damage was between £40 and £50; this was later amended to just under £400.

The mill was advertised for sale on July 11th 1883, when it was described as having spinning rooms, weaving shed, warehouse, dyehouse, and other trade premises, with machinery valued to the tenants at £1,275 5s; also cottages and land in excess of 9 acres. The premises were let on a ninety year lease to Mr. Eli Moorhouse, at a rent of £150 a year, from 1 January 1851. The 50 workers were given a treat by Eli Moorhouse in January of both 1887 and 1888. Eli Moorhouse died at Grove House on 29 November 1888 aged 67; he had begun his working career at Hunger Hill, later moving to New Mill where he developed his business at Ing Nook.

A sale of raw materials and yarn was advertised to take place on 10 March 1890; with the mill premises, cottages and machinery being offered for sale by private contract. They were advertised again in November of the same year, but still did not sell. In November 1896, they were again offered for sale, Lot 1 was the 2 stone built mills, large weaving and finishing sheds, dyehouse, warehouse, offices, store-room, engine and boiler houses, chimney and reservoir; plus the water wheel, steam engine, boiler and fly-wheel; also 2 cottages and almost 6½ acres of land. Lot 2 was Grove House, which had 3 reception rooms and a kitchen on the ground floor, with another kitchen, cellars etc. in the basement, and six bedrooms with a bathroom and lavatory on the first floor. The mill was bought for £725; the house for £790.

It is likely that the buyers of both the mill and the house were Bower Roebuck & Firth, who began their business at Bridge mill, Holmfirth in 1896. They moved to Ing Nook, which they renamed Glendale mill, and became a limited liability company in 1899, giving a treat to their workers in January 1900, when they reported that they had enjoyed a good share of trade in the previous year, and were gradually making a name for themselves. The Firth part of the partnership was fairly short lived, as by 1906 the company name had changed to Bower Roebuck & Co Ltd. Mr. Richard Bower died at his home Grove House, on 23 January 1907. The *Yorkshire Textile Directory* said in 1910, that Bower Roebuck & Co, made worsted cloth on 60 looms, and had additional premises at 5 St. George's Square, Huddersfield. The firm installed electric lighting in the mill in 1911.

The company continued production at the mill throughout the 1920s and '30s, until in 1937 the business and mill were sold to W.E. Yates of Bramley, Leeds, although the name Bower Roebuck remained unchanged. Due to the Second World War, in 1941 the Government were looking to make savings of fuel and power, and were making efforts to concentrate production in fewer premises. Production at Glendale ceased on 1 February 1942, and was moved to the parent company in Leeds, along with some of the workers; but most people were able to find alternative employment in other local mills.

Production returned to Glendale mill in 1945, which was the year that Yates' sold Bower Roebuck to Troydale Industries, who would later sell the company to Messrs. Otten of Germany; in 1975 they became part of the Scabal Group. Many alterations and improvements to the mill took place in the late 1940s, '50s and '60s.

A severe thunderstorm occurred on Saturday 29 May 1948; lightening struck the chimney of Glendale mill shortly after 4pm, bringing a large number of bricks down into Sheffield Road. The road was closed until around midday on Sunday to allow steeplejacks to repair the damage. The company began a major expansion programme in 1979 that caused some concern amongst the residents of New Mill, as it included erecting new modern buildings on land previously unused. Some people expressed concern that the new building had a white roof, until the company explained that the colours had been decided by the Kirklees Planning Committee.

Heavy rain on 30 July 2002 brought flash floods to New Mill; the premises at Bower Roebuck were flooded to a depth of 3 feet, inflicting severe damage on buildings, machinery and stock, amounting to around £5,000,000.[15] Fortunately, as the company's owners were prepared to repair and refurbish the plant, and replace the necessary machinery; production is continuing into the 21st Century. The mill is equipped with modern Dornier looms, capable of weaving 450 picks a minute, and is producing similar quantities of cloth with six weavers, to the amount produced in the 1950s and '60s with around 40 weavers.

Sude Hill mill

Standing on the rising ground between Penistone Road and Sude Hill on the outskirts of New Mill, the origins of this mill are obscure although, by comparison with Glendale mill, fairly recent. The enclosure map of the area dated 1838 shows buildings that could be a mill, as does the 6inch Ordinance Survey map of 1853, but neither marks the use in any way, although the 6inch map does show the dam higher up and across Penistone Road with the outlet stream running in the direction of the mill. The earliest definite information on the mill's existence is from the will of John Armitage of Wooldale who, on his demise in 1840, left Holling House and Sude Hill mill to his niece Ann Armitage, the daughter of John's late brother William. The mill was also one of those in the district that were closed by the 'Plug Riots' on 17 August 1842.

The census of 1851 shows that the occupant of the mill was Andrew Mellor a woollen yarn manufacturer, who employed 9 men, 5 women and 8 children. An auction of machinery was advertised to take place at the mill on 26 July 1855, consisting of 4 pairs of spinning mules, probably hand operated as none are described as self-acting, with a total of 1,802 spindles. The occupant of the mill was still Andrew Mellor, who may, or may not have been the owner of the mules. Several rooms in the 4 storey mill were advertised to be let in 1856; the mill had a 30ft diameter water wheel 2ft 3in wide, with a steam engine and boiler of 8hp. The advertisement claimed that the rooms were 'well adapted for spinning machinery'.

One person who took advantage of the opportunity was George Booth who is listed in *White's Directory* in 1857 as a woollen manufacturer at Sude Hill. George Booth had joined forces with George Pitts by 1861, when they were trading as Booth & Pitts. There was a fire at the mill in February 1861; which was then used for teazing, scribbling carding and spinning wool. Discovered at 2am, the fire was thought to have started in the teazing room, but strong winds had fanned the flames in the direction of the main mill, which was also well ablaze. The Unity brigade were sent for, but by the time they arrived the roof of the mill had collapsed, and the contents of the buildings were reduced to ashes. Nearby houses were also threatened, but were saved due to the efforts of the fire brigade, helped by neighbours.

The mill was originally built as a two storey building, but had been increased to four storeys about

Sude Hill mill. © A.J. Brooke

1855. The owner of the mill was Mr. C. H. Macaulay of Brighouse, who had married Ann Armitage (see above), after her first husband, John Atherton, had died. Damage was estimated to be between £1,000 and £2,000, which would be only partly covered by insurance. The mill was rebuilt, and the firm now named George Booth & Co. continued their business, giving a treat to their 60 workers at the Duke of Leeds Hotel in New Mill on 4 February 1865. The meal was followed by singing and dancing.

Booth's were still in the mill in October 1877 when, about 2pm on Friday 5th, a 15 year old boy called George Haigh was holding a drive belt that Sam Booth was repairing. The belt caught round the boy's hand and carried him up and round the shafting, banging his head against the beam above. The engine was stopped and the boy extricated; Mr. W. Pinck surgeon, said that the boy had broken both thighs, one foot was badly bruised, one elbow had a compound dislocation and the skin and flesh were badly lacerated. His head was battered, but the skin was not broken. George had vomited blood several times indicating that he also had internal injuries. He was taken from the mill to his home, where he told his father that it was a pure accident, and that no-one was to blame. He died from his injuries at 6.15pm. The inquest jury returned a verdict of accidental death.

Booth, Pitt & Co was one of the companies in the area who closed their mill during the strike and lockout of 1878, discussed in Chapter 5. The company undertook scouring, milling and finishing work for Jonathon Thorp & Sons of Dobroyd mill after their disastrous fire in 1888. This was in return for the help that they had received from Thorp's after the fire at Sude Hill in 1861. The firm were trading as William Pitt & Co. in 1890 when their lease on the mill expired.

The mill was advertised to let in May 1890, described as a 4 storey mill 27yds by 15yds; plus a second 4 storey mill 27yds by 8yds, with an abundant water supply. A large sale of machinery was advertised to take place on 19 June consisting of machinery covering all the processes of turning raw wool into dyed and finished cloth. An obituary was printed in the *Holmfirth Express* of 18 April 1925, for Mr. Richard Mitchell aged 81, who had been born in New Mill. He had helped his father in the fulling mill at Sude Hill from the age of eight, eventually becoming a fulling miller himself and working for Booth Pitt & Co. until they closed in 1890. John H. Butterworth and Alfred Capper were trading as fustian cutters at the mill, but their partnership was dissolved in 1896, after which Butterworth traded on his own for a time.

The 25 inch Ordinance Survey map of 1904 marks the mill as 'disused'; Holmes Taylor & Co. submitted plans for a new dyehouse and store-shed in February 1905, which the council turned down in the following month as the sewage works could not deal with trade effluent.

An Indenture dated 14 April 1919, shows that Fred Lawton, of Claremont, Holmfirth, bought Sude Hill mill for £1,000; Fred Lawton & Son moved their business from Bridge Mill Holmfirth, to Sude Hill later in the year. The company made various alterations and extensions to the premises during their tenure. They became a member of the Allied Textile Companies by 1968; but their last advertisement for staff at Sude Hill appeared in the *Holmfirth Express* in 1975. An advertisement for a machinist at Sude Hill mill appeared in the Holmfirth Express in August 1976, for Miss Julie Fashions, but no more information has come to light on that company.[16] In 2010 the mill was partly occupied by New Mill Knitting Co, which had a limited workforce.

Reliance works / mill

Standing in the triangle of land between, and at the junction of, Penistone Road and Springwood Road; the 6 inch Ordinance Survey map of 1853 shows a small dam just below the road junction with a building below that, but does not mark its usage. In 1857 the building was known as Spring Mill and had a water wheel, the building was being used as a malt kiln at that time. A young, unnamed girl, who was playing there in August 1857, tried to ride on the wheel as it revolved and was drowned.

The 25 inch map of 1893 shows a larger building and marks it as a malt house; whereas in the New Mill Council minutes of 1895 it is recorded as Reliance Rug Works, which was occupied by Holmes, Taylor & Co. who may have had a connection with John Holmes of Stanley Rug Co. at Tenterhill mill. In 1898 New Mill Council agreed to allow Holmes Taylor & Co to remove a wooden shed from Messrs. Haigh's of Jackson Bridge and rebuild it at 'Stanley Mill' Sudehill. The *Yorkshire Textile Directory* of 1910 records that Holmes, Taylor & Co. were still occupying the works that year, and had a branch in Castleford; but they were not mentioned in subsequent years.

The YTD gives the occupants as Marshall, Lodge & Co, manufacturing worsteds and woollens in 1915; and A.F. Hirst & Co, commission weavers in 1916. Graham & Potts occupied the premises from at least 1920 to the mid 1930s. Eddison Taylor & Booth, Estate Agents, compiled an inventory of the premises and machinery in 1920. They describe the building as being a 3 storey mill 64ft long by 48ft wide. On the ground floor was the engine house with a 28hp gas turbine, and a storeroom; the first floor housed 15 looms; the second floor also housed 15 looms and a mending room with 4 mending tables. They calculated the value of the buildings, land and water rights at £1,750; and the value of the plant and machinery at £2,065.[17] New Mill council received an application from the tenants of the mill in 1936 for an electricity supply to be installed, which could have been submitted by Graham & Potts, but the name of the applicant is not given.

The *Yorkshire Textile Directory* records that Hirst & Read (Textiles) Ltd. were using the premises in 1957, manufacturing woollen and worsted coatings, costume cloths, flannels, serges, suitings, tweeds, and velours. They had been in business since 1947, but the entry does not say where. Their last entry in the directory was in 1960.

The buildings and dam have since been dismantled, and the site is much overgrown.

New Mill Dyehouse

Standing in Dyehouse Bottom, off Fulstone Road, to the north of New Mill Church, the buildings are clearly shown on the 6 inch Ordinance Survey map of 1853. The dyehouse and cottage run from north to south, with a dam to the east and a stream flowing downhill to the west. The buildings are still there, but the dam wall has been dismantled. An advertisement appeared in the *Huddersfield*

Examiner dated 30 October 1896: George Wimpenny Auctioneers were advertising the sale of 2 horses along with various carts that belonged to Ramsden Brothers Dyers, 'who have sold the premises', but apart from those premises being in New Mill, gives no other information. Whether it refers to this dyehouse or not is unknown.

Notes

1 Upper House/Over House mills.
  W.C.R. 5 Sept. 1818; 28 May 1794; 24 July 1818, 5 Sept. 1818; 5 Oct. 1796; 28 Oct. 1807;, 30 May,1821; 30 Oct. 1822; 5 June 1839; 11 March 1842; Kirklees Archive KC6/1/33 1853 and 1854; Huddersfield Chronicle, 6 Sept. 1862

2 Hepworth/Doctor Mill/Dyehouse
  Deed EH448.536, 1791; W.C.R. 10 April 1795; 15 Jan. 1808; 29 March 1822; 19 April 1822, 10 May, 21 Jun. 1822; 14 May 1824; 20 Oct. 1843; Leeds Mercury, 4 May 1850; Hudds. Chron. 18 April 1857; 19 Aug. 1865; Hudds. Ex. 18 Jan. and 18 July 1868; H'firth Exp. 1 Jan. and 21 May, 1887.

3 Other Hepworth Properties
  W.C.R. 10 Apr. 1733; 11 Dec. 1778

4 W.C.R. 5 June1822; Huddersfield Chronicle, 10 Dec. 1853

5 W.C.R. 26 Oct. 1821.

6 W.C.R. 18 June 1828, 22 Jan. 1830, 1 June, also 2 Sept. 1831.

7 Dobroyd mill
  W.C.R. 18 Oct. 1799, 16 Oct. 1814; Kirklees Archive, KC6/1/33 1853; Hudds. Chron. 23 July 1859; 26 May, 24 Nov. 1860; Hudds Ex. 2 Jan. 1860; 6 March, also 8 May 1869; 7 Dec. 1872; 13 Sept. 1873; 7 July 1883; 17 July 1886; 15 May 1897;15 July 1899; H'firth Exp. 23 June, 21 July, 1 Sept. 1888; 19 Jan. 1895; 13 Feb. 1897.

8 Holmfirth Express, 3 June 1905; 5 Jan. 1907; 3 Feb. 1917, 21, 28 June, 1919; 25 May, 1968; 12 Oct. 1929; Hudds. Ex. 11 May, 6 July 1907; Yorks. Text. Directory, 1923 and 1928; H'firth Exp. 21 Dec. 1957; 25 May 1968; 8 July 1971; National Monuments Record Centre documents, Dobroyd mill; H'firth Exp. 14 Dec. 1979; 20 June 1980, 15 Oct. 1982; 14 Jan 1983.

9 Lee mill
  W.C.R. (2) 22 Mar. 1822; 10 May 1822; 21 Mar. 1828; Leeds Intelligencer, 8 Oct. 1836; W.C.R. 7 Feb. 1837; Hudds Chron. 24 Dec. 1853; 29 March 1856; . 8 Nov. 1862; 14 Dec. 1867; Hudds. Ex. 28 July 1857; Yorks. Fact. Times, 7 Nov. 21 Nov. 1890; H'firth Exp. 1 Feb. 1890; 28 Aug. 1909; Hudds. Ex. 17 Aug. 1912.

10 H'firth Exp. 16 Oct. 1915, 3 Aug. 1918; 24 Nov. 1934; Kirklees Archive, UHO New Mill, 19 June 1929;24 April 1935; 23 Jan. 1936; Anecdotal evidence, 2010; H'firth Exp.13 Jan. 1989; 21 July 1951; 18 Aug. 1973; 4 July 1975; 6 Feb. 1981; 6 Sept. 1996.

11 Jackson Bridge mill
  W.C.R. 30 May 1759; 8 Feb. 1777; 19 May 1784; 15 Jan. 1790, 19 Oct. 1791; 19 Sept, 29 Oct. 1806; 15Sept. 1809; 16 Oct. 1814; 15 March 1816; Kirklees Archive, KC6/8/37 16 June 1801, 8 Feb. 1822; KC6/1/33 1853; W.C.R. 21 Nov, 12 Dec. 1834; 21 Aug. 1835 25 Oct. 1837; 2 Mar. 1838; 8 Oct. 1847; Hudds Chron. 11 May, 10 Oct. 1861; 2 Jan. 9 July 1864; 17 Nov. 1866; Kirk. Arch. KC6/8/37 1864; Hudds. Ex. 5 July, 15 Nov. 1879; 26 May 1888; H'firth Exp. 9 June 1888; 27 Oct. 1919.

12 Midge/Scholes/Valley mills
  W.C.R. 1 May 1806; 3 Oct. 1817; Kirklees Archive, KX321, 12 Aril 1834; KC6/1/33 1853; KC6/1/5 19 June 1856; Hudds. Ex.13 Mar. 1869; 25 March 1871; 10 May, 13 Dec. 1873; 30 April 1881; 15 Nov. 1884; 28 Aug. 1886; 2 June 1888; Yorks. Text.Directory, 1910 and subsequent years; Anecdotal evidence given to me by JT Knitting Ltd. in 2010.

13 Tyas mill
  W.C.R. 27 Apr. 1743; 2 Jun. 1756; 29 Spr. 1785 2 entries; 28 March 1794; 4 June 1817; 3 June 1818; 25 Feb. 1831.

14 Wildspur mill
  Leeds Mercury, 23 Oct. 1847; Hudds. Chron. 22 Feb 1851; 8 March 1869; 10 Aug. 1872; Kirklees Archive KC6/1/33, 1853; Hudds.Ex.11 July 1857; 10 Oct. 1857; 23 July, 10 Dec. 1859; 13 May 1871; 10 Nov. 1883; 5 Jan. 1884; 23 Oct. 1886; 6 Oct. 1888; 15 May 1897; 15 July, 1899; H'firth Exp. 22 Jan. 1887, 4 Feb. 1888; Kirklees Archive, UHO New Mill, 15 Dec. 1897; KC28/1-6; Holmfirth Express, 24 Dec. 1987, and 8 Jan. 1988.

15 Ing Nook/Glendale mill
  W.C.R. 9 Jan. 1540; 30 Oct. 1805; 10 Oct. 1806; 21 Oct. 1808; 22 Jan, 20 Aug. 1830; 25 April 1834; 20Oct. 1843; 9 May 1845; Halifax Guardian, 8 April 1837; Leeds Mercury, 20 Aug. 1842; 6 Jan. 1849; Hudds. Chron. 9 Dec. 1854; 11 April 1857; 22 Jan. 1859; 15, 22 Oct. 1870; Hudds. Ex. 8 Aug. 1868; 30 June 1883; 8 Dec. 1888; 1 Mar. 1890; 4 Feb. 1900; Holmfirth Express, January 1887 and 1888; 8 Nov. 1890; 14 Nov. 1896; 29 April 1942; 26 Jan. 1907; 11 Feb. 1911; 29 June 1979; 27 June 1986; Mar. 1988; Textile Manufacturer, May 1899; Bower Roebuck – Site/Company History; August 2001; Kirklees Archive, KC28/1-6; Hudds Daily Ex. 31 May, 1948.

16 Sude Hill mill
  W.C.R. 6 March 1840; Leeds Mercury, 20 Aug. 1842; Hudds. Chron. 21 July 1855; 31 May 1856; 11Feb. 1865; Hudds. Ex.16 Feb.1861; 10 May, 7 June 1890; Hudds. Weekly News, 13 Oct. 1877; H'firth Exp. 10 Apr. 1925; Textile Manufacturer, June 1896; Kirklees Archive, UHO New Mill, 15 Dec. 1897; Kirklees Archive, UHO New Mill, 22 Feb, 29 Mar. 1905; West Yorks. Deeds Registry, Vol. 26, p. 1269 no. 485.

17 Reliance works/mill
  Huddersfield Chronicle, 27 Aug. 1857; Kirklees Archive, KHY29/4/1/3 9 Aug. 1898; KC501/13, 20 Dec. 1920.

Chapter 13

Wooldale to Mytholmbridge

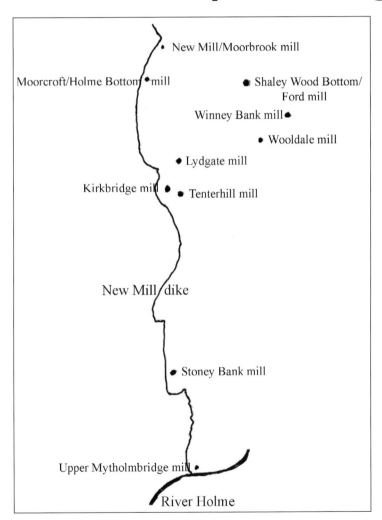

Winney Bank mill

This mill stands in the hamlet of Winney Bank between Wooldale and Cinder Hills. The 6inch Ordinance Survey map of 1853 shows the buildings at Winney Bank being in a three sided square, the left arm of the square being the mill; with a dam apparently built within the hollow square.

In 1832 Benjamin Bates dyer of Winney Bank paid £74 12s to James Bates of Millhouse Wooldale,

Winney Bank mill, after rebuilding. © the Author

and £104 1s 8d to William Bates cloth merchant of Winney Bank, for a one third share in his late father's (John Bates) property: the house at Winney Bank, a house at Wood Bottom Wooldale with a barn, stable, outbuildings, dyehouse, dam, watercourses etc. Also a house with a dyehouse and reservoir at Shaley Wood, plus several closes of land. In April of the following year, Thomas England of Huddersfield paid £300 to Benjamin Bates for his one third share in the properties.

An advertisement appeared in the *Leeds Mercury* on 15 June 1839 offering: 'Room and Power to let in the mill with immediate availability; with a dwelling house having 3 ground floor rooms, four good lodging rooms and good cellars, with Barn, Mistal and outbuildings. Also room and power for 1 pair of mules, and two rooms for the finishing of cloth in Winney Bank mill, with gig and brushing mill ready for use; also, to be sold, a good 8hp steam boiler'. Applications were to be made to Mr. Benjamin Bates, Wood Bottom, near Winney Bank, Holmfirth. The mill was advertised again in May 1840, when it was described as being 3 storeys high, 16 yards long and 10½ yards wide, with a steam engine and reservoir. Machinery was also available: 1 willow or teazer, 3 scribblers, 3 carders, 3 billies; 2 double and 1 single fulling stocks, also 1 driving stock; all in excellent condition. Applications could be made to Mr. James Bates at Winney Bank; or William Bates or Benjamin Bates at Wood Bottom.

A report in the *Leeds Mercury* on Boxing Day 1840, said that: 'A person by the name of Barrowclough, alias Cockin, who has long been a very suspicious character, was taken into custody last Thursday week charged with stealing a quantity of leather straps from the mill of Mr. Bates at Winney Bank near Holmfirth. Part of the stolen goods were found in his house; on being taken to the magistrates Barrowclough implied that some of his neighbours were also involved. On investigation this proved to be entirely false. He was brought to court on the 19th and committed to trial at the Quarter Sessions.'

The mill was again advertised as being available for rent in 1845; in addition to the mill and its machinery the occupant could also take 2 houses with outbuildings, and around 20 acres of land. The advertisement also stressed that the mill was within 1½ miles of 6 excellent beds of coal, and only a mile from Holmfirth. Whether anyone took the mill is not known.

James Bates died on Wednesday 4th September 1867; he had been a sub inspector of Factories for the area since the implementation of the Act appointing inspectors in the mid 1830s. The mill was advertised for sale as part of a large sale of property in Holmfirth, Shepley and Skelmanthorpe, to be auctioned on 22 September: Lot 5 was Winney Bank house and a close of land; also a one third share in the building formerly used as a woollen mill, with the engine and boiler house and other buildings, dam and vacant ground. The mill had obviously fallen into disuse at this time, and in February 1883 Wooldale Council recorded that it was in a dangerous condition. In September of that year they said that the most dangerous parts of the building must be demolished.[1] The mill has since been restored as a two storey building, and converted to living accommodation.

The Wakefield Court Roll recorded on 29 January 1796 that the Messuage at West Nelly also known as Nellroyd had a **Dyehouse**. It was mentioned again in 1803 and in several subsequent entries.

Shaley Wood Bottom / Ford mill

Built in the 1850s the earliest information about the mill is a report in the *Huddersfield Examiner* dated 20 February 1858, when Charles Whitehead, a wool washer of Totties, who worked for Mr. Alfred Wood, a knitting wool and worsted manufacturer at Ford mill, was injured at work. On 26 January he was piecing some lappings on the washing rollers when the fingers of his left hand became caught. The manager Mr. John Horn managed to free his hand, but the flesh had been torn from the fingers. Whitehead was taken to Mr. Morehouse surgeon of Stoney Bank who dressed the wounds before sending Whitehead to the Infirmary. The press report said that 'mortification set in and lock jaw supervened on the 8th'. Whitehead died on Sunday 14th leaving a widow and five children. The inquest jury returned a verdict of accidental death.

In December 1859, Alfred Wood was charged by Mr. Bates the Factory Inspector with working Sarah Brook and Elizabeth Lawton, both under 18, without entering their names in the mill's book of workers, and without having them examined by a Surgeon. Mr. Wood told the bench that Lawton's name was entered in the book of workers kept at the mill, and this charge was dropped; but he pleaded guilty to the other charges, and was fined 40s plus costs in each case, a total of £4 18s.

A father and son both called John Audsley broke into the mill through the roof on 2 November 1860 and stole worsted yarn to the value of £20. Mr. Wood discovered the break-in the following morning and went straight to Holmfirth Railway Station where he saw the Audsley's put some packages on a train and buy tickets to Bradford. He followed them, and finding the packages of yarn in a dealer's warehouse in Bradford he got the police who took charge of the packages, and charged the Audsley's with theft. The magistrates committed the two men for trial in York, but refused bail. This was not the first time that goods had been stolen from the mill.

Occupancy of the mill changed, David Bower and Mark Bailey took over the mill, they were Woollen manufacturers; however, by 1863 they had decided to part company and dissolved their partnership on 11 April. On 20 April, John Cartwright caught his hand in a drive belt and was taken up and round the shafting. His right hand was torn off, and the arm was fractured in several places. He was taken to Huddersfield Infirmary where, on the following day, Mr. Rhodes a surgeon, amputated the arm. The report concluded: 'considering the nature and extent of the injuries, the sufferer is at present doing well'.

The mill was offered for sale by private contract in October of the same year, along with the house and land; the sale of Bower & Bayley's machinery was advertised to take place at the mill on 18 November, comprising a horizontal steam engine, boiler, both nearly new, with a steam condenser made for the engine and boiler but never fitted; beaming machine and winding on frame, bobbin winding machine, 14 power looms, plus extra beams and many sundries. The machinery appears to have sold, but the boiler and steam engine, along with the shafting, stayed in the mill, presumably bought by the owner of the building. About three weeks after that sale the premises were advertised 'To Let', and were described as a building 73½ft long by 36ft wide and 10½ft high under the beams, recently used as a weaving shed, and included a nearly new 10hp steam engine and boiler. With a dwelling house, cottage, mistal, stable, outbuildings, 1½ acres of land and a well stocked garden. Apply George Tinker & Son, Auctioneers, Holmfirth.

The next occupants of the building were Charles Hoyle & Co, whose fortunes seem to have faired little better than those of either of their predecessors, as the premises and their machinery were advertised for sale on the instructions of their assignees in July 1868. The description of the premises is almost identical to the previous sale, except that the amount of land appears to have increased from 1½ to 11 acres. The machinery shows that Hoyle's started their manufacturing process with raw wool and took it through to woven cloth, as they had a spiked willey, scribbling condenser, spinning mules, warping woofs, balloon and winding on frame, and 6 10quarter power looms. The building was next used for making shoddy and mungo, as an advertisement appeared in September 1874 advertising the farm of 11 acres, and the mill recently used for rag grinding, with a plentiful supply of water from 2 reservoirs, to be let with immediate access. Whether this attracted an occupant is not known, but is doubtful as in the following year the boiler, steam engine, rag grinding machine and shoddy cleaner were advertised for sale.

By 1877 the mill was occupied by Messrs. Senior and Charlesworth. On 14 March a 16 year old girl called Annie Booth, who lived just up the road in Totties, was cleaning a stationary spinning mule and had her arm through a wheel when the overlooker, who could not see the girl, set the machine in motion mutilating Annie's arm. She was taken home where she was seen by Dr's Trotter and Pinck, who sent her to the Infirmary. It was thought that she would not lose her arm. Senior & Charlesworth dissolved their partnership in 1877 and also ceased trading. Their machinery was advertised in the Huddersfield Chronicle of 23 June 1877 for sale on 27 June, consisting of a rag grinding machine, 1 scribbler, 1 spiked willow, a shoddy cleaner, 2 narrow 2box power looms, a weighing machine and some yarn and waste.

It is possible, although not certain, that the owner of the mill from being built was the same Mr. Alfred Wood, who worked the mill with different partners, or alternatively rented the property out. The next occupants were Wood & Burtt who were spinners of knitting wools, and eventually became part of J. J. Baldwin & Partners, and subsequently Paton & Baldwin. Wood & Burtt carried out several alterations and enlargements to the premises from 1885, when they asked permission from the council to divert the road, and then close it temporarily in the following year to enable a new boiler to be installed. The company advertised for builders to supply tenders for a new warehouse in May 1888; the successful firm were Thorpe & Mallinson. In October of that year Amos Ellis of Wooldale who worked for them as a labourer, was ascending a ladder with a large stone on his back. When he reached the top Sam Crosland and Alex Kaye were helping Ellis put the stone down when the ladder broke, pitching all three to the ground some 25 feet below. Crosland and Kaye were only slightly injured, but Ellis fell on his head; he was taken home where he was seen by Dr. Trotter who said that it was no use taking Ellis to the Infirmary as his injuries were fatal. Ellis died at 7pm the same evening.

Wood & Burtt's number of employees was gradually growing, they gave a treat to 80 people in 1887; this had risen to 90 in 1888. There was a fire at the mill on 25 May 1906, which broke out around 11.30pm; neighbours with buckets formed a chain to ferry water across the road from a stream to the mill, and hoses were attached to the council water main, but the fire had a good hold and a strong wind was blowing. Holmfirth fire brigade were quickly on the spot, but the fire was too big for them to tackle alone, so Huddersfield brigade were contacted who arrived with their steam powered engine 'Phyllis' about 1.30am. They had difficulty obtaining a water supply and had to pump water from a dam about 175 yards away. The fire was out by 4.30am, and although the dyehouse, willeying room, scouring room and engine house were destroyed, the main mill and warehouse was still intact. It was thought that it would be at least two weeks before a temporary engine could be installed, putting some 200 people out of work until then. Damage was estimated at between £4,000 and £5,000, which was insured. The cause of the fire was not given. The company submitted plans for rebuilding the mill in August of the same year, followed in December by plans to build a new dyehouse, dye-shed and cotton dryer screen, plus alterations and extensions to the offices, which were all passed.

The body of Arthur Batty landlord of the Bay Horse at Hade Edge was found when the police dragged the mill dam on Thursday 2 April 1908. Before taking the Bay Horse, Mr. Batty had been a pork butcher in Holmfirth, but there were no indications of any difficulties that would have caused him to commit suicide. The inquest jury returned a verdict of 'suicide while of unsound mind'.

The *Yorkshire Textile Directory* for 1910 recorded that Wood & Burtt made hosiery and knitting yarns and had 4,000 spindles. More new buildings followed in 1912, along with the installation of a sprinkler system that was connected to the water main. Mr. Fred Barrowclough the mill's cashier discovered a fire at the mill at 9.25pm on Thursday 18 August 1914. He raised the alarm, and with the help of Mr. A. Wood plus E.H. and G.E. Burtt and others, connected the firm's hosepipe to the water main and sprayed water onto the fire. The Holmfirth Council brigade attended, but the fire had been put out before they arrived. It was fortunate that the fire was discovered so early as there was a large amount of wool in the warehouse, but little damage was done. The mill was able to resume full production on the following morning.

Due to the number of buildings in which the sprinkler system had been installed, it was found to be necessary to increase the size of the water main to 6 inches in 1920. Edwin Henry Burtt died in May 1922, at the age of 73. He had moved from Lincolnshire to Holmfirth when he was around 20 years old, going into partnership with Mr. Alfred Wood about 1890. The erection and alteration of buildings continued into the 1930s; full details can be found in the minutes of the council.

Another serious accident occurred at the mill in December 1937, when Mr. George Bailes aged 49 of Lydgate, fell 18 feet down the flue of a fuel economiser into red-hot soot and was burned to death. It took rescue workers three hours to recover his body, which was burned beyond recognition. The Coroner returned a verdict of 'accidental death'.

In 1941 the council gave Wood & Burtt permission to extend their wool warehouse; and more interestingly, to build an Air-Raid Shelter. The company continued production at the mill into the 1960s, their last advertisement for staff appearing in the Holmfirth Express during 1966. After leaving Ford Mill, Paton & Baldwin concentrated production at their plant in Denby Dale Road, Wakefield, from where they were advertising for staff in 1975. The United Box Company were using part of Ford mill in 1978, when they were advertising vacancies for 16 to 18 year olds; other companies were also using different parts of the complex. A fire broke out in the premises used by United Box Company in the early hours of Sunday 7th November 1982, fire fighters managed to restrict damage to the one building, allowing other companies to continue their operations unhindered. This fire appears to have been the beginning of the end for the mill, the Council accepted a plan in July 1984 to demolish the industrial buildings and allow the site to be developed for housing.[2]

Wooldale mill

In the nineteenth century there was a small mill in Little Lane Wooldale, it stood on what is now the children's playground, with a dam covering the land that was between the mill and the road through the village; this has since shrunk to a small pond. The water supply comes from an underground source at Cliff. A rather indistinct photograph of the building is reproduced here, which probably dates from the late nineteenth or possibly the early twentieth century.

It has not been possible to determine which, if any, of the following information actually refers to this particular building. There were also several other buildings in the area that were used for textile processes. All the information on these various premises comes from the Wakefield Court Rolls; by following the repetition of names, or the description of premises, I have grouped certain ones together to give a progression of owners and/or occupiers. The precise location of the various premises is not certain.

An entry in the Court Roll on 26 September 1823 records a transaction between James Preston

'Wooldale mill' photograph provided by Mr. & Mrs. Cartwright.

and George Augustus Preston, both of Wooldale, involving various houses and lands including a Dyehouse with another building newly erected and used as a Corn Mill, occupied by James Preston.

William Carr of Bolton Abbey surrendered on 29 April 1844 Wooldale Hall, with barns, stables and outbuildings; also another dwelling house with a cottage, barn stable and mistal and another building adjoining intended as a mill with the reservoir attached. Also the Blue Dyehouse with vats, pans and other apparatus, and also that close of land called the Croft, 3 roods 34 perches, occupied by Charles Ewart. To the use of Henry Alcock of Skipton.

The Court Roll for 1846 records that on 25 September, James Preston a blue dyer of Holmfirth, paid £370 to Henry Alcock of Skipton for Wooldale Hall, with Barns, stables, outbuildings gardens and orchard with a close of land called the Rabbit/Rubbish Garth 2 roods 5 perches occupied by Daniel Hellawell or his undertenant Mr. Cuttell, and a dwelling house with a cottage, barn, stable, mistal and fold, also the building intended as a mill with the reservoir attached, and the blue dyehouse with vats, pans and other apparatus. The money was supplied by Mr. Edward Milner of Ashton-under-Lyne, as a mortgage. He transferred the mortgage to William Marvel Ashton of Duckinfield Cheshire, on 16 October 1846.

The roll for 1824-5 records on 8 July that John Farrar had use of a Stove in Wooldale, and that Benjamin Bates had the use of a Dyehouse. On 19 August Benjamin Bates bought 202sq.yds of land which was part of a close called the Croft containing a cottage, dyehouse and garden that were newly erected. In April 1844 the roll records that there was a stove and dyehouse in Wooldale belonging to Benjamin Bates; and also a mill plus another building.

An entry dated 14 March 1788 records a Messuage at Wooldale Town End occupied by Joseph Heap that had a dyehouse; and mentions fields called the Old House Close, Wheat Croft and Kirk Royds. Sales of this property are also recorded on later dates, with the same description.

John Tinker the younger of Hepworth paid £765 in November 1827, to James Haigh clothier of Hogley, John Woodhead dyer of Upperthong, and Robert Smith fancy cloth manufacturer of Grange, Kirkburton, who were the assignees of John Wood merchant, dealer and chapman of Wooldale; for 3 cottages with a barn, stable, raising shop, garden and other outbuildings at Wooldale Town End late in the possession of George Roberts George Goddard and William Sykes, and now of John Mellor and William Sykes. Plus 2 closes of land called the Croft and the Near Croft.

Lewis Fenton of Underbank paid £475 to the assignees of John Wood bankrupt merchant, dealer and chapman, in October 1829 for the dwelling house with barn, stable, pressing shop and other outbuildings at Wooldale, and land containing 1 acre, 1 rood 18 perches, along with 2 cottages.

Samuel Harper Walker, son of Samuel Walker deceased, of Stainland, applied to the Court on 6 March 1840, for a licence of Heriot for a dyehouse at the top of a close called the Upper New Croft, along with 3 closes of land and 3 cottages. Walker also paid 10s. each to Miles Netherwood, woolstapler of Deighton, and Mary Pontefract widow of Gamaliel Pontefract, to take over their interest in the properties. On 17 April 1840 Joseph Broadhead, who was the occupier of the dyehouse, paid £340 to Samuel Harper Walker who was a worsted top spinner from Stainland, for the dyehouse, land and 2 of the cottages.

There is a record of a dwelling house with a stove and dressing shop at New Gate in Wooldale occupied by Jonathon Wadsworth, 17 March 1826.

The court roll for 1910 records in March 1911, that George Elliott Booth sold a dressing shop at Sunny Brow Wooldale to Jane Harrop Sykes.

New Mill / Moorbrook mill

Built as a Corn mill, the early information comes from the Wakefield Court Rolls. An entry in the roll dated 29 October 1456 records that:

> *William Moorehous and Richard Castell came here in court and took from the lord three parts of two mills within the graveship of Holme, of which one is called Cartworthmylne and the other Nwemylne, and John Sykes came here in court and took from the lord the fourth part of the two mills, to have and to hold the two mills with their appurtenances to the aforesaid William Richard and John from the feast of St Michael the Archangel last past before the date of this court until the end of the term of seven years next following and fully completed. Paying thence to the lord annually during the whole term abovesaid 76s 8d for rent/farm at the feasts of Easter and St. Michael by equal portions etc. And the lord will repair and keep up the said mills during the aforesaid term at his own costs and expenses except for Cogges and Spyndils etc.*

In 1461 the fee farmer became Elias Burton, who was paying a total of £4 per year to the lord in rent; and in 1486 the fee farmers were Nicholas Littlewood, John Hynchecliff and John Coldwell, who paid £4 8s 4d per year rent; made up of 33s 4d for the *Nwemylne*, and 55s for *Cartworthmylne*. By the late 18th century the corn mill at New Mill does not seem to have been doing very much, if any, business. The miller in 1785 was John Green, he and his wife raised a mortgage on the two closes of land separated by the mill dam and two houses built on the land, but there is no mention of the mill. Two years later John Green and his wife were living in Sheffield, they passed the land, dam and houses to John Batye of Crosland Hill a gentleman, who was one of the mortgagees.

Due to the existence of Ing Nook mill, it was not until 1804 that the New mill was converted from being a corn mill to having scribbling engines installed. The owner of the mill in the early months of 1817 was George Green of Dalton Innkeeper, he passed 'All that building at New Mill used as a scribbling mill, plus 2 cottages and 2 closes of land known as the Carr and the Dam Ing' to John Dickinson butcher, Jonas Walker the elder, John, Jonas the younger and Emas Walker, all of whom were also the occupants of the premises.

A document written in 1835 gives an Abstract of Title, beginning with John Green of New Mill borrowing £700 as a mortgage from John Firth. In December 1835 John Firth and George Green (son of John Green deceased) rented out the mill, with its water wheel, going gear etc. to Jonathon

New Mill/Moorbrook mill. © A.J. Brooke

Sandford of Dyson's mill Holmfirth, Iddo Wood of Parkhead and John Tinker of Prickleden, for a term of 21 years from 1 May 1836. In 1838 the three were given permission to erect at their own expense, on the Dam Ing, a 'good and substantial building to be used as a mill, not exceeding 22yds in length, 13yds in width, and of a height that the three considered proper'; without paying any additional rent for it during the remainder of the 21 years.

Jonathon Sandford relinquished his half share in all the mill buildings and land to Tola Wood of Park House Upperthong, Jonathon Wood the younger and Edmund Littlewood both of New Mill, on 25 November 1843. Iddo Wood died in 1844, leaving his share of the New mill, plus all his property at Parkhead to be shared between his friend John Harpin the younger, and Iddo's two brothers Tola and Palti. The three beneficiaries sold a half share in the mill and land to David Wood of Hillhouse Lane Bottom in Cartworth, in 1845. The Holme Reservoir Commission records the owner of the mill in 1853 as George Green, and the occupants as Tola Wood, Jonathon Wood and David Wood, with Edmund Littlewood.

George Green senior had died by 1854, leaving the mortgaged mill to his son George Green junior who subsequently arranged to sell it to Charles Lockwood of Belgreave Fulstone for £1,300, which more than covered the mortgage and any accrued interest.

Charles Lockwood became the owner and occupant of the mill in September 1857. He possibly built a new weaving shed, into which he installed power looms in the following year. The firm began trading as Lockwood & Markham in 1858; The Markham connection is unclear, but was possibly Mrs. Lockwood's maiden name. They based their price structure for weaving on the rates paid by another [unnamed] local company who were making similar qualities. Early in 1859, the weavers asked for pay rates to be increased in line with those of another manufacturer who was making entirely different qualities. Because they had urgent orders to fulfil, the firm agreed to a temporary increase, but when the firm attempted to reduce rates back to those originally agreed, the weavers objected and in excess of 30 came out on strike in May 1859, claiming that the company wanted to reduce the amount paid for weaving a particular quality of cloth from 30s to 22s. [Strike pay at that time was 7s per week]. Lockwood & Markham maintained that the proposed reduction amounted to five percent, rather than the thirty percent claimed by the weavers. The differences were resolved, and the weavers were back at work by 2 July, when the *Examiner* correspondent suggested that 'Strikes were becoming unpopular in the Holmfirth district'.

During the strike, a fire was discovered in the stove at the mill around 1am on 19 June, wool waste that had been put to dry had ignited. Neighbours attempted to put out the fire but were unsuccessful. The Unity Brigade was able to stop it spreading to other parts of the mill. Damage to the building and its contents was estimated at £150. The stove was the only part of the building not covered by insurance. In October of the same year Eliza, the 21 year old daughter of Jonathon Brook of Sudehill, was helping Woofenden the foreman, to repair a broken drive belt by holding a light for him when her clothing became caught in the wheels of the machine, drawing one leg into the cog-wheels. After stopping the machine it took almost 15 minutes to release her. She also received injuries to her arm, neck and head. She was taken to the Infirmary where her leg was amputated above the knee; she remained in hospital until she died on October 15th. The Coroner severely reprimanded Woofenden for exposing the woman to danger, but the jury still returned a verdict of 'accidental death'.

Another fire at the mill was spotted by a policeman just before 1am on the morning of 10 July 1860. He and the firer, who lived nearby, forced an entry into the building known as the 'weaving shed', which was actually a two-storey building 135ft long by 78ft wide. They removed books and papers and, helped by neighbours, they began removing pieces of cloth, 4 skeps of woollen yarn, and other goods. The Unity brigade was sent for; meanwhile a double bucket chain was formed to try to fight the fire; however, their efforts were unsuccessful, and the fire spread throughout the entire building. The looms on the upper storey began falling through the blazing floor, and eventually the roof collapsed. The Unity brigade was unable to save that building, but concentrated their efforts on stopping the fire spreading to the nearby 4 storey spinning mill. 48 looms, 3 pairs of mules, 2 other machines and a large quantity of shafting and gears were lost besides pieces of cloth etc. The report suggested that the damaged building had been built about three years previously, hence the speculation that it was built just after Lockwood's bought the mill. Damage estimates varied between £7,000 and £12,000; and 100 people were put out of work. Later in the year Charles Lockwood entertained around 100 guests at the 'rearing supper' held at the Shoulder of Mutton Inn, New Mill on 10 November 1860, to celebrate the rebuilding of the part of the mill damaged by the fire. The workpeople had been idle since the fire, and were said to be eagerly anticipating the return to work.

John Cartwright aged 34 died in Huddersfield Infirmary on 28 April 1863 from injuries received while he was standing on a wooden frame trying to untangle a strap wrapped around the moving main drive shaft near the ceiling of the room, when his hand became caught and he was drawn up towards the shaft. His hand being torn off he dropped to the floor, sustaining a compound fracture of his right arm and a fractured thigh. He cried out "Lord, have mercy upon me", and when Mr. John Lockwood went into the room a few minutes later Cartwright said to him "This is a serious thing for me, I am killed; be kind to my wife and family". The surgeon Mr. King was sent for and attended to the injuries before sending Cartwright to the Infirmary, where, shortly after he arrived, the damaged arm was amputated. He seemed to be improving but on Tuesday 28th his condition deteriorated and he died that night. The jury returned a unanimous verdict of 'accidental death', remarking that the deceased should have had the engine stopped before attempting to put the strap to rights.

Steam engines relied on coal, Charles Lockwood also owned coal pits in Fulstone, and in 1864 some of them became flooded. He employed two men to drain the water by digging 'drive ways'. The men had dug into the hillside, and knew that they were nearing the flooded workings, when the water broke through and carried them along the tunnel holding their breath for some 70 or 80 yards, before the water turned off down another drive way leaving them gasping for breath and nursing their wounds. They had suffered cuts and bruises from colliding with rocks, but were said to be recovering.

Walter Fawcett, a 17 year old, was fettling a condenser engine in August 1865 with the help of another lad. The drive belt had been thrown off the drum and hung loosely at the side of the engine. They had to kneel on part of the machine in order to clean it, and Fawcett found that the strap was in his way, so he kicked it backwards with his foot and it engaged with the pulley on the drive shaft, caught his foot and carried him round the shafting. An Engineer in the room had the mill engine stopped and Fawcett was taken down. Dr. Morehouse was called but his injuries were too severe to allow him to recover; he died a few hours later.

Charles Lockwood agreed in 1866, to employ William Green, a scribbling engineer of New Mill, for five years and pay him £8 every four weeks, and also to allow Green to live rent free in the cottage that he was then renting, which was presumably part of the mill premises. In view of the wages paid to other scribbling engineers at the time, the amount mentioned plus a rent free house seems particularly generous.

In March 1872 Lockwood's charged Benjamin Taylor, a weaver, with breach of contract. Taylor had worked for Lockwoods for seven or eight years, and on 21 March had complained to his foreman that the warp in his loom was so difficult to weave that he could not make a wage from it. The firm agreed to put him on a time rate of £1 per week, which Taylor accepted. He worked until Thursday 28th March, which was the day before Good Friday and the mill would be closed until Monday; but he did not return to work on either Monday or Tuesday so the foreman went to Taylor's house and asked him to return and finish the piece, which Taylor refused to do. The foreman then gave Taylor formal notice to return to work, but Taylor had not done so. In evidence, Taylor said that he had been offered the time rate to weave the piece 'until he was stall'd,' and as no notice was required, when he was stall'd he left. Taylor's counsel argued that the initial contract ended when Taylor was offered the time rate, and therefore no period of notice was required; wages had been paid on the 28th, the start of the Bank Holiday and the end of that working week. The bench said that the offer of £1 a week had been 'quite an act of favour' to Taylor, and ordered him to return and finish the piece.

The firm gave a treat to all their workers at the Shoulder of Mutton New Mill, on Saturday 19 October 1872, when 200 men sat down to a substantial supper, and the 130 women enjoyed a knife and fork tea. The occasion was to celebrate Charles Lockwood's second son Arthur attaining his majority, the workers presented him with a gold Albert, chain and seal.

In 1885, Charles Lockwood leased part of the New mill to his sons Arthur Lockwood, Charles Markham Lockwood and Bernard Ambrose Lockwood, on a yearly basis at a rent of £600 per year. The agreement contained a stipulation that the building should be kept in good repair, and that the outside should be pointed and painted every three years. The agreement also contains a schedule of plant and machinery with a total value of £5,715 13s 7d. On the termination of the agreement an independent assessor was to be appointed to assess the value at that time. Any shortfall was to be made good by the sons. Insurance documents for all the mill buildings and the machinery dated 25 December 1886 show that the buildings were insured for £4,028, while the plant and machinery was insured for a total of £9,028. The new firm traded as Charles Lockwood & Sons; giving a treat to their 43 workpeople in January 1888.

The mill was built on the left bank of New Mill dike, where the land gradually rises towards Greenhill Bank, the road to Totties and Scholes. Part of the rising ground had been dug away to accommodate a weaving shed, so that a good part of the shed's back wall was below ground level. At the top of the rising ground was a row of houses that fronted onto Greenhill Bank, with a grass slope between the houses and the mill. These houses, whose back doors opened onto the sloping ground, also belonged to Charles Lockwood. For some undefined reason, the drive shaft for the fast looms inside the shed ran along the outside of the back wall, fully exposed and about 28 to 30 inches above ground level and some 22 inches away from the wall.[3]

A family, also called Lockwood, lived in one of the houses; the mother was Mary Ann Lockwood, a 45 year old widow who had seven children. On Monday 23 April 1888, two of the children Eliza Ann aged 12 or 13, and Lilly 10, were playing at 'Pig and Stick' on the sloping ground. One of them hit the Pig so that it struck the back wall of the weaving shed and dropped to the ground between the rotating shaft and the shed. Lilly went to retrieve it and her clothes became caught on the shaft, twisting her round and round; Eliza went to help her sister, but she also became caught on the shaft. Mrs. Lockwood ran to try to free her daughters and she too became caught by the shafting.

The shafting was stopped and Lilly was the first to be released, her injuries were slight. Eliza and her mother were freed by cutting their clothing, all three were then carried into their home, where Doctors Hornblower, Morehouse and Trotter attended to their injuries before they were transferred to Huddersfield Infirmary, Mrs. Lockwood and Eliza were taken in a spring cart, while Lilly was taken in a cab. They were accompanied by Dr. Hornblower, and Mrs. Lockwood's eldest daughter. Mrs. Lockwood was unconscious, but Eliza talked throughout the journey, which took about 1½ hours. Mrs. Lockwood, whose face and head had come into contact with the roof and wall of the weaving shed, died at 2am the following day without having regained consciousness; Eliza Ann, whose left hand had been severed above the wrist, her right leg broken in several places, and had many bruises covering her body, died several hours after her mother at 11am the same morning. They were subsequently buried at Linthwaite Church. Lilly, whose injuries were less severe, was expected to make a recovery.

At the inquest, Lockwood's maintained that the land behind the weaving shed was mill property, and was not a recreation area for the residents of the houses. Mr. Prior the Factory Inspector read the relevant part of the Factory Act: 'every part of the mill gearing shall either be securely fenced, or of such construction to be equally safe to every person employed in the factory as if it were securely fenced'. Mr. Meller the solicitor who was representing the firm, said that the shaft did not need to be fenced as no-one employed at the mill ever went near it. Mr. Prior said that he had ordered that the shafting be fenced off. The inquest jury said that they considered that the shafting should have been boxed in when it had been erected six months previously; despite this, they returned the usual verdict of 'accidental death'.

Ben Ainley discovered a fire in the stove in January 1890, he raised the alarm and workmen using the mill's own fire engine pumped water from the dam to extinguish it. Damage was estimated at around £30. Two more tragedies occurred on the 17 August 1894: Ben Booth a wool grinder aged 58, returned home at ten past eleven in the evening, and went to the closet at the back of the house. When he did not return his son went to look for him and noticed that the rail between the closet and the mill dam was lying on the grass. He informed PC Wincup, and they found Mr. Booth's body in the mill dam; there were no marks of violence on the body. The jury found that Mr. Booth had died accidentally, and recommended that a proper fence should be erected. On the same day, William Castle aged 40 a woollen weaver at the mill, was found hanged at home. Mrs. Castle said that she had left him in bed that morning as he was not going to work, and would have a lie in. About 11.20am she sent their son to wake his father, he came running back downstairs saying that his father had hung himself. She knew of no reason for her husband to be depressed, but added that both his brothers had had to be watched through depression. The jury returned a verdict of 'death by hanging, with no evidence to show the deceased's state of mind at the time'.

Business was very difficult in the 1880s and 90s; in 1899 Chas. Lockwood & Sons machinery was advertised for sale 'due to declining business', there was a considerable quantity of it: 10 condenser sets, 6prs. mules, 4 twisting frames, plus a range of machines for preparing worsted yarn; 18 fast looms and 36 slow looms; a range of machinery for wet and dry finishing; and for dyeing loose wool as well as spun yarn.

The mill was offered for sale by auction on 30 May 1905, but was withdrawn as bidding failed to reach the reserve. The 25 inch O.S. map of 1906 marks the mill as 'disused'. The premises were again offered for sale in May 1906 when they were described as: A 5 storey mill 72ft by 42ft; weaving shed 73ft 6in by 63ft 6in; 3 storey fulling mill 59ft by 27ft; 2 storey finishing mill; double shed, willey shed, tentering shed, dyehouse etc. 2 boilers, fuel economisers, condensing beam engine with a 24ft flywheel.

The mill was eventually bought by Moorhouse and Brook Ltd. who changed its name to Moorbrook mill. They are listed in the *Yorkshire Textile Directory* for 1912 as manufacturers of plain and twill Vicunas, dress coatings, serges etc. with 2,000 spindles and 80 looms. They also had premises in Bradford. The company made various alterations to the premises, installing a new mill engine, which was named 'Marjorie' by Miss Marjorie Moorhouse, daughter of F.W. Moorhouse. An innovation in 1918 was the installation of an 'open air dining room' on the premises. The firm said that they would stop the mill engine twice a day for 20 minutes each time to allow workers the opportunity for rest and relaxation in the open air. They thought that this would lead to a happier and healthier workforce, reducing the amount of productivity lost due to illness.

A fire broke out in the boiler room at the mill in the early hours of Sunday 24 August 1947. Mr. A.E. Creswell a passing motorist noticed smoke coming from the boiler house at 3am. He went to a telephone box and 'phoned the fire brigade, and then went to a house across from the mill where he saw a light. Mrs. Rosie Turton told him where Mr. Arnold Beaumont the mill manager lived and Mr. Creswell went and woke him up. Before fire brigades from Holmfirth and Huddersfield arrived, the boiler house roof had collapsed, but the fire did not spread to any other buildings. The boiler flues had been cleaned out on the Saturday afternoon and evening, and there was a large container of soot in the room, but this was not the cause of the fire. Employees worked throughout Sunday clearing up the debris, supported with food and drinks by nearby residents. The boiler was not badly damaged, and normal work was able to resume on the Thursday morning. The report offers no suggestion as to the cause of the fire.

Various renovations, alterations and extensions were carried out during the 1950s and '60s, including new buildings for the teazing, winding and warping departments, installation of an electricity sub-station, reconstruction of the old mill, and a new wool store.

Vandals throwing stones smashed 8 roof lights on 4 February 1983, causing damage to the value of £640. Fire broke out in the dry finishing department during the small hours of 26 April 1988. The alarm was raised by police at 1.30am, and 50 firemen from Holmfirth, Huddersfield, Skelmanthorpe and Dewsbury fought the blaze, preventing it from spreading to other parts of the mill; although the dry finishing department would be unable to function for some time to come. The resulting damage was estimated at £500,000. The cause of the blaze was thought to be an electrical fault.

A company using the name Yorklyde were using the mill in 1999; they were described as 'an upmarket textile group' making fine cloths, scarves and travel rugs from wool, cashmere and camel hair. The Company Chairman was Mr. Charles Brook; they had other premises in Sowerby Bridge, three factories in Scotland and one in Newton Abbot, Devon. Nationally they employed 450 people, but were finding business difficult and were trying to reorganise with the minimum of redundancies.[4] The mill has recently been completely demolished and replaced by housing.

Lydgate mill

Situated on the Holmfirth to New Mill road, virtually opposite Lydgate Chapel, this mill was built in the later part of the nineteenth century. The earliest occupant of the mill that has come to light is in March 1897. This was Herbert Hinchliffe, who was described as a Woollen Waste Opener, making Shoddy and Mungo from waste. Herbert's brother George Hinchliffe aged 18, was cleaning a Garnet machine on Friday 19th, while the large drum, known as the Swift, was in motion. George's fingers became caught between the Swift and one of the smaller rollers called the Fancy crushing them. He was taken to the Infirmary where his fingers were amputated but, as with Charles Whitehead at Ford Mill, Lockjaw set in and he died on the 24th. At the Inquest, Tom Hinchliffe, another brother, said that it was necessary to have the Swift in motion while cleaning the machine. The jury returned the verdict that 'the deceased had died from injuries accidentally received'.

The mill was advertised to let in June 1901, suitable for a Mungo manufacturer, with boiler, engine and shafting, along with a house, a large garden, six acres of land, plus stabling and hay loft. Rent would be about £60. Application should be made to J.W. Mellor or W.J. Lockwood, at Lydgate. The advertisement was repeated in January 1902.

The *Yorkshire Textile Directory* records the occupants of the mill in 1910 as Albert Mallinson &

Sons, manufacturers of Linsey aprons, shirtings, skirtings etc. Their last entry in the Directory is in 1920, but the mill was advertised in April 1919 to be sold by auction, when the tenants are given as Taylor Brothers; and Mr. Sam Tinker, with part unoccupied. The mill was bought for £730 by an unnamed buyer. The *YTD* for 1920 shows that Wimpenny & Co. Ltd. were occupying space in this mill in addition to Holme Bottom mill; their last entry in the directory was in 1926. Graham & Pott Ltd. expanded into this mill during the late 1920s and early '30s, but in May 1935 they asked the council for a reduction in their rates as Lydgate mill had been closed and empty since 7 March.[5] An entry in the *YTD* for 1967 lists D. & R. England (Hudds) Ltd. as occupants of the mill. They had 200 looms and were making fine worsted suitings and trouserings; there are no subsequent entries for them.

Moorcroft / Holme Bottom mill

This mill stood between New Mill dike and Huddersfield Road on the New Mill side of the junction with Holme Lane. Constructed in the early 1790s an advertisement in the *Leeds Mercury* in July 1794 offered the mill 'To let for a term of years and can be entered immediately'. It went on to describe the mill as 'All that new erected scribbling mill situate and being at Moorcroft in Holmfirth', with 3 double scribbling engines, 3 carding engines, 2 slubbing billies and a teazer for mixing wool. The mill is well supplied with water and the building and machinery nearly new. Three stocks could be connected to the water wheel for the milling of cloth. The building was 59ft long, 31ft wide, 4 storeys high. Application was to be made to Mr. Thomas Morehouse of Moorcroft who will show the premises. The mill was built and owned by the Morehouse family of Stoney Bank; John Morehouse of Stoney Bank passed, on his death in 1826, a one-third share in Moorcroft mill to his daughter Mary Elizabeth Morehouse Hobson, of Mitham Bridge.

George Morehouse who lived in Moorcroft, died in 1836, leaving his one-third share in the mill to his [apparently illegitimate] son George Morehouse Hebblethwaite. The mill was occupied at that time by Joseph Roberts, also William, John and Joseph Hirst. Later in that year the Hirst family seem to have relinquished their tenure of the mill as it was leased for a term of 21 years to Joseph Roberts clothier, of Holmroyd Nook Honley; Jonathon Brook engineer, of Paddock; John Roebuck clothier, of Totties; Thomas Crookes clothier, of Miry Lane Bottom; and Joshua Booth clothier, of New Mill. The owners of the mill at that time are given as John Hobson of Mytholmbridge, who was the husband of Mary Elizabeth Morehouse; Cookson Stephenson Floyd and Mary his wife of Thorp Heys; and George Morehouse Hebblethwaite known as George Morehouse; in addition to the mill, the lease included a cottage at the mill and 2,000sq.yds of land.

George Morehouse Hebblethwaite passed the use of Moorcroft House and its 24 acres of land to Sydney Morehouse of Fulstone in 1839, for a term of 21 years. George died the following year, and in his will he left the house to Sydney Morehouse; leaving his one-third share in the mill to Cookson Stephenson Floyd. This entry in the Court Rolls names the mill as 'Moorcroft mill also known as Holme Bottom mill'.

In 1842 John Hobson of Mytholmbridge sold his one-third share in Holme Bottom mill to Thomas Iveson of Holmfirth for £100; the occupants of the mill at that time were virtually the same as in 1836, except that Jonathon Brook has been replaced by Jonathon Booth. Francis and Jarvis Roebuck were occupying part of the mill in 1848, but were in financial difficulties, as in February of that year they assigned all their goods to the benefit of their creditors.

A fire was discovered at the mill on 7 March 1851, by a man passing through New Mill who smelled burning, and traced it to the stove at the mill. He went to the White Hart Inn and got the 30 or 40 people in there to help him to put the fire out by throwing buckets and cans of water into the building. The hot iron floor of the stove turned the water into steam, which helped to put out the fire in about 20 minutes. The mill which was owned by 'a company of proprietors' was insured; but, due to an oversight, the stove was not. About 250lbs of wool was damaged or destroyed.

The Reservoir Commissioners give the owners of the mill in 1853 as Cookson Stephenson Floyd, and Mr. & Mrs. George Smirthwaite; the occupiers were Joseph Roberts, Jonathon Booth, John

Roebuck and Joshua Booth. The mill was advertised 'to let' in July and September 1857, described as a commodious fulling and scribbling mill with a steam engine and boiler, and some machinery; Joshua Booth was still using part of the mill. It was still to let in December 1858.

A one third share in the mill was advertised for sale in September 1866, the occupants of the mill at that time were John and William Hirst, who held a 19 year lease from 1 October 1862. A fire was discovered at the mill about 3am on Tuesday 9 Nov. 1869, the alarm was given and efforts were made to douse the flames, but without success. Fire engines from Holmfirth and Thongsbridge attended but they were unfortunately unable to save the building; the roof and floors of the four storey mill collapsed but left the walls standing. The occupant of the mill was John Hirst who was a yarn spinner; damage was estimated at £2,500, and was only partly covered by insurance. The cause of the fire was not known. A salvage sale of machinery was advertised to take place in February 1870, including the high pressure horizontal steam engine that had been slightly damaged, a steam boiler with safety valve, and metal plates and beams that were probably the remains of the stove. The owner of the property was Mrs. Cookson Stephenson Floyd of Holmfirth.

The mill and machinery were advertised for sale in October 1881, the sale was held on 12 October. Lot 1 was the rebuilt mill, reservoir and goits occupied by John Seddon, with steam engine, boiler and water wheel; along with 5 60inch condenser sets, 5prs mules, plus a willow and other machines for manufacturing yarn. The buildings had been erected within the last six years, and the steam engine, boiler and shafting were new. The advertisement also pointed out that the mill was near to local collieries. Lot 2 comprised 4 cottages at Town End, occupied by Alfred Cartwright, Lydia Greaves, Mrs. Kaye, and one unoccupied. The mill does not appear to have been sold, as it was offered again in July 1882.

John Seddon was still using at least part of the mill in 1882, but had fallen on hard times as a sale of his stock of some 20,000lbs of yarn, wool, shoddy, mungo, flocks, cotton etc. along with tools and other sundries, was ordered to be held on 9 May by his assignees. He did not go out of business immediately, as his assignees ordered the sale of his machinery to be held on 28 July 1882, which consisted of the condenser sets, spinning mules and willow mentioned earlier, along with a Fearnought, a cotton breaker with dust tin and pipe, a pattern loom and a warping woof and creel.

In 1883 the mill was again advertised 'to let' in August of that year, anyone interested should apply to S. Wimpenny, Auctioneer. The mill was then advertised for sale in October 1883; one of its attributes being that it was 'a short distance from collieries'. The mill was bought by the Tinker family of Hepworth, with Mr. Henry Thorp as a partner. Beaumont, Son & Co. were renting at least part of the mill in 1888 when they offered to carry out some manufacturing for Jonathon Thorp's of Dobroyd mill after their disastrous fire in August.

A company called Halstead & Co. were using the mill in 1895; in April of that year they asked the Fulstone Local Board for permission to use mains water for manufacturing. The board would not permit that but, in September, they offered to allow Halstead's to use the surplus water from the reservoir at a cost of one shilling per thousand gallons. This was presumably the water that ran down the reservoir's overflow, as it was pointed out to Halstead's that it would not be available when the level of the reservoir dropped; whether Halstead's agreed to this arrangement is not recorded. The board seem to have monitored the situation however, as in September 1897 they recorded their anger and dismay when they found that Halstead's had been using the mains water supply to fill their boiler between March and September.[6] The *Textile Manufacturer* recorded in February 1898 that the partnership between William Halstead, William Shaw, Thomas H. Rayner and James Halstead, trading as Halstead & Co. yarn spinners, had been dissolved. The company reappeared as Shaw, Rayner & Sykes later in the year.

Fire broke out in Feb. 1903, damage about £200. Some space in the mill was advertised as being to let in 1905. A fire was discovered at the mill at 12.15 midday on 5 February 1907. It was put out by workpeople with the help of workers from Kirkbridge mill. Damage was estimated at between £150 and £200. The *Yorkshire Textile Directory* of 1910 lists Shaw Rayner & Sykes as spinners of Woollen, Angola and Drugget yarns; they also undertook commission spinning on their 2,780 spindles. The name of the company changes to T.H. Rayner & Sons in the 1915 directory.

Thomas Rayner bought the mill in 1916; Bamforth & Booth, plus other companies were tenants in the mill along with T.H. Rayner & Sons in 1917. The Wimpenny name reappears at the mill in 1920 as Wimpenny & Co. Ltd, manufacturers of woollens, costumes and mantlings. The *Yorkshire Textile* Directory for that year shows that they had taken over the spinning plant of 2,780 spindles from T.H. Rayner & Sons, and had installed 30 looms. The directory also contains the last entry for Rayner's. Wimpenny's were using this mill, along with Lydgate mill until 1926; after they left the mill was probably empty for some time, as the 25inch O.S. map of 1932 marks the mill as 'disused'.

Dobroyd Mills Co. Ltd. were using this mill solely for storing wool from at least 1936, with all the processing being carried out at Dobroyd. This continued until around 1960, when it was decided that the mill's chimney would have to be demolished as it was unsafe.[7] The survey carried out by the Royal Commission for Historical Monuments in 1985 noted at that time that the mill had also been demolished and the stone reused to construct houses.

Kirkbridge mill

There were eventually three mills in this area, the first mill stood on the eastern side of Kirkbridge Lane, between the lane and the river. The earliest mention of the mill comes in the Wakefield Court Roll of 1732, although it had possibly been in existence for some years before that. The owner of the mill at that time was Abraham Radcliffe of Almondbury, who also owned Mytholmbridge Upper mill, and property at Wooldale Townend. The occupant of the mill, which was used for 'grinding wood', was Joseph Battye. Radcliffe let the mill to Joshua Wilson of Holmfirth for 21 years from 2 February 1733.

Kirkbridge mill. © A.J. Brooke

The 1794 roll records that the owner of the mill at that time was Thomas Radcliffe of Georgetown, South Carolina, who on 1 May 1795, passed the use of the water mill for rasping, grinding and chipping of Dyeing wood, known as Kirkbridge mill with its dams, goits, wheels, wheel-races, grinding stocks, rasping and chipping engines, to George Armitage of Honley and James Harrop of Holmfirth, along with the dwelling house, garden and two crofts. This mill formed part of the large holding of property and land that included Mytholmbridge mill, also owned by Thomas Radcliffe. The object of the mill was to prepare the roots and/or wood from several plants that were used to provide the colours with which to dye wool or cloth.

The *Leeds Mercury* advertised the sale of a moiety or half share in the mill, which was occupied by Robson and Harrop, on 4 October 1800. This was possibly bought by Marley Hobson a drysalter, of Scotland Road Liverpool; recorded in the Wakefield Court Roll in April 1803.

The Reservoir Commissioners record the owners of the mill in 1853 as the Trustees of Charles Radcliffe deceased, and others; and the occupants of the mill as Joseph and Samuel Mellor. The mill had by then become a conventional woollen mill, and the Mellors' were also occupying Upper Mytholmbridge mill.

The premises were to be extended further when a co-operative venture eventually set up their business. A meeting was held at National School New Mill on 1 April 1861, attended by 300 to 400 people, to discuss forming a company to spin cotton yarn to be run on the basis of a co-operative. There were a number of co-operative ventures already established in Lancashire, which had taken their inspiration from the formation of the Rochdale Pioneer Co-operative Society that was established in that town in 1844. One of the first speakers was a Mr. Mellor of Ripponden who described how a company formed on similar lines was prospering in his area. The name of the new company would be the New Mill Cotton Spinning Company (Limited). Mr. William Moorhouse (coal merchant) proposed that the company should have a working capital of £30,000, made up from the sale of 6,000 £5 shares; this mirrored the financial model of at least one other co-operative venture already in existence. The proposal was seconded by Mr. Eli Moorhouse manufacturer, and supported by Mr. Paterson also of Ripponden, who was able to give much information on the rise, progress and prosperity of similar companies already established in the Rochdale area. A subscription list was opened, to which at least one hundred people subscribed for shares in the venture.

An advertisement inviting people to buy £5 shares in the new company appeared in the *Huddersfield Examiner* on 20 April 1861. It was not necessary to pay for the shares outright, they could be bought over a period by paying a minimum of 2s 6d per share each month. Shareholders and anyone interested in the company were requested to attend a meeting at New Mill National School on 1 June at 5pm when the proposed rules and regulations of the company would be read, discussed and passed. In the meantime, a meeting was held at New Mill on 3 May to appoint a board of Directors for the new company; Mr. Crosland said that it was necessary to elect people who had the experience to enable them to carry out their obligations. The President was Mr. John Mills Preston; the other members of the board were Joseph Roberts, Thomas Crosland, William Greaves, William John Morehouse, William Holden, John Seddon, Arthur Bennett and Sydney Jubb. Mr. Paterson of Ripponden said that it had been found in other companies being run on similar lines that there was a diminishing of class prejudice, and that the workpeople would have a better insight into the costs and difficulties encountered in business that should reduce, if not eradicate, the number of strikes. A meeting was held in Holmfirth on 23 May, when those attending were told that it was the new company's intention to build a mill in Holmfirth at some time in the future; although it was initially necessary to establish the first one at New Mill.

At the meeting in New Mill on 1 June it was announced that 800 shares had been taken up. The main business was the discussion of the proposed rules of the company. The one that led to a prolonged discussion was the distribution of profits; this was so protracted that the meeting was adjourned to be reconvened a week later. Some thought that 10 percent of profits should be paid to shareholders, and the remaining 90 percent should be placed as capital in the company, to the benefit of the workers. It was suggested that this would ensure a constant supply of good workmen, would encourage the production of provident habits, and would give workers the opportunity to become shareholders in the company in their own right. Others were afraid that unless the shareholders had all the profits, the shares would not be taken up. After a two hour discussion it was decided that 'the workers should be content with "permanent employment and good wages", and that the shareholders should get all the profits – great or small'. The President, Mr. Preston, said that they were looking for a site on which they could build their mill so that production could commence.

A meeting was held in Honley on 20 June, when the audience were told that the company envisaged eventually building mills in Holmfirth and Honley, in addition to the one in New Mill. It was also announced that the co-operative now had 600 members, and a capital of almost £12,000. At a meeting at New Mill National School on 28 June, Mr. Preston said that they had received details of several sites for the mill, the two favourite sites were Kirkroyds and Kirkbridge. The newspaper reported that the majority at the meeting were in favour of Kirkroyds; this was followed within days by a correction saying that the majority actually preferred Kirkbridge.

A meeting at Holmfirth on 9 August was told that Friendly Societies were looking to cooperatives as being good businesses for investing their capital, as they felt that the returns from such ventures were greater. At a meeting in Honley in late August, Mr. Preston said that almost half the required capital of £30,000 had now been subscribed. The company also had a branch in Thurlstone collecting money for shares. They held a soiree in New Mill on 30 December 1861, when some 300 people took tea. Mr. Bennett urged people to support the company, pointing out the benefits to working people to be had from cooperation. Mr. J. Woodhead of Huddersfield sounded a cautionary note by pointing out the scarcity of raw cotton due to the American Civil War; which was to continue until 1865.

Trade for all branches of the textile industry proved to be extremely difficult over the next few years, particularly for cotton, as America in addition to being one of Britain's principal markets, was also the premier source of supply; although business did gradually improve as imports from sources of raw cotton, other than America, increased. An indication of the affect that the American Civil War had on Britain's cotton industry can be had from an article in the *Huddersfield Chronicle* in May 1862, which reported that the Lancashire mills normally employed about 300,000 people, of which, at that time, 50,000 were unemployed and 200,000 were on short time, with little prospect of an early improvement in their circumstances. Questions were asked in Parliament; the headline for an article in the *Huddersfield Chronicle* in June 1862 asked 'What is to be done to get cotton?', as there was little immediate prospect of increasing the amounts of cotton being grown in India and elsewhere.

Special collections were taken in churches and chapels to help desperate families in Lancashire, which were repeated in November of that year. Unsurprisingly, announcements from, and meetings of, the Newmill Cotton Spinning Company were non-existent until 1866, when they held a ceremony at Kirkbridge mill to mark the laying of the foundation stone for the new premises. This was carried out by the then President Mr. S. Wimpenny, Auctioneer, of Holmfirth, with an engraved Silver trowel and Mahogany mallet. He said that the depression in trade, the American Civil War and the cotton famine had prevented them making the progress that they had originally expected. They had bought 2 acres of land on the western side of Kirkbridge Lane opposite the original mill, and a number of cottages at Kirkbridge. After the ceremony the Wooldale Band led a procession to the National School in Sudehill, where 500 people took tea.

It was reported that the company had 300 paying members at that time. The premises, which were the second mill in the district to be built for processing cotton fibre rather than wool, were completed during the following year; but it does not seem that NMCSCo ever used them, as an advertisement appeared in the *Huddersfield Examiner* on 20 July 1867, for Room and Power to let at Kirkbridge, with a large shed 100ft by 82ft; upper room 24ft6in x 82ft; low room 24ft x 72ft; willey room 15ft x 30ft; scouring room 9ft x 30ft; drying room over boiler, and if required a warehouse, and a room suitable for a dyehouse with a good supply of water. Mr. Mellor, who was using the original mill, would show the premises. For rent etc. apply to Mr. S. Wimpenny, Auctioneer, Holmfirth. This advertisement ran weekly until 7 September, but with little, if any, success.

The premises were advertised for sale in October 1868, with the addition of an Engine House with a steam engine partly fixed and a steam boiler, plus a warehouse offices and outbuildings. Also 3 cottages occupied by Jonathon Holmes, Richard Littlewood and Samuel Barden. At the auction on 21 October, the highest bid was £1,750, whereas the total cost of the premises was £3,300. £2,800 of shares had been taken up by prospective shareholders, of which £2,000 had already been subscribed. The mill was advertised for sale again in June 1869 and in May 1870, but did not sell.

After the failure of the third attempt, the newspaper reported that two £5 shares in the company changed hands for the price of 'a glass of drink', the type of drink was not specified. The report continued: 'It has been said more than once that "the Devil has got his feet amongst this Kirkbridge business". If that is true it argues well for the cause, as we know from good authority that Satan is not likely to work against himself'. A notice appeared in the *Huddersfield Examiner* in November 1870, asking all creditors of the company to forward details of amounts owing to them to either Mr. S. Wimpenny Auctioneer of Holmfirth, or Mr. Samuel Wibberley, cloth finisher of Hinchliffe Mill, who was the liquidator, before 1 January 1871. The outcome must have been satisfactory to the majority of creditors at least, as there were no formal bankruptcy proceedings.

The Mellor family continued to occupy the original mill into the 1860s; in 1864 Hugh Mellor decided to give up the yarn business and his unwanted machinery was advertised to be sold on 15 August, consisting of: 1 scribbling engine, 1 carder, 1 nearly new piecing machine, 1 billey, 1 mule, and 2,000lbs of wool and cotton mixed ready for Angola yarn. Mr. Mellor was in partnership with Jonathon Moorhouse as Mungo dealers, this came to an end on 1 October of the same year.

Henry Pontefract, whose primary place of business had been at Stoney Bank mill until 1860, then appears to have split his manufacturing between Smithy Place mill at Brockholes and Kirkbridge. He had a small amount of machinery at Kirkbridge, which was advertised to be sold on 6 May 1867, consisting of 1pr of mules, 1 billey and 1 willow.

John and Thomas Crosland, who were trading as John Crosland & Sons, yarn spinners, were using the mill by 1872, when Jane Castle aged 14 worked for them as a piecer. She was cleaning a machine on the morning of 8 February when the second finger of her left hand became caught in moving cogs and was amputated. She was taken to Huddersfield Infirmary for treatment. Crosland's had bought a feeding machine from David Horsfall, machine maker of Crosland Moor. Crosland's refused to pay for the machine for seven months and then asked Horsfall to take the machine away as it did not meet their expectations. Horsfall took them to court to enforce payment and won the case. Crosland's had run into financial difficulties by June 1883, and were in liquidation in September of that year when their machinery was put up for sale, consisting of: 5 condenser sets, 4prs hand mules, 1 shake willey, 1 tenter-hook willey, 1 waste cleaner; dye cisterns, hydro extractor, wringing machine, and 6,750lbs of yarn.

The premises were put up for sale on 18 June 1885, as Lot 22 in the auction of property that had been owned by Thomas Radcliffe. The mill, cottages and land were bought by Mr. F. Learoyd for £400, who also paid £85 for Lot 23, a plot of land across New Mill dike from the mill. The mill was again offered for sale by auction on 7 September 1886, but was withdrawn due to lack of interest. Allen Hinchliffe was the occupier of the premises in both years, but his tenancy appears to have ended by March 1887 when the mill was advertised to let.[8]

The incoming tenant was probably Edwin Holmes a twine manufacturer, who bought the mill, and subsequently sold it with its steam engine, boiler, water wheel, reservoir, yard, dwelling houses and 3roods 31 perches of land to Robert Walker a farmer of Pell Lane Wooldale for £350. Robert died on 25 October 1894, leaving the mill to his brother Edward Walker. Edward died on 9 October 1895, leaving the mill to his son Joseph, who took possession of it on 14 February 1896.

Graham and Barnfather became tenants of the mill in 1889, two Ledgers are held in Kirklees Archive department showing details of the machinery that they bought and giving its cost prices; the catalogue numbers are KC501/12 and 13. Amongst this machinery were 6 Sowden looms at £42 each, and two slow looms at £10 each; these they sold in 1895 making an overall loss of £50 on the Sowden looms, and a loss of £8 10s on the two slow looms, but they had used them all for at least five years.

The firm's weavers went on strike on 18 March 1890 and asked the Weavers Association for help to settle the dispute. Graham and Barnfather had been setting up their business at Kirkbridge and looking for weavers at the same time that F. Turner & Sons were giving up their business at Bridge mill, consequently the weavers moved *en masse* from one firm to the other. Turner's had lowered weavers wages when work was scarce, promising to raise them when orders improved. Graham & Barnfather employed the weavers at the lower rates, and continued to do so despite a rising market and other manufacturers increasing wage rates. Mr. Gee of the W.A. contacted the firm on behalf of the weavers and resolved the problem. The following week the *Yorkshire Factory Times* reported that the matter was settled, but added a cautionary note by saying that work may not always be as plentiful as it was at present, and that if employers found in the future that they again needed to cut their prices it was likely that wages would also be reduced.

Graham & Barnfather sued France, Eastwood & Co cloth finishers of Brockholes for £15 10s 2d The dispute was referred to Mr. J.H. Kaye of Kaye & Crowther of Longwood, who found that £11 5s 7d was due to Graham & Barnfather, but that this should be reduced to £6 19s 6d, as a piece of cloth valued at £4 6s 1d had been returned to Graham & Barnfather by France, Eastwood's. A counter claim was submitted by France, Eastwood & Co for £16 7s 2d, but Mr. Kaye found that only 13s 9d of this was actually owing. Judgement was entered in accordance with these findings, and, in addition, costs were awarded against France, Eastwood & Co.

Edwin Holmes was still using part of the mill, and had also constructed a rope walk on the flat ground across the dike from the mill. Graham & Barnfather submitted plans to New Mill Local Board in 1897 to build a new finishing room, and in the following year Edwin Holmes applied to build a new shed at the mill. Mr. Prior, the Factory Inspector, took John Holmes rope and twine manufacturer, to court in August 1894 for employing children under 18 without having a surgeon's certificate. Lister Ramsden aged 14 and Fred Bailey aged 13 had been employed at the rope works since 19 August 1893, but did not have surgeon's certificates. Mr. Prior then went to the recently erected Tenterhill mill round the corner in Tenterhill Lane, where he found Martha Bailey, Eunice Kaye and Hugh Holmes working at Stanley Rug Co, also owned by John Holmes, without surgeon's certificates. Mr. J.H Bentley of Kidd & Bentley Solicitors appeared for Mr. Holmes; he said that Mr. Holmes employed formen who were responsible for attending to 'matters of detail' such as surgeon's certificates. Mr. Prior pointed out to the bench that it was the employer who held the responsibility of obtaining the certificates. The bench imposed fines of 5s plus 11s 6d costs in each case; a total of £4 2s 6d.

A fire started in the rope works about 8pm on Monday 13 November 1899, caused by a lighted candle falling over and setting fire to yarn while the manager Hubert Holmes, and John Lockhead an employee, were examining the yarn. While efforts were made to put out the fire using buckets of water, the church bell was rung to alert local fire brigades. The Holmfirth Council brigade arrived about an hour after the fire had started and ran out a hose, but they had little to do as the bucket line had been very successful. The Unity brigade and the brigade from Bridge mill also attended, but were not needed. Damage, which was not insured was estimated to be around £100.

Joseph Walker sold the mill for £180 on 23 May 1905 to Arthur Lockwood, son of Charles Lockwood, who had owned New Mill mill and Lee mill. Arthur then sold it to Hiram Haigh, who owned the Queen Carriage Company, Zetland Street, Huddersfield for £125 in 1908.

Wright Hinchliffe & Co. who were dyers, moved into the dyeworks at Kirkbridge in 1907, they were undertenants of Graham & Barnfather, to whom they paid £100 a year rent. There is a letter in the file at Kirklees Archive detailing the repairs and renewals carried out by Hinchliffe's from 1909 to the end of 1911. New Mill council were surprised, to say the least, when they discovered in 1915 that Wright Hinchliffe & Co. had been using mains water free of charge for all their dyeing processes, which they had obtained via Graham & Barnfather. Hinchliffe's then moved from Kirkbridge to the dyehouse at Prickleden, Holmfirth, which, by then, had been renamed Valley Dyeworks.

H.H. Seddon was using the dyeworks in 1916 and 17, in addition to their premises in Lockwood, but this appears to have been a temporary arrangement. Graham & Barnfather had become Graham & Pott Ltd. by 1917, and were making fancy worsted suitings, coatings, trouserings and serges on their 58 looms. The 1918 edition of the 25inch O.S. map shows that the original mill on the east side of Kirkbridge Lane had disappeared along with the rope-walk. In 1918 Stocks & Mallinson had moved from the dyehouse at Lords mill Honley, to Kirkbridge Dyeworks, and were there until 1925.

An entry in the Minute Book of the local branch of the National Union of Textile Workers records on 23 January 1923 that Messrs J. Eagleton had employed a union member without having first made an application to the union; the entry does not record what action, if any, was taken by either the union or the employer.

Graham & Pott Ltd. added a yarn shed to the mill in 1927, and submitted an application to the Council to build new offices and a press room in 1928; E. Holroyd & Son of The Banks, Honley, submitted an estimate for building the office and press room of £950 excluding heating and interior decorating. As this estimate was preserved, they were probably the successful applicants.

Although trade in the 1930s started very slowly, as discussed in Chapter 5, things apparently improved for Graham & Pott as, in addition to Kirkbridge, they were also using Reliance Works on Penistone Road and Lydgate mill for a time. There were two robberies at the mill in the late 1940s, early 1950s. An unspecified amount of cloth was stolen in 1949 valued at £2,000; and two years later in 1951 65 pieces were stolen on 27 May, valued at £12,000.

Employees were given redundancy notices in January 1968, the firm was part of the Lancashire and Yorkshire Tulketh Group, and production was to be moved to Wellington Mills, Oakes; with the offices moving to Crowther & Vickerman at Crosland Moor. It was expected that the changes would have taken place by early March.[9] The mill has since been demolished and replaced with housing.

Tenterhill mill

Built about 1890 by the Holmes family for manufacturing hearth rugs, this building stood in Tenterhill Lane virtually alongside Kirkbridge mill. It was a stone built 4 storey mill about 20yds long and 12yds wide. The ground floor was used for storing hemp and jute warps, woollen rags and finished twine from the rope works. The first floor was used for storing finished rugs; and the top two floors were weaving rooms. There was a mill dam built alongside Tenterhill and behind Kirkbridge that held water supplied by the stream that runs from Wooldale past Lydgate mill and these two mills on its way to join New Mill dike. John Holmes was trading from this mill as Stanley Rug Co. and, in common with other rug manufacturers, had difficulty in finding weavers to make 'pegged' or 'rag' rugs on handlooms. By 1898 they had been joined by another rug firm called Jubilee Rug Co. who were also advertising for weavers. They were using part of the mill until at least 1900, but there is no mention of them after that year.

On Wednesday 19 February 1902 a fire broke out at the mill. It was discovered by Mrs. Castle a waste sorter, on the ground floor of the mill at 7.15am. She raised the alarm and the 20 women weavers, who were working upstairs, hurriedly left the building. Mr. John Holmes had left earlier that morning to catch a train to Sheffield, but his son Hubert and the men from the rope works fought hard with buckets of water trying to extinguish the flames, but the fire had too firm a hold. Ben Lockwood had left the mill when the alarm was raised and arrived at Holmfirth fire station at 7.40am. Fireman Whitworth and two others set out immediately with hoses; they were apparently on foot, as they received a valuable lift from a horse belonging to Councillor Brook, allowing them to reach the mill before 8am. The nearest hydrant was some 300 yards from the mill, but the hoses were able to get water onto the flames. The Unity brigade, and the fire engine from Charles Moon's at Stoney Bank mill also attended, and took water from the mill dam but they were unable to save the building, the roof and part of the walls collapsed about 8.30am. The cause of the fire was thought to be either overheating of hemp warps placed on steam pipes to dry, or alternatively, spontaneous combustion in the bags of waste. Damage to buildings and stock was estimated at over £3,000, which was only partly covered by insurance. The mill appears to have been rebuilt in the same year, as an advertisement appeared in the *Holmfirth Express* in January 1903, offering two dwelling houses at Tenter Hill with outbuildings for sale by auction, one house was occupied by Mr. Edwin Holmes, the other had been lately occupied by Mrs. Sarah Morehouse, along with 13 closes of land. Also the rug weaving mill and warehouse occupied by Stanley Rug Co; and another 2 closes of land occupied by Jonathon Haigh. The auction took place on January 22nd, the whole sold for £1,350 to an unnamed buyer. The *Yorkshire Textile Directory* for 1911 records that the Stanley Rug Company also had premises at Orch mills Belinda Street Hunslet Leeds, Perseverance mill east Ardsley near Wakefield, and Corporation mill Marshgate, Doncaster. The last entry for the firm at Tenterhill mill was in 1931.[10]

Stoney Bank mill

In 1759 George Morehouse paid £390 to The Reverend John Stott of Horbury for Stoney Bank and nine closes of land, that were occupied at that time by Thomas Morehouse. Baines' *Yorkshire Directory* records that in 1822 a Thomas Morehouse, tanner was still living at Stoney Bank, but it may not have been the same person. The *Wakefield Court Roll* of 1826 lists the occupant of Stoney Bank mill as Thomas Morehouse, who passed 3 parts from a total of 4 parts in the mill to George Morehouse, Sarah Morehouse and John William Morehouse, who were presumably Thomas's brothers and sister.

Seven years later, in 1833, J.W. Morehouse passed his quarter share in the house plus the fulling and scribbling mill occupied by Jonas Hobson, to his daughter Ellen Elizabeth Morehouse on her 21st Birthday. The mill was some distance from the house, being beside New Mill dike; water was taken from the dike a few yards downstream of Kirk Bridge, and transferred to the mill via a long goit. White's Directory of 1838 gives Henry James Morehouse Surgeon and author of the *History of Kirkburton and the Graveship of Holme*; Thomas Morehouse Tanner, and William Jonathon Morehouse Scribbling Miller as being residents in the house; and John Mellor woollen manufacturer in the mill.

The mill was one of those visited by 'Plug Rioters' on 17 August 1842, who drained the mill's boiler by drawing the plug, and also opened the shuttles, emptying the mill dam so that the boiler could not be refilled. William John Morehouse possibly took a mortgage on the mill in 1844 from William Holt of Horbury; but he had stopped working the mill by 1849, when an advertisement appeared in the *Leeds Mercury* of 27 January offering the mill to let with immediate possession, and described it as being within 5 miles of Huddersfield, and close to a station on the Huddersfield and Holmfirth railway. The mill was 4 storeys high, having a water wheel with 30ft of fall and a large reservoir, also a 16hp steam engine; 7 fulling stocks, 2 washing machines and a dryer, 4 scribbling engines, 4 carders, 4 billeys and rooms for mules; also a dyehouse with 3 pans supplied with excellent spring water, and a coal pit within a hundred yards of the mill. Attached to the premises were one small dwelling house, 4 cottages and 3 acres of good land. The premises could be viewed by contacting Mr. J. Morehouse surgeon, of Stoney Bank, or Messrs. Bradley & Son land agents, of Richmond Yorkshire would supply any further particulars.

The new tenant was Henry Pontefract who, from the 1851 census returns, employed a total of 78 people, 60 men, 4 women, 10 boys and 4 girls. In 1852 Pontefract was summoned by John Bates of Winney Bank, Factory Inspector, for employing five young persons under 18 years of age after 6pm on 26 February. They were R. Robinson, Mary Schofield, Sarah Lockwood, Ann Lockwood and J. Richard Owen. Mr. Pontefract pleaded guilty; Mr. Bates said that he was prepared to abandon four of the five charges provided that the defendant was prepared to pay the expenses of those cases, and urged the bench to exact the maximum penalty of £5 plus costs on the fifth case. The bench

Stoney Bank mill. © A.J. Brooke

decided to impose a fine of £2, plus costs for all five, making a total of £5 9s. The Holme Reservoir Commissioners record the owners of the mill in 1853 as George Morehouse, William Jonathon Morehouse, also Thomas Bradley snr, and Christopher Lonsdale Bradley, who were probably the land agents in Richmond; the occupier was still Henry Pontefract.

A fire was discovered in the stove at the mill on 2 December 1853, the alarm was raised and a good number of people attempted to put out the flames using buckets and other utensils, but considerable damage was done to the building. It was thought that the fire could have resulted from recent cleaning of the boiler flues, allowing the stove to become overheated. No estimate of the damage was available. The report concludes: 'Where were all the long talked of Fire Engines?' The Reservoir Commissioners marked the mill as 'not rated' in 1854, but do not say why. It would possibly be due to the fire of the year before, as stoves were usually built over the boiler house in a building separated from the main mill, because of the possibility of fire; but could be due to the mill not working as repairs were not completed. There was a second fire in the stove discovered about 7am on Thursday 24 August 1854. On this occasion people with buckets were able to put out the flames before much damage was done, despite there being a large quantity of wool put to dry in the stove. Damage was estimated at between £15 and £20.

1856 brought the end of the Crimean War, a cause of much rejoicing throughout the country, and many manufacturers provided treats to their workers to mark the occasion. Mr. Jonathon Morehouse gave an (unspecified) amount of money, to which the workers added their 'proportion'. A meal was provided in a room at the Duke of Leeds Hotel in New Mill, where the men had 'a good substantial supper of Roast Beef and Plum Pudding'; and the women had 'an excellent tea'.

A haystack containing about 14 tons of hay belonging to Henry Pontefract caught fire on the evening of 28 August 1857. Again, a large number of people with buckets of water managed to put the fire out, but much of the unburned hay would only be fit for use as cattle bedding. It was thought that the hay had been stacked before it was properly dry, causing spontaneous combustion. The stack was valued at around £50.

By 1859 Henry Pontefract had entered into a partnership with James Richard Owen; they were trading as Pontefract & Owen. Was it possibly the same J. Richard Owen named as one of the five young persons who were working beyond their permitted hours in 1852, or perhaps his father? A fire was discovered at 2am on the morning of September 2ⁿᵈ 1859 by a woman living near the mill. The fire bell was rung bringing a large number of people to help and the Unity brigade was sent for, but the 4 storey mill was soon enveloped in a mass of flames. At 4am the roof fell in with a tremendous crash; the flames 'completely illuminating the sky' to the extent that it was visible from Huddersfield, where the Inspector of night police Ramsden White alerted the Lancashire & Yorkshire engine and Armitage Bros, but as no call for their services arrived they returned home. Several hours' later news that the mill had burned to the ground reached the town. The fire was thought to have started in woollen waste on the second floor; damage was estimated at between £4,000 and £5,000, not all of which was insured. The fire seems to have had a devastating effect on Henry Pontefract, ending his tenancy. The remnants of machinery and stock at the mill and also at the farm were advertised to be auctioned on 26 October. At the mill the amount of saleable machinery was small, there was 1 scribbler, 1 billey, 1pr mules, a rag shaking machine, a spiked willow, 1 pattern loom, a brushing mill, also dyewares, some sundries including 33 pieces of English Oak 12ft 6in long by 5½ inches by 6 inches for water wheel arms, 2 warping woofs with creels, 1 urine barrel on wheels, and 'a very neat Phaeton lined with brown plush'. There was also a large quantity of wrought and cast iron salvage from the fire. At the farm there were 8 milch cows 5 of which were in calf, a yearling stirk, a grey 4 year old Draught mare 16 hands, 2 narrow wheeled carts, a plough, harrow, straw chopper, turnip slicer, plus standing crops.

In November 1859 the entire premises were advertised for sale as the 'Stoney Bank Mill Estate', with a handsome newly erected family residence with lawns and gardens, plus the mill site and the materials remaining, which included some buildings not destroyed by the fire, and 12½ acres of land. The auction took place on 8 November, but the property was not sold. The house and mill were then offered for sale by private treaty as one Lot or two in April 1860, but do not appear to have sold as the owner of the property in November 1860 was still Mr. C.L. Bradley.

The mill must have become useable during 1860, as it was occupied, at least in part, in November of that year by George Hey. Another occupant by 1863 was Eli Wimpenny, who gave a treat for his 160 workpeople to celebrate the completion of the new 'spacious' mill. Access to the mill became restricted in early December 1865 due to a cart road to the mill being closed by debris after the collapse of the original railway viaduct between Brockholes and Thongsbridge. The viaduct was a wooden structure some 200 yards long and 90 feet high; work to replace it with stone had begun about a year previously, carried out by Wadsworth's of Holmfirth, with the line being kept open but operating a single track system over the viaduct. Thirteen stone pillars had been built and the timber supports removed on that part of the viaduct. On Saturday 2 December sixty to seventy men had been occupied building, plate laying, removing the old structure and other tasks, while 14 passenger trains and 1 goods train carrying 200 tons of coal had used the line. Around 5.45am on Sunday the 3ʳᵈ, William England a miller who lived at Scar End was awoken by the noise of the collapse. He described hearing a 'clap, clap, clap' as one stone pillar fell against the next throughout the length of the viaduct and, on looking out, seeing the valley filled with 'lime and smoke'. He and Abraham Littlewood ran to Brockholes Station to get them to stop any trains. Besides blocking the cart road, the debris also blocked the goit carrying water to Knutton's Corn mill at Mytholmbridge.

On Saturday 8 September 1866 a young man named Hoyle got his hand caught in the rollers of a condenser, badly mutilating it. He was taken to the Infirmary for treatment. Rebuilding the viaduct was a protracted task; it was not until the 19ᵗʰ of February 1867 that the first train, carrying goods, crossed it. The reopening of the line was initially set for March 1ˢᵗ, but was delayed until Monday March 11ᵗʰ, when despite heavy snow, hundreds of people gathered at Holmfirth Station for the ceremony. A dinner to celebrate the reopening of the viaduct was held at the Victoria Hotel, Holmfirth, in late February 1867.[11]

Eli Wimpenny had gone into partnership with a Mr. Bowes, and in 1873 they were trading as Wimpenny & Bowes when Mr. Wimpenny was a witness at the bankruptcy hearing of James Mettrick of Hinchliffe Mill mill, having bought Mungo from Mettrick. The part of the mill used by Wimpenny & Bowes was advertised to be let 'as a going concern, or otherwise' in October 1881. Anyone interested could contact Eli Wimpenny at the mill, or Ramsden, Sykes and Ramsden in Huddersfield.

Arthur John Wiley and Edward Rowley were partners in business at the mill during 1881; besides having premises at Stoney Bank they also had an office or showroom at Lion Chambers in Huddersfield. In July of that year they had debts of £8,000, and were also in partnership with Edward Longworth of Deighton in the firm of Longworth, Wiley & Rowley which was manufacturing at Field Mill Leeds Road, with an office/showroom at 3 Brook St. Huddersfield. This company was also in bankruptcy with debts of £18,000. At their bankruptcy hearing Wiley and Rowley said that their failure had largely been caused by the failure of Longworth's company.

Early in 1883 James Coldwell had entered into partnership with six others, and set up business as woollen manufacturers at Stoney Bank. Each partner had contributed £50 to the firm's capital; the business continued until July of that year when dissolution took place. Coldwell and a man called O'Regan took over the business trading as Coldwell, O'Regan & Co, and repaid £30 to each of the other former partners, giving them 12 month Promissory Notes for the balance. A man called George Moorhouse put £50 into the firm with the intention of becoming a partner, and although a partnership agreement was drawn up it was never signed. The firm was in financial difficulties by mid 1884, with a bankruptcy hearing taking place in August when Moorhouse was very vague about his involvement with the Company. Coldwell, O'Regan & Co had previously had dealings with Brook Thornton and Samuel Green who had set up a company trading as Thornton & Green, but their partnership had ended on 12 March 1884, with Samuel Green continuing in business as S. Green & Co. James Coldwell's hearing was adjourned as the judge wanted more information on Coldwell, O'Regan & Co's involvement with S. Green & Co Ltd.

John William Horsfall dyer, was using part of the mill in July 1884 and was also in financial trouble. He filed a petition for bankruptcy on 21 July 1884, with his public examination being held on 15 August. A dividend of 3s 4d in the £ would be paid to creditors in March 1885.

The mills were empty in October 1886, when the mill buildings with the engine, boiler and shafting, formerly occupied by Eli Wimpenny were advertised to let along with the dwelling house and 12 acres of land. This was a difficult period for business due, at least in part, to the American Civil War and several other factors. The mills appear to have stayed empty, as they were advertised again two years later, and the *Yorkshire Factory Times* also commented in July 1889, that they were still empty due to the depressed state of trade. The mills were offered for sale in July 1893, when they were described as one 5 storey mill 117ft 3in by 44ft 6in, with a beam engine; one 3 storey mill plus attic 182ft by 42ft 6in; fulling room, boiler house, water wheel, dyehouse 89ft by 22ft 6in, 2 storey willey shed 73ft by 12ft 3in, stone built office, chimney, outbuildings, yard, goits etc. and 4 cottages in the mill yard. Also 5 closes of land with the stone residence, stable and outbuildings, occupied by Hewley Graham Esq.

The next occupant of the mills was Charles Moon who was a Woollen and Angola yarn spinner, he possibly moved in and began trading during 1895 rather than before that, as he gave a treat to his 70 workers in February 1896, which was recorded as being their first. The *Yorkshire Textile Directory* of 1910 records that the firm had 6,000 spindles. Charles Moon died at his home at Blackpool's South Shore on 21 July 1912. He was succeeded by his son who was also called Charles, but the firm's name became Charles Moon's Executors until 1925, when they became known as Charles Moon's Successors Ltd. The firm remained in business until January 1978, when it was announced that they would be closing at the end of March after a total of 107 years in business, which would result in their

45 employees being made redundant. They gave as the principle reason for closure the high cost of safety guards for their carding machines, which they said would cost between £3,000 and £3,500 each, that the Factory Inspectorate was insisting should be fitted. This brought a vehement response from the Inspectorate who insisted that the necessity for closure was due to bad management[12].

An advertisement appeared in the *Holmfirth Express* in October 1982 for B & C Motorcycles' spares and repairs, who were using part of the premises. Marion and Kenneth Moorhouse had bought the premises in 1978, and submitted plans to Kirklees Council to convert the site to housing, which was turned down. They had since been trying to secure funding to convert the buildings into individual industrial units, but had not succeeded. In late 1994 or early 1995 they again applied to Kirklees Council for permission to demolish the mills and use the site to build houses, this was granted in April 1995. The reason given by the council for their change of mind was that, in common with the vast majority of mills, the floors were soaked in oil; mainly due to the over enthusiastic way that many operatives lubricated the moving parts of their machines daily, thus rendering the buildings uninsurable due to the increased risk of fire.

Notes

1   Winney Bank mill
     W.C.R. 31 Oct. 1832; 12 April 1833; Leeds Mercury, 16 May 1840; 26 Dec. 1840; 17 May 1845; Hudds Chron. 7 Sept. 1867; 10 Sept. 1870; Kirk. Arch. UHO Wooldale, 8 Feb. also 20 Sept. 1883.

2   Shaley Wood Bottom/Ford mill
     Hudds Ex. 24 Dec. 1859; 17 Nov. 1860; Hudds Chron. 18 & 25 Apr. 17 Oct. 14 Nov. 5 Dec. 1863; Hudds Ex. 20 June, 1868; 19 Sept. 1874; 14 Aug. 1875; Hudds Chron. 17 March 1877; Kirk. Arch. KMT 4, 14 Dec. 1885, 16 Aug. 1886; Hudds Ex. 5 May, 27 Oct. 1888; also H'firth Exp. 26 May and 2 June 1906, 4 April 1908; Yorks. Fact. Times, 20 Aug. 1914; H'firth Exp. 20 May 1922; 11 Dec. 1937; 12 Nov. 1982; 13 July 1984.

3   New Mill/Moorbrook mill
     W.C.R. 29 Oct. 1456, 14 Oct. 1461, 8 Dec. 1486; also H.J. Morehouse, Kirkburton and Graveship of Holme; p. 148 footnote; W.C.R. 4 June 1817; Kirklees Archive, KC6/8/22; W.C.R. 2 Dec 1843; 11 Oct.1844; 18 April 1845; Kirk. Arch. KC6/1/33 1853; KC6/8/22; Hudds Ex. 21, 28 May, 4 June, 2 July, 1859; 25 June 1859; Hudds Chron. 22 Oct. 1859; 14 July and 17 Nov. 1860; Hudds Ex. 2 May 1863; Hudds Chron. 24 Dec. 1864; 26 Aug. 1865; Kirk. Arch. KC6/8/21; Hudds Chron. 13 Apr. 26 Oct. 1872; Kirklees Archive, KC6/8/24.

4   Hudds Ex. also H'firth Exp. 28 April 1888; 11 Jan. 1890; Hudds Ex. 28 Aug. 1894; Kirk. Arch. KC6/8/24, 1899; H'firth Exp. 3 June 1905; Kirk. Arch. KC6/8/24, May 1906; H'firth Exp. 1 Jan 1913; 4 May 1918; 30 Aug. 1947; 11 Feb. 1983; also 29 Apr. 1988; 15 Jan. 1999

5   Lydgate mill
     Hudds Ex. 27 Mar. 1897; 15 June 1901, 4 Jan. 1902; H'firth Exp. 29 March, 12 April 1919; Kirk. Arch. UHO New Mill, 9 May, 1935.

6   Moorcroft/Holme Bottom Mill
     W.C.R. 15 Dec. 1826; 15 Aug. and 26 Oct. 1836; 21 Aug. 1840; 22 Apr, 24 June1842; Leeds Merc. 12 Feb. 1848; Hudds. Chron. 15 March 1851; Kirk. Arch. KC6/1/33 1853; also Hudds Chron. 11 July, 19 Sept. 1857; 11 Dec. 1858; 22 Sept. 1866; 13 Nov. 1869; Hudds Ex. 22 Jan. 1870; 24 Sept. 1881; 29 April, 24 June and 22 July 1882; Kirk. Arch. UHO Fulstone 10 Apr, 23 Sept. 1895, Sept. 1897.

7   Kirk. Arch. UHO New Mill, Nov. 1898; Worker 9 Feb. 1903; Hudds. Ex. 1 Apr. 1905; H.firth Exp. 9 Feb. 1907, 20 Feb. 1915; 12 Ocr. 1918; 20 Aug. 1960.

8   Kirkbridge mill
     W.C.R. 2 Feb. 1733; 19 May 1736; 1 May 1795; 29 April 1803; Kirk. Arch. KC6/1/33 1853; Hudds Ex./Chron. 6, 20 Apr; 11, 25 May; 8, 15, 22 29 June; 17, 31 Aug. 1861; 4, 11 Jan. 17 May, 28 June 1862; 10 Mar. 1866; 27 Apr. 20 July 1867; 10, 31 Aug. 1868; 12 June 1869; 21, 28 May; 19 Nov. 1870; Hudds. Chron. 13 Aug. 1864; 6 May 1865; 27 April 1867; Hudds Ex. 10 Feb. 1872; 12 July 1873; also 29 Sept. 1883; 30 May 1885; 28 Aug. 1886; 12 March 1887.

9   Kirk. Arch. KC6/8/23 Abstract of title of Arthur Lockwood, 1905; Yorks. Fact. Times, 21, 28 March 1890; Hudds Ex. 4 Feb. 1893; H'firth Exp. 18 Aug. 1894; 18 Nov. 1899; Kirk. Arch. KC6/8/23; KC501/13; also UHO New Mill 15 Feb. 1915; KC 28/2 (NUTW); KC501/12a (Holroyd); H'firth Exp. 12 Feb. 1949, 2 June 1951; 13 Jan. 1968.

10   Tenterhill mill
     H'firth Exp. 18 Aug. 1894; 19 Dec. 1896; 3 Sept. 1898; 9 Sept. 1899; 10/17 Mar. 1900; Kirk. Arch. KMT4 20 Feb. 1902; H'firth Exp. 22 Feb. 1902; 10 Jan. 30 May 1903; 25 Feb. 1911.

11   Stoney Bank mill
     W.C.R. 30 May 1759; 15 Dec. 1826, 7 Sept. 1833; 22 Nov. 1844; Leeds Mercury, 20 Aug. 1842; 27 Jan. 1849; Hudds Chron. 20 Mar. 1852, Hudds Ex. 10 Dec. 1853, 26 Aug. 1854; Kirk. Arch. KC6/1/33 1853 and 1854; *Hudds Chron.* 14 June 1856; *Hudds Ex.* 5 Sept 1857, 3, 10, Sept 1859; *Hudds Chron.* 22, 29, Oct 1859, 21 Apr. 1860, 30 Apr. 1863, 9 Dec. 1865; *Hudds Ex.* 15 Sept. 1866; *Hudds Chron.* 23 Feb 1867.

12   *Hudds Ex.* 1 Nov 1873, 23 July & 1 Oct. 1881, 15 Mar. & 16 Aug. 1884; *London Gazette*, 13 June, 1, 15, 25, 29 July, 19 Sept. 1884, 17 Feb. 27 Mar. 1885; *Hudds Ex.* 16 Oct 1886, 27 Oct 1888, 1 July 1893, *Holmfirth Express*, 15 Feb. 1896, 13 Jan 1978; 10 Oct. 1982; 18 Nov. 1994; 31 Mar. 19 Apr. 1995.

CHAPTER 14

Mytholmbridge to Honley

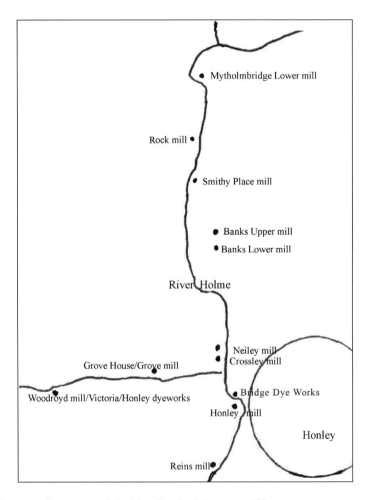

River Holme – Lower Mytholmbridge mill

Originally known as Brigg Royd mill, there is a suggestion that there was a mill on the site in the mid sixteenth century, although no documentation exists to support it. This mill stood some three or four hundred yards downstream from Upper Mytholmbridge mill, but on the opposite (left) bank. The house and mill dam still exist, while the site of the mill buildings is now used as part of the area for caravans. In 1626 the house and land were acquired by Richard Horsfall, who paid £240 for them to John Ramsden.

The land from Upper Mytholmbridge through Brockholes to Smithy Place and beyond over which the river flows, while not being flat, does not fall at the same rate that it does along many other parts of its length, which has caused problems from time to time. John Armitage who was working Lower Mytholmbridge mill in the 1790s raised the level of the weir that diverted water to his mill dam, which raised the water level in that part of the river back to Upper Mytholmbridge, stopping the water wheel of the upper mill from turning; that problem is discussed in the section on Upper Mytholmbridge mill in Chapter 11.

In 1808 a similar problem occurred, although it was the wheel at Lower Mytholmbridge that was stopped due to the height of the weir at Smithy Place mill being raised about two feet by Richard and Joseph Haigh who, along with Benjamin Carter were occupants of Smithy Place mill. The distance from the tail race of Lower Mytholmbridge to the goit carrying water to Smithy Place dam was 485 yards; the fall of the river over that distance being only some 18 to 20 inches. The problem recurred from time to time, until in 1847 William Green Armitage, who was the owner and occupier of Lower Mytholmbridge, sued James Robinson of Smithy Place mill for raising the level of the weir again. The problem would diminish over time as steam engines replaced water wheels as the main source of power.

Lower Mytholmbridge was offered to be let by ticket for a period of fourteen or twenty-one years in 1836, when it was described as a fulling and scribbling mill plus a farmhouse occupied as two dwellings by Henry Pinder and Thomas Greenwood, along with 5 closes of land. There were also three cottages occupied by Elias Pinder, Charles Mitchell and George Armitage. The owner of the property was Joseph Green Armitage, who was then living at Thick Hollins, Meltham. Ten years later the mill was offered for sale in February 1846, when it was described as just being a fulling mill, along with the farm, cottages and land. It was not sold at that time, as a memorandum of agreement between William Green Armitage and Lord Dartmouth, dated 7 March 1848, shows that Lord

Lower Mytholmbridge mill. © A.J. Brooke

Dartmouth agreed to purchase the mill, houses and land for £1,800; he also had an option to buy the machinery in the mill if he wished to do so. It would appear that Lord Dartmouth chose not to buy the machinery as it was offered for sale by order of William Green Armitage in July 1848.

The flood of 1852 caused little or no structural damage to the mill, but water did get inside the buildings and damaged machinery and yarns belonging to J. and G. Robinson; the dyehouse at the mill also suffered damage. The stocks in the fulling mill were badly damaged, along with the washing machine; several pieces of cloth belonging to G. & G. Booth, and cloth belonging to G. Bashforth was also damaged; also a double arched bridge spanning the river near the mill was washed away. Robinsons submitted a claim for damage to goits, machinery and stock totalling £315 11s, which was reduced to £139 4s; the inspectors added the claims from Robinsons at Thongsbridge, Lower Mytholmbridge and Smithy Place together, and treated them as one claim, making it difficult to determine how much of this claim was actually paid out. Booth's submitted a claim for damage to machinery and stock for £96 15s 6d which was agreed by the inspectors, but only £60 3s 3d was paid. The registered owner of the mill in 1853 was The Earl of Dartmouth, with the occupants listed as George Robinson, George Booth and Charles Bashforth. George Booth was in partnership with his son, also called George; the flood seems to have had a devastating effect on their business, as they dissolved their partnership on 22 September 1853, and their assignees ordered that their scribbling machinery, dyehouse and stove fittings, and work tools should be sold by auction in early December of that year.

Two thirteen year old girls called Hannah Kinder and Mary Moss were employed as piecers by Sam Mellor who was using part of the mill in 1858. On 31 May they went up to a room on the fourth floor of the mill where Thomas Wood and another man were installing machinery. The girls were attracted by a drive shaft that appears to have been at about waist height and was turning. The shaft was unfenced, but was due to be fenced off that day. Wood saw them near the shafting and sent then away, saying that if they returned he would thrash them. Around two hours later the girls went back into the room, and unseen by Wood returned to the revolving shaft. Their skirts became caught by the shaft which made them scream, alerting the two men. Wood went to help the girls while the other man went to stop the water wheel. The girls were being carried round the shaft, which was far enough from the wall not to throw them against it, and was held up from the floor by carriage slips that caught against their feet and legs. Wood broke the slips nearest to the girls to avoid more injuries and, with the help of the proprietor Mr. Mellor, took them off the shafting after it stopped. Mr. Mellor said that he could see that one of the girls had broken her leg, as the end of the bone had broken through the skin of her thigh. Both girls were seen by a surgeon who sent Hannah to Huddersfield Infirmary, where she underwent an operation to repair the compound fracture of her right thigh; any injuries that Mary received did not require further treatment. Hannah was still in hospital on 12 June when her thigh began to haemorrhage badly and she subsequently died. At the inquest Mary Moss said that they were both 'short timers' [meaning part timers]; they had gone into the room on the fourth floor "to play", while the Slubber for whom they worked was fettling his machine to start another run. Mr. Mellor said that Moss had told him that they were playing with the shaft when their dresses caught. The jury returned a verdict of 'accidental death'.

There was a violent thunderstorm in the district on the evening of Monday 18 July 1859. Large hailstones fell in the Mytholmbridge area smashing around 1,000 panes of glass, probably affecting both the upper and lower mills; other mills and buildings in the district were similarly damaged.

The question of ownership of designs was a topic that raised its head from time to time. Samuel Mellor brought a court case against Tom Mellor, one of his designers, charging him with embezzling 8lbs of patterns of fancy cloth that Tom had designed. Tom had signed an agreement that he would keep all aspects of his employer's business, including designs, secret. Several designers employed by other manufacturers gave evidence that they also retained samples of all the cloth that they designed. An abusive argument developed between the advocates appearing for the two sides that became so heated that the magistrate, Captain Armitage, threatened to leave the court. The question as to whether the design ultimately belonged to the designer or the manufacturer was not determined and the case was dismissed.

In March 1865 Samuel Mellor was in financial difficulty, he conveyed all his goods to Matthew William Cliffe, wool merchant of Huddersfield, George Greenwood, cloth finisher of Thongsbridge, and Frederick Shaw, card maker of Huddersfield to be used to the benefit of his creditors. The *Huddersfield Chronicle* that reported this occurrence also carried an advertisement that Lower Mytholmbridge mill with its machinery was to be let. Anyone interested should apply to James Robinson, Smithy Place mill.[1]

The next occupants of the mill were John William France and George Beaumont, who signed a lease in 1866 for 14 years, agreeing to pay £425 a year rent to James Robinson for the mill, dyehouse, warehouse and cottages, also the house and land. On the 10 November 1866 it was reported that Mr. J.W. France had given a treat to their 87 workers at the Royal Oak, Thongsbridge, to celebrate his recent marriage. The meal was followed by speeches, dancing and glee singing. Heavy rains about two weeks later flooded the land around the mill and raised the level of the river to the point where the water wheel was in back water and would not turn; however, the mill buildings were only slightly affected. France and Beaumont had ordered a new boiler from Holt's of Folly Hall in 1867, which was transported to Mytholmbridge by traction engine. Mrs. Kinder, the wife of the keeper of Smithy Place Bar, demanded a toll of 1s per wheel for the traction engine rather than the usual 3d. Holt's brought a case against the Kinders' to recover the overcharge, which Kinders' maintained was justified by local regulations as the traction engine was a broad wheeled vehicle. Holt's argued that national legislation restricted the charge to 3d per wheel. After much debate, the bench ruled that Holt's should receive a refund of 3s and also awarded costs against the Kinders', a total cost of 16s. The partnership between France and Beaumont was dissolved on 5 March 1869, with John Wm. France continuing in business on his own trading as John France & Son.

The census of 1871 suggests that France was employing 100 workers at that time. Mr. France applied to the Patent Office in London in October 1872, to patent his invention of an "improved means or apparatus for promoting the combustion of fuel". The company seem to have been in financial difficulties by February 1873, the first meeting of creditors was held on 19 February; with all creditors being asked to supply details of debts before 24 June 1873. James Robinson leased 'All that woollen mill with the cottage, warehouse, dyehouse and other conveniences called Lower Mytholmbridge mill' plus the house, to Joseph Blackburn of Huddersfield for a term of 14 years from 1 April 1873, at a rent of £425 a year. John William France contested the bankruptcy order against himself; but failed to get it rescinded. The deficit was in the region of £12,000; in May 1874 Joseph Blackburn agreed to buy France's business for £5,800, to which J.W. France would add £200. This would allow payments to creditors of 10s in the £; the firm then becoming known as Blackburn and France. The partnership between Blackburn and France was terminated on 28 January 1876, when J.W. France left the company; the name was changed to J. Blackburn & Co. but did not prosper, as Joseph Blackburn filed for bankruptcy at the Bankruptcy Court in Huddersfield in May 1877. His estimated liabilities were thought at that time to be around £12,500, but the debts were later published as being £7,478, while his assets amounted to £5,120. Mr. Beaumont Taylor was appointed receiver, and the creditors agreed to accept 9s in the £ to be paid in three instalments at 4, 6 and 9 months. A sale of Blackburn's machinery for preparing and spinning yarn; weaving, scouring and finishing cloth, was held in July 1877, which also including a large quantity of wool and office furnishings.

C. & A. Mellor & Co. were occupying the mill by January 1887, when they gave a treat to their 120 workpeople at the Royal Oak, Thongsbridge; the meal was followed by speeches, songs and dancing. The engine tenter at the mill discovered at 8.30pm on Thursday 30 June 1887, that some hanks of yarn which had been hung in the stove to dry were in fact burning. He raised the alarm, and as some staff were still working they responded quickly, some going to other mills to alert their fire brigades, and some starting to fight the fire. Brigades from Smithy Place, Thongsbridge mill and

Bridge mill soon arrived; these were followed by the Unity brigade, Ribbleden mill, John Brooke's at Armitage Bridge, and one from Milnsbridge, but these were not needed, as by the time they arrived the roof of the stove had collapsed, and its contents of between 4,000 and 6,000lbs of yarn plus some pieces of cloth were burned. There was a possibility that the fire could have spread to the main mill, but this was avoided. The damage, which was not quantified, was covered by insurance.

The title of the company had changed to Sykes, Mellor & Co by 1890. In March of that year the weavers of fast looms, who were dissatisfied with their rates of pay, began leaving work as they downed their warps. They did not have a negotiated pay scale, but were being paid 75 percent of the rates paid to slow loom weavers for each quality of cloth, and the firm were wanting to reduce the rate to two thirds, rather than three quarters, which caused the strike. The weavers' union became involved and the strike was settled by 20 March. The total number of employees gradually diminished, probably due to the difficult trading conditions experienced by all manufacturers. The firm employed 180 people in 1887; this dropped to 150 by January of 1888, and was down to 120 by early 1893. Sykes, Mellor & Co were coming to the end of their lease in 1893, and had apparently decided not to renew it, as the mill, for scribbling, dyeing and finishing, along with the weaving shed, steam engine, boiler and some machinery, plus the house, farm buildings and land, were advertised to be let in April of that year; applications were to be made to W.B. Robinson, at Smithy Place mill. Sykes, Mellor's lease actually expired in November 1893, when they advertised the sale of a large quantity of machinery to be held at the mill on 8 November.

The next occupants of the mill were J. & J. Lancaster, who had moved from Thongsbridge mills, although when they moved in unclear. The firm was run by two brothers, who dissolved their partnership in May 1896, Mr. James Lancaster continued the business as its sole owner, trading as J. Lancaster & Son, dyers and finishers. The workers presented Mr. Charles H. Lancaster with a clock to mark his marriage to Miss Greenwood of Thongsbridge on 1 June 1899. James Lancaster announced that the mill would be closed on the day of the wedding, and the firm would provide a trip for the workpeople to wherever they wanted to go, on whichever Saturday they chose. The company continued in business at the mill for many years, making several changes and additions to the premises during the 1920s, including a new boiler house, a tenter house and a new scouring room. Mr. James Lancaster died at his home, Mytholmbridge House, on Sunday 3 March 1935, at the age of 83; by which time the lane leading from the main road through Hagg Wood to the mill had been named Lancaster Lane. The company continued to be run by James Lancaster's two sons, Brook and Arnold. In the flood of 29 May 1944, the weaving shed was damaged, the rest of the mill was flooded and there were considerable deposits of sludge. Further extensions to the mill took place in the 1950s, and the company continued trading into the 1970s, with their last advertisement for staff appearing in the *Holmfirth Express* in 1970.[2]

Rock mill

This mill stood across the New Mill road from Rock Terrace in the centre of Brockholes. From an article in the *Huddersfield Examiner* in 1877 it was originally built as a three storey Cotton mill in 1865, making it one of only two mills in the district that were originally built as Cotton mills rather than Woollen mills. The first occupants of the mill were Turner & Bower cotton spinners, who moved from Huddersfield. A flood on Friday 16 November 1866 affected the ground floor of the mill, but being forewarned, all moveable goods had been taken to the upper floors. The flood waters did trap 24 workpeople in the mill for several hours until it subsided sufficiently to allow them to leave. The water left a heavy deposit of mud behind when it finally withdrew.

Two more storeys were added to the mill in 1867 making it five storeys high. On Saturday 23 November, Edmund Priestley of Neiley, one of the workmen carrying out the alteration, was helping to position some heavy shafting when it slipped, trapping his hand and completely severing his thumb. Two other men working on the shafting received head injuries that were not serious. Some planks placed below the shafting had stopped it from falling further, allowing the people working below to move away uninjured. There had been several accidents during the course of the alterations, but none had been fatal. By October 1868 the name of the company had changed to Bower & Smith, a fire broke out in the boiler house around 11.40pm on Thursday 8 October, the engine tenter raised the alarm and the prompt attendance of the fire engine from Mellor's of Thongsbridge confined the blaze, restricting damage to an estimated £70. Engines from Shaw's of Crossley mills and Brooke's of Armitage Bridge also arrived, but were not needed.

The occupant of the mill in 1877 was Samuel Smith who was a cotton spinner, he employed John Johnson a 21 year old from Honley as a stripper and grinder. On Friday 22 October Johnson was helping another man to crane bales of cotton through a warehouse door that was about 12 yards above ground level. Johnson leaned out of the doorway attempting to grab a bale to pull it towards the doorway, but missed it and fell to the ground, landing on his head and arms, badly cutting his forehead. The *Huddersfield Chronicle* reported on the following day that Johnson had been taken to Huddersfield Infirmary for treatment.

A disastrous fire occurred at the mill on 8 December 1877, it broke out on the fourth floor of the five storey mill at 1pm on the Saturday afternoon, just as the mill was about to close. The mill buzzer was sounded, and the fire engine from James Robinson & Sons arrived within about 5 minutes. The main building was about 70 yards long and 20 yards wide, there was a square tower attached to one side of that building that contained a staircase and also rooms used for spinning and doubling. Attached to the other side of the square tower were the carding room, warehouse and other buildings around the mill yard. Fire engines from Thongsbridge and John Brooke & Sons of Armitage Bridge also attended, and were followed by engines from Joseph Turner & Sons Bridge mills, J.T. Taylor & Co of Ribbleden mill, and the Unity brigade. The valve of a nearby gasometer was opened to prevent an explosion. The close proximity of the River Holme ensured a plentiful supply of water, but within 45 minutes of the outbreak the roof of the main building had collapsed, to be followed by a part of the side wall; fortunately none of the fire fighters were injured. Within 2 hours the main building was completely destroyed, but the square tower and the other buildings were saved by firemen continually spraying them with water to keep them cool. The mill buildings were

Rock mill. © A.J. Brooke

owned by Mr. Joseph Turner of Fitzwilliam St. Huddersfield, and were fully insured. The machinery and materials within the mill were owned by Mr. Samuel Smith and were partly, if not wholly, insured; but the 180 men and women who worked at the mill were put out of work Although the mill was rebuilt, Samuel Smith did not restart his business; instead, a sale of cotton machinery, which had come from the undamaged buildings at the mill, was advertised to take place on 13 November 1878, along with quantities of salvaged shafting and gearing, 200 tons of Iron and 10cwt of Brass, that had obviously come from the damaged part of the mill.

The next occupants of Rock mill were Joseph Sykes & Co. worsted manufacturers, who also moved to Brockholes from Huddersfield. Caroline Stancy of Milnsbridge was employed by the firm as a weaver, and had moved with them from Colne Road to Brockholes in late January 1880. Stancy brought an action against the firm in the County Court, in July, for £4 0s 9d which she claimed was due to her in unpaid wages. All the weavers, both men and women had made a demand for higher wages, which the company had turned down. They would have finished their warps on the old terms and then left, but in consequence of Mary Bray starting a new warp at the old rates, all the weavers, with the exception of Bray and one other woman, left work on 30 March. Stancy said that she dared not have carried on working. The judge pointed out to her that there was one person who had dared to stay. Stancy replied that the woman would never be forgotten for her action, and would never be able to work in any other mill. The strikers had met with Mr. Sykes on the Monday evening after they had walked out; he refused to pay them any outstanding wages, or to allow them to resume work. Since then all but five of the weavers had returned to work at the mill, presumably at the old rates. Mr. Sykes would not allow Stancy to resume work, but did pay her the wages that were due to her at the time she had walked out.

Joseph Sykes died in January 1882, and the running of the firm was taken over by Mr. Elon Crowther in partnership with Mr. Alfred Sykes. Elon Crowther had previously been in business with his brother William at Falls Lane mill Marsden, and at Crimble mills Golcar. The firm installed a system of Electric lighting in the mill by November 1882. They used a Gulcher low tension arc system in combination with Crookes Incandescent lamps, utilising three 2,300 candle power arc lamps, and 40 incandescent lamps run from a No. 4 Dynamo driven by a 10hp steam engine working at 150rpm. The firm said that the light was perfect for colour matching, and was 'far superior to gas lights'. At that time they were not able to give comparative costs between using gas lights and the new system.

The mill was again affected by flooding on the night of 29 January 1883, the night watchman realised that the level of the river was rising, and was coming into the mill so rapidly that he was unable to get out and warn neighbours. The water filled the cellars and rose to a height of around three feet inside the large shed; the weaving, mending and finishing sheds were also flooded, doing much damage to cloth and machinery. Some bales of wool were carried by the water over a four foot high wall and floated off downstream. The water gradually subsided, but rose again around 9am the following morning, when a newly paved road had to be broken up to allow the water to run off. The problem was caused by alterations being carried out at one of Lord Dartmouth's properties, which, the report said, was being looked into by the owners of the mill and Lord Dartmouth's land agent.

The firm was charged by the Factory Inspector with employing 14 young people after 6pm on 21 February 1884. They were presumably all female, as they were mending, knotting and burling. Mr. Alfred Sykes pleaded guilty to all the charges, and the bench imposed fines of 10s plus costs in each case, a total of 20 guineas [£21].

A 17 year old beamer named Harry Heeley of Brockholes Lane was working at the mill on Monday 1 February 1886. The *Daily Examiner* of 2 February reported that Heeley was up a ladder holding one end of a drive belt for a warping balloon that he and another person were attempting to repair; and that the belt had become wrapped around the moving drive shaft, drawing Heeley with it, mutilating his limbs and body. The *Weekly Examiner* of 6 February in reporting the inquest gave a different version of events. Joseph Bayliff overlooker, of Berry Brow told the inquest that the strap needed a new lace to join the two ends together; as he did not have one he sent a lad to get one, but the lad returned empty handed. After telling two lads to each hold one end of the strap Bayliff went to the mill office and got a new lace. One of the two lads told the court that Heeley was standing on the bottom of a ladder holding the two sides of the strap together. Heeley had not been asked to do this by anyone. After Bayliff returned and began preparing the lace, Heeley started ascending the ladder backwards while still holding the strap sides together. Heeley's clothing became caught by the revolving shaft and drew him towards and round it. Bayliff said that he heard no cry, but turned round to see Heeley being carried around the shafting.

The mill was the first in the district to install emergency switches to stop the engine, which worked by breaking a glass panel and pushing a button, so that the engine was stopped quickly. James Smith a tuner from Thurstonland said that he had released Heeley from the shafting; his legs and arms were broken in several places, his feet were torn off and his forehead was broken in. Heeley's body along with the severed parts were taken to his home to await inspection by the coroner and inquest jury. The jury returned a verdict of 'accidental death', and added that no blame could be attached to anyone else.

The number of people employed by the company in the late 1880s is difficult to quantify; in 1887 the firm gave a treat to 150 people in the mill dining room in mid January, followed by a treat to 180 people at the end of that month. The Factory Inspector Mr. Prior brought an action against the firm for employing four young people after the permitted hours. Mr. A. Sykes pleaded guilty to the charges, but said that as they employed 700 workers it was impossible to inspect every department in the mill. Mr. Sykes also said that he had not known that the youths were employed in the mill, two of them, who were employed in the heald making department, had been engaged by the man in charge of that department; the third was employed in the pattern room, while the fourth had no right to be in the mill at all. He also pointed out that it was the practice in some mills to employ young persons longer during the week and allow them time off on Saturdays. The bench imposed fines of 20s plus costs in each case.

In April 1891 thirteen year old Phyllis Crowther a learner burler, somehow became entangled in the machinery of a pumping engine, which broke her right leg so badly that it had to be amputated. The press report said that she was 'going on as well as could be expected'. Later that year on 13 October, the engine tenter Abraham Drury was found dead in the engine room with an oilcan in his hand, and his head smashed in. It was assumed that he had been oiling the engine when a segment of a gear wheel hit and killed him.

All the employees at the mill were given a return train ticket to Liverpool and a new half-crown [2s 6d] by Mr. Elon Crowther in April 1895, in celebration of his son J.D. Crowther reaching the age of 21. Two trains left Holmfirth on the morning of 27 April, one at 5.10am, the second at 5.25am taking 850 people including friends, arriving in Liverpool at 7.55am and 8.20am. Some crossed the Mersey on the Ferry to visit New Brighton, others looked around the docks or visited the Mersey Tunnel, and looked around the city, before catching the trains home. There was a meeting in the mill dining room on the Monday to offer a vote of thanks to the firm.

In August 1897, the company presented the village with a playground for the children of Brockholes to enjoy, in celebration of Queen Victoria's Diamond Jubilee, when everyone also enjoyed a free tea. The local council who, in common with many other public bodies, were contemplating installing generating equipment for electricity, paid a visit to Rock mill in February 1900 to inspect their system, which by then had been installed for over seventeen years. The council minutes do not record whether or not the councillors were favourably impressed.[3]

The *Yorkshire Factory Times* reported in March 1900 that some of the weavers were dissatisfied with their rates of pay, and had obtained a list of the rates paid by firms in Huddersfield from the

Weavers and Textile Workers Union. The weavers at Rock mill had asked the union to represent them in a meeting with the firm's management on 8 March, but the meeting was postponed as only a small number of the weavers employed at the mill were trade union members. The YFT urged more of them to join the union.

Joseph Sykes & Co. registered as a Limited Company with a nominal share capital of £25,000, in December 1900. The Directors of the company were Mr. Elon Crowther, Mr. J.D. Crowther, Mr. Alfred Sykes and Mr. A.H. Sykes. In May 1907, the Rivers Board complained that the firm were not properly treating effluent from the mill before allowing it to enter the river. They did concede that Sykes' were not the only company guilty of this; there were some 15 or 16 other mills upstream from Brockholes who were also guilty of the same offence. Joseph Sykes' said that they would install better equipment to deal with the problem.

The Yorkshire Textile Directory recorded the company, in 1910 and 1912, as being woollen and worsted spinners and manufacturers, with 8,000 spindles and 230 looms. The firms of Joseph Sykes & Co. Ltd., Learoyd Bros. Leeds Road, Huddersfield, and A Crabtree & Co. of Colne Valley, amalgamated in 1920 to form the group known as Huddersfield Fine Worsteds, although they continued to trade independently.

A quantity of yarn in a storeroom was damaged in 1921, by sewage getting into the room through a manhole cover in the floor. The firm maintained that the problem lay in a blocked main sewer in the village, which the council refuted. A protracted campaign for compensation against the council got nowhere.

One of the weavers at Rock mill, Sam Ainley, died at his loom on 21 September 1921, at the age of 58. The Coroner recorded that he had died of natural causes. Mr. Elon Crowther died at his home in Brockholes on 4 April 1927, he was 79.

Fire broke out at the mill on 15 April 1939, in some waste stored under a warehouse. Holmfirth fire brigade had the blaze under control within 10 minutes of arriving. Only slight damage occurred. The Yorkshire Textile Directory for 1942-43 shows that the number of spindles had increased to 8,500, but the number of looms had fallen to 106.

The mill was affected by the flood on 29 May 1944, which left large quantities of sludge throughout the ground floors of all the buildings, and caused sections of the roofs to collapse in the single storey sheds. It also washed away some parts for new machinery that was in the process of being installed. Two fires broke out at the mill in 1951, the first was in a wool storage shed and occurred on 4 May, the mill's own fire brigade fought the blaze until the Holmfirth fire engine arrived. The fire was contained within the storage shed, but the worsted combing department, which was next to the store room, suffered water damage. The total cost of that fire was estimated at £3,000. The second fire occurred on 20 June, and was in the wool drying stove, which overheated. This was put out by the Holmfirth fire brigade; no estimate of the damage was given.

A tragic and distressing accident occurred at the mill in June 1953, when a five year old boy was crushed to death. John Muir Normington was making his way home from school to Oakes Avenue Brockholes. The entrance to the mill was some twelve or more feet wide, with a high, solid, heavy wooden gate that opened and closed using an electric motor. The gate travelled along a steel track that was set into the roadway, and it moved, from memory, almost silently. The gate was controlled from within the time office which was on the left, or New Mill side of the gateway. Between the gate and the office was a corridor to admit pedestrians to the mill, each wall of this corridor had windows to permit those in the office to observe vehicles arriving and leaving, but the windows did not go down to the ground. If John was near the corridor wall, he would be below the sill of the window, and out of the sight of the person operating the gate. He must have stood directly in the path of the gate and been crushed by it as it closed. John had been seen near the gate only two days earlier, and had been warned of its danger. After the accident a mirror was attached to the wall opposite the office to enable anyone inside the office to see the full opening.

The firm continued in business until 1969, by which time Huddersfield Fine Worsteds had become part of the Illingworth Morris Group, who were based in Bradford. It was announced in February of that year that Joseph Sykes & Co. Ltd. would close at the end of March. The sale of all the plant and machinery was advertised to take place on 17 and 18 September 1969. The mill buildings were demolished during late 1974 and '75; at 9.45am on 14 December 1974 a thirty foot high boundary wall of the mill collapsed into the car park of the Rock Inn next door, damaging 2 cars, a telephone kiosk and a bus shelter, fortunately no-one was injured; the mill's chimney was felled at 10.15am on Sunday 9 February 1975. There were no plans to develop the site at that time, it was to be cleared and left.

There were differences of opinion between Kirklees Council and the residents of Brockholes on how the site should be developed. As with many other former industrial sites in the district the council favoured continued industrial usage; whereas the local residents wanted housing. Several plans were put forward and abandoned, until in 1984 a plan to build around 30 industrial units and some 50 houses was adopted and passed on 30 November. [4]

Smaller Textile Enterprises in Brockholes

A company by the name of Holme Valley Textiles Ltd. had a single entry in the *Yorkshire Textile Directory* in 1952, when they were at Providence mill, Brockholes; the Managing Director and Secretary was Mr. Vernon Longbottom. They were yarn spinners with 2,000 spindles, and also weavers. No further information on either the company or the whereabouts of Providence mill has emerged.

Magdale Spinning Co, woollen spinners moved from Lords mill to premises in New Mill Road Brockholes in 1957, and were still there in 1971.

Riverside Mending Co. were using premises in New Mill Road Brockholes in 1964, when they advertised in the *Holmfirth Express* for experienced worsted and woollen menders. They were there until around 1969, when they took over the premises at Lane End Holmfirth from Holmfirth Mending Co.

Smithy Place mill

Standing a few hundred yards downstream from Rock mill was Smithy Place mill and dyehouse. It was considerably older than Rock mill, having been built in the late eighteenth century. Giving evidence to the inquiry held in 1811 into the water dispute between Lower Mytholmbridge and Smithy Place mills, Joseph Kaye said that he had gone to Smithy Place mill in 1780, when he was 6 years old, to work for a member of the Brooke family who also held premises in Honley at that time, prior to their eventual move to Armitage Bridge. The mill was clearly built and running in 1780. The first evidence of a problem with the river's water level above Smithy Place was in 1789 when Giles Gartside occupied at least part of the mill, he placed planks on top of the weir at Smithy Place which raised the level of the water upstream and flooded land used by Robert Bradley. Gartside was ordered to remove the planks from the weir; his reason for raising the water level was to increase the amount of water in the mill dam, possibly because he had built a new dyehouse with three vats, three coppers and two dyepans, and felt that he needed more water. In addition to Giles Gartside, other occupants of the premises in 1805 and '06 were Richard and Joseph Haigh and Ben Carter, who had taken over from John Carter the elder; also Firth Gartside and William Booth Gartside had a lease on a dyehouse, with their dyehouse machinery being driven by the mill's water wheel.

Joseph Green Armitage who was the owner of Lower Mytholmbridge mill, complained that on 9th or 10th May 1808 the Haigh's and Carter had raised the height of the weir at Smithy Place by between 6½ and 8 inches, raising the water level at Lower Mytholmbridge by 2¾ inches above the bottom of their water wheel, virtually stopping it from turning which, due to the slowing of the current, also allowed greater amounts of sand and gravel to be deposited in that part of the river.

The matter went to court in 1811, resulting in the defendants, Haigh's and Carter, being ordered not to raise the level of their weir; but the problem continued spasmodically for a number of years.

Joshua Robinson, who was using part of the mill by 1833, replied to the Government Inquiry into the employment of children and said that the mill was used for scribbling and carding wool, also fulling cloth, but that he did not regard himself as a manufacturer, as the work he did was for the country domestic manufacturers; no spinning or weaving was carried out on the premises. He thought at that time that the mill had been erected in 1791; it was powered by a 12hp water wheel and in times of drought partly by a 7hp steam engine. The firm employed a total of 18 people: 1 girl under 10, 1 boy and 3 girls under 12, 1 boy and 1 girl under 14, all earning 3s 6d per week; 1 boy and 1 girl under 16 each earning 5s 6d per week; 1 boy under 18 earning 7s per week; 2 men under 21 earning 15s, and 1 woman under 21 earning 6s per week; 5 men over 21 were also earning 15s per week. The children were provided by the slubbers and the engineer, who also paid them. Everyone was employed on piece rates; the mill had no set hours, workers set their own hours, which were less on Saturdays. The mill had no set meal times, but the machines were stopped during them. With regard to holidays, Mr. Robinson, said that the staff had "as many as they think proper", they never asked for holidays and were not paid for them. The firm only employed one set of children, as they did not think it necessary or practical to employ more. "No children were healthier on earth or look better than children that work in domestic mills". Corporal punishment was not sanctioned and not used; all children under 12 were employed as piecers. No suggestions were offered to the enquiry about parliament regulating the hours of work in mills and factories.

An indenture dated 20 Sept. 1836 adds to the history of the mill by relating that, in September 1789, Harry Cumbray had loaned John Gartside £1,200 for the messuage and land at Smithy Place, formerly owned by Giles Gartside and then by Firth and William Booth Gartside, later by Mrs. Harriet Gartside, also Joseph Scholefield and Messrs. Swift and Taylor, but in 1821 by Joshua Robinson. Also the scribbling and fulling mill at Smithy Place late in the possession of William Brooke, then of Swift and Taylor, and currently of Joshua and John Robinson; and the dyehouse lately occupied by William Booth Gartside, but now by Joshua Robinson. Joshua Robinson had then raised the mortgage on the properties to £3,000, borrowed from a Mr. Joshua Ingham in 1827; the purpose of the 1836 indenture was to transfer ownership of this mortgage to Mr. John Wood.

John Robinson acquired a poor reputation amongst some of the working class community of the area in 1841, when a large number of people went to Smithy Place Sunday School on Sunday 28 March to hear a sermon preached by Mr. Joshua Bray, at which a collection was to be taken for the benefit of the wife and family of a Chartist supporter named Clayton who had been committed to prison. The people were unable to gain access to the building, as John Robinson had written to the key-holder instructing him to keep it locked. The report describes Robinson as 'pious'. The meeting transferred to the Socialist meeting room in Honley, who readily agreed to allow the meeting to go ahead. The paper's correspondent suggested that the inscription over the door of the Sunday school that read: "To do good is our aim" should be removed.

The problem with water levels in the river recurred in 1847 when William Green Armitage of Lower Mytholmbridge brought a court action against James Robinson of Smithy Place and George Robinson of Thongsbridge for raising the height of the weir at Smithy Place to the point where the water wheel at Lower Mytholmbridge was stopped from turning. Mr. Sydney Morehouse was appointed as arbitrator; he called meetings at the White Hart Inn Holmfirth in March 1847 and in succeeding months, to take evidence. John Hirst, who had worked at Lower Mytholmbridge, said that in 1843 he had accompanied Mr. Armitage to inspect the weir at Smithy Place and found it had been raised by six to eight inches. John Carter, who was 69 in 1847, said that he had worked with his father at Smithy Place mill from being 13 years old until he was 29. He said that they put planks on top of the weir that were only removed if they were expecting heavy rain to prevent them being washed away. On occasions when Mr. Armitage had threatened legal action they would be taken off, but would be replaced when they thought that the problem had been forgotten. John Carter said that he remembered Smithy Place mill being built, prior to that the river had flowed without hindrance to Banks mills, but after the weir at Smithy Place was built sand and gravel had tended to block the outflow of water from the tail goit of Lower Mytholmbridge mill. There was also evidence that the water wheel at Smithy Place mill, which was originally 15 feet in diameter, had been replaced with one that was 18 feet in diameter. The level at which the water hit the wheel would probably also need to be higher, which would possibly mean increasing the height of the water in the mill dam. The eventual solution to the problem is not recorded.

John Robinson, mentioned above, described as a dyer, dealer and chapman who occupied part of Smithy Place mill, was declared bankrupt on 12 November 1847, and was ordered to appear at the Bankruptcy Court in Leeds before Mr. William Scrope Ayrton on 27 November and 18 December 1847 to make a full disclosure of his estate. The *Leeds Mercury* of 27 November 1847 advertised the dwelling house with outbuildings, garden and grounds, along with the recently erected dyehouse with machinery, also the cart shed, barn, stable and other outbuildings all occupied by John Robinson to be sold by auction on 8 December. The *Leeds Intelligencer* dated 22 January 1848 reported that the premises at the mill formerly used by John Robinson were to be let to Isaac Beardsell of Hagg House, who had previously been in business in Holme. The assignees of Robinson called a meeting of his creditors to give them the opportunity to assent to or dissent from proceeding with a suit in the Prerogative Court in York, as John Robinson was one of the executors named in his father's will. The Bankruptcy Court announced in March 1848 that a first dividend, amounting to 3d in the £ was available to be paid to creditors. There do not appear to be any details of subsequent dividends, but the Bankruptcy Court in Leeds said it would sit on 3 December 1849 to take the last examination of John Robinson, and if no-one objected he would be discharged. His Certificate of Conformity was issued by the court on 31 December 1849. Isaac Beardsell was established in the mill by 1849, when he advertised for a pattern weaver and designer.

The flood of 1852 affected several firms who were using parts of Smithy Place mill. The flood waters rose to between eight and nine feet within the mill buildings, causing a considerable amount

Part of Smithy Place mill showing the dam. © A.J. Brooke

of damage and destruction to machinery, raw materials and finished cloth. Martin and Frederick Heap submitted a claim totalling £102 5s, which was reduced by the inspectors to £90, but there is no indication of any money being paid (claim no. 8). Isaac Beardsell submitted a claim for damage to buildings, machinery and stock totalling £981, the inspectors reduced this to £699 18s, with a total of £385 5s 4d being paid (claim no 246). The inspectors combined claims made by James and George Robinson for Lower Mytholmbridge mill for damage to buildings machinery, stock and land totalling £315 11s, which was reduced to £139 4s; with a claim made by them plus Isaac Beardsell, Joseph Heap & Sons, John Littlewood & Sons, also Mark and Frederick Heap and George Booth, for damage to Smithy Place mill totalling £545 10s, which was reduced to £380 3s; and a claim from J & G Robinson for damage to Thongsbridge mill buildings, machinery, dams, goits and stock totalling £803, which was reduced to £463. The totals of the reduced amounts was £982 7s, of which £623 8s 9d was paid (claim nos. 297, 298, and 300). James Robinson submitted a claim for a dyehouse and stock destroyed at Smithy Place totalling £878 4s, which was not reduced by the inspectors, but only £605 3s 6d was paid (claim no 313). A separate claim was submitted by J & G Robinson and John Littlewood & Son, for damage to buildings machinery and stock at Smithy Place totalling £300, which was reduced to £241, with only £14 5s 1d being paid for labour (claim no. 315). The Holme Reservoir Commissioners list the owners of Smithy Place mills in 1853 as James & George Robinson, who were the trustees of their father Joshua Robinson's estate; The occupants of the mill are listed as James & George Robinson; Joseph, Jonathon, George, Jonathon junior, Joshua and Robert Heap; Isaac Beardsell and George Noble Nelson; John and Lupton Littlewood.

The economist and politician Richard Cobden, who was an advocate of free trade and one of the founders of the Anti Corn Law League, had been invited to address a gathering at the annual Soiree of the Holmfirth Mechanics Institute in February 1853, and was to stay at Hagg House as the guest of Isaac Beardsell and his family. On his way to Hagg House Mr. Cobden called at Smithy Place mill, and was presented with an address by the workmen, most of whom were in the employ of Messrs. Beardsell & Co. The address expressed the gratitude of the workers for Mr. Cobden's efforts to repeal the Corn Laws, and his 'advocacy of the principles of peace and mutual good will among nations'. Mr. Cobden gave a speech in reply.

An article printed in the *Huddersfield Chronicle* on 13 August 1853 about the Sunday school at Smithy Place said that James Robinson and Isaac Beardsell had spared no effort, pecuniary or otherwise, to keep it open. Between 90 and 100 children were receiving instruction in reading, spelling, writing etc. with the organisers providing books and materials at their own expense. Isaac Beardsell had been heavily involved with the non denominational Sunday school in Holme before moving to Hagg, it is understandable that he would continue his interest in the education of children after moving. He was also a regular member of the congregation at the Unitarian Church in Upperthong Lane Holmfirth.

Snow was lying on the hills around the district in November 1853, which was melted by heavy rain that fell on the 25th of the month, resulting in some flooding of the area that affected the mill and dyehouses at Smithy Place. Shuttles at the head of the mill dam had been left open allowing water to rush in and fill the dam to overflowing. A large dyepan in the dyehouse belonging to Isaac Beardsell that had only been set a few weeks previously was displaced; and the rooms on the ground floor of the mill were also flooded to a good depth causing damage to materials stored there.

Workpeople in the Brockholes area held their Annual Gala at Robin Rocks on Saturday 5 August 1854. There were sports and games, and the Kirkburton 'Old Band' provided music for dancing, with the revelries continuing until dusk. The report laments that "Galas' seem to be on the wane in the district, and are not so well attended as formerly".

In May 1856 John E. Brigg brought a case against Isaac Beardsell and his partner George Noble Nelson, for infringing an agreement limiting the finishing of Mohair cloth in the style known as the Whirlpool Mohair Finish to cloth owned by Brigg. The design and finish of the cloth had been registered by Brigg in the Design Office in London in April 1855. Brigg's counsel produced various samples of cloth, which he argued were all the same Whirlpool Mohair Finish, even though they had been obtained from several of Beardsell's customers; while counsel for Beardsell and Nelson argued that the finish on them was different. The judge found that all the samples were essentially the same, and ordered that, for the time being, this finish should be restricted to cloth owned by Brigg.[5]

Two brothers, Allan and George Armitage were charged with assaulting Richard Batley the engineer at the mill on 4 May 1857. The father of the Armitage brothers had been the engineer at the mill until the beginning of May when he had been dismissed, and Batley was promoted to his post, albeit at a lower salary. The brothers had abused Batley on the Saturday night, and had threatened a more severe assault on the Monday. After leaving work on Monday evening Batley was knocked down, kicked on his side and head and flung into a hedge by the brothers. A man called Arthur Hey had accompanied Batley and was able to corroborate Batley's evidence. The bench imposed fines on each of the brothers of £1 for the assault, £3 11s for the damage done to Batley and 9s costs, a total of £5 each. If they were unable to pay they should each be sent to Wakefield gaol for two months with hard labour.

Isaac Beardsell unexpectedly died at his home, Hagg House, on Friday 18 June 1858 after a short illness; he was 52 years old. This was only about 1 year and 5 months after the death of his father James, who was 92. Isaac's obituary said that as a manufacturer of fancy woollen cloth he was the most accomplished in the district; also he had contributed greatly to the increased skill and knowledge in dyeing techniques. In view of the court case of May 1856, there is a certain irony in recording that almost six months after his death Isaac was awarded a Patent for improvements in the finishing of Mohair cloth and other textiles, and for improvements in the machinery. A consequence of Isaac Beardsell's death was that his partner George Noble Nelson filed for bankruptcy in late August 1858. There were liabilities of £16,670; net assets amounted to £6,878; trade creditors were owed £3,400, Mr. Noble of Leeds was owed £9,188 in loans and accrued interest. Losses on imports of wool from Australia amounted to £11,300. Mr. Nelson offered a dividend of 8s in the £, after much discussion the creditors agreed that they would accept 9s in the £. The meeting was adjourned to allow George Nelson to consider the proposal. The report ends with the comment from the Chairman at the meeting saying: 'this is a commercial community, and is supposed to be composed of men of business; and yet the partner in a well known business says that he knows nothing about that business and has not seen a balance sheet for six years'. From Isaac Beardsell's account of the way that he conducted business as a partner in James Beardsell & Sons, the remark about the lack of a balance sheet does not ring true. Hagg House, which Isaac Beardsell had bought in 1844, was advertised to be sold by auction on 15 December 1858, presumably as part of the bankruptcy proceedings; it was announced on 3 December that the property had been bought privately by Mr. Godfrey Mellor of Thongsbridge who was a personal friend of Isaac Beardsell.

John Robinson the former dyer had, since his bankruptcy, moved to Huddersfield. He committed suicide by cutting his own throat in January 1862. The newspaper report said that he had suffered from 'gradual disorganisation of the brain' over the previous three months. George N. Nelson continued in business at Smithy Place mill, but did not fare particularly well, as his goods were assigned to creditors on 1 September 1863; they ordered that his machinery for converting loose wool into yarn, dyeing, weaving, scouring and finishing cloth, large stocks of dyewares, raw materials and yarns, should be sold by auction on 17 and 19 September.

James Robinson gave evidence to the *Enquiry into the Pollution of Rivers* in 1866, saying that he employed between 100 and 120 workers, and that the water used for dyeing was brought in by pipes as water from the river was polluted by Ochre. The firm had lost in the region of £2,000 from damage sustained in the flood of 1852, which was at least partly responsible for the bed of the river being around 12 inches lower than it had been forty years previously. The mill was also affected by the flood in November 1866, when, as at Rock mill, the river left heavy deposits of mud and silt on the floors of buildings.

Henry Pontefract had moved from Stoney Bank mill after the fire there in 1859, and was using part of Smithy Place mill. By 1867 he was experiencing financial difficulties, and his assignees ordered that his equipment for scribbling and carding wool, plus 19,000lbs of materials and two dyepans should be auctioned in May. This sale was to be followed on the same day by the sale of 9 spinning mules, but the name of their vendor is not given.

Mary Haigh was a 25 year old weaver who worked at Robinsons earning around 15s per week. She was married to William Haigh who was a stone delver, and they had a four year old daughter. Haigh spent most, if not all, of his earnings on drink. On Friday 14 January 1870 he had come home about 10pm and argued with his wife, hitting her twice on the head and kicking her. She went to bed complaining that her head hurt, and had died around 3am. William Haigh was committed for trial at the Assizes.

Harriet Boothroyd was injured at the mill on 5 July 1871, when a large steam pipe fell and hit her on the head. She was unconscious for two hours, after regaining consciousness she was taken home in a vehicle. A firm of cloth finishers called Thornton, Dodson & Co. had been using part of the mill; the partners dissolved their partnership in May 1872, which was followed by an advertisement for the sale of their machinery on 19 June. They had possibly not been in business very long, as some of the machinery was described as being 'nearly new'.

On 6 June 1875 the members of the mill's fire brigade were joined by the brigades from Barbers Holmbridge, the Unity brigade, Turners of Bridge mill, Mellors of Thongsbridge, Brook's of Meltham Mills, Messrs. Ridleys, the Spinks Mire mill brigade, and the Liverpool, London & Globe brigade from Huddersfield, to attend a special service at Brockholes Church to remember 24 year old Ernest Cheetham, a member of Robinson's brigade, who had died on 23 May.

Brook Beardsell, the eldest son of Isaac, had started a company at Smithy Place mill, and was trading as Beardsell Brothers. One of his employees was 17 year old Harpin Knowles, who was found hanged in the mill on 19 June 1876. At the inquest witnesses said that they had seen him in the mill on the afternoon of the day that he died, but no-one could offer an explanation for him dying. The jury returned a verdict of 'death by hanging'. Another employee of the firm died in 1883; twelve year old Joe Hobson went to get two buckets of water from the mill dam for weavers to wet their weft bobbins in, but failed to return. Friend Boothroyd a tuner, went to look for the lad, and found one of his buckets on the dam bank. He lifted the shuttle to release the water from the dam and discovered the boy's body. Allen Jenkinson said that he had seen the boy near the dam, but had not heard him fall in. The jury returned a verdict of 'accidental drowning'.

Brook Beardsell was in debt in 1884, with liabilities of £13,172 15s 8d; his assts totalled £1,182 2s 6d. He was declared bankrupt on 29 July 1884, his creditors accepted a settlement of 1s 9d in the £, and the examination was closed. Brook's younger brother Thomas was still living at Hagg House, and had been a partner in Joseph Mellor & Sons of Thongsbridge, but had retired from there. Thomas had taken responsibility for a portion of the debts of Beardsell Brothers; he also was declared bankrupt on 27 August 1884 with liabilities of £5,201 16s 5d, and assets of £661 13s 2d. His bankruptcy examination was also closed at the same time as his brother's.

Abel Coldwell & Sons were using part of the mill by 1887, when they gave a treat to their 80 employees in a room at Honley Corn Mill on 15 January, by permission of Messrs. Mitchell & Bower. The number of Coldwell's employees had risen to around 100 in 1891 and '92, after which time there is no further mention of them.

Joseph Robinson, who was the son of James Robinson, worked at the mill, but at Abel Coldwell & Sons, rather than with his father. He died on Sunday 11 Dec. 1892 at the age of 41, which could be the reason that the firm of Abel Coldwell & Sons disappeared.

France, Eastwood & Co, who were cloth finishers also took space in the mill in 1887, they gave their first treat to the workforce in January 1888 at the Royal Oak, Thongsbridge. William Hay Robinson a yarn spinner was using part of the mill in 1888. In October of that year Mr. Robinson found the body of 70 year old George Woodhead of Wooldale, who was one of his workers, floating in the mill dam. As there were no marks of violence on the body it was assumed that he had drowned himself.

A Joseph Silverwood was using part of the mill in 1890, he was a cloth manufacturer. Whether he had any connection to Henry Silverwood who had been at Upper Mytholmbridge mill in the 1880s is not known. Joseph Silverwood appears to have been finding business difficult, as his 18 looms and ancillary equipment were advertised to be sold by auction on 5 November 1891.

In 1894 James Robinson & Sons had bought some bags of waste yarn from Moses Harris of Spitalfields London valued at £146, but Mr. Robinson refused to pay for them as he said they were not of the same quality as the ones he had seen, which resulted in the matter being taken to court. Mr. Robinson had gone to Harris's premises and looked initially at two bags of worsted waste; he then looked at a third bag that was of a lower quality then the first two. There were more bags in the Lot that Mr. Robinson did not inspect, although he was given the opportunity to inspect all the bags if he wished to do so, but accepted the seller's comment that the unopened bags were of similar quality to the ones that he had seen. Mr. Robinson maintained that he had bought the goods by sample, whereas Harris's argued that he had not bought by sample, but had inspected the goods before buying them. The judge agreed with Harris's, saying that as Mr. Robinson had chosen not to inspect every bale, the responsibility was his. The Jury found for Harris's and ordered Mr. Robinson to pay the full price for the goods plus the costs of the case.

The Factory Inspector Mr. J.D. Prior summoned W.H. Robinson Yarn Spinners in 1896, for employing boys under 16 without a surgeon's certificate of fitness. Prior had visited the mill on 21 August as a boy had met with an accident, which it was Prior's duty to investigate. He also found that Brook Hirst had been employed there for a considerable length of time without a certificate; John Fearne had worked there for a shorter time, but without the necessary certificate. The firm were fined 8s plus costs in each case. Prior had also visited James Robinson & Sons, where he found that two girls under 16 were employed without the necessary certificates. Edith Beaumont had worked there almost 18 months, while Alice Earnshaw had been there for a shorter period. Robinson's were fined 20s plus costs in the case of Beaumont, and 10s plus costs in the case of Earnshaw.

In 1897 France, Eastwood & Co were charged with employing 3 youths without certificates of fitness. Mr. Prior said that the firm did not appear to keep a register of employees, but one of the youths had been there for over one year, one for six months and the third for about four or five months. In their defence the firm said that the lads had obtained certificates for the firm at which they had originally worked, and that France, Eastwood & Co had not realised that new certificates should be obtained when the lads came to work for them. The bench imposed a fine of 20s plus costs in each case.

A company trading as Eastwood's who were dyers and finishers, and appear to have had no connection to France, Eastwood & Co, had taken premises in the mill from 16 May 1894, agreeing to pay James Robinson £300 per year rent in quarterly instalments. They had fallen into arrears, and in 1896 Robinsons had issued a distress warrant against Eastwood's in an attempt to redress the balance. Robinsons had also bought the machinery from Eastwood's for £553, and were leasing it to them in a further attempt to address Eastwood's problems, but Eastwood's still fell behind with their payments. In 1899 Eastwood's had agreed to pay the rentals at a monthly rate of £30, but still the payments were not maintained. It was eventually agreed that Eastwood's would pay £10 per week; when this arrangement failed Robinsons withdrew the supply of motive power and steam from Eastwood's part of the mill, prompting Eastwood's to apply to the Court for an injunction ordering Robinsons to restore it. Robinsons contended that the last arrangement had put an end to the original tenancy, permitting them to re-enter the premises. The judge agreed with this opinion and dismissed the case.

A man called Ernest Hinchliffe detected a smell of burning coming from the mill at about 5.30pm on Saturday 16 Sept. 1905. Along with Charles Reckitts, who lived in the mill yard, he connected a hosepipe to the Batley Corporation water main, and by 6.30 they had extinguished a fire in a blowing machine at the mill. Damage, which was estimated to be about £50, was covered by insurance. The Mungo, Shoddy and Merino side of Robinson's business suffered a more serious fire on 1 August 1909. A policeman discovered the fire during the early hours of Sunday Morning in the rag grinding room at the mill. Along with some workpeople they set up three hoses, but the fire had a firm hold. Huddersfield fire brigade, with their steam powered engine 'Phyllis', arrived after the roof had collapsed. The fire was extinguished after two hours, but the rag grinding room and a large quantity of stock were destroyed. Damage was estimated at £3,000.

 A succinct advertisement appeared in the *Holmfirth Express* in April 1909: 'Wanted Jerry lads, apply Robinsons Brockholes'. This related to the cloth finishing side of Robinsons business; 'Jerry' is the term used by cloth finishers for the cropping machine with a rotary blade, that was referred to in machinery sales advertisements of the nineteenth century as a 'perpetual'. The person in charge of operating a machine was known as the 'head ender', whereas the assistant was the 'tail ender'; Jerry lads would be tail enders. There seems to be no other evidence of this term being used in print.

The *Yorkshire Textile Directory* of 1910 gives the occupants of the mill as James Robinson & Sons, dyers, fullers, finishers, shoddy and mungo manufacturers; along with W.H. Robinson & Co. who were spinners of woollen and Angola yarns. The Directory for 1916 also includes W. Cheetham & Co. worsted manufacturers, who were in part of the mill until 1920.

Shortly before midnight on 16 February 1916, a fire was discovered in one building at the mill. A strong wind was blowing, which fanned the flames resulting in the roof of the building collapsing shortly before the arrival of the Huddersfield fire brigade. The direction of the wind blew the flames away from adjacent building helping to limit the damage, which was estimated at several thousands of pounds and was insured. The cause of the outbreak was not given. On discovering the fire the mill buzzer was sounded, which alarmed a number of the residents in Brockholes, as, due to the war, the sounding of buzzers was used to warn the population of the approach of Zeppelin airship bombers.

Entries in the *Yorkshire Textile Directory* for W.H. Robinson disappear after 1930, whether they moved to other premises, went out of business, or just stopped advertising is unclear. Their name reappears at Smithy Place in 1947 and continues until 1952; the firm moved premises in 1951, or possibly late 1950, to Yew Tree mill at Hinchliffe Mill.

A company named Zeta Textiles who were dyers of woollen and worsted yarns and cloth were using part of the mill by 1954, they may have been an offshoot of James Robinson & Sons, as the telephone number was the same for both companies. Zeta Textiles were listed in the YTD until 1971.

A fire broke out in a building that was separate from the main mill on 15 May, 1970. Brigades from Holmfirth, Huddersfield, Meltham and Skelmanthorpe attended and the blaze was brought under control within 45 minutes. The cost of the damage was estimated to be in the region of £30,000. A fire at the mill on 2 June 1983 caused between £40,000 and £50,000 damage to bales of wool and synthetic fibres stored in a single storey building. Holmfirth fire brigade had the blaze under control within 20 minutes, but were called back several times during the day to deal with fires breaking out in different bales within the store room. James Robinson & Sons last advertisement for staff appeared in the *Holmfirth Express* in 1982; the date of their closure is unknown, but the mill was demolished around 1991. A plan to build 40 two storey terrace houses and 7 detached houses on the site was submitted to Kirklees Council in 1996.[6]

Banks and Lower Banks mills

Standing downstream from Smithy Place, Banks and Lower Banks mills were on the land between the Woodhead and Sheffield Turnpike roads. The earliest information on them comes from an Indenture dated 1 January 1768, between William Walker of Crownest Halifax; to Joseph Armitage and Joseph Jagger of Honley. Each of the three should contribute equally to the cost of building a 'Mill or Mills for the crushing and pressing of Rapes with sufficient Granaries storehouses and other buildings and improving the Fulling mill there now standing'. The estimated cost of doing these things was £500. Armitage and Jagger were to rent the premises from Walker by paying him the equivalent of the interest that his share of the money would have earned had it been invested, plus a fee of £5 per hundred, for the term of 42 years. The fulling mill with the house, barns and other buildings was already rented to Joseph Jagger; the previous occupant had been Abraham Roberts. The indenture also includes permission to build 'a Rasp or other engine on the premises for cutting, clipping, rasping or grinding Dyeing wood'. Power for the new Rape mill was to be taken from the water wheel in the fulling mill. The occupant of the mill house in 1768 was Benjamin Townsend.

The mill was slightly affected by the flood of 4 February 1852, J. Haigh & Son submitted a claim for damage to the mill dam and the water wheel totalling £67 6s, which was reduced by the inspectors to £50. The claim was marked 'disallowed' and nothing was paid; claim no.306. The Holme Reservoir Commissioners give the owner of the mills in 1853 as Anne Walker; the occupants of the upper mill were William Joseph Haigh and Richard Haigh; the occupant of the lower mill was William Cross Robinson.

The occupant of the lower mill, used for corn and animal feed, had become Joseph Sutcliffe in February 1856, when it was broken into and a quantity of bran, sharps and pig meal were stolen. The thieves were followed towards Honley, as one of the stolen sacks had a hole in it, leaving a trail, and also a large easily distinguished footprint showed regularly. However, no-one had been arrested prior to the report being published in the *Huddersfield Chronicle* on 9 February.

Richard, George, John and William Haigh trading as John Haigh & Co. fulling millers, dissolved their partnership in March 1860. In March 1864, William Haigh sued a man called Holroyd in the County Court for not returning 10 skeps valued at £4. Holroyd produced a receipt from Haigh, showing that the skeps had in fact been returned. Haigh also claimed £21 in damages from John Brook a carrier from Scholes. Haigh had been returning to Honley from Huddersfield market in November 1855 when he passed Brook who was walking a cow back to his home. Haigh bought the cow, which appeared to be healthy, from Brook and took it home. The following day the cow appeared to be sick and had since infected his other cows. Haigh had to have medical help with his herd for the next month. After much evidence from both sides the jury decided that Brook had not given Haigh a warranty with the animal, therefore Haigh could not claim damages. Haigh was ordered to pay the full costs of the case.

Two slubbers, Ben Baxendale and Jonathon Kilburn were charged in August 1866 with leaving work without giving fourteen days notice. There was some discussion in court as to whether the way in which the requirement for notice was displayed in the mill and administered by the company was actually legal. The bench advised the two slubbers to return to the mill and complete the work that they had begun; and also advised Haigh's to get a better notice, saying that they would not convict on the existing one.

A fire broke out at the fulling mill at 2am on Saturday 30 May 1868. The press gave two accounts of how it was discovered, the *Huddersfield Chronicle* reported, on 6 June, that a fuller, who was sleeping at the mill, was awoken by the smell of smoke, discovered the fire and went to wake his brother who was asleep in an adjoining house. After they had informed the Haigh family the brothers began moving pieces of cloth from the mill, and furniture from the house. The *Huddersfield Examiner* records on the same day that the fire was seen by a navvy who was walking along Sheffield Road towards New Mill, who raised householders to help him to put it out. It is possible that both reports are correct. The fire brigade from James Shaw & Co. of Crossley and Neiley mills attended, but much of the mill was destroyed. The fire brigade were able to save two spinning rooms and the mill house; the damage was estimated to be between £2,000 and £3,000. No explanation of how the fire occurred was given. The lower, meal mill was not affected. An advertisement appeared in the *Huddersfield Chronicle* in April 1869 for the house, farm buildings, meal mill, 8 cottages, 'the remaining portions of the woollen mill', and around 55 acres of land commonly known as Banks mill to be let. Applications were to be made to John Smith Land Agent, of Lightcliffe near Halifax. Attempts were also made to sell the land and property in the 1880s, and in the 1890s it was turned into a Pleasure Gardens.

The *Holmfirth Express* carried a report on 6 August 1898 about the Bank Holiday weekend from 30 July to 1 August: Clayton West Band had played on the Saturday, followed by a fire work display and a "mechanical but lifelike" parachute descent in the evening. Honley band had given 2 concerts of sacred music on the Sunday afternoon and evening, and also played on the Monday. The gardens, covering some fifty acres, had been designed and constructed by Mr. J.W. Mellor. There was a shallow boating lake covering some 5 acres, with a second lake being constructed later. The rest of the land was laid out with lawns, flowerbeds, paths, and water falls in the streams feeding the lakes. Bathing was allowed on Sunday mornings in one of the lakes. Hot houses sold bouquets of flowers, buttonholes and bedding plants. There were also swings and Donkey rides; and dancing to a small band. A novelty was the Hotchkiss Bicycle Railway, real bicycles that were fixed to a track.

The 25 inch Ordinance Survey map of 1892 shows the main mill buildings and the mill pond, but their use is not marked; the lower mill is shown as a Corn mill. The 1906 map shows the main mill buildings with the gardens alongside, and the lower mill is marked 'disused'. The maps of 1918 and 1932 show the continuing development of the pleasure gardens, with the lower mill still marked as 'disused' on both maps.

The Mellor family sold the Pleasure Grounds to Mr. Fred Thompson of Blackpool in 1943 for £8,790. During the war it had been used as a military base and was consequently rather dilapidated. Thompson installed a miniature railway, the two boating lakes, one of which was especially for children, and a Ghost Train plus several other rides. There was also a dance hall and catering facilities; in total he had spent in the region of £20,000. The site was advertised for auction in April 1949 and attracted two bids, the highest was for £7,500; the property was withdrawn. The land was eventually sold to Brook Motors, whose main factory was on St. Thomas' Road, Huddersfield. They built a factory on the site that opened in 1958.[7] The site continues to be used for industrial purposes.

Neiley and Crossley mills

Standing on the right bank of the River Holme these two mills were next to one another only a few hundred yards upstream from Honley Bridge. Both mills were in the possession of the Shaw family until about 1860. The earlier of the two mills is Crossley mill, the precise date of building is unclear, it came into the occupation of David Shaw, Son & Co. in 1819, but had been built some time earlier. In his response to the government's enquiries into the conditions in mills and factories in 1833 David Shaw said that since 1819 Crossley mill had been powered by a 4hp water wheel and a 24hp steam engine that they brought into use if and when water was scarce. A total of 47 people were employed at Crossley mill: 2 girls and 1 boy under 10 years of age, 3 girls and 2 boys under 12 years, 3 girls and 3 boys under 14 years, all earning 4s per week; 7 boys earning 6s 10½d and 1 girl earning 5s who were under 16, 3 boys under 18 earning 8s 8d, 3 males under 21 earning 20s 4d, 20 men over 21 some earning 20s 9d and others earning 24s. Nineteen boys and nine girls relied on the people that they worked under for their wages. The working day during summer began at 5.30am and ended at 7.30pm, in winter the hours were from 6am to 8pm. The reasons given for the alteration of times was to save expense incurred by having to light the mill, prevention of fire, and the convenience of the workpeople. The working day on Saturday was three hours shorter than during the week. Workers were allowed half an hour for breakfast, one hour for dinner, and half an hour for tea; Machinery was only stopped for the midday meal, not the half hour breaks, this was supposedly for the benefit of the fulling department, which employed only adult men. The firm paid for a doctor to attend a worker who had been injured at work, but not in other cases; they would give relief to needy families due to accident or illness; whether this was an advance on future earnings is not known. Workers were allowed two days holiday at Christmas, one or sometimes two days at Whitsuntide, two half days on 14 and 15 May, and three days in September, besides other half days during the year when they were unable to run the machinery due to lack of water. In

Part of Crossley/Neiley mills. © A.J. Brooke

answer to the question about Parliament regulating and reducing the number of working hours the firm said that working less than 12 hours a day would be injurious to manufacturers and operatives alike, and would be a boon to foreign manufacturers who could run their machinery for as long as they wanted. Shaw's also gave some statistics for Neiley factory, which had been built in 1825, its original use was not given, but it had been used as a woollen mill since 1831. Power was supplied by a 40hp steam engine; 155 people were employed in this mill, 1 boy and 1 girl under 10 each earning 4s; 6 boys under 12 earning 4s 8d, and 7 girls under 12 each earning 4s 1¾d; 20 boys under 14 earning 5s 5¼d, 4 girls under 14 earning 4s 6d; 13 boys under 16 earning 6s 7½d, 5 girls under 16 earning 5s 1d; 9 boys under 18 earning 8s 5d, and 6 girls earning 5s 6d; 9 males under 21 earning 14s 6d; a total of 74 men over 21, 52 of them could earn 52s 4d in a full week of 69 hours, the other 22 earned 21s per week. Answers to the other questions were exactly as those for Crossley mill.

The survey of properties in Honley carried out in 1838 and published in 1843 for rating purposes shows that Neiley mill was owned by the Executors of David Shaw, and the occupants were D. Shaw, Son & Co, which was being run by David Shaw's eldest son Benjamin Ledger Shaw; the owner of Crossley mill was Sarah Waddington and the occupant is given as Benjamin Ledger Shaw. The mills appear to have been stopped from working on Monday 13 August 1842 by 'Plug Rioters' supporting the Chartist movement. The report gives no specific details of damage done; the usual action was to draw the drain plug from the mill's boiler forcing the engine tenter to withdraw the fire to avoid an explosion. At some mills or factories they also lifted the dam shuttles to allow the dam to empty, prolonging the period of enforced idleness. These actions had little effect, if any, on overall production, but inevitably affected the immediate earnings of the workers, whose interests the rioters were supposed to be promoting.

The Factory Inspector charged William Dawson, a slubber who worked at D. Shaw, Son & Co, with working Hannah Slater, who was under 13 years of age, for more than nine hours on 25 June 1844. Dawson admitted the offence and said that the girl had only been employed for that day due to his regular piecer being ill; he was fined £1 plus costs. Charles Slater, the girl's father, was charged with failing to send Hannah to school for her two hours education on that day. The girl's mother appeared and pleaded that the day in question was the only day that Hannah had missed school. The bench fined the father 5s plus 10s costs.

On 7 Aug. 1847 about 1pm, Thomas Thornton a 40 year old weaver at the mill, decided to treat his work colleagues, who were returning to work after their midday meal, to a display of his oratory skills. He stood on the parapet of Honley Bridge; unfortunately he had imbibed a quantity of liquid refreshment and was unable to maintain his balance, falling headlong into the river some 20 feet below. On being rescued it was found that he had badly damaged one leg, which would keep him from working for some time and allow him to ponder the advisability of his action.

Textile manufacturers were finding trading to be very difficult in the late 1840s, Shaw's, and probably other manufacturers, had cut the length of the working day from 11 hours down to 8 by November 1847. An advertisement in the *Huddersfield Chronicle* of 2 November 1850 announced the first show of the 'Honley Association for Promoting and Encouraging of the Keeping and Rearing of Good Bred Pigs amongst the Labouring Classes', to be held in Honley on 9 November, from 12noon to 4pm. Prizes ranged between 5s and £1, plus Rosettes. The '*Chronicle*' of that date said that Mr. B.L. Shaw was to let off a quantity of land for 'the encouragement of spade husbandry and cottage comfort. Mr. Shaw is the largest millowner in Honley and his proposal to the labouring classes coming directly after the announcement of the pig show, is proof that he is desirous to afford facilities by which the labouring classes can feed their pigs at the lowest possible cost'.

The lack of orders for cloth continued into the 1850s, in May 1852 Shaw's had laid off many workers, with others working short time; Dickinson & Platt cloth finishers were using part of the mill, and were mainly occupied with 'country work' for self employed weavers. In October 1852 the *Huddersfield Examiner* reported that many of the mills in Honley were only partially employed. 'There is little doing at the large works of D. Shaw, Son & Co; and latterly that little has been made less by Messrs. Dickinson & Platt's removal to Huddersfield.' The paper did give a small ray of hope by reporting that: 'Mr. Charles Lawrence, foreman for 20 years in the machine making department at Shaw's, has taken over the machinery and workshop and is to carry on the business'. This would allow at least some of the men from that department, who had been laid off for some time, to return to work. They were able to make boilers, steam engines and many machines used in woollen cloth manufacture.

The flood of February 1852 had a much less severe effect on premises in the Honley area, water entered Crossley/Neiley mills, and the watchman went to the upper storeys of the mill to keep dry. The flood waters also washed away the Toll Gate that was opposite Crossley mill, close to the bottom of Gynn Lane. The Trustees of David Shaw submitted a claim for damage to machinery and stock totalling £525 12s 5½d, which was subsequently marked 'claim withdrawn'. Claim no 238.

In July 1852 the wife of the engine tenter at Crossley/Neiley mills was attempting to wean her suckling child, and was suffering from the fullness of her breasts. She was attempting to draw off some of her milk using a tobacco pipe when her husband came into the room. He thought that he could improve on the method by attaching a thin tube to the vacuum pump on the mill's 100hp engine, and attaching the tobacco pipe to the other end. He then sent for his wife, who sat down and had her breasts emptied much more quickly. The '*Examiner*' correspondent was given a live demonstration of the procedure on the Thursday morning.

The firm of D. Shaw, Son & Co. virtually stopped trading in 1852; this was the year that Benjamin L. Shaw died, with the running of the business being taken over by his two half-brothers Foster Shaw & James Shaw. The machinery was still in the mill, some of it eventually being used by Kellett

& Scott and other firms. 'A man from Lindley' was using some of the looms in February 1853, but his weavers walked out on Tuesday 22ⁿᵈ dissatisfied with their rate of pay. They were weaving 'plain broads' with a mohair weft, and were being paid 3d per 10ft string for weaving 20 picks per inch; the weavers maintained that they could only earn between 6s 0½d and 7s 6d per week. Within a week the dispute was settled and the weavers returned to work with a 25 percent increase in their pay rates.

Business began to improve during the latter part of 1852, by January 1853 James Shaw had started a new company and had posted bills for between 40 and 50 weavers. In May of that year James Shaw appealed against the amount levied against the mills by the overseers for the poor rate. Rather than enter into complicated legal procedures, the court advised the two sides to get together and reach an amicable agreement, which they did. The Reservoir Commissioners listed the owner of Crossley mill, in 1853, as Robert Walker Waddington, the occupant was given as James Shaw; as Neiley mill had no water wheel it was not included in the statistics.

Although business was increasing, not everyone was reaping the benefits. Charles Lawrence, foreman machine maker for D. Shaw, Son & Co, who had started his own business after Shaw's had closed in October 1852, advertised a large quantity of new and second hand machinery for sale on 28 May 1853, apply to Charles Lawrence at the mill. The advertisement was repeated in November of the same year. The *Huddersfield Chronicle* of 6 May 1854 carried an advertisement for an auction of machinery at Neiley mill on 15 May, which was very similar to that which Charles Lawrence had been trying to sell the year before. Ownership of the machinery was not given, but neither machine making, nor the name of Charles Lawrence appears at the premises after that date.

An accident occurred at Crossley mill on 8 February 1854; Matthew Fretwell was oiling shafting bearings when his clothing became caught and he was dragged round, crushing his body between the shafting, the ceiling and the wall of the room. The shafting was stopped as quickly as possible and Fretwell extricated. He had many injuries to his body, and two broken legs, also much of his clothing had been torn from him. A Doctor was called, but he died about 30 minutes later. A 43 year old gas fitter named James Lodge who was married with 8 children, was working on a gas pipe under the floor of Neiley mill when a plug in the end of the supply pipe became dislodged. Mr. Lodge was immediately overcome by the fumes; he was taken outside and a Doctor was sent for. Although Lodge was unconscious there were times when he was seen to be breathing; the Doctor attempted to give him Brandy, but this failed to revive him and he was carried home where he died the following day. He had previously suffered a similar experience at the mill around one year earlier. The inquest jury returned a verdict of 'Inhaling gas while repairing a gas pipe'.

On Saturday 23 January 1858 there were rumours circulating in the district that a major bankruptcy had occurred, on the Monday it became known that it was James Shaw of Honley, who was the present controller of the old and once respected firm of D. Shaw, Son & Co. The firm's liabilities were said to be in the region of £30,000. At a creditors meeting on Tuesday 2 February the total liabilities were £21,690 17s 5d; the assets amounted to £7,577 8s 7d, leaving a deficit in excess of £14,000. When examined, James Shaw said that he had entered business in January 1852; having no money of his own he said that he had borrowed £12,000 on the estimated value of the machinery in the mills; the value of the machinery at the time of his bankruptcy was £8,000, and £5,800 of that mortgage was still owed. Other losses included interest owed on loans, losses on speculation in railway shares, bad debts in Huddersfield, and depreciation of machinery. Shaw had known that he was insolvent for two or three years; he attributed his failure to: differences in the premiums paid on policies for life assurance compared with their current value; interest paid on loans and bank accounts; losses on railway shares; bad debts; cash taken for household expenses, and depreciation of machinery. At the second creditors meeting held one week later on 9 February 1858, Shaw said that he could not meet the demands of the creditors to pay 7s 6d in the £ on his debts. It was shown that Shaw had been 'commercially rotten' for years and had resorted to all sorts of devices to keep himself from sinking. A motion was put to declare Shaw bankrupt but no-one would second it, eventually it was decided to wind up the estate under a deed of assignment. The assignees chosen were Wright Mellor, J,T, Taylor, Law Hepponstall, and J. Barwick of Yorkshire Bank. A large portion of the machinery in Neiley mill was to be sold in June 1858; a report on 12 June said that it had been sold privately.

In August 1858, Sarah Ann Kaye who was a burler at the mill, was 'grassing' a piece in a field next to the mill when Amos Pinder, who was intoxicated, tried to take improper liberties with her. When she got free, Pinder threw a stone at her. In court he was fined 2s 6d plus 18s 6d costs; if he was unable to pay he was to be imprisoned for two months.

A one sixth share owned by Foster Shaw and James Shaw in Neiley mill, was to be auctioned on 10 November 1858, when the premises were described as a 5 storey high Woollen mill 40yds long and 17yds wide, with an engine house; also the boiler house building 3 storeys high 16yds by 11yds, plus the 'new end' 2 storeys high 12 yds by 11yds; and the weaving shed 70yds by 13yds. A building 4 storeys high 12yds by 5yds used as storage and offices. The gas-house and wool drying stoves. A fire-proof building 2 storeys high 80yds by 7yds; stables and porter's lodge. Also the building used for hand raising, steam brushing and teazing, plus the steam engine, boiler, shafting and going gear.[8]

A fire was discovered in a drying stove shortly before 6pm on 26 January 1859. It was fortunate that it was discovered then, as the mill closed at 6pm. Workmen put out the fire using buckets of water; the damage was said to be 'trifling'. It was thought that the fire had been caused by a spark from a lamp. Robert Walker Waddington and William Henry Waddington, who lived in Liverpool and were the owners of Neiley mill issued a notice in January 1859, to the effect that in addition to the buildings, they also owned all the shafting and gearing in the buildings and some of the machinery. Why they felt the necessity to issue the notice is not stated. Around 2,000 panes of glass in the mills were broken by large hailstones during a violent thunderstorm on the evening of 18 July 1859, which also affected other premises in Holme Valley.

The fire bell at the mill was rung just before 9pm on Monday 21 November 1859, bringing 'hundreds' to the mill, but there was no equipment available to fight the fire, 'not even a bucket'; the fire engine was again out of order. When buckets were found the mill dam was empty. The door to the room where the fire had started was locked, and was only burst open with difficulty. It was then found that large bales of wool had been stacked just inside the door. The people present worked very hard for one hour to get the fire under control. The floor of the room was covered with teazed wool and cotton that had been oiled; the seat of the fire was beside a teazing machine, therefore it was assumed that the cause was friction in the machine due to a lack of oil on the machine, which had happened before. Damage was limited to 'a few pounds'. Neighbours said that the mill used to be the leader in the district for fire prevention, but it was now one of the worst.

A company named Kellett and Scott cloth manufacturers were using part of the mill by January 1861, when they gave a treat to their 40 women workers at the Jacobs Well Inn; in August of the following year they formed part of a party of 300 from the mills who went on a trip to Hollingworth Lake. Some enjoyed excursions onto the lake, while other promenaded on the bank, surprised to see such a 'great mill dam'. They arrived back in Honley about 10pm. The firm of Beaumont Kaye & Co. cloth dressers, were originally using part of Reins mill, but had moved to "Shaw's Factory" by January 1860. The partners were John Beaumont, George Beaumont, David Liversedge and Thomas Gledhill in June 1863, when they dissolved their partnership, and appear to have ceased trading.

Mr. William Arnold, boiler manufacturer of Huddersfield, was delivering a new boiler to the mill in February 1864 using a traction engine. After delivering and unloading the boiler, the traction engine went back through the toll bar without the wagon that had carried the boiler. Some of the workmen from the mill yoked themselves to the wagon and pulled it through the toll bar in an attempt to avoid the charge, which the toll bar keeper objected to. William Arnold refused to pay the toll for the cart, and the matter went to court. After hearing the evidence the bench ordered that the 5s toll should be paid, and added 12s in costs.

The firm of Kellett & Scott seem to have ceased trading in the early 1860s; Charles Kellett then went into partnership with William Henry Kellett, and the firm became Charles Kellett & Son. They assigned all their goods to their trustees: Joshua Moore, George Mallinson and Samuel Rhodes, all wool staplers in Huddersfield, for the benefit of their creditors on 28 June 1865.

Police Constable Morley spotted a fire in a large shed at the mill early on the morning of Monday 10 July 1865. He raised the alarm, bringing a large number of people with buckets and cans to put out the flames. Thirteen bags of wool and shoddy were totally destroyed, the damage was estimated at £300, and was not insured. The mill's fire engine was still out of order.

On 4 October 1865, Joseph Fothergill, the 13 year old son of Thomas Fothergill of New St. Honley, who worked in Crossley mill, got his right hand caught in a machine. His fore finger was torn off and his other fingers on that hand were badly crushed. His hand was so far into the machine that it took 15 minutes to release the boy so that he could be taken home.

Another fire occurred at the mill, in a drying stove, on 1 February 1866, it was seen by someone across the river at Banks, who alerted the night watchman. He rang the alarm bell bringing a crowd of people to the mill. The mill's fire engine was got out, but 'as usual' it was not working, and a good half hour was lost before it was of any use at all. Someone went to alert the fire crew at Brooke's mill at Armitage Bridge, which was quickly put to work after it arrived, but the building was completely gutted. No estimate of the damage was given. Both mills suffered some disruption and damage to the ground floor rooms from flood waters in November 1866, in common with Rock and Smithy Place mills upstream.

In 1872 David Schofield of Honley set up in business at the mill with Joseph Sykes of Fitzwilliam Street Huddersfield as cloth finishers, they had a three year partnership. Schofield left the firm in 1875, and his place was taken by Thomas Heaton a cloth miller of Thirstin Honley; but their partnership was dissolved on 1 Aptil 1876, when their business also closed. Their finishing machinery was sold in January 1877 for £49 7s.

Crossley mill was advertised for sale by auction on 12 May 1873, as Lot 13 in a large sale of land and property in Honley. The name of the previous owner is not given. It was described as a stone built 3 storey mill with shafting and going gear; also the dyehouse, cottages, outbuildings, yards and gardens, plus 5acres, 1 rood, 24 perches of land.

Despite the financial difficulties of the Shaw family in the 1850s and the problems that it had created for other manufacturers, James Shaw had continued in business. He was again in difficulty in November 1876, when the first meeting of his creditors was held on the 23rd of that month at Learoyd, Learoyd and Morrison, Solicitors of Buxton Road Huddersfield. Shaw was adjudged bankrupt on 7 December 1876, details being published in the *Huddersfield Examiner* of 6 January 1877. Total liabilities amounted to £14, 464 8s 3½d, he had £4,112 12 10d in assets, leaving a total deficiency of £10,351 15s 5½d. The Auctioneer Henry Tinker was appointed as Shaw's trustee. The business had been started by David Shaw, who was the father of Benjamin Ledger Shaw by his first wife, also Foster Shaw and James Shaw by his second wife. After the death of the father, B.L. Shaw had taken over the business with a silent partner named Samuel Brown Hargreaves. After the death of his half brother Benjamin in November 1872, James Shaw said that he had bought the machinery for £12,000 with a loan to that amount. Before the death of S.B. Hargreaves, Shaw had repaid £7,000 of the loan. The outstanding debt of £5,000 was transferred from Hargreaves to James Shaw's son James Hargreaves Shaw. In addition to that debt, Shaw said that his son had loaned him a further £2,000 on 31 March 1868, plus an additional £3,500 in January 1874. As security for these loans Shaw had taken out a life policy for £5,000 on 27 July 1874. Since that date Shaw had borrowed money from the Insurance Company using the policy as collateral. The large quantity of Shaw's machinery at the mills was advertised for sale by auction on the morning of Wednesday 31 January 1877; there was also a small sale in the afternoon of that day comprising the finishing machinery from Heaton & Sykes. The sale of 30,000lbs of yarn, wool and mungo was arranged for

Thursday 1 February, to be followed by the sale of the gas making plant, steam and water piping, plus the contents of the mechanic's shop and the office furnishings on Friday 2 February. The *London Gazette* reported on 15 October 1878, that the whole of Shaw's assets had been realised for the benefit of creditors, and a dividend of 2s 6d in the £ had been paid. This closed the bankruptcy proceedings.

Josiah France was using part of the mills in April 1878, when he advertised for a tuner for his Dobcross looms. John Hey had been using a dyeworks at the mills, but which one is debatable. He advertised the plant for sale as a going concern in Neiley mill in the 'Private Contract' section of the *Huddersfield Examiner* in March 1884, but failed to find a buyer. The machinery was subsequently advertised for sale by auction on 12 May in the same year because he was giving up business, but at Crossley mill.

C.E. Bousefield was using part of the 'Shaw factory' in June 1885, when a boy called Fred Brook spotted a fire about 11pm on the 16th. Brook told Thomas Beetham the engine tenter, who lived on the premises. The mill's own fire engine was put to use, followed by the engine from Robinson's of Smithy Place mill, and the one from Brooke's at Armitage Bridge. The fire, which was thought to have started due to some wool placed in the boiler house becoming overheated, was out by 2am. Damage was estimated to be around £1,000.

In July 1889 the *Yorkshire Factory Times* reported that all the firms in Honley were very busy, and that the village was wearing a healthy and prosperous look. It continued: 'The only regrettable matter noticeable is the tendency to employ boys where formerly men were employed; and women taking the place of men in weaving'. Confirmation of this tendency was contained in the paper's edition of 30 August of the same year when they reported that H.B. Harrison & Co, who were dyers and finishers, had locked out about seventeen men who worked in their dyehouse and had asked for higher wages. They had each been earning 18s a week, with the exception of one man who had the additional responsibility of looking after the washing machine and was paid £1 per week. Harrison's had told the men that their jobs could be done by young men for 15s per week and laid them all off. Harrison's had moved into the dyehouse around 1 October 1888, taking a ten year lease on the property at a rent of £200 a year, payable in quarterly instalments. This was a particularly low rent for a property the size of Neiley mill, but contained a condition that Harrison's should in addition, spend at least £1,500 on building a new shed, and repairing and renovating the existing buildings, which they had done. It would seem, however, that Harrison's considered that trading conditions were not sufficiently buoyant to permit them to trade successfully for the remainder of the lease. An auction sale of the unexpired portion of the lease was advertised to be held on 11 March 1891, with the sale of their machinery to follow one hour after the sale of the lease.

Neiley mill contained a bone boiling plant for the manufacture of size and manure, which had been used by William Barker who had died. The premises consisted of a three-bedroomed house, plus a 2 storey building used as a grinding mill and engine house; a second 2 storey building used as store rooms, size boiling sheds, a three stall stable and loose box, chimney shaft, cart shed and other buildings. All the necessary machinery and equipment were already installed. The premises were auctioned on 4 October 1892, and were bought by Wright Charlesworth Littlewood, who had premises at Thirstin mill in Honley; he never moved into Neiley mill however, the reasons for this are explained in Chapter 15 under Thirstin mill.

Most, if not all, of Neiley mill appears to have been empty from 1893; advertisements were placed at regular intervals in the local press for around ten years with no signs of success. Cooper & Liversedge, who were originally in premises in Huddersfield, were using Neiley dyeworks by April 1906, when they sued Crosland Marsh spinners, of Bridge mill for £2 7s for work done. Crosland Marsh submitted a counter claim for £2 11s 9d, the £2 was claimed as compensation for dyeing done by Cooper & Liversedge that had been off shade, the 11s 9d was claimed for an overcharge of ½d per pound for dyeing done. The judge found for Cooper and Liversedge and awarded them

Aftermath of the fire 3 June 1914. Collection of A.J. Brooke
Original photograph taken by C.E. Exley of Honley

£1 15s 3d. The *Yorkshire Textile Directory* of 1910 records the tenants of Neiley mill as Herbert Scholefield & Co. woollen and worsted spinners and manufacturers; B.T. Cave Ltd. woollen, Angola and commission spinners with 2,400 spindles; and Cooper, Liversedge and Wood Ltd. wool, cotton and waste dyers, who were using Neiley dyeworks.

In 1913 Scholefield's upset nearby residents when they installed a noisy gas engine, the local council ordered them to fit a silencer to it. Allen Thornton & Son Ltd. eventually became the owners of Neiley mill. It is likely that they bought it at auction on 3 May 1909, when it was sold for £600. Neiley mill was gutted by fire in June 1914. All three firms were in the five storey mill, Cooper, Liversedge & Wood were on the ground floor, with the other two firms occupying the four upper floors. The fire originated in a mule-gate of Scholefield's on the third floor of the mill about 8.30am; the Huddersfield fire brigade arrived at 9.05, followed one minute later by the Unity brigade from Holmfirth. The five storey mill was completely destroyed, but Scholefield's offices and Crossley mill next door were not affected as there was only a light breeze. The Unity brigade went home after midnight, but water was still being played on the ashes the following morning. After the fire, Herbert Scholefield & Co and B.T. Cave moved to Bradshaw mill in Honley. Some rebuilding took place, but not to the height of five storeys.

Tom Liversedge, the founder of the original dyeing firm, which was on Leeds Road in Huddersfield, had died in 1897 at the age of 64; Joseph Cooper, who became the managing director of Cooper, Liversedge & Wood, died in early October 1922. He was president of the Huddersfield Master Dyers and Finishers Association at the time of his death. The firm continued using Neiley mill until around 1968, which was the last year that they advertised for staff.

Allen Thornton & Son were using part of Crossley mill in 1887, when the Honley Local Board cautioned them for causing a smoke nuisance; the firm registered as a Limited Liability Company in 1903. Allen Fox of Concord Place Honley, was engine tenter at the mill, he was oiling shafting in a wooden shed that contained a winding off frame at about 8.50am on Wednesday 27 April 1904. He was alone in the building, and the report said that it was assumed that his coat had been caught by the drive shafting drawing him up to the shaft. He became caught on a beam, and part of the roof had to be removed before he could be released. Dr. Dyson was called, he found that Fox had no broken bones, but had suffered considerable bruising. He was later said to be recovering satisfactorily. Both mills suffered some flooding but no structural damage in the May 1944 flood.

Thornton's made various alterations and additions to the premises during their tenure, including the conversion of a wartime air-raid shelter into lavatories in 1947. A fire started in the mill's engine house about 8.40pm one day in early June 1961; flames were soon shooting through the roof of the three storey building. Eight workmen used extinguishers until the Holmfirth brigade arrived, followed by appliances from Huddersfield, Slaithwaite and Skelmanthorpe. The fire was under control by 10.30pm, but the brigade from Brighouse stood by all night damping down. Allen Thornton's employed about 80 people and were, by this time, part of the same group as W. Greenwood & Sons, Perseverance mill Holmfirth. A director said that they hoped to be able to carry on working, which they did.

Thornton's continued in business until 1984; despite the general increase in trade, they had recently been laying off their 73 employees and were expected to close on 25 May. The premises were subsequently let in units, Kirklees Dyers and Finishers were established in the mill by 1987, and Airedale Textiles Ltd. was using part of the mill in 1988. Airedale Textiles had a small fire in the flue of a drying machine in January 1994, which Holmfirth fire brigade had under control within ten minutes of arriving. Both these companies eventually closed, to be replaced by non textile businesses.[9]

Lud Hill Dike – Woodroyd mill / Victoria Dyeworks

Standing on the left of Gynn Lane above the bend and the railway bridge, the earliest information on this mill is in 1854, although it was already established by then. The mill was operated by John Haigh, described as a woollen spinner, who was possibly the brother of George A. Haigh corn miller who owned Grove House mill lower down Gynn Lane. The manager of Woodroyd mill was Henry Pearson, who had worked for John Haigh for three years in 1854, suggesting that the mill was already established by 1851. Most of the work at the mill seems to have been 'country work', that is commission work for small producers such as self employed weavers.

George Lodge & Sons of Fenay Bridge had sent both wool and cotton to Woodroyd to be spun, which Lodge's sold to Samuel Hallas of Mirfield. Hallas complained that the yarn received from Haigh's mill did not match the weight-note. Henry Pearson was charged with theft, he claimed that Hallas's had made a mistake in the weight. It emerged that there had been a fire at the mill in December, and Haigh had ordered Pearson to burn the waste that was lying about; but Pearson persuaded Haigh to allow him to sell it. After several hearings, Pearson was acquitted of the felony, but was fined £20 for embezzlement. The court determined that Haigh was not implicated. The incident appears to have ruined Haigh's business at the mill, as the machinery in the mill plus the water wheel and the cottages were advertised to be let on 25 March 1854. Application should be made to John Haigh of Hall Ing, or George Haigh of Grove house.

The next tenants were Joshua and James Hanson woollen spinners, an application for their bankruptcy was filed on 26 March 1858. They were ordered to appear for examination in Leeds on 24 April and 20 May, to make full disclosure of their estate. Haighs had also brought an action against Hansons for unpaid rent, the sale of their machinery and other effects was advertised to take place on Wednesday 7 April. The machinery may have been sold on that date, but many of the smaller items were advertised to be sold at Chapel Hill 'removed from Woodroyd mill for convenience of sale' on 11 May 1858. The bankruptcy case continued in Leeds into 1861, and included not only the business accounts, but the personal accounts of both Joshua and James Hanson. The premises were advertised to be let in January 1859, when they were described as a 5 storey mill plus loft 86ft by 36ft. A sale of yarn was advertised to take place at the mill on 18 August 1861 in distress for rent,

Woodroydmill/Victoria dyeworks. © A.J. Brooke

but the vendor is not named. This was possibly connected to Hanson's, but could equally refer to a subsequent tenant. In addition to the yarn, the sale included growing crops of Oats, Hay grass and Barley that were close to the mill, suggesting that it was Haighs who had instigated the sale.

In January 1869 a company called Hebblethwaite & Haigh were advertising for a pattern weaver with knowledge of design. The advertisement also said that 'room and power' or condensers and mules were available to rent. Another sale of yarn and machinery in distraint for rent was advertised to take place in March of the same year but the vendor is not named, this could have been Hebblethwaite & Haigh as their name does not appear again.[10] The 1871 census records the building as a woollen mill, but unoccupied.

A company called Whiteley Brothers occupied the mill in 1877. Thomas Stephenson, a married man with 5 children, was a designer at the firm. He worked in a shed that was separate from the main mill with a 23 year old single woman named Mary Haigh. Stephenson was under notice to leave the firm and had made several attempts to take hold of Haigh, which she had resisted. On the Friday afternoon they had been measuring pieces, Stephenson had grabbed her and thrown her onto the measuring table when he committed an indecent act. Haigh screamed, but no-one had heard her due to the noise of machinery. Stephenson was committed for trial at the assizes.

Ellis Lee Adamson was timekeeper at the mill in 1878, on the evening of 14 December he had gone to the Railway Hotel at Honley Bridge. Joe Moss, a millhand, was also there, he said that he wanted to gamble, but no-one responded. He then said several times that Adamson was the timekeeper at Woodroyd; Adamson eventually asked Moss "What business was that of his?" Adamson said that Moss then attacked him, kicking him several times on the legs, which was corroborated by several witnesses. Moss, in his evidence, denied wanting to gamble, and that after saying that Adamson was the timekeeper at Woodroyd Adamson had pushed him twice, which was why he had retaliated. He called one witness to corroborate his evidence. The bench fined Moss 2s 6d plus expenses.

A serious fire broke out at the mill in October 1880, when Whiteley Brothers were still the tenants. John Batley the engine tenter had left the mill at 10.15pm on Wednesday 27th, but had been woken at 11.50pm by the driver of a railway shunting engine continuously blowing his whistle. On looking out Batley saw that the mill was on fire, he went to the mill and sounded the buzzer, which brought the brigades from Neiley, Thongsbridge, Smithy Place and Armitage Bridge mills. Snow lay on the ground and was also falling heavily, which delayed the fire crews reaching the mill. The fire was well established and the roof and floors of the 6 storey mill collapsed before the first engine arrived. Also the bridge connecting the main mill to the finishing place and boiler house was in flames. The fire crews concentrated on saving the finishing place and boiler house, and managed to save some cloth from the finishing place, but everything in the 6 storey mill was lost. Damage was estimated at £10,000 to £12,000.

The following month Thomas and Arthur Whiteley were sued by Benjamin Bailey a rag merchant of Kirkstall Road Leeds. He sued them for £11 19s 1d for wages and expenses that he said he was owed. Bailey had been engaged by the brothers in December 1879 to buy rags for them at 30s per week to cover wages and expenses. Whiteley Brothers had paid £6 9s 1d into court to cover wages, but disputed the other £5. 10s. After a lengthy discussion the judge ordered Whiteley's to pay Bailey £7 9s 1d plus the costs of the case.

A dyehouse was to be built at the mill in 1882, Edward Holroyd & Sons of Banks Honley were overseeing the work, and they put an advertisement in the *Huddersfield Examiner* in March of that year inviting builders and other trades to tender for the work. No occupant of the new dyehouse was indicated; also the name of Whiteley Brothers disappears from the records around 1881.

It is possible that the new dyehouse was for Thomas Littlewood who, along with other members of his family, was operating a dyeing and finishing business at the mill by the 1890s. The 1892 25inch Ordinance Survey map marks the premises as Victoria Dyeworks rather than Woodroyd mill.

On 2 June 1892 the body of John Moss, a 57 year old quarry owner of Concord Street Honley was found in the mill dam. He had been suffering from heart disease and depression, and had said that he 'would be better off dead'. A newspaper in his house had a handwritten note on it saying that he could be found "in Mr. Littlewood's dam". The inquest verdict was suicide.

The *Textile Manufacturer* recorded in May 1895 that the partnership between France Littlewood, Fred Littlewood, Charles E. Littlewood and Tom E Littlewood trading as Tom Littlewood dyers and finishers at Victoria Dyeworks, and Charles Littlewood & Co. fancy worsted manufacturers at Prospect mill Honley, was dissolved on 1 May. Charles E. Littlewood left the partnership, the other three continued to run the companies. The worsted manufacturing business appears to have been short lived, as no further references to it have appeared. Thomas Littlewood dyers and finishers were in financial difficulties by August 1900, when a creditors meeting was held on the 8th. Their liabilities totalled £10,122 4s 8d, with assets of only £1,058 1s 8d, leaving a deficit of £9,064 3s. A deed of assignment was executed, with W.H. Armitage accountant, being appointed as trustee, and the five largest creditors being appointed a Committee of Inspection. A preliminary announcement of sale appeared in the *Huddersfield Examiner* on 11 August 1900, which said that the machinery and stock in trade from Victoria dyeworks, Grove mill and Hollin Hall Farm would be sold in the near future. Subsequent advertisements gave details of the sales at Victoria dyeworks and Hollin Hall farm, but Grove mill was not mentioned. The horses, carts, lurries and other implements at the farm were to be sold on 10 September, with the machinery and stock at Victoria dyeworks being sold on 19 September. A separate advertisement for the sale of the buildings at Victoria dyeworks, along with the boiler, steam engine, shafting and going gear was advertised to take place on the 18th. The name of the owner of the buildings was not mentioned, but this was not part of the realisation of assets of the Littlewood's. The *Yorkshire Factory Times* dated 21 September reports that the dyeworks were withdrawn from the auction, the highest bid of £1,200 being below the reserve price. The paper subsequently reported that the premises had been sold privately to an unnamed buyer. A report in the *Huddersfield Examiner* in February 1901, said that a second and final dividend of 8d in the £ would be paid in T. Littlewood's bankruptcy. This brought the total repaid to creditors to 2s 2d in the £.

The private buyer for the dyehouse was possibly William Brook & Sons of Slaithwaite who were using Victoria dyehouse by 1903, and had changed the name to Honley dyeworks by 1906. The council complained to them about smoke nuisance in August 1915. The head of the firm, Mr. Edwin Brook died on 12 April 1922. His obituary recorded that the firm had begun in Hepworth, and had moved to Slaithwaite in the late 1880s. After his death the name of the company was changed to Edwin Brook & Co. Ltd.

On 2 September 1929, Joe North climbed a ladder to a platform from which he could fix a drive belt around a 14inch pulley on the shafting to drive a piece-squeezing machine. His clothing caught in the shafting and he was whirled around and battered against the beams of the ceiling. He was flung off before the shafting, which was unfenced, could be stopped, but was found to be dead. Brook's were fined £25 plus 10s costs for failing to fence the shafting. The firm continued to use the dyeworks into the 1970s. Anecdotal evidence suggests that they were eventually taken over by Quarmby and Sykes, and the entire business moved to Meltham in 1979, but there do not appear to be documents in the public domain to support this.

In September 1982, workmen, who were possibly demolishing the buildings, cut through a gas main that burst into flames igniting beams and floorboards. Appliances from Holmfirth and Huddersfield attended. The site has since been used for housing.[11]

Grove House / Grove mill

Situated towards the bottom of Gynn Lane on the southern, New Mill, side of the road, this mill appears to have been built in the 1840s. The original owner of the mill was George Armitage Haigh, who was living at Gynn View Gynn Lane in 1841 and is described as a coal merchant; whereas in 1851 he was living at Grove House Gynn Lane and is described as a corn miller and coal owner. He was reputed to have moved from Gynn View due to the construction of the Huddersfield to Penistone railway, because the embankment obscured his view down into the valley.

The 1851 census records George Armitage Haigh, plus his wife Mary and their six children Thomas, Samuel, Edward, Joshua, Charles and Eliza Ann, along with a servant named Emma Banks as living in Grove House. Ten years later Thomas was married, he and his wife Ruth and their two children lived in a cottage that had been added to the main house, but there was no connecting door at that time.

There was also a stone saw mill close to Grove House, situated just off Gynn Lane at a bend in

Grove mill, copied from C.A. Haigh Letterhead. Collection of A.J. Brooke.

the track leading to the house. The occupants of the premises in the early 1850s were Bower, Brown & Co. On Monday 3 July 1854 two men were raising a block of stone weighing around 3 tons. When the stone was a few feet from the ground the iron spring broke, as did the 18inch by 8inch wooden beam supporting the jenny. The stone, along with one man and the jenny fell to the ground, narrowly missing Mr. Bower who was near the crane. The man who fell was injured, but not fatally. In February 1865 the premises were advertised to be let or sold.

The stone mill was occupied in May 1866, but the name of the occupant is not recorded, when the wooden framework carrying the machine for winding up blocks of stone broke with a great crash. Thomas Brook, who was working the machine, was thrown into the bottom of the pit along with the machine and its frame. Mr. Brook was initially thought to have been killed, but by the Friday there were hopes that he may recover. It was advertised for sale again in January 1867 along with a dwelling house, and was described as being 'contiguous to Mr. George A. Haigh's brewery'. The final occupant appears to have been Andrew Bell, who was in liquidation in May 1871.

In addition to the brewery and other premises at Grove House, George A. Haigh also owned the Coach and Horses public house in Honley; it was advertised to be let with immediate possession in February 1895, along with the croft stables and other conveniences. Potential occupants should apply to G.A. Haigh at Grove House. The 1861 census records him as a common brewer and miller, indicating that the coal business had either been taken over by another member of the family, or that it had been abandoned. The opening of the railway line in the 1850s opened the opportunity for better quality coal from the Barnsley district to be brought into the area quickly and more cheaply. G.A. Haigh died in April 1870, one of the stipulations in his will was that the mill and other property should be sold within seven years.

A sale was advertised to take place on 4 March 1873, which included the corn mill, brewery, malthouses, drying kiln, dwelling house with gardens and outbuildings, the occupant at the time was Edward Robertshaw; also 6 cottages and several closes of land. They were bought by Henry Mitchell of Holmfirth who was an established miller, but had no interest in the brewery side of this business. The brewery plant, wagons, carts, beer barrels etc. were advertised to be auctioned on 16 April 1873. Some building took place between 1873 and 1881, particularly a three storey mill 63ft by 35ft 9inches. This, along with the original 3 storey mill plus attic, the former brew house, 2 malt houses, and various other buildings including the dwelling house occupied by a Mr. Joseph Sykes, were advertised for sale in March 1881; but were possibly withdrawn due to lack of interest, as the property did not change hands. The property was advertised for sale again in March 1889, and was withdrawn at £3,500. It was subsequently advertised to be let, but was eventually bought by Thomas Littlewood in 1891 for £3,750, who changed the use to dyeing and finishing.

From letters written in 1980 by Edna & Albert Mosley to their grand children, Littlewoods used this mill mainly for the bleaching and stoving of white cloth for tennis and cricket clothing. This cloth was woven in Bradford, and before 1920 Littlewoods transported the cloth daily by horse and cart, taking pieces of finished cloth, folded and wrapped back to the manufacturers, and collecting pieces for finishing; a round trip of 28 miles. They had two horses, named Duke and Kruger, which were used on alternate days to pull the cart. The firm acquired a motor lorry with a covered back in the 1920s to replace the horse and cart.

As mentioned in the details of Victoria dyeworks, Littlewoods also had a worsted manufacturing business trading as Charles Littlewood & Co. which was in one of the mill buildings, along with David France & Co. who were making patterned cloths woven on hand looms; there was also a company named Holmes Heaton who were millwrights and farriers occupying the ground floor. During the 1890s this building was renamed Prospect mill, but appears to have reverted to being part of Grove mill after the turn of the century.

All Littlewoods 150 employees (from both companies) were taken on a trip to Southport on 2 September 1892, arriving there at 10am, they spent the day visiting the town's Centenary Exhibition, the Winter and Botanic gardens, and strolling on the sand until 6.45pm when they left for home, arriving back in Honley at 9.30pm. Mrs. Littlewood gave a treat to all the workers of a substantial tea and concert at Moorbottom Congregational Sunday School in March 1894, followed by a ball in the Co-op. Hall, to celebrate the coming of age her son Thomas Edgar Littlewood. The concert included items from the Arlon Prize Quartet Party and various other soloists; after which a large number went to the Co-op Hall and spent the night dancing, with refreshments being served at intervals. The party broke up around 4.30am the following morning.

In early July 1900, a party of students from Huddersfield Technical College visited Littlewoods dyehouse at Victoria dyeworks, and the finishing plant at Grove mills; after these visits they moved on to visit the bobbin works of Gledhill and Roberts, who made the bobbins that carried the weft in shuttles. The financial difficulties of the company in August 1900, discussed previously in the information on Victoria dyeworks, for some unexplained reason did not affect the business at Grove mills, which continued with the finishing of white cloth. In April 1912, the council approved Littlewoods plan to install a generator at the mill to produce electricity. Eventually, power from the generator could be diverted from use at the mill to supply power to light the streets of Honley if required. The firm also finished Donegal tweeds, and made some patterned cloths of their own, including designing, weaving and finishing the cloth to make the blazers for the students attending Holme Valley Grammar School after it opened in 1933.

Finishing of white cloth for sports wear was superseded in 1939 by a demand for white cloth to make overalls for munitions workers. The cloth needed to be white because it readily showed any spillages of gunpowder and reduced the possibility of explosions; and secondly, it needed to be made from wool due to the lack of any form of heating in the munitions factories. A third requirement was that the cloth should be virtually shrink proof, which Littlewoods managed to achieve by treating it with an enzyme. After the war 'drip dry' cloths came on the market and put an end to the white wool cloth trade.

Littlewoods turned to finishing double jersey double knit circular knitted cloths which came from knitting factories in Leicestershire. The firm ran a daily collection and delivery service between Honley & Leicester. Littlewoods continued in business until 1964 or '65; in November of that year H. Fisher (Plastics) were granted change of use for the premises from dyeworks to plastic manufacturing, they were using the premises until 1995. Other companies to use parts of the mills were Boothroyd Rugs, who moved from Thongsbridge mill to Grove mills in 1966 until at least 1971; Berjo Engineering were also using part of the mills between 1966 and 1970. Holmes Heaton & Co. moved into premises in 1970, renaming it New Grove Works, and were there until at least 1978. After Fisher Plastics moved out in 1995, Kirklees permitted housing to be built on the site.[12]

River Holme – Bridge Dyeworks Honley

These premises stand on the left bank of the river Holme between the left hand bend where the river leaves the New Mill road and the right hand bend where it runs under Honley Bridge. James Beaumont, who was established in Scissett from the 1860s, applied to build the premises at Honley in 1880, Honley Local Board passed the plans in August of that year. It seems that someone other than Beaumont's was also using the dyeworks in the early years; by order of Fred Carter Accountant, a liquidation sale of dyewares including Indigo, Logwood and Vitriol, plus a brown horse called Bob, 2 carts, a wagonette, and harnesses, was advertised to take place 27 September 1883, but the owner is not named. The premises were definitely the property of Beaumont's. A fire was discovered in a drying shed at the works at 1.45 am on 6 October 1908. The fire brigade put it out within 1 hour; damage was estimated to be around £100. The *Yorkshire Textile Directory* for 1912, list the company as dyers of loose cotton and wool, and also spun yarns. The last advertisement for staff at Honley appeared in the Holmfirth Express in 1972; an application for change of use of part of the premises was refused by Kirklees due to the lack of off-road loading space. The premises were still standing in 2010, but had been split into a number of units that were occupied by a variety of companies.[13]

Honley mill

This mill stands on the right bank of the river, a few yards downstream from Honley Bridge. Mary Jagger wrote in her *History of Honley* published in 1941 that there were records in existence showing a corn mill in Honley in 1344. Unfortunately, these records appear to have been lost, as neither West Yorkshire Archives, the Dartmouth Estate, nor Yorkshire Archaeological Society have any trace of them.

The earliest information found on the premises comes from a document relating to the sale of a dyehouse at Deanhouse in November 1767, when David and Matthew Hampshire of Netherthong borrowed £250 from James Thornton corn miller of Honley, the interest rate on the loan was 4½ percent per year. Honley mill is indicated on Jeffries map published in the 1770s, and in 1796 it was a Corn mill and Scribbling mill, with I. & T. Thornton as the tenants. The *Dartmouth Terrier*, which can be seen at the Dartmouth Estate Offices in Slaithwaite, records in 1805 that it was a large Water Corn and Scribbling mill, with a dwelling house and sundry other outbuildings, to which Lord Dartmouth had contributed £400 towards its renovation. The occupants were still I & T Thornton, who were paying a rent of £110 per year.

A copy of a letter written in June 1806 suggested that the rent, which had been set in 1798, should be increased by £5 per year. Thornton's asked that the increase should be dated from 1802, the date of their existing lease, rather than being backdated further. Sarah Thornton described as a scribbling miller, was to appear at the Court House in Wakefield on 28 October 1828, as an insolvent debtor, she had originally been in partnership with her husband, and then, after his death, began to run the business on her own account. Since losing the tenancy of the mill she was described as a widow and labourer; at the hearing in Wakefield she was discharged.

The tenancy was taken over in 1828 by Isaac Dickinson, the mill was described as having 3 floors with 3 pairs of grindstones plus the scribbling engines, driven by two water wheels. The rent had increased to £120 a year. The *Leeds Mercury* advertised a sale of machinery to take place at the mill on 20 April 1829, including scribbling and carding engines plus slubbing billies, millstones and a variety of other articles suitable for scribbling and corn millers, plus a cart and a horse, but does not name

Honley mill. © A.J. Brooke

the vendor; which was presumably not Isaac Dickinson as in November of that year he was allowed £58 10s for putting the mill into tenantable repair. It is possible that Isaac took a partner, as the firm of Armitage & Dickinson had failed by 1832, when the mill was again said to be in a dilapidated state; the *Terrier* recorded in June 1834 that the premises had been let to Thomas Hinchliffe and John Heap for 14 years at a rent of £125 a year, 'they doing all the repairs and leaving the same in good repair at the end of the term and also leaving the water wheel, the upright and going gears, the shuttles and all other work in and about the mill which have been lately done at the said Earl's expense'.

John Bates the Factory Inspector charged Hinchliffe & Heap with offences against the Factory Act in February 1836, these were: irregularly keeping time books, working children without medical certificates, and working children under 11 years of age longer than the permitted number of hours; the firm admitted the offences. Mr. Bates said that he would not press for conviction on the first two charges, but it was 'his bounden duty for the protection of children' to press for penalty on the third. Hinchliffe and Heap were fined 1s plus 1s 6d costs; the magistrates said that they would be more harsh if the firm should appear again. The fines were given to Honley Church Sunday School by the magistrates.

Thomas Hinchliffe of Honley and John Heap of Oldfield dissolved their partnership on 10 May 1841, Thomas Hinchliffe was to carry on the business on his own. The mill had a 12hp steam engine by 1848, which consumed about 100 cart loads of coal per year; the water wheel also gave a similar rate of power. A fire was discovered in the wool drying stove shortly after 6pm on 3 April 1849. The engine from D. Shaw & Co. was in action within a few minutes, and the engine from John Brooke & Sons of Armitage Bridge also attended, but as it had further to travel the fire was under control before it arrived. Damage, which was insured, was estimated at less than £100. Joseph Hinchliffe, one of the partners in the firm, was prosecuted in November 1850 for having 900lbs of wool waste that he could not account for. The waste should have been returned to the manufacturers for whom Hinchliffe was spinning. Inspector Kaye, Sub-inspector Earnshaw and Constable Taylor entered the mill without a warrant, and found the waste stored in the top floor of the mill, also in the billy gate of the second floor and in the engine house. It consisted of coppins, willey locks, runnings off and shoddy. Hinchliffe's attempted to burn the evidence before it could be taken away. The defendant said that the waste was 'teazing muck' which he was allowed to keep, Noah Taylor, a partner, said that the wool was justifiably retained. The prosecution called manufacturers who identified the waste as theirs, and said that it was the custom of the trade to return waste with scribbled wool or yarn. Tom Brooke of John Brooke & Sons appeared as a defence witness and said that Hinchliffes always returned the correct amount of waste when they did work for him, he did not require the return of willey-locks. The magistrates fined Joseph Hinchliffe £20, but refused to prosecute his partners.

The flood of February 1852 affected the mill; the report in the *Huddersfield Examiner* said that 'flood waters penetrated the power loom room on the ground floor, and part of a scribbling mill'. *The scribbling and fulling mill belonging to Mr. Thomas Hinchliffe is in a complete wreck at the bottom part, 5 billies, 3 pairs of mules and fulling stocks have been broken down.* Whoever owned the power looms did not submit a claim for damage. Thomas Hinchliffe & Sons, who were the scribbling millers and fullers, submitted a claim for damage to the buildings, goit, machinery and stock totalling £38 10s, which was reduced by the inspectors to £11 10s, but only £5 appears to have been paid (claim no 270). Standing alongside the turnpike road at the junction of the Holmfirth and New Mill roads, was a house, warehouse, stove and dyehouse belonging to Benjamin Mellor, these were flooded, with many bales of wool, dyewares and yarns being carried away, but again, there is no evidence of a claim.[14]

The Reservoir Commissioners give the owner of Honley mill as The Earl of Dartmouth, and the tenant as Thomas Brooke junior, in 1853. James and William Bean were charged with stealing 8cwt of coal from Thomas Brook of Honley mill in May 1856. On Thursday 8 May Mr. G.W. Joyce coal agent, had employed the Bean brothers to deliver a railway truck load of coal from Honley Station to the mill. He did not authorise them to put any of the coal into sacks. The Station Master W.L. Sharp said that he saw Wm Bean and a younger brother place a sack of coal on top of a loaded cart. He asked George Tylburn to watch the cart. Tylburn saw William Bean leave the sack of coal on a wall beside another sack, before delivering the coal to the mill. Oh his way back Bean collected the two sacks of coal, leaving one at Mrs. Boothroyd's and taking the other to his own house. Mrs. Boothroyd said that she had been in the habit of buying coal from Bean. John Laycock, engine foreman at the mill, said that he had never given Bean permission to remove coal on the understanding that it would be returned later. William Bean was sent to Wakefield House of Correction for 14 days. The case against James Bean was delayed for 1 week due to the absence of a witness; however, the witness could only say that he had seen James Bean walking beside the coal cart. James was discharged.

In April 1865 Allen Firth drove his cart through a field to get to Honley mill, avoiding the toll gate, he was then summoned and charged with evading the 4d toll. His defence was that he had been told that the road through the field was the regular route used by people going to the mill. To make an example to others, the bench fined Firth 1s plus the 4d toll and the expenses of the case, a total of 11s 10d.

Joseph Pontefract had been using part of the mill since at least 1864; in April 1868 Joseph and Henry Pontefract, both of Honley, assigned their goods to Trustees, who were Thomas Brooke of Armitage Bridge, John Davies of Leeds and Abraham Knight of Huddersfield. The sale of 2,750lbs of yarn was advertised to take place in March 1871, plus household furnishings and effects.

An 11 year old reacher-in called George Chambers was taken to Huddersfield Infirmary in November 1871, having had his right thumb caught between cog wheels and crushed. The thumb was amputated close to his hand.

Hannah and Eliza Taylor were mother and daughter who both worked at Honley mill. They were charged with stealing half a hundredweight of coal from the boiler house at the mill in March 1872. PC Henry Yates saw Hannah take the coal and put it in her apron; she was then joined by her daughter. Hannah was sentenced to one month's imprisonment with hard labour in Wakefield; as the evidence against Eliza was doubtful she was discharged.

Dean & Hey, who had been using part of the mill for over a year, combined with James Mellor of Reins mill to take all the employees to Scarborough for the day on Saturday 20th July 1872. A company named T.M. Tolson & Co were using part of the mill in August 1877, and had presumably been there for some time; a sale of their machinery consisting of 3 condenser sets, 2 pairs of hand mules and various sundries, plus 22,000lbs of materials was advertised to take place on 9 August.

A small fire was discovered by PC Smith in the stove used by James Beaumont fancy wool dyer, one morning in December 1878. PC Smith raised the alarm bringing neighbours with cans and buckets who fought the fire and put it out. Damage was estimated at around £10 which was not insured. It was thought that the fire had started due to a sheet of flocks becoming overheated.

The corn mill was still operating in 1887 and also had a Bone Grinding mill, Ellis Lockwood the miller, was told by the Honley Local Board inspector to stop storing corn in the same room as bones. Part of the Corn mill was used by Honley and District Fanciers Society for their show on Saturday 7th November 1896, when there were almost 500 exhibits of poultry, pigeons, cage birds, rabbits and cats.

In January 1903, Ellis Lockwood & Sons sued a farmer and cattle dealer from Newsome named Paul Mellor for £6 14s for Indian corn and bean meal which, they said, had been delivered to Mellor on 20 February 1902. Mellor disputed this and said that he had bought and paid for goods from Lockwood's on several occasions since then. The judge said that he was not satisfied that the goods had been delivered, and ordered Lockwood's to pay the costs of the case. Garnet Ellis Lockwood was crushed in the cogs of a machine at the mill in January 1903. Tom Lockwood, Garnet's brother, who also worked at the mill but was not present when the accident happened, said that his brother had worked there for 6 or 7 years and was used to operating the machine, which was used for dressing oats. Tom also said that if someone became caught in the machine it was not possible for them to escape even if help was available, as the only way to stop the machined was to stop the mill engine. Garnet was found by Ben Littlewood a clerk at the mill; he was caught between two bevelled cogs. The machine was stopped and Littlewood, with the help of Frank Oldroyd a joiner, managed to force the cogs to reverse by using iron bars releasing Lockwood, who was found to be dead. The inquest jury returned a verdict of 'accidental death'.

A factory inspector said that a second staircase was needed to the upper floor of the mill in January 1904, in case of fire. The Council then inspected it and found that access to the top floor was through a trap door. That floor was occupied by John Thornton who made hearth rugs, and employed 20 people. Mr. Thornton was told by the council to remove the trap door. The council maintained that as less than a total of 40 people were employed in the building the Act did not apply, therefore no second staircase was necessary. The corn mill was occupied by Samuel Drake corn millers by July 1918, and has been in the tenure of the Drake family since then.[15]

Reins mills

The oldest mill on this site, which is a few hundred yards downstream from Honley mill, is the three storey mill that stands alongside the river, behind the single and two storey buildings. The precise date of building is not known, the earliest information comes from the *London Gazette* of 8 January 1847, reporting that William Bottomley of Reins mill had been declared Bankrupt on 28 December 1846, and was ordered to attend Leeds Bankruptcy Court on 22 January and 9 February 1847 to make a full disclosure of his estate. The *Leeds Mercury* subsequently carried an advertisement on 31 March 1847 offering the mill for sale and describing it as 'newly erected'. The machinery for scribbling carding, slubbing and spinning wool into yarn was described as being 'nearly new' in 1847, when it was advertised to be sold by auction on 11 August. The mill was again advertised to be sold, by order of the assignees of William Bottomley, on 27 March 1848, when it was described as the newly erected and spacious woollen mill, with steam engine, boiler, shafting and going gear, also workshops with spinning room over, adjoining the mill; the occupants of the premises were Godfrey Berry and William Haigh. In May 1848 the *London Gazette* announced that William Bottomley's creditors would receive a first dividend of 2s in the £.

The mill was again advertised to be sold in March 1849, the only difference in its description from a year before being that it was now with vacant possession, and was currently owned by William Greenwood. The flood of February 1852 obviously affected the area, but the newspaper reports do not give any specific details of damage to Reins mills, although it is reasonable to assume that water, sludge and debris entered the ground floors of the buildings.

The failure of the Shaw family business at Neiley/Crossley mills and in Huddersfield that had become public knowledge on Saturday 23 January 1858, affected many other business in the area. One business that was severely affected was that of Beaumont, Kaye & Co. cloth finishers of Reins mill. Mr. Joseph Kaye was one of the partners in the firm, which had suffered considerably by the failure. On the morning of Monday 25th Mr. Kaye was on the platform at Honley Station waiting for a train to Huddersfield, and had been talking to someone about the failure when he seemed to stagger and then fell to the ground and died. The report concluded 'It is surmised that he died heartbroken'. Beaumont, Kaye & Co had left Reins mill by 1860 and moved to 'Shaw's factory', whether they were in Crossley mill or Neiley mill is not known, but they were there for a number of years.

Benjamin and James Mellor owned at least part of Reins mill in 1865, when James leased Benjamin's share for £220 per year. A fire broke out at the mill around midnight on Monday 13 September 1869; it was spotted by a passer by who saw a glow through a window. He raised the alarm and Mr. Mellor and neighbours fought the fire with buckets of water. The fire had started by spontaneous combustion in some waste, only slight damage was caused. James Mellor gave his workers a day trip to Scarborough in July 1872, in conjunction with Dean & Hey of Honley mill; in May of the following year Mellor was in liquidation, and his machinery was advertised for auction.

Reins mill. © the Author.

Benjamin Mellor advertised the mill to let with the steam engine, boiler, and machines for preparing yarn and weaving cloth in March 1874. A firm named Dean & Hey were using the mill in the following year; by 1880 they had erected two new sheds on the premises. The name of the company became Charles Dean shortly afterwards; he seems to have had a good rapport with his workers who presented him with a black marble clock on his 38th birthday, and E. Croft paid tribute by saying that Mr. Dean and the workpeople had a cordial relationship despite there being a weaver's strike in the area. A firm of bobbin makers called Dodson & Kenyon moved into the mill in 1888 and installed a new steam engine, which was christened 'Princess Ida'. In May of the following year Dodson & Kenyon dissolved their partnership. A fire was discovered in the stove used by Charles Dean & Sons at 9.20pm on 11 February 1890 by a millhand who lived nearby. Local people attempted to put out the fire using buckets of water taken from a tank in the mill yard. After the arrival of fire brigades from Brooke's of Armitage Bridge, and G. Shaw & Sons of Milnsbridge, the fire was brought under control. The cause of the fire was attributed to 'overheating', and damage was estimated at £200, which was insured. Another new weaving shed and other plans for enlarging the mill took place in 1891. Charles Jubb aged 32, was putting up a partition in the dyehouse in November 1896, when he fell into a 3ft. deep dyepan containing chrome water that was virtually at boiling point. He managed to climb out, but died from shock a few days later. The firm were probably finding trade difficult in the late 1890s, as were many other manufacturers, registering as a limited liability company in 1898.

On 25 May 1899 some children were playing on the bank of the river near to the mill when 5 year old Alice Ann Boothroyd fell into the water. A youth named George Lockwood saw the incident and told Robert Berry the dyer for Chas. Dean & Sons Ltd, who, despite the fast flowing current, went into the river and rescued her. After a short time she seemed to have fully recovered.

The company went into voluntary liquidation in July 1900, with debts of £7,026 10s 2d, and assets of £1, 827 3s 1d. The company owned the premises, which were advertised for sale by auction on 31 July 1900. In addition to the original 3 storey mill used for scribbling and spinning, there was a newly erected 2 storey worsted mill 113ft by 30ft, a second 2 storey building 137ft by22ft used for finishing and warehousing, a new weaving shed, a stone built dyehouse, boiler house with 2 drying stoves over, engine house, blacksmith's shop, 2 cottages, a yard and conveniences. A note at the end of the advertisement said 'A considerable amount of money has recently been expended in the erection of the new weaving shed and worsted mill'. A large quantity of machinery and stock were also advertised to be sold by auction on the 8th and 9th of August 1900. Creditors were asked to submit details of debts owed to them to W.H. Armitage, the appointed trustee, before 31 May 1901. Another meeting of creditors was eventually called for 17 February 1903, to explain how the business had been wound up. Due to the firm being a Limited Liability Company, it was the company that had gone bankrupt, not Charles Dean himself. This allowed him to start a new business in his own name in Huddersfield. He was trading from premises in Cloth Hall Street and was styled as a woollen and worsted manufacturer in October 1903, when he was again in financial difficulties. At a meeting of creditors it was disclosed that he had liabilities of £2,664 19s 6d; his assts amounted to £1,603 4s 4d, leaving a deficit of £1,061 14s 11d. Dean was ordered to execute a Deed of Assignment; the Trustee was again Mr. W.H. Armitage, and the three largest creditors were appointed as a committee of inspection.

In October 1901 the *Yorkshire Factory Times* reported that the mill had been empty since Chas. Dean & Sons Ltd had left; it was currently being refurbished and Alfred Armitage formerly of Clough House mill Birkby was to take it over. A second report on 13 December 1901 said that the repairs were almost completed and the mill would soon reopen. Alfred Armitage registered the firm as a limited liability company on 7 February 1902, the directors were A. Armitage and C.T. Ensor. The YFT announced on 21 February that the firm had moved into the mill, which they were leasing from Mr. W. Brook. There was a dispute between the company and their weavers in June 1902 resulting in the weavers walking out on the 13th. The strike continued into October of that year, despite attempts by officials of the Weavers and Textile Workers Union to mediate between the two sides. Alfred Armitage & Co. Ltd. moved from Reins mill in 1904 taking much of their machinery with them. A machinery sale was advertised to take place on 20 October 1904 'due to the removal of the business', but the vendor was not named. As the machinery is described as 'new and fitted in 1902', it was obviously from Armitages.

David France & Co. was using the mill in 1905 manufacturing Fancy Worsteds. The employees enjoyed a trip to Liverpool on Saturday 27 June 1914, they arrived in the city by 9am, leaving for home at 7.30pm and arriving back in Honley at 10.30pm. David France died at his home in late August 1916, at the age of 58. He left his eldest and youngest sons running the company; his middle son being in the Army. The firm were using the mill until around 1928.[16]

Sykes, Marsden & Co. were using the mill between 1931 and 1952, manufacturing worsted coatings. R.L. Robinson, mungo and shoddy manufacturers, were using the mill by 1934, they had moved from the family mill at Smithy Place, and were in Reins mill until 1935, when they moved to Thongsbridge mill. Norman Marsh, previously manager of Greenwoods at Digley mill, moved to Reins mill after Greenwoods closed in December 1936, bringing some of his former staff with him. He was occupying part of the mills until 1969 or 1970. A.C. Wickman & Co were using part of the mills from 1942, they suffered some water damage in the flood of 29 May 1944.

Messrs. Airey who were rug manufacturers, weaving wool hearth rugs on Dobcross looms, were using the original three storey mill by 1948. They had changed the firm's name to Holme Rug Co. by 1950, and continued in business until the mid 1970s. A company named S. Marsden Worsted Mills Ltd. were using part of the mills by 1952, they renamed their part of the mills Huddersfield Road Works. Honley Worsted Mills, who had 60 looms, were using Huddersfield Road Works by 1956; whether they had any connection to S. Marsden is not known. The number of looms rose to 71 during the 1960s, they were commission weavers, and advertised that they could weave worsteds, woollens, baratheas, blazer cloths, boucles, clericals, flannels, gabardines, overchecks, serges, suitings, vicunas, twills and velours. They were using the mill until 1970 when, as part of the Illingworth Morris group of companies, they were merged with James Sykes & Son Ltd. Stafford Mills, Milnsbridge, where 30 of their existing employees would be employed, the other 20 would loose their jobs.

Other non-textile companies using the mills were: Habasco International, importers of basketware from 1975 until they moved to Bankfield Road, Huddersfield; Holme Valley Patterns, engineering pattern makers, in 1977; Gelpack, makers of plastic bin-liners and food packs, in 1981; Simplast Ltd. plastics manufacturers, who had a fire in their boiler house causing damage estimated at £40,000 in January 1986; also Crowther & Shaw refrigeration engineers in 1992. Much of the premises have since become disused and are still standing, but empty.

Notes

1 Lower Mytholmbridge mill
Kirk. Arch. KC315/3/15 6 Nov. 1626; KC485 1796; KC165/121 1 Aug. 1808, 20 Feb. 1847; Leeds Mercury 24 Sept. 1836; Leeds Arch. WYL 219/306/1 7 Mar. 21 July 1848. Hudds Chron. 7 Feb. 1852;Kirk. Arch. T/H/F 36 claim no 297, claim no 314; KC6/1/33; *Hudds Ex.*24 Sept. 5 Nov. 1853. *Hudds Chron.* 12 June 1858; *Hudds Ex.* 23 July 1859; *Hudds. Chron.* 9 Apr. 1864, 25 March 1865

2 Kirk. Arch. KC642 Box 1, 18 Sept 1866; *Hudds Chron.* 10 and 24 Nov. 1866; 2 Nov. 1867; *London* Gazette, 8 June 1869, 1 Nov. 1872, 4 Feb. 17 June, 1873; Kirk. Arch. KC642 Box 1 17 June 1873; Hudds Ex.14 and 21 Mar. 2 and 9 May 1874; London Gazette, 1 Feb. 1876; Hudds. Weekly News, 19 May and 9 June 1877; Huddersfield Chronicle, 23 June 1877; H'firth Exp. 15 Jan, 2 July 1887; Yorks Fact. Times, 21 March 1890; H'firth Exp. April 1893; Hudds Ex. 4 Nov. 1893; Text. Manfr, May 1896; H'firth Exp. 3 June 1899; Kirk. Arch. UHO Holmfirth, 1923, 1926, 1928; Hudds Ex. 9 Mar. 1935; Kirk Arch. Holmfirth Council flood records 1944.

3 Rock mill
Hudds Chron. 24 Nov. 1866; 30 Nov. 1867; Hudds Ex.10 Oct. 1868; Hudds Chron. 23 June 1877; Hudds Ex. 15 Dec. 1877, 26 Oct. and 9 Nov. 1878; 31 July 1880; 15 Apr. 25 Nov. 1882; 3 Feb. 1883; 26 Apr. 1884; H'firth Exp. 22 Jan. and 5 Feb. 1877; Hudds Ex. 19 Feb. 1887; 25 April 1891; H'firth Exp. 17 Oct. 1891; Hudds Ex. 4 May 1895; 14 Aug. 1897.

4 Kirk. Arch. KMT4 Honley, 22 Feb. 1900; Yorks. Fact. Times, 2 and 9 March 1900; Hudds Ex. 1 Dec. 1900, 4 May 1907; Kirk. Arch. KC693 Box 1, 1920; UHO Honley Feb. 1921; H'firth Exp. 24 Sept. 1921; Hudds Ex. 9 April 1927; Kirk. Arch. UHO Holmfirth, 17 Apr. 1939; Council flood records, May 1944; H'firth Exp. 23 June 1951; 27 June, 1953; 1 Feb. 1969; Hudds Ex. 14 Dec. 1974; H'firth Exp. 14 Feb. 1975, 4 May 1979, 8 May 1981, 18 Nov. 1983, 12 Oct. 1984, 1 Feb. 1985.

5 Smithy Place mill
Kirk. Arch. KC 165/121 1780-1811; Supplementary Report into the Employment of Children in Factories and as to the Propriety and Means of Curtailing the Hours of their Labour, Part 1; (25 March 1834); Kirk. Arch. KC 642 Box 1 20 Sept. 1836; Northern Star, 3 Apr. 1841; Kirk. Arch. KC165/121 20 Feb. 1847; London Gazette, 16 Nov. 1847, 18 Jan, 10 Mar, 2 May, 14 Sept. 1848, 4 Jan. 1850; Hudds Chron. 7 Feb. 1852; Kirk. Arch. T/H/F/36, T/H/F/45; KC6/1/33 1853; Hudds Chron. also Hudds. Ex. 5 Feb. 1853; Hudds Chron, 3 Dec. 1853; 12 Aug. 1854; 10 May 1856.

6 Hudds Chron. 17 Jan. 1857; Hudds Ex. 16 May 1857, 26 June 1858; London Gazette, 21 Jan. 1859; Hudds Ex. 28 Jan. 1862, Hudds Chron, 5, 12 Sept. 1863; 24 Nov. 1866; London Gazette, 22 Apr. 1867; Hudds Ex. 27 Apr. 1867; Hudds Chron, 22 Jan. 1870; 8 July 1871; Hudds Ex. 1 June 1872; 12 June 1875; 23 Dec. 1876; 14 July 1883; 16 Aug. 1884; 31 Jan. 1885; H'firth Exp. 22 Jan. 1887; 28 Jan 1888; Hudds Ex. 27 Oct. 1888; 31 Oct. 1891; 17 Dec. 1892; 27 Apr. 1895; Hudds Ex. 23 Sept 1905; H'firth Exp. 7 Aug. 1909; 19 Feb. 1916; 23 May 1970; 10 June 1983; 5 Jan. 1996.

7 Banks and Lower Banks mills
Kirk. Arch. KC165/368 1 Jan. 1768; T/H/F/36, KC6/1/33 1853; Hudds Chron. 10 Mar.1860; 19 Mar. 1864; 4 Aug. 1866; 10 Apr. 1869; H'firth Exp. 8 Jan. 1949.

8 Neiley and Crossley mills
Supplementary Report into the Employment of Children in Factories and as to the Propriety and Means of Curtailing the Hours of their Labour, Part 1; (25 March 1834). Kirkl. Arch. KC333/17/6 1838; Leeds Mercury, 20 August 1842; Leeds Times, 13 July, 1844; Leeds Mercury, 14 Aug. 1847; Hudds Chron. & 9 Nov. 1850; 15 May 1852; Hudds Ex. 22 May 1852; Kirk. Arch. /H/F/36; Hudds Ex. 3 July 1852; Hudds Chron. 6 Feb, 3 Mar, 7 May 1853; Kirk. Arch. KC6/1/33 1853; Hudds Chron. 11 Feb. 1854; Hudds Ex. 27 October 1855; Hudds Chron. 30 Jan. 6 and 13 Feb; 5, 26 June, 7 Aug, 23 Oct. 1858; 29 Jan; 26 Nov. 1859;

9 Hudds Ex. 23 July 1859; Hudds. Chron, 12 Jan. 1861; 23 Aug. 1862; 5 Sept. 1863; 20 Feb. 1864; 15 July 1865; Hudds Ex. 7 Oct. 1865; Hudds Chron. 3 Feb, 24 Nov. 1866; Kirk. Arch. KC642 Box B 1872 & 1875; Hudds. Ex. 26 Apr. 1873; Genealogical Information on the Shaw family kindly supplied by Mr. P Sanderson; London Gazette, 10 Nov. 12 Dec. 1876, 9 Jan. 27 Mar. 21 Aug. 1877; 1 Feb 15 Mar. 1878; Hudds. Ex. 6 & 20 Jan. 1877; 17 Apr. 1878; Hudds. Chron. 26 Apr. 1884; Hudds Ex. 20 June 1885; Yorks. Fact. Times, 19 July and 30 Aug. 1899; Hudds Ex., 17 Sept. 15 Oct. 1892; H'firth Exp. 6 June 1914. Hudds Ex. 14 Oct. 1922; Huddersfield Local History Library, Holmfirth Council records of flood 1944; Text. Manfr 28 Oct. 1903; Hudds Ex. 30 Apr. 1904; Worker, 8 May 1909; H'firth Exp. 3 June 1961; 25 May 1984; 3 July 1987; 14 Apr 1988; 14 Jan. 1994.

10 Woodroyd mill/Victoria dyehouse
Hudds Chron. 11, 25 March, 22 April, 13 May 1854; London Gazette, 30 March, 3 April, 8 May, 28 May, 9 July, 1858; 28 Oct, 29 Nov. 1859; 31 Jan. 1860; 26 March 1861. Hudds Chron. 3 April, 8 May 1858; 1 Jan. 1859, 10 Aug. 1861; 2 Jan. 1869, 20 Mar. 1869.

11 Hudds Ex. 10 Mar. 1877, 28 Dec. 1878, 30 Oct. and 20 Nov. 1880; 4 Mar. 1882; 11 June 1892; London Gazette, 7 May 1895; Hudds Ex. 11 Aug, 18 Aug, 1 Sept. 1900; Yorks. Fact. Times, 21 Sept. also 16 Nov. 1900; Kirk. Arch. UHO Honley 7 Sept. 1903, 23 Aug. 1915; H'firth Exp. 20 May 1922, 26 Oct. 1929, 24 Sept. 1982.

12 Grove House/Grove mill
Census returns 1841, 1851; 1871; Hudds Ex. 8 July and 28 Oct. 1854, 19 May 1866, 5 Jan. 1867, 6 May 1871; 15 Feb. and 12 Apr. 1873; 16 Mar. 1881, 16 Mar. and 6 July 1889; Kirk. Arch. KC206/14 1980; Hudds Ex. 3 Sept. 1892; 17 Mar. 1894; 7 July 1900; Kirk. Arch. UHO Holmfirth, 10 Nov. 1965; H'firth Exp. 11 June 1966, 12 Aug. 1994, 8 Dec. 1995.

13 Bridge Dyeworks
Kirk. Arch. UHO Honley Local Board, 16 Aug. 1880; Holmfirth Express, 10 Oct. 1908, 15 Mar. 1985.

14 Honley Mill
W.C.R. 7 Nov. 1767; Kirk. Arch. KC161/1-3 1806 Letter Books; London Gazette, 7 Oct. 1828; Leeds Mercury, 25 Oct. 1828; 4 April 1829; Dartmouth Terrier, 1828, 1829 Nov, 1834 June; Halifax Guardian, 6 Feb. 1836; Leeds Mercury, 12 June 1841, 7 Apr. 1849, 16 Nov. 1850; Hudds Ex. 7 Feb, 1852, Kirk. Arch. T/H/F36, also KC6/1/33;

15 Hudds Chron. 24 May 1856, 15 Apr. 1865; London Gazette, 17 Apr. 1868; Hudds Ex. 18 Mar. 1871; Hudds. Chron. 11 Nov. 1871, 23 Mar. and 27 July 1872; Roberts family papers 9 Aug. 1877; Hudds. Ex. 28 Dec. 1878; 28 Jan. 1903; Kirk. Arch. KMT4/UHO Jan. 1904; Holmfirth Express, 6 July 1918.

16 Reins mill
Leeds Mercury, 7 Aug. 1847, 11 Mar. 1848; 31 Mar. 1849; Hudds Chron. 30 Jan. 1858; Kirk. Arch. KC315 Box 2, 5 Oct. 1865; Hudds Chron. 18 Sept 1869, 27 July 1872; Hudds Ex. 10 May 1873. 28 Mar. 1874, 24 Mar. 1883, 1 Dec. 1888, 15 Feb. 1890; Kirk. Arch. UHO Honley, 23 Feb. 20 July 1891, 14 Nov. 1896; Text. Manfr, May 1889, June 1898; Yorks. Fact. Times, 2 June 1899; H'firth Exp. 14 July 1900; Hudds. Ex. 21 July, 29 Sept. 1900; London Gazette, 21 May 1901, 16 Jan. 1903; Yorks. Fact. Times, 5 Sept, 17 Oct. 1902; Hudds Ex. 1 Oct. 1904, 4 July 1914, 2 Sept. 1916.

CHAPTER 15

Honley and the Mag Valley

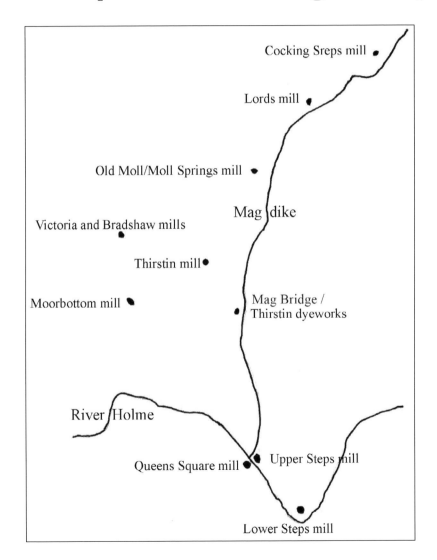

Cocking Sreps mill

Lords mill

Old Moll/Moll Springs mill

Mag dike

Victoria and Bradshaw mills

Thirstin mill

Moorbottom mill

Mag Bridge /
Thirstin dyeworks

River Holme

Queens Square mill   Upper Steps mill

Lower Steps mill

Queens / Victoria mill

A draft Indenture drawn up in 1836 shows that George Beaumont and James Stocks, both of Honley, purchased 1 acre 1 rood and 33 perches of land at Fisher Green from Sarah Waddington of Liverpool at a cost of £352, on which they built a mill. The buildings are shown on the plan that accompanies the Valuation survey carried out in 1838 and published in 1843, in which Beaumont and Stocks are listed as owners and tenants of the property. The census return of 1851 lists James Stocks of Fisher Green as a manufacturer employing 39 adults and 12 children, made up of 17 men, 22 women, 10 boys and 2 girls. In July of that year the mill was advertised for sale as one lot in a large property sale, possibly owned by George Beaumont. The mill was described as:

> '*All that capital Mill called Victoria Factory; the northern end of the mill built by Beaumont & Stocks, also the spacious building 3 storeys high, erected by the late Mr. Beaumont in 1845 to the west and adjacent to the original part and communicating with it; with the steam engine and boiler each 10hp installed in 1845. Also land on 3 sides of the mill, with the buildings a total of 3roods 29 perches'.*

The 6inch Ordinance Survey map of 1853 marks the buildings as Queen's Mill, but all other documents refer to it as Victoria Mill.

The early 1850s were a difficult time for business, with many mills on short time. The *Huddersfield Examiner* of 23 October 1852, carried a report on the state of trade in Honley, in which it said 'That portion of the [Victoria] mill that has been standing [idle] a while is getting into work and will employ a few more hands, but these will be few in comparison with the many that have been thrown out of work at the larger mills'.

The workers' treat had become a tradition by 1853, and was continued despite the difficult conditions of the time, although with one notable difference, which is demonstrated in the report of the treat at Victoria mill. The *Huddersfield Chronicle* reported on 15 January 1853 that 70 workers employed by Mr. Marsden at Victoria mill sat down to a substantial supper in a large room at the mill. 'The meal was provided *at the joint expense of the master and the workers*, and was accompanied by home brewed beer. During the week, workmen at several other mills have had tea parties, *at their own expense*, at the several public houses in the village'.

The mill was offered for sale on 19 October 1853, described as 4 storeys high, 49ft by 36ft, 'well lighted', with engine and boiler houses, also land totalling 2,376sq.yds, which would afford the erection of another mill and weaving sheds. The owner of the mill was James Stocks. On the 13th, six days before the auction, there was a small fire in some waste yarn belonging to Joseph Marsden, thought to have been caused by spontaneous combustion; damage was estimated at £10. The mill was not sold, and was offered 'for sale or to let' on October 29, with machinery at valuation if required. A quantity of broad and narrow power looms, several hand looms and other pieces of machinery allied to weaving were advertised for sale by auction on 1 March 1854; the name of the vendor was not given. Joseph Marsden was still occupying part of the mill in March 1858 when he brought charges against Robert Haigh, a weaver working at home, for robbery. Marsden had gone to Haigh's house accompanied by a Police Constable and had found warps, weft and other yarns that should not have been there. Haigh had a warp in his loom that should have gone to Midge mill at Scholes. Haigh was sentenced to three months imprisonment with hard labour.

Joseph Pontefract was using part of the mill in 1859, when he and Joseph Marsden gave a joint treat to their 80 workers at the Wheatsheaf Inn Honley on 12 January. The same month, Jonathon Roebuck, a linsey-woolsey maker and dealer of Choppards, was charged by the woollen inspector R.H. Kaye, with having a number of yards of linsey-woolsey and a few old coppins and bobbins in his possession suspected to be the property of Joseph Marsden, and which Marsden identified. Roebuck produced invoices for the materials from Hezekiah Haigh, who had been given them in payment of rent arrears. The case was dismissed.

Mary Ann Dyson was prosecuted by Joseph Marsden in July 1859 for leaving his employment without finishing a warp that she was working on. After hearing the evidence against her, Dyson decided to return and finish the warp, and to pay the 8s expenses of the case. In August of the same year a man named Ben Carter brought a case against Marsden's for injury sustained by his 15 year old son, also called Ben Carter, in October 1858. The boy was a layer-on for Ben Sanderson, a slubber working for Joseph Pontefract, and was earning 6s 9d per week. Pontefract was renting room and power from Marsden, who was responsible for the shafting and gearing. Ben was piling up slubbings when his foot slipped through a hole in the boxing of the drive shaft. He had been under the care of Dr. Lees for six weeks, the father said that the Doctor's bill came to £2 12s 6d. Dr. Edward Lees said that he had removed three toes from Carter's foot, and had attended him on 53 occasions. The slubber Ben Sanderson, and his employer Joseph Pontefract, both said that Marsden was aware of the hole in the boxing. The jury found Marsden guilty of gross negligence, and awarded the boy £15 damages.

John Littlewood & Sons were using part of the mill in August 1861, when they gave a treat to 100 people on the occasion of Lupton Littlewood's wedding. His bride was the sister of the wife of G.W. Farrar of Cliff House, and Mag Bridge/Thirstin Dyeworks. Lupton Littlewood and G.W. Farrar were both elected members of the new Local Board in 1864. Richard Mellor gave a treat to his 60 workers, plus a similar number of friends on Saturday 21 January 1865, to celebrate the completion of a new spacious weaving shed at the mill; but it was apparently not spacious enough, as seven years later, in September 1872, it was being enlarged. A fire was discovered in the willowing room used by Richard Mellor on 9 June 1868; the room was just a few yards from the mill dam, and the fire was extinguished in about 30 minutes by neighbours using buckets. Damage was estimated to be around £20. Lupton Littlewood was head of John Littlewood & Sons in November 1872, when he presided over a treat for several hundred people when Richard Littlewood married Miss Hirst. The men had their meal in a beerhouse near to the mill, while the women had theirs in a large room at the mill. After the meal everyone assembled in the large room for the speeches and toasts.

A building in Huddersfield known as Littlewood's Buildings had one side facing the Cloth Hall, and the other facing onto Sargentson Street. Richard Mellor was using the top floor of this building, and had a large number of pieces of cloth stored there. In July 1876 a beam gave way and the floor collapsed, causing a considerable amount of damage to the entire building. The lower floors were occupied by William Roberts of Hinchliffe Mill, and Jonas Hobson & Co of Holmbridge, both firms also had pieces stored in the building. Due to the collapse, all the cloth would have to be refinished.

A fire broke out in the kitchen of Richard Littlewood's house near the mill at around 1am on the morning of 30 April 1879. The mill buzzer was sounded, and Robinson's fire engine 'Britannia' from Smithy Place mill arrived and put out the fire by 3am. Damage was estimated to be around £100. A large quantity of machinery, presumably belonging to Richard Mellor, was offered for sale on 11 January 1886. The Mellor name disappears from this mill after that date.

John Littlewood & Sons were accused of breaching the Factory Act in April 1888. Mr. Prior the Factory Sub-Inspector had visited the factory on 9 April and found a woman weaver working after the permitted time. Littlewood's were fined 20s plus costs. The mill was advertised for sale in May 1890, due to Littlewood's giving up business. It was described as a 4 storey mill 49ft by 36ft, 2 storey spinning mill 29ft by 16ft 3in, weaving shed, beaming shed with pattern weaving room over, 35hp steam engine and boiler. This was followed by a sale of loose mill furnishings, 10,000lbs of raw materials and yarn, and a large quantity of machinery for preparing and spinning yarn, and turning that yarn into cloth in July 1890.

Paul Wallace, a worsted spinner was using part of the mill in 1890; he was in financial difficulty by November, as his machinery was offered for sale by auction in distraint for rent. Thomas Wood Dearnley had started in business at the mill in January 1889 and, in common with many others at that time, was finding trading conditions difficult. He had originally intended to go into partnership with his brother George Frederick Dearnley; but had borrowed £210 from his wife, sold their household furniture to his father-in-law for £213, and set up on his own trading as Dearnley Brothers. In July 1891 he had liabilities of £2,396 16s 7d; his assets amounted to £836 13s 8d, leaving a deficit of £1,560 2s 11d. Mrs. Dearnley appears to have become very disillusioned or even disgruntled by April of that year, as she instructed the auctioneer Frank Smith to advertise the sale of their household furniture at their Magdale home. The sale was set to take place on 27 April 'due to declining housekeeping', the advertisements appearing in the Huddersfield Examiner on the 18th and 25th of the month.

A 25 year old woman named Annie Taylor was found drowned in the mill dam on Saturday 14 April

1894. She had left home the previous evening; her brother Turner Taylor had found a note from her at 12.20am on the Saturday morning saying that she would be found 'in Lupton Littlewood's dam' and that no-one else was to blame. He took the note to the police, and PC Satchwell went with Turner to the dam where they found a shawl on the bank, that her father subsequently identified as Annie's. There was no sign of the woman at that time, but early the following morning the dam was dragged and her body recovered. The inquest jury returned a verdict of 'Suicide while temporarily insane'.

The premises were advertised for sale again in April 1895, by which time it had been extended. The buildings were described as the 4 storey mill plus attic 49ft by 36ft; 2 storey plus attic spinning mill 91ft by 41ft; 2 storey fire proof willey room 29ft by 16ft 6in; weaving shed 108ft by 64ft; beaming shed with pattern weaving room over; engine house, boiler house with stove over, chimney. Plus the 35hp steam engine and boiler. Lot 2 comprised 2,578sq.yds of building land fronting onto Cross/ Gib Lane. At some time between 1895 and 1906 the premises became divided, with Victoria mill being the original premises onto Meltham Road; and the L shaped premises onto Bradshaw Road being renamed Bradshaw mill. The 25inch Ordinance Survey map of 1906 marks the premises on Bradshaw Road as an Iron Works. The *Yorkshire Textile Directory* records that Sykes and Schofield were using part of the mill in 1910, the company's name had changed to T.H. Sykes & Co in 1911, and they were using the premises until 1916. A firm of Angola yarn spinners named Sellers, Lister & Co. of Bradley mills sued T.H. Sykes & Co. in July 1912, for non payment of £15 8s 8d for yarn supplied. Sykes & Co said that they had not paid for the yarn because it was faulty, and they submitted a counter claim against Sellers, Lister & Co. of £9 6s 5d for bobbins that Sykes & Co had returned to Sellers, Lister & Co that had not been credited. Sellers, Lister & Co argued that Sykes & Co should have informed them within seven days of receiving the yarn that it was faulty, which they had not done. The judge decided that Sykes & Co. should pay the money that they owed to Sellers, Lister & Co. less the amount owed to them for bobbins returned.

A company called Gledhill Bros. moved into the mill in 1916, and advertised for women weavers, warpers, winders and menders, also 2 lads for reaching in. They also had premises in Huddersfield. They were using Victoria mill until 1923. Victoria Textiles Ltd. who were rayon warpers, winders and sizers were using the mill from 1935. Walter Shaw was the Managing Director and Company Secretary. They were also using premises in Upper Mytholmbridge mill in the 1950s trading as W. & O. Shaw. Their last entry in the YTD for Victoria mill appeared in 1963.

The premises were bought by Lodge's Supermarkets of Huddersfield in 1965 and were used as a grocery warehouse for some years. During the 1980s the premises became a restaurant, eventually being taken over by John Copley and Dennis Clarke who were trading as 'The Silk Mill Restaurant' in the 1990s.[1]

Bradshaw mill

This building stands on Bradshaw Road, just above the junction with Meltham Road, and was originally part of Victoria mill. The premises seem to have been divided at some time between 1895 and 1906, although why, and by whom, is unclear. The split had occurred before 1906, as the 25inch Ordinance Survey map printed in that year marks the building as an Iron Works. The *Yorkshire Factory Times* reports a fire that occurred on 4 March 1909 as happening at Victoria mill, but the company involved was John Shaw & Sons who were machine makers, making it likely that they were in the Iron Works rather than the mill. Tom Lockwood, who lived in Bradshaw Road, saw sparks coming from the roof of the building and raised the alarm. He and others attempted to douse the fire with buckets of water; they were soon joined by Honley fire brigade with their hand hose cart, and by 10.10pm the fire was out. The cause of the fire was thought to be due to overheating of the necks of buffing machines; the machines and the building's roof sustained damage estimated to be around £125, which was fully insured.

Herbert Scholefield & Co. moved from Neiley mill after a severe fire there in 1915, and was using

Bradshaw mill until around 1923. B.T. Cave Ltd. were also homeless after the fire at Neiley mill and moved into Bradshaw mill trading as B.T. Cave Successors Ltd, but were only there for one year.

A serious fire occurred at the mill on Saturday 14 May 1924, completely gutting the building and causing damage estimated at £20,000. The mill had been working as usual on the Saturday morning, but there was no-one in the building during Saturday afternoon. Smoke was seen coming from the windows of the lower floor around 3pm. Before the fire brigade arrived, several people including PC Jones tried to put out the fire using the mill's hose pipe, but to no avail. The roof of the mill had collapsed before the fire engine arrived at 3.25pm. The fire brigade were able to prevent the fire spreading to other buildings, but the interior of the mill was completely destroyed. The mill was at least partially rebuilt, and was being used by G. W. Smith, commission weavers from 1936 until at least 1971.[2]

Moor Bottom mill

Situated on Moor Bottom Road on the corner of what is now the entrance to Roundways, this was a weaving shop that came into existence during the 1940s, possibly before the end of the Second World War, but definitely before May 1948, when Moorbottom Manufacturing Company were advertising for male weavers. The company were listed in the *Yorkshire Textile Directory* between 1950 and 1958 as weavers of plain and fancy worsted suitings and overcoatings. The premises seem to have been empty from 1958 until the West Riding County Council announced in January 1960 that they were to buy the premises and convert them into an Ambulance Depot.[3]

Thirstin mill

Originally the site of a dyehouse, the mill was built in 1790. The first recorded occupant was Thomas Hinchliffe, who replied to the Factory Commissioners questionnaire in 1833. He said that since its erection the mill had alternated between being occupied and empty, and 'it is now in a very poor condition, wanting to be made entirely over again'. The power came from a water wheel, or from a steam engine, both supplied about 3hp. The water to drive the wheel came from 'Thirsting Springs' and was sufficient to drive the wheel for 'perhaps a quarter of the year'. He had a total of 8 workers, 2 boys under 12, 1 boy and 1 girl under 14, all earning 4s per week; 1 male under 18 earning 7s, 1 male under 21 earning 8s and 2 men over 21 each earning 20s per week. The working day was from 6am to 8pm in summer, and from 7am to 8pm in winter. No answer was given to the question about working less time on Saturdays. The workers were allowed a half hour break for breakfast, one hour for dinner, and half an hour for 'drinking'. Hinchliffe's answer to the question about stopping the machinery at meal times was 'Yes, sometimes; and at other times the scribblers have to run at mealtimes when one is employed in laying-on'. They had a half day holiday at Shrovetide, one day at Easter, one day at Whitsuntide, three days at Honley Feast and three days at Christmas; none of them with pay.

The Survey and Valuation carried out in 1838, published in 1843, shows that Benjamin Ledger Shaw was the owner and occupier of the mill at that time. There was also a smaller mill nearby that was also owned by B.L. Shaw called Brow mill, which was occupied by John Dyson. This building eventually became part of Thirstin mill. An auction sale of over 50 lots of land and property belonging to the Shaw family was advertised to take place on 26 May 1852. Lot 1 was Thirstin mill, 2 storeys high 73ft 6in by 32ft together with going gear, a new 26ft diameter water wheel, reservoir and yard. Also a 2 storey house occupied by James Radcliffe, and a small dyehouse situated between the reservoir and mill occupied by Jonathon Roebuck. Bidding for this lot failed to reach the reserve and it was withdrawn. Thirstin mill, the dyehouse and Old Moll mill were advertised to let separately or together in May 1853. All the property was owned by the Shaw family, application to be made to Mr. James Shaw, Market St. Huddersfield, who had succeeded his half brother Benjamin. Some rebuilding probably took place during the next five years, a sale advertisement in April 1858 describes the mill as being 2 storeys 33yds by 10yds 'of recent construction', and having a good water wheel and small steam engine.

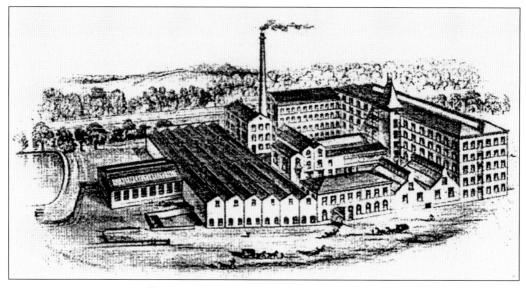

Thirstin mill, taken from Letter Head. Collection of A.J. Brooke

A 52 year old tailor named Charles Thornton left home early on the morning of 31 May 1853, and drowned himself in the mill dam. His clothing was found on the bank about 4am, but there was no sign of him. His body was eventually found in the deepest part of the dam by Saville Oldfield. At the inquest, held at the Commercial Inn, it emerged that for a long time Thornton had 'led an intemperate and unhappy life', and had been heard to say that he wished to die. The jury returned a verdict of 'temporary insanity brought on by excessive drinking'.

A 44 year old single woman from Austonley called Grace Hinchliffe was taken by friends to Abraham Mellor, the Relieving Officer for Holmfirth on Sunday 16 January 1859. She was said to be 'low in spirits', and was also ill. Mellor took her to the Workhouse in Honley, where he saw her again on the Monday in company with Edward Lees the surgeon who thought that he could 'do her good'. An old woman who slept in the room that Hinchliffe was put in was asked to keep an eye on her. Hinchliffe became agitated on the Monday evening and got out of bed three times during the night. The third time was at 4.50am on the Tuesday morning when she went downstairs. The older woman followed her and tried to take her back upstairs, but Hinchliffe broke away and escaped by throwing herself through a closed window. The woman raised the alarm and others got up and went to look for Hinchliffe, but did not find her. Joseph Whitworth Assistant Overseer, heard about the incident at 8am; he sent word to Hinchliffe's brother and also went to look in Thirstin mill dam some 200 to 300 yards away, where he found Hinchliffe drowned. He then informed the police, got Hinchliffe out of the dam and taken back to the workhouse. At the inquest John Hinchliffe, brother of the deceased, said that his sister had two children aged 19 And 16 and had lived in Mosley, but had returned to Austonley. He said that the 19 year old son was afraid that his mother would harm herself, she was 'wick' in the eyes, but had said nothing remarkable. The Coroner made some strong criticism about the condition of the workhouse and the quality of care given to the poor of Honley, saying that the workhouse was a disgrace to the Huddersfield Union. The jury returned a verdict of 'temporary insanity'.

Presumably due to James Shaw's financial problems, Thirstin mill was in the hands of the Yorkshire Banking Company's Huddersfield Branch in 1860, when Philemon Armitage agreed to lease the mill from them, together with the cottage and outbuildings, reservoir, garden and land for seven years at a rent of £50 per year, subject to John Dyson, who was using part of the mill, retaining his tenancy. Armitage was to have the first year's rent waived to allow him to carry out necessary improvements.

Armitage's property, including a 4hp steam engine and boiler, various machines for processing loose wool into yarn, and 700lbs of 'scribbled Alpaca extracts', was advertised to be sold by auction under a Deed of Assignment in May 1862; this seems to have signalled his demise, as there is no subsequent record of his business.

Thomas Shaw a linen draper of Berry Brow, and Elliott Hirst also of Berry Brow, were trading as Thomas Shaw & Co. yarn spinners and manufacturers, in part of the mill in October 1864. Wright Taylor was working for them as a slubber, and left the firm without giving the required 14 days notice. He subsequently appeared in court charged with neglect of work. After hearing the evidence, Mr. Learoyd his counsel, recommended him to return to work and complete the notice period. The firm was in financial difficulty in July 1866, when they dissolved their partnership; and completed a Deed of Assignment on 11 July, conveying their goods through their trustees, who were James Chadwick a merchant of Manchester, William Lawton, Bank Manager of Huddersfield, and William Whiteley machine maker of Lockwood, to the benefit of creditors. A dividend was paid to their creditors in May 1867.

Several members of the France family were using the mill around 1870, Nathan France, Benjamin France and Charles Henry France trading as Benjamin France & Sons, had lodged a list of their debts and liabilities, plus a statement of their property and credits with the Office of the Chief Registrar of Bankruptcy in London. They had also issued a Deed of Composition dated 30 December 1869, in which they agreed to pay 6s in the £ to their creditors. This was to be paid in two equal instalments on 30 April and 30 August 1870; the final instalment being guaranteed by James Robinson of Smithy Place, and Josiah France, who was living at Well Hill. He is recorded in the 1871 census as a manufacturer employing 160 people, whether this was at Thirstin mill, or at Neiley mill where he was in 1878, is unclear. George France, working as a cloth finisher, was also using part of the mill in 1870, but soon found himself in financial difficulty. A Committee of Inspection ordered that his machinery, including a tentering machine and a hydraulic press, should be sold on 28 September of that year. The advertisement said that all the machines were new within the last 9 months.

A company named Dearnley & Denham were using part of the mill in 1870; they also used a barn a short distance from the mill in which shoddy and waste were stored. A fire broke out in the barn on Saturday 13 August, neighbours managed to get a horse and its harness out, but the roof of the building collapsed, and the wool, shoddy and some chickens that roosted in the barn were burned. No estimate of the damage was given.

The part of the mill used by Benjamin France & Sons was offered for sale by private treaty in March 1872, applications were to be made to Mr. Charles France of Thirstin. The premises were re-advertised for sale by auction on 17 June, and finishing machinery, which from the advertisement could include at least some of the machines from George France, was advertised to be sold on 8 July 1872.[4] Benjamin France died in early September 1873; in addition to his manufacturing career, he had been an active member of Honley Congregational Sunday School. John William France also went into liquidation in November 1873, the case appears to have been brought by his sister Emma who was a spinster living in Longwood, who was dissatisfied with her inheritance from their father's estate. J. Robinson of Smithy Place mill had guaranteed John William France in business for the amount of £1,100. In return France had given Robinson the deeds to some property at Townend Honley and on Honley Moor. After France's default, Robinson took charge of the property which, he found, was not equal to the amount of money that he had paid out, neither was he able to sell it. Robinson applied to the court in April 1875 for permission to sell the property, which was granted. John William France appears to have been working for Wrigley's at Cocking Steps mill in August 1884, when he led the funeral procession of Mr. George Henry Wrigley.

Denham & Dearnley were still using part of the mill 1874, when they applied to Honley Local Board to make several alterations to their premises, which were passed. By 1876 the name of the company had become Dearnley & Drury. On Saturday 29 December 1877 Mr. Dearnley gave notice to their weavers that they intended to reduce the prices paid for weaving worsted warps by 1d per string, and that in the case of 2 beam warps, the price would be reduced by 2d per string. In common with other manufacturers in the area Dearnley & Drury had been paying the rates agreed after the strike of 1872, which the weavers wished to continue. During the next week the weavers attempted to negotiate, offering to accept a reduction of 1d per string on 2 beam warps, but leaving single beam warps at their current rate, but Mr. Dearnley refused to negotiate and 55 weavers were set to come out on strike on Thursday 3 January. Four, who had downed their warps that day actually walked out, however, Mr. Dearnley met the weavers again that evening and accepted the weavers' terms, allowing everyone to carry on working from Friday morning. Around 25 of the firm's looms had 2 beam warps at the time. Later that year between May and July 1878, manufacturers throughout Holme Valley were trying to reduce weaving rates, which the weavers vehemently resisted. Unable to reach a collective agreement, each manufacturer individually negotiated agreements with their weavers. Dearnley & Drury continued their occupation of the mill until 1885, when they gave a treat to some 250 employees, but their name disappears from the records after that date.

Wright Littlewood, a tripe and bone boiler for manufacturing Size and Glue, was using premises in the mill in 1884; he came to the notice of the Local Board in July of that year for carrying out unauthorized extensions. Later that year Littlewood was also in danger of polluting the mill dam with effluent from his plant. There was also a tripe and bone works at Neiley mill, which Littlewood bought in October 1892 intending to move there from Thirstin. On the morning of 10th October 1892 Littlewood, who was 43, married with 5 children, went to his works at Thirstin, about 100 yards away from his house; he returned home at 7.20am, and went upstairs. Mrs. Littlewood heard a scream; she went upstairs where she found that Littlewood was trying to cut his throat with a knife. Mrs. Littlewood took the knife from him, and then discovered their 16 year old daughter, who was described as 'a cripple', in her own bed with her throat cut. Littlewood was arrested, taken to Huddersfield Police Station, and charged with murder. At his trial in the Assize Court on 17 December, it was said that had the incision Littlewood made in his own throat been slightly lower he would have succeeded in his attempted suicide. The jury returned a verdict of 'Guilty, but Insane'. He was sent as a 'criminal lunatic' to Armley, to be detained at His Majesty's pleasure.

Eastwood Brothers had been using the mill since 1891, and possibly earlier, in August 1895 they applied to Honley Local Board to erect a new dyehouse and 12 privies, which was passed. Work on the project was stopped when Eastwood's broke open the council's sewer without permission; but they were given permission to continue on 10 April 1896. The majority of Local Authorities maintained, at that time, that their sewage treatment plants could not handle industrial effluent. On the evening of 21 May 1896 the workpeople at the firm presented H.H. Eastwood with a marble clock and a gentleman's dressing case to mark his attainment of his majority. Also as part of the celebrations, the firm took all the employees to Blackpool for the day on Saturday 27 June. The train left Honley station at 5am, arriving in Blackpool at 8am. After spending the day enjoying the pleasures of both the town and the beach, the company left Blackpool at 8pm, arriving back in Honley at midnight.

The controversy over the treatment of trade effluent continued within the Local Board until, in September 1899, Eastwood's were informed that their sewer carrying trade effluent would be disconnected on 26 October, and that a separate sewer would be installed for sewage. Eastwood's then commenced a High Court action against the council, the council minutes of November 1899 record that they were awaiting the judgement in the case of Peebles v Oswaldtwistle Council, which would set a precedent. In February 1901 the decision went against the council, but Honley council still maintained that they could not deal with trade effluent and appealed the decision, but failed. The council minutes of January 1902 record that they decided not to continue with the case. In November 1902 Eastwood's planned to build a new weaving shed, which involved them buying a small area of vacant land next to the mill that they thought had a value of between £10 and £15. The council however, asked for £50 for the land, Eastwood's offered £30, which the council refused to accept. During the ensuing weeks the disagreement between the two sides was aired in the pages of the *Huddersfield Examiner*, resulting in Eastwood's abandoning the scheme.

In January 1908, 19 year old David Garside of Bankbottom Netherton was working as a feeder on a garnet machine. His left hand became drawn into the mechanism of the machine and later had to be amputated. He was claiming compensation for the injury, which the judge allowed as it was caused while the machine was being operated correctly. Garside was awarded a weekly payment of 10s. The *Yorkshire Textile Directory* of 1912 records that Eastwood Bros. were manufacturers of worsteds and woollens, with 3,300 spindles and 85 looms. At that time they were employing between 200 and 220 people, but in March of that year they had to lay off all but 20 of them due to a coal strike. The firm continued in business through the First World War, and at some time between the two World Wars their share capital was bought by Dobroyd Mills Company of Hepworth, although Eastwood's carried on using their own name. The YTD of 1942-3 records that the firm then had 7,500 spindles and 113 looms. The name of Eastwood Bros. disappeared after the Second World War, and was replaced by that of Dobroyd Mills Co. who continued to use the mill until around 1969

Two companies were using parts of the mill in 1976, one was G.R. Knitwear, the second company was A1 Spinners and Doublers. A serious fire occurred at the mill on 15 June 1976, a fireman who attended the blaze described it as 'one of the most serious fires in the Huddersfield area for years'. Sarwan Singh Purewal one of the directors of G.R. Knitwear, was accused of causing the fire, and admitted responsibility for it. The buildings were owned by Jack Brook builders, and were occupied by a variety of companies.

A company called Taylor & Whiteley Ltd. were using some premises at Thirstin in 1977 when they were advertising for staff; they moved to Newtown Honley in August of that year. A plan was submitted to Kirklees Council in 2000 to demolish all the buildings on the site and build 29 houses. The buildings have gone, but no houses have appeared.[5]

Mag Brook – Cocking Steps / Wrigley's mill

Although often referred to as being at Netherton, the buildings of this mill are on the Honley side of the river, beside Cocking Steps Bridge. There is a deed in the Wakefield Deeds Registry showing that James Rawcliffe, a fulling miller at Spinks Mire mill Meltham, bought land at Honley Wood Bottom in 1790, and built the mill in the following year. He also built a weir to direct water to the mill dam, which caused problems for John Beaumont of Lower Hall mill. Rawcliffe was ordered to lower the weir by 4 feet in 1792. The premises were advertised to be let in March 1810, when they were described as 3 storeys high, with 2 rooms 12yds by 8yds and 3 rooms 16yds by 12yds, with a good water wheel, a stove in the middle of the buildings, being very eligible for cloth or cotton manufacture; and were still owned by James Rawcliffe.

John Wrigley bought the premises from Rawcliffe in 1812. John Hirst was the occupant of Lower Hall mill in 1832, and brought a case against Wrigley's for again raising their weir to a level that stopped the water wheel at Lower Hall mill. Wrigley's replied to the Parliamentary enquiry into the conditions in mills and factories in 1833; saying that the premises were used for scribbling carding, slubbing, milling or fulling and finishing of cloth; that they had used the premises for just over 20 years, but it had been built before that by the person from whom they bought it. The mill was equipped with both water and steam power, the water coming from the 'River Mag'. The water wheel delivered 10hp, while the steam engine delivered 30hp. John Wrigley & Sons used two thirds of the power, with the other one third being allocated to Robert Wrigley, but since June 1832 Robert Wrigley's machinery had stood idle because the Union had told all his employees to stop work. A total of 56 people were employed at the mill, 30 of them were paid by time, the other 26 were employed on piece rates. All those under 21 were better off on time rates, whereas some of those over 21 could earn more on piece work. 14 children were employed as piecers in the slubbing

Cocking Steps mill. © A.J. Brooke

department, more than half of them worked for a parent, they were all paid by their slubber. Work started at 6am until 8pm in Summer, and at 6.30am to 7.30pm in Winter, but on Saturdays the mill closed at 5pm. The workers had 30 minutes for breakfast at 8am, 1 hour for dinner at 12 noon, and 30 minutes for 'drinking' at 4.30pm. The machinery only stopped at dinner time. If work stopped for up to 2 hours due to a breakdown of machinery, the lost time would be made up by shortening the dinner hour; if the stoppage was longer than 2 hours the time was not made up and was considered a loss to both masters and men alike. The firm had about 8 days holiday a year, but no days or dates are given. About half of the men employed on fixed wages were allowed holiday pay, while the rest were not, in accordance with the agreements made when the men were employed. Deductions in pay would be made if someone was more than thirty minutes late for work. Wrigley's had never tried to employ a second group of children to allow part time education, in common with several other manufacturers they said that they did not know the same number of children anywhere who were more healthy than those that worked in their mill. Their child employees had instruction given in reading, writing and accounts two nights each week by one of the masters, and were 'every way better in health and conduct than the children who are not allowed to work in the mills, but run about at their own pleasure'. They also said that had the firm employed a second group of children, the majority of parents could not afford to lose half their child's wage, which for children under 12 would go down from 4s to 2s per week. To do so would force the family onto Parish relief. Wrigley's did not sanction the use of corporal punishment; they did think that children under twelve made better feeders for slubbing machines than older children, but apart from that it was not necessary to employ children under 12. In answer to the question about government regulation of working hours Wrigley's said that adoption of the Ten Hours Bill would be attended with a great loss to the working classes, and particularly so to the small manufacturers, who would lose one sixth of their work time, which would make them uncompetitive against the large employers who, because of their unlimited resources could increase their output whenever they felt it necessary.

The dispute between Robert Wrigley and the Union tainted the view that the press had of the whole Wrigley family. In November 1833 the *Halifax Guardian* labelled them as 'strenuous opponents of the union', while the *Voice of the West Riding* described them as 'deadly enemies of the unions'. These comments possibly arose from an incident that occurred on Tuesday 5 November. A group of non-union workmen were in the house of one of Wrigley's overlookers in Netherton, which was attacked by a number of men who broke the windows and did other damage. The attack was repeated the following day, when the workmen escaped from the house by means of a trap door; but a young son of the overlooker was seriously injured, which incensed other members of the community. The local Constabulary rounded up ten of the group of attackers, who, at the time the report was written, were confined awaiting examination by the magistrates.

Robert Wrigley brought a case for assault against his brother William, James Dawson overlooker, Benjamin Wood a slubber and Benjamin Lees, that was due to be heard in the early part of 1834 at York Assizes; the alleged assault having taken place on 9 October 1833. Robert Wrigley rented one third of the mill from his brother William; his machines were erected in the same rooms, and alongside those of his brother. Robert was three years in arrears with his rent and insurance premiums; and for the last eighteen months he had not contributed to the cost of running the mill engine. The defendants said that on the day in question Robert had come to the mill at 2pm, that he was drunk and was operating machinery in a dangerous manner. Rather than work his own machines, he attempted to stop the rest of the mill from working by removing the governor rod from the mill engine when it was running, and opening the engine's steam inlet valve to maximum. He had to be forcibly removed from the premises; had he not been removed, the mill engine and other machinery would probably have been destroyed, and the lives and livelihoods of the sixty or so employees put in jeopardy. Although copies of statements from witnesses exist, there is no indication that the case ever got to court. It is possible that Robert Wrigley was advised by his Solicitor not to proceed with the case.

Plug rioters caused some disruption at the mill on Monday 15 August 1842, as they passed through the district on their way to Huddersfield. Mr. James Wrigley had previously given a piece of land in Netherton for the erection of an Independent Chapel and Sunday School. The completed building was opened by the Rev. James Pridie of Halifax, on Wednesday 10 May 1843. It had cost a total of £208 to build, which had been raised by public subscription.

After a visit to the mill by James Bates the Factory sub-inspector, the firm were charged with not having an upright drive shaft securely fenced, for which they were fined £5 plus costs; and for employing two young persons without surgeon's certificates, they were fined 20s plus costs. David Bradley a slubber at the mill was also charged for employing his son without a surgeon's certificate, and for not sending the boy to school, he was fined 10s plus costs.

A fire was discovered in the stove at the mill on the morning of 11 May 1853; girls working in a nearby room smelled the smoke and raised the alarm. The workers realised that using large amounts of water would probably damage the large number of finished pieces of cloth stored in the room below the stove. They extinguished the fire by taking buckets and containers of water into the stove and immersing the wool in them.

The mill was closed on Wednesday 6 July 1853 to allow workers who wished to do so, to attend the funeral of Mr. John Sykes of Honley, who had been with the firm for 23 years and was well liked and respected. 46 workmen joined with members of the Order of Ancient Druids in the funeral procession. The funeral of 85 year old Martin Wimpenny who had worked for the firm for over 50 years as a cloth miller, took place on 19 December 1855. Upwards of 150 mourners including employers, workpeople and friends attended. An accident took place at Honley Station in August 1859, John Beardsell, a cart driver at Wrigley's for 12 years, had taken his cart to the station and filled it with coal. He was helping a friend to fill his cart when a truck that they had emptied was rolled away and a full truck was rolling into position. Mr. Beardsell was in a stooping position when he was hit by the full truck, knocking him onto the rails. One of the truck wheels ran over him severing his head from his body. He left a wife and four small children.

James Albert Wrigley, the second son of James Wrigley, reached the age of 21 in August 1860.

The workpeople enjoyed a meal of roast beef and plum pudding provided for them in a large warehouse at the mill. Speeches, Toasts and Glee singing followed the meal. David Schofield a cloth finisher, was walking alongside the mill buildings in October 1864 when a stone weighing 10 to 12lbs fell from some scaffolding, hitting him on the head and shoulders, cutting him severely. He was seen by two local surgeons, who confined him to bed.

William Wrigley married Miss Dewhirst of Aspley in March 1865. The firm gave a treat to the male workers of a substantial English dinner in the Oddfellows' Hall, while the women were treated to a 'plentiful repast' in the school room, where they had an excellent dish of tea with the very agreeable addition of "brown cream" [Rum]. A second wedding feast took place in November 1865, to celebrate the wedding of James Albert Wrigley. 130 men were entertained in the Oddfellows' Hall, and 130 women in the Independent Schoolroom.[6]

A fire was discovered in the stove around 8.30pm on the evening of 1 June 1866. A large number of workpeople and neighbours formed a bucket chain and fought the blaze, which was subdued in around 20 minutes. The origin of the fire was thought to be due to missing mortar in the flue, allowing flames to ignite the drying wool. Damage was estimated at £120. Wrigley's were one of the firms to give evidence to the enquiry into the pollution of rivers in 1866. Mr. Joseph Wrigley junior said that they burned about 2,000 tons of coal a year in Cocking Steps and Dungeon mills. The river bed did not appear to have risen perceptibly, which he attributed to their practise of throwing ashes into deep holes in the river bed. He justified this by saying that if they did not dispose of ashes in the river they would have to destroy good land by heaping up the ashes, as there were no nearby quarries where they could dump them. Water for manufacturing purposes came from a borehole or streams on their land rather than from Mag Brook, although they sometimes took water from the Brook on Saturday nights or early mornings, when it ran clearest. Waste water from dyepans and other processes was turned into Mag. Brook. Mr. Wrigley also said that water polluted with Ochre [which often came from abandoned coal pits] was one of the worst pollutants for cloth manufacturers.

Another fire occurred in the stove on the evening of 19 July 1867. Millhands were working until 8pm, then the doors were locked for the night. A passer-by saw the fire at 9.30pm and raised the alarm; the engine tenter blew the mills buzzer, summoning workers and neighbours. The contents of the stove were well alight, but the flames were soon quelled. Due to its construction the stove building was fire-proof, preventing the fire from spreading. Damage amounted to £130.

There was a catalogue of accidents at the mill in the 1870s. Thirteen year old Henry Rowbottom was employed as a piecer at the mill; in October 1871 he was walking through the jenny gate in the mule spinning room when he slipped and fell. He put his hand out and his fingers became caught between the cogs of one of the mules, removing two of them. He was taken to Huddersfield Infirmary for treatment. All the machinery in the mill came to a standstill about 7am on the morning of Monday 12 August 1872, due to the mill boiler having burst.

John Hodgkinson & Son who were cloth dressers had been using the mill since 1871, and possibly earlier; James Whitehead aged 17 of Honley, who worked for Hodgkinson's, was lifting two rollers onto his shoulders on Thursday 30 December 1875, when he overbalance and fell backwards into a dyepan full of boiling water, scalding his back, thighs and arms. He was taken to Huddersfield Infirmary where he died at 11pm on New Year's Eve. Another fatal accident occurred in July 1877, when John Bloor a painter, was standing on a step ladder in the open third floor doorway of the crane hoist painting a fan light, when he overbalanced and fell to the ground, landing on his head. He died from his injuries 40 minutes later. In both these incidents the inquest juries returned the usual verdict of 'accidental death'. Joah Gledhill aged 51, was night watchman at the mill. On the morning of Sunday 7 October 1877 he was found dead in the road outside the mill at about 10.30am. His death was attributed to natural causes.

Henry Wrigley died, aged 61, at Craiglands Hydropathic Establishment in Ilkley on 7 March 1883, having apparently jumped from a third floor window. He was buried at South Crosland church.

The only part of Cocking Steps mill still standing, after conversion to apartments. © the Author.

Joseph Sykes aged 65, was cleaning a brushing machine while it was running shortly before 1pm on Saturday 1 December 1883. His hand became caught in some cog wheels that were normally covered, but Sykes had removed the cover. His hand was badly lacerated; the mill sent him to the Infirmary where two of the fingers on his right hand were removed. In the ensuing days his hand became swollen and inflamed, his arm was amputated on Friday 7th, but Mr. Sykes continued to decline and died on Monday 10th. At the inquest it was said that notices were posted in the mill about cleaning machines when they were in motion. Again, the jury returned a verdict of accidental death.

Mr. James Wrigley died aged 84, at his home Field House in Netherton in April 1893, having been retired for many years. Mr. James Taylor had retired in late September or early October 1906 at the age of 77, having worked for James Wrigley & Sons for 64 years. A ceremony was held at the mill on 1 January 1907 to present Mr. Taylor with an inscribed walking stick and a purse of money. In his response to the speeches made by members of the Wrigley family, Mr. Taylor said that he was happy to have had the health and strength to carry on working for so long, and he looked forward to using the walking stick on his walks around the district.[7]

The *Yorkshire Textile Directory* suggests that John Hodgkinson & Sons were tenants in the mill until 1917; a company named G.F. & L. Eastwood, manufacturers of woollen and worsted suitings and overcoatings were using part of the mill between 1928 and 1930. They had 42 looms, plus their own dyeing and finishing plant. James Wrigley & Sons last entry in the YTD was also in 1930; a company trading as Netherton Spinning Co. were listed as tenants from 1933, they had 7 Condenser sets and 6 spinning mules in 1962, and were still using the mill in 1971. The site has since been converted to housing.

Lords / Woodbottom mill

Originally built with money provided by Lord Dartmouth, hence its name; George Beaumont told the Factory Commissioners in 1833 that the mill was built in 1792 as a scribbling, carding and fulling mill, with slubbing being added around 1802, and cloth finishing about 1820. However, there is a note in documents in the possession of the National Monuments Record Centre in Swindon that reads: '*1788, Lords mill is in land excluded from the Manor of Honley enclosure award*'; suggesting that it was already in existence by that date. There is also a water wheel marked on Jeffries map published in 1775, that could denote Lords mill. The mill stands on the right bank of Mag Dike [or Brook], only yards downstream from Cocking Steps Bridge. The 'Dartmouth Rentals' record the rent for the mill and land in 1799 as being £7 5s per annum, and the tenant as William Elmsall, who was the Land Agent. By 1804 the rent for the house and mill was £5 5s, tenanted by William Elmsall; the rent for the land was £3 3s, tenanted by George Beaumont.

Fire broke out in the mill during the night of 10th to 11th May 1809; it was discovered around 2am, but had such a hold that the building collapsed before help arrived. In common with other properties in which Lord Dartmouth had an interest, the building was fully insured, ensuring that it was rebuilt. In 1828 it was described as 'A scribbling and fulling mill on three floors, built from stone and slate, driven by water and an 18hp steam engine. A detached outbuilding with a carding and slubbing billy in it. A stone and slate dwelling house at 6 rooms, Barn and Stable. This mill is leased in the name of William Elmsall for 27 years from 1.8.1806, at the annual rent of £5 5s'.

In his answers to the questionnaire in 1833 George Beaumont said that all the processes apart from fulling were powered by the steam engine, which was only 12hp; with the fulling mill being driven by the 9hp water wheel. Beaumont employed 48 people: 3 boys under 10 earning 3s 6d each, 6 boys under 12 earning 5s each, also 1 girl earning 4s; 6 boys under 14 earning 6s 6d each, and 1 girl earning 5s; 9 boys under 16 earning 7s 6d, and 1 girl earning 6s; 4 boys under 18 earning 12s each; 11 men over 21 earning 20s per week each, and 2 women over 21 earning 15s each; also 4 men over 21 working on piece rates who earned an average of 19s each in a 72 hour week. 9 of the children were paid by the person for whom they worked, all the rest were paid by George Beaumont. The working day started at 6am to 7.30pm, except on Saturdays when the mill closed at 5pm. Machinery was stopped at mealtimes: 15 minutes for Breakfast at 8am; one hour for dinner from 12.30pm; and 15 minutes for 'Drinking' at 5pm. Workers were allowed 3 days holiday at Christmas, half a day at Shrovetide, 2 days at Easter, 2 Days at Whitsuntide, and 3 days at Honley Feast in September; no pay was given for holidays. Workers were not fined for lateness or non-attendance. The firm did not employ, or sanction, the use of corporal punishment. Children under 12 were employed as piecers or layers on, and 'watching the knives used in finishing'. In answer to the question about Parliament regulating factory hours, George Beaumont said: 'I am of opinion that the children in our mill are not injured at all by working eleven and a half hours per day; and, if there must be a reduction in time, there must, of course, be a reduction in the wages'.

Lords mill was also visited by Plug rioters on 13 August 1842, on their way to Huddersfield. The rioters gathered in the centre of Huddersfield, and were dispersed by mounted soldiers. One man, employed at Lords mill, received a fairly serious injury from a sword-cut to his head. He was taken to the Infirmary, and despite rumours that he had died, was later allowed to go home.

In June 1837 George Beaumont, who was then living at West House, signed a 21 year Lease to run from 1 August 1837, for the Scribbling, Carding and Fulling mill, also the warehouse at the back of the mill, and the buildings in front of same wherein dyepans are erected and fixed; plus the dam, goits and water wheel. The rent had risen to £125 a year. George Beaumont died around 1848; he had appointed his wife Charlotte and his two sons as executrix and executors of his will. Charlotte Beaumont took over the running of the mill. In early March 1849, fire broke out in the stove at the mill; the fire engine from Shaw's at Neiley, which was named 'Hercules' was sent for and quickly arrived drawn by four horses. The report said that, at that time, the machine was well maintained and the men regularly drilled. The fire engine from Brooke's of Armitage Bridge also arrived, but their hose burst. A correction was printed in the following week's paper, pointing out that the burst occurred when the crews were comparing their engines after the fire had been extinguished; 'there being a strong spirit of rivalry between the firemen of the two firms'.

Remains of Lords mill, from the west. © the Author

Andrew Cartwright was charged, in May 1853, with trespassing on Hannah Beaumont's land. The workmen at Lord's mill had been in the habit of crossing her field on their way to work. Hannah Beaumont had recently come into possession of the field, and had initially diverted the road, before altogether stopping its use. The occupiers of the mill had been advised by Lord Dartmouth's Land Agent to remove any obstacles and continue to use the road. In view of the continuous use of the road for between 30 and 40 years the Bench dismissed the case.

George Henry Brook a Woolstapler of Huddersfield, John Haigh Coal Master of Woodroyd Honley, and Frederick Shaw Card maker of Huddersfield, who were presumably the main creditors of Charlotte Beaumont, had taken over the machinery and trade fixtures and furnishings, along with the running of the mill, in November 1849. They agreed to pass the lease for the mill to the Heap family free of charge, provided that Heaps would take the machinery etc. at valuation, and also indemnify the three from future debts.[8]

Heaps signed a lease in May 1854 agreeing to take the mill for 30 years at £145 a year rent; they were also committed to spending £2,000 on repairs to the mill within one year. By 1860 Heap Brothers had also taken William Henry Walker into partnership and were trading as Heap & Walker. Richard Ross Heap left the partnership in November 1860, leaving Edward Heap, Allen Heap and William H, Walker as partners. William Walker was riding through Berry Brow towards Honley on Horseback in November 1861; he was described as 'riding furiously' when he collided with a cab being driven in the opposite direction. Walker was thrown from his horse, the splashboard and shafts of the carriage were broken, and two men were thrown from the 'dickey'. The passengers in the cab, Mr. McWaterhouse and his wife, described as a '20 stone giantess' were returning from a concert in Holmfirth. The report added that it was only Mrs. McWaterhouse's weight that stopped the cab from overturning. The McWaterhouses had to walk the last two miles to their home.

A company named David Carter & Co. machine makers were using part of the mill in 1861. A notice appeared in the *Huddersfield Chronicle* of 7 September 1861 saying that Tom Carter had no connection with the firm other than being employed on a weekly wage; with no authority to contract any debt on behalf of the firm. The partnership was dissolved on 1 October 1861, leaving David and Charles Carter in the business. They also had a business in Chapel Hill Huddersfield that traded as David Carter & Co; the partners were David and Tom Carter, and John Lisle. That partnership was dissolved on 25 November 1861, with David Carter leaving. The machinery at Lords mill belonging to the firm was advertised for sale by auction on 31 January 1862, and also included some partly completed machines.

In April 1865, William Walker was returning home in a carriage after visiting a relative in Longwood when the horse took fright and bolted, jerking the reins from Mr. Walker's hands. Unable to control the vehicle he was thrown onto the roadway, sustaining some seriously deep cuts to his head and rendering him unconscious. The horse jumped a wall smashing the carriage to pieces, but was apparently entirely unhurt. Mr. Walker received medical treatment, and had to stay in Longwood for a few days before recovering sufficiently to allow him to return home. Mr. Walker went with the supporters of Netherton United on a rail excursion to Hull in late July 1866. The train for the return journey was 28 carriages long and carrying 855 people, when it collided with goods wagons at Crofton near Wakefield. Mr. Walker was found with severe injuries including broken ribs. He was thought to have left the train after the crash and had fallen some 30 feet from a bridge. He was brought back to his home and placed under the care of Dr. Dyson. The remainder of the party arrived back in Netherton at 4am, they should have returned at 11pm.

The firm gave a treat to their 110 workers plus 40 friends at the Foresters Arms on Tuesday 21 January 1868, of Roast Beef followed by Plum Pudding. The mill was fully employed despite the recession. It was possibly around this time the large weaving shed that stood alongside the river was built. In July of the same year, the mill's steam engine broke down with a tremendous crash. The 'weigh balk' was broken in two, five of the six spokes of the flywheel were broken, and one wall of the engine house was smashed. The 16hp engine was calculated to be doing 70hp of work. 100 people became unemployed.

Heap and Walker gave a treat to their workers in August 1871 with a trip to Liverpool; the firm also sold tickets to other firms whose workers went on the same train, one firm that also went was James Blakeley & Sons of Netherton who were joiners. The pleasure of the day was somewhat marred by a large number of people, many of whom were from Sowerby Bridge, invading the return train for Huddersfield and refusing to leave it. Only around one third of the intended passengers had managed to board the train; the rest were brought back by various trains, arriving in Huddersfield between 3 and 4am on the Sunday morning.

William Walker lived at Crosland Hall; also living in part of the house were three sons and two daughters of the late Joshua Heap. Mrs. Walker's day room was also furnished with a bed, since she had an affliction that meant that she should lie down during the day. In May 1872, Jesse Carter, blacksmith for Crosland mill, was repairing the inside of the shutters in that room; it was necessary for them to be closed during the repairs so the gas lights in the room were being lit. Eliza Gill of Netherthong, a housemaid, was lighting the burners of a gasolier with a candle. She lit the first burner, when she came to the second there was a loud explosion due to a gas leak. The clothing of Mrs. Walker, Eliza, and Jesse Carter was set alight; and eight year old Ben was blown down a passage, cutting his head open. The casualties were rescued by Joseph and David Heap, and had their burns treated by Dr. Haigh. The room was badly damaged and other windows in the house were broken.

Allen Heap left the partnership in 1874, assigning his interest to John & Joseph Heap. Levi Broadbent, who was a stoker at the mill, was charged with assaulting John Sykes, a bobbin turner of Netherton on 19 April 1875. Sykes had been going home, and had overtaken Broadbent who was with Robert John Porritt. Broadbent asked Sykes why he had heaved a stone at his dog; Sykes replied that he had not touched the dog. Broadbent then said that Sykes was a "damned liar" and that "he was going to give it to him". Broadbent, who was drunk, then struck Sykes twice, and said to Porritt that "he would give Sykes two black 'een' before he got home". The county magistrates fined Broadbent 5s plus 12s costs.

Heaps renewed the lease on the mill in November 1884, the signatories being Allen, John, Joseph and David Heap. They seem to have been in financial difficulties by late 1885, when the premises were advertised to be sold by auction on 5 January 1886, with Heap's being described as the 'late occupiers'. Their machinery was also advertised to be sold by auction on 17 February 1886.

The mill was unoccupied in 1886; by 1890 G.W. Oldham, who was using Old Moll mill had some interest in Lords mill, as he advertised for a night watchman for both premises. Lord Dartmouth sold the mill and 21 acres 3 roods, 31 perches of land to George William Oldham Silk Dyer of The Stubbings, Netherton, for the sum of £3,700 in 1897. A sale of surplus machinery at both Lords mill and Moll springs dyeworks was advertised to take place on 1 December 1902 consisting principally of finishing machinery, but also included 2 horses, 2 sprung lurries and a coal cart. The reason for the sale was said to be 'to make way for new'. G.W. Oldham seem to have concentrated their production in Moll Springs dyeworks from around 1907.

The 25 inch Ordinance Survey map of 1906 marks the large weaving shed that had been built alongside Mag dike as Lords mill and also 'disused'; with the original mill and buildings downstream from it being marked as Mag Valley Dyeworks; by late 1907 the entire premises were not being used. On Tuesday 19 January 1909 Robert Armitage aged 33 was accused of stealing a large quantity of brass fittings from Lords mill on the 15th that belonged to Mr. Oldham. Willie Jubb the engineer at the mill said that the mill had been closed for a year with the machinery left inside. He had visited the premises on 9 January and found everything in order; but in response to information received on the 15th he went to the mill and found 3 doors forced open and the locks broken off; two windows had also been smashed. He saw that many brass fittings from machines had been either unscrewed or smashed off; copper tubes had been removed, and brass fittings from the shafting had also been removed. He estimated that it would cost £100 to make good all the damage. Arthur Sheratt a clerk at Oldham's went to Lords mill and followed footprints through Spring Wood, where he saw a grey pony and shandy come out of a field being driven by three men, who had some sacks on the cart. It was later found that Armitage had hired the grey pony and shandy from John Regan a lodging house keeper of High St. Huddersfield for 4s for the day. Armitage had taken the metal to Thomas E. Taylor marine store dealer of Firth Street and asked Herbert Castle an assistant in the shop, to buy them. Castle weighed the goods and bought them for £2 16s. When arrested Armitage told the police that he had bought the goods from two men that he did not know for 25s. He was committed for trial at the Assizes.

Another sale of finishing machinery was advertised to take place at the mill on 13 December 1909, the vendor was not named, but was presumably G.W. Oldham. The Yorkshire Textile Directory for 1910 shows G.W. Oldham as only occupying Moll Springs Dyeworks.

Stocks and Mallinson dyers, were using at least part of the mill between 1912 and 1915; J & A Liversedge dyers were occupants in 1918. T.H. Hoyle & Sons, who were also dyers, were using the mill in 1924, when they submitted plans for a garage; they moved to Steps mill in 1927. Mitchell & Shaw dyers, were installed in the premises by 1930; they changed the name of the company to W.L. Shaw & Sons Ltd. in 1948. The mill was advertised to be sold by auction on 24 April 1946, when the dyehouse was still occupied by Mitchell & Shaw; J. W. Turner (Netherton) Ltd. who were chandlers, occupied the former 115ft by 55ft weaving shed, plus its 42ft by 30ft annexe and offices. There was also the 4 storey mill, 2 stoves and offices, along with some land. The whole produced a gross rent of £190 a year.

Heywood Yarns were using some of the mill in 1950, they moved to Deanhouse mill in 1957. A fire broke out on the top floor of the 4 storey mill on the afternoon of Friday 1 August, 1952. Mr. Roy Lindley, a 23 year old director of Magdale Spinning Co. who occupied the top two floors was working alone on the top floor supervising two carding machines and a pair of spinning mules, when flames came up from one of the carding machines. He tried to put out the fire using an extinguisher, but was unsuccessful. As the flames spread along the floor he escaped via a trapdoor to the floor below and then to the ground floor, warning others as he went. He then rang the fire brigade. The two lower floors were occupied by Magdale Textiles owned by Mr. R.H. Brook of Honley, who also owned the building. Mr. Brook, his son Hubert and Harry Lee a workman, began evacuating yarn from the building, but were forced to abandon their efforts due to the rapid spread of the fire. Fire Brigades from Huddersfield, Holmfirth and Meltham attended, and brought the fire under control within two hours. Two thirds of the roof had collapsed, as had half of the top floor, allowing machinery to fall through to the floor below. Every floor in the building had suffered severe damage. Mr. Brook said that the building and his 15 looms on the two lower floors were covered by insurance. A spokesman for the Fire Service said that production would be able to restart fairly soon in the least affected part of the building.[9]

Both companies continued using the mill, Magdale Spinning Co. were there until 1957 when they moved to Brockholes; Magdale Textiles being there for longer, their last advertisement for staff in the *Holmfirth Express* was in 1964, but their last entry in the *Yorkshire Textile Directory* came in 1967. W. L Shaw & Sons Ltd. was still listed by the YTD as using Mag Valley Dyeworks in 1971, before moving to Mag Bridge/Thirstin dyeworks the following year, where they joined forces with T. Lees & Co. Ltd.

Old Moll mill / Moll Springs dyeworks

Situated around 200 yards towards Honley alongside Old Moll Road from Lords mill, but on the opposite side of the road, this mill was probably built in the 1840s. It was owned by the Shaw family, and was offered for sale along with Thirstin mill in 1853, either separately or together. Not having a plentiful supply of water, Old Moll mill relied on steam power. The mill was advertised in June 1855 to be let, with a 20hp steam engine driving three fulling stocks; also a dyehouse equipped for dyeing loose wool and woven pieces. Application, in both instances, to be made to James Shaw, John William St. Huddersfield. A more determined effort to find a tenant was made in September 1857, when it was advertised as 'A large and commodious dyehouse 62ft by 43ft, containing 9 stone cisterns and 4 wrought iron pans. The water, with which the dyehouse is amply supplied in all seasons, is both pure and excellent, and was some time ago examined by an eminent analytical chemist who reported it to contain most valuable qualities and to be unsurpassed in Yorkshire for Dyeing purposes'. Even this does not appear to have provided a tenant, as in April 1858 the whole premises were advertised to be sold along with Thirstin mill. The occupant of the foreman's house at Old Moll was George Owen.

At the bankruptcy examination of James Shaw held in Leeds in June 1858, it emerged that George Owen had worked for the Shaw family for 28 years, from the days of D. Shaw Son & Co. James Shaw had told Owen that he owned both Thirstin and Old Moll mills, but had never told him that they were mortgaged. Thinking that James Shaw was a man of substantial means, Owen had installed his own machinery in the mill, and had also accepted bills from Shaw to a total of £5,688. When Shaw had brought Owen another bill at the end of 1857, a time when many textile merchants were failing, Owen had asked Shaw what the outcome would be if anything happened to Shaw and the bills were called in, as Owen was unable to honour them. Shaw replied that in the event of his death, his estate would receive £10,000 from an insurance policy. At the time of Shaw's bankruptcy Owen still held bills for £1,232, that he had no means of honouring. At the hearing George Owen said: "It has ruined me; I have had to call a meeting of my creditors and offer an assignment".

Two companies were occupying the mill by January 1866, when a fire was discovered in the stove shortly after 6pm on the 13th. A man went to Brooke's at Armitage Bridge to alert their fire brigade, which arrived at Old Moll around 20 minutes later; while workers attacked the fire with buckets of water. The intensity of the blaze coupled with the strength of the wind proved too great, and the building was gutted, with all the wool on the lower floor belonging to Mr. Wm Taylor, and the silk on the upper floor belonging to H & J Oldham, being destroyed. Damage was estimated to be in the region of £240. The damage had been repaired by early October 1866, when Oldham's gave a

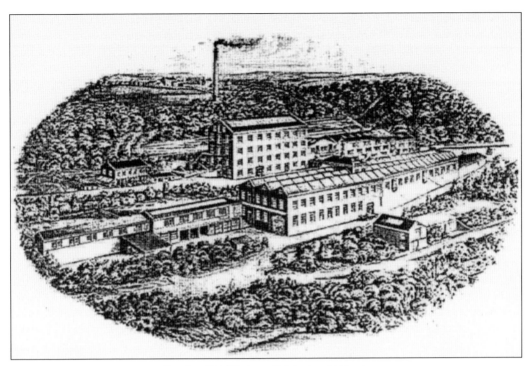

Drawing of Moll Springs mill. Collection of A.J. Brooke

'rearing supper' to between 70 and 80 guests, including neighbours and contractors, to celebrate the reopening of the premises. The meal was followed by singing and dancing.

Joseph Greenwood was using part of the mill by 1867; smoke was seen coming from a room used by him at 9pm on Sunday 1 September by workers from the mill who, with the help of neighbours, put out the flames using buckets of water. The fire was in some shoddy, and was thought to have started by spontaneous combustion. Damage was estimated at around £70. B. & J. Donkersley, cloth dressers, were also using part of the mill in 1868, when, in spite of the recession, they were said to be fully employed. The census of 1871 records Joseph Greenwood, who is described as a woollen manufacturer and landowner living in Honley, as employing a total of 39 people, 24 men, 7 boys and 8 women. An undivided moiety or half share in the mill was offered for sale in February 1872, when the tenants were given as Joseph Greenwood, B & J Donkersley, and Oldham's, the premises were described as 'a newly erected scribbling, spinning, finishing and weaving mill 4 storeys plus attic, 96ft by 48ft; with engine and boiler houses and drying stove. 3 storey stone built willow house with warehouse and drying room over; dyehouse, 2 cottages, cart shed and stables, plus land and woodland'.

The district was suffering from a shortage of coal in 1873; G.W. Oldham was reported to be looking for coal on his land in February of that year, and in March the *Huddersfield Examiner* reported that the high price of coal was having a serious effect on trade in the area, with some mills beginning to work short time, and to have abandoned Saturday working. High prices were also affecting people's ability to buy coal for domestic use.

Huddersfield and West Yorkshire Designers Association held an exhibition at the Victoria Temperance Hall, Buxton Road, Huddersfield on Saturday 17 September 1880, showing designs created in the district over the last 40 to 50 years. The exhibits covered a wide range, including book marks, pictures, table cloths, shawls, Indian style fabrics in cotton, besides worsteds and woollens. There were numerous fancy waistcoatings, also suitings that were similar in design to those produced in the 1880s, but were of a considerably higher quality. The only modern goods on display were from Smith & Co. of Old Moll mill, consisting of a number of imitation tapestry curtains, 4 yards long and 68 inches wide, that retailed at £6 a pair. They were made from wool and spun silk, but did not have the feel or appearance of woollens.

After visiting Victoria mill on 9 April 1888, Mr. Prior the Factory Sub-Inspector went on to Old Moll mill, where he found 3 youths, Albert Knutton 14, Joshua Hirst 16, and Joe Hall 15, had been working for 10½ hours, rather than the 10 hours permitted by the Factory Act. Mr. G. W. Oldham said that if he had erred, he had done so in ignorance of the law. The bench fined him 10s plus costs for each offence. G.W. Oldham advertised for a night watchman for both Old Moll mill and Lords mill in June 1890, at a wage of 20s per week. Oldham's workpeople gathered in a warehouse at the mill on 25 August 1894 to present Harry Oldham, G.W. Oldham's second son, with an inscribed French marble clock, in recognition of his forthcoming marriage on August 29th.

Henry Bamford had taken some space in Old Moll in 1890 for his silk throwing business. He had formerly been connected with the family business at Bent Lee Meltham, which had gone into liquidation. Henry himself was in financial difficulties by 1897, the first meeting of his creditors was called for 31 January 1898, and an auction sale of his machinery, stock-in-trade and office furnishings was advertised to take place on 9 February. At his examination in early February, Bamford had liabilities totalling £5,031 12s 10d, with Assets of £774 17s 2d; leaving a deficit of £3,953 11s 9d. Bamford said that he had been in business for a total of 22 years, mostly as a partner at Wm. Bamford & Sons, Meltham. After the failure of that firm he had set up his own business at Old Moll mill, which he funded with a bank overdraft guaranteed by his father-in-law. Annual profits averaged between £200 and £300, with his living expenses for each year being around the same amount. His downfall seems to have been caused by his association with a man named Norton, to whom Bamford had lent money totalling around £3,000, to fund various projects. Bamford had raised the money by selling stocks, giving accommodation bills, and taking money from the business. The returns that he had received from Norton's schemes had been negligible. The *London Gazette* announced on 11 April 1899, that creditors would be paid a first and final dividend of 1s 3½d in the £ on 21 April 1899.[10]

Thomas Hargreaves aged 45, a foreman dyer for Oldham's, had been found dead in the dam at the mill on the morning of 15 June 1898. His wife told the inquest that she had last seen him on the evening of Tuesday 14th, when he had said that he was going to bed. He had apparently left the house, via the kitchen window, before 7.30am on the Wednesday morning. Mrs. Hargreaves said that her husband seemed to be in his normal state of mind and body; although he had complained of 'weakness' for about 3 months, she had not contemplated the possibility of him taking his own life. Harry Oldham said that Hargreaves had been a good steady worker who had earned good wages, but had recently complained of feeling unwell. Hargreaves had seen Dr. Clarke, who had said that he was run down and had prescribed a tonic. The Jury returned a verdict of 'found drowned, with no marks of violence', and, 'he had probably committed suicide while temporarily insane'.

All the firm's employees enjoyed a trip to Scarborough on 7th July 1900, to celebrate the recent marriage of George T. Oldham. The train travelled via Goole and Hull; some of the party got out at Bridlington, but the majority went on to Scarborough, arriving there in the late morning. Various attractions were visited, including the 18th Century Convict Ship moored in the Harbour; the Castle, Oliver's Mount and Scalby Mills. The Group left Scarborough at 8pm, returning via the same route, arriving back in Honley at 1.30am on the Sunday morning.

Honley Urban District Council wanted to install a generating plant for electricity to supply the area's homes and businesses with power in 1902. At a council meeting in October, G.T. Oldham voiced concern about the project, saying that in partnership with his father at the mill, they were one of the largest rate payers in West Ward, and he opposed the application to be allowed to raise £4,800. His reason for the opposition was that in common with the majority of manufacturers in the area, he already generated his own supply of electricity that was sufficient for the firm's needs; and he doubted whether, without the business element, the project would be successful.

G.W. Oldham was interviewed at the mill on 1 May 1907, marking a double celebration. Mr. Oldham was 77 years old on 30 April, and it was the firm's Golden Jubilee on 1 May. Born in Derby, Mr. Oldham had carried on the trade of Silk Dyer from his father and grandfather. After moving to Huddersfield, he and his brother Henry had formed a partnership and began dyeing Silk in a small dyehouse at Spring Vale, Big Valley, Netherton, in 1857. They moved to Old Moll mill in 1862 because they were afraid that the construction of the railway branch line between Lockwood and Meltham would affect their supply of clean water. Henry Oldham left the partnership in 1872. When they had moved to Old Moll the two brothers were the entire workforce of the firm, as well as being the masters. 45 years later they employed between 110 and 120 workers. To mark the double celebration Mr. Oldham was presented with a silver Rose Bowl by the workforce. G.W. Oldham died at the age of 84, at his home 'Stubbings' in Netherton on 12 May 1914; the firm was already being run by G.T. Oldham, who continued to do so. G.T. Oldham was Chairman of Honley UDC in 1921, when he offered to transfer ownership of Old Moll Road which, up to that time, had been a private road, to the Council. The Council said that they would be pleased to accept his offer after a formal deed had been drawn up.

Two members of the workforce were each rewarded for 50 years service in 1928 by being presented with a mahogany chiming clock and a cheque for £50. The first went to William Pearson of Moorbottom Road Honley in June who, it was said, had never been late for work; the second was to Tom North foreman dyer, of Top Row, Armitage Bridge in November.

The name of the firm was changed in 1935 when it became Moll Springs Dyeing Co. Ltd.; G.T. Oldham was still the Managing Director. He died on 12 February 1938, his place being taken by his son G. H. Oldham. It was announced in December 1939, that the firm would close at the end of January 1940, with the loss of between 40 and 50 jobs. The closure of the mill could be regarded as being an early casualty of war, the reason given was that G.H. Oldham was now an Army Major who was in charge of an anti-aircraft company, and was unable to fulfil those duties and run the dyeing company. However, the buildings were occupied, presumably by Oldham's, when the three storey dyehouse on the site caught fire in the early hours of 15 November 1944, and was discovered by Arthur Skelton who worked there. The building was well ablaze when the fire brigade arrived, but the firemen extinguished it within 2 hours of arriving. They also managed to prevent the fire from spreading to the adjoining five storey mill and other buildings; but all the machinery in the dyehouse and stocks of wool and felt on the upper floors of that building were destroyed. G.H. Oldham died at the age of 53 on 5 January 1953, less than six months after selling the mill complex to David Brown Tractors of Meltham.

Central Woodworking Machinery Co. was using the premises during the 1980s. Some alterations had taken place; the Royal Commission for Historical Monuments survey carried out in 1985 listed a 2 storey stone built building 150ft by 20ft, plus a 3 storey section.[11]

Mag Bridge / Thirstin dyeworks

This dyehouse stands just upstream of Mag Bridge, the earliest information comes from the Dartmouth Estate to the effect that Joseph Robinson leased the dyehouse from Lord Dartmouth in 1796. The trustees of Clitheroe School complained in 1805 that water on their estate had been diverted to provide water for a steam engine, and was depriving another dyehouse of sufficient water to drive their water wheel. From the Dartmouth Letter Books, the Dartmouth Land Agent noted in 1806 that there was sufficient water to meet the needs of all users.

The premises were offered for sale by auction on 8 December 1847, described as a dwelling house with gardens, along with the recently erected commodious dyehouse, with vats, pans, boilers and other dyeing utensils, water wheel, stable, cart shed and other outbuildings. All occupied by John Robinson.

The premises were eventually bought by G.W. Farrar and his brother Thomas, although possibly not in 1847; they were using the dyehouse by the mid 1850s, trading as Farrar Brothers. George Farrar gave evidence to the Enquiry on River Pollution held in Huddersfield in November 1866. At that time he employed 26 people, and used in the region of 126,000 gallons of water in a twelve hour day, which they obtained from springs of pure water near the dyeworks, rather than river water that was polluted. They dyed both loose wool and woven cloth, either blue or black. They used very little soap, as they did not wash the loose wool, but they did wash the cloth. The water leaving the dyeworks was polluted to a greater or lesser extent. Ashes from the boilers were used to repair the roads, surplus ashes were put into the stream; they had received no complaints about their dealings with the stream. Night soil was spread onto their land around the works. The used dyewares were also spread onto the land. They used around 400lbs of Indigo each year, which dyed about 1,000lbs of wool per day.

A young man named Charles Hellawell who worked as a dyer at Mag Bridge appeared in court on 8 August 1871 charged, in conjunction with a 14 year old boy named Joseph Bower, with indecently assaulting Mrs. Ann Haigh, a 66 year old mother of 16 children, who lived in Netherton. Mrs. Haigh was returning home through Scar Top Wood after visiting one of her daughters at Reins when she encountered the two who, after making indecent remarks to her, threw her to the ground. She called for help, her cries were heard by George Taylor a neighbour, who said that when he arrived Mrs. Haigh was laid on the ground with a boy kneeling on either side of her and her clothing was turned up over her head. Hellawell had been before the court on 13 July accused of indecently assaulting a five year old girl; who, due to her young age and inexperience, was unable to give positive details of her ordeal. That case had been dismissed due to lack of evidence. The bench committed Hellawell to six months imprisonment, saying that they regretted their inability to pass a sterner sentence; Bower was fined £5, if unable to pay he would serve 2 months imprisonment.

All the firm's employees, plus the workers from Gledhill and Roberts bobbin makers, of Grove mill, enjoyed a day trip to Hull on 22 July 1876. The train left Honley at 6am arriving in Goole at 8am, where they transferred to river steamers for the journey to Hull, which also took about 2 hours. After looking around the docks and the town, the party left to return by the same means, arriving in Honley at 11pm.

Farrar Brothers were in financial difficulty by 1866, a receiving order was made on 24 February, with a date of 18 March being set for the first meeting of creditors. The brothers were adjudged bankrupt on February 26th. The *Huddersfield Examiner* of 27 February carried an advertisement for the sale of 9 horses, 4 milch cows, 2 stirks and 1 calf, also various lurries and carts, plus a variety of farm implements, due to the bankruptcy. The advertisement had been placed by the Official Receiver, but without consultation with any of the creditors, who objected to it. This sale did not take place. At the creditors meeting it emerged that the firm's liabilities amounted to £9377 19s 11d; with assets of £7969 9s 1d; leaving a deficit of £1,408 10s 10d. The personal financial status of the brothers was also given, with George William Farrar having liabilities of £2,010 19s 3d, with assets of £688 18s 2d, leaving a deficit of £1,322 1s 1d; Thomas Farrar's assets exceeded his liabilities. The brothers cited bad trade, and losses due to claims, as the reasons for their bankruptcy. Mr. W. H. Armitage was appointed as Trustee, with Mr. B. Allen, Mr. G. Bedforth and Mr Holroyd being appointed as a committee of inspection. The creditors agreed to accept 12s in the £ in settlement of the debts, this was to be paid in four payments of 3s in the £ at 3 month intervals, the first payment being due of 7 June 1886. Additionally, G.W. Farrar was ordered to pay a dividend of 7s 8½d in the £ to his personal creditors on 30 July 1886.

Edward Taylor a weaver spotted a fire at the dyeworks on 27 October 1886 at about 11.45pm. He raised the alarm, and neighbours who formed a bucket chain managed to extinguish the fire in around one hour. 33 pieces of cloth were destroyed, and there was also damage to the buildings; the cost of the fire was estimated to be around £1,000.[12]

Lupton Littlewood of Victoria mill was G.W. Farrar's brother-in-law, as he had married George

Farrar's wife's sister. William Schofield an accountant was the father-in-law of George Crosland Farrar, G.W. Farrar's son. Littlewood and Schofield bought the dyeworks from the receiver by agreeing to pay the settlement of 12s in the £ to the creditors. They paid the first amount in June 1886 in cash, and gave promissory notes for the subsequent payments; these were actually paid by cheque from Farrar Bros. bank account. Schofield and Littlewood drew up a lease in November 1886 between themselves and G.W. Farrar that set a rent of £330 a year for the premises, plant and machinery. George William Farrar continued to run the dyeworks with the help of his son George Crosland Farrar; Thomas Farrar was excluded from the business. G.W. Farrar paid himself £5 per week and his son George £4 per week from 1886. After Schofield began taking a close interest in the running of the business in early 1889 G. W. Farrar's wage was reduced to £3 a week, but George's was unchanged. G. W. Farrar also signed the company's cheques until March 1889, but from that date they were signed 'per pro' [on behalf of] Farrar Bros. by George Crosland Farrar, and countersigned by William Schofield. Although Schofield was closely connected with the running of the business, he took no form of remuneration from it. At one point he sold part of the premises, the money being paid into the company's bank account and used by it.

In late 1891 the firm was again in financial difficulties, a receiving order was made on 17 December 1891, with the first meeting of creditors being set for 7 January, followed by a public examination in the County Court on 23 January 1892. The firm had liabilities of £9,076 8s 11d, with Assets of £1,257 6s 10d leaving a deficit of £7,819 2s 1d. George W. Farrar said that he again attributed their failure to 'bad trade', also the serious rise in the price of coal, the heavy encumbrances with which his property was burdened, and the severe losses suffered in the fire in late 1886. An auction sale of three 'Lots' of property was advertised to take place on 19 January. The first lot was the dyeworks buildings, which were stone built with grey slate roofs, along with the steam engine, machinery and other fixtures. Also 3 cottages, coach house, stables, mistal and barn. Lot 2 was Cliffe House, the home of G.W. Farrar, with the grounds, gardens and 6½ acres of land. Lot 3 was the old Thirstin dyeworks on Thirstin Road that was being used as a warehouse at that time. Lots 1 and 2 were withdrawn at the auction as the reserve was not reached; the fate of lot 3 is unknown. Although the lease had been drawn up in late 1886 setting a rent of £330 a year for the premises, no rent had been paid, neither had any been requested until 16 December 1891, the day before the receiving order was issued, when Schofield and Littlewood issued a distraint order on Farrar Brothers for £1,284 4s 11d for unpaid rent. An enquiry was held on 2 April 1892 into the involvement of Schofield and Littlewood in the business and, despite their claims to the contrary, the court decided that they also shared responsibility for the company's debts.

The company continued in business trading as Farrar & Co, they were listed in the *Yorkshire Textile Directory* for 1910 as Indigo wool and cloth dyers. Herbert Mallilieu, a Director at Farrar's, was a passenger on a train on Sunday 26 April 1914 that was bringing many supporters back from the F.A. Cup Final played at Crystal Palace the day before. The train came to a standstill on an incline north of Finchley Road Station as the engine did not have sufficient power to pull the seventeen coaches up the hill. The train was split, leaving the rear half stationary inside a tunnel. The engine that was sent to assist struck the rear of the stationary carriages with some force, smashing 23 panes of glass in windows, and causing cuts and shock to some passengers. Mr. Mallilieu was slightly injured, suffering a bruised elbow; Mr. T Littlewood of Grove House, and Mr. Albert Littlewood of Honley were also passengers on the train, but were unhurt.

A strike by carters' in Holmfirth began on Monday 27 April 1914, and lasted until Friday 1 May, disrupting many businesses. Striking carters formed picket lines and were turning back carters who had chosen to work, affecting coal deliveries to homes and businesses. Farrar and Co closed their business for the duration, making 40 employees idle. The police eventually placed constables at intervals along main roads to stop pickets from interfering with those still working. A meeting was held on the Friday, when both sides agreed that, with immediate effect, a man in charge of a cart with a single horse would be paid 25s per week, while a man in charge of a cart pulled by two horses would be paid 27s 6d a week Both these rates were to be increased by 6d a week from the first payday in August. Herbert Mills was a teamer for Farrar's, and lived at Farrar's Fold at Thirstin. He had taken his cart to Walter Greenwood's cloth finishers at Perseverance mill Holmfirth, on Tuesday 12 February 1918, when he was taken ill and died. He had been receiving treatment for a medical condition. An ambulance took his body to his home address.

Farrar & Co. had been taken over by Tom Liversedge & Sons Ltd. of Canal Bank Works, Leeds Road, Huddersfield, at some time between 1918 and March1928, when Tom Lees bought Thirstin dyeworks and the Farrar business from Liversedge's for £3,500. Tom Lees had been using the dyehouse at Dobroyd mill near Hepworth from at least 1923, and transferred the plant and machinery from Dobroyd to Thirstin. The firm became a Limited Company from 7 June 1928. Mr. Tom Lees died in late April or early March 1940; Mr. Ernest Parry was appointed a Director of the company at that time, and was appointed Company Chairman on March 9th. The company continued to trade as Tom Lees & Co Ltd. until 1975, when it was taken over by the firm of W.T. Johnson of Moldgreen and renamed DP Dyers. Mag dike was in flood on 30 July 2002, when flood waters invaded the dyeworks. No structural damage occurred, but DP Dyers lost half a day's production due to the need to dry the electric motors on the machines. The company were still in business in 2010, when they had 14 employees.[13]

Upper and Lower Steps Mills

Mary Jagger wrote in her *History of Honley* that in 1344, in addition to a corn mill, there was also a 'walk' or fulling mill in the district; also, that in 1569 Sir Robert Stapylton sold land at Honley that included woods, a corn mill, a walk mill and other estates together with the royalties, to Sir John Kaye of Woodsome. Although there are no documents available to be able to authenticate these claims, they are possibly correct. The first documentary evidence comes in 1707 from the Dartmouth Estate, regarding the lease of a Fulling Milne at Meltham from Joseph Radcliffe to James Roberts of Steps Milne and Joseph Roberts of Dungeon Milne, for a term of 21 years at £11 per year rent. James and Joseph Roberts were also signatories to an agreement between the owners and fee farmers of fulling mills not to mill cloth on Sundays between 6am and 6pm. This was in response to concerns voiced nationally by the Church that weavers and fullers throughout the country were working on Sundays when they should have been in church. The agreement also included details of the prices to be charged for fulling cloth, which were: pieces up to 18yds in length 6d; between 18 and 30yds 8d; and over 30yds 12d. A mill is depicted on Jeffries map of 1775, at the end of a long goit, and on a bend in the River Holme, which is in the position of the lower mill. The upper mill was built at the end of the mill dam that served it, between Mag Dale Road and the river Holme. The precise date of building is not known, but it was in existence in the 1790s, when Mary Jagger maintained that the first Sunday School in Honley was held there.

The Land Tax returns for 1781 record that in that year Joseph Roberts paid £1 7s for the property. Joseph appears to have died before 1789, as Widow Roberts of Steps was responsible for Land Tax in that year. In 1792, Mrs. Roberts had the fulling mill and the farm called Healdy Butts, when she paid 12s for the farm; Edward and Benjamin Haigh were the tenants of the fulling mill, they paid £2 tax for a newly erected wheel for 'engeons'.

The fulling mill was advertised in the *Leeds Mercury* to be let in May 1795, it was described as being 'in excellent repair' with two streams of water, three water wheels, six fulling stocks and three drivers, with room for more to be set up; also a house, barn and other outbuildings, and 'nine days work of land', which would be equivalent to about nine acres. Anyone interested in renting the mills should apply to Mrs. Roberts of Steps. [A 'day's work' was calculated on the basis of the amount of land that could be ploughed in one day by a man with a team of Oxen, which was roughly one acre. It should be borne in mind that teams of Oxen only worked from dawn to midday, after which they were turned out to graze].

William Beaumont & Co were using the lower mill and Healdy Butts farm in 1797, when they paid land tax of £1 7s 11d for the mill, and 13s 10d for the farm. Edward Haigh also paid 18s land tax for 'engeons'. The buildings were insured with the Royal Exchange Insurance Co. in 1800: Steps mill was insured for £600, and Upper Steps mill for £200.

William Beaumont and his partners Richard Beaumont and Stephen Vickerman, were experiencing financial difficulties in 1802, when they assigned their goods to J. Whittaker dyer of Lane, Joseph Tolson woolstapler of Wakefield, John Dickinson woolstapler of Huddersfield and Jonathon Senior of Farnley Tyas.

The upper mill was being used for cotton spinning by William Bailey the elder of Batty Mill, Kirkheaton, Richard Brown of Hillhouse, and William Bailey the younger of Honley. They dissolved their partnership in April 1803, allowing William Bailey the elder to leave. The two remaining partners trading as William Bailey & Co assigned their lease on the upper mill and the cotton machinery to Sylvester Sykes and Joshua Ingham bankers, as security for a loan of £2,500 in October 1803. The dissolution of their partnership was advertised in the *Leeds Mercury* in March 1805, along with the sale of their machinery, by private contract, as it stood on the premises. The machinery was described as being 'entirely new and fully complete...for every part of the spinning business on a moderately extensive scale'. The Land Tax Returns for 1805 cite William Beaumont as being responsible for Steps mill, the Farm, Engeons, and the Cotton Factory.

The *Leeds Intelligencer* of 24 November 1806, told a rather tragic story: 'On Friday se'nnight [this comes from the same 'stable' as fortnight, so 'a week last Friday'] the 14th, in the evening, Steps mill near Honley was discovered to be on fire; the flames soon extended over the whole, which, with the machinery etc. was entirely consumed. The overlooker whilst he was endeavouring to save the property of his employers, lost his own. For the fire communicated to the house in which he lived, and destroyed all his furniture'.

The Dartmouth Letter Books record on 16 May 1807, that the two mills were leased for a period of 21 years to William Beaumont, from May Day 1804 at a rent of £250 a year; plus £100 a year for the house, garden and land. The amounts that the mills were insured for was increased to £1,200 for Steps mill and £500 for the Upper mill. Beaumont was rebuilding the fire damaged mill with the help of a loan of £1,400 from W. Ingham, who was to receive half the profits from the mill for two years in recompense. In October 1807, a letter from the Land Agent recommended that as it was so impressive it should be insured immediately, even though it was not finished. After visiting the finished mill a year later, the Land Agent recommended that as the new mill was larger than the original, and in every way better, the new [1804] lease should be re-dated from May Day 1808.

A notice of William Beaumont's Bankruptcy appeared in the *Leeds Mercury* in March 1827, he was required to attend the court on 13 and 17 March, also 10 April for examination. The *London Gazette* carried two notices on 11 May, firstly asking all creditors to prove their debts by 21 May, and to appoint another assignee to replace the one who had refused to act. There was obviously disagreement amongst the creditors as to the course of action to be followed, as the second notice called a meeting on 4 June 1827 to give all the creditors and the assignees the opportunity to discuss whether or not (a) Beaumont's goods and machinery should be sold, (b) the assignees should run the business for the benefit of the creditors, or (c) permission for the assignees to appoint a manager, an accountant or other workers. The outcome of the discussions is not known, but the firm continued in business.

The Dartmouth Terrier recorded in 1828 that: A large stone and slate scribbling and slubbing mill of three floors, driven by three wheels, a weaving shed built by the tenant six years ago, had been leased to Beaumont and Ingham for 21 years from Mayday 1808 at £250 per year rent. The mill was re-let from Mayday 1829 to Joshua Beaumont, Enoch Vickerman and Benjamin Vickerman, for 14 years at £400 a year.

Beaumont & Vickerman replied to the Factory Commissioners questionnaire regarding the condition in factories and mills in 1833. They said that the mill was used for scribbling, fulling and finishing of woollen cloths; that it had been built in 1807, and was powered by a 20hp water wheel. They employed 57 persons, 52 of which were male. They had 12 boys and 1 girl under 12, each earning 3s 6d per week; 6 boys and 1 girl under 14, earning 4s 2d; 7 boys under 16 earning 7s 8d, and 2 girls under 16 earning 5s 6d; 5 boys under 18 earning 12s 6d; 3 males under 21 earning 7s 6d; 19 men over 21 earning 21s and 1 woman over 21 earning 6s. Six men were paid on piece rates, all the rest on time rates. 4 slubbers, 1 willower, 8 feeders, 12 piecers and 3 millers were dependant on the person for whom they worked for their wages. The hours of work in summer were 6am to 7.30pm, and from 7.30am to 9pm in winter; the mill worked fewer hours on Saturday, making a 69 hour week. Employees were allowed three half-hour meal breaks, when machinery was stopped; apart from the fulling mills which ran continuously. In answer to the question on holidays, the firm said: 'say 8 or 10, and more if they require them, by asking for liberty'; all holidays were unpaid. They had never tried to recruit a second set of children, and did not permit corporal punishment. Children of ten years and above were employed in the scribbling and slubbing departments. No answer was given to the question on parliament regulating factory hours.[14]

Vickermans summoned George Heaton and Abraham Taylor, both of Honley, for wilful trespass by using a private road without permission on 8 February 1840. Witnesses were called to prove that the road had been gated for at least 60 years; Vickermans also employed a person to look after the bar, and carts that did not have permission to pass were charged 3d toll. Heaton had gone through the gate without paying, but on his return he found the gate locked and refused to pay the toll. He returned later with Taylor and they broke the staple of the lock with a hammer. The bench fined them 6d damages, plus a penalty and expenses, a total of 23s 6d.

The mill was visited by plug rioters on Monday 13 August 1842, who stopped the mill from working by drawing the boiler plug. Around March 1842, a number of young men at the mill formed themselves into a Society for Mental Improvement, which was a trend at that time; there were Mental Improvement Societies in many towns. Pressure was brought to bear on the members of this society reportedly by their parents, arguably under a degree of duress from the employers, suggesting that they would be discharged if they continued to meet. The sentiment expressed by the complainants was that "they had enough to do to mind their work!" The employers that were against the trend were principally Wesleyans, which is surprising as it was the non-conformists who were the instigators of the Sunday School movement to teach children to read and write. Benjamin Vickerman set up his own business at Taylor Hill and left the partnership at Steps in October 1844. Enoch Vickerman and Joshua Beaumont continued, trading as Beaumont & Co.

Lower Steps mill.c. 1958 © A.J. Brooke

Powerloom weavers at the mill went on strike in late March 1848, because Beaumont & Co. was paying 1d per string less than other manufacturers in the area. The dispute continued into mid March and probably longer, as a copy of a letter sent to Ben Haigh in Ohio in June said: "there has been a great turnout at Steps and another at Dungeon'. The press did not give a date for the end of the strike, or details of its outcome. Normal relationships had been restored by 24 January 1850 when the firm gave all their women employees a tea and all the men a supper, in a room at the mill. After the meal, a brass band and a party of glee singers added to the entertainment.

The Census return for 1851 shows Enoch Vickerman as employing 138 men and 155 women at the mill. On the evening of 6 June 1851 a young man named William Clay tried to stop the scribbling engine that he was tending by using his foot to remove the drive belt from the drum, rather than by using the 'throwing handle'. His foot was caught by the moving belt and taken round the drum, causing a fracture just above his ankle. Clay was attended to by Mr. Lee the surgeon, before being taken home. Mr. Lee told the reporter that in his experience 18 of every 20 accidents involving machinery were due to carelessness by the operators.

The mill appears to have been virtually untouched by the flood waters of 1852; The Holme Reservoir Commissioners recorded in 1853 the owner of the mills as the Earl of Dartmouth, and the occupiers as Enoch Vickerman and Joshua Beaumont.

A cart driver called Farrand went to see Mr. Vickerman in April 1854, to apply for a job that someone had told him was vacant. Mr. Vickerman offered to employ him at 16s per week, his current wage, and Farrand gave one week's notice to Bentley & Shaw's brewers of Lockwood. On the evening of the day that Farrand had given notice, Vickerman sent him a note saying that after speaking to Mr. Beaumont, he realised that the vacancy no longer existed. Farrand then experienced difficulty in obtaining employment elsewhere, and was claiming £5 in lost wages from Vickerman. After hearing the evidence, the judge ordered that Vickerman should pay Farrand 1 week's wages of 16s, plus the costs of the case.

The firm gave a treat in January 1855, possibly just to the men, as it was held at the Coach and Horses in Honley. After the meal, "the time was spent in interesting discussions on the war and other things connected therewith". The following year the firm gave orders to the landlords of the Coach and Horses and the George & Dragon to provide treats for their employees to celebrate peace in the Crimea on May 29th.

Joshua Beaumont's son Alfred married Mary Hirst of Wilshaw in October 1858. A celebration was held after the couple returned from Honeymoon in December. The men had a dinner at the George & Dragon, and were entertained by Bailey's Quadrille Band, while the women had tea in a large room at the mill. After the meals, the men joined the women in the large room at the mill, which could accommodate 1,000 people, and was lit by 60 gas burners, where festivities were continued.

In common with several other mills in Holme Valley, Steps mills had several thousand panes of glass smashed by giant hailstones during a thunder storm on the evening of Monday 18 July 1859. In October 1859 a young man named Michael Tynan was sent by his employer William Crabtree, into the flue of the boiler at the mill to clean it. Being dissatisfied with the result, Crabtree made Tynan clean it for a second time. It was suspected that Tynan was under the legal age to be allowed to clean flues, and Crabtree and Tynan appeared in Court in early November. In an attempt to appear to be the injured party, Crabtree charged Tynan with stealing two bags of soot; the solicitor appointed to defend Tynan refused to do so, instead he insisted that Crabtree should be charged with knowingly employing a person below the legal age for sweeping chimneys. Crabtree was adamant that when Tynan came for the job he had said that he was 22 years old, and produced two witnesses who corroborated that story. In court, Tynan insisted that he was only 16 years old, having had his sixteenth birthday in August of that year; also, that he had cleaned as many as sixteen chimneys in a day. The bench dismissed the case.

Mr. Enoch Vickerman died at the age of 64 in Harrogate, where he had gone in an attempt to regain his health, in early October 1861. The mill was closed on the day of his funeral. The death brought the Beaumont and Vickerman partnership to an end. In June 1862 Joshua Beaumont put a notice in the Huddersfield newspapers requesting that anyone who owed any debt to the late firm of Beaumont and Vickerman should pay it immediately, and anyone who had an outstanding account owed to them by the firm should advise Mr. Beaumont so that it could be paid.[15]

Despite the depression in the industry in 1867-8, Joshua Beaumont & Co. was still in full production. 200 workpeople were given a treat in January of that year in the burling room at the mill; an interesting fact to emerge from the account is that all the firm's powerloom weavers were women. Allan Green worked as a cloth dresser at the mill in 1871, on Saturday 13 May his five year old daughter Emma was playing with a group of children near the mill, who missed her and raised the alarm. George Brook, who also worked at the mill, went to the mill dam, found her and brought her out, but she was already dead. It was thought that she had been trying to reach something in the water and had fallen in and drowned, which was the verdict returned by the inquest jury.

Mr. Thomas B. Platt had been working at Steps mill, in June 1872 his furniture was advertised for sale as he was leaving the district. He actually emigrated to the United States and settled in Iowa, where he died on 27 February 1875. He had travelled to a nearby town on business, but missed the last train home. He set out to walk along the railway track, which was common practise in that part of the country. His badly mutilated body was found on the track the following day; he was not thought to have been knocked down by a train, but to have died from some other cause, fallen onto the track, and been subsequently run over by a train. Doctors who examined his body said that he had died either from heart disease or the intense cold, death had taken place some hours before he was run over as no blood had been spilled.

Alfred Beaumont trading as Joshua Beaumont & Co. filed a petition for liquidation in the County Court in Huddersfield in early March 1881. The initial report suggested that he had liabilities of around £65,000; but at the creditors meeting held on 28 March his total liabilities were given as £48,312 14s 6d, with assets of £26,108 3s 1d, leaving a deficit of £22,204 11s 5d. The creditors agreed to liquidation by arrangement rather than bankruptcy, which permitted the firm to continue trading. Various sales were advertised to take place during the ensuing weeks: the farm implements, livestock and hay at Steps farm were to be auctioned on 25 May; with the auction sale of furniture at Parkton Grove on 6 July, and a sale of machinery at Steps mill being advertised for 10 October. Joshua Beaumont & Co. continued in business, becoming a Limited Liability Company in 1899.

Business was difficult in 1900 when the firm's weavers, who were still all women, agreed to accept a reduction in their rates of pay. Reduced wages being better than no wages. The summer of 1901 was hot with little rain, the *Huddersfield Examiner* commented, in August, on an offensive effluvia coming from the mill dam due to the scarcity of water. Possibly to give the workpeople the benefit of 'sweet airs and pleasant views' Mr. G.P Armitage, the managing director of the firm, invited all the workpeople to tea at his home, Storthes Hall, on Sunday 25 August. What must have been a veritable convoy of wagonettes started from Honley Bridge at 2 in the afternoon, travelling via Huddersfield and Kirkburton to arrive at the hall at 4pm. Tea was served on the lawns in front of the house at 4.30pm, after which the party lined up for a group photograph. There were games of cricket and bowls to be enjoyed by some, while others looked round the flower beds and the kitchen garden. Kirkburton Brass Band provided musical entertainment, which encouraged some to dance. After thanking Mr. Armitage for his generosity and kindness, the party left for home at 7.30pm, arriving back in Honley at 9.30. Joshua Beaumont & Co. Ltd. continued trading at Steps mill until 1927 when there was a fire, after which their name disappears from the records.

Later in that year T.H. Hoyle & Sons dyers moved into the Lower mill from Mag Valley Dyeworks at Lords mill. They installed a new (larger) boiler, despite having been given prior warning by Honley UDC that they would be liable for the repair of any damage done to Steps Bridge.

A large quantity of cloth was stolen from the mill in October 1947; the police followed the lorry carrying the cloth, five men were arrested, the sixth, who was the driver, managed to escape. The five were remanded in custody to appear at the quarter sessions. Another break-in occurred in January 1964, when Kevin Collins who lived in a caravan at Elland Hall farm stole 8 pieces of cloth valued at £760. On his appearance in court on Monday 27 January, he pleaded guilty to the charge and was remanded to appear at the quarter sessions.

The company was bought by Denisons (Wilsden) Ltd. who were also dyers and finishers, in 1967, but continued trading under the original name. On Christmas Eve 1967 two men stole 6 pieces of Gabardine cloth from Hoyle's. Richard Parker of Upper Brow Road Paddock had broken in, while Brian Newbold of Meltham Road Netherton kept watch. When questioned they said that they had committed the offence because 'they were desperately short of money for Christmas'. Parker was sent to prison for 6 months, while Newbold was fined £50, and ordered to pay £100 in restitution. Hoyle's continued using the mill into the 1970s; by 1979 the buildings were occupied by Honley Dyeing Co, whose parent company was Brook Dyeing Co. of Bottoms mill, Holmfirth.[16]

Upper Steps mill was used by the tenants of the lower mill as an integral part of the factory until around 1900. B & W Donkersley cloth finishers, were also using part of the upper mill in the 1880s until they advertised a sale of their machinery to take place at the mill on 12 December 1887. The Ordinance Survey map of 1906 marks the premises as 'disused'; part of it was demolished in 1916. The remaining part was used by Josiah France's as the works canteen for some years, this has now been converted to housing.

Queen's Square mill

Built sometime prior to 1848, this mill, in keeping with its neighbour Upper Steps mill, was part of Steps mills and used by the occupants of that mill until around 1881. when Josiah France moved from Neiley mill into here and it became known as Queen's Square mill. In 1883 a number of employers, including Josiah France, in Huddersfield and the surrounding areas, posted notices in their weaving sheds outlining a new pay structure to commence from 26 March, which would result in weavers earning less pay. From the beginning of March weavers began leaving work as they downed their warps, until on the 14th there were some 2,000 weavers either on strike or locked out in the area. The dispute continued for several weeks, until a meeting of weavers was called to be held in Huddersfield Town Hall on 4 May to consider an ultimatum from the employers. A large number of weavers attended the meeting, at the end of which a ballot was taken. The total number of votes cast was 1,040, of which 850 voted to accept, 186 voted to reject, and 4 papers were spoiled. It was estimated that, due to the strike, there were then around 4,000 people unemployed; work resumed on 7 May.

Penelope France, Josiah France's daughter, married Dr. D. Winder in April 1888. The workpeople presented the couple with a centre-piece for their dining table. To celebrate the event the firm took all the workers to Scarborough for a day in September. A special train left Holmfirth at 5am, calling at all the stations to Huddersfield before setting out for Scarborough where they arrived at 8.55am. Each man was given 2s to spend and each woman and juvenile 1s. Three men missed the train back, but managed to get a later train; one of them got off that train in Normanton to slake his thirst and was left behind. Two years later the firm treated everyone to a trip to Southport. The train left Honley at 5.15am arriving in Southport 3 hours later. After a second breakfast many went to the promenade and were dismayed to find that the sea was still a half mile walk away. The day was spent enjoying the town and its sights, before leaving at 8pm. One man waited on the wrong platform and forlornly watched the Honley train pull out. He managed to arrange to travel with another excursion that was coming in the right direction, but was then faced with getting back to Huddersfield. Most people arrived back in Honley at 11.30pm; the lone traveller finally arrived home in the early hours of Sunday.

The firm registered as a Limited Liability Company in October 1899, the directors were J. France, W.H. Lord, J.C. Lord and T. Senior. Josiah France died at his home Parkton Grove, on 24 June,

Queens Square mill. © A.J. Brooke. Also shows Upper Steps mill on right of Queens Square.

1905. Business improved around the turn of the century, and in 1906 'Josiah's', as they had become known, were very busy and working overtime when they introduced the new 4-box, 100 picks per minute looms.

The women weavers were dissatisfied with their rates of pay and working conditions in 1908, beginning in June discussions between the women and the employers took place, but with Mr. Gee of the National Union of Textile Workers as go-between. In October the firm offered the women a weekly time rate of 20s per week rather than the 22s per week that they had asked for. The women accepted the offer subject to certain conditions that were put to the employers, one was that the women should not be responsible for drawing new warps through the healds and slays. The weavers met at the Railway Hotel in Honley on 3 November, when the male pattern weavers agreed to accept an increase of 6d per hour to time spent drawing twistings through on looms woven by women. The men hoped that the offer would be backdated to the time when the suggestion was first made. Twisters at the mill went on strike on 27 April 1914 in protest at the dismissal of some of their colleagues, which disrupted the working of some 30 weavers for several days.

Josiah France Ltd. was taken over by Salt's Ltd. of Saltaire in January 1954; Josiah's had a workforce of 375 people at that time. The last advertisement for staff appeared in the *Holmfirth Express* in 1975. The paper subsequently reported that the canned drinks arm of Ben Shaw's, Suncharm Ltd. had moved into premises at the mill in August 1978. They had previously been in premises in Brockholes. The mill has since been split into units and its buildings considerably altered.[17]

Notes

1   Queen's/Victoria mill
    Kirk. Arch. KC165/368 1836; KC311/17/6 1838; Hudds Chron. 19 July 1851, 8 Oct. 1853; Hudds Ex. 15 & 29 Oc, 26 Nov. 1853; Hudds Chron. 11 Feb. 1854; 16 Mar. 1858, 15, 22, Jan. 13 Aug. 1859; 17 Aug. 1861, 10 Dec. 1864; Hudds Ex. 28 Jan 1865 also 7 Sept. 1872, 13 June 1868, 29 July

1876 3 May 1879, 9 Jan 1886, 12 May 1888; 3 May, 12 July, 1 Nov. 1890; 11 and 18 July, also 18 April, 1891; 21 Apr. 1894, 13 Apr. 1895; Yorks. Fact. Times, 11 Mar. 1909; H'firth Exp. 20 July 1912; 3 June 1916; 24 Oct. 1959; Kirk. Arch. UHO Holmfirth 13 Apr. 1965; H'firth Exp. 16 Feb. 1990.

2   Bradshaw mill
Yorks. Fact. Times, 11 Mar. 1909; Yorks. Text. Diry, 1915 and 1923; Hudds Ex.31 May 1924; Kirk. Arch. UHO Honley Jan. 1937; Yorks. Text. Diry, 1971.

3   Moor Bottom mill
H'firth Exp. 1 May 1948; Kirk. Arch. UHO Honley 13 Jan. 1960.

4   Thirstin mill
Supplementary Report into the Employment of Children in Factories and as to the Propriety and Means of Curtailing the Hours of their Labour, Part 1; (25 March 1834). Kirk. Arch. KC311/17/6; Hudds Ex. 15 May 1852, 21 May 1853, 24 Apr. 1858; 4 June 1853; HuddsChron. 22 Jan. 1859; Kirk. Arch. KC1061 Box 8 1860; Hudds Chron. 24 May 1862, 8 Oct. 1864, 2 Feb. 27 Apr. 1867; London Gazette, 11 Jan. 6 Sept. 1870; Hudds Chron, 20 Aug, 24 Sept. 1870, 9 Mar, 8 and 15 June, 6 July, 1872.

5   Hudds Ex. 6 Sept. 8 Nov. 1873, 10 Apr. 1875, 5 Jan 1878; 31 Jan. 1885; Kirk. Arch. UHO Honley, July 1884; Hudds Ex. 8 Nov. 1884; H'firth Exp. 15 Oct. 1892; Kirk. Arch. UHO Honley, 19 Aug. 1895; Hudds Ex. 24 May 4 July 1896; Kirk. Arch. UHO Honley 18 Sept. 23 Oct. 6 Nov. 1899, 27 Jan. 1902; Hudds Ex. 1,8,29 Nov. 1902, 25 Jan. 1908; Worker, 9 Mar. 1912; H'firth Exp. 16 Jan. 12 Mar. 25 June 1976 8 Sept. 2000.

6   Cocking Steps/Wrigley's mill
Deeds Registry Wakefield, DC:133:577 1790; Kirk. Arch. KC165/338 1792+; Leeds Mercury, 3 Mar. 1810; Supplementary Report into the Employment of Children in Factories and as to the Propriety and Means of Curtailing the Hours of their Labour, Part 1; (25 March 1834). Kirk. Arch. KC !65/341 22 Mar. 1834; Leeds Mercury, 20 Aug. 1842; 13 May 1843; 20 Oct. 1845; Hudds Chron. 14 May, 9 July 1853; 22 Dec. 1855; 6 Aug. 1859; 18 Aug. 1860; 8 Oct. 1864; 18 Mar, also 25 Nov. 1865.

7   Hudds Chron. 14 May, 9 July 1853; 22 Dec. 1855; 6 Aug. 1859; 18 Aug. 1860; 8 Oct. 1864; 18 Mar, 25 Nov. 1865; 9 June, 3 Nov. 1866; 27 July 1867; Hudds Ex. 28 Oct. 1871; Hudds Chron. 17 Aug. 1872; Hudds Ex. 1&8 Jan. 1876; 7&14 July, 13 Oct. 1877; 10&17 Mar. 8&15 Dec. 1883; 30 Aug. 1884; 15 Apr. 1893; Hudds Daily Ex.2 Jan. 1907.

8   Lords/Woodbottom mill
Dartmouth Estate Office, Slaithwaite, Dartmouth Terrier 1805, 1828; Dartmouth Rentals, p.135, 1799, 1804; Supplementary Report into the Employment of Children in Factories and as to the Propriety and Means of Curtailing the Hours of their Labour, Part 1; (25 March 1834); Leeds Mercury, 20 Aug. 1842; West Yorks. Archive Leeds, WYL219/25 1849 & 1853; Leeds Mercury, 10 Mar. 1849; Hudds Chron. 7 May 1853.

9   West Yorks. Archive Leeds, WYL219/29; Hudds Chron. 23 March, 7 Sept, 16 Nov. 7 Dec. 1861, 25 Jan. 1862; Hudds Ex. 15 Apr. 1865, 4 Aug. 1866, 25 Jan. 11 July 1868, 19 Aug. 1871; 1 June 1872; Kirk. Arch. KX248 (25) 1874; Hudds Ex. 1 May 1875; Kirklees Archive KX248 (26) 1884. Hudds Ex. 12 Dec. 1885; 2 & 30 Jan. 1886; 28 June 1890; 22 Jan. 1902; 11 Dec. 1909; H'firth Exp. 23 Jan 1909; Kirk. Arch. UHO Honley, 18 Aug. 1924; H'firth Exp. 6 Apr. 1946, 15 July 1950; Hudds. Ex. 2 Aug. 1952

10   Old Moll/ Moll Springs mill
Huddersfield Examiner, 28 May, 10 Dec. 1853, 30 June 1855; Huddersfield Chronicle, 5 Sept. 1857, 24 Apr. 26 June, 1858, 20 Jan. 1866; Hudds Ex. 6 Oct. 1866, 7 Sept. 1867, 10 Feb. 1872, 15 Feb. 8 Mar. 1873, 24 Apr. 1880, 12 May 1888, 28 June 1890; 1 Sept. 1894; London Gazette, 21 Jan. 11 Feb. 24 May 1898, 3 Mar. 11 Apr. 1899.

11   Huddersfield Examiner, 22 Jan. 19 Feb. 18 June, 1898; 14 July 1900; 18 Oct. 1902; 4 May 1907; 16 May 1914; 29 Jan. 1921; 9 June 24 Nov. 1928; Holmfirth Express, 19 Feb. 1938; 30 Dec. 1939; Hudds Ex. 18 Nov. 1944; H'firth Exp. 10 Jan. 1953; 22 Apr. 1983.

12   Mag Bridge/Thirstin Dyeworks
Kirk. Arch. KC161/1-3 Dartmouth Estate letter books, 1805-6; Leeds Mercury, 27 Nov. 1847; Hudds Chron. 3 Nov. 1896, 12 Aug. 1871; Hudds Ex. 29 July 1876. London Gazette, 26 Feb. 2, 9, 30 Mar. 7, 14, 18 May, 1 June, 13, 20 July, 3 Dec. 1886; 4 Nov. 1887; Hudds Ex. 27 Feb. 20 Mar. 30 Oct. 1886.

13   London Gazette, 22 and 25 Dec. 1891; 12, 19, 17 Feb. 1892; 17 Feb. 1893, Hudds Ex. 2, 9, Jan. 2 Apr 1892; Hudds Chron. 23 Jan. 1892; Hudds Ex. 2 May 1914; 16 Feb. 1918; Minute Books of Tom Lees & Co. 1928, and 1940; also Anecdotal evidence from Mr. Parry junior.

14   Upper and Lower Steps mills
Jenkins & Ponting, p.306; Deeds Registry Wakefield, EI281:395 1802; Leeds Mercury, 9 Apr. 1803, 9 Mar. 1805; Leeds Intelligencer, 24 Nov. 1806; Kirklees Archive, KC161/1-3 1807-8; Leeds Merc. 3 Mar. 1827; Dartmouth Estate Office, Dartmouth Terrier, 1828 -29; Supplementary Report into the Employment of Children in Factories and as to the Propriety and Means of Curtailing the Hours of their Labour, Part 1; (25 March 1834);

15   Halifax Guardian, 29 Feb. 1840; Leeds Times, 21 Jan. 1843; Leeds Mercury, 3 Oct. 1846, 1 and 15 Apr. 1848, 5 Feb. 1850; Hudds. Chron. 14 June 1851; Kirklees Archive, KC6/1/33 1853, Hudds Chron. 3 June 1854; Hudds Ex. 13 Jan. 1855; Hudds Chron. 24 May 1856, 16 Oct. 11 Dec. 1858; 5 Nov. 1859; Hudds Ex. 12 Oct. 1861, 28 June 1862.

16   Hudds Chro., 25 Jun. 1868; Hudds Ex.20 May 1871, 22 June 1872 and 10 Apr. 1875; Hudds Chron, 5 Mar., 2 Apr. 1881, Hudds. Ex. 21 May, 25 June, 1 Oct. 1881, London Gazette, 11 Mar. and 21 June, 1881; Yorks. Fact. Times, 16 Nov. 1899; Hudds. Ex. 17 and 31 Aug. 1901, 9 Apr. and 8 Oct. 1927; H'firth Exp. 1 Nov. 1947, 1 Feb 1964, 16 Sept 1967, 6 Jan. 1968; 10 Aug. 1979.

17   Queen's Square mill
Huddersfield Examiner, 17 Mar. 12 May 1883; 21 Apr. 22 Sept. 1888; 2 Aug. 1890; Textile Manufacturer, 31 Oct. 1899; Yorks. Fact. Times, 26 June, 26 Oct. 17 Nov. 1908; Hudds Ex. 2 May 1914; Holmfirth Express, 9 Jan 1954, also 11 Aug. 1978.

GLOSSARY

Angola yarn – A mixture of wool and cotton fibres, used in the warps of woollen cloths. Popular with woollen manufacturers in the mid nineteenth century as it gave a strong fibre at reduced cost to all wool, which allowed them to compete with foreign manufacturers.

Batten – The part of a loom that moves forwards to 'beat up' the weft against the cloth, and backwards to allow the next pass of the shuttle. It has boxes on the end to hold the shuttles, and carries the 'slay'.

Beam – holds the warp threads, suspended at the rear of the loom.

Billey (slubbing billey) – first machine in the process of turning slubbings into spun yarn.

Brushing and Steaming Mill – Steams the cloth to raise the fibres, and then brushes both sides of the cloth with rotary brushes to remove bits before the cloth is cropped.

Burler or Mender – Carried out by women and girls, originally referred to as Burlers; they repaired weaving faults, unfastened knots and stitched the yarn into the weave to enable the cloth to be cropped without being cut, these women later became known as Menders. Burling, the removal of any foreign matter from the cloth, was then carried out usually by older women whose eyesight was less keen than it had been.

Burring machine – Used to remove burrs (seed heads etc.) from raw wool before it was scribbled and carded. Needed principally for imported wools.

Card clothing – Wire teeth fixed into a strong backing, can be used for hand carding fibre prior to spinning, or fixed to the drums of scribbling and carding machines. Also used on raising gigs.

Carding and Scribbling machines – The process that follows Teazing/Willowing. Scribbling separates course fibres from finer ones, and starts the straightening process, Carding straightens the finer fibres.

Cassimere/Kerseymere – fine woollen cloth, very popular until replaced by Worsted cloths.

Condenser – machine that combines the processes of scribbling and carding, and produces a filmy web of fibre that is then processed by the slubbing billy.

Crabbing machine – the cloth is passed firstly through a tank of boiling water followed by a tank of cold water, to set the required tension in the cloth.

Currency – L.s.d. to £. p. 2.4d = 1p (240d and 100p both £1). 12d make 1shilling or 5p. 10s make 50p, 20s. make £1.

Dewing machine – sprays fine jets of water onto the cloth to assist in the conditioning process.

Drying Stove – room used to dry died yarn or scoured cloth, often built over the flues carrying the smoke and other exhaust gasses from the boiler to the mill's chimney. Prone to fires due to overheating.

Fearnought – type of Willey/Willow machine for cleaning dust, dirt, seeds and burrs from fleeces. Presumably made by a particular machinery manufacturer.

Fulling stocks – wooden hammers originally driven by a water wheel to pound woven cloth, imitating the action of the feet of the fuller or 'walker'. This gives the cloth greater bulk, but shrinks both the length and width.

Garnet – machine for opening hard waste to be made into shoddy or mungo.

Grinding frames – for grinding rags in the making of shoddy and mungo

Healds – Frames holding looped wires through which the individual warp threads are passed.

The sequence of raising and lowering these frames determines the design of the cloth.

Hydro Extractor – also known as a Wuzzer; an industrial spin drier, can be open topped or lidded.

Jacks – 'L' shaped arms on the side of looms that raise and lower the healds.

Jacquards – Punch card system used on looms to raise and lower wires or healds to enable patterned cloth to be woven.

Knopping – making an ornamental loop or tuft in yarn.

Left/Right bank of a river – this is determined by the direction of the flow of water, and assumes that the reader is facing in the same direction.

Lewis Cross-cutting machine – Early cropping machine where the blade travelled across the width of the cloth, necessitating stopping the machine to reposition the blade and the cloth after each pass.

Loom – Means of weaving cloth, originally hand operated; the first mechanised loom was invented in 1785, with modifications and improvements being made in 1813, 1821 and 1822, and continually thereafter. Used increasingly by Holme Valley manufacturers from 1850s onwards. The width of power looms is measured in 'quarters'- nine inches/quarter yard. e.g.a 10quarter loom is 90 inches or 7ft 6in. wide.

Milling machine – Replaced fulling stocks.

Moiety – a half share in a property.

Moiter – machine for shredding rags in making shoddy and mungo.

Moser – Raising gig with wire teeth made by the Moser company

Mungo – Reclaimed fibre from rags with a shorter staple than Shoddy.

Overlooker – The person in charge of a process or department; also known as a Foreman.

Perpetual – Cropping machine, the rotary blade is wider than the cloth, and is placed across the cloth, allowing the piece to run continuously. Replaced hand cropping and the Lewis cross-cutter.

Piecing machine – rejoins the ends of broken threads.

Press – large machine used at the end of the finishing process to give the cloth a better texture and appearance.

Raddle – A shorter, portable version of the slay used to keep the strands of yarn in position when transferring a warp from the warping wall or woof to a beam.

Raising gig – used to raise the fibres in cloth to achieve a brushed finish. Originally fitted with Teazles, later with card clothing.

Shoddy – Reclaimed fibre from rags, used mostly in woollen cloths to add bulk at a more reasonable cost than using new wool.

Shoddy cleaner – process to remove the colour from shoddy before incorporating it into a woollen yarn.

Slay – a long closed comb fastened to the top of the batten on looms. One warp thread is passed through each space between the teeth to keep them in the correct order.

Slubbing Billy – machine that converts the filmy web from the condenser into a loose rope-like roving ready for the spinning mule

Spinning Jenny – a means of spinning multiple yarns simultaneously. The moving part or 'jenny' draws out the fibres before they are twisted into a yarn.

Spinning Mule – incorporates the actions of the spinning jenny and Arkwright's water frame.

Tappet looms – the healds are raised and lowered by tappet arms controlled by a series of cams rather than by jacks. Restricts the number of healds that can be used.

Teazing machine, Willey or willow – used to separate fibres of a fleece, also to remove dust, knots, tangles etc. and unwanted foreign matter. The name willow or willey came from clothiers using willow wands to beat the fleece over a lattice of sticks.

Teazles – Spiky seed pod of the Teazle plant, used to straighten fibres ready for spinning and for raising the nap on cloth before cropping. Was eventually superseded by card clothing.

Tenter posts/stands – Rows of stone or wooden poles with rods containing hooks suspended between them from which newly woven cloth that had been washed was hung to dry. Originally in fields, but when drying stoves began to be built many tenter posts were moved inside the stoves. Origin of the saying 'on tenter hooks'.

Tentering Machine – Replaced tenter posts. An endless belt carried the stretched cloth between rows of hot steam pipes to dry it. Considerably speeded up the drying process.

Thrums and Nippings – Thrums are the unwoven ends of a warp left in the loom after the woven piece is removed, they are used to fasten the new warp to. After being drawn through the healds they are removed and processed as waste to be re-spun. Nippings are short lengths of yarn, and are treated in a similar way.

Tops and Noils – Long staple wool is known as Tops and is used for spinning Worsted yarn. The shorter staple wool that is left after the Tops have been combed out, and is not suitable for Worsted, is used for spinning Woollen yarn, and is known as Noils.

Tuner – The person who erects, adjusts and repairs looms.

Twisting frame – Twisted two, or in the case of knitting wools three, single threads together to form a two or three ply yarn.

Warp Drying Balloon – Large open latted drum around which warp threads would be wound to dry after being sized. Also permitted the making up of a warp before rolling onto a beam ready for the loom.

Warping Woof – Framework made from wood or iron with holes drilled to allow wooden pegs to be placed in them. The warp threads would be wound between the pegs until the required length was reached. They can then be taken for sizing, or be wound onto the warp beam.

Winding-on frame – used to transfer a warp from the warping balloon to the beam that would then be fitted into the back of the loom

Witch – controlled multiple healds in a handloom, and allowed the weaver to change the position of the healds with one simple action 'as if by magic'.

Dyewares prior to the introduction of Analine dyes:

American Bark: possibly the bark of Wild Cherry tree, used by American Indians.
Camwood: red African wood.
Cudbear: a purplish-red dye obtained from orchil lichens
Fustic: from the wood of *Chlorofora tinctoria*, or *Cotinus coggyria*
Lac: made from the droppings of the Cochineal Beetle, from India or China.
Logwood: a leguminous West Indian tree, *Heamatoxylon campechianum.*
Madder: root of a climbing plant, gives a red dye.
Peachwood, comes from Nicaragua
Sanders: heartwood of the Indian sandalwood tree, gives a red or purplish dye.
Mordants: - used to fix the colour when dyeing fibres or fabric. Using different mordants with a dye can produce different shades.
Alum: double sulphate of Aluminium and potassium.
Argol bichrome, potassium hydrogen tartrate.
Blue Vitriol: Copper Sulphate.
Copperas: iron sulphate, forms green crystals
Oxalate of Tin: oxalate is found in Sorrel and Rhubarb leaves.
Soda Ash: caustic soda

BIBLIOGRAPHY

Aikin J., *A Description of the Country from Thirty to Forty Miles around Manchester;* (Manchester, 1795; reprinted by David & Charles, 1968).

Aldcroft D.H. (Ed.), *The Development of British Industry and Foreign Competition 1875-1914: Studies in Industrial Enterprise;* (London, 1968).

Allen G.C., *British Industries and their Organisation;* London, 1959.

Baines E., *An account of the Woollen Manufacture of England;* New edition, 1970. Gives details of methods and problems associated with early power looms.

Benham W. Gurney, (trans. & ed), 'The Red Paper Book of Colchester' (1902), in G.W. Hilton, *The Truck System, 1465-1960;* (Connecticut, 1960).

Binfield K. *Writings of the Luddites;* Baltimore, 2004.

Binnie G.M., *Early Victorian Water Engineers,* (London, 1981).

British Labour Struggles: Contemporary Pamphlets 1727 – 1850, *The Factory Act of 1819; The Factory Act of 1833; The Factory Education Bill 1843; (New York 1971).*

British Parliamentary Papers, Industrial Revolution, Factories 1876, Book 4.

Brooke A.J. *The Handloom Fancy Weavers, 1820-1914;* (Honley, 2007).

Brooke A.J. *The Social and Political Response to Industrialisation in the Huddersfield area, 1790-1850;* Unpublished Thesis, 1988.

Carpenter K.E. (Ed.), *Prelude to Victory of the Ten Hours Movement: Two Speeches, One Letter and a Report, 1844; (New York, 1972).*

Carpenter K.E. (Ed.), *Richard Oastler: King of the Factory Children, Six Pamphlets 1835-1861;* (New York, 1972).

Carpenter K.E. (Ed.), *Trade Unions in the Early 1830s;* (New York, 1972).

Carpenter K.E. (Ed.), *The Spread of Machinery: Five Pamphlets 1793-1806;* (New York, 1972).

Catling H., 'The Evolution of Spinning' in Jenkins J.G., *The Wool Textile Industry in Great Britain;* (London, 1972).

Clapham J.H., *The Woollen and Worsted Industries;* (1907).

Cowgill John, *A Historical Account of the Luddites;* (1862).

Crump W.B., Ghorbal G., *History of the Huddersfield Woollen Industry;* Hudds., 1935.

Crump W.B., Hargrave E., *Trade Notices, Newspaper Advertisements and Extracts;* Thoresby Society, Vol. 32. 1931.

Cunningham, *Growth of English Industry and Commerce;* 1907 and 1910.

Deane P. and Cole W.A., *British Economic Growth 1588 – 1959,* 2nd Edn; Cambridge, 1968.

Defoe D., *A Tour Through the Whole Island of Great Britain;* 2 vols. (London, 1928).

Drummond J.C. and Wilbraham A. *The Englishman's Food: Five Centuries of English Diet;* Pimlico Edition, (London, 1991).

Ellis P., 'The Techniques of Weaving', in Jenkins J.G. (Ed.), *The Wool Textile Industry in Great Britain;* (London, 1972).

Evans E.J. *The Forging of the Modern State: Early Industrial Britain, 1783-1870;* 3rd Edn. (Harlow, 2001).

Fisher D.J.V., *The Anglo-Saxon Age c400-1042;* (London, 1973).

Fitton R.S. & Wadsworth A.P., *The Strutts and the Arkwrights, 1758-1830;* (1973).

Fogarty M.P., *Prospects of the Industrial Areas of Great Britain;* London, 1945.

Giles C. & Goodall I.H., *Yorkshire Textile Mills 1770 – 1930;* (HMSO London, 1992).

Habbakuk H.J. & Postan M. (Eds.), *The Cambridge Economic History of Europe,* Vol. VI, 'The Industrial Revolution and Beyond'; Part I, (1964).

Haigh E.A.H. (Ed.), *Huddersfield a Most Handsome Town;* (Huddersfield, 1992).

Hammond J.L. & Hammond B., *The Skilled Labourer,* 1760-1832; (London, 1933).

Hartwell R.M., *The Causes of the Industrial Revolution in England;* London, 1967.

Heaton, Prof. H., *The Yorkshire Woollen and Worsted Industries: from the earliest times to the Industrial Revolution;* Oxford, 1965.

Heaton H., 'Yorkshire Cloth Traders in the United States, 1770-1840', in *Publications of the Thoresby Society,* XXXVII, iii, (1944).

Hinchliffe J.M., *Mills of the Upper Holme Valley;* Unpublished Dissertation, 1973.

Homans Geo. C., *English Villagers of the Thirteenth Century;* (New York, 1970).

Horn Pamela, *Children's Work and Welfare, 1780-1890;* (Cambridge 1994).

Hornsey Ian S., *A History of Beer and Brewing;* Cambridge, 2003.

Jagger M., *History of Honley;* (Honley, 1914).

Jenkins D.T. & Ponting K.G., *The British Wool Textile Industry 1790-1914;* (London, 1982).

Jenkins D.T., *The West Riding Wool Textile Industry 1770-1835: A Study of Fixed Capital Formation;* (1975).

Jenkins J.G., *The Wool Textile Industry in Great Britain 1790-1914;* (1972).

Kerridge E., 'Wool Growing and Wool Textiles in Medieval and Early Modern Times', in Jenkins J.G., *The Wool Textile Industry in Great Britain;* (London, 1972).

Landes D.S., 'Technological Change and Development in Western Europe, 1750-1914', in Habakkuk H.J., and Postan M., (Eds.), *The Cambridge Economic History of Europe,* Vol. VI, Parts 1 & 2. (Cambridge, 1965).

Laybourn K., *A History of British Trade Unionism c. 1770-1790;* (Stroud, 1992).

Laybourn K. *Britain on the Breadline: A Social and Political History of Britain 1918-1939;* (Stroud, 1990).

Lean Garth, *Brave Men Choose;* (London, 1961.)

Lipson E., *The History of the Woollen and Worsted Industries;* (London, 1965).

Mayhall J., *Annals of Yorkshire,* 3 vols; (1876 approx.).

McCord N. *The Anti-Corn Law League 1838-1846;* 2nd Edn, (London, 1968).

Morehouse H.J. *History of the Parish of Kirkburton and the Graveship of Holme;* Huddersfield 1961 facsimile edition 1984.

O'Gorman F., *The Long Eighteenth Century: British Political and Social History 1688-1832;* (1997).

Peel Frank, *The Risings of the Luddites;* 1st Edn. 1880, also 1895, and 1968.

Peel Frank, *Spen Valley, Past & Present;* (1893).

Roth Ling, *Yorkshire Coiners;*

Rule J., *The Labouring Classes in Early Industrial England, 1750-1850;* (1986)

Seward D., 'The Wool Textile Industry 1750-1960' in Jenkins J.G., *The Wool Textile Industry in Great Britain;* (London, 1972).

Sigsworth E.M. and Blackman J.M., 'The Woollen and Worsted Industries', in Aldcroft D.H. (Ed.), *The Development of British Industry and Foreign Competition;* 1968.

Stansky P. *The Victorian Revolution: Government and Society in Victoria's Britain;* (New York, 1993).

Stevenson J., *Popular Disturbances in England 1700 – 1870,* 2nd Edn; London, 1992.

Sykes D.F.E., *The History of Huddersfield and the Valleys of the Colne, the Holme, and the Dearne.* Facsimile Edn., (Holmfirth, 1986).

Thompson Dorothy, *The Chartists: Popular Politics in the Industrial Revolution;* (Aldershot, 1984).

Thompson E.P., *The Making of the English Working Class;* (London, 1980).

Thorpe Judi, *Marsden Children;* (Huddersfield 2010).

Tufnell E.C., *Character, Object and Effects of Trade Unions 1834;* (New York, 1972).

Turner Ben, *About Myself 1863-1930;* Humphrey Toulmin, 1930.

Turner Ben, *Short History of the General Union of Textile Workers: Established Dewsbury 1875; Huddersfield 1881;* (Heckmondwyke, 1920).

Wickson R., *The Community of the Realm in Thirteenth Century England;* (London, 1970).

Wild M.T., 'The Yorkshire Wool Textile Industry', in Jenkins J.G. (Ed.), *The Wool Textile Industry in Great Britain;* (London, 1972).

Journals and Reports

Carus-Wilson E.M., 'The Aulnage Accounts: A Criticism', *Economic History Review,* Vol. 2; (Jan., 1929).

Carus-Wilson E.M., 'An Industrial Revolution of the Thirteenth Century', *Economic History Review,* Vol. XI, (1941), reprinted in *Essays in Economic History,* Vol. 1, (1961).

Clapham J.H., 'The Decline of the Handloom in England and Germany', *Bradford Textile Journal,* (1905).

Clapham J.H., 'Industrial Organisation in the Woollen and Worsted Industries of Yorkshire', *Economic Journal,* XVI; (1906).

Clapham J.H., 'The Transference of the Worsted Industry from Norfolk to the West Riding', *Economic Journal,* XX; (1910).

Clapham J.H., 'Some Factory Statistics of 1815-16', *Economic Journal,* XXV; (1915).

Crump W.B., 'The wool textile industry of the Pennines, in its physical setting', *Journal of the Textiles Institute,* Vol. 26 (1935).

Heaton H., 'Benjamin Gott and the Anglo-American Cloth Trade', *Journal of Economic and Business History,* 2, (1929-30).

Heaton H., 'Non-Importation, 1806-1812', *Journal of Economic History,* Vol. 1, No. 2. (1941).

Navikas Katrina, 'The search for "General Ludd": the mythology of Luddism', *Social History,* Vol. 30, No. 3; (2005).

Randall J., 'The Shearmen and the Wiltshire outrages of 1802: Trade Unionism and Industrial Violence', *Social History,* VII, 2, (1982).

Smith Simon D., 'British Exports to Colonial North America and the Mercantile Fallacy' *Business History,* Vol. 37 No. 1, (1995).

Maps

Honley Enclosures Map, 1788.

HMSO, 6 inch Ordinance Survey maps published c.1853; 25 inch Ordinance Survey maps printed 1893, 1906, 1918 and 1930.

Jeffries T., *The County of York;* surveyed in 1767, 68, 69, 70. Published in 1770,

Teesdale H., *Map of Yorkshire;* surveyed 1827 – 28, published 1835

INDEX OF PERSONAL AND COMPANY NAMES

Early Court Rolls
Addam of Heppeworth 8,
Hannah of Wlvedale 8,
John of Wlvedale 8
John Towler 11,
Jordan the Milner 9,
Adam his son 9,
Nicholas Kenward 11,
Moorehouse William 9,
Nicholas the Millener 8,
Richard of Scholes 8,
Richard of Birkes 8,
Richard of Byrton 9,
Richard son of Michael 9,
Richard Child 9,
Richard del Bothe 9,
Thomas Coldwell 11,
William Dernilee 11,
William de Forrester 9,
William Strekeyes 9,
William de Thwong 8,
William Hynchecliff 11,

A
A1 Spinners and Doublers 315,
Ackroyd Jonathon 144,
Adams D. & Co. Ltd. 127,
Adams William 219,
Adamson Ellis Lee 295,
Addy Edward Brook 71,
Ainley Ben 253,
Ainley Mr. 196,
Ainley Sam 276,
Airey Messrs. 305,
Alcock Henry 248,
Alderson Charlie 94,

Allen B. 328,
Allied Textiles Group 186, 241,
Allison John 184,
Allison & Exley 231,
Allott Bryan 103, 177,
Allott Martin 11, 136,
Allott Robert 177,
Allsop Charles Kevin 156,
Anders Henry William 168,
Anglo Yarn Spinners Ltd. 136,
Arkwright Richard 14, 15, 23,
Armitage Alfred 305,
Armitage Allan 281,
Armitage Ann 240,
Armitage Ann Elizabeth Green 101,
Armitage Captain 270,
Armitage Edgar 182,
Armitage Edward 238,
Armitage George 182, 238, 258, 269, 281,
Armitage G.P. 334,
Armitage Henry 169,
Armitage James Green 99, 100,
Armitage John 101, 130, 194, 209, 238,
	239, 269,
Armitage Joseph 284, 285,
Armitage Joseph Green 99, 100, 269, 277,
Armitage Martha 130,
Armitage Robert 323,
Armitage Tom 101,
Armitage Philemon 312, 313,
Armitage Thomas 130,
Armitage William Green 269, 270, 278,
Armitage William & Co. 111,
Armitage W.H. 118, 191, 296, 304, 328,
Armitage Alfred & Co. Ltd. 305,
Armitage Ann & Son 210,

Armitage Bros. 265,
Armitage & Clelland 181,
Armitage & Dickinson 300,
Armitage & Norton 191,
Arnold William 290,
Askham William 80,
Ashton William Marvel 248,
Atherton John 240,
Atkinson Law 19,
Atkinson Elizabeth 210,
Atkinson Richard 210,
Audsley John 245,
Ayre Mr. 94,
Ayrton William Scrope 279,

B

Baddeley Bros. Ltd. 69, 175,
Bailes George 247,
Bailey Benjamin 296,
Bailey Fred 261,
Bailey Mark 245,
Bailey Martha 261,
Bailey William 331,
Bailey, Mettrick & Wakefield 145, 174,
Bailey William & Co. 331,
Baldwin J.J. & Partners 246,
Bamford Henry 326,
Bamford William & Sons 326,
Bamforth & Booth 257,
Banks Emma 297,
Barber & Co. 117, 178,
Barber Annie Rachel 89,
Barber Benjamin Wilson 123,
Barber Edmund 88,
Barber Fanny 87, 88,
Barber Firth 117, 204,
Barber Firth & Co. 117, 118,
Barber George 117,
Barber Gibbon Mrs. 105,
Barber Henry 87,
Barber J & Sons 39,
Barber John 87, 88, 89 92, 95, 105, 117,
    124, 203,
Barber John Wilson 123,
Barber Joseph 79, 85, 86, 87, 88, 112, 116,
    117, 203,
Barber Joshua 86, 87, 88, 106, 117, 118, 150,
Barber Joshua Thristle 89, 91, 101, 119, 121,

Barber Percy 108,
Barber Sarah 89,
Barber Thomas 87, 121, 122,
Barber Thomas & Co. 121,
Barber William Henry 89,
Barber Joshua & Co. 86, 117,
Barber Joshua & Sons 124,
Barber W.H. & J. 42, 68, 89, 94, 101, 112,
    118, 180, 202,
Barden Samuel 260,
Barker J.H. & Co. 224,
Barker & Moody 224,
Barker William 92, 292,
Barnes & Taylor 191,
Barramatch Fabrics 91,
Barrowclough Abraham 201,
Barrowclough Fred 247,
Barrowclough Joseph & Sons 190,
Barrowclough Thomas 227,
Barrowclough Mr. Alias Cockin 244,
Barwick J. 290,
Bashforth Charles 65, 117, 118, 123, 144,
    270,
Bashforth G. 270,
Bashforth William 117, 144,
Bates Benjamin 243, 244, 248,
Bates James 33, 171, 234, 243, 244, 245, 317,
Bates John 88, 198, 244, 263, 301,
Bates Tim 111,
Bates William 244,
Bates J.S. & J. 165,
Bateman Mr. 61,
Batley George 207,
Batley Herbert 202,
Batley James 207, 208,
Batley John 296,
Batley Lewis 206, 208,
Batley Richard 281,
Batley William 183,
Batley J. & Sons 183,
Batt Edward Alfred 203,
Batty Abigail 106,
Batty Arthur 247,
Batty Betty 101,
Batty Charles 93,
Batty Edward 11, 136,
Batty George 83, 106,
Batty George & Bros. 129,

Batty James 83, 136,
Batty John 83, 106, 150,
Batty Jonathon 83, 136,
Batty Joseph 136,
Batty Joshua 54, 83,
Batty Thomas 83, 136,
Batty William 54, 83,
Battye (girl) 172,
Battye Ann 137,
Battye Charles 61, 62,
Battye Edward 156,
Battye George 141, 150,
Battye Henry 131,
Battye Hobson & Co. 132,
Battye James 82, 137, 150,
Battye John 105, 226, 232, 233, 234, 249,
Battye John Stocks 226,
Battye Jonathon 150, 233,
Battye Joseph 83, 130, 146, 257,
Battye Mr. J. 180,
Battye J. & Bros. 83,
Battye Mary 137,
Battye Richard 226,
Battye Sarah Jane 180,
Battye Thomas 106, 120, 137,
Battye Tom 83,
Battye T & Bros. 84,
Battye William Walter 100,
Battye William W. 132, 150,
Battye W.W. & Sons Ltd. 68, 132,
Battye v Battye 226,
Bayliff Joseph 275,
Baxendale Ben 285,
Bean James 301,
Bean William 301,
Beardsell Alfred 82, 84,
Beardsell Brook 282,
Beardsell Charles 46, 83, 178,
Beardsell Charles & Sons 81, 83, 84,
Beardsell Hannah 49
Beardsell Henry 96,
Beardsell Isaac 37, 46, 178, 210, 234, 279, 280, 281,
Beardsell James 8, 47, 83, 84, 85, 92,
Beardsell John 317,
Beardsell Jonas 237,
Beardsell Jonathon 82,
Beardsell Joseph 46, 85, 93,

Beardsell Luke 85,
Beardsell Lydia 19,
Beardsell Martha 85,
Beardsell Mary 45, 47, 49,
Beardsell Peter 37, 50, 144,
Beardsell Rachel 49,
Beardsell Ruth 49,
Beardsell Sarah 49,
Beardsell Thomas 282,
Beardsell William 181,
Beardsell William Henry 84,
Beardsell & Co. 54, 280,
Beardsell Bros. 282,
Beardsell J. & Co. 66,
Beardsell James & Sons 50, 81, 83, 95, 281,
Beattie T. 186,
Beaumont Ann 144,
Beaumont Alfred 333, 334,
Beaumont Arnold 254,
Beaumont Charlotte 320,
Beaumont Edith 283,
Beaumont Fred 181,
Beaumont George 208, 271, 290, 307, 319,
Beaumont Hannah 321,
Beaumont James 299, 302,
Beaumont Joe 1674,
Beaumont John 133, 144, 159, 196, 290, 315,
Beaumont Joshua 331, 332, 333,
Beaumont Lucy 160,
Beaumont Richard 331,
Beaumont Robert 119,
Beaumont William 330, 331,
Beaumont & Co. 333,
Beaumont & Coldwell 155,
Beaumont James & Sons 71,
Beaumont Joshua & Co. 334,
Beaumont Kaye & Co. 290, 303,
Beaumont, Son, & Co. 223, 256,
Beaumont & Stocks 308,
Beaumont & Vickerman 331,
Beaumont William & Co. 331,
Beckitt John 133,
Bedford Thomas 162,
Bedford William 237,
Bedforth G. 328,
Beeley Mr. 74,
Beeston Mary 210,
Beetham Thomas 292,

Beever John 169,
Beever John & Sons 169,
Beever Mary Ann 200,
Bell Andrew 298,
Bennett Arthur 258, 259,
Bennett James 100,
Bentley J.H. 261,
Bentley Robert 89,
Berry Dr. 145,
Berry Godfrey 193, 303,
Berry Nathaniel 193,
Berry Robert 304,
Bilcliff Edward 209,
Bilcliffe Thomas 164,
Bill Charles Horsfall 210,
Biltcliffe Ellen 213,
Binswell Ltd. 160,
Birkhead T. 191,
Birkhead Thomas & Sons 186, 191, 192, 228,
Blackburn & France 271,
Blackburn Joseph 271,
Blackburn J & Co. 271,
Blakeley James & Sons 322,
Bloor John 318,
Blyth Mr. 26,
Booth Annie 246,
Booth Ben 253,
Booth Edward 11, 186,
Booth F. 132,
Booth George 239, 270, 280,
Booth George Elliott 249,
Booth George & Co. 240,
Booth James Alfred 119,
Booth James 80, 220, 229,
Booth John 55, 144, 229, 237,
Booth Jonathon 255, 256,
Booth Joseph 95, 96, 120,
Booth Joshua 220, 255, 256,
Booth, Lockwood & Co. 105,
Booth Martha 229,
Booth Phillip 139,
Booth Mr. 200,
Booth Sam 240,
Booth G. & G. 270,
Booth & Pitts 239,
Booth Pitt & Co. 240,
Boothroyd Alice Ann 304,
Boothroyd Friend 282,

Boothroyd Harriet 282,
Boothroyd Jack Irvin 203,
Boothroyd Joseph 212,
Boothroyd Joshua 89,
Boothroyd Richard 158,
Boothroyd William 152, 201,
Boothroyd Rugs 69, 203, 299,
Boothroyd S. 190,
Boothroyd Mrs. 302,
Bottomley William 303,
Bourne Daniel 14,
Bousefield C.E. 292,
Bower Ben 181,
Bower & Co. 156,
Bower David 245,
Bower Elizabeth 233,
Bower Henry 179, 181,
Bower H. & Son 39,
Bower James 179, 198,
Bower John 133, 156, 159, 160, 179, 226,
Bower John William 198,
Bower Jonas 179,
Bower Jonathon 139, 179,
Bower Luke 233,
Bower Mr. 298,
Bower Richard 18, 107, 156, 179, 238,
Bower William 179,
Bower & Bailey 245,
Bower Brown & Co. 298,
Bower John & Sons 131, 139, 140, 157, 159, 160,
Bower Richard & Co. 156, 180,
Bower Roebuck & Co. Ltd. 44, 71, 238,
Bower, Roebuck & Firth 191, 238,
Bower & Smith 273,
Bowes James 211, 212,
Bowes Mr. 266,
Bowskin Thomas 122,
Boythe Henry 196,
Bradbury James 95,
Bradley Christopher Lonsdale 264, 265,
Bradley David 317,
Bradley Robert 277,
Bradley Thomas 264,
Bradley & Son 263,
Bradshaw Benjamin 188,
Bramall George 181,
Bray B. & Son 152,

Bray John 82, 105, 144, 150, 162, 165,
Bray Joseph 161, 162, 165, 177, 237,
Bray Joshua 278,
Bray Lydia 177,
Bray Mary 274,
Brearley Charles 82,
Brierley Fred 145,
Brierley Tom Scott 173,
Brierley, Chester & Co. 173,
Brierley & Co. 173,
Brierley & Wall 174,
British Design Knitters 158,
Britton Rugs Ltd. 160,
Broadbent John 96,
Broadbent Joseph 184, 188,
Broadbent Levi 322,
Broadbent Joseph & Sons 188, 189,
Broadhead Bros. 157,
Broadhead David 93,
Broadhead James 93,
Broadhead Joseph 92, 229, 230, 249,
Broadhead Joseph & Co. 66, 93,
Broadhead & Mason 93,
Broadhead William 102,
Broadhead v Morehouse 104,
Broadhurst Rev. Joseph 92,
Brooke James & Son 18,
Brooke Charles 153,
Brooke John 165, 199,
Brooke John & Sons 180,
Brooke Thomas 301, 302,
Brooke William 278,
Brook Arthur Wilkinson 118,
Brook Benjamin 125, 152,
Brook & Brownson 118,
Brook Charles 123, 126, 153, 254,
Brook David 52, 88, 124,
Brook Edward 125,
Brook Edwin 297,
Brook Eliza 251,
Brook Elizabeth 152, 156,
Brook Emily 213,
Brook Emor 158,
Brook Fred, 108, 292,
Brook George 66, 88, 334,
Brook George Henry 321,
Brook Henry 227,
Brook Hubert 324,

Brook James 107, 150, 151, 152, 153, 156,
    158, 172, 189,
Brook J. 105,
Brook John 150, 152, 285,
Brook Jonas 123,
Brook Jonas & Bros. 122, 123, 124, 125, 126,
Brook Jonathon 150, 152, 251, 255,
Brook Joseph 123, 153,
Brook Joshua 150, 151, 152, 219,
Brook Lydia 151,
Brook Mabel Francis 126,
Brook Ruth 158,
Brook R.H. 324,
Brook Sarah 245,
Brook Thomas 298, 301,
Brook W. 305,
Brook Councillor 262,
Brook Edwin & Co. Ltd. 297,
Brook Dyeing Co. 335,
Brook James & Bros, 189,
Brook James & Sons 188, 189,
Brook John & Sons 168, 169, 175, 273,
Brook William & Sons (Dyers) Ltd. 120, 220,
    297,
Broomfield Engineering Co. 229,
Brown Ann 233, Brown Joseph 328,
Brown Richard 82, 233, 331,
Brown William 88, 182,
Brown & Blackburn 207,
Brown David Corporation 229,
Brown David Tractors 327,
Brownson Thomas 118,
Buchanan Mr. 200,
Burleigh Lord 7,
Buckley James 171,
Buckley Jonathon 201,
Buckley Walter 171,
Bullock George 182,
Burton Elias 249,
Burtt Edwin Henry 247,
Burtt G.E. 247,
Butterworth Benjamin 106, 107, 146, 162,
Butterworth Edward 54, 107, 112, 116, 117,
Butterworth Henry 140,
Butterworth Herbert 174,
Butterworth J. 108,
Butterworth John H. 240,
Butterworth Jonathon 106,

Butterworth Joseph 107, 146, 171, 172,
Butterworth Julia Ann 172,
Butterworth Matthew 106, 107, 133,
Butterworth Richard Woofenden 107,
Butterworth Robert 107, 111, 146,
Butterworth Samuel 140,
Butterworth Sarah 107,
Butterworth Thomas 107,
Butterworth Tomas Herbert 108,
Butterworth William 138, 140, 142, 145,
Butterworth & Co. 106,
Butterworth H. & S. Ltd. 68, 70, 108, 140, 142,
Butterworth Joseph & Sons 107,
Butterworth & Roberts 91, 111, 112,
Butterworth & Sons 110, 111,
Butterworth S. & Son 108,
Butterworth T. & Sons 107,
Butler Mr. 204,
Byrom John 136,

C

Campbell Thomas 85,
Capper Alfred 240,
Carr William 220, 248,
Carter Ben 308,
Carter Benjamin 269, 277,
Carter Charles 322,
Carter David 321,
Carter Fred 299,
Carter Hannah Mary 125,
Carter Jesse 322,
Carter John 146, 277, 278,
Carter Tom 321,
Carter Messrs 184,
Carter David & Co. 322,
Cartwright Alfred 256,
Cartwright Andrew 321,
Cartwright Ann 65,
Cartwright Rev. Edmund 17, 19,
Cartwright John 164, 245, 251,
Cartwright Jonas 138,
Cartwright Moorhouse 132,
Cartwright William 25,
Cartwright & Co. 192,
Cartwright & Sons 132,
Castell Richard 9,
Castle Alfred 199,

Castle George 186-7,
Castle G.W. Ltd. 69, 170,
Castle Herbert 323,
Castle Jane 260,
Castle John 187,
Castle Mary 187, 200,
Castle Mrs. 253, 262,
Castle Tommy 75,
Castle William 235, 253,
Cave B.T. Ltd. 293, 311,
Cave B.T. Successors Ltd. 311,
Century Steel 196,
Chadwick Benjamin 195,
Chadwick James 313,
Chadwick William 237,
Chambers George 302,
Chambers Joseph 197,
Chambley Jonathon 97,
Chambley J. Sons & Co. 97,
Chapman Benjamin 112,
Chapman William 126,
Charlesworth David 86,
Charlesworth George 107,
Charlesworth James 79, 87,
Charlesworth John 18, 38, 112,
Charlesworth Jonathon 106, 153,
Charlesworth Joseph 86,
Charlesworth Joshua 86, 88, 138,
Charlesworth J. & Sons 86, 87, 177,
Charlesworth J. and H. 129,
Charlesworth George 39, 152,
Charlesworth Hirst 227,
Charlesworth Mary 192,
Charlesworth Mary Ann 87,
Charlesworth Miss 223,
Charlesworth Mr. 26, 134,
Charlesworth Nellie 160,
Charlesworth Richard 209,
Charlesworth Thomas 184,
Charlesworth Thomas Lister 87,
Chatterton Elizabeth 88,
Chatterton Joseph 88,
Chester John 173
Cheetham Ernest 282,
Cheetham W & Co. 284,
Choppards Mill Co. 151,
Churchill Winston 41,
Clapham John 158,

Clay William 333,
Clarke Dennis 310,
Clarke Dr. 326,
Cliffe Matthew William 210, 271,
Clough Bros. 132,
Clough John 50,
Clough Mary (Mally) 45,
Coats Crafts 158,
Cobbett William 33,
Cobden Richard 66,
Coldwell B. 129,
Coldwell Harry 98,
Coldwell James 266,
Coldwell John 137, 249,
Coldwell Paul 204,
Coldwell Abel & Sons 282,
Coldwell, O'Regan & Co. 266,
Collins Kevin 335,
Cooks Hannah 196,
Cooks John 196,
Cooper Joseph 293,
Cooper & Liversedge 292,
Cooper Liversedge & Wood 69, 293,
Copley John 310,
Copley Marshall & Co. 44, 236,
Corfield J. 143,
Cottage Knitwear Ltd. 225,
Crabtree A & Co. 276,
Crabtree William 333,
Crag Rats Theatre Co. 165,
Craven Sarah 106,
Craven Thomas 106,
Crawshaw Mr. 236,
Cree T.S. 39,
Creswell A.E. 254,
Croft E. 304,
Cromack Charles 151, 152,
Crompton Samuel 2, 16,
Crompton William 95,
Crookes Henry 194,
Crookes Thomas 255,
Crosland James 137,
Crosland John 82, 260,
Crosland Joseph 158,
Crosland Marsh 142,
Crosland Sam 246,
Crosland Thomas 258, 260,
Crosland T.P. 199,

Crosland John & Sons 260,
Crossley John 172,
Crowther Elon 274, 276,
Crowther George 59, 60,
Crowther J.D. 275, 276,
Crowther Phyllis 275,
Crowther William 274,
Crowther & Shaw 305,
Crowther & Vickerman 262,
Crump & Ghorbal 209,
Cumbray Harry 278,
Cuttell Abel 162, 164, 167, 168, 238,
Cuttell John 79, 80, 103,
Cuttell Joseph 162, 165,
Cuttell Joshua 32, 162, 171,
Cuttell Joshua & Bros. 162,
Cuttell Joshua & Sons 163,
Cuttell William 188,
Cuttell Mr. 248,

D
DAC (Yorkshire) Co. Ltd. 229,
Dark R.H. & Co. 68, 69, 129,
Darnley Angela 204,
Dartmouth Lord 269, 270, 274, 301, 319,
    323, 327, 333,
Davies John 302,
Davies L.R. 160,
Davis John & Co. 174,
Davis Dyers Ltd. 174,
Dawson James 317,
Dawson Thomas 158,
Dawson William 237,
Day John 238,
Day, Watkinson & Co. 154,
Dean Charles 304, 305,
Dean Charles & Sons 304,
Dean & Hey 303, 304,
Dearnley George Frederick 309,
Dearnley Mr. 314,
Dearnley Mrs. 309,
Dearnley Thomas Wood 309,
Dearnley Bros. 309,
Dearnley & Denham 313,
Dearnley & Drury 314,
Defoe Daniel 2,
Denisons (Wilsden) Ltd. 335,
Dennison Mr. H. 66,

Dennison & Sharman 224,
Depledge John 137,
Devenish Mrs. Kathleen 71,
Dewhirst Miss 318,
Dickinson Frank 171,
Dickinson Isaac 301,
Dickinson John 170, 171, 249, 331,
Dickinson Joseph 171,
Dickinson William 147, 170, 171,
Dickinson & Platt 288,
Dickson Nathaniel 167,
Dodson & Kenyon 304,
Dobroyd Mills Co. 224, 315,
Dobroyd Mills Co Ltd, 225, 257, 267, 315,
Dollive Fred 98,
Donkersley John 83,
Donkersley J.W. 125,
Donkersley B. & J. 235,
Donkersley B. & W. 335,
Donnolly A.F.J. 213,
Dore (Dorr) Samuel 22,
Dover Woollens Ltd. 160,
Downing J.W. 39,
Downtry/Daintry/Daltry 133,
D.P. Dyers 71, 330,
Drake Samuel & Sons 211, 303,
Dransfield Thomas 209, 210,
Drury Abraham 275,
Duckett Brian 175,
Dunkley J. R. 81,
Dunsley Heating Appliance Co. 127,
Dyson Mrs. Elizabeth 135,
Dyson Dr. 294, 322,
Dyson George 62, 104,
Dyson John 221, 311, 312,
Dyson Major John 133, 135,
Dyson Jennett Henry 135,
Dyson Joseph 133, 135,
Dyson Mary Ann 308,
Dyson Thomas 194, 195,
Dyson Mr. and Mrs. 73,

E

Eagleton J Messrs. 262,
Earnshaw Police Constable 189,
Earnshaw Abraham 236,
Earnshaw Alice 283,
Earnshaw Benjamin 146,

Earnshaw D. 211,
Earnshaw James 103,
Earnshaw John 88, 104, 106, 146, 236,
Earnshaw Joseph 198,
Earnshaw Joshua 104, 144,
Earnshaw Rev. Joshua 106,
Earnshaw J. & Sons 104,
Earnshaw Lawrence 15,
Earnshaw Tedbur 104,
Earnshaw Mr. 196,
Earnshaw Sub-Inspector 301,
Eastwood's 283,
Eastwood Benjamin 194,
Eastwood Edmund 194, 211,
Eastwood H.H. 314,
Eastwood James 136, 194,
Eastwood Jonas 96,
Eastwood Joshua 196,
Eastwood William 201,
Eastwood Bros. 225, 314, 315,
Eastwood G.F. & L. 319,
Eddison, Taylor & Booth 241,
Eddlestone Thomas 138,
Eddlestone William 138,
Elders International Wool (U.K.) Ltd. 143,
Ellis Amos 246,
Ellis J. & T. 107,
Ellis John 167,
Ellis Jonathon 124,
Ellis Robert & Son 124,
Ellis & Co. 162,
Elmsall William 320,
England G.W. 183,
England James 231,
England Thomas 244,
England D. & R. (Hudds) Ltd. 255,
England F. & Sons 183,
England William 265,
Ensor C.T. 305,
Ewart Charles 248,
Exley George 179, 227,

F

Fairburn Mary Taylor 195,
Fallas Elizabeth 177,
Fallas James 177,
Fallas John 161, 177,
Fallas Joseph 234,

Falshaw Mr. 58,
Farrand Mr. 333,
Farrar Elizabeth 138,
Farrar George 47, 65, 66, 137, 138, 139,
     144, 156, 328,
Farrar George Crosland 329,
Farrar G.W. 309, 327,
Farrar James 137,
Farrar James Hobson 66, 138,
Farrar John 248,
Farrar John Hobson 137, 138,
Farrar Hobson 47,
Farrar Mary 138,
Farrar Sarah 144,
Farrar Thomas 137, 226, 230, 327,
Farrar & Co. 329,
Farrar George & Co. 138, 226,
Fawcett Walter 251,
Fearne John 283,
Fearnlea Mending Co. 127,
Fein W. & Sons Ltd. 143, 196,
Fenton James Crosland 100,
Fenton Lewis 249,
Firth Allen 302,
Firth John 106, 136, 249,
Fisher Mr. 173,
Fisher Plastics 299,
Fitton Benjamin 234,
Fitton Charles 'Ancient' 189,
Floyd Aaron 230,
Floyd Cookson Stephenson 255, 256,
Floyd Mary 255, 256,
Foster Joseph 25,
Fothergill Joseph 291,
Fothergill Tomas 291,
Fox Allen 293,
Fozzard Charles 96,
Fozzard Edward 161,
France Benjamin 313,
France Charles Henry 313,
France Emma 313,
France George 313,
France James 80,
France John 92,
France John William 271, 313,
France Josiah 43, 292, 313, 335, 335,
France Nathan 313,
France Penelope 335,

France Benjamin & Sons 313,
France & Beaumont 271,
France, Eastwood & Co. 261, 282, 283,
France David & Co. 298, 305,
France John & Son 271,
Fretwell Matthew 289,
Furniss Alice 95,
Furniss George 95,
Furniss John 66, 95,
Furniss Mrs. L. 95,
Furniss Ruth 95,
Furniss William 95,

G
Gamma Beta Holdings Ltd. 112, 229,
Gardiner James 85, 124,
Garlick Abel 47, 81,
Garlick Solomon 47, 81,
Garside David 315,
Gartside Benjamin 86,
Gartside Firth 86, 87, 101, 277, 278,
Gartside George 53, 171, 177, 178, 179,
     180, 181,
Gartside Giles 277, 278,
Gartside Hannah 162,
Gartside Harriet 278,
Gartside J. & G. 32,
Gartside John 113, 177, 178, 278,
Gartside Mary 86, 179, 180,
Gartside Mrs. 53,
Gartside William 86, 177,
Gartside William Booth 277, 278,
Gee Mr. 142, 173, 261, 336,
Gelpack 305,
Gibson Mr. 145,
Gill Alfred 204,
Gill Eliza 322,
Gleadall Charles 218, 220,
Gledhill Joah 318,
Gledhill Thomas 290,
Gledhill Walter 192,
Gledhill Bros. 310,
Gledhill & Brook 69, 181, 183,
Gledhill Mark & Sons Ltd. 214,
Gledhill & Roberts 328,
Gledhill Walter & Son 192,
Goddard George 113, 249,
Goddard John 113, 225, 231,

Goddard Jonathon 113, 221,

Goodman John 234,

Gott Benjamin 24,

G.R. Knitwear 315,

Graham Hewley 266,

Graham Mr. 141,

Graham & Barnfather 261,

Graham & Pott 42, 241, 255, 262,

Greame Henry 106,

Greame John Earnshaw 107,

Greasley W.H. 19,

Greaves Lydia 256,

Greaves Roland M. 174,

Greaves William 258,

Green Allan 334,

Green Anthony 106, 107,

Green Benjamin 85, 102, 103,

Green Christopher 99, 120,

Green Edmund 85, 95,

Green Emma 334,

Green George 249, 250,

Green Hurst 108, 109,

Green James 85,

Green John 103, 249,

Green Joseph 99,

Green Samuel 266,

Green S. & Co. 266,

Greensmith John 150,

Greenwood Frank 98,

Greenwood George 161, 190, 191, 198,
    210, 271,

Greenwood Joseph 97, 98, 325,

Greenwood Joseph Albert 98,

Greenwood Joseph Benjamin Hepworth 98,

Greenwood J.F. 136,

Greenwood Lucy (nee Green) 98,

Greenwood Miss 272,

Greenwood Thomas 269,

Greenwood William 303,

Greenwood J. Sons & Co. 94, 97, 99, 305,

Greenwood, Senior & Greenwood 191,

Greenwood Walter & Sons 68, 135, 136,
    191, 294, 330,

Gudgeon Christopher 219,

H

Habasco International 305,

Hadfield Eric Ltd. 174,

Hadfield Eric (Yarns) Ltd. 174,

Hadfield John 237,

Hadfield Moses 146,

Haigh Ann 156, 328,

Haigh Ben 333,

Haigh Benjamin 151, 330,

Haigh Charles 181, 297,

Haigh David 188, 226,

Haigh Dr. 322,

Haigh Edward 297, 330, 331,

Haigh Eliza Ann 297,

Haigh George 19, 146, 226, 240, 285, 294,

Haigh George Armitage 297, 298,

Haigh George Roberts 184, 188,

Haigh Hezekiah 308,

Haigh Hiram 261,

Haigh James 113, 156, 248,

Haigh John 85, 144, 156, 230, 285, 294, 321,

Haigh John Roberts 184,

Haigh Jonathon 263,

Haigh Joseph 269, 277,

Haigh Joshua 297,

Haigh Keith 225,

Haigh Martha 156,

Haigh Mary 282, 295, 297,

Haigh Matt. 206,

Haigh Nicholas 11, 136,

Haigh Peter 233,

Haigh Richard 113, 269, 277, 285,

Haigh Robert 308,

Haigh Ruth 297,

Haigh Samuel 151, 187, 297,

Haigh Sarah 188,

Haigh S. 199,

Haigh Thomas 11, 103, 136, 144, 151,
    156, 297,

Haigh Thomas Mellor 185,

Haigh Webster 156,

Haigh William 194, 224, 225, 282, 303,

Haigh William Joseph 285,

Haigh J. & Son 285,

Haigh John & Co. 285,

Haigh James Ltd 186,

Haigh W. & Son 127,

Hall Joe 326,

Hall Joshua 59,
Hall Robert 165,
Hallas Robert & Co. 66,
Hallas Samuel 294,
Halliday John 220,
Halstead James 256,
Halstead William 256,
Halstead & Co. 256,
Hammond Joshua 188,
Hampshire David 146, 300,
Hampshire Matthew 146, 300,
Hampshire Jonas 226,
Hanson James 294,,
Hanson Joshua 294,
Hardy Thomas 120, 218, 226, 232,
Hardy William 120,
Hargreaves Elizabeth 100,
Hargreaves James 15, 23, 100,
Hargreaves John 167,
Hargreaves Samuel Brown 291,
Harrison David 120,
Harrison H.B. & Co. 292,
Harrop James 137, 258,
Hargreaves Mrs. 326,
Hargreaves Robert 188,
Hargreaves Thomas 326,
Harmer Rev. James 22,
Harpin John 59, 116, 117, 122, 130, 131,
     171, 200, 230, 250,
Hartley Sidney and Mrs. 73-5,
Hastings Charles 100,
Hatfield Joseph 237,
Hebblethwaite & Haigh 295,
Heap Allen 321, 322, 323,
Heap Alexander 84,
Heap David 322, 323,
Heap Edward 194, 321,
Heap Frederick 66, 280,
Heap George 280,
Heap John 194, 219, 301,323,
Heap Jonathon 28, 280,
Heap Joseph 219, 220, 226, 232, 248, 280,
     322, 323,
Heap Joshua 220, 280, 322,
Heap Mark 66, 194, 280,
Heap Martin 280,
Heap Richard Ross 84, 85, 321,
Heap Robert 280,

Heap Sarah 220,
Heap William 219,
Heap Rev. W. H. 213,
Heap R.R. & A. 85,
Heap John & Sons 194,
Heap Joseph & Sons 280,
Heap Joshua & Sons 66,
Heap & Walker 321, 322,
Heathcote John 138,
Heathcote Mary 138,
Heaton George 332,
Heaton Thomas 291,
Heaton & Sykes 291,
Hebblethwaite George Morehouse 255,
Hebblethwaite H. 81,
Heeley Harry 274, 275,
Hellawell Charles 328,
Hellawell Daniel 248,
Hellawell Mr. 172,
Helm H. 174,
Hemmingway (boy) 211,
Hepponstall Law 290,
Hepworth David 120,
Hepworth Iron Co. 231,
Heward Betty 84,
Heward Caleb 82,
Heward Edward 82,
Hey Arthur 281,
Hey George 265,
Hey John 292,
Heywood John Pemberton 219,
Heywood Yarns 196, 323,
Hill Charles 122,
Hill Edward 88,
Hinchliff Cassandra 87, 88,
Hinchliff Charles 219,
Hinchliff David 153,
Hinchliff Elkanah 55,
Hinchliff Henry 219,
Hinchliff James 88,
Hinchliff John 153,
Hinchliff Sarah Ann 153,
Hinchliff William 153,
Hinchliffe Aaron 79,
Hinchliffe Abraham 189,
Hinchliffe Allen 260,
Hinchliffe Allen & Sons 129,
Hinchliffe Ann 218,

Hinchliffe Charles 102,
Hinchliffe David 177, 180,
Hinchliffe Ely 150,
Hinchliffe Ernest 283,
Hinchliffe Fanny 145,
Hinchliffe George 144, 152, 158, 159, 164, 254,
Hinchliffe G.H. 169,
Hinchliffe Grace 312,
Hinchliffe Hannah 160,
Hinchliffe Herbert 231, 254,
Hinchliffe Hugh 88,
Hinchliffe James 80, 137, 144, 145,
Hinchliffe Jill M. 161,
Hinchliffe John 26, 121, 133, 165, 217,
    218, 219, 220, 237, 312,
Hinchliffe John & Co. 218,
Hincliffe John & Sons 238,
Hinchliffe Jonas 79,
Hinchliffe Jonathon 234,
Hinchliffe Joseph 144, 152, 301,
Hinchliffe Mark 102,
Hinchliffe Mary 144,
Hinchliffe Sarah 144,
Hinchliffe Tom 254,
Hinchliffe Thomas 311,
Hinchliffe James & Sons 190.
Hinchliffe Thomas 237, 301,
Hinchliffe & Heap 301,
Hinchliffe Thomas & Sons 124, 131, 301,
Hinchliffe & Taylor 156,
Hinchliffe Wright & Co. Ltd. 68, 142, 261,
Hinchliffe Z. & Sons Ltd. 112, 225,
Hinchliffe & Horncastle 165, 166, 167,
Hinchliffe Mill Cooperative Society Ltd. 170,
Hirst Abraham 112, 194,
Hirst Brook 283,
Hirst Charles 235,
Hirst Edmund 133,
Hirst Edward 93,
Hirst Edward & Sons 39, 224, 231, 233,
    235, 236,
Hirst James 89, 153, 184,
Hirst Jane 93,
Hirst John 52, 95, 96, 203, 218, 255, 256,
    278, 315,
Hirst Joseph 255,
Hirst Joshua 96, 326,
Hirst J.B. 117,

Hirst George 58, 61, 65, 96, 203,
Hirst Hannah 96,
Hirst Lewis 69,
Hirst Mary 96, 333,
Hirst Miss 309,
Hirst Matthew 133,
Hirst Reuben 89,
Hirst Thomas 94,
Hirst William 233, 255, 256,
Hirst A.F. & Co. 241,
Hirst & Read (Textiles) Ltd. 241,
Hobson Ely 150,
Hobson Firth 83,
Hobson George 103, 210,
Hobson Joe 282,
Hobson John 52, 137, 209, 210, 255,
Hobson Jonas 104, 209, 210, 263,
Hobson Jonathon 209,
Hobson Joseph 210,
Hobson Leonard 214,
Hobson Mary Elizabeth Morehouse 255,
Hobson Marley 258,
Hobson Thomas 209,
Hobson William 83,
Hobson Jonas & Co. 309,
Hobson L. (Rugs) Ltd. 214, 215,
Hobson's Choice 205,
Hodgkinson John & Sons 318, 319,
Holdam William 218,
Holden William 258,
Holesworth James 146,
Hollingworth Allen 83,
Hollingworth Brook 154,
Hollingworth Fred & Son 127,
Hollingworth James 97,
Hollingworth John 131,
Hollingworth Mary H, 90,
Hollingworth Sam. 206,
Hollingworth Mr. 195,
Holme Rug Co. 305,
Holme Valley Dyeworks Ltd, 142,
Holme Valley Patterns 305,
Holme Valley Textiles Ltd. 277,
Holmes Brian 137,
Holmes C. 127,
Holmes Edwin 260, 261, 263,
Holmes Francis 230,
Holmes Frank 141,

Holmes Henry 139, 230,
Holmes Hubert 261, 262,
Holmes Hugh 261,
Holmes Isaac 230,
Holmes James 182, 230,
Holmes James Francis 139,
Holmes John 261, 262,
Holmes Jonas 226,
Holmes Jonathon 230, 260,
Holmes Joseph 230,
Holmes Thomas 230,
Holmes William 230,
Holmes, Heaton & Co. 298, 299,
Holmes James & Sons 139, 141, 230,
Holmes Taylor & Co. 241,
Holmfirth Dyers Ltd. 175,
Holmfirth Motor Co. 182,
Holroyd Edward & Sons 206, 262, 296,
Holroyd F. 172,
Holroyd John 221,
Holroyd Joseph 94,
Holroyd Mr. 285,
Holt John 133,
Holt William 263,
Holt, machine makers 271,
Honley Dyeing Co. 335,
Honley Worsted Mills 305,
Horn John 245,
Hornblower Dr. 253,
Horncastle James 146, 165, 171,
Horncastle, Buckley & Co. 171,
Horrocks William 19, 209,
Horsfall David 260,
Horsfall John William 212, 266,
Horsfall Richard 268,
Horsfall William 24, 25,
Howard Caleb, 79, 82,
Howard D. 184,
Howard Edward 82,
Howard John 79, 153,
Howard Moses 79,
Hoyle Charles & Co. 246,
Hoyle Ely 66, 1161, 162,
Hoyle James 211, 234,
Hoyle Joshua 66, 124, 179, 211,
Hoyle Sarah 146,
Hoyle T.H. & Sons 323, 334,
Huddersfield Fine Worsteds 276, 277,

Hudson John 161,
Hudson Joseph 199,
Hudswell Anne 167,
Hunt Henry 27,
Hutchinson & Hollingworth 97, 111, 220,
Hynchecliff John 106, 249,

I

Ibbotson Sarah 165,
Illingworth Morris group 277, 305,
Ingham Joshua 278, 331,
Ingham W. 331,
Irving John 162,
Iveson Thomas 144, 325,

J

Jacomb William 61,
Jagger Mary 11, 300, 330,
Jagger Joseph 284, 285,
Jenkinson Allen 282,
Jessop George 130, 165,
Jessop Noah 89,
Johnson John 234, 274,
Johnson W.T. 330,
Jones Police Constable 311,
Jowitt Joseph 219,
Jowitt Thomas 156,
Joyce G.W. 301,
JT Knitting 225,
Jubb Charles 304,
Jubb Sydney 258,
Jubb Willie 323,
Jubilee Rug Co. 262,
Julie Miss Fashions 241,

K

Kay John 15,
Kaye Alex 246,
Kaye David 82,
Kaye Elizabeth 150,
Kaye Eunice 261,
Kaye Humphrey 150,
Kaye Sir John 11, 330,
Kaye J.H. 261,
Kaye Joseph 277, 303,
Kaye R.H. 308,
Kaye Sarah Ann 290,

Kaye Thomas 133,
Kaye William 84,
Kaye Mr. 134, 234,
Kaye Mrs. 256,
Kaye & Barnfather 141,
Kaye C.T. & Co. 141,
Kaye & Crowther 261,
Kaye Levi & Co. 165,
Kaye & Messenger Ltd. 69,
Kaye & Rhodes 124,
Kaye Inspector 301,
Keeling Mr. 26,
Kellett Charles 291,
Kellett William Henry 291,
Kellett Charles & Son 291,
Kellett & Scott 288-9, 290, 291,
Kenion John 86,
Kenion/Kennion/Kenyon Widow 86,
Kenyon Eli 113,
Kenworthy Harry 70,
Kenworthy James 196,
Kidd Mr. 157,
Kidd & Bentley 261,
Kidd & Jessop 227,
Kilburn Jonathon 285,
Kilner Jeremy 155,
Kinder Hannah 270,
Kinder Jonathon 137,
Kinder William 92,
Kinder Mrs. 271,
King Dr. 251,
Kirk John 66,
Kirk Joseph 137,
Kirk & Mellor 66,
Knight Abraham 302,
Knight Allen 126,
Knowles Harpin 282,
Knowles Joseph 162,
Knutton Albert 326,
Knutton John 211,
Knutton Mary 210,

L
de Lacy Henry 8,
Lancashire & Yorkshire Tulketh Group 262,
Lancaster Arnold 272,
Lancaster Brook 272,
Lancaster Charles H. 272,

Lancaster James 67, 272,
Lancaster J. & J. 201, 272,
Lancaster J. & Son Ltd. 69, 272,
Larder Thomas 135,
Lawrence Charles 288, 289,
Lawson Henry 199,
Lawton & Co. 173, 174,
Lawton C. 183,
Lawton David 84,
Lawton Elizabeth 245,
Lawton Fred 145, 241,
Lawton William 313,
Lawton Fred & Sons 191, 241,
Lawton George, Son & Hoyle 145,
Laycock John 302,
Leake Edmund 79,
Leake Edward 79,
Leake John 79,
Leake Joseph 79,
Leake Rachel 79,
Leake Sarah 79,
Leake Thomas Wain 79, 80,
Leake William 79,
Learoyd F. 260,
Learoyd Bros. 276,
Learoyd, Learoyd & Mallinson 291,
Learoyd Mr. 313,
Leather George 57, 58, 59, 61, 63, 64,
Leather George & Son 57,
Lee Dr. 333,
Lee Harry 324,
Lee James 206,
Lee Joseph 120,
Lees Benjamin 317,
Lees Dr. Edward 309, 312,
Lees Tom & Co. 224, 324, 330,
Lehane, MacKenzie & Shand Ltd. 91,
Leigh William 210,
Lewis James 22,
Lindley Mr. 55,
Lindley Roy 323,
Lisle John 322,
Littlewood Abraham 161, 162, 265,
Littlewood Albert 329,
Littlewood Ben 303,
Littlewood Charles E. 296,
Littlewood Elizabeth 162,
Littlewood Edmund 250,

Littlewood France 296,
Littlewood Fred 296,
Littlewood Hannah 162,
Littlewood Henry 194,
Littlewood Hiram 194,
Littlewood John & Sons 66, 280,
Littlewood John 92, 160, 168, 169, 280,
Littlewood Joshua 59, 61, 161, 165, 166,
    167, 168,
Littlewood Lupton 280, 309, 328,
Littlewood Mary 92, 162,
Littlewood Mr. 234,
Littlewood Nathan 75,
Littlewood Nicholas 249,
Littlewood Mrs. 314,
Littlewood Rachel 110,
Littlewood Richard 260, 309,
Littlewood T. 329,
Littlewood Tom E. 296, 299,
Littlewood Thomas 150, 160, 296, 298,
Littlewood Wright Charlesworth 292, 314,
Littlewood Tom 296,
Littlewood Charles & Co. 296, 298,
Littlewood John & Sons 309,
Littlewood's Ltd. 214,
Liversedge David 290,
Liversedge Tom 293,
Liversedge J. & A. 323,
Liversedge Tom & Sons Ltd. 330,
Lockhead John 261,
Lockwood Ann 263,
Lockwood Arthur 252, 261,
Lockwood Ben 164,
Lockwood Bernard Ambrose 252,
Lockwood Bros. 39, 191, 228,
Lockwood Chas. & Sons 39, 252, 253,
Lockwood Charles 159, 250, 251, 252, 261,
Lockwood Charles Markham 252,
Lockwood Eliza Ann 252, 253,
Lockwood Ellis 302,
Lockwood Garnet Ellis 302,
Lockwood George 304,
Lockwood James 227, 235,
Lockwood John 232, 251,
Lockwood Kenyon 227,
Lockwood Lilly 252, 253,
Lockwood Mary Ann 252, 253,
Lockwood Sarah 100, 263,

Lockwood Tom 302, 310,
Lockwood Vavince 125,
Lockwood William 117, 123, 124, 130, 156,
Lockwood W.H. 182,
Lockwood W.J. 254,
Lockwood & Sons 302,
Lockwood & Turner 132,
Lockwood & Markham 250,
Lodge James 289,
Lodge Walter 201,
Lodge George & Sons 294,
Longbottom J. &J.W. 69,
Longbottom Vernon 277,
Longworth Edward 266,
Longworth, Wiley & Rowley 266,
Lord Jane 219,
Lord J.C. 335,
Lord W.H. 335,
Lovett William 27,
Lumb James 174,
Lumb & Thompson 154,

M

Macauley C.H. 240,
McWaterhouse Mr. & Mrs. 321,
Magdale Spinning Co. 277, 323,
Magdale Textiles 324,
Makin Mary 230,
Malkin Thomas 230,
Mallilieu Herbert 329,
Mallinson George 291,
Mallinson Albert & Sons 254,
Marsden Alfred 213,
Marsden Alice Jane 200,
Marsden Eliza 62,
Marsden John 144, 237,
Marsden Jonas 144,
Marsden Joseph 150, 153, 220, 308,
Marsden S. Worsted Mills Ltd. 305,
Marsh Crosland 292,
Marsh John 139,
Marsh Mr. H, 109,
Marsh Norman 99, 305,
Marshall Lydia 213,
Marshall Thomas 210,
Marshall William 219,
Marshall, Lodge & Co. 241,
Marston William 226,

Martin Mary 156,
Martin Dr. Thomas 156,
Martin Dr. Thomas Haigh 156,
Martin William Day 65, 156,
Mathewman John 103,
Matthewman Richard 136,
Mayhall J. 179,
Meake Rev. Robert 8,
Meller Mr. R, 80, 253,
Mellor Abraham 312,
Mellor Andrew 239,
Mellor A.P. 185,
Mellor Benjamin 66, 138, 168, 184, 185,
    301, 303, 304,
Mellor Catherine 151,
Mellor Charles Alfred 200, 201, 202,
Mellor Edwin 210,
Mellor Friend 169,
Mellor George 25, 117,
Mellor Godfrey 197, 198, 205, 281,
Mellor Hugh 260,
Mellor James 302, 303,
Mellor John 198, 249, 263,
Mellor Jonathon 151,
Mellor Joseph 123, 130, 150, 198, 199,
    210, 211, 258,
Mellor Joseph R. 185, 257, 260,
Mellor Joshua 210,
Mellor J.W. 254, 286,
Mellor Mr. 258,
Mellor Paul 302,
Mellor Richard 309,
Mellor Samuel 52, 210, 258, 270, 271,
Mellor T. 232,
Mellor Thomas 197, 198, 199, 201, 270,
Mellor William 66,
Mellor Wright 290,
Mellor B. & Sons Ltd. 69, 186,
Mellor Benjamin & Sons 185,
Mellor Godfrey & Sons 198, 199, 201,
Mellor Joseph & Sons 66, 205, 282,
Mellor Josh & Sons 195,
Mellor Thomas & Sons 200,
Mellor C. & A. & Co. 271,
Mellor Messrs. 198,
Messenger Messrs. 71,
Metcalfe Cuthbert 158,
Metcalfe Leonard 158,

Metcalfe Richard 158,
Mettrick H. 182, 183,
Mettrick James 107, 266,
Mettrick Jonathon 236,
Midgeley Frederick 102,
Midgeley F.W. 91,
Midgeley John 101,
Midgeley Jonathon 101,
Miles Thomas 95,
Mills Herbert 330,
Milner Edward 248,
Milner Thomas 125,
Milnes John 219, 229,
Mitchell Charles 269,
Mitchell Henry 298,
Mitchell John 232,
Mitchell Jonathon 232,
Mitchell Joseph 233,
Mitchell Richard 240,
Mitchell & Bower 282,
Mitchell & Shaw 323,
Moll Springs Dyeing Co. 327,
Moody Captain (Royal Engineers) 62, 63, 64,
Moon Charles 263, 266,
Moon Charles Executors 266,
Moon Charles Successors Ltd. 267,
Moorbottom Manufacturing Co. 311,
Moore Joshua 291,
Moorhouse Benjamin 217, 218,
Moorhouse Christopher 113, 217, 218,
    220, 230,
Moorhouse Daniel 151,
Moorhouse Elizabeth 218,
Moorhouse Eli 235, 238, 258,
Moorhouse F.W. 254,
Moorhouse George 151, 170, 171, 266,
Moorhouse James 100, 150, 220, 221, 229,
    230, 231, -
Moorhouse John 94, 150, 151, 170, 218,
    232, 233,
Moorhouse Jonathon 151, 221, 235, 260,
Moorhouse Joshua 53, 133, 140, 164, 170, 171,
Moorhouse Joseph 146, 170, 171,
Moorhouse Ken. 127,
Moorhouse Kenneth 267,
Moorhouse Marion 267,
Moorhouse Marjorie 254,
Moorhouse Mary 151,

Moorhouse Matthew 170, 220, 221, 229, 230,
Moorhouse Samuel 100, 101,
Moorhouse Sydney 54,
Moorhouse Thomas 150, 151,
Moorhouse Tom & Co. 151,
Moorhouse William 170, 217, 218, 221,
  230, 258,
Moorhouse & Brook Ltd. 253,
Moorhouse Bros. 221,
Moorhouse Chris. & Co. 231,
Moorhouse & Dickinson 170,
Moorhouse John & Sons 228,
Morehouse Ellen Elizabeth 263,
Morehouse George 255, 263, 264,
Morehouse Dr. Henry James 108, 177,
  208, 236, 245, 252, 253, 263,
Morehouse John 255,
Morehouse John Clare Earnshaw 104,
Morehouse John William 263,
Morehouse Jonathon 264,
Morehouse Joshua 135, 179,
Morehouse Mary Beatrice 105,
Morehouse Mrs. 235,
Morehouse Sarah 263, 263,
Morehouse Sydney 135, 234,235, 255, 278,
Morehouse Thomas 106, 107, 255, 263,
Morehouse William John 258,
Morehouse William Jonathon 263, 264,
Morley Police Constable 291,
Morton George 180, 234,
Morton James 58,
Mosley Albert and Edna 298,
Moss Joe 295,
Moss John 296,
Moss Mary 270,
Motley James 150, 151,
Motley Joseph 150, 151,
Motley Thomas 146, 150, 151, 156,
Moxon Joseph W. 172,
Moxon's Huddersfield 112,
Musgrave Ven. Charles 208,

N
Naylor Herbert Hirst 111,
Nelson George Noble 280, 281,
Netherton Spinning Co. 319,
Netherwood 142,
Netherwood Miles 249,

Newbold Brian 335,
Newton Arthur Blencoe 150,
Newton Isaac Parker 150,
Newton Mary 156, 213,
Newton William 196,
Noble James 17,
Norcliffe Joseph Brook 89,
Norcliffe & Jessop 89,
Norhill Yarns 127,
Normington John Muir 276,
Normington Michael 161,
Norris William 219,
Norris William John 208,
North Ben 16,
North British Rayon Co. 126, 193,
North Tom 327,
Norton Mr. 326,
Norton William 36,

O
Oastler Richard 19, 33, 37,
Oldfield Saville 312,
Oldham G.H. 327,
Oldham George T. 326, 327,
Oldham George William 323, 327,
Oldham Harry 326,
Oldham Henry 327,
Oldham John 219,
Oldham H. & J. 234,
Oldroyd Frank 303,
O'Regan Mr. 266,
Owen George 324,
Owen James Richard 263, 265,
Oxley Mr. 234,

P
Parker Richard 335,
Parker Robert 219,
Parkhead Textiles 146,
Parkin Inspector 189,
Parry Ernest 330,
Paterson Mr. 258,
Paton & Baldwin 246, 247,
Paul Lewis 14,
Peace Thomas 219,
Pearson Albert 206,
Pearson William 327,

Peebles v Oswaldtwistle Council 314,
Peel Robert 28,
Pickering Edith 204,
Pinck W. Dr. 240, 246,
Pinder Amos 290,
Pinder Elias 269,
Pinder Henry 269,
Pitt & Co. 39,
Pitts George 239,
Pitt William & Co. 240,
P.J. Textiles 205,
Place Francis 27,
Platt K.K. 135,
Platt Thomas B. 334,
Pogson Abraham & Bros. 127,
Pogson Messrs. 66,
Pogson John 154,
Pole Charles 160,
Pole Sir Peter 160,
Pollitt & Wigzell Ltd. 111, 123, 125,
Pontefract Gamaliel 249,
Pontefract Henry 260, 263, 264, 281, 302,
Pontefract Joseph 302, 308,
Pontefract Mary 249,
Pontefract & Owen 265,
Porritt Richard 168,
Porritt Robert John 322,
Porter David 59, 63,
Porter George 58, 63,
Preston Arthur 147, 172, 174,
Preston Augustus George 248,
Preston James 247,
Preston John Mills 258, 259,
Preston Joseph 161,
Preston Julia Ann 174,
Preston Walter 172, 174,
Preston Whitfield 202,
Price Jonathon 160,
Pridie Rev. James 317,
Priest Benjamin 144,
Priestley Edmund 272,
Prince James Turner 88,
Prior J.D. 91, 191, 201, 261, 275, 283, 309, 326,
Priestley A. Vickerman 202,

Q
Queen Carriage Co. 261,
Quinn Bridget 201,
Quinn John 190,

R
Radcliffe Abraham 257,
Radcliffe Charles 210, 258,
Radcliffe James 122, 311,
Radcliffe John 209,
Radcliffe John & Sons 154,
Radcliffe Joseph 330,
Radcliffe Lucretia Constance 210,
Radcliffe Thomas 209, 212, 258, 260,
Radcliffe William 187,
Ramsden James 100,
Ramsden John 268,
Ramsden Lister 261,
Ramsden Robert 156, 179,
Robert Ramsden & Co. 157,
Ramsden Bros. Dyers 242,
Ramsden, Sykes & Ramsden 266,
Rankin R.W. 142,
Ratcliffe Richard 12,
Rawcliffe James 315,
Rayner Joseph 100,
Rayner Thomas H. 256,257,
Rayner T.H. & Sons 257,
Reckitts Charles 283,
Regan John 323,
Rennard & Gartside 196,
Rhodes Mary Ann 100,
Rhodes Samuel 291,
Rhodes Thomas 141, 212,
Rhodes Wright 52,
Rhodes Dr. 245,
Richardson John 171,
Ridgwick Eli 102,
Riley Donald 69,
Riley Geoffrey 69,
Rimmington Elizabeth 144,
Rimmington James 137,
Rimmington John 137,
Riverside Mending Co. 277,
Roberts Abraham 285,
Roberts Arthur Henry 111,
Roberts Ben 238,
Roberts David 133, 137,

Roberts Elizabeth 138,
Roberts Ely 144,
Roberts George 83, 135, 168, 188, 249,
Roberts Gordon 111, 112,
Roberts Green 135,
Roberts Hannah 111,
Roberts G. & H. Ltd. 111, 112,
Roberts Henry 111,205,
Roberts Hugh 138,
Roberts James 330,
Roberts John 83, 110, 111, 112, 135, 167,
Roberts John William 82,
Roberts Jonas 188,
Roberts Jonathon 110, 111, 113, 131, 133, 135,
Roberts Joseph 106, 135, 168, 208, 218,
    237, 255, 256, 258, 330,
Roberts Mrs. Joseph (widow) 330,
Roberts Mary 110,
Roberts Miss 89,
Roberts Mr. 199,
Roberts Nathaniel 226,
Roberts Richard 17,
Roberts Samuel 111,
Roberts Thomas 133,
Roberts William 110, 133, 135, 309,
Roberts W.E. 108,
Roberts & Sandford 133,
Robertshaw Edward 298,
Robertshaw Joseph 234,
Robinson George 66, 198, 270, 278, 280,
Robinson James 66, 67, 198, 270, 271,
    278, 280, 281, 282, 313,
Robinson John 131, 278, 279, 327,
Robinson Joseph 282,
Robinson Joshua 32, 197, 278,
Robinson R. 263,
Robinson R.L. 69, 71, 202, 203, 305,
Robinson W.B. 272,
Robinson William Cross 285,
Robinson W. H. 112, 282, 283, 284,
Robinson James & Sons 273, 283,
Rochdale Pioneer Cooperative Soc. 258,
Rodgers John 93,
Roebuck Eli 99, 100,
Roebuck Emma 204,
Roebuck Francis 255,
Roebuck George 220,
Roebuck Jarvis 255,

Roebuck John 61, 99, 100, 255, 256,
Roebuck Jonas 99,
Roebuck Jonathon 99, 308, 311,
Roebuck Joseph 156,
Roebuck Mrs. (widow) 220,
Roebuck William 99. 100,
Rollinson G. 133,
Rollinson William 173,
Rowan Weavers/Rowan Yarns 158, 165,
Rowbottom Henry 318,
Rowley John 233, 236,
Rowley Edward 266,
Rowley Stephen 236,
Ryder James 7,

S
Sadler M.J.
Salts Ltd. Saltaire 336,
Sanders J. 171,
Sanderson Abraham 82,
Sanderson Andrew 147,
Sanderson Ben 308,
Sanderson Edward 125,
Sanderson George 198,
Sanderson Jessie 164,
Sanderson Jonathon 107,
Sanderson Nancy 107,
Sanderson Samuel 107,
Sandford Jonathon 123, 134, 144, 165, 250,
Sandford Samuel 133, 135,
Sandford William 144, 164, 165,
Sandford William & Son 165,
Sandy Jonas 226,
Sarwan Singh Purewal 315,
Satchwell Police Constable 310,
Saxton Jonathon 151,
Schofield David 291, 318,
Schofield Mrs. Dorothea 69,
Schofield John 26,
Schofield May 263,
Schofield William 329,
Schofield & Kirk 181,
Schofield & Littlewood 329,
Scholefield Herbert & Co. 293, 310,
Scholefield John 26, 156, 161, 162, 278,
Seddon John 185, 256, 258,
Seddon H.H. 262,
Seedhill Schofield Finishing Co. Ltd. 214,

Sellers E.H. & Sons Ltd. 228,
Sellers Lister & Co.
Senior Amos 232,
Senior Benny 206,
Senior George Henry 195,
Senior John 162,
Senior Jonathon 331,
Senior Sarah 162,
Senior Mrs. 189,
Senior T. 335,
Senior William 226,
Senior & Charlesworth 246,
Settle Police Constable 235,
Shackleton John 144,
Shackleton Richard (Dick) 75,
Shackleton Tamer 73,
Shackleton William 187, 229,
Sharman C.J. & Co. 224,
Sharp W.L. 301,
Sharpe Daniel & Son 57, 58, 63,
Sharpe Joseph 58,
Sharpe Thomas 139,
Shaw Benjamin Ledger 287, 288, 311,
Shaw David 286,
Shaw Fred 94,
Shaw Frederick 210, 271, 321,
Shaw Foster 288, 290,
Shaw James 88, 116, 117, 288, 290, 311,
Shaw John 220,
Shaw Jonathon 161,
Shaw Joseph 234,
Shaw Nathaniel 209,
Shaw Robert 116,
Shaw Samuel 120,
Shaw Thomas 313,
Shaw Walter 310,
Shaw William 95, 152, 220, 256,
Shaw Messrs. 219,
Shaw's Ben Suncharm Ltd. 336,
Shaw D. & Co. 32, 234,
Shaw D. & Sons 83,
Shaw David, Son & Co. 286, 287, 288, 289,
Shaw G. & Sons 304,
Shaw John & Sons 310,
Shaw James & Co. 285, 312, 324,
Shaw Thomas & Co. 313,
Shaw W.L. & Sons Ltd. 323, 324,
Shaw W.O. Ltd. 214, 310,

Shaw Rayner & Sykes 256-7
Sheard C.W. 206,
Sheard Bros. 206,
Shepherd J.R. 205,
Sheratt Arthur 323,
Shore John 145,
Shore William 227,
Silk Mill Restaurant 310,
Silverwood Henry 211, 212, 283,
Silverwood Joseph 283,
Simplast Ltd. 305,
Skelton Arthur 327,
Slater Charles 288,
Slater Hannah 288,
Smith Frank 309,
Smith George 220,
Smith G.W. 311,
Smith James 94, 213, 275,
Smith Janet 213,
Smith John 286,
Smith Robert 249,
Smith Samuel 273, 274,
Smith Selwyn 165, 208,
Smith William 200,
Smith & Co. 326,
Smith Police Constable 302,
Smirthwaite George 255,
Smirthwaite Mrs. 255,
South James 126,
Spivey Thomas 197,
Spring Lane Woollen Mill 127,
Spring Lane Woollen Spinners 127,
Spurr Henry Mr. & Mrs. 103,
Stag Bethel Earnshaw 158,
Stanley Benjamin 230,
Stanley Mary 230,
Stanley Rug Co. 241, 262, 263,
Stancy Caroline 274,
Stapylton Sir Robert 11, 330,
Starbrook George 102,
Starkey George 79,
Starkey Mr. 227,
Stead William 137,
Stephen John Ltd. 205,
Stephenson Cookson 112, 225, 229,
Stephenson Thomas 295,
Stephenson William 165, 230,
Stocks Ben 97,

Stocks James 307,
Stocks & Mallinson 262, 323,
Storthes John 208,
Stott Rev. John 263,
Stumpe William 2,
Sturgis John 219,
Sutcliffe Joseph 285,
Swallow Joseph 137,
Swallow Joshua 219,
Swift & Taylor 278,
Sykes Alfred 39, 274, 276,
Sykes A.H. 276,
Sykes D. 198,
Sykes D.F.E. 30,
Sykes Edmund 86, 112,
Sykes H.B. 152,
Sykes James 134,
Sykes Jane Harrop 249,
Sykes John 9. 198, 249, 317, 322,
Sykes Joseph 67, 291, 298, 319,
Sykes George 57,
Sykes Sylvester 331,
Sykes Walter 235,
Sykes William 133, 135, 170, 249,
Sykes & Co. 142,
Sykes James & Son Ltd. 305,
Sykes Joseph & Co. 69,
Sykes Joseph & Co. Ltd. 274, 276, 277,
Sykes, Marsden & Co. 305,
Sykes, Mellor & Co. 272,
Sykes & Schofield 310,
Sykes T.H. & Co. 310,
Sykes Wm. & Co. 129, 130, 152, `182,
Sylvester Terry 127,

T

Tait John 58, 73,
Tait Hellen 74,
Tait Lydia 73,
Tattersall William 227,
Taylor Abram 236,
Taylor Abraham 151, 158, 332,
Taylor Annie 309,
Taylor Beaumont 271,
Taylor Ben 226, 227,
Taylor Edward 328,
Taylor Eliza 302,
Taylor Enoch 24,

Taylor George 137,
Taylor Hannah 302,
Taylor James 319,
Taylor Rev. John 137,
Taylor John 156,
Taylor John Thorpe 158, 172,
Taylor J.T. 290,
Taylor Joseph 226,
Taylor Martha 151,
Taylor Sarah Ann 111,
Taylor Thomas E. 323,
Taylor Turner 310,
Taylor William 232, 324,
Taylor William Chapman 109,
Taylor Wright 313,
Taylor Bros. 255,
Taylor J.T. & Co. 39, 172, 181, 273,
Taylor & Whiteley Ltd. 315,
Taylor Police Constable 301,
Thewlis Able 88, 164,
Thewlis & Co. 179,
Thewlis George 156, 179,
Thewlis G. & Sons 164,
Thewlis Joshua 137,
Thewlis Nathan 54, 66, 179,
Thewlis Nathan & Co. 179,
Thewlis v Farrar 139,
Thompson Fred 286,
Thornbank Tweeds 204,
Thornhill Thomas 33,
Thornton Benjamin 146,
Thornton Brook 266,
Thornton Charles 312,
Thornton James 146, 300,
Thornton John 182, 303,
Thornton Sarah 300,
Thornton Allen & Co. Ltd. 69, 71, 136,
Thornton Allen & Son 293, 294,
Thornton & Co. 202,
Thornton, Dodson & Co. 282,
Thornton & Green 266,
Thornton John & Co. 129,
Thornton I & T. 300,
Thornton Thomas 288,
Thorp Henry 182, 223, 256,
Thorp Hubert 223,
Thorp Jonathon 180,
Thorp Jonathon & Sons 181, 221, 236, 240, 256,

Thorp Jonathon (Successors) Ltd. 225,
Thorp Sarah 159,
Thorpe Dr. 160,
Thorpe Elizabeth 151,
Thorpe George 144,
Thorpe Jonathon 59,
Thorpe Jonathon & Co. 61,
Thorpe Jonathon & Sons 233,
Thorp & Mallinson 246,
Thristle Elizabeth 121,
Thwaite Isaac 226,
Tilscher O. & Sons 215,
Tinker Albert 119,
Tinker Arthur 101, 191,
Tinker Bros. 101,
Tinker Charles 119,
Tinker Mrs. Charles 119,
Tinker Charley 119,
Tinker Ebenezer 158,
Tinker Francis 220,
Tinker George 79, 80, 84, 101, 189, 224, 230,
Tinker George & Son 151, 191, 246,
Tinker Henry 291,
Tinker Hezekiah 237, 238,
Tinker John 96, 119, 212, 214, 220, 248, 250,
Tinker Joseph 229, 230,
Tinker Mary E. 213,
Tinker Sam 255,
Tinker Tedbur 84, 96,
Tinker Uriah 231,
Tinker A.T. & S. 220,
Tinker T. & J. 68, 84, 101, 119, 212,
Toepler Paul & Co. 122,
Tolson Joseph 331,
Tolson T.M. & Co. 302,
Topham Christopher 160,
Townend John Tackherd 225,
Townsend Benjamin 285,
Trotter Dr. 89, 98, 111,172, 181, 221, 235, 246, 253,
Troydale Industries 238,
Tudor Henry 151,
Turf Horse Clothing Co. 214,
Turner Alice 213,
Turner Ben 5, 120, 173,
Turner Fred 211,
Turner H.G. & Co. 160,
Turner James 161, 221,

Turner John 161,
Turner Joseph 161, 274,
Turner Jonathon 160, 166,
Turner Thomas 192,
Turner William 161,
Turner v Turner 161,
Turner & Bower 272,
Turner F. & Sons 261,
Turner Joseph & Sons 89, 117, 145, 180, 190, 222, 273,
Turner J.W. (Netherton) Ltd. 323,
Turton Emma 160,
Turton Rosie 254,
Tyas A.L. 172,
Tyas Christian 233,
Tyas John 233,
Tylburn George 302,
Tynan Michael 333,

U
United Box Co. 247,

V
Varley John 79,
Varley Mary 79,
Vautry William 218,
Vickerman Benjamin 331, 332,
Vickerman Enoch 331, 332, 333,
Vickerman Stephen 331,
Vickerman B. & Sons Ltd. 91, 201, 202, 206,
Victoria Carpet Co. 155,
Victoria Textiles Ltd. 214, 310,
Villiers Charles 28,
VM Fabrications 133

W
Waddington Robert Walker 289, 290,
Waddington Sarah 287, 307,
Waddington William Henry 290,
Wadsworth (girl) 167,
Wadsworth W. & Co. 190, 204, 265,
Wadsworth Edward 204,
Wadsworth John 237,
Wadsworth Jonathon 249,
Wagstaff (girl) 171,
Wagstaffe John 136,
Wagstaff Joseph 226,

Wagstaffe Thomas 187,
Wagstaffe & Turner 174,
Wainhouse Edward 208,
Walker Anne 285,
Walker Ben 322,
Walker Edward 260,
Walker Edwin & Co. 195,
Walker Emas 249,
Walker John the 10,
Walker John 208, 249,
Walker J.C. 84,
Walker Jonas 249,
Walker Joseph 260,
Walker Joshua 218, 219,
Walker Robert 260,
Walker Samuel 152, 217, 249,
Walker Samuel Harper 249,
Walker Walter 194,
Walker William 284, 285,
Walker William Henry 321, 322,
Walker Mr. 196,
Walker Mrs. 322,
Wallace Paul 309,
Wallaces Grocers 69,
Waller R.C. 169,
Warewright George Ltd. 127,
Waterhouse John 194,
Wathews Dr. J.W. 127, 174,
Watkinson James Brook 155,
Watkinson James & Son, 152, 153, 154,
    181, 191,
Watkinson James & Sons Ltd. 155, 157,
    158, 159,
Watkinson T.B. 154, 157,
Webster Hannah 160,
Webster Mary 221,
Webster Thomas 160,
Weller Sam & Sons Ltd. 193,
Wells James 92,
Wentworth Margaret 187,
Wentworth Thomas 196,
West John 11, 136,
West Rev. James 162,
Westwood Yarns 155, 156,
Whitaker Ann 137,
White Police Constable 221,
White Ramsden Police Inspector 265,
Whitehead Abraham 31,

Whitehead Charles 245, 254,
Whitehead Elizabeth 151,
Whitehead James 318,
Whitehead Sarah 151,
Whitehead Thomas 151, 204,
Whiteley Ann 95,
Whiteley Arthur 296,
Whiteley Charles F. 109,
Whiteley Charles Henry 109,
Whiteley Mrs. C.H. 109,
Whiteley Dyson 94,
Whiteley Mrs. F. 109,
Whiteley George 202,
Whiteley Hannah 95,
Whiteley Henry 108,
Whiteley James 95,
Whiteley John 62, 92, 93, 95,
Whiteley John Dyson 94,
Whiteley Joseph 58, 95,
Whiteley Thomas 109, 296,
Whiteley William 313,
Whiteley Bros. 295, 296,
Whiteley & Green 68, 108, 109,
Whiteley's machine makers 22, 140
Whitworth Fireman 262,
Whitworth Joseph 312,
Wibberley Samuel 260,
Wickam B.W.D. 132,
Wickman A.C. Ltd. 69, 305,
Wilberforce William 33,
Wild Mary 123,
Wiley John 156,
Wiley Arthur John 266,
Willis Mr. 69,
Wilson Benjamin 153,
Wilson Dr. 214,
Wilson George 12, 125,
Wilson John 153,
Wilson Joshua 257,
Wylson Anthonye 196,
Wimpenny & Bowes 107,
Wimpenny Boothroyd 201,
Wimpenny Eli(y) 107, 146, 151, 162, 265,
    266,
Wimpenny Ebenezer 162,
Wimpenny John 113, 120,
Wimpenny Joseph 159, 172,
Wimpenny Joshua 96,

Wimpenny Martin 317,
Wimpenny Maude E. 69,
Wimpenny S. 181, 256, 259, 260,
Wimpenny Uriah 88,
Wimpenny William 159,
Wimpenny H. & S. 117,
Wimpenny & Co. Ltd. 255,
Wimpenny & Bowes 266,
Winchcombe John 2,
Wincup Police Constable 253,
Winder Dr. D. 335,
Wood Abraham 146,
Wood Alfred 157, 245, 246, 247,
Wood Ben 124,
Wood Benjamin 317,
Wood Charles 235,
Wood David 250,
Wood Elizabeth 133,
Wood Ellen 134,
Wood Harriet Annie 202,
Wood Iddo 130, 250,
Wood James 95, 234, 235,
Wood John 87, 249, 278,
Wood Jonathon 250,
Wood Joseph 159,
Wood Joseph B. 157,
Wood Palti 130, 250,
Wood Robert 184,
Wood Samuel 233,
Wood Sarah 87,
Wood Thomas 270,
Wood Tola 130, 250,
Wood & Burtt 246, 247,
Woodcock John 62,
Woodcock Jonathon 61,
Woodcock Joshua 98,
Woodhead Absolom 195,
Woodhead Daniel 195, 203-4,
Woodhead George 282,
Woodhead J, 259,
Woodhead Joe 105,
Woodhead John 188, 204, 249,
Woodhead Joseph 164, 187,
Woodhead Joshua 121, 184, 188, 199,
Woodhead Matthew 188,
Woodhead Richard 184, 188, 237,
Woodhead Sarah 203,
Woodhead Thomas 103,

Woodhead William 188,
Woodhead George & Sons 201,
Woodhead John & Son 204,
Woodhead John Ltd. 69, 71, 136, 202, 206,
Woodhead William & Sons 188,
Woodhead family 131,
Woodhead Mr. 196,
Wodehede Thomas 196,
Woodhouse John 198,
Woofenden David 120,
Woofenden Joseph 133,
Woofenden Richard 162,
Woofenden Mr. 251,
Wordsworth Sarah 137,
Wormald John 200,
Worsley Jonathon 9,
Wrigley George Henry 313,
Wrigley Henry 318,
Wrigley James 317, 319,
Wrigley James Albert 317, 318,
Wrigley Joseph 318,
Wrigley Harrop 122,
Wrigley John 315,
Wrigley Robert 315, 316,
Wrigley William 317, 318,
Wrigley J. & Sons 32, 315, 319,

Y

Yates Henry Police Constable 302,
Yates W.E. 44, 238,
Yorklyde 253,
Yorkshire Fine Woollen Spinners Ltd.
    135, 204, 225,

INDEX OF SUBJECTS AND PLACES

A

Abstract of Title 249,
Aire and Calder Navigation Canal 57,
Air Raid Shelter 247, 294,
Albert mill 66, 69, 184-186,
Albion mill 69, 136, 203-205, 206, 225,
Alma mill 205-207,
Almondbury 8, 10, 100, 209, 257,
Ambulance Depot 311,
America 22, 33, 50, 52, 53, 259,
    American Civil War 266,
    American War of Independence 19, 23, 259,
Angola Yarn 260, 284, 293, 310,
Angora wool 196,
Annals of Agriculture 29,
Annual Suspending Acts 24,
Anstey Leics. 25,
Anti-Corn Law Associations 28,
    Anti-Corn Law League 28, 280,
Arlon Prize Quartet Party 299,
Armitage Bridge mills 155, 180, 195,
    Armitage Bridge mill fire brigade 272,
        273, 291, 296, 301, 304, 320, 324,
Armley Mills, Leeds 195,
    Armley Prison 314,
Arunden 9, 150,
Ashton-under-Lyne 248,
Aspley, Hudds. 210,
Austrian Troops 23,
Austonley 85, 87, 95, 100, 168, 178, 312,
    Austonley/Bank End mill 61, 62, 66, 84,
        89, 99-101, 121, 191, 212,
    Austonley Tithe 1847 101, 110,

B

Bailey's Quadrille Band 333,
Baines' Yorkshire Directory 263,
Bake-house 170,
Balance Sheet 212,
Bank Bottom Cartworth 86, 87, 112,
Bank Bottom Netherton 215,
Bankend 160, 165,
Banks The, Honley 262, 291, 296,
Banks, Lower Banks mills 284-286,
Bank House, Meltham 158,
Bankruptcy 188, 191,
    Bankruptcy Court Hudds. 271,
    Bankruptcy Court Leeds 279,
Bank Top House, Austonley 99,
Barnsley 53, 133, 151, 298,
Barnside, Hepworth 165, 219, 220,
Batley 39,
    Batley Corporation 84, 85, 91, 284,
Batty's Dam 83,
Batty's/Farrar's Upper and Lower mills
        136-144,
Batty mill Kirkheaton 331,
Bay Horse Inn Hade Edge 247,
Beaming 6,
    Beaming Frame 190, 219, 226, 245,
    Beaming Shed 310,
Beans 211,
Bedford cord 109, 160,
Beever's Overture Band 227,
Belgreave, Fulstone 250,
Bent, Wooldale 218,
Bent Lee Meltham 326,

Bentley Grange 9, 177,

Berry Brow 67, 313,

Beverley 1,

Bevin Boys 43,

Bilberry/Lum(b) Bank mill 61, 62, 66, 67, 92-94, 95, 98, 99, 100,
   Bilberry Reservoir 57, 58, 59, 60, 62, 70, 84, 87, 93, 150,
   Bilberry Res. Embankment 58, 98,
   Bilberry Res, Valve Pit 58,

Binns 156,

Birkacre nr. Chorley 23,

Birkby 39,

Birks House, Burnlee 230,

Birdsedge 39, 223, 235,

Birmingham 45, 188,

Birth Certificates 189,

Blackburn 15,

Blackpool 202, 222, 266, 286, 314,

Black Sike 218,
   Black Sike mill 56, 122, 128,
   Black Sike Dike 66-7, 122, 123, 127,

Bleaching 298,

Blenders 196,

Blue Dyehouse 122, 248,
   Blue Dyer 248

Board of management 109,

Bobbin 5,
   Bobbin Winding machine 168, 190, 211, 219, 220, 226, 245,

Boilers 328, 327,

Boiler House 154, 158, 168, 172, 195, 199, 200, 210, 233, 238, 245, 254, 273, 290, 296, 304, 308, 310, 325,

Bolling Hall Bradford 219,

Bolton Abbey 248,

Bonded Warehouse 236,

Bone Boiling Plant 292, 314,

Booth House Holmfirth 5, 111, 113, 120,

Botany Wool 46, 221,

Botham Hall 152,

Bottoms 69, 84, 125, 184,

Bottoms mill 37, 68, 70, 90, 116-120, 121, 140, 144, 150, 160, 200, 214,

Bowling Green 228,

Bowshaw Whams Reservoir 57, 150, 217, 218, 219,

Bradford, Yorks. 18, 29, 41, 42, 100, 141, 193, 213, 245, 254, 277, 298,

Bradford-on-Avon 3,

Bradley Mills Hudds. 189, 310,

Bradshaw Mill Honley 310, 310-311,
   Bradshaw Road 310,

Braithfurthe 11, 105,

Bramley Leeds 44, 238,

Bretton 137,

Brewery 298,

Brick Making 35,

Bridge Dyeworks Honley 71, 299-300,

Bridge Lane Holmfirth 69,

Bridge Mills 11, 18, 55, 56, 89, 101, 108, 117, 124, 135, 155, 186-192, 198, 200, 201, 222, 228, 238, 240, 261,
   Brigg mill 187,
   Bridge mill fire brigade 145, 157, 238, 272, 273,
   Bridge Mill Bottom 184,
   Bridge Mill Wood 192,

Bridge Tavern/Commercial Inn Holmbridge 103,

Bridlington 326,

Brigg Royd mill 268,

Brighouse 119, 293, 293,

Brighton 53,

Briscombe Glos. 22,

Bristol 89,

Brockholes 11, 135, 213, 264, 269, 275, 276, 324, 336,
   Brockholes Church 282,
   Brockholes Lane 274,
   Brockholes Station 264,

Brookfield mills, Kirkburton 160,

Brook St. Huddersfield 169, 266,

Broom Head Hall, Ecclesfield, 137,

Brow Bottom/Brownhill mills 54, 81, 82-85, 96, 97, 101, 124, 214,
   Lower Brow Bottom mill 46, 54, 82, 85,

Brow mill Honley 311,

Brown Hill 110, 150,
   Brown Hill Lane 83, 85,
   Brown Hill Reservoir 82-3, 85, 91,

Brushing mill 244, 265, 319,

Buckskin 50,
   Buckskins striped 50,

Builders yard 174,

Burling 46, 140, 210,
   Burlers/Menders 225,
   Burling Chamber 99,

Burnham, Norfolk 177,
Burnlee Holmfirth 5, 68, 116, 117, 120,
    123, 161, 162, 171,
    Burnlee/Bottoms Dyehouse 56, 122-3,
    Burnlee Road 124, 130,
Burring machine 211, 222,
Byrton (Kirkburton) 9,

C

Camel Hair 196,
Canal Bank Works Leeds Rd. Hudds. 330,
Carders 196,
Carding 2, 14, 16, 50, 106, 116, 128, 138,
    151, 156, 164, 177, 184, 188, 210, 218,
    226, 228, 273, 278, 282, 303, 315, 319,
    Carding Machine/engine 14, 16, 144,
    151, 153, 154, 157, 164, 168, 185, 197,
    204, 219, 221, 226, 238, 260, 263, 300,
Card Maker 321,
Carlisle 28,
Carr, Shepley 220,
Carr Green, Austonley 112,
    Carr Lane, Austonley 113,
Cartmell Lancs. 73, 75.
Carriage Slips 270,
Cartworth 8, 9, 10, 110, 124, 133, 146,
    152, 156, 158, 161, 165, 168, 170, 219,
    Cartworth Mill 9, 10, 177, 249,
    Cartworth Moor 150,
    Cartworth Vestry Minutes 104,
Cashmere fibre 196,
Cassimere 3, 12, 48, 50,
Castleford 160,
Cavalry Twill 109,
Cawthorne Lanes 233,
Chapel-en-le-Frith 85,
Chapel Hill Hudds 294, 322,
Charlestown, S. Carolina 209, 210, 212,
Chartist Movement 27, 287,
Cheshire 28,
Children 30,
Cinder Hills 38, 227, 243,
Chancery Court 104, 158, 161, 201, 235,
    Chancery suit 226,
Chicken Rearing 219,
Chief Registrar of Bankruptcy 313,
Choppards 9, 18, 150, 151, 152, 156,
    Choppards mill 150-152,

Church Terrace, 181,
    Churchyard Holmfirth 181,
Civil Defence 70,
Claremont Holmfirth 241,
Clarence mill Holmbridge 68, 88, 90, 91,
    112, 205,
Clayton West 36, 186,
    Clayton West Band 286,
Cleckheaton 119,
Cleethorpes 94, 98,
Cliffe House Honley 309, 329,
Clitheroe School 327,
Cloth Dresser 318,
Cloth Finisher 260, 282, 303, 313,
Cloth Hall St. 305,
Clough House Slaithwaite 170,
Clough House mill, Birkby 305,
Coach & Horses Inn Honley 298, 333,
Coal Pits 251,
    Coal Owner 297, 321,
Cocking Steps mill 32, 313, 315-319,
    Cocking Steps Bridge 315, 320,
Colne Valley 55,
Colwyn Bay 183,
Combination Acts 36,
    Combination Acts repeal 17, 36,
Combing machines 223,
Commercial Inn Honley 312,
Commission Weavers 241,
Committee of Inspection 191, 212, 296,
    313,
Committee of the Masters 38,
Concord Place Honley 293,
Condenser/sets 14, 165, 181, 190, 191,
    198, 201, 206, 211, 223, 233, 246,
    251, 253, 256, 260, 264, 295, 319,
Conscription 43,
Cook's mill, Thongsbridge 196, 197,
Cooperative Hall Honley 299,
Cooperative Supermarket 186,
Cooper Lane dyehouse 146,
Copthurst 150,
Corn Laws 27, 28, 48, 164, 280,
Corn Mills 8, 11, 177, 181, 182, 187, 188,
    196, 197, 209, 211, 229, 248, 249, 286,
    298, 300, 302, 303,
    Corn miller 294, 297, 300,
Costume cloths 233,

Cotswolds 2,
Cotton 256, 293,
  Cotton trade 19,
  Cotton Mills 30, 272,
  Cotton spinners 33, 123,
County Bridge 179, 184,
County Court Huddersfield 329, 334,
Country Work 152,
Craiglands Hydropathic Establishment
  Ilkley 318,
Creditors Meeting 189, 191, 328,
Crimble mills Golcar 274,
Crimean War 88, 107, 153, 179, 264,
  Crimea 158, 172, 333,
Crofton nr. Wakefield 322,
Cromford Derbys. 15,
Croppers/Shearmen 8, 22, 23, 24,
  Cropping/Shearing Frame 22, 23,
  Cropping Machines 22, 25,
Crosland Edge 120,
  Crosland Hall 322,
  Crosland Hill 249,
  Crosland mill 322,
  Crosland Moor 25, 83, 260,
Cross 153,
Crossley/Neiley mills Honley 18, 32, 68,
  71, 98, 234, 285, 286-294, 296, 310,
  311, 313, 314, 335,
Crossley/Neiley fire brigade 273, 301,
  320,
Crown Bottom, Holmfirth 181,
Crownest Halifax 284,
Cumberworth 86, 154,
Cunliffe Committee on Currency and
  Foreign Exchanges 41,
Curling Machine 223,
Customs Authority 236,
Cuttell Bottom Holmfirth 147, 170, 171,
  184,
  Cuttell mill Underbank 32, 162,

D
Daisy Lee, Scholes 218,
Dalry nr. Glasgow 112,
Dalton 89, 249,
Damhouse 161, 166, 168,
Damhead Hinchliffe Mill 11, 67, 68, 113,
Darlington 158,

Dartmouth Estate Office 300,
  Dartmouth Letter Books 331,
  Dartmouth Rentals 320,
  Dartmouth Terrier 300, 331,
Deadmanstone 137,
Deal, Kent 45,
Dealers 188,
Dean Dike Hepworth 221, 224,
Deanhouse Dyehouse 196, 300,
Deanhouse mill 143, 193-196, 323,
  Dean Clough, Honley 193,
  Dean Dike 193, 196,
  Deanhouse Workhouse 235,
Deed of assignment 84, 191, 211, 296,
  305, 313,
  Deed of Composition 313,
  Deed of Covenant 123,
  Deeds Registry, Wakefield 219, 315,
Denby Dale 225,
  Denby Dikeside 86,
  Denby 139,
Derby 53,
Dewsbury 39, 57, 106, 195, 254,
Digley mill, 66, 94, 97-99, 305,
  Digley Dike 57, 87, 92, 95, 98, 101,
  Digley Lower mill 58, 61, 65, 95, 96-97,
  99, 100, 203,
  Digley Reservoir 71, 94, 99,
  Digley Upper mill 50, 51, 54, 66, 81, 84,
  85, 95-96, 97, 101, 214,
Discipline in mills 31,
Distaff and Spindle 4, 17,
Distress Warrant 153,
District Medical Officer 207,
Dobb Dike 61, 103,106,
  Dobb Lane 106,
  Dobb mill/Dyehouse 102, 103-105,
Dobcross 96, 111,
  Dobcross Looms 21, 305,
Dobroyd mill 181, 204, 218, 221-225,
  233, 256, 330,
  Dobroyd Wood 221,
Doctors evidence 32,
  Doctors to examine Children 33,
Doeskin Looms 232,
Domestic Service 35,
Donegal Tweeds 299,
Dornier looms 239,

Doubling 273,

Dover Mill 9, 127, 140, 157, 158-160, 172,

Dressing shop 152, 163, 249,

Drive belts 251,

Drought 52,

Druids Hall, Holmfirth 154,

Dry Finishing 186, 253, 254,

Drysalter 187, 258,

Dry Houses/Drying Stove 7, 46, 47, 85,
    99, 100, 113, 120, 122, 123, 138, 150,
    151, 153, 154, 158, 159, 167, 168, 172,
    179, 185, 188, 189, 190, 195, 197, 199,
    200, 208, 210, 212, 219, 220, 221, 235,
    238, 240, 244, 248, 249, 253, 255, 256,
    259, 263, 264, 270, 276, 290, 291, 298,
    301, 304, 317, 320, 324, 325,

Drying Kiln 102, 187, 188, 229, 298,

Duchy Court, Lancaster 103,

Duckinfield Cheshire 248,

Dunford Bridge 53,
    Dunford Road 71, 162, 170, 174,

Dungeon mill Lockwood 318, 330,

Duke of Leeds New Mill 211, 240, 264,

Dunsley, 156,

Dyehouse 7, 46, 47, 96, 97, 100, 101, 113,
    120, 129, 138, 144, 146, 150, 151, 152,
    153, 158,160, 161, 165, 168, 172, 173,
    174, 181, 183, 193, 195, 197, 208, 210,
    211, 212, 214, 220, 221,224, 226, 231,
    233, 235, 238, 245, 246, 247, 248, 249,
    253, 259, 262, 263, 270, 271, 277, 279,
    280, 292, 296, 297, 299, 301, 304, 311,
    314, 323, 324, 325, 327, 330,

    Dyehouse Bottom New Mill 241,

    Dyehouse Machinery 206, 228, 277, 329,

    Dyeing 47, 50, 140, 253, 272, 296, 298,

    Dye Cisterns 260,

    Dye Pans 160, 211, 220, 233, 238, 263,
    277, 280, 282, 304, 318, 324, 327,

    Dyers 185, 186, 228, 272, 284,

    Dyewares 265,

    Dyeworks 329,

    Dyeing Wood 285,

    Dye vats 160, 161, 277, 327,

Dynamo 222,

Dyson's mill – see Perseverance mill.

E

East Anglia 13, 17,

East Midlands 25,

Eccup Reservoir 57,

Edgerton 238,

Edwardthorpe, Darfield 225,

Egyptian cotton 236,

'Elbie Dustless Dusters' 208,

Electric Lighting 108, 274,
    Electric Motors 156,

Elephant & Castle Inn 138, 144, 145, 167,
    180, 189, 200,

Elland Hall Farm 335,

Ellis Pond 98,

Elmwood, Netherthong 195,
    Elmwood Hospital 120,

Emley show 71,

Empire Register 99,

Employers Federation 43,

Employment of Children Act 1903: 35,

Enclosure Awards 232,

Engineering 41,

Engine House 154, 158, 172, 179, 195,
    219, 233, 238, 245, 246, 260, 290,
    292, 294, 304, 308, 325,

    Engine Tenter 273, 275, 288, 292, 293,
    296, 318,

England 29, 88,

Enquiry into the Pollution of Rivers 281, 328,

Europe/European 28,

Everlasting Tweeds 119,

Exley, Halifax 106,

F

Factory the, Holme 81-82,

Factory Commissioners 19, 87, 96, 99,
    116, 134, 137, 152, 156, 165, 166, 170,
    177, 311, 319, 331,

    Factory Acts 186, 326,

    Factory Act 1819: 30, 90,

    Factory Act 1833: 33-4, 79, 92, 96, 99,
    108, 301,

    Factory Act 1844: 34, 142, 191, 236,
    253, 309,

    Factory Inspectors 27, 33-34, 88, 90,
    159, 164, 165, 198, 204, 213, 224, 234,
    236, 253, 261, 263, 267, 274, 275, 283,
    288, 301, 303,

Factory Sub-inspector 191, 202, 245,
    309, 317, 326,
    Factory Superintendent 171,
Falls Lane mill Marsden 274,
Fancy Mixture cloths 50, 51,
    Fancy Woollens 160, 281,
    Fancy Worsteds 129, 305,
Farrar's Lower mill 51,
    Farrar's Upper mill 51,
Farnley Tyas 233, 331,
Fartown 59,
Far Underbank 162,
Fearnought/Pickwick mill 126, 192-193,
    Fearnought machine 157, 197, 222, 256,
Feast of St. Luke the Evangelist 9,
Fenay, Almondbury 229,
Ferry Bridge 75. 294,
Field End 85, 86, 102,
    Field End Corn mill 102-3,
    Field End Lane 102,
    Field mills Leeds Road Hudds. 195, 266,
Field House Netherton 319,
Finishers 185, 186, 213, 228, 272, 284, 296,
    Finishing 50, 140, 166, 240, 244, 272,
        298, 299, 304, 315, 319, 325, 332,
    Finishing Machinery 206, 228, 313,
    Finishing Mill 253,
    Finishing Room 185, 238, 261, 274, 296,
Fire Bell 124, 154, 179, 222,
Fire Brigades 70, 117, 143, 254, 282, 304,
    Fire Engines 108, 195, 256,
        Also lack of 123,
    Fire Extincteurs 157, 185,
    Fire Insurance 180,
First Sunday School in Honley 330,
First World War 109, 155, 158, 315,
Firth St. Huddersfield 323,
Fisher Green, Honley 307, 308,
Five Lane Ends 137,
Fixby Hall 33,
Flanders 23,
Flashouse/Flushouse 99,
Flocks 256,
Floods 55-75,
    1738: 55,
    1777: 55-56,
    1852: 56-66, 72-75, 93, 102, 179, 197-8,
        210, 279-280, 281, 285, 288, 301, 333,

1866: 66-67, 204, 281, 291,
1944: 67-70, 119, 204, 276,
1946: 70-71
2002: 71, 239, 330,
Flood Relief Committee 1852: 65, 66, 100,
    127, 138, 188, 198,
    Flood Relief Fund 60, 65,
Folly Hall Huddersfield 271,
Frame Knitters 24,
France 23, 41, 88,
French Revolution 23,
Friendly Societies 36, 259,
Frisian 1,
Fly Shuttle 5, 13, 15,
Food riots 23,
Ford Gate Hinchliffe Mill 69,
Foresters Arms 322,
Friendship Inn 182,
Frizer 210,
Fullbeck Hall, Lincs. 100,
Fuller(s) 7, 186, 284,
    Fullers Earth 6,
Fulling 10, 12, 46, 116, 166, 171, 177,
    315, 319, 332,
    Fulling Mills 6, 10, 11, 12, 16, 21, 85,
        87, 92, 100, 120, 137, 150, 151, 153,
        157, 158, 165, 166, 170, 177, 187, 196,
        197, 209, 210,211, 218, 221, 222, 223,
        236, 237, 240, 253, 256, 263, 270, 278,
        285,
    Fulling Miller 93, 95, 211, 236, 285,
        301, 315,
    Fulling Stocks 6, 21, 93, 100, 138, 151,
        153, 154, 169, 171, 172, 191, 193, 194,
        218, 231, 233, 238, 244, 263, 270, 301,
        324, 330,
Fulling Milne at Meltham 330,
Fulstone 236,

G

Gainsborough 230,
Garden of Remembrance Cemetery Road 192,
Garnet machine 254,
Gartside Estate 180, 182,
Gaslight Co. 124,
George Inn, Upperbridge 161,
George & Dragon Honley 333,
Georgetown S. Carolina 258,

General Union of Weavers and
   Textile Workers 40, 41,
Germany 41, 48,
Gig Mill 22, 23,
Gilds 1-2,
Gilling machines 223,
Glass Houghton 99,
Glendale/Ing Nook mill 11, 44, 191, 236-
   239, 249,
Glossop 52, 61,
Gloucester 29,
Golcar 152,
Gold Standard 41,
Good Bent 67,
Goole 326, 328,
Goose Green 144, 146, 152,
Government Select Committee 23,
Grange, Kirkburton 249,
Graveship of Holme 8, 10, 232,
Great Exhibition 1851: 83,
Great Spring Wood 160,
Great War 1914-18: 40,
Greenfield Road 130,
Green Gates Farm 62,
Greenhill Bank 237, 252,
   Greenhill Lane 235,
Green Lane mill 18, 32, 156-158, 159,
   165,
Green Owlers 92, 94, 98,
Grimsby 98,
Grind stones 182, 300,
   Grinding mill (sugar) 182,
   Grinding mill (wood for dyeing) 257,
   Grinding mill (Bones) 292, 302,
   Grinding Stocks 258,
Grocery Shop and Post Office
   Thongsbridge 202,
Grove House New Mill 238,
Grove House Honley 297,
   Grove House mill Honley 19, 203, 294,
   296, 297-299, 328,
Gulley 152, 189,
Gynn House Honley 113,
   Gynn Lane Honley 288, 294, 297,
   Gynn View Gynn Lane 297,

H
Hadfield, Derbys. 136,
Hade Edge 21,
Hagg 209,
   Hagg House 51, 54, 279, 280, 281,
Hall Ing 294,
Hall Sunday School 67,
Halyfax(e) 1,
Hallifax 2,
Halifax 7, 141, 145, 173, 194, 210, 219,
   Halifax Act 2-3,
   Halifax Gibbet 7,
   Halifax Guardian 317,
   Halifax Joint Stock Banking Co. 89,
Hammond Royd Wood 168, 169,
Handlooms 19, 82, 308,
   Handloom Weaver 5, 19, 37,
Hand spun yarn 16,
Hares Fur 196,
Hartshead Moor 25,
Harrogate 182, 334,
Hattersley Loom 21,
Hawes, 158,
Healds 19,
   Heald making 275,
Healders and Twisters Trade
   and Friendly Society 36,
Healdy Butts Farm 330,
Health and Morals of Apprentices Act
   1802: 30,
Hebble Dike 188,
Height Linthwaite 188,
Helayhowsse 12. Healey House 123, 153,
Hepworth 209, 218, 219, 227, 236, 248,
   297,
   Hepworth Endowed School 223,
   Hepworth Iron Co. 192,
   Hepworth/Doctor mill/Dyehouse 219-
   220,
Hey nr, Thongsbridge 208,
   Hey Gap 145,
Higgin Dike 152, 161,
   Higgin Bridge Holmfirth 67,
High Burton 229,
High St. Huddersfield 323,
Hill, Holmfirth 125, 146, 162, 164,
Hillhouse, Cartworth 103, 106, 112, 116,
   Hillhouse Lane Bottom 250,

Hillsborough, Sheffield 137,

Hinchliffe Mill 11, 39, 62, 66, 83, 84, 105, 106, 116, 117, 119, 131, 138, 140, 150, 167, 168, 260, 309,

Hinchliffe Mill Cooperative Socy. 170,

Hinchliffe Mill Methodist Sunday School 67,

Hinchliffe Mill mill 54, 68, 105-109, 111, 266,

History of Kirkburton and the Graveship of Holme 263,

History of Honley 300,

Hogley 113, 120, 249,

Hogley Green 120,

Hollin Brigg House 105,

Hollin Hall Farm 296,

Holling House 239,

Hollingworth Lake 290,

Hollow Gate Holmfirth 69, 144,

Holmbridge 39, 67, 68, 80, 85, 86, 87, 88, 89, 178, 202, 309,

Holmbridge Dyehouse 88, 91, 101,

Holmbridge mill 42, 84, 85-91, 101, 102, 108, 117, 118, 121, 153, 178, 200,

Holmbridge Parish Church 67, 103,

Holme Bottom/Moorcroft mill 255-257,

Holme Lane New Mill 255,

Holme 45, 51, 52, 54, 70, 82, 84, 85, 95, 96, 168, 178,

Holme Banks 38, 46, 50, 51, 82, 85, 86, 101, 279,

Holme Banks Wood 96,

Holme (Liberal) Club 82,

Holme Electric Company 81,

Holme Fields 106,

Holme House 45, 47, 51, 81,

Holme Woods 9,

Holm Rentals 79, 80,

Holme Reservoirs Act 57, 63,

Holme Reservoir Commissioners 57, 58, 59, 60, 63, 88, 93, 94, 103, 107, 138, 139, 151, 153, 156, 158, 167, 171, 179, 198, 210, 218, 221, 224, 232, 235, 238, 250, 258, 264, 285, 289,

Holme Sunday School 51, 81,

Holme UDC 81, 99,

Holme Bottom mill New Mill 223, 225,

Holmfirth 10, 26, 37, 38, 39, 42, 50, 53, 55, 56, 57, 62, 67, 68, 70, 71, 86, 89, 103, 111, 113, 120, 121, 139, 150, 153, 156, 157, 158, 160, 161, 162, 164, 171, 177, 188, 189, 193, 196, 199, 208, 211, 222, 227, 229, 244, 245, 247, 248, 251, 257, 258, 259, 265, 298, 321,

Holmfirth Council 69, 81, 91, 108, 126, 127, 174, 191, 193, 203, 214,

Holmfirth Dyers Ltd. 175,

Holmfirth Express 91, 94, 135, 142, 146, 155, 157, 169, 174, 182, 183, 203, 206, 208, 220, 222, 225, 233, 240, 241, 247, 263, 267, 272, 277, 284, 286, 299, 324, 336,

Holmfirth Fire Brigade 169, 202, 206, 225, 228, 246, 247, 254, 256, 261, 276, 284, 294, 324,

Holmfirth Fire Station 160, 262,

Holmfirth Flood Relief fund 60, 64,

Holmfirth Literary and Philosophical Society 45,

Holmfirth Local Board 125, 208,

Holmfirth Magistrates Court 189,

Holmfirth Mechanics Institute 280,

Holmfirth Mending Co. 147,

Holmfirth mill 18, 32, 53, 55, 57, 86, 87, 177-183, 184, 202, 221,

Holmfirth Parish Church 55, 56, 108, 117,

Holmfirth Parish Council 143, 170,

Holmfirth Patent Wool Co. 181,

Holmfirth Police Court 160, 169,

Holmfirth Prosecution Society 169, 200,

Holmfirth Relieving Officer 312,

Holmfirth Station 153, 164, 168, 245, 265, 275,

Holmfirth Sunday Schools 67,

Holmfirth Temperance Band 164, 189,

Holmfirth Town Hall 40, 159, 172, 189, 191,

Holmfirth Wesleyan Burial ground 57,

Holmroyd Nook, Honley 255,

Holme Styes mill 83, 150,

Holme Styes Reservoir 57, 60, 64, 150, 152, 162,

Holme Valley 39, 55, 67, 81, 97, 208,

Holme Valley Grammar School 299,

Holme Valley Theatre 174,

Holme Valley Textiles Ltd. 277,

1st Holme Valley Scout Group 183,

Hong Kong 136,
Honley 11, 12, 19, 71, 83, 98, 150, 165,
    191, 211, 234, 258, 259, 273, 278, 284,
    285, 287, 288, 291, 292, 299, 301, 321, 331,
    Honley Band 286,
    Honley Bridge 12, 67,
    Honley Congregational Sunday School 313,
    Honley Church Sunday School 301
    Honley Corn mill 282, 300-303,
    Honley Dyeworks 297,
    Honley Fire Brigade 310,
    Honley Local Board 293, 299, 309, 313, 314,
    Honley Local Board Inspector 302,
    Honley Mills 12,
    Honley Moor 313,
    Honley Rentals 196,
    Honley Station 301, 303, 314, 317,
    Honley survey and valuation 308, 311,
    Honley Wood 9,
    Honley Workhouse 312,
    Honley Wood Bottom 315,
Honley and District Fanciers Society 302,
Honley Dyeing Co. 335,
Hoobram House 92, 95, 98,
    Hoobram Bottom 61,
    Hoobram Hill 66,
    Hoowood 92,
Hope Bank 71,
Horbury 56, 161, 162, 263,
Hotchkiss Bicycle Railway 286,
House of Commons 27,
Huddersfield 3, 8, 18, 20, 25, 26, 27, 28,
    29, 38, 45, 47, 51, 53, 64, 68, 73, 84,
    89, 94, 100, 110, 119, 120, 123, 151,
    160, 189, 196, 209, 210, 218, 227, 244,
    259, 263, 265, 281, 291, 294, 303, 317,
    320, 321, 322, 331, 334,
    Huddersfield Banking Company 52, 64,
    65, 164,
Huddersfield Bankruptcy Court 118,
    Huddersfield Boiler Association 206,
    Huddersfield Building society 69,
    Huddersfield Bye-laws 1913: 35,
    Huddersfield Cloth Hall 8, 45, 46, 47,
    48, 50, 51, 52, 104,
    Huddersfield Chronicle 122, 131, 139, 144,
    164, 167, 172, 179, 184, 189, 210, 231, 246,
    259, 273, 280, 285, 288, 289, 308, 321,

Huddersfield Corporation 94, 99,
Huddersfield Examiner 122, 123, 146,
    156, 161, 182, 185, 219, 225, 241, 245,
    258, 259, 272, 274, 275, 285, 288, 291,
    292, 296, 297, 301, 308, 315, 325, 328,
    334,
    Huddersfield Fire Brigade 206, 225, 228,
    246, 254, 284, 293, 324,
    Huddersfield Infirmary 93, 154, 156,
    157, 164, 194, 195, 198, 205, 206, 211,
    245, 246, 251, 253, 260, 270, 302,
    Huddersfield Market 285,
    Huddersfield Market Charter 8,
Huddersfield Masters Association 173,
    Huddersfield Master Dyers and Finishers
    Association 293,
    Huddersfield Technical College 299,
    Huddersfield Town Hall 335,
    Huddersfield to Penistone Railway line 57,
    Huddersfield Police Station 314,
    Huddersfield Weekly News 154,
    Huddersfield to Woodhead Turnpike
    Road 186, 190, 196, 207, 215,
    Huddersfield Woollen and Worsted
    Federation 43,
Huddersfield & District Cloth Pressers
    Benevolent and Burial Society 36,
Huddersfield and West Yorkshire
    Designers Association 325,
Huddersfield Road Works, Honley 305,
Hull 7, 33, 326, 328,
Hunger Hill 238,
Hussars 27,
Huthersfield 2,
Hydraulic Press 191, 313,
Hydro Extractor/Wuzzer 181, 220, 260,

I

Illustrated London News 70,
Indian Corn 211,
Indigo mill 211,
    Indigo Vats 211,
Industrial Revolution 13,
Ing Holme 80,
Intake Lane End 161,
'Integrity' Fire Engine 94,
Inquest 127,
1832 Inquiry into the Employment of
    Children in factories 30, 31-33,

Iron Oxide 224,
Iron and Steel 41,
Iron Works 3`10,

J
Jack Lane End 161,
Jackson Bridge 71, 221, 225, 234, 241,
　Jackson Bridge Mill 224, 229-231,
Jacobs Well Inn Honley 290,
Jacquard looms 223,
Jane Wood Dyehouse 160-161,
Jeffries map 320,
Jenny Gate 318,
Jerry lads 284,
Job Creation Scheme 43,
Joiner's shop 174, 182, 195, 212,

K
Keighley 18, 158,
Kersey 3, 7, 12, 50,
　Kerseymere 3,
Kettlethorpe 209,
Kilnhouse Bank 82, 87, 116, 203, 204,
King's Head Inn, Holmfirth 190,
Kings mill, Huddersfield 55-6,
Kirk Bridge New Mill 71, 182, 259, 263,
　Kirkbridge Lane 71, 257, 259,
　Kirkbridge Dyeworks 262,
　Kirkbridge mill 142, 210, 257-262,
Kirkburton Parish Register of Baptisms 9,
　Kirkburton Brass Band 334,
　Kirkburton 'Old Band' 280,
　Kirkburton, Rector of 103,
Kirklees Archive 193, 196, 261,
　Kirklees Council 133, 136, 144, 160,
　170, 196, 267, 277, 284, 315,
　Kirklees Dyers and Finishers 294,
　Kirklees Planning Committee 239,
KirkRoyds New Mill 259,
Knitting Wool 245, 246,
Knutton's Corn mill 265,

L
Lambswool 204,
Lancashire 13, 15, 33, 66, 67, 258,
Lancashire & Yorkshire Fire Engine 265,
Land Tax 330, 331,
Lane Independent/Congregational chapel
　51, 69,

Lane Village Holme 79,
Lane End Holmfirth 147, 277,
Larch House, Cartworth 139,
Lawnmower 22,
Layers-on 30,
Lee mill 39, 191, 192, 225-229, 261,
Leeds 2, 3, 14, 18, 23, 28, 29, 33, 39, 42, 57,
　100, 139, 150, 151, 294,
　Leeds Bankruptcy Court 303,
　Leeds Intelligencer 153, 162, 167, 188,
　279, 331,
　Leeds Mercury 138, 177, 188, 219, 238,
　244, 255, 258, 263, 279, 300, 303, 330, 331,
　Leeds Waterworks Company 57,
Leicester 28,
Leigh 15,
Leominster 14,
Lepton 174,
Letters of Credit 52,
Licence of Heriot 158, 171, 229, 233, 249,
Lido Swimming Pool 145,
Lightcliffe nr. Halifax 286,
Lincoln 2,
　Lincolnshire 247,
Lindley 39, 120, 152,
Linsey 255,
　Linsey-Woolsey 308,
Linthwaite 134,
　Linthwaite Church 253,
Lion Arcade Chambers Hudd. 195, 211,
　Lion Chambers Hudds. 266,
Little Lane Wooldale 247,
Littlewood Buildings Sargentson St.
　Hudds 104, 201, 309,
Liverpool 52, 53, 88, 100, 275, 305, 307, 322,
Local Authorities 43,
Lockwood 71, 75, 89, 262,
　Lockwood mill 67,
London 45, 46, 47, 48, 53, 89, 129, 130, 200,
　236,
　London Gazette 163, 168, 212, 292, 303,
　328, 331,
Long Ing, Austonley 86, 112,
　Long Ing 233,
　Long Walls, Austonley 103,
Longwood 188, 322,
Loom 5, 6,
　See also Power Looms

Lords/Woodbottom Mill Honley 9, 262, 320-324,

Lower Damhouse 162, 165, 166,

Lower Dover mill 162,

Lower Hall mill 315,

Lower mill 39, 47, 55, 66, 68, 108, 111,
    127, 131, 136-144, 185, 196,

Lower Mytholmbrige mill 66, 67, 69, 197,
    198, 209, 214, 268-272, 277, 278,

Lower Netherhouse Farm 131,

Luddism 26,
    Luddite 25, 26, 27,

Luke Lane 213, 215,

Lum Bank Holme 92,
    Lumb Bank, Wooldale 184,

Lydgate 247,
    Lydgate Chapel 254,
    Lydgate mill 254-255, 262,

M

Machine Makers 321,

Mag Bridge 327,

Mag Bridge/Thirstin Dyeworks 309, 324,
    327-330,

Mag Dale Road 330,

Mag Dike Honley 67, 71,

Mag Valley Dyeworks 323, 334,

Maidstone 45,

Main Gate Hepworth 219,

Malmesbury 2,

Malthouses 298,

Manchester 23, 27, 28, 33, 45, 52, 53, 61,
    67, 199, 210,

Manorial/Soke mills 8, 209,

Manor of Wakefield 8, 11, 230,

Mantle cloths 233,

Manufacturers Associations 40, 41, 48,

Marble Hall 153,

Mark Bottoms 189,
    Mark Bottoms Wood 188,

Market St. Holmfirth 183,

Marsden 24, 29, 119, 184, 187, 188, 225,

Married Women Weavers 39,

Masons Arms Underbank 164, 167,

Meal Hill, Holme 47,
    Meal Hill road 81,

Mechanics shop/Motor Garage 182,

Meltham 92, 96, 119, 120, 123, 160, 196,
    225, 284,

Meltham Fire Brigade 324,
    Meltham Mills 96, 123,

Meltham Road Honley 310,

Meltham Road Netherton 335,

Mending/knotting/burling 274,

Mending Room 182, 241, 274,
    Mending Tables 213,

Merino Yarns 204, 284,

Mersey Tunnel 275,

Military Uniforms 155,

Mill Hill Holmfirth 162, 177, 178,

Millhouse Wooldale 243,

Milling 21, 46, 240, 315,
    Milling Machine 191, 211, 223,

Millstones 300,

Mill Wood 233,

Milnsbridge 59, 60, 187, 238,
    Milnsbridge fire brigade 272, 304,

Mirfield 119, 195, 200,

Miry Lane Thongsbridge 203, 204, 207,
    Miry Lane Bottom 255,

Mohair cloth 281,

Moiter/Waste Grinding Machine 111, 222,

Moldgreen 330,

Moorbottom Honley 130,
    Moorbottom Congregational church 299,
    Moorbottom mill 311,

Moorbrook mill 253,

Moorhouse Bank 233,

Moorside Farm 218, 219,

Mortgagees and Subscribers 57, 60,

Moser raising gig 223,

Mosley Lancs. 312,

Mottram 15,

Mount Pleasant Holmfirth 108,

Mule: see 'Spinning mule'.

Mungo 107, 183, 221, 246, 254, 256, 260,
    266, 284,

Muslin Hall 235,

Mytholmbridge 84, 177, 210, 255, 265,
    Mytholmbridge House 272,
    Mytholmbridge Upper mill 51, 65, 101,
    119, 208-215, 255, 258, 269, 283,

N

Nabb 158, 162,
    Nabb House 169,
    Nabb Dyehouse 146,

Napoleonic Wars 19, 23, 27,
National Association of Textile Trade
  Unions 43,
National Charter Association 27,
National Insurance 43,
National Monument Record Centre 320,
National School New Mill 258, 259,
National Society of Dyers and Finishers 40,
National Strike 42,
National Union of Textile Workers 42,
  186, 262, 336,
National Wool and Allied Industries
  Council 41,
National Wool Textile Industrial Council 41,
Neiley 272,
Netherthong 26, 168, 180, 196, 198, 199,
  201, 300, 322,
  Netherthong Local Board 199, 206,
Netherton 211, 315, 317, 322,
  Netherton Independent Chapel 317,
  Netherton Independent School Room 318,
  Netherton Oddfellows Hall 318,
  Netherton United 322,
New Brighton 275,
New Chapel Penistone 221,
Newdoorstones Holmfirth 172,
New Fold Holmfirth 37, 45, 232,
  New Fold Mill 144-146, 164, 173,
Newgate Wooldale 184, 249,
New Hagg 194,
New House Austonley 113,
  Newhouse Upperthong 162,
New Inn Hinchliffe Mill 88, 107,
New Mill 9, 10, 11, 18, 54, 71, 234, 238,
  239, 255, 258, 259, 285,
  New Mill Church 241,
  New Mill Cotton Spinning Co. (Ltd.) 257-260,
  New Mill Council 228, 241,
  New Mill Dike 57, 71, 209, 252, 255,
  260, 262, 263,
  New Mill Knitting Co. 241,
  New Mill Local Board 261,
  New Mill/Moorbrook mill 10, 11, 39,
  224, 226, 233, 249-254, 261,
  Newmillwater 236,
New Mill Road Brockholes 277,
New Road 186, 199,
Newton Abbott Devon 254,

Newtown, Holmfirth 177, 183, 226,
  Newtown mill 183-184,
New Zealand 172,
Nippings 221,
Noble Worsted Combing machine 17,
Norland 92, 95,
Normanton 53, 335,
Norridge Bottom Holmfirth 69, 147, 177,
  Norwich Upperthong 184,
Northern Dozens 3,
Northrop Loom 21,
Notched Shuttle Stick 5,
Nottingham 15, 28,
  Nottingham Review 25,
Nuisance Inspector 118, 182, 207,

O
Oakes Avenue Brockholes 276,
Oaklands Holmfirth 174,
Oakwell House, Birstall 218,
Ochre (Iron Oxide) 281, 318,
Office furnishings 191,
Official Receiver 328,
Oldfield 301,
Oldham 65,
Old Jane 160,
Old Mill Court Hepworth 202,
Old Moll/Moll Springs mill/Dyeworks 98,
  191, 311, 323, 3243-327,
  Old Moll Road 324,
Old Sick Club, Holmfirth 152,
Old Tan Yard, Digley Road 91,
Open Air Dining Room 254,
Order of Ancient Druids 317,
Osney Abbey Oxfordshire 2,
Ossett 25, 104,
Ottiwells mill Marsden 24, 25,
Out-menders 191,
Overlooker/Foreman 31, 246, 251, 275, 317,
Ox Lee 218,

P
Paris Scholes 227,
Parish Apprentices 29,
  Parish Relief 30, 32,
Parliament 23, 66, 189, 287,
  Parliamentary Reform Act 27, 48,
Park the 233,

Parkhead 69, 123, 124, 126, 250,
    Parkhead mill/dyeworks 130-131,
Park House 130, 250,
Parkton Grove House 334, 335,
Parliament 259,
Patent Office 271,
Pattern looms 191, 206, 223, 256, 265,
    Pattern Room 275,
    Pattern Weaver 279, 294,
    Pattern Weaving Room 309, 310,
Peacock Inn Holme 79, 80,
Pegged Rugs 182,
Pell Lane Wooldale 260,
Penistone 53, 119, 159,
    Penistone Bypass 43,
    Penistone Road 239, 241,
People's Charter 27,
Perseverance mill/Dyson's mill 68, 107,
    123, 133-136, 137, 191, 250, 294,
Peterloo Massacre 27,
Pick Measures 38,
Picturedrome Cinema 174,
Piecer/Piecener 18, 30, 31,
    Piecing machines 154, 226, 260,
Pig and Stick 252,
Pingle/Lower Dover mill 161-162, 165,
Plastic Bobbins 205,
Pleasure Gardens 286,
Plug Riots 28, 239,
    Plug Rioters 194, 237, 263, 287, 317,
    320, 331,
Pocklington Canal 57,
Pog Ing 168,
Pontefract Quarter Sessions 12,
Poor Guardians 29,
Poor Harvests 23,
Potato famine Ireland 28,
Poultry farming 174,
Power Looms 19, 123, 124, 154, 164, 168,
    181, 190, 191, 201, 206, 211, 212, 218,
    219, 220, 223, 226, 231, 232, 235, 245,
    246, 251, 253, 272, 283, 308, 324,
    Power Loom Weavers 38, 154, 333,
    Power Loom Weavers Association 107,
    141, 154, 164, 173,
Press Shop 123, 144, 152, 168, 208, 220,
    221, 249,
Preston 15,

Prickleden 133, 136, 156, 174, 226, 250, 262,
    Prickleden House 183,
    Prickleden mill, 89, 200, 212,
Promissory Notes 266, 329,
Prospect mill Honley 296, 298,
Providence mill Brockholes 277,
Pumping Engine 275,
Purchase Tax 203,
Puttees 119, 213,

Q
Quarter Sessions 244,
Queen's Award to Industry 225,
Queen's Mill in Holnefrith 11, 177,
Queens mill Honley 308,
Queen St. Mission Hudds. 213,
Queens Square mill 43, 335-6,
Queen Victoria's Diamond Jubilee 275,
Quick Wood, Saddleworth 137,

R
Rabbit Hair 130, 196,
Raddle 5,
Rag Pullers 129,
    Rag Grinding machine 246,
    Rag Grinding room 284,
    Rag Merchant 296,
    Rag Shaking machine 265,
Railway Viaduct 265,
Raising Shop 146, 152, 249,
    Raising gig 223, 244,
Railway Hotel onley 295,
Rake Dike Holme 61, 79, 81, 82, 84, 85,
    87, 91, 101,
    Rake mill 21, 79-81, 96,
Rakes Dike Hepworth 219, 221, 224,
Ramsden, 79,
    Ramsden Dike 84,
Ramsgate Lodge, Cumberland 158,
Rapes, crushing and pressing 284,
    Rape mill 285,
Rasping and Grinding mill 210, 258,
Rawfolds Mill Cleckheaton 25,
Rearing Supper 190, 251, 325,
Receivership 233,
Reins Honley 328,
    Reins mill 69, 99, 290, 303-306,

Reliance Works/Mill 241 262,
  Reliance Rug Works 241,
Repeal of the Corn Laws 28,
Reservoir 150, 208,
Ribbleden Valley 55, 57,
  Ribbleden mill 145, 158-9, 161, 167,
    169, 170-175, 191, 215,
  Ribbleden mill fire brigade 165, 272, 273,
  Rippledens 170,
  Rivelin Dike 170,
Richmond Yorks 263,
Riots 24,
Ripponden 258,
Rivers Board 98, 213, 276,
  River Pollution Act 214,
River Holme 57, 70, 71, 106, 177, 184,
    196, 209, 286, 330,
  River Ribble 152, 174,
Robin Rocks Brockholes 280,
Rochdale 192, 258,
Rock mill 39, 67, 69, 213, 272-277,
  Rock Inn Brockholes 277,
  Rock Terrace 69, 272,
Room and Power 18, 123, 141, 142, 198,
    204, 244, 259, 295, 308-9,
Rope Walk 261,
Rotcher, Holmfirth 207,
Round Bottom/Riverside mill 66, 68, 70,
    127-130,
  Round Bottom Close 127,
  Round Bottom Ironworks 127,
Round Green, Silkstone 99,
Roundways Honley 311,
Roving 22,
Royal Commission for Historical
  Monuments survey 327,
Royal Engineers 62,
Royal Exchange Insurance Co. 331,
Royal Oak, Thongsbridge 190, 200, 210, 271, 282,
Rugby 53,
Rug Weavers 169, 182, 305,
  Rug Weaving mill 2
Rye Bank Wood 233,

S
Saddleworth 52, 96, 97, 118,
St. Peter's Fields Manchester 27,
St. Thomas' Road Hudds. 286,

St. Thomas' Square Hinchliffe Mill 67,
Sands Holmfirth 165,
  Sands House Holmfirth 203,
Sandygate, Scholes 218, 230,
Sanitary Inspector 168,
Sardinia 88,
Scammonden 139,
Scarborough 111, 165, 222, 302, 303, 326, 335,
Scar Fold Holmfirth 69,
  Scar End 265,
Scar Top Wood 328,
Scholecroft Farm, Holme 108,
Scholes 21, 31, 55, 165, 219, 221, 225,
    226, 233, 236, 252,
  Scholes/Midge/Valley mills 231-233, 308,
  Scholes Moor 55,
School St. Holmfirth 183,
Scotland 254,
Scotland Road Liverpool 258,
Scouring 21, 214, 240,
  Scouring House 122, 246, 259, 272,
  Scouring/Washing machinery 191, 206,
    211, 221, 223, 231, 263, 270, 292,
  Scour Pans 161, 211, 220,
Scribbling 14, 16, 29, 99, 106, 116, 123,
    128, 138, 140, 151, 153, 156, 164, 166,
    171, 174, 177, 188, 226, 239, 272, 278,
    282, 303, 304, 315, 319, 325, 331, 332,
  Scribblers 196,
  Scribbling Engines 16, 124, 144, 151,
    154, 171, 180, 194, 197, 202, 204, 210,
    219, 226, 228, 231, 236, 238, 244, 249,
    255, 256, 260, 263, 265, 270, 300, 333,
  Scribbling Engineer 252,
  Scribbling Mills 16, 18, 79, 87, 100, 120,
    137, 150, 151, 157, 158, 161, 162, 165,
    166, 170, 184, 188, 193, 197, 221, 229,
    237, 249, 255, 263, 269, 300,
  Scribbling Miller 79, 188, 263, 301,
'Seak' pits 180,
Seal-skin 89,
Second World War 21, 43, 109, 155, 165,
    186, 238, 311, 315,
Selas Incandescent Lights 142,
'Serious Riot' 194,
Serge 119, 155, 124,
Shaley Upperthong 116, 130, 161, 171, 230,

Shaley Wood Totties 244,
　Shaley Wood Bottom/Ford mill 245-247,
　　254,
Shaw Bank Wood 96,
Shearing Frames: see Cropping/Shearing
　Frames
Sheffield 22, 28, 53, 67, 144, 249, 262,
　Sheffield Road 239, 285,
Shelley Woodhouse mill 16,
Shepley 39, 103, 245,
　Shepley Lane Head 194,
　Shepley turnpike road 221,
Shipbuilding 41,
Shittlington 208,
Shoddy 107, 183, 221, 246, 254, 256, 284,
　313,
　Shoddy Cleaner 246,
Short Time Committees 33,
Shoulder of Mutton Inn New Mill 227, 251, 252,
Shrinkers 186,
Siemens electric machine 220,
Silk Dyer 323,
Silkstone 237,
Sizing machine 168, 232,
　Sizing Shop 179,
Skelmanthorpe 119, 160, 225, 245, 254,
　284, 294,
Skipton 18, 248,
Slaithwaite 79, 119, 120, 160, 220, 225,
　233, 294, 297, 300,
Slaughter House 170,
Slubbers 30, 116, 139, 153, 270, 316, 317,
　Slubbing 99, 106, 116, 138, 156, 177,
　　180, 184, 182, 219, 303, 313, 315, 316,
　　320, 331,
　Slubbing Billy 14, 89, 124, 151, 154,
　　180, 197, 204, 219, 226, 231, 238, 244,
　　255, 260, 263, 265, 300, 301, 319,
Smithy Place Bridge 69, 269,
　Smithy Place mill 31, 32, 54, 67, 85,
　　112, 194, 197, 198, 211, 260, 269, 270,
　　277-284, 292, 309, 313,
　Smithy Place mill fire brigade 271, 296,
　Smithy Place Sunday School 278,
　Smithy/Smith's Shop 182,
Snowgate Head Hepworth 220,
Soay Sheep 1,
Socialist's Hall 40,

Society for Mental Improvement 332,
Somerset 23,
Southdown wool 46,
South Lancashire 27, 28,
Southowram 226,
Southport 298, 335,
　Southport Centenary Exhibition 298,
Southwark London 137,
Sowerby 92,
　Sowerby Bridge 111, 254, 322,
Spinks Mire mill Meltham 315,
Spinners 5, 15, 30, 159, 204, 246, 294,
　313,
　Spinning 2, 14, 18, 29, 50, 99, 116, 123,
　　128, 140, 151, 153, 157, 166, 185, 218,
　　228, 239, 273, 278, 303, 304, 325,
　Spinning Frames 225,
　Spinning Jenny 15,
　Spinning mill 171, 251, 310,
　Spinning Mules 16, 17, 124, 151, 154,
　　157, 164, 168, 191, 201, 204, 211, 220,
　　225, 226, 231, 234, 238, 239, 244, 246,
　　251, 253, 256, 260, 265, 282, 295, 301,
　　319,
　Self-acting Mule 17, 181, 190, 206, 211,
　　223, 231, 233, 246,
　Spinning Room 238, 263, 285, 303, 318,
　Spinning Wheels 4,
Spitalfields London 283,
Sprinkler System 225, 247,
Spring Bank House 88, 124,
Spring Bottom, Netherthong 106, 196,
Spring Grove, Austonley 100,
Spring Lane 124,
　Spring Lane mill 85, 122, 123-127, 130,
　　160, 182, 193,
Spring Mill 241,
Spring Vale Big Valley Netherton 327,
Springwood road New Mill 241,
Spring Wood Netherton 323,
Stables 153,
Stafford mills Milnsbridge 305,
Stagwood Hill 150, 196,
Stainland 249,
Stalybridge 184,
'Stanley mill' Sudehill 241,
Statham 53,

Steam Boiler 152, 158, 169, 171, 172, 189, 195, 204, 206, 211, 212, 220, 231, 233, 238, 239, 244, 245, 246, 253, 254, 256, 260, 272, 288, 290, 296, 303, 304, 309, 310, 313, 318,

Steam Engine 144, 152, 156, 158, 166, 168, 169, 171, 172, 177, 195, 204, 206, 212, 220, 221, 231, 233, 238, 239, 244, 245, 246, 251, 253, 254, 256, 260, 263, 269, 272, 278, 286, 287, 288, 290, 296, 303, 304, 309, 310, 311, 313, 315, 320, 322, 324, 329,

Steam power 16, 152, 156, 324,

Steaming and Brushing mill 186,

Steps, Honley 11, 12,

Steps Mills, Upper and Lower 202, 322, 330-335,

Stockinet 119, 191, 214, 222, 223, 233,

Stockport 45, 47, 130,

Stone Cisterns 324,

Stoney Bank 245,

Stoney Bank mill 18, 107, 260, 263, 263-267, 281,

Stone Sawmill 297,

Storths Hall 209,

Storthes Hall 334,

Stove/Stoving: see Drying Stove

Street Trading 35,

Strikes 23, 154, 227, 250, 333,

Strike Pay 42,

Stubbin 93, 116,

Stubbin Clough 111,

The Stubbings Netherton 232,

Sude Hill 221, 251,

Sude Hill mill 37, 192, 223, 239-241,

Sunday Schools 31, 34, 92,

Sunny Brow Wooldale 249,

Surrey Iron Railway 57,

Survey of Graveship of Holme 177,

Swanbank mill 165-170, 182, 202,

Swanbank Wood 165, 168, 169,

Sycamore Inn Wooldale 213,

T

Taiwan 136,

Taking-in Steps 6,

Taylor Hill 332,

Taylor Hill mill 196, 201, 202,

Teazing machine 142, 157, 190, 222, 225, 255,

Teazing Room 168, 172, 222, 239, 254,

Teazer 119,

Teazing mill 137,

Ten Hours Bill 316,

Tentering 21, 22, 46,

Tenter Hooks 7,

Tentering House 171, 253, 272,

Tentering Machine 21, 140, 156, 191, 223, 311,

Tenter Posts 7, 140,

Tenterhill Lane 261,

Tenterhill mill 182, 261, 262-3,

Textiles 41,

Textile Manufacturer 118, 128, 256, 296,

The Factory, Holme 81-82,

The Factory Marsden 29,

Thick Hollins 99, 269,

Thirstin Dyeworks 71, 224,

Thirstin old Dyeworks 329,

Thirstin mill 225, 292, 311-315, 324,

Thongsbridge 69, 84, 88, 132, 203, 207, 208, 210, 236, 237, 256, 264, 281, 282,

Thongsbridge Bone and Size Works 207-208, 211,

Thongsbridge mills 18, 69, 71, 91, 117, 190, 195, 196-203, 205, 206, 210, 272, 299, 305,

Thongsbridge Mill-dam 206,

Thongsbridge mill fire brigade 271, 273, 296,

Thongsbridge Railway Station 208, 210,

Thongsbridge Mill Spinning Co. 202,

Thorp Heys 255,

Throstle 16,

Throstle Nest Marsden 29,

Thrum Hall, Soyland 137,

Thrums 221,

Thurlstone 259,

Thunderstorm 199,

Thurstonland 194, 208, 275,

Toll Gate 288, 302,

Tom mill Holmfirth 184, 187,

Totties 139, 227, 233, 245, 246, 252,

Towngate Holmfirth 69, 72, 177, 181, 182,

Townend Honley 313,

Traction Engine 159, 290,

Trades Unions 36-43,

Trades Union Conference 27-28,

Treadmill 164,
 'Truck' payment by 28,
Turkey 88,
Tweeds 214, 233,
Twister 160,
  Twisting Frame 190, 211, 223, 253,
Tyas mill 233-234,
Typhus 65,

U

Ulnage 12, 37,
  Ulnager 12,
Underbank 161, 162, 164, 249,
  Underbank mill 144, 162-165, 168,
Unemployment 41,
  Unemployment pay 41,
Union St. Huddersfield 227,
United States 41,
Unity Fire Brigade 88, 98, 108, 117, 124,
  125, 128, 139, 145, 154, 157, 165, 179,
  180, 181, 189, 200, 206, 211, 222, 238,
  239, 251, 261, 263, 265, 272, 273, 293,
  Unity Fire Office 167,
Upper Bottom, Austonley 92, 95,
Upperbridge Holmfirth 62, 69, 86, 127,
  136, 144, 146, 156, 160, 162,
Upper Brow Road Paddock 335,
Upper Damhouse 162,
Upper Holme Bottom mill 203,
Upper House/Over House mills 21, 217-219,
  Upper House Dike 57,
Upper Mytholmbridge mill: see
            Mytholmbridge Upper mill
Upper/Prickleden mill/Valley Dyeworks 11,
  67, 68, 70, 142, 174, 262,
Upperthong/Overthong 11, 26, 54, 120,
  125, 130, 133, 146, 168, 184, 249,
  Upperthong Lane 26, 165, 171,
  Upperthong Local Board 125, 132, 140,
    183, 185, 201,
  Upperthong Valuation 123, 146,
Urine Pots 6,
  Urine Barrel on wheels 265,
Uttley nr. Keighley 158,

V

Valley mill New Mill: See Wildspur mill
Valley Theatre/Cinema 69, 70, 174,
Victoria Carpet Co. 155,
Victoria Bridge Holmfirth 57, 69, 180,
  Victoria Hotel Holmfirth 124, 266,
  Victoria Park Holmfirth 67,
  Victoria Square 69, 170,
  Victoria Street 139, 167, 205,
Victoria/Victoria Inn 66-7, 68, 69, 70, 71,
  84, 135,
  Victoria mill H'firth 62, 68, 119, 131,
  Victoria Ironworks 132,
Victoria/Queens mill Honley 214, 307-310,
  326, 32,
Victoria Temperance Hall Buxton Road
  Huddersfield 326,
Vitriol (Sulphuric Acid) 111,
Voice of the West Riding 317,

W

Wagon & Horses Inn Holmfirth 38,
  Wagon & Horses Inn Holmbridge 102, 103,
Wakefield 2, 10, 92, 137, 171, 208, 219,
  229, 231, 302, 331,
  Wakefield Assizes 83,
  Wakefield Court House 300,
  Wakefield Court Rolls 7, 8, 9-10, 11, 55,
    79, 92, 95, 96, 99, 102, 103, 105, 112,
    116, 120, 133, 136, 146, 150, 153, 156,
    160, 162, 165, 168, 177, 186, 187, 188,
    209, 217, 219, 220, 221, 229, 233, 236,
    245, 247-249, 255, 258, 263,
  Wakefield Prison 164, 221, 302,
  Wakefield Record Office 195,
Wakefield & Halifax Journal 170,
Wall Street Crash 43,
War bonuses 40,
Ward Place 156,
Warehouse 122, 138, 146, 153, 154, 158,
  169, 185, 190, 200, 204, 208, 212, 225,
  226, 228, 231, 233, 238, 259, 271, 273,
  301, 304, 320, 325,
Warp Beam 5
Warp Beaming Frame 164, 211,
Warp Drying Balloon 154, 164, 232,
Warping 6, 254,
  Warping Balloon 168, 190, 191, 211,
    219, 220, 223, 246,

Warping Woof and Creel 5, 219, 223, 246, 256, 265,

Warp Threads 5, 19,

Warrington 15,

Wash (Urine) 221.

  Wash barrel 221,

  Wash cisterns 161,

Washing machine: see Scouring

Washford, Somerset 122,

Washpit Mill 9, 142, 152, 156, 157, 181, 191,

Waste cleaner 260,

Waterloo 27, 67,

Water power 16, 156, 231, 320,

  Water Corn mill 187,

  Water mill for Rasping and Grinding 258,

  Water Wheel 79, 80, 87, 96, 99, 102, 106, 109, 116, 120, 131, 134, 138, 141, 150, 152, 154, 156, 157, 160, 161, 166, 169, 170, 171, 177, 188, 197, 212, 221, 223, 233, 238, 239, 241, 256, 260, 263, 269, 271, 278, 285, 286, 294, 300, 311, 315, 320, 327, 330, 331, 332,

Waterproofers 186,

Water Street Hinchliffe Mill 18, 70, 87, 106,

  Waterside 69, 110,

  Upper Waterside 113,

Weavers 250,

  Weavers Association 227, 261,

  Weavers and Textile Workers Union 40, 276, 305,

  Weavers Union 19,

Weaving 6, 50, 128, 140, 274,

  Weaving Chamber 6,

  Weaving machinery 185,

  Weaving Rooms 182,

  Weaving Shed 154, 160, 165, 192, 225, 228, 235, 238, 246, 251, 253, 272, 304, 308, 309, 310, 314, 322, 324, 331,

  Weaving Shops 195, 208,

Weeting 6,

Weft Room 192, 228,

  Weft Threads 5,

Weighing Machine 181,

Wellhouse 117,

Well Hill Underbank 169,

  Well Hill Hepworth 220,

  Well Hill Honley 313,

Wellington Inn Burnlee 124,

Wellington Mills Oakes 262,

West House Honley 320,

West Indies 33,

Westminster 29,

West Nelly/Nellroyd 245,

West of England 2, 3, 36,

West Riding 1, 10, 16, 25, 28, 36, 42, 45, 50, 53,

  West Riding Assize Court 182,

  West Riding County Council 186, 311,

  West Riding Medical Officer 208,

  West View 172,

West Yorkshire 18, 27,

  West Yorkshire Archive 300,

  West Yorkshire Archaeological Advisory Service, Wakefield 153,

West Riding of Yorkshire Power Loom Weavers Association 39,

Westwood Yarns 155,

Wet Finishing 21, 253,

Wheatclose 106,

Wheatsheaf Inn Honley 308,

Whipcords 109,

Whirlpool Mohair Finish 280, 281,

White's Directory 239,

White Gate Head, Soyland 161,

White Hart Inn Holmfirth 72, 123, 164, 171, 182, 278,

  White Hart Inn New Mill 255,

White's Directory 263,

White Walls Austonley 92,

Whitley 230,

Whitsuntide 67,

Whit Walks 67,

Wickens, Upperthong 26,

  Lower Wickens 188,

Wigan 14,

Wildspur mill 39, 44, 54, 224, 225, 231, 233, 234-236,

Willey/Willow machine 151, 181, 204, 219, 226, 233, 244, 246, 256,

  Shake Willey 260,

  Spiked Willow 265,

  Tenter Hook Willey 260,

  Willow House 153, 154, 158, 195, 235, 246, 253, 259, 309, 310, 325,

Willeyers and Fettlers Union 40,

Wiltshire 24,

Winchester 1,
Winding Department 254,
  WindingFrames 223,
  Winding-on Frame 220, 245,
  Winding off frames 223,
Windsor 53,
Winney Bank mill 18, 21, 243-245,
  Winney Bank House 245,
Woad 211,
Wood, Upperthong 137, 161, 177,
Wood Bottom Wooldale 244,
Woodhead 45, 53, 156,
  Woodhead Road 51, 71, 102, 132, 135,
  Woodhead Tunnel 67,
Woodhouse Hudds. 137,
Wood Leigh Ribbleden Hill 174,
Woodleigh, Brighouse 203,
Wood Nook 221,
Woodroyd mill/Victoria Dyeworks 19,
  294-297, 298, 321,
Wool and Allied Textile Employers
  Council 43,
Wool Chapmen/Drivers/Staplers 2, 3, 123,
  150, 156, 188, 218, 249, 321,
Wooldale 9, 18, 21, 125, 150, 152, 161,
  182, 209, 226, 238, 239, 243, 262,
  Wooldale Brass Band 172, 259,
  Wooldale Cliffe 233,
  Wooldale Hall 248,
  Wooldale Local Board 180, 181, 207, 211,
  Wooldale Mill 247-249,
  Wooldale Townend 200, 248, 257,
Woollen trade 19,
  Woollen Mill 245, 258,
  Woollen/Woollens 208, 214, 222, 223,
  241, 284, 293,
  Woollen Waste 179,
Woolley nr, Mottram Cheshire 187,
Wool Grinder 253,
Wool Hearthrugs 305,
Woolwich Dockyard 53,
Wool Textile Executive 44,
Wool washer 245,
The Worker 213,
Workhouses 29,
Workshops Regulations Act 1867: 34,
Worstead, Norfolk 17,
Worsteds 208, 214, 222, 241,

Worsted Comb/Combing 17, 276,
Worsted Drawing machine 223,
Worsted cloth 38, 119,
Worsted fibres 17, 245, 293,
Worsted manufacturer 274, 284,
Worsted mill 304,
Worsted Spinner 309,
Worsted Spinning Frames 223,
Worsted trade 19,
Worsted Yarn 17, 223, 245,
Wringing machines 233, 260,
Wuzzing 3,
  Wuzzing Holes 3,

Y

Yarn Ready Reckoner 156,
  Yarn Store 165,
Yateholme 84,
Yew Tree 86, 106, 108,
  Yew Tree mill 91, 98, 229, 284,
York 1, 187,
  York Assizes 227, 245, 317,
  York Weavers Charter 1164: 1,
  York Gaol 79, 100,
Yorkshire 14, 66,
  Yorkshire Archaeological Service 196,
  Yorkshire Archaeological Society 300,
  Yorkshire Banking Corporation 89, 290,
  312,
Yorkshire Factory Times 39, 98, 118, 191,
  213, 227, 261, 266, 275, 292, 305, 310,
Yorkshire Penny Bank 69,
Yorkshire Textile Directory 91, 98, 109,
  119, 126, 127, 130, 132, 146, 155, 157,
  165, 173, 174, 183, 186, 192, 193, 195,
  196, 202, 204, 214, 215, 224, 228, 231,
  236, 238, 241, 247, 253, 254, 257, 263,
  266, 276, 277, 284, 293, 296, 299, 310,
  311, 315, 319, 323, 324, 329,

Z

Zeppelin Airships 284,